Cloud Security:

Concepts, Methodologies, Tools, and Applications

Information Resources Management Association
USA

Volume IV

Published in the United States of America by
IGI Global
Engineering Science Reference (an imprint of IGI Global)
701 E. Chocolate Avenue
Hershey PA, USA 17033
Tel: 717-533-8845
Fax: 717-533-8661
E-mail: cust@igi-global.com
Web site: http://www.igi-global.com

Library of Congress Cataloging-in-Publication Data

Names: Information Resources Management Association, editor.
Title: Cloud security : concepts, methodologies, tools, and applications /
   Information Resources Management Association, editor.
Description: Hershey, PA : Engineering Science Reference, [2019] | Includes
   bibliographical references.
Identifiers: LCCN 2018048047| ISBN 9781522581765 (hardcover) | ISBN
   9781522581772 (ebook)
Subjects: LCSH: Cloud computing--Security measures.
Classification: LCC QA76.585 .C5864 2019 | DDC 004.67/82--dc23 LC record available at https://lccn.loc.gov/2018048047

British Cataloguing in Publication Data
A Cataloguing in Publication record for this book is available from the British Library.

The views expressed in this book are those of the authors, but not necessarily of the publisher.

For electronic access to this publication, please contact: eresources@igi-global.com.

List of Contributors

Table of Contents

Section 2
Development and Design Methodologies

Section 3
Tools and Technologies

Volume II

Section 4
Utilization and Applications

Volume III

Section 5
Organizational and Social Implications

Section 6
Managerial Impact

Section 7
Critical Issues and Challenges

Section 8
Emerging Trends

Preface

The constantly changing landscape of Cloud Security makes it challenging for experts and practitioners to stay informed of the field's most up-to-date research. That is why Engineering Science Reference is pleased to offer this four-volume reference collection that will empower students, researchers, and academicians with a strong understanding of critical issues within Cloud Security by providing both broad and detailed perspectives on cutting-edge theories and developments. This reference is designed to act as a single reference source on conceptual, methodological, technical, and managerial issues, as well as to provide insight into emerging trends and future opportunities within the discipline.

Cloud Security: Concepts, Methodologies, Tools, and Applications is organized into eight distinct sections that provide comprehensive coverage of important topics. The sections are:

1. Fundamental Concepts and Theories;
2. Development and Design Methodologies;
3. Tools and Technologies;
4. Utilization and Applications;
5. Organizational and Social Implications;
6. Managerial Impact;
7. Critical Issues and Challenges; and
8. Emerging Trends.

The following paragraphs provide a summary of what to expect from this invaluable reference tool.

Section 1, "Fundamental Concepts and Theories," serves as a foundation for this extensive reference tool by addressing crucial theories essential to the understanding of Cloud Security. Introducing the book is "Curtailing the Threats to Cloud Computing in the Fourth Industrial Revolution?" by John Gyang Chaka and Mudaray Marimuthu: a great foundation laying the groundwork for the basic concepts and theories that will be discussed throughout the rest of the book. Section 1 concludes and leads into the following portion of the book with a nice segue chapter, "Approaches to Cloud Computing in the Public Sector" by Jeffrey Chang and Mark Johnston.

Section 2, "Development and Design Methodologies," presents in-depth coverage of the conceptual design and architecture of Cloud Security. Opening the section is "A Multi-Dimensional Mean Failure Cost Model to Enhance Security of Cloud Computing Systems" by Mouna Jouini and Latifa Ben Arfa Rabai. Through case studies, this section lays excellent groundwork for later sections that will get into present and future applications for Cloud Security. The section concludes with an excellent work by Rekha Kashyap and Deo Prakash Vidyarthi, "A Secured Real Time Scheduling Model for Cloud Hypervisor."

Section 3, "Tools and Technologies," presents extensive coverage of the various tools and technologies used in the implementation of Cloud Security. The first chapter, "CCCE: Cryptographic Cloud Computing Environment Based on Quantum Computations" by Omer K. Jasim, Safia Abbas, El-Sayed M. El-Horbaty, and Abdel-Badeeh M. Salem, lays a framework for the types of works that can be found in this section. The section concludes with "Keystroke Dynamics Authentication in Cloud Computing" by Basma Mohammed Hassan, Khaled Mohammed Fouad, and Mahmoud Fathy Hassan. Where Section 3 described specific tools and technologies at the disposal of practitioners, Section 4 describes the use and applications of the tools and frameworks discussed in previous sections.

Section 4, "Utilization and Applications," describes how the broad range of Cloud Security efforts has been utilized and offers insight on and important lessons for their applications and impact. The first chapter in the section is "Cloud Computing and Cybersecurity Issues Facing Local Enterprises" written by Emre Erturk. This section includes the widest range of topics because it describes case studies, research, methodologies, frameworks, architectures, theory, analysis, and guides for implementation. The breadth of topics covered in the section is also reflected in the diversity of its authors, from countries all over the globe. The section concludes with "Necessity of Key Aggregation Cryptosystem for Data Sharing in Cloud Computing" by R. Deepthi Crestose Rebekah, Dhanaraj Cheelu, and M. Rajasekhara Babu, a great transition chapter into the next section.

Section 5, "Organizational and Social Implications," includes chapters discussing the organizational and social impact of Cloud Security. The section opens with "Impact of Technology Innovation: A Study on Cloud Risk Mitigation" by Niranjali Suresh and Manish Gupta. This section focuses exclusively on how these technologies affect human lives, either through the way they interact with each other or through how they affect behavioral/workplace situations. The section concludes with "Trust Management in Cloud Computing" by Vijay L. Hallappanavar and Mahantesh N. Birje.

Section 6, "Managerial Impact," presents focused coverage of Cloud Security in a managerial perspective. The section begins with "The Collaborative Use of Patients' Health-Related Information: Challenges and Research Problems in a Networked World" by Fadi Alhaddadin, Jairo A. Gutiérrez, and William Liu. This section serves as a vital resource for developers who want to utilize the latest research to bolster the capabilities and functionalities of their processes. The chapters in this section offer unmistakable value to managers looking to implement new strategies that work at larger bureaucratic levels. The section concludes with "Smart Healthcare Administration Over Cloud" by Govinda K. and S. Ramasubbareddy.

Section 7, "Critical Issues and Challenges," presents coverage of academic and research perspectives on Cloud Security tools and applications. The section begins with "A Comparative Study of Privacy Protection Practices in the US, Europe, and Asia" by Noushin Ashrafi and Jean-Pierre Kuilboer. Chapters in this section will look into theoretical approaches and offer alternatives to crucial questions on the subject of Cloud Security. The section concludes with "Privacy Preserving Public Auditing in Cloud: Literature Review" by Thangavel M., Varalakshmi P., Sridhar S., and Sindhuja R.

Section 8, "Emerging Trends," highlights areas for future research within the field of Cloud Security, opening with "Advances in Information, Security, Privacy, and Ethics: Use of Cloud Computing for Education" by Joseph M. Woodside. This section contains chapters that look at what might happen in the coming years that can extend the already staggering amount of applications for Cloud Security. The final chapter of the book looks at an emerging field within Cloud Security in the excellent contribution "Emerging Cloud Computing Services: A Brief Opinion Article" by Yulin Yao.

Although the primary organization of the contents in this multi-volume work is based on its eight sections, offering a progression of coverage of the important concepts, methodologies, technologies, applications, social issues, and emerging trends, the reader can also identify specific contents by utilizing the extensive indexing system listed at the end of each volume. As a comprehensive collection of research on the latest findings related to using technology to providing various services, *Cloud Security: Concepts, Methodologies, Tools, and Applications* provides researchers, administrators, and all audiences with a complete understanding of the development of applications and concepts in Cloud Security. Given the vast number of issues concerning usage, failure, success, policies, strategies, and applications of Cloud Security in countries around the world, *Cloud Security: Concepts, Methodologies, Tools, and Applications* addresses the demand for a resource that encompasses the most pertinent research in technologies being employed to globally bolster the knowledge and applications of Cloud Security.

Chapter 82

Examining the Contributing Factors for Cloud Computing Adoption in a Developing Country

Winfred Yaokumah
Pentecost University College, Ghana

Rebecca Adwoa Amponsah
Hightel Consults Ltd, Accra, Ghana

ABSTRACT

The growth in cloud computing adoption is phenomenal in organizations worldwide due mainly to its potential to increase productivity and enhance efficiency in business operations. However, cloud adoption is very low in many organizations in the developing countries. To gain insights into organizations' behavioral intention and usage behavior of cloud computing, based on the Extended Unified Technology Acceptance and Use Theory, the current study investigated the effects of technological, organizational, and environmental factors on cloud adoption in organizations. Using samples from five industry sectors and by employing the Structural Equation Model, the study found that facilitating conditions, habit, performance expectancy, and price value had positive and significant effect on behavioral intention to use cloud computing. But, effort expectancy, social influence, lack of motivation, and inadequate security were found to be barriers to cloud adoption. These findings could contribute toward better formulation of planning guidelines for successful adoption of cloud computing.

INTRODUCTION

The growth in cloud computing adoption and implementation is phenomenal in small, medium and large sized organizations worldwide. Cloud computing is an on-demand self-service technology platform that enables users to access computational resources anytime and anywhere (Bamiah et al., 2012). It offers businesses increased productivity and efficiency in data management. In particular, cloud computing

DOI: 10.4018/978-1-5225-8176-5.ch082

provides computing resources (including hardware, software, infrastructure, and platform) to various organizations; relieving them from owning such resources, but rather use the resources to achieve business objectives (Masrom & Rahimli, 2015). A recent organisational study reveals that 85.80% of the participants support cloud computing technology; 97.63% mention its usefulness; whereas 95.26% recognize service quality and security as the key factors in the adoption of cloud computing (Alsanea & Barth, 2014). According to Cloud Security Alliance (CSA), adoption of cloud computing is increasing rapidly because it enhances efficiency in business operations (CSA, 2011) and many organizations find cloud services flexible to use, affordable, and scalable (Aharony, 2015). Thus, it requires minimal capital expenditure (Masrom & Rahimli, 2015) and can be implemented gradually (Bildosola et al., 2015).

Therefore, cloud computing has become a suitable option for many organizations. The International Data Corporation (IDC), a worldwide cloud information technology (IT) infrastructure tracker, analyst and forecaster, provides a five-year (2015 to 2019) forecast of cloud computing. According to IDC, the total spending on cloud IT infrastructure (servers, storage, and Ethernet switches) grew by 24.1%, amounting to $32.6 billion in 2015; the annual growth rate on public cloud IT infrastructure was 29.6%; while the traditional IT infrastructure deployment recorded a decline of -1.6% (IDC, 2015). This report indicates an increasing adoption rate of cloud computing technologies while showing drastic decline in traditional IT infrastructure. Comparatively, cloud computing provides cost reduction on IT infrastructure and maintenance; improves communication and scalability; promotes business continuity; offers reliable backup and recovery services; provides automatic software integration, quick deployment, and unlimited storage; and provides easy access to information, expert service, and convenience (Hemlata, 2015). Owing to its substantial advantages, the technology is being embraced by many organizations and countries worldwide (Bildosola et al., 2015; Gantz et al., 2012; Omar, 2015).

Regardless of its numerous benefits, cloud computing has faced outright rejection (Sultan, 2010) and has been openly and strongly criticized (Armbrust et al., 2010). Zhou et al. (2012) mention lack of knowledge, poor internet connectivity, security of cloud services, lack of trust, and interoperability with existing systems as barriers to cloud adoption. Shimba (2010) points out that technical, policy, and organizational obstacles may prevent companies from adopting cloud computing services. Similarly, Yeboah-Boateng and Essandoh (2014) identify top management support, trainability, competence of cloud vendors, resistance to new technology, and compatibility with existing IT infrastructure as the key factors affecting cloud computing adoption in organizations. Notwithstanding the challenges, the benefits derive from the use of cloud computing seem to outweigh the limitations, hence its massive implementation trend worldwide (IDC, 2015).

However, recent findings indicate that cloud adoption rate is relatively low in some developing countries (Alismaili et al., 2015; Omar et al., 2015; Senarathna et al., 2016; U.S. Department of Commerce, 2016). Organizations in the developing countries need to benefit from cloud technology in order to realize increased productivity and enhanced efficiency in businesses operations. This therefore heightens the need for a deeper research into each of the cloud computing adoption factors (technological, environmental and organizational), focusing on consistent theoretical lenses, to determine factors hindering cloud adoption in developing countries, and hence offer guidelines for organizations planning to adopt cloud technology.

Accordingly, based on the extended Unified Technology Acceptance and Use Theory (UTAUT2), the goal of this study is to investigate the factors that influence the adoption of cloud computing in the context of a developing country, in particular Ghana. In order to achieve the objective of this study, three research questions are formulated: (a) what is the impact of technological factors on the adoption of cloud computing? (b) to what extent do organizational factors impact the adoption of cloud computing? and (c) what impact has environmental factors have on the adoption of cloud computing?

LITERATURE REVIEW

According to National Institute of Standards and Technology (NIST, 2011), cloud computing has five essential characteristics, three main service models, and four deployment models.

Essential Characteristics

Cloud computing has five essential characteristics including on-demand self-service, broad network access, resource pooling, rapid elasticity, and measured service. On-demand self-service enables delivering of computing capabilities (such as server time and network storage) automatically to cloud computing consumers without any interaction of the service providers (Gutierrez et al., 2015). Broad network access is the capabilities of cloud consumers to access the available infrastructure through standard mechanisms that promote the use of heterogeneous thin or thick client platforms (e.g., mobile phones, tablets, laptops, and workstations) (Zissis & Lekkas, 2012). Resource pooling involves cloud resources that are pooled to serve various consumers using a multi-tenant model. This mean assigning and re-assigning of both physical and virtual resources (such as storage, processing, and memory) to customers can be done dynamically based on their demands without having any control of the location of the resource (Lee, 2015). Rapid elasticity is the capabilities of the cloud system to quickly and automatically release the pooled resources to the appropriate customers on demand in any quantity at any time (Gutierrez, 2015; Lee, 2015). Measured service is the capability of monitoring, controlling, reporting, and providing transparency of cloud service utilization to both provider and consumer automatically (Lee, 2015).

Service Models

Cloud computing has three main service models, which are Software as a Service (SaaS), Platform as a Service (PaaS), and Infrastructure as a Service (IaaS). Software as a Service (SaaS) allows a consumer to use the pooled resources (applications) hosted on the cloud infrastructure through various client devices using web browsers or program interfaces (Lee, 2015). Platform as a Service (PaaS) provides the cloud consumers access to deploy the applications developed or acquired on the cloud infrastructure (Gutierrez, 2015). In this case, the consumer does not manage the infrastructure (network, servers, operating systems, or storage), but can have access to some configuration settings related to the application. Infrastructure as a Service (IaaS) is where the consumer, to some extent, is granted access and control over cloud infrastructure such as operating systems, storage, deployed applications and other networking modules like the host firewalls (Lee, 2015).

Deployment Models

NIST (2011) outlined four basic models cloud systems can be deployed. According to Sen (2013), these deployment models are based on who provides and who accesses the service. The deployment models include private cloud, public cloud, community cloud, and hybrid cloud. Private cloud services are provided solely for an organization and are managed by that organization or a third party (Sen, 2013). These services may exist either on-site or off-site. Public cloud services are opened to the general public and owned by an organization selling the cloud services, for example, Amazon cloud service (Williams, 2012). Community cloud services are shared by several organizations for supporting a specific community that has shared concerns (e.g., mission, security requirements, policy, and compliance considerations). These services may be managed by the organizations or a third party and may exist on or off the organisation's premises. A special case of community cloud is the Government or G-Cloud (Sen, 2013). This type of cloud computing is provided by one or more agencies (service provider role), for use by all, or most, government agencies (user role). Finally, hybrid cloud is the composition of different cloud computing infrastructure (public, private and community) (Gutierrez, 2015). An example of the hybrid cloud is the data stored in private cloud of a travel agency that is manipulated by a program running in the public cloud.

Theoretical Background

Previous studies, many of which were based on developed countries, have been conducted to investigate the factors that impacted the adoption of cloud computing. Most of these studies used various technology acceptance theories and models to validate the findings. For instance, Gutierrez et al. (2015) conducted a survey in United Kingdom to determine the influential factors of a manager's decision in adopting cloud computing technology using the Technology-Organisation-Environment (TOE) framework. The study identified competitive pressure, complexity, technology readiness and trading partner's pressure as the most significant factors for cloud adoption decision (Gutierrez et al, 2015). A study in India found similar results. Based on the integrated Technology Acceptance Model - Technology Organization and Environment (TAM-TOE) model, Hemlata et al. (2015) investigated the determinants of cloud computing adoption in India. Data were collected from 280 IT companies and the results identified relative advantage, compatibility, complexity, organizational readiness, top management commitment, and training and education as key determinants that affect cloud computing adoption; while competitive pressure and trading partners' support were identified as the main intention to adopt cloud computing (Hemlata et al., 2015). Stieninger et al (2014) and Oliveira et al (2014) both used integrated Diffusion of Innovations Theory (DOI) and TOE frameworks to identify cloud computing adoption factors. Shiau and Chau (2015) investigated students' behavioral intention of adopting cloud computing in the classroom environment by employing multiple acceptance models including Theory of Reasoned Action (TRA), Theory of Planned Behavior (TPB), TAM, Service Quality (SQ), Self-Efficacy (SE), Motivational Model (MM), and Innovation Diffusion Theory (IDT).

The UTAUT model proposed by Venkatesh has also been used in studies on technology adoption. The model consists of performance expectancy (the degree to which an individual believes that adopting a technology will help to increase work performance); effort expectancy (the degree of ease associated with the use of the technology); social influence (the degree to which an individual perceives others to believe that one should use a new technology); facilitation condition (the degree to which an individual believes that an organizational and technical infrastructure exists to support the use of the system); and behavioral intention (the degree to which a person has formulated conscious plans to perform or not to perform some specified future behavior) (Venkatesh, et.al., 2012). In 2012, Venkatesh proposed a new version of UTAUT model known as UTAUT2. The purpose of the new model is to validate behavioral intention of technology acceptance from the context of the consumer (Venkatesh et al. 2012).

The UTAUT2 model extended the former UTAUT by adding three new constructs as determinants of behavioral intention. The new constructs include hedonic motivation, price value, and habit. Hedonic motivation is the enjoyment or happiness resulting from using a new technology (Brown, Venkatesh, & Goyal, 2014). Price value refers to the cost associated with the purchase of devices and services, which users have to bear (Venkatesh, et.al. 2012). Habit is the degree to which a person has a regular tendency to perform or not to perform some specified future behavior (Venkatesh, et.al. 2012). Thus, UTAUT2 model contains seven constructs with three moderation factors: Age, gender, and experience.

Conceptual Model and Hypotheses

This current study employs UTAUT2 as an appropriate and a suitable model because of its comprehensiveness, validity, and the reliability of its constructs (Francisco et al, 2015). Studies that used UTAUT2 model obtained a better explanation power than other technology acceptance models such as TAM and TRA (Francisco et al, 2015). This current study utilises all the seven constructs on the UTAUT2 model. In addition, the perceived security construct has been added to measure the degree of confidence organizations have in adopting cloud computing. The eight constructs are considered to have influence on an organization's use behavior (actual use) of cloud computing mediated through behavioral intention to adopt cloud computing (see Figure 1). Moreover, two constructs, facilitating conditions and habit, are hypothesized to have direct influence on the actual use of cloud computing. Thus, the UTAUT2 model will help explain the factors that organizations consider when deciding on adopting cloud computing. In line with the previous studies (Gutierrez, 2015; Lee, 2015; Tornatzky & Fleischer, 1990) and the questions this study addresses, the eight constructs (factors) have been categorized into three: technological, organizational, and environmental.

Technological Factors

The technological aspects of cloud computing that influence its adoption could be categorized as (1) relative advantage – this is a degree to which a perceived innovation is regarded as being improved or better than the original knowledge it is intended to replace (Rogers, 2003; Yeboah-Boateng & Essandoh, 2014), (2) compatibility – the capability of companies to easily deploy and integrate applications onto the cloud infrastructure with no or just few technological challenges (Yeboah-Boateng & Essandoh, 2014), (3) trialability – the ability of users to undergo pilot studies (trial) to understand and embrace the new technology (Rogers, 2003; Wu et al, 2013), and (4) complexity – this entails whether users find it very complex and uncertain when migrating from the they are system already conversant with (Gartner, 2012; Morgan & Conboy, 2013).

Figure 1 shows three technological factors and their influence on behavioral intention (BI) to use cloud computing. Performance expectancy (PE) describes an organization's belief that adopting cloud computing technology would help achieve increase work performance and productivity. Performance expectancy indicators include perceived usefulness, relative advantage, and extrinsic motivation. Previous studies indicated that performance expectancy has direct influence on behavioral intention (Jati & Laksito, 2012; Ir & Lisandy, 2014; Venkatesh et. al., 2012). Moreover, the price value (PV) is the cost associated with the purchase of devices and services, which the organization has to bear (Venkatesh, et.al. 2012) when adopting cloud computing. The price value (PV) includes the cost involved in using cloud services as compared to the traditional computing (such as purchasing software, platforms, and any computing infrastructure required by the organization). According to Venkatesh et al. (2012), PV has direct significant impact on consumer's technology use. Effort expectancy (EE) is how easy or difficult it is for a user to use a particular technology (Nguyen et al., 2014; Venkatesh et. al., 2012). This can also be referred to as perceived ease of use and complexity in TAM and IDT models respectively (Davis, 1989; Rogers, 1962). Some studies have validated effort expectancy's direct influence on behavioral intention (Nguyen et al., 2014; Venkatesh et. al., 2012; Venkatesh et. al., 2003). The hypotheses of the three technological factors are, therefore, stated as follows:

H1: PE has positive and significant influence on BI of adopting cloud computing.
H2: EE has positive and significant influence on BI of adopting cloud computing.
H3: PV has positive and significant influence on BI of adopting cloud computing.

Organizational Factors

This indicates the influential factors within the organization with regards to the technology being adopted. Achieving successful technology acceptance depends on taking into account individual traits, such as cognitive appraisal, personal innovativeness, openness to experience as well as support from top management (Aharony, 2015; Lee, 2015; Yeboah-Boateng & Essandoh, 2014). The organizational factors consist of facilitating condition (FC) and hedonic motivation (HM). FC is the degree to which the organization believes it has the required organizational structure in connection with the use of the new technology. This construct is also described in previous models. For example, in TAM it has been described as perceived behavioral control (Davis, 1989) and in IDT as compatibility (Rogers; 1995). The second organizational factor is HM, which plays a significant role in determining an organization's perception of adopting a new technology. HM represents the joy or fun a person gets in using a new technology (Brown & Venkatesh 2005; Venkatesh et. al. 2012). Studies in information systems revealed that HM has direct influence on a consumer's technology acceptance and use, which is an important determinant of behavioral intention (Bhatiasevi, 2015; Chong & Ngai 2013; Lewis et al. 2013; Nguyen et. al. 2014; Raman & Don, 2013; Venkatesh et. al. 2012; Yang & Forney 2012).

H4: FC has positive and significant influence on BI of adopting cloud computing.
H5: FC has positive and significant influence on Actual Use (USE) of cloud computing.
H6: HM has positive and significant influence on BI of adopting cloud computing.

Environmental Factors

This involves the social impact from the industrial segment, which may include competitors (Tornatzky & Fleischer, 1990), government, market uncertainty (Lee, 2015), trading partners and customers, and regulatory policy compliance (Aharony, 2015). Security and legal issues are identified as the major environmental factors of cloud computing adoption. Issues regarding data jurisdictions, data confidentiality, and security risks were very important to most companies since they do not know where their data is being stored, the legislation around the jurisdiction, and the data protection or governance procedures put in place.

The environmental factors include security (SE), social influence (SI), and habit (HB). SE is the extent to which organizations trust that their cloud service providers would protect their sensitive data.

Also, SI is the influence posed by the social environment that has direct impact on an organization as to whether to or not to use a new technology. These factors include subjective norm, social influence, and image. Research indicated that SI has direct influence on consumers' behavioral intention (Ir & Lisandy, 2014; Venkatesh et. al., 2012). Moreover, HB is the extent to which people tend to perform behaviors automatically because of learning (Venkatesh et al. 2012). Studies affirmed habit's significant effect on behavioral intention to adopt and use a new technology (Nguyen et. al., 2014; Ir & Lisandy, 2014; Venkatesh et al., 2012). The hypotheses involving the three environmental factors are as follows:

H7: SE has positive and significant influence on BI of adopting cloud computing.
H8: SI has positive and significant influence on BI of adopting cloud computing.
H9: HB has positive and significant influence on BI of cloud computing adoption.
H10: HB has positive and significant influence on Actual Use (USE) of cloud computing.

Finally, Behavioral Intention (BI) is the degree to which a person has formulated conscious plans to perform or not to perform some specified future behavior (Venkatesh et al., 2012). In this study, BI is used to describe the organization's greatest desire to adopt and implement cloud technology, while use behavior (USE) on the other hand describes the passion of using cloud technology in daily life. According to Venkatesh et al. (2012), behavioral intention has direct effect on use behavior of a technology, therefore, leading to the following hypothesis.

H11: BI has positive and significant influence on Actual Use (USE) of cloud computing.
H3: PV has positive and significant influence on BI of adopting cloud computing.

METHODOLOGY

Research Design, Sampling and Data Collection

A research method involved the techniques and instruments used in collecting data for a study (Bryman & Bell, 2015). This study used quantitative with a cross-sectional survey where questionnaires were distributed to targeted respondents within different organizational sectors in order to quantitatively ascertain the effect of various factors on cloud computing behavioral intention to adopt and the actual use behavior of cloud computing. An exploratory research was initially conducted to identify an appropriate theoretical technology adoption framework upon which to base the current study. The study adopted both convenience and random sampling methods. Convenience sampling enabled samples to be chosen based on availability and accessibility (Yilmaz et al., 2015). The two sampling methods were used to get access to respondents across the country, from particular study centers (convenience sampling) and from organizations (random sampling).

The sample consisted of middle and top level managers from different industry sectors who were involved in decision making in their organizations regarding both IT and business strategies. The questionnaires were self-administered specifically to employees of selected organizations in five regional capitals. Moreover, the questionnaires were given to postgraduate students in some selected universities who were offering distance and sandwich courses and fall within the targeted sample. The students se-

Figure 1. Conceptual model of behavioural intention and use of cloud computing

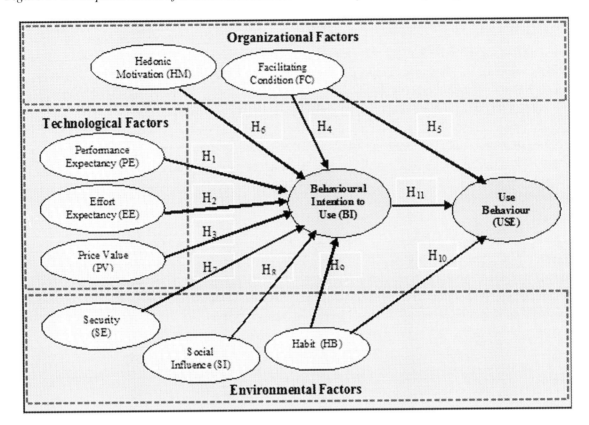

lected were managers working with organizations and at various levels of management. These students were contacted at their study centers in the respective regional capitals. This, therefore, provided ease of access in collecting data that represent organizations across the country. A total number of 500 questionnaires were administered, out of which 264 were obtained, amounting to 52.8% useful responses.

Instrument, Measures, and Data Analysis

A 70-item questionnaire instrument was adapted from Venkatesh UTAUT2 model (Venkatesh et. al, 2012) because it has been identified to have a better explanation power than other technology acceptance models (Francisco et al, 2015). This instrument has been tested, confirmed, and used by many researchers (Francisco et al, 2015; Lian, 2014; Mathur & Dhulla., 2014). The constructs consisted of 2 endogenous variables, 9 exogenous variables, and 1 variable acted as both endogenous and exogenous variable. The questionnaire was divided into two parts. The first part gathered information about the respondents' demographic data – gender, age, educational level, industry, and basic knowledge about cloud computing, while the second part asked questions about the variables in the study. The constructs consisted of (a) facilitating condition (7 items), (b) performance expectancy (9 items), (c) effort expectancy (9 items), (d) social influence (7 items), (e) price value (7 items), (f) hedonic motivation (3 items), (g) habit (4 items), (f) behavioral intention (6 items), and (i) Actual use (3 items) (see Table 1). Moreover, the model was modified to suite the context of the current study by adding one more construct, security

Table 1. Adapted items used to measure the constructs

Performance Expectancy	
PE1	We find cloud computing technology useful to our company.
PE2	Using cloud service would enable us to accomplish tasks more quickly.
PE3	Using cloud service would improve our job performance, operational efficiencies and effectiveness.
PE4	Using cloud service would increase our company's productivity.
PE5	Cloud computing allows us to use the latest versions of technologies.
PE6	Cloud computing would make data-intensive computing faster.
PE7	Cloud computing provides reliable, relevant and accurate information and services relating to my task anytime.
PE8	Cloud computing would enhance our company's data storage capacity.
PE9	Overall I think using cloud computing would be advantageous for our business.
Hedonic Motivation	
HM1	Using cloud computing is very educative.
HM2	Using cloud computing helps overcome difficult challenges.
HM3	Using cloud computing is entertaining.
Effort Expectancy	
EE1	Learning to use facilities on the cloud will be easy.
EE2	We have a great deal of opportunity to try various types of cloud services before we use them.
EE3	Our interaction with cloud systems would be clear and understandable.
EE4	It would be easy for us to become skillful at using any cloud system.
EE5	Working with cloud computing is complicated; it is difficult to understand what is going on.
EE6	It takes too much time to learn how to use any cloud service to make it worth the effort.
EE7	We would prefer to use systems installed on our computer rather than using online services.
EE8	Using cloud services is very complex to us.
EE9	We would need some training before we can use any cloud service.
Social Influence	
SI1	There are many facilities in cloud services that will enhance our business strategically.
SI2	It is easy for our customers to switch to another company that has signed up with cloud services.
SI3	People who influence our business and our behavior think that we should use cloud services.
SI4	Joining the cloud would expose us to a collaborative cloud community.
SI5	Friend's and customers suggestions and recommendations will affect our decision to use cloud services.
SI6	We would switch to the cloud platform because the people we do business with use cloud services.
SI7	Our customers think that we should use the cloud services.
Habit	
HA1	The use of cloud services has become a habit for us.
HA2	The use of cloud services has become part of our daily activities.
HA3	We must use cloud services.
HA4	Using cloud applications has become regular to us.

continued on following page

Table 1. Continued

Facilitating Condition	
FC1	We have the resources necessary to use cloud services.
FC2	We have the knowledge necessary to use cloud services.
FC3	Cloud services are compatible with the technologies used in the nature of our work.
FC4	In order to use cloud services we do not need to technically change anything.
FC5	Can get help from the cloud providers and other cloud users when we have difficulties using the cloud platforms.
FC6	Using cloud services is entirely within our control.
FC7	We have enough Internet experience to use online services.
Price Value	
PV1	Cloud computing decreases our capital expenditure.
PV2	Cloud computing decreases the investment in new IT infrastructure.
PV3	Cloud computing eliminates the cost of licensing new software.
PV4	Deployment process of cloud computing involves a slight amount of time and effort.
PV5	Cloud computing eliminates the cost of upgrading systems.
PV6	Cloud computing decreases the cost of system maintenance.
PV7	The pay-as-you-go model of payment makes cloud computing an attractive solution.
Behavioral Intention	
BI1	Cloud computing has been discussed formally and it is part of our (IT) strategy.
BI3	We intend to continue using cloud services in the future.
BI5	We will always try to use cloud applications in my daily life.
BI6	We plan to continue to use cloud infrastructure frequently.
BI1	We will often use cloud service in the future.
BI3	We will recommend others to use cloud computing.
Actual Use (Use Behavior)	
USE1	We are currently using cloud computing service.
USE2	We intend to continue using cloud services in the future.
USE3	We plan to continue to use cloud infrastructure frequently.
Security	
SE1	Cloud computing would keep our sensitive data secure.
SE2	Using cloud service is something we do without fear.
SE3	We trust our cloud service provider for our data protection.

(3 items). All the variables were measures on a 5-point Likert scale ranging from 1 (strongly disagree) to 5 (strongly agree).

The study employed Partial Least Squares – Structural Equation Modelling (PLS-SEM) using Warp-PLS 5.0 (developed by Ned Kock, 2012) software to analyse the collected data and to examine the hypothetical framework. PLS-SEM is the statistical approach for the simultaneous analysis of hypothetical frameworks (Byrne, 2010). PLS-SEM tests and evaluates the relationships between constructs presented in a conceptual model (Hair et al., 2012).

DATA ANALYSIS

The assessment of the conceptual model using PLS-SEM analysis was performed in two steps; assessment of the measurement model and the assessment of the structural model (Chin, 2010; Hair et al., 2012; Hair, Ringle, & Sarstedt, 2011). The assessment of the measurement model was performed to examine the validity and reliability of the relationship between the latent variables and the associated observable variables, while the assessment of the structural model was done to estimate the relationships between the constructs (Chin, 2010; Hair et al., 2011).

Assessment of the Measurement Model

The model used in this study has ten reflective constructs: (a) facilitating condition (FC), (b) performance expectancy (PE), (c) effort expectancy (EE), (d) social influence (SI), (e) price value (PV), (f) hedonic motivation (HM), (g) security (SE), (f) habit (HA), (i) behavioral intention (BI), and (j) Actual use (USE). Apart from the behavioral intention (BI) and the actual use (USE), all the constructs were exogenous variables. The actual use (use behavior) was an endogenous variable, whereas behavioral intention was both an exogenous and an endogenous variable. The reflective measurement model assesses the reliability and validity, which are generally conducted by evaluating the composite reliability (CR) and the average variance extracted (AVE) (Chin, 2010; Hair et al., 2011).

Firstly, the indicator and construct reliability were assessed to estimate the reliability of the reflective measurement model for the structural equation modelling (SEM). Indicator reliability was evaluated by inspecting the loading of each indicator on its associated latent construct. According to Gotz et al. (2010) and Hair et al. (2011), the loading should be higher than 0.7 to be regarded an acceptable indicator of reliability. In order to assess the construct reliability, CR and the Cronbach's alpha coefficients (Chin, 2010; Gotz et al., 2010) were considered. However, CR is more suitable for PLS-SEM as Cronbach's alpha is susceptible to the number of items on the construct (Hair et al., 2011). Table 2 shows the assessment results of the measurement model, which indicated high internal consistency and reliability. Observably, all the indicator loadings were higher than 0.7, the CR ranged from 0.793 to 0.942 and the Cronbach's alpha ranged from 0.711 to 0.930. Thus, the indicator and construct reliability were within the acceptable range.

Secondly, the convergent and discriminant validity were considered to validate the reflective measurement model (Gotz et al., 2010; Hair et al., 2011). For the AVE values to be acceptable, the latent variables should be greater than 0.5 (Chin, 2010; Hair et al., 2011). AVE measures the amount of variance in a latent variable through its indicators (Chin, 2010).

Table 2 indicates that the AVE values of all of the constructs used in the measurement model were higher than 0.506. Also, all loadings were higher than 0.7. Therefore, the convergent validity of the measurement model was acceptable. Moreover, the discriminant validity is the extent to which each construct is distinguished from other constructs in the model (Chin, 1998). The test of discriminant validity implies that the AVE of each construct should be higher than the highest squared correlation of the construct of any other latent variable in the model, and that the loading of an indicator with its associated latent variable must be higher than that with other latent variables (Chin, 2010; Hair et al., 2011). Table 3 presents the comparison of the square root of AVE for each construct with its correlation with another constructs. These results indicate acceptable discriminant validity of the measurement model.

Table 2. Results of the measurement model evaluation

Construct/Indicators	Factor Loading (> 0.7)	CR (> 0.7)	Cronbach's Alpha	AVE(> 0.5)
Performance Expectancy		0.942	0.930	0.643
PE1	0.780			
PE2	0.844			
PE3	0.837			
PE4	0.853			
PE5	0.746			
PE6	0.803			
PE7	0.798			
PE8	0.810			
PE9	0.830			
Effort Expectancy		0.793	0.711	0.507
EE1	0.759			
EE2	0.744			
EE3	0.733			
EE4	0.749			
EE5	0.715			
EE6	0.710			
EE7	0.749			
EE8	0.785			
EE9	0.746			
Social Influence		0.868	0.821	0.591
SI1	0.741			
SI2	0.778			
SI3	0.752			
SI4	0.787			
SI5	0.780			
SI6	0.793			
SI7	0.819			
Facilitating Condition		0.823	0.747	0.506
FC1	0.736			
FC2	0.781			
FC3	0.751			
FC4	0.736			
FC5	0.763			
FC6	0.778			
FC7	0.747			

continued on following page

Table 2. Continued

Construct/Indicators	Factor Loading (> 0.7)	CR (> 0.7)	Cronbach's Alpha	AVE(> 0.5)
Hedonic Motivation		0.863	0.762	0.678
HM1	0.820			
HM2	0.852			
HM3	0.796			
Price Value		0.869	0.823	0.588
PV1	0.789			
PV2	0.742			
PV3	0.782			
PV4	0.780			
PV5	0.795			
PV6	0.721			
PV7	0.761			
Habit		0.896	0.842	0.688
HA1	0.900			
HA2	0.911			
HA3	0.720			
HA4	0.853			
Behavioral Intention		0.871	0.800	0.633
BI1	0.798			
BI2	0.866			
BI3	0.865			
BI4	0.823			
Use Behavior		0.805	0.732	0.592
USE1	0.798			
USE2	0.863			
USE3	0.885			
Security		0.802	0.727	0.576
SE1	0.746			
SE2	0.774			
SE3	0.847			

Note: Loadings and cross-loadings are unrotated.

Assessment of the Structural Model

Table 4 summarizes the model fit indices, namely Average R squared (ARS), Average Path Coefficient (APC), Average Variance Inflation Factor (AVIF), and the Tanenhaus GoF. According to Tenenhaus et al. (2005), APC and ARS should be significant at 5% while AVIF should be less than 5. Table 4 indicates that both ARS and APC are significant at 0.001 and AVIF is 1.762. These show evidence of good fit.

Table 3. Results for discriminant validity

Constructs	Performance Expectancy (PE)	Effort Expectancy (EE)	Social Influence (SI)	Facilitating Conditions (FC)	Hedonic Motivation (HM)	Price Value (PV)	Habit (HB)	Behavioral Intention (BI)	Actual Use (USE)	Security (SE)
Performance Expectancy	**0.802**									
Effort Expectancy	0.178	**0.712**								
Social Influence	0.393	0.315	**0.769**							
Facilitating Conditions	0.439	0.181	0.384	**0.711**						
Hedonic Motivation	0.653	0.386	0.512	0.387	**0.823**					
Price Value	0.380	0.264	0.446	0.428	0.501	**0.767**				
Habit	0.455	0.341	0.427	0.561	0.404	0.332	**0.829**			
Behavioral Intention	0.543	0.172	0.361	0.580	0.428	0.453	0.543	**0.796**		
Actual Use	0.572	0.163	0.367	0.540	0.486	0.461	0.551	0.704	**0.769**	
Security	0.535	0.274	0.350	0.608	0.481	0.385	0.546	0.511	0.536	**0.759**

Note: Square roots of average variances extracted (AVEs) shown on diagonal in bold.

Table 4. Model fit and quality indices

Index	Value/Thresholds
Average R Square (ARS)	0.621***
Average Adjusted R Square (AARS)	0.615***
Average Path Coefficient (APC)	0.188***
Average Block VIF (AVIF)	1.762 / acceptable if <= 5, ideally <= 3.3
Tanenhaus GoF	0.584/ small >= 0.1, medium >= 0.25, large >= 0.36

Moreover, the overall fit of the model is assessed with the Tenenhaus GoF, which is the Geometric mean of the average communality and average R^2 for endogenous variables (Hwang et al., 2015; Tenenhaus et al., 2005). Tenenhaus GoF guidelines proposed that GoF of 0.1, 0.25 and 0.36 represent small, medium and large fit respectively (Kock, 2013). The model obtained a GoF of 0.584, which was remarkably greater than the cut-off of 0.36 for large fit. Based on these results, it can be concluded that the proposed model has good fit with the data and measures well.

On the basis of the analyzed results from the assessment of the measurement model, the questionnaire used was considered valid and reliable in assessing the model. The R-square (R^2) measure of endogenous constructs and the path coefficients should be evaluated as part of a preliminary assessment of the structural model (i.e., inner model) and the hypothetical framework (Chin, 2010; Hair et al., 2011). The path coefficients must be significant, whereas R^2 is highly dependent on the research area. Chin (1998) suggested 0.67, 0.33, and 0.19 as substantial, moderate, and weak measures for R^2 respectively. In the present study, overall, the R^2 of behavioral intention (intention to use cloud computing), which was a dependent variable, was 0.64 and that of Actual Use (use behavior) of cloud computing was 0.70.

The path coefficients of the paths leading from facilitating condition (FC) to actual use (USE), facilitating condition (FC) to behavioral intention (BI), performance expectancy (PE) to behavioral intention (BI), price value (PV) to behavioral intention (BI), habit (HB) to behavioral intention (BI), habit (HB) to actual use (USE), and from behavioral intention (BI) to actual use (USE) were significant with an associated p values lower than 0.05 ($p < .05$). On the other hand, the paths from effort expectancy (EE) to behavioral intention (BI), social influence (SI) to behavioral intention (BI), hedonic motivation (HM) to behavioral intention (BI), and security (SE) to behavioral intention (BI) were not significant. These results are illustrated in Figure 2 and Table 5.

The effect size (f^2) is another measure that verifies whether the effects indicated by the path coefficients are low, moderate, or high, represented by 0.02, 0.15, and 0.35 respectively (Cohen, 1988). Effect size indicates whether the effect of a specific independent latent variable on a dependent latent variable is substantial (Chin, 2010). Table 5 indicates that the effect of behavioral intention on actual use was high 0.497; whereas those of facilitating condition on actual use and facilitating condition on behavioral intention were moderate (between 0.153 and 0.155); and those of effort expectancy on behavioral intention, social influence on behavioral intention, hedonic motivation on behavioral intention, performance expectancy on behavioral intention, price value on behavioral intention, habit to behavioral intention, habit on actual use, and security on behavioral intention were small (between 0.011 and 0.135).

Another important measure of the predictive capability of each endogenous construct in the model is the Stone–Geisser's Q^2. The Q^2 assesses the prediction capability of the model (Hair et al., 2011; Hair

Figure 2. Assessment results of the structural model

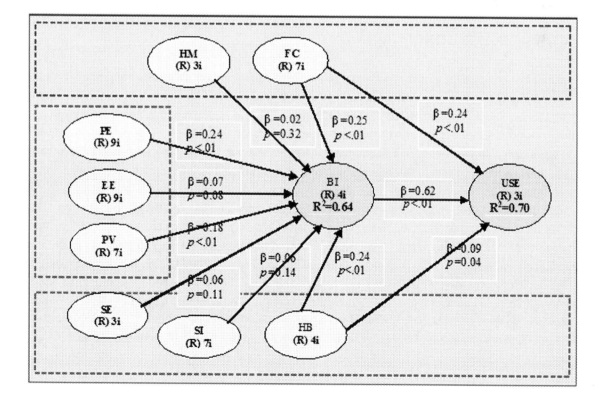

Table 5. Hypotheses testing results

Hypotheses	Path Coefficient (β)	*p*-Value	Effect Size	Support
H1 Performance Expectancy (PE) → Behavioral Intention (BI)	0.238**	<0.001	0.130	Yes
H2 Effort Expectancy (EE) → Behavioral Intention (BI)	0.071	0.079	0.012	No
H3 Price Value (PV) → Behavioral Intention (BI)	0.182**	<0.001	0.088	Yes
H4 Facilitating Condition (FC) → Behavioral Intention (BI)	0.252**	<0.001	0.153	Yes
H5 Facilitating Condition (FC) → Use Behavior (USE)	0.238**	<0.001	0.155	Yes
H6 Hedonic Motivation (HM) → Behavioral Intention (BI)	0.024	0.318	0.011	No
H7 Security (SE) → Behavioral Intention (BI)	0.061	0.112	0.032	No
H8 Social Influence (SI) → Behavioral Intention (BI)	-0.055	0.137	0.021	No
H9 Habit (HB) → Behavioral Intention (BI)	0.242**	<0.001	0.135	Yes
H10 Habit (HB) → Actual Use (USE)	0.089*	<0.038	0.050	Yes
H11 Behavioral Intention (BI) → Use Behavior (USE)	0.617**	<0.001	0.497	Yes

* Significant at 0.05 ** Significant at 0.001

et al., 2012). The predictive relevance of the construct can be confirmed when the value of Q^2 is greater than zero. WarpPLS automatically provides the Q^2 value for each endogenous latent variable (Kock, 2012). The analysis yielded a Q^2 value of 0.536 for behavioral intention to cloud computing and 0.703 for actual use of cloud computing. Therefore, each factor has a high predictive capability in achieving behavioral intention and actual use of cloud computing.

DISCUSSION AND CONCLUSION

This paper investigated the effect of technological, organizational, and environmental factors on intention to use and the actual use (use behavior) of cloud computing in Ghanaian organizations using the structural equation model. The effects of three technological, two organizational, and three environmental factors were considered essential predictors of behavioral intention to use and the use behavior of cloud computing. In particular, one technological factor, effort expectancy; one organizational factor, hedonic motivation; and two environmental factors, social influence and security, were found to have no significant influence on intention to adopt cloud adoption. Overall, our results indicated that performance expectancy, price value, facilitating condition, and habit exerted significant but varying effects on behavioral intention to use cloud computing. Facilitating condition exerted the greatest influence on behavioral intention to use cloud computing, followed by habit, performance expectancy, and price value. But the effect of effort expectancy, social influence, hedonic motivation, and security were not significant. Moreover, the examination of the direct effect of facilitating condition on actual use, and the behavioral intention and actual use was significant, while the effect of habit on actual use was minimal.

Previous studies on cloud adoption highlighted the effects of technological, organizational, and environmental factors on behavioral intention to use and the actual use of cloud computing. Some previous studies have highlighted the role of performance expectancy (Akbar, 2013; Bhatiasevi, 2015; Dhulla & Mathur, 2014; Hashim & Hassan, 2015; Venkatesh et al., 2012), price value (Dhulla & Mathur, 2014; Venkatesh et al., 2012), facilitating conditions (Akbar, 2013; Yang & Forney, 2013), and habit (Akbar,

2013) with regards to intention to use cloud computing. The results of our study were consistent with these earlier studies. However, we did not find the effect of effort expectancy, hedonic motivation, social influence, and security to be significant in the Ghanaian context. These findings contradicted previous studies on the factors of adoption cloud computing (Hashim & Hassan, 2015; Dhulla & Mathur, 2014; Yang & Forney, 2013; Venkatesh et al., 2012). Thus, effort expectancy, lack of social influence, lack of motivation, and perception of inadequate security serve as barriers to cloud computing adoption in the Ghanaian context.

Concerning our analysis regarding facilitating conditions, the result indicated that in Ghana, there were availability of the required facility (thus, resources, knowledge, system compatibility, and enough internet experience) to support the use of cloud services. Also, organizations believed that cloud computing would give them relative advantages such as usefulness, quick task accomplishment, performance improvement, efficiency and effectiveness, use of latest technology, and provision of reliable and accurate information. However, organizations perceived the use of cloud services as very complex, difficult to understand; requiring a lot of effort and skill. Moreover, social influence from other organizations and customers on the use of cloud computing has been minimal. Also, there was lack of competitive environment where customers might switch to other companies that use cloud services. Perhaps, this might be due to generally low level of cloud adoption among many organizations.

Furthermore, organizations indicated that cloud services would decrease their capital expenditure and investment in new IT infrastructure; eliminate the cost of upgrading systems, and the cost of system maintenance. While organizations believed they must use cloud services, the greatest challenge was lack of trust in cloud platform with regards to protection of sensitive data. In addition, organizations' behavioral intention and the actual use of the services contributed most significantly to the model. Base on these findings, organizations seemed to have the intention, resources, and the desire to use cloud services once other factors such as education, adequate training, trust, data security and data protection measures are put in place.

This study has important implications for both practice and theory. Due to the relative infancy of cloud technology in many developing countries, previous studies had not adequately explored factors underlying cloud adoption in the Ghanaian context. Therefore, identification of these factors is valuable to organizations planning to adopt cloud computing, assisting them in overcoming implementation barriers. Besides, the results revealed the importance of facilitating conditions, habit, performance expectancy, and price value for achieving successful adoption of cloud computing. These four factors had the greatest effect on the intention to use cloud computing. These findings can contribute towards better formulation of planning system guidelines for successful adoption of cloud computing in Ghana and in other developing countries that share similar technological, social, and environmental conditions. Though this study was limited to a developing country, the findings could serve as a reference for comparison with other developing countries as a result of the similarities in organizational, environmental, technological developments. Future study could explore cloud computing in other developing countries and compare the results with that of the developed nations.

ACKNOWLEDGMENT

We are very grateful to the reviewers and the editor of this paper for their time, insightful comments and suggestions.

REFERENCES

Aharony, N. (2015). An exploratory study on factors affecting the adoption of cloud computing by information professionals. *The Electronic Library, 33*(2), 308–323. doi:10.1108/EL-09-2013-0163

Akbar, F. (2013). *What affects students' acceptance and use of technology? Senior Honors Thesis* [master's thesis]. Carnegie Mellon University, Pittsburgh, United States.

Alismaili, S., Li, M., & He, Q. (2015). A multi perspective approach for understanding the determinants of cloud computing adoption among Australian SMEs. *Proceedings of the Australasian Conference on Information Systems*. Retrieved from https://acis2015.unisa.edu.au/wp-content/uploads/2015/11/ACIS_2015_paper_99.pdf

Alsanea, M., & Barth, J. (2014). Factors Affecting the Adoption of Cloud Computing in the Government Sector: A Case Study of Saudi Arabia. *International Journal of Cloud Computing and Service Science, 3*(6). Retrieved from http://iaesjournal.com/online/index.php/IJ-CLOSER/article/view/6811

Ambrust, & ... . (2010). A view of cloud computing. *Communications of the ACM, 53*(4), 50–58. doi:10.1145/1721654.1721672

Bamiah, M., Brohi, S., Chuprat, S., & AbManan, J. L. (2012). A study on significance of adopting cloud computing paradigm in healthcare sector. *Proceedings of the 2012 International Conference on Cloud Computing Technologies, Applications and Management (ICCCTAM)* (pp. 65-68). IEEE.

Bhatiasevi, V. (2015). An extended UTAUT model to explain the adoption of mobile banking. *Information Development, 10*(7), 1–16.

Bildosola, Río-Belver, R., Cilleruelo, E., & Garechana, G. (2015). Design and Implementation of a Cloud Computing Adoption Decision Tool: Generating a Cloud Road. *PLoS ONE, 10*(7), 308–323. doi:10.1371/journal.pone.0134563 PMID:26230400

Brown, S. A., & Venkatesh, V. (2005). Model of adoption of technology in households: A baseline model test and extension incorporating household life cycle. *Management Information Systems Quarterly, 29*(3), 399–426.

Brown, S. A., Venkatesh, V., & Goyal, S. (2012). Expectation confirmation in technology use. *Information Systems Research, 23*(2), 474–48. doi:10.1287/isre.1110.0357

Brown, S. A., Venkatesh, V., Kuruzovich, J. N., & Massey, A. P. (2008). Expectation Confirmation: An Examination of Three Competing Models. *Organizational Behavior and Human Decision Processes, 105*(1), 52–66. doi:10.1016/j.obhdp.2006.09.008

Bryman, A., & Bell, E. (2015). *Business research methods* (4th ed.). New York, U.S.: Oxford University Press.

Byrne, B. M. (2010). *Structural equation modeling with AMOS*. New York: Routledge, Taylor & Francis.

Chin, W. W. (1998). The partial least squares approach for structural equation modeling. In G. A. Marcoulides (Ed.), *Modern methods for business research. Methodology for business and management*. Mahwah, NJ: Lawrence Erlbaum Associates.

Chin, W. W. (2010). How to write up and report PLS analyses. In V. E. Vinzi, W. W. Chin, J. Henseler, & H. Wang (Eds.), *Handbook of partial least squares*. London, New York: Springer. doi:10.1007/978-3-540-32827-8_29

Chon, A. Y. L., & Ngai, E. T. W. (2013). What influence travellers adoption of a location-based social media service for their travel planning? *Proceedings of PACIS '13*. Retrieved from http://aisel.aisnet.org/pacis2013/210

Cloud Security Alliance. (2011). Data Centric Protection in the Cloud (White Paper). Retrieved from https://cloudsecurityalliance.org/wp-content/uploads/2011/11/DataCentricProtection_intheCloud.pdf

Cloud Security Alliance (CSA). (2015). *Establishes Cloud Data Governance Working Group and Releases Governance Framework*. Retrieved from https://blog.cloudsecurityalliance.org/2015/06/04/csa-establishes-cloud-data-governance-working-group-and-releases-governance-framework/

Cohen, J. (1988). *Statistical power analysis for the behavioral sciences* (2nd ed.). Hillsdale, New Jersey: Lawrence Erlbaum Associates.

Consulting, C. B. (2012). *Cloud computing Virtualización en España 2012–2015*. Retrieved from http://carlosborrasdelahoz.com/?p=272

Consulting, C. B. (2012). El cloud computing y su situación en España. Retrieved from http://carlosborrasdelahoz.com/?p=180

Davis, F. D. (1989). Perceived usefulness, perceived ease of use, and user acceptance of information technology. *Management Information Systems Quarterly, 13*(3), 319–340. doi:10.2307/249008

Davis, F. D., Bagozzi, R. P., & Warshaw, P. R. (1989). User acceptance of computer technology- a comparison of 2 theoretical-models. *Management Science, 35*(8), 982–1003. doi:10.1287/mnsc.35.8.982

Dhula, T. V., & Mathur, S. K. (2014). Adoption of cloud computing by tertiary level students – a study. *Journal of Exclusive Management Science, 3*(3). Retrieved from https://www.scribd.com/doc/218098160/Adoption-of-Cloud-Computing-by-Tertiary-Level-Students-A-Study

Francisco, L. C., Iviane, R. L., & Francisco, J. M. R. (2015). User behavior in QR mobile payment system: The QR Payment Acceptance Model. *Technology Analysis and Strategic Management, 27*(9), 1031–1049. doi:10.1080/09537325.2015.1047757

Gantz, J. F., Minton, S., & Toncheva, A. (2012, April 5). *Cloud computing's Role in Job Creation. IDC*. Retrieved from http://news.microsoft.com/download/features/2012/IDC_Cloud_jobs_White_Paper

Gartner (2012). *Worldwide software-as-a-service revenue to reach $14.5 billion in 2012*. Gartner press release. Retrieved from http://www.gartner.com/newsroom/id/1963815

Gotz, O., Liehr-Gobbers, K., & Krafft, M. (2010). Evaluation of structural equation models using the Partial Least Squares (PLS) approach. In V. E. Vinzi, W. W. Chin, J. Henseler, & H. Wang (Eds.), *Handbook of partial least squares*. London, New York: Springer. doi:10.1007/978-3-540-32827-8_30

Gutierrez, A., Boukrami, E., & Lumsden, R. (2015). Technological, Organisational and Environmental factors influencing managers decision to adopt cloud computing in the UK. *Journal of Enterprise Information Management, 28*(6), 160–170. doi:10.1108/JEIM-01-2015-0001

Hair, J. F., Ringle, C. M., & Sarstedt, M. (2011). PLS-SEM: Indeed a silver bullet. *Journal of Marketing Theory and Practice, 19*(2), 139–151. doi:10.2753/MTP1069-6679190202

Hair, J. F., Sarstedt, M., Ringle, C. M., & Mena, J. A. (2012). An assessment of the use of partial least squares structural equation modelling in marketing research. *Journal of the Academy of Marketing Science, 40*(3), 414–433. doi:10.100711747-011-0261-6

Hashim, H. S., & Hassan, Z. B. (2015). Factors that influence the users' adoption of cloud computing services at Iraqi Universities: An empirical study. *Australian Journal of Basic and Applied Sciences, 9*(27), 379–390.

Hemlata, G., Hema, D., & Ramaswamy, R. (2015). Understanding determinants of cloud computing adoption using an integrated TAM-TOE model. *Journal of Enterprise Information Management, 28*(1), 107–130. doi:10.1108/JEIM-08-2013-0065

Hwang, H., Takane, Y., & Tenenhaus, A. (2015). An alternative estimation procedure for partial least squares path modelling. *Behaviormetric Society of Japan, 42*(1), 63–78.

International Data Corporation. IDC (2015). *Worldwide SaaS and Cloud Software 2015–2019 Forecast and 2014 Vendor Shares.* Retrieved from https://www.idc.com/getdoc.jsp?containerId=257397

Ir, L.D.H., & Lisandy, A.S. (2014, August 3). Factors affecting the use behavior of social media using UTAUT2 model. *Proceedings of the First Asia-Pacific Conference on Global Business, Economics, Finance and Social Sciences.* Retrieved from http://globalbizresearch.org/Singapore_Conference/pdf/pdf/S471.pdf

Jati, J. N., & Laksito, H. (2012). Analysis of factors affecting interest utilization and use of *e-ticket* system: Empirical study on travel agents in Semarang. *Diponegoro Journal of Accounting, 1*(2), 1–15.

Kock, N. (2012). *WarpPLS 3.0 user manual.* Texas: ScriptWarp Systems.

Lee, H. T. (2015, May). *Regression Analysis of Cloud Computing Adoption for U.S. Hospitals: A dissertation for applied management and decision science* [doctoral dissertation]. Walden University, Minneapolis, United States.

Lewis, C. C., Fretwell, C., Ryan, J., & Parham, J. B. (2013). Faculty use of established and emerging Technologies in Higher Education: A Unified Theory of Acceptance and Use of Technology Perspective. *International Journal of Higher Education, 2*(2), 22–34. doi:10.5430/ijhe.v2n2p22

Lian, Yen, D. C., & Wang, Y.-T. (2014). An exploratory study to understand the critical factors affecting the decision to adopt cloud computing in Taiwan hospital. *International Journal of Information Management: The Journal for Information Professionals, 34*(1), 28–36. doi:10.1016/j.ijinfomgt.2013.09.004

Masrom, M., & Rahimli, A. (2015). Cloud Computing Adoption in the Healthcare Sector: A SWOT Analysis. *Canadian Center of Science and Education, 11*(10). doi:10.5539/ass.v11n10p12

Mathur, S. K., & Dhula, T. V. (2014). Factors influencing professionals' decision for cloud computing adoption. *International Journal of Research in Advent Technology, 2*(4). Retrieved from https://www.researchgate.net/publication/262488625_Factors_Influencing_Professional_Decision_for_Cloud_Computing_Adoption

Morgan, L., & Conboy, K. (2013). Factors affecting the adoption of cloud computing: an exploratory study. *Proceedings of the 21st European Conference on Information Systems.*

National Institute of Standards and Technology - NIST. (2011, October 25). *Final Version of NIST Cloud Computing Definition Published.* Retrieved from http://www.nist.gov/itl/csd/cloud-102511.cfm

Nguyen, T. D., Nguyen, T. M., Quoc-Trung, P., Sanjay, M. (2014). Acceptance and Use of E-Learning Based on Cloud Computing: The Role of Consumer Innovativeness. In *Computational Science and Its Applications – ICCSA 2014* (pp. 159–174). Springer International Publishing Switzerland 2014.

Nyembezi, N., & Bayage, A. (2014). Performance expectancy and usage of information systems and technology: Cloud computing. *International Journal of Education and Science, 7*(3), 579–586.

Oliveira, T., Manoj, T., & Espadanal, M. (2014). Assessing the determinants of cloud computing adoption: An analysis of the manufacturing and services sectors. *Journal of Management Processes and Information Systems, 51*(5), 497–510.

Oliveira, T., & Martins, M. F. (2011). Literature review of information technology adoption models at firm level. *The Electronic Journal Information Systems Evaluation, 14*(1), 110–121.

Omar, A., Jacques, O., & Gwamaka, M. (2015). Cloud computing adoption for business development: A TOE perspective. *Proceedings of the 9th IDIA conference, IDIA2015,* Nungwi, Zanzibar (pp. 463–476). Retrieved from http://www.developmentinformatics.org/conferences/2015/papers/33-abrahams-ophoff-mwalemba.pdf

Raman, A., & Don, Y. (2013). Preservice teachers acceptance of learning management software: An application of the UTAUT2 model. *International Education Studies, 6*(7), 157–164. doi:10.5539/ies.v6n7p157

Rogers, E. M. (1962). *Diffusion of innovations.* New York: Free Press.

Rogers, E. M. (1995). *Diffusion of innovations* (4th ed.). New York: Free Press.

Rogers, E. M. (2003). *Diffusion of innovations* (5th ed.). New York, NY: Free Press.

Sen, J. (2013). Security and Privacy Issues in Cloud Computing. In *Architectures and Protocols for Secure Information Technology Infrastructures.*

Senarathna, I., Yeoh, W., Warren, M., & Salzman, Scott. (2016). Security and Privacy Concerns for Australian SMEs Cloud Adoption: Empirical Study of Metropolitan vs Regional SMEs. *Australasian Journal of Information Systems.* Retrieved from http://journal.acs.org.au/index.php/ajis/article/viewFile/1193/721

Sharmand Consulting Engineers. (2003). *Methods of Urban Development Realization.* Tehran: Municipalities Organizations Press.

Shiau, W. L., & Chau, P. Y. K. (2016). Understanding behavioral intention to use a cloud computing classroom: A multiple model comparison approach. *Information & Management, 53*(3), 355–365. doi:10.1016/j.im.2015.10.004

Shimba, F. (2010). Cloud computing: strategies for cloud computing adoption. *Masters dissertation. Dublin institute of technology*. Retrieved from http://arrow.dit.ie/cgi/viewcontent.cgi?article=1028&context=scschcomdis

Stieninger, M., Nedbal, D., Wetzlinger, W., Wagner, G., & Erskine, M. A. (2014). Impacts on the organizational adoption of cloud computing: A reconceptualization of influencing factors. *Procedia Technology, 16*, 85–93. doi:10.1016/j.protcy.2014.10.071

Sultan, N. (2010). Cloud computing for education: A new dawn? *International Journal of Information Management, 30*(2), 109–116. doi:10.1016/j.ijinfomgt.2009.09.004

Tenenhaus, M., Esposito Vinzi, V., Chateline, Y.-M., & Lauro, C. (2005). PLS Path Modelling. *Computational Statistics & Data Analysis, 48*(1), 159–205. doi:10.1016/j.csda.2004.03.005

Tornatzky, L., & Fleischer, M. (1990). *The process of technology innovation*. Lexington, MA: Lexington Books.

U.S. Department of Commerce for International Trade Administration Industry & Analysis. (2016). 2016 Top Markets Report Cloud Computing: A Market Assessment Tool for U.S. Exporters. Retrieved from http://trade.gov/topmarkets/pdf/Cloud_Computing_Top_Markets_Report.pdf

Venkatesh, V., Morris, M. G., Davis, G. B., & Davis, F. D. (2003). User acceptance of information technology: Toward a unified view. *Management Information Systems Quarterly, 27*(3), 425–478.

Venkatesh, V., Thong, J. Y. L., & Xu, X. (2012). Consumer acceptance and use of information technology: Extending the unified theory of acceptance and use of technology. *Management Information Systems Quarterly, 36*(1), 157–178.

Williams, B. (2012). *The economics of cloud computing: An overview for decision makers*. Indianapolis, IN: Cisco Press.

Wu, Y., Cegielski, C. G., Hazen, B. T., & Hall, D. J. (2013). Cloud computing in support of supply chain information system infrastructure: Understanding when to go to the cloud. *Journal of Supply Chain Management, 49*(3), 25–41. doi:10.1111/j.1745-493x.2012.03287.x

Yang, K., & Forney, J. C. (2013). The moderating role of consumer technology anxiety in mobile shopping adoption: Differential effects of facilitating conditions and social influences. *Journal of Electronic Commerce Research, 14*(4), 334–347.

Yeboah-Boateng, E. O., & Essandoh, K. A. (2014). Factors influencing the adoption of cloud computing by small and medium enterprises in developing economies. *International Journal of Emerging Science and Engineering, 2*(4), 13–20.

Yigitbasioglu, O. M. (2015). The role of institutional pressures and top management support in the intention to adopt cloud computing solutions. *Journal of Enterprise Information Management, 28*(4), 579–594. doi:10.1108/JEIM-09-2014-0087

Yilmaz, F. G. K., Yilmaz, R., Ozturk, H. T., Sezer, B., Karademir, T., & Lin, W. (2012). Cyberloafing as a barrier to the successful integration of information and communication technologies into teaching and learning environments. *Computers in Human Behavior*, *45*, 290–298. doi:10.1016/j.chb.2014.12.023

Zhou, T., Geller, M. A., & Lin, W. (2012). An observational study on the latitudes where wave forcing drives Brewer-Dobson upwelling. *Journal of the Atmospheric Sciences*, *69*(6), 1916–1935. doi:10.1175/JAS-D-11-0197.1

Zissis, D., & Lekkas, D. (2012). Addressing cloud computing security issues. *Future Generation Computer Systems*, *28*(3), 583–592. doi:10.1016/j.future.2010.12.006

Zista Consulting Engineers. (1993). *The evaluation of the city comprehensive plans in Iran*. Tehran: Planning & Budgetary Organization Press.

This research was previously published in the International Journal of Enterprise Information Systems (IJEIS), 13(1); edited by Madjid Tavana, pages 17-37, copyright year 2017 by IGI Publishing (an imprint of IGI Global).

Chapter 83
Trust Management in Cloud Computing

Vijay L. Hallappanavar
KLE College of Engineering and Technology, India

Mahantesh N. Birje
Visvesvaraya Technological University, India

ABSTRACT

Cloud computing is a model for enabling everywhere, suitable, on-demand network access. There are a number of challenges to provide cloud computing services and to accomplish this, it is necessary to establish trust across the cloud, between the user and the service provider. It is becoming increasingly complex for cloud users to make distinction among service providers offering similar kinds of services. There must be some mechanisms in the hands of users to determine trustworthiness of service providers so that they can select service providers with confidence and with some degree of assurance that service provider will not behave unpredictably or maliciously. An effective trust management system helps cloud service providers and consumers reap the benefits brought about by cloud computing technologies. Hence the objective of this chapter is to describe existing mechanisms that are used to determine a trust worthiness of a cloud service, various models that are used for calculating a trust value and method to establish trust management system.

INTRODUCTION

Cloud computing is a model for enabling ever-present, suitable, on-demand network access to a shared pool of configurable computing resources, e.g., networks, servers, storage, applications and services that can be rapidly provisioned and made available easily with minimal management effort or service provider interaction described by Siani (2012). Cloud environments provide several benefits such as reduced expenses and simplicity to service providers and service requesters. The cloud computing provides hardware and systems software resources on remote datacenters, as well as Internet gives access to the services based upon these resources. These resources dynamically scale up to match the load, using a pay-per resources business model. The significant features of cloud computing are elasticity,

DOI: 10.4018/978-1-5225-8176-5.ch083

multitenancy, maximal resource utilization and pay-per-use. Figure 1 shows an abstracted view of the cloud computing environment with the interacting parties.

Virtualization or job scheduling techniques unifies the shared pool of resources. A host computer runs an application known as a hypervisor which creates one or more virtual machines, which simulate physical computers so faithfully, that the simulations can run any software, from operating systems, to end-user applications, Siani Pearson (2012). At hardware level processors, hard drives and network devices, are located in datacenters, independent from geographical location, which are accountable for storage and processing needs. Above this, the combination of software layers, the virtualization layer and the management layer, allow for the effective management of servers. Virtualization is an important element of cloud implementations and is used to provide the essential cloud characteristics of location independence, resource pooling and rapid elasticity. Differing from traditional network topologies, such as client–server, cloud computing can offer robustness and alleviate traffic congestion issues. The management layer can monitor traffic and respond to peaks or drops with the creation of new servers or the destruction of unnecessary ones. The management layer has the additional ability to be able to implement security monitoring and rules throughout the cloud. Figure 2 shows the basic diagram of this layout.

Cloud can worsen the damage on traditional frameworks for privacy that globalization has already started. For example, location of the data is critical from a legal point of view. But in the cloud, information might be in multiple places, might be managed by different entities and it may be difficult to know the geographic location and which specific servers or storage devices are being used. It is currently difficult to discover and meet compliance requirements, as existing global legislation is complex and includes export restrictions, data retention restrictions, sector- specific restrictions and legislation at state and/or national levels. Legal advice is required, transborder data flow restrictions need to be taken into account, and care must be taken to delete data and virtual storage devices when appropriate.

High security is one of the major obstacles for the adoption of computing as a utility as the sensitive applications and data are moved into the cloud data centers. This unique attributes, however, poses many novel tangible and intangible security challenges such as accessibility vulnerabilities, virtualization

Figure 1.

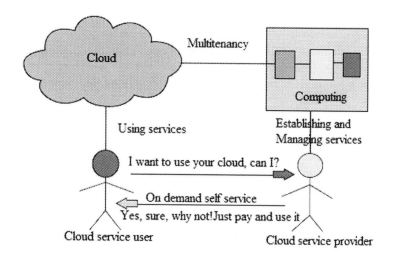

Figure 2.

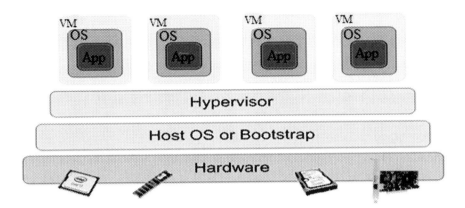

vulnerabilities, and web application vulnerabilities. These challenges relate to cloud server having physical control of data, relate to identity and credential management, relate to data verification, tempering, integrity, confidentiality, data loss and theft. To protect private and sensitive data that are processed in data centers, the cloud user needs to verify:

1. The real exists of the cloud computing environment in the world;
2. The security of information in the cloud; and
3. The trustworthiness of the systems in cloud computing environment.

There are many issues related to privacy, security and trust. The Table 1 lists those issues.

Table 1. Issues related to privacy

SL. NO	SECURITY	PRIVACY	TRUST
1.	Gap in Security	Lack of User Control	Lack of consumer trust
2.	Unwanted Access	Lack of Training and Expertise	Weak Trust Relationships
3.	Vendor Lock-In	Unauthorized Secondary Usage	Lack of Consensus about Trust Management Approaches to be used
4.	Inadequate Data Deletion	Complexity of Regulatory Compliance	
5.	Compromise of Management Interface	Addressing Transborder Data Flow Restrictions	
6.	Backup Vulnerabilities	Legal uncertainty	
7.	Isolation Failure		
8.	Missing Assurance and Transparency		
9.	Inadequate Monitoring, Compliance, and Audit		

TRUST MANAGEMENT

Trust plays a vital role in our social life. Trust between people can be seen as a key component to facilitate coordination and cooperation for mutual benefit as shown in Figure 3. Social trust is the product of past experiences and perceived trustworthiness. Based on our feelings in response to changing circumstances, we constantly modify and upgrade our trust in other people. Trust is formed and supported by a legal framework, especially in business environments or when financial issues are involved. The framework ensures that misbehavior can be punished with legal actions and increases the incentive to initiate a trust relationship. The legal framework decreases the risk of misbehavior and secures the financial transactions.

With the rapid growth of global digital computing and networking technologies, trust becomes an important feature in the design and analysis of secure distributed systems and electronic commerce. However, the existing legal frameworks are often focused on local legislation and are hard to enforce on a global level. The most popular examples are email spam, software piracy and a breach of warranty. Particularly, because legal regulation and control cannot keep pace with the development of electronic commerce, the extant laws in conventional commerce might not be strictly enforceable in electronic commerce. In addition, resorting to legal enforcement in electronic commerce might be impracticably expensive or even impossible, such as in the case of payment transactions.

This increases the importance of trust between interacting digital entities. People do not believe that the legal framework is able to provide the needed trustworthiness for their digital relationships. It has been a critical part of the process by which trust relationships are required to develop in a digital system. In particular, for some emerging technologies, such as MANET (Mobile Ad Hoc Networks), P2P (Peer-to-Peer) computing, and GRID virtual systems, trust management has been proposed as a useful solution to break through new challenges of security and privacy caused by the special characteristics of these systems, such as dynamic topology and mobility.

Establishing a trust relationship in digital networking environment involves more aspects than in the social world. This is because communications in the computing network rely on not only relevant human beings and their relationships, but also digital components. On the other hand, the visual trust impression is missing and need somehow to be compensated. Moreover, it is more difficult to accumulate accurate information for trust purposes in remote digital communications where information can be easily distorted or fake identities can be created. The mapping of our social understanding of trust

Figure 3.

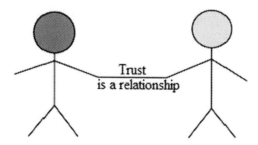

into the digital world and the creation of trust models that are feasible in practice are challenging. Trust is a special issue beyond and will enhance a system security and personal privacy. Understanding the trust relationship between two digital entities could help selecting and applying feasible measures to overcome potential security and privacy risk.

DEFINITION OF TRUST

The trust can be defined as an entity A is considered to trust another entity B, when entity A believes that entity B will behave exactly as expected and required. Thereinafter, an entity can be considered trustworthy, if the parties or people involved in transactions with that entity rely on its credibility. The notion of trust in an organization could be defined as the customer's certainty that the organization is capable of providing the required services accurately and infallibly.

A certainty which also expresses the customer's faith in its moral integrity, in the soundness of its operation, in the effectiveness of its security mechanisms, in its expertise and in its abidance by all regulations and laws, while at the same time, it also contains the acknowledgement of a minimum risk factor, by the relying party. The notion of security refers to a given situation where all possible risks are either eliminated or brought to an absolute minimum given by Zissis (2012).

Trust management is considered as one of the key challenges in the adoption of cloud computing with the accelerated growth of acceptance of cloud computing. Trust management and security are ranked among the top 10 obstacles for adopting cloud computing given by Armbrust (2009). This is because of challenging issues such as privacy, security and dependability described by Cavoukian (2009). In addition, the highly vibrant, distributed and non transparent nature of cloud services makes trust management even more challenging. An effective trust management system helps cloud service providers and consumers reap the benefits provided by cloud computing technologies. With the given benefits of trust management, numerous issues related to general trust assessment mechanisms, distrusted feedback, poor identification of feedback, privacy of participants and the lack of feedback integration need to be addressed. Traditional trust management approaches such as the use of Service-Level Agreement (SLA) are inadequate for complex cloud environments. The vague clauses and unclear technical specifications of SLAs can lead cloud service consumers to be unable to identify trustworthy cloud services. Hence different types of trust management techniques and models are designed in order to make use of the benefits of cloud computing.

Trust management is an effective approach to assess and establish trusted relationships. It is originally developed to overcome the issues of centralized security systems, such as centralized control of trust relationships (i.e., global certifying authorities), inflexibility to support complex trust relationships in large-scale networks and the heterogeneity of policy languages. Policy languages in trust management are responsible for setting authorization roles and implementing security policies. Authorization roles are satisfied through a set of security policies, which themselves are satisfied through a set of credentials. The Figure 4 gives the relation between different cloud entities and need of trust for a cloud service provider to attract the cloud users. The cloud broker and cloud auditor are the interfaces between user and provider.

Figure 4.

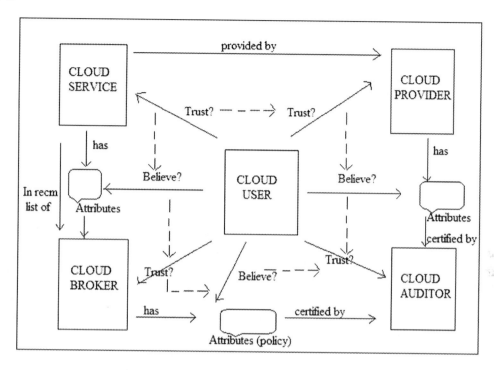

IMPORTANCE OF TRUST MANAGEMENT

Cloud Computing has a lot of research focus in recent years and it provides a virtual framework for sharing of resources. In such a distributed environment, an entity has the advantage of using collection of resources. The idea of virtual framework is not appealing to some entities because of the risk of being associated with the notion of sharing resources or services. Hence such entities prefer to use their own closed box resources for the reason of the sensitivity and the vitality of data or information. This is not just costly for the individual entities but also an inefficient way to utilize resources. To use cloud computing more effectively, trust issues must be addressed and trustworthy domains must exist where an entity can use resources or deploy services safely. In such a scenario the user/consumer and the resource provider does not have complete control over each other. The user/consumer expects good Quality of Service from a trustworthy service provider. The service provider expects the cloud resources to be protected and it allow the cloud resources to be utilized by a trustworthy consumer. To accomplish this it is necessary to establish trust across the cloud, between the user and the service provider as explained by Manuel (2008) shown in Figure 5.

An important goal of trust management in cloud resources is to establish faith and confidence on resource providers in the internet based distributed environments. Trust is a complex subject involving an entity's belief in honesty, competence, trustfulness and reliability of another entity. In most of the existing distributed heterogeneous networks, trust between a consumer and a service provider is established based on identity and reputation. This identity-based trust model is concerned with verifying the authenticity and authorization of an entity. This however does not ensure consistency, promptness of service and Quality of Service, resulting in loss to the consumers. This difficulty is overcome in

Figure 5.

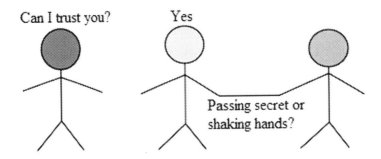

reputation-based trust management. Reputation of an entity is a measure derived from direct or indirect knowledge of the entity's earlier transactions. In this model, a certification process verifies the consistency of services offered by a service provider. The consumers who have had transactions with the service providers provide feedback on various aspects of the services provided by the service providers. The feedback received for a service provider from various consumers is aggregated over a period of time. This forms the reputation of the specific service provider and the consumer first confirms the behavior of the service provider as being trustworthy or not, before proceeding to use the service provider. This ensures Quality of Service for the consumer. This scheme is very suitable in a cloud environment where entities are distributed geographically.

The companies like e-bay, Amazon have implemented the reputation based trust management system for e-transactions and it helps them to improve the quality of service based on the user's feedback value. The effectiveness of a reputation based trust management system depends on the trust model behind the system.

TRUST MANAGEMENT CHARACTERISITICS IN CLOUD

The characteristics of trust management defined by Noor (2013) which allow the cloud users to adopt cloud are authentication, security, privacy responsibility, virtualization, cloud consumer accessibility.

- **Authentication**: This characteristic refers to the techniques and mechanisms that are used for authentication in a particular cloud. Cloud consumers have to establish their identities every time they attempt to use a new cloud service by registering their credentials, which contain sensitive information. This can lead to privacy breaches if no proper identity scheme is applied for the cloud service consumers.
- **Security**: There are three security levels in a particular cloud: the Communication Security Level (CSL), the Data Security Level (DSL), and the Physical Security Level (PSL). CSL refers to communication techniques such as Secure Socket Layer (SSL), etc. DSL refers to data replication techniques for data recovery. Finally, PSL refers to physical security techniques such as hardware security.

- **Privacy Responsibility**: The privacy responsibility can be categorized into two different privacy responsibility categories: the cloud service provider privacy responsibility category and the cloud service consumer privacy responsibility category.
- **Virtualization**: This characteristic refers to techniques that are used for virtualization. There are two virtualization levels in a particular cloud: the Operating System level and the application container level. Virtualization techniques allow the cloud service provider to control and manage the underlying cloud environment, whereas the cloud service consumers have control on their virtual machines which include the storage, the process, and even the selection of some network components for communication.
- **Cloud Consumer Accessibility**: This characteristic refers to techniques and mechanisms that are used for cloud service consumers to access cloud services such as Graphical User Interfaces, Application Programming Interfaces, command-line tools, etc.

TASKS OF A TRUST MANAGEMENT SYSTEM

This section describes the three tasks of trust management system. It begins with the initialization of trust relationships, and then identifies different means to observe the trustee's behavior during the actions. Finally, actions to take based on the new experience are discussed as described by M'armol (2011). The Figure 6 shows all the three tasks.

Figure 6.

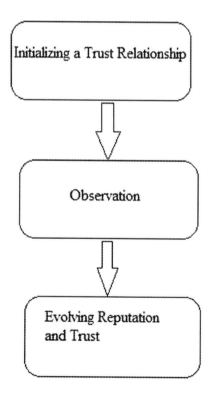

Initializing a Trust Relationship

Sometimes partners can be selected with traditional out-of-band means like word of mouth, but in a highly dynamic and possibly automated environment a discovery service of some sort is necessary. The lack of background information even if the recommending party is known to be honest and knowledgeable, their statements may be useless if the principles are not known by the same name by the recommender and the receiver, or if the principles behind the recommendations are not comparable to those of the receiver.

Recommendations remain an attempt at communicating reputation information between communities. There are three requirements for a successful reputation system:

- The entities must be long-lived and have use for reputation.
- Feedback must be captured, distributed and made available in the future.
- The feedback must be used to guide trust decisions.

The first property implies some problems that newcomers have with reputation systems. Besides having the problem of finding a trustworthy information provider, they must gain a reputation themselves. The usability of reputation information from outside sources is not limited to choosing a partner. It can also be considered as a factor in the trust estimate of a partner, along with their locally gathered reputation based on first-hand experience. Initially, as there is no local information about the partner's behavior, external reputation information may hold considerable weight in a trust decision. Besides reputation systems, various kinds of authentication and credential systems may help determine an initial level of trust through e.g. membership in a group with a good reputation. The Web Services standard WS-Trust approaches authorization and authentication via security tokens requested from on-line servers. A hybrid public key infrastructure model is proposed to ease the delegation of trust, in the sense of allowing third parties to produce credentials usable for authorization trust management in the target system.

A trust management system also tends to have some sort of a default value to assign to complete strangers. This value represents the system's general tendency to trust, or its trust propensity. This default may be raised or lowered based on a general view of the world the system operates in. If the average partner seems to be a somewhat unreliable opportunist, the trust propensity may be reduced. On the other hand, if the system operates in an environment of honest cooperation, the trust propensity may be increased. As the initial trust value is even at best based on the experiences of others with the partner, it may prove to be a poor estimate. Observing the partner's actions and updating their local reputation based on the observation strengthens the system against misplaced expectations.

Observation

Observation can be done in two different roles:

1. Either as an active participant of collaboration or
2. As an outsider, a silent third party.

In the first case, the actions of the observed are seen through a personal context, which gives more depth to the analysis. The principles and research in the field of intrusion detection can be put to use in observing users or partners in a trust management system. The traditional approach to intrusion detection looks at system calls or network traffic, while application-level intrusion detection adds "insider" understanding to the analysis by being aware of the particular applications observed.

We can divide intrusion detection into two main approaches. Anomaly detection attempts to model normal behavior, often by learning from experience gained during an observation period and considers abnormalities potential signs of an attack. The second approach, misuse detection, constructs models to match the attacks instead. While such specifications are less likely to yield false positives than detecting previously unseen behavior in general, keeping them up to date is problematic—only known attacks can be detected.

Specification-based anomaly detection shows some promise, but building specifications of normal behavior may not be feasible for all applications. It has been applied to network protocols, and could maybe find a place in the field of Web Services. On the other hand, misuse intrusion detection would also miss some attacks due to not knowing them beforehand. The idea of preventing policy-breaking or otherwise suspicious activity is not new. Access control lists have for long prevented users without specific identity tied privileges from accessing certain files or services, and policy languages can be used to further limit access according to other constraints. They can also be used to lower the resources allocated for a slightly risky task which is not considered to be in direct conflict with policy, and as mentioned earlier, the task can be allowed to proceed normally, but under tighter observation as with trust decisions. Similar adjustments could be based on trust instead of more static, pre-set constraints. Besides detecting suspicious activity, an observation system could be used as a witness of "normal" behavior. Good experiences lead to better or at least more "certain" reputation in many reputation systems where the users themselves act as witnesses. On the other hand, if a reputation estimate includes a measure of confidence, i.e. how certain the estimate is, a lengthy period of observation showing behavior in agreement with the current reputation may be taken as increased confidence in the reputation estimate.

Evolving Reputation and Trust

The evolution of reputation stands at the heart of a trust management system. Translating experience into updates in reputation seems to largely be work in progress. As the user's reputation is updated based on their actions, information about the changes can be sent as recommendations to reputation systems spanning larger communities, such as those used by the local reputation system to estimate the initial reputation of newcomers. The information can then be used to adjust the user's reputation in the target community as well. This requires that the recommendation includes a representation of the user's identity that is recognized in both communities. It is noteworthy that the reputation changes communicated across systems are not an objective truth by our definition, and the updates involve agreements on how the information is dealt with.

TRUST MANAGEMENT TECHNIQUES

Establishing trust is one of the most challenging issues in emerging cloud computing area. It is becoming increasingly complex for cloud users to make distinction (with respect to trustworthiness) among service providers offering similar kinds of services. There must be some mechanisms in the hands of users to determine trustworthiness of service providers so that they can select service providers with confidence and with some degree of assurance that service provider will not behave unpredictably or maliciously. There are different types of trust management techniques to support the consumers in selecting trustworthy CPs as listed in Figure 7:

- **SLAs:** In practice, one way to establish trust on CPs is the fulfillment of SLAs. A service level agreement (SLA) is a legal contract between a cloud user and a cloud service provider as shown in Figure 8. SLA validation and monitoring schemes are used to quantify what exactly a CP is offering and which assurances are actually met. In Cloud computing environments, customers are responsible for monitoring SLA violations and informing the providers for compensation. The compensation clauses in SLAs are written by the CPs in such a way so that the customers merely get the advantage of applying for compensation (e.g., service credits) due to SLA violation. This problem arises for not having standardized SLAs for the stakeholders in Cloud computing marketplace. Although, the problem is addressed by industry driven initiative for establishing standardized SLAs, this initiative is far from implementation in practice.

Figure 7.

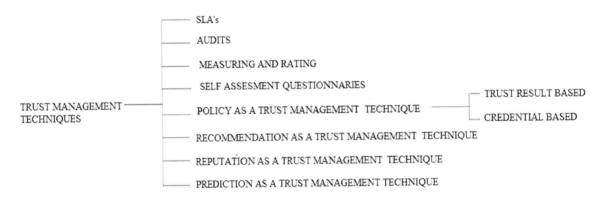

Figure 8.

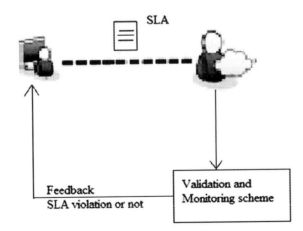

- **AUDITS:** CPs use different audit standards to assure users about their offered services and platforms as shown in Figure 9. For example, Google lists SAS 70 II and FISMA certification to ensure users about the security and privacy measures taken for Google Apps. The audit SAS 70 II covers only the operational performance (e.g., policies and procedures inside datacenters) and relies on a highly specific set of goals and standards. They are not sufficient to alleviate the users' security concerns and most of the CP's are not willing to share the audit reports, which also leads to a lack of transparency.

- **MEASURING AND RATINGS:** Recently, a Cloud marketplace has been launched to support consumers in identifying dependable CPs. They are rated based on a questionnaire that needs to be filled in by current CCs as shown in Figure 10. In the future, Cloud Commons aims to combine consumer feedback with technical measurements for assessing and comparing the trustworthiness of CPs. Furthermore, there is a new commercial Cloud marketplace named SpotCloud that provides a platform where CCs can choose among potential providers in terms of cost, quality, and

Figure 9.

Figure 10.

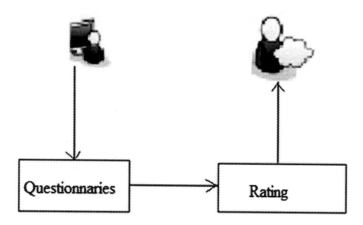

location. Here, the CPs' ratings are given in an Amazon-like "star" interface with no documentation on how the ratings are computed.

- **SELF-ASSESSMENT QUESTIONNAIRES:** The CSA (Cloud Security Alliance) proposed a detailed questionnaire for ensuring security control transparency of CPs – called the CAIQ (Consensus Assessment Initiative Questionnaire). The Figure 11 shows the cloud providers answering the questionnaires. This questionnaire provides means for assessing the capabilities and competencies of CPs in terms of different attributes (e.g., compliance, information security, governance). However, the CSA metrics working group does not provide any proposals for a metric to evaluate CAIQ yet. This is necessary for comparing the potential CPs based on the answered assessment questionnaire stored in the STAR. Furthermore, the information stored in the STAR repository can be checked against the CCM (Cloud Control Matrix). This will provide the assurance whether services offered by the CPs comply with the industry-accepted security standards, audits, regulations, control frameworks or not.

POLICY AS A TRUST MANAGEMENT TECHNIQUE (PocT)

Policy as a trust management technique (PocT) is one of the most popular and traditional ways to establish trust among parties and has been used in cloud environments, the grid, P2P systems, Web applications and the service-oriented environment. PocT uses a set of policies, each of which assumes several roles that control authorization levels and specifies a minimum trust threshold in order to authorize access. The trust thresholds are based on the trust results or the credentials.

For the trust-results-based threshold, several approaches can be used. For instance, the monitoring and auditing approach proves Service-Level Agreement (SLA) violations in cloud services (i.e., if the SLA is satisfied, then the cloud service is considered as trustworthy and vise versa). The entities credibility approach specifies a set of parameters to measure the credibility of parties while the feedback credibility approach considers a set of factors to measure the credibility of feedback.

Figure 11.

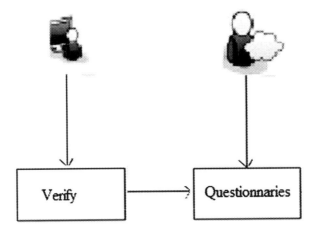

- SLA can be considered as a service plan (i.e., where the service level is specified) and as a service assurance where penalties can be assigned to the cloud service provider if there is a service-level violation in the provisioned cloud services. SLA can establish trust between cloud service consumers and providers by specifying technical and functional descriptions with strict clauses.
- The entities credibility (i.e., the credibility of cloud services) can be measured from qualitative and quantitative attributes such as security, availability, response time, and customer support.
- The feedback credibility can be measured using several factors such as cloud service consumers' experience (i.e., the quality of feedback differs from one person to another).

For a credential-based threshold, PocT follows either the Single- Sign-On (SSO) approach where the credentials disclosure and authentication take place once and then the cloud service consumers have an access approval for several cloud services, or the state machine approach where the credentials disclosure and authentication take place for each state of the execution of cloud services. Credentials are generally established based on standards such as the X.509v3, the Simple Public Key Infrastructure (SPKI) or the Security Assertion Markup Language (SAML). The digital certificates perspective can be used to define the credential term where a trusted third party (i.e., certificate authority) is required to certify the credential. However, not all credentials require a trusted certificate authority for establishing identities such as the Simple Public Key Infrastructure (SPKI) credentials where the certificate authority is not required.

Figure 12 depicts how PocT is arranged to support trust management in the cloud environment. A cloud service consumer x has certain policies Px to control the disclosure of its own credentials Cx and contains the minimum trust threshold Tx. Tx can either follow the credentials approach or the credibility approach, depending on the credibility assessment of the cloud service provider y (denoted Ry) to determine whether to proceed with the transaction. In contrast, the cloud service provider y also has certain policies Py to regulate access to its cloud services (e.g., IaaS, PaaS, SaaS), to control the disclosure of its own credentials Cy, and contains the minimum trust threshold Ty. Similarly, Ty can either follow the credential approach or the credibility approach, depending on the credibility assessment of

Figure 12.

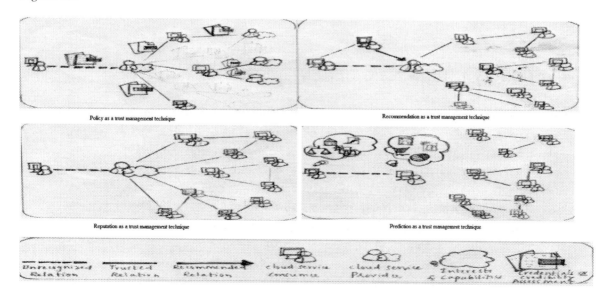

the cloud service consumer x (denoted Rx). If both trust thresholds are satisfied (i.e. Tx and Ty), the relation between the cloud service consumer x and provider y is considered as a trusted relation (i.e., T r (x, y) = 1 as shown in Eq. (1)).

$$T\,r\,(x,\,y) = 1\ if\ Cx \geq Ty \Leftrightarrow Cy \geq Tx\ or\ Ry \geq Tx \Leftrightarrow Rx \geq Ty$$

0 otherwise   (1)

RECOMMENDATION AS A TRUST MANAGEMENT TECHNIQUE (RecT)

Recommendation as a trust management technique (RecT) has been widely used in the cloud environment, the grid and the service-oriented environment. Recommendations take advantage of participant's knowledge about the trusted parties, especially given that the party at least knows the source of the trust feedback. It is well known in social psychology theory that the role of a person has a considerable influence on another person's trust assessment if a recommendation is given. Recommendations can appear in different forms such as the explicit recommendation or the transitive recommendation. An explicit recommendation happens when a cloud service consumer clearly recommends a certain cloud service to her well-established and trusted relations (e.g., friends). A transitive recommendation happens, on the other hand, when a cloud service consumer trusts a certain cloud service because at least one of her trusted relations trusts the service. *Figure 12 depicts the RecT approach where the cloud service consumer x has a trusted relation with another cloud service consumer z.* Essentially the cloud service consumer z recommends consumer x to cloud service provider y, or x transitively trusts y because there is a trusted relation between z and y. In other words, because the cloud service consumer x trusts the other cloud service consumer z, it is more likely that x will trust the recommended relation (i.e., the cloud service provider y), T r (x, y | T r (z, y)) = 1 as shown in Eq. (2).

$$T\,r\,(x,\,y\,|\,T\,r\,(z,\,y)) = 1\ if\ T\,r\,(z,\,y) = 1$$

0 otherwise   (2)

REPUTATION AS A TRUST MANAGEMENT TECHNIQUE (RepT)

Reputation as a trust management technique (RepT) is important because the feedback of the various cloud service consumers can dramatically influence the reputation of a particular cloud service either positively or negatively. RepT has been used in the cloud environment, the grid, P2P as well as the service-oriented environment. Reputation can have direct or indirect influence on the trustworthiness of a particular entity (e.g., cloud service). Unlike RecT, in RepT, cloud service consumers do not know the source of the trust feedback, because there are no trusted relations in RepT. There are several online reputation-based systems such as the auction systems where new and used goods are found and the review systems where the consumer's opinions and reviews on specific products or services are expressed. Figure 12 depicts how RepT supports trust management. The cloud service consumer x has a certain minimum trust threshold Tx and the cloud service provider y has a set of trusted relations T r(y) = {r1, r2, . . ., ri} (i.e., other cloud service consumers), which give trust feedback on the cloud service provider T f (y) = {f1, f2, . . ., fn}. This feedback is used to calculate the reputation of y, denoted as Rep(y), as shown in Eq. (3). The cloud service consumer x determines whether to proceed with the transaction based on the reputation result of y. The more positive feedback that y receives, the more likely x will trust the cloud service provider y.

$$Rep(y) = (\sum\nolimits_{x=1}^{|T f (y)|} T f (x, y)) / |T f (y)|$$ (3)

T r (x, y) = 1 i f Rep(y) ≥ Tx

0 otherwise (4)

PREDICTION AS A TRUST MANAGEMENT TECHNIQUE (PrdT)

Prediction as a trust management technique (PrdT) is very useful, especially when there is no prior information regarding the cloud service's interactions (e.g., previous interactions, history records). The basic idea behind PrdT is that similar minded entities (e.g., cloud service consumers) are more likely to trust each other. Figure 12 depicts how PrdT works to support trust management. The cloud service consumer *x* has some capabilities and interests (denoted *ix*) represented in a vector space model by binary data, *ix* = (*i*1, *i*2, . . ., *ij*), and a certain minimum trust threshold *Tx* is used to determine whether to trust the other cloud service consumers. Similarly, the cloud service consumer *y* also has some capabilities and interests (denoted as *iy*) represented in a vector space model by binary data, *iy* = (*i*1, *i*2, . . ., *ik*), and a certain minimum trust threshold *Ty* is also used to determine whether to trust the other cloud service consumers. The similarity between these two vectors (i.e., *ix* and *iy*) can be calculated using a similarity measurement such as the cosine similarity, as shown in Eq. (5). The more similar these capabilities and interests are, the more likely that the cloud service consumer *x* will trust *y*.

$$sim(ix, iy) = (ix \cdot iy) / (\|ix\|.\|ix\|)$$ (5)

$$T r (x, y) = 1 \; i f \; sim(ix, iy) \geq Tx \Leftrightarrow sim(ix, iy) \geq Ty$$

0 *otherwise* (6)

TRUST AND REPUTATION MODELS

The following section explains the different types of trust and reputation models, challenges and solutions in trust and reputation models and strength and weaknesses of the models:

- **Different Types of Trust and Reputation Models:** Ensuring security in a distributed environment such as P2P networks is a critical issue nowadays. Nevertheless, it is in those kind of scenarios in which entities can enter or leave the community whenever they want, where traditional security schemes cannot always be applied. Specifically, the use of a PKI (Public Key Infrastructure) may be unacceptable within highly distributed systems. Therefore, modeling concepts like trust and reputation may result very helpful and useful when trying to gain a certain level of security and confidence among inter-operating entities. The following section discusses the different types of trust management models defined by M´armol (2011) which are listed in Figure 13.

- **Common Challenges and Solutions in Using Trust and Reputation Models:** Trust and reputation management in P2P networks provides several benefits to electronic interactions between users, like a minimum guarantee of benevolent behavior of another interacting peer. Nevertheless, this kind of systems also has several common issues and challenges that need to be addressed when developing such mechanisms.

Modeling Trust and Reputation

One of the first things to face when developing a new trust and reputation model, or when analyzing an existing one is the way of modeling precisely that: trust and reputation. Thus, some models use bayesian networks like BNBTM, while others use fuzzy logic like PATROL-F, or even bio-inspired algorithms as is the case of TACS, TDTM and AntRep. Other models, however, just give an analytic expression to compute trust for example, GroupRep. Each way of modeling trust and reputation has its own advantages and drawbacks. For instance, fuzzy logic allows us to model concepts like trust, reputation or recommendations in a manner closer to the way humans understand them. However, fuzzy logic will be difficult to scale to larger problems because it consists of important limitations with conditional possibility, the fuzzy set theory equivalent of conditional probability. Bio-inspired mechanisms have demonstrated a high adaptability and scalability in dynamic scenarios such as P2P networks. However, in some cases, their indeterminism and approximation techniques can lead to choose a malicious peer as the most trustworthy one, discarding another clearly benevolent who could be selected. Analytic expressions are

Figure 13.

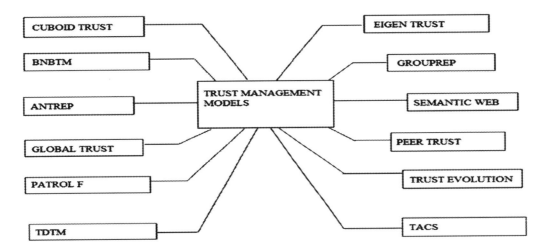

most of the times easy to read and understand, but they may not take into consideration all the possible factors involved in the evaluation of trust and reputation for a certain participant in a P2P network since they need to manage those factors explicitly, while other approaches effectively deal with them in an implicit way. Finally, Bayesian networks provide a flexible mechanism to represent multifaceted trust in many contexts of each others' capabilities (providing different services or carrying out several tasks, for instance). It also allows to efficiently combining different aspects of trust. One drawback is, however, that the approach can be computationally intensive, especially when the variables being studied are not conditionally independent of one another.

Contextualized Trust and Reputation

Another important concept managed in many trust and reputation models is what is commonly known as the context. Since a peer can be very trustworthy and benevolent when supplying a service or performing a task but, at the same time, very fraudulent or malicious when dealing with another service or task, it is not fair to identify it as fully trustworthy or untrustworthy. That is why several models like CuboidTrust, BNBTM, PeerTrust, PATROL-F or TACS include a context factor or distinguish in one or another way the trust placed on a peer depending on the task or service it is requested to supply or perform.

P2P Networks Dynamism

Not many models take into account the intrinsic dynamic nature of P2P networks (i.e. nodes entering and leaving the community whenever they want) when modeling trust relationships. Furthermore, only a few ones among the discussed models like CuboidTrust, EigenTrust, TACS and PeerTrust present experiments dealing with this issue as well as with the fact that also the behavior of peers may be dynamic, i.e., peers are not always benevolent or malicious. And how fast and accurate a model can react against these behavioral changes is an important feature that every trust and reputation model should consider. Therefore, every trust and or reputation model for P2P networks should consider three basic scenarios:

- A static one, where the topology of the network does not change along the time. This is the simplest scenario where trust and reputation models should work efficiently.
- A dynamic one, where the topology changes along the time, with nodes joining and leaving the network. This scenario could be used in order to test the reaction of a trust and reputation model against changes in the size and topology of the network, and the specific nodes composing it. This kind of experiment also allows testing how the model faces the topic of newcomers and deals with some threats like the Sybil attack
- An oscillating one, where the behavior of the nodes changes along the time, so they can be benevolent and become malicious and vice versa. Finally, this scenario would show if the model has a quick and accurate response or not against sudden behavioral changes of nodes trying to cheat. A good trust and reputation model should identify immediately these fluctuations and react consequently.

Collusion

There are also some security threats related to trust and reputation systems which are not completely considered in every model. For instance, only PeerTrust, CuboidTrust and EigenTrust explicitly treat the problem of collusion among malicious nodes. A collusion consists of several malicious nodes joining in order to increase their reputation values by fake rating themselves and, on the other hand, decrease the reputation of current benevolent peers by giving negative recommendations about the latter, as it can be observed in Figure 14.

It is not easy to overcome this problem, especially when the percentage of nodes forming the collusion is quite high. Actually, any of the studied models is completely resilient against this kind of attack. The solution is to try to minimize its global impact by punishing every node in the network which is known to belong to the collusion. There are even variants of this attack, like a set of nodes providing good services but rating positively other malicious peers and negatively other benevolent ones.

Identity Management (Sybil Attack)

It is a fact that cannot be obviated when designing and developing a new trust and reputation model since many deficiencies and weaknesses can emerge from an inaccurate management of identity. One of the most common problems related to identity management in trust and reputation schemes is what is known as Sybil attack. In a Sybil attack the reputation system of a P2P network is subverted by creating a large number of pseudonymous entities, using them to gain a disproportionately large influence. A reputation system's vulnerability to a Sybil attack depends on the cost of generating new identities, the degree to which the reputation system accepts inputs from entities that do not have a chain of trust linking them to a trusted entity, and whether the reputation system treats all entities identically.

Figure 15 shows the steps followed in a Sybil attack and some other attacks related to identity management in trust and reputation models. These steps are:

Figure 14.

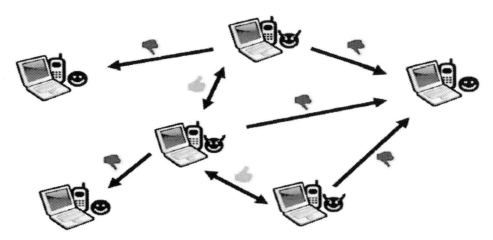

Figure 15.

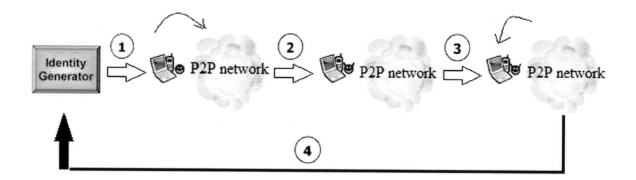

Step 1: An entity joins the community with a new identity, looking like being a trustworthy peer.

Step 2: At a certain moment (probably after gaining some reputation in the system), this entity swaps her goodness and becomes malicious, obtaining thus a greater self profit.

Step 3: Once the system has detected her behavioral change and has identified her as a malicious participant, she leaves the network.

Step 4: Finally, she generates a new identity and enters again the system, repeating the process indefinitely.

Strengths and Weaknesses of the Trust Models

After describing various types of trust and reputation models over P2P networks it is necessary to highlight strengths and weaknesses of those models. The Table 2 lists the strengths and weaknesses of the trust models.

TRUST MANAGEMENT SYSTEM FOR CLOUD COMPUTING

TM systems allow relying parties/entities to reliably represent their capabilities and competence of the underlying systems in terms of relevant attributes. In cloud computing, multiple attributes and trust information from multiple sources and roots are needed to be taken into account when selecting trustworthy cloud providers. TM system for cloud computing should be able to combine multi-attribute based trust derived from multiple sources and roots: soft (e.g., user feedbacks or reviews) and hard trust (e.g., certificates or audits).

Attributes for Trust Assessment in Cloud Computing

During the trust assessment phase, multiple attributes need to be taken into account to ensure reliable decision making in any application scenario. This is particularly true for cloud computing environments, where multiple attributes (e.g., security, compliance, availability) are important for reliably determining the quality level of cloud providers. The Qos parameters are discussed briefly below and which is mentioned in Table 3:

Table 2. Strengths and weaknesses of the trust models

SL. NO	TRUST MODEL	STRENGTH	WEAKNESS
1.	CUBOID TRUST	It shows good outcomes against above scenarios and it also considers the problem of collusion	• Direct trust or direct experiences are not given a differentiated treatment • The score takes discrete values in the set {-1,1} instead of continuous ones in the interval [-1,1]
2.	EIGEN TRUST	• It shows good outcomes against above scenarios and it also considers the problem of collusion • Moreover, it also takes into account the Sybil attack	To consider pretrusted peers there is not always a set of peers that can be trusted by default, prior to the establishment of the community
3.	BNBTM	Manages trust in different contexts, which can be combined to form an overall opinion of the trustworthiness of a peer	It only deals with three discrete valuations for a transaction
4.	GROUPREP	It provides the distinction among trust between groups of peers, between groups and peers, and only between peers	It is missing a global trust value for a peer as a result of the combination of the three previous ones
5.	ANTREP	It has ability to easily adapt to the dynamix topologies of P2P networks	It just provides a mechanism to distribute reputation evidences, not to assess those evidences
6.	SEMANTIC WEB	It clearly distinguishes between direct trust and indirect trust or reputation, and also between the trust given to a peer as a service provider and as a recommender	Searching all the paths connecting two agents may lead to some scaliability problems
7.	GLOBAL TRUST	It clearly distinguishes between direct trust and indirect trust or reputation, and also between the trust given to a peer as a service provider and as a recommender	Searching all the paths connecting two agents may lead to some scaliability problems
8.	PEER TRUST	• It shows good outcomes against above scenarios and it also considers the problem of collusion • It also introduces a context factor to distinguish the trust given to a peer for different	It does not distinguish between the confidence placed on a peer when supplying a service or carrying out a task, and when giving recommendations about

Table 3. Qos parameters

QoS+ Parameters	Who Provides the Information?	How to Derive the Information?
SLA	CPs, CBs, CCs, CCas	Standardized SLAs
Compliance	CAs, CSA	Audit Standards, CCM
Portability Interoperability Geographical Location	CPs	SLAs
Customer Support	CCs, CPs, CBs, CCas	SLAs, User Feedback
Performance	CBs, Independent Third-Party, CCs, CPs	Measurement, User Feedback
Federated IdM	CPs	SLAs
Security	CSA, CPs, CAs	CSA CAIQ, Certificate-Based Attestation mechanism, Audits
Service Deployment Models Serviice Delivery Models	CCs, CBs, CRs	Context Dependency and Similarity Techniques

- **SLAs**: The entities that are providing services are required to follow standardized SLA, e.g., proposed by Cloud Computing Use Cases community. The SLA specification of CPs then can be assessed based on the compliance to the standardized format. This compliance is further factored into trust assessment of CPs. The information regarding the SLAs is considered to be direct, as these agreements are usually between the corresponding entities (e.g., CCs and CPs, CPs and CBs, CPs and CCas).

- **Compliance**: CPs use audit standards as an assurance for the existence of technical (e.g., security) and organizational controls related to their offered services. The CAs assess these controls and issue certificates for the CPs based on the assessment reports. Otherwise, the information about those controls is provided by CPs in the STAR repository and can be checked against the CCM initiated by CSA. The results about the audit compliance can be obtained directly from the CPs or indirectly from the CSA.

- **Portability, Interoperability, and Geographical Location**: The information regarding these parameters is directly obtainable from the CPs. The existence of terms and clauses related to these parameters documented in the SLAs are the valid form of information in this case.

- **Customer Support**: CPs usually provides assurances about terms and clauses related to "customer support" in their SLAs. CBs and CCas are also required to include similar terms in their SLAs for their respective consumers (e.g., CPs or CBs or CCs). The SLA-based terms and clauses can be complemented by considering experiences from the existing consumers and factor into overall trust computation of CPs or CCas.

- **Performance**: In Cloud computing environments, the information about the performance related parameter (e.g., availability, latency, bandwidth, and elasticity) is obtained using service monitoring technologies. CPs and CBs usually provide the application for monitoring such parameters which are usually used after the service provisioning contract. CCs also can hire the independent third-party brokers (if required) to monitor those parameters before provisioning the services. In this case, the monitored or observed data regarding the performance parameters can be compared among the potential providers or with the agreed data stated in the SLAs to validate them. The validation result (i.e., success or failure) or the comparison of performances then may influence the evaluation of trustworthiness of CPs.

- **Security**: CCs want to know about the existence of certain security controls when outsourcing their IT resources to the cloud. The CSA initiated CAIQ, a self-assessment questionnaire designed for the CPs to document their security controls, to increase transparency between the providers and consumers by publishing it in a public repository. Moreover, CPs host services in trusted virtualized platforms using the trusted computing (TC) technology. In a distributed service environments (e.g., Cloud computing), consumers can learn about the security or non-security related behavior of the software components running on those platforms using remote-attestation mechanism.

- **User Feedback**: Feedback, recommendation, reviews from the consumers are valuable for service selection in e-marketplaces. This concept is also adapted in Cloud marketplaces (e.g., CloudCommons, SpotCloud) where CCs share their experiences about the cloud services they provisioned. The information about their experiences may appear as quantitative (e.g., satisfaction score) and/or qualitative (e.g., reviews) forms. Consumers' experiences can be used to evaluate the CPs as a whole or with respect to each QoS+ parameter.

- **Service Deployment and Delivery Models**: Trust models are usually context-specific and it is important to consider in the TR models for service selection in Cloud environments. The service delivery models and service deployment models should be factored as a contextual parameter in trust models. Hence, the context dependency and similarity techniques are considered complementary for the trust models in Cloud environments.

DEPENDENCE OF CLOUD ENTITIES ON SOURCES OF EVIDENCE FOR TRUST JUDGEMENT

The trust relations with various cloud entities are dependent on various sources of evidence and the derivation of a source of evidence is dependent on some trust relations either.

Properties for TM Systems in Cloud Computing

TM systems require specific properties to incorporate those attributes for trust establishment in a cloud marketplace.

Multi-Faceted Trust Computation

The computation of trust should consider the QoS+ Parameters for TR models, which refer to the competencies and capabilities of a service provider in certain aspects, for instance, providing security measures, accreditation, bandwidth or customer support. Integrating these different aspects brings up multi-faceted challenges regarding computation of trust, which are as follows:

- **Multi-Criteria:** The assessment of the trustworthiness of an entity should consider all relevant parameters, which usually means to take into account multiple parameters describing different qualities of a service (composition) or its provider. Especially the aggregation of objective parameters (e.g., expert ratings or real-time measurements) and subjective parameters (e.g., recommendations by other consumers) is a major challenge.
- **Multi-Root:** When integrating multiple parameters into a TR model, one has to consider that the quantitative or qualitative information, being factored into the trust establishment process, can be derived from different roots. Furthermore, one has to consider that those roots might have very different characteristics; for instance, information derived from a trusted platform module (TPM) or certificates provided by a property attestation authority (sometimes referred to as hard trust) need to be handled differently from trust information derived from user feedback (sometimes referred to as soft trust). Therefore, the combination of information from different roots poses another major challenge.
- **Multi-Context:** As a single service provider may offer different services that require different competencies, a computational model should be able to reflect the context in which a service provider has established trust. In Cloud computing, the different context can refer to different service delivery models. For example, a service provider might be trustworthy in delivering SaaS but not PaaS or IaaS. Moreover, if a trust model is able to consider that an entity has different trust values in different contexts, the model should be able to reason about the overall trustworthiness of an entity, or about the trustworthiness of a newly deployed service (e.g., based on the knowledge which components that are already used in other contexts are re-used for the new service).

Customization and Aggregation

Another issue that is relevant when selecting or designing of trust or reputation mechanism relates to how much customization should be supported and where should the trust values be aggregated:

- **Trust Customization (Global Reputation vs. Local/Subjective Trust Values)**: When trust is derived from different parameters, it is possible to consider subjective interests and requirements that are dependent on the entity evaluating the trustworthiness of a service provider. This leads to a local trust value. However, a global trust value is independent from who evaluates trustworthiness of a service provider. On the one hand, the local trust values provide means for considering the preference of each user in detail. Customization allows users to define the parameters relevant for trust establishment from their point of view, to weight the parameters according to his preferences and to consider which sources of information the user believes to be more trustworthy. On the other hand, service providers might be more interested in the calculation of a global trust (or reputation) value, as this might be more directly influenced and observed by the companies.
- **Trust Aggregation (Centralized vs. Decentralized)**: Usually, there are two different fundamental approaches to store and aggregate trust-related information. The first one is to host the information in a centralized repository, the other is to use decentralized approach. Both have distinct advantages and disadvantages: In centralized trust models – requiring a trusted third party – users cannot manipulate the data except by providing ratings to the central system. The aggregation methodology can be kept secret and the individual ratings of an entity are published or distributed. However, the trusted authority hosting the centralized repository may manipulate the results and represent a single point for attacks. Decentralized trust models do not require a trusted third party; however, one has to trust in the mechanisms which are used for distributing the ratings and to consider the costs for distributing the ratings among the entities. The latter can be solved by applying algorithms that aggregate the individual ratings by only communicating with an entity's local neighborhood. A disadvantage of decentralized models is that preserving privacy is much harder as more information is distributed between the participating entities.

Trust Evaluation

For complex, distributed environments (e.g., Cloud computing) we introduce a categorization of mechanisms that are relevant for trust evaluation that – to the best of our knowledge – have not been discussed in this context before:

- **Black Box Approach**: Following this approach, the trustworthiness of an entity or a service is evaluated taking into account only the observed output, for example by only considering user feedback. Models in this class treat the service as a black box, and do not require any knowledge about the internal processes and components of the service.
- **Inside-Out Approach**: Following this approach, the trustworthiness of an entity or a service is derived based on the knowledge about the architecture of the service and the trustworthiness of its components.

- **Outside-In Approach:** A model that is following this approach requires knowledge about the internal architecture of a service and its components as input as well as information stating the observed behavior of the overall service. The goal of this kind of model is to derive the trustworthiness of internal components of a service composition based on its external behavior. This is far from trivial, but can be successful when some components are re-used in multiple services and if certain errors in the behavior of the service composition can be backtracked to the originating component.

Transferring Trust Between Contexts

As stated above, customer trust in a service provider depends on the specific application context or the scope of interaction. Transfer of trust across those contexts is a significant challenge for trust and reputation systems. Consider, for example, a service provider offering an email service and a video rendering service – both belonging to the SaaS category. Both application contexts require different competencies, for example spam protection and storage for the email context, whereas for video rendering context, latency, bandwidth and parameters dealing with performance matters (e.g., response time, CDN (Content Delivery Node) facilities, etc.) are important. Here, transferring trust established in one context (email) to the other one (video rendering) is not a trivial task, and could, for instance, be supported by combining the outside-in and the inside-out evaluation.

Attack Resistance

As soon as the influence of trust and reputation models on the decision of customers will grow, the interests in manipulating those values in Cloud environment will grow accordingly. A number of different attacks e.g., playbooks, proliferation attacks, reputation lag attacks, false praise, whitewashing, sybil attacks, etc. against trust and reputation systems are present. These types of attacks will also be of concern when designing trust and reputation system for Cloud computing environments. Thus, attack resiliency is a central design goal for developers of these kinds of systems.

Transparent Trust Representation

The derived trust values or reputation scores must be transparent to and comprehensible enough for the consumers, so that they can easily and confidently make trust-based decision. To make the trust values transparent and comprehensible, users need to be supplied with an intuitive representation of trust together with enough information regarding the relevant parameters.

SUMMARY

Trust management that models the trust on the behavior of the elements and entities would be especially useful for the proper administration of cloud system and cloud services. Trust plays an important role in commercial cloud environments. It is one of the biggest challenges of cloud technology. Trust enables users to select the best resources in a heterogeneous cloud infrastructure. Security is one of the most important areas to be handled in the emerging area of cloud computing. If the security is not handled properly, the entire area of cloud computing would fail as it mainly involves managing personal sensitive information in a public network. Also, security from the service providers point also becomes imperative in order to protect the network, the resources in order to improve the robustness and reliability of those resources. Hence the need of trust management techniques and models became important.

REFERENCES

Armbrust, M., & Fox, A. (2009). *Above the Clouds: A Berkeley View of Cloud Computing*. UC Berkeley Reliable Adaptive Distributed Systems Laboratory.

Bradai, A., & Hossam, A. (2012). Enforcing Trust-based Intrusion Detection in Cloud Computing Using Algebraic Methods. *International Conference on Cyber-Enabled Distributed Computing and Knowledge Discover*. IEEE. 10.1109/CyberC.2012.38

Cavoukian, A. (2008). *Privacy in the clouds*. Identity Journal Limited.

Firdhous, M., Ghazali, O., & Hassan, S. (2011). Trust Management in Cloud Computing: A Critical Review. *International Journal on Advances in ICT for Emerging Regions*.

Habib, M. S., Hauke, S., Ries, S., & Habib. (2012). Trust as a facilitator in cloud computing: a survey. *Journal of Cloud Computing: Advances, Systems and Applications*.

Huang, J. & Nicol, D. (2013). Trust mechanisms for cloud computing. *Journal of Cloud Computing: Advances, Systems and Applications*.

Hwang, K. (2010). *Trusted Cloud Computing with Secure Resources and Data Coloring*. IEEE Computer Society.

Khalid, G., Ghafoor, A., Irum, M., & Shibli, M. A. (2013). Cloud Based Secure and Privacy Enhanced Authentication & Authorization Protocol. *Procedia Computer Science*, *22*, 680–688. doi:10.1016/j.procs.2013.09.149

Khan, M. K., & Malluhi, Q. (2010). *Establishing Trust in Cloud Computing*. IEEE Computer Society.

Paul, Selvi, & Ibrahim. (2011). A Novel Trust Management System for Cloud Computing - IaaS Providers. *Journal of Combinatorial Mathematics and Combinatorial Computing*, *79*, 3-22.

Pearson, S. (2012). *Privacy, Security and Trust in Cloud Computing. HP Laboratories, HPL-2012-80R1*. Springer.

Zeadally & Yu. (2013). Trust Management of Services in Cloud Environments: Obstacles and Solutions. *ACM Computing Surveys*, *46*(1), Article 12.

Zissis, D., & Lekkas, D. (2012). Addressing cloud computing security issues. *Future Generation Computer Systems*, *28*(3), 583–592. doi:10.1016/j.future.2010.12.006

This research was previously published in Security Solutions for Hyperconnectivity and the Internet of Things edited by Maurice Dawson, Mohamed Eltayeb, and Marwan Omar, pages 151-183, copyright year 2017 by Information Science Reference (an imprint of IGI Global).

Section 6
Managerial Impact

Chapter 84
The Collaborative Use of Patients' Health-Related Information:
Challenges and Research Problems in a Networked World

Fadi Alhaddadin
Auckland University of Technology, New Zealand

Jairo A. Gutiérrez
Auckland University of Technology, New Zealand

William Liu
Auckland University of Technology, New Zealand

ABSTRACT

The advancement in the field of information and communication technology has generated a great deal of information that was not possible to access earlier. Healthcare systems are one of the most beneficial applications using wireless medical sensor technologies, which can facilitate patient care within homes, hospitals, clinics, disaster sites, and the open environment. The integration and sharing of such information can contribute significantly to a better understanding of patients' health conditions and therefore to improving the quality of healthcare provided to them. However, in order to achieve sufficient levels of collaborative use of information among healthcare-related practitioners, there is a need to overcome a number of issues such as privacy and interoperability, among others. This chapter discusses two of the main challenges encountered before healthcare information systems can collaboratively share patients' records, namely privacy and interoperability.

DOI: 10.4018/978-1-5225-8176-5.ch084

INTRODUCTION

With the advancement in information and communication technologies (ICT) it has become easier for healthcare providers to collect and make use of patients' information promptly. These advancements have created new methods to manage patients' information through the digitization of health-related information, and have contributed significantly towards improving the health care provided to patients at lower costs. Recently, the healthcare sector has shown a growing interest in information technologies. The amount of health-care records is rapidly growing in detail and diversity and it is increasingly collected outside traditional medical record-keeping systems such as within mobile devices, wearable sensors and home wireless networks (Mamlin & Tierney, 2016). Almost half (48 percent) of healthcare providers polled in a PricewaterhouseCoopers survey said that they had integrated consumer technologies such as wearable health-monitoring devices or operational technologies like automated pharmacy dispensing systems with their IT ecosystems (Compton & Mickelberg, 2014). For instance, IoT and WSN technologies nowadays are considered as a potential solution for healthcare applications. Different researchers focus on designing wireless sensor networks for healthcare monitoring system (Vo, Nghi, Tran, Mai, & Le, 2015).

The Internet of Things (IoT) is another technology paradigm which is becoming adopted in various applications in the healthcare domain (Islam, Kwak, Kabir, Hossain, & Kwak, 2015). IoT refers to an enormous number of sensors and sensor-enabled devices deployed to collect data about their environment, which frequently includes data related to people. IoT is fundamentally a network of networks with the internet as a backbone. It associates diverse sensors, actuators, and computing systems and communications to provide intelligent services to society (Bandyopadhyay, Balamuralidhar, & Pal, 2013). The automatic exchange of information between two systems or two devices without any manual input is the main objective of the Internet of Things (Borgohain, Kumar, & Sanyal, 2015). The adoption of the IoT concept grants significant help toward collecting and accessing information that was not accessible before in real time. Areas, which are fast adopting this technology, include industrial monitoring, structural monitoring, environmental monitoring, vehicle telematics, home automation and healthcare (Rghioui, L'aarje, Elouaai, & Bouhorma, 2014). Healthcare systems are one of the most beneficial applications using wireless medical sensor technologies, which can assist with patient care within homes, work at hospitals, clinics, disaster sites and the open environment(Kumar & Lee, 2012; Yang et al., 2014). Several research groups and projects have started to develop health monitoring systems using wireless sensor networks such as CodeBlue (Karla Felix Navarro & Lim, 2009), LiveNet (Sung & Pentland, 2004), CareNet (Jiang, et al., 2008), and Lifeguard (Montgomery, et al., 2004). Such applications generate massive amount of patients' health-related data forming leading to a field of big data analytics. The term "Big Data" refers to a large amount of data that traditional database systems cannot process. Big data is a large amount of data that requires new technologies and architectures so that it becomes possible to extract value from it by capturing and analysis process (Katal, Wazid, & Goudar, 2013). Data from various sensors, hospitals and social networking sites are rich source of information for big data (Victor & Lopez, 2016). The healthcare sector has generated huge amounts of data that has huge volume, enormous velocity and vast variety. Such data also comes from various new sources, as hospitals today tend to implement electronic health record (HER) systems (Patel & Patel, 2016). Big data analytics have started to play a vital role in the evolution of healthcare practices and research. It provides tools to accumulate manage and analyse huge volume of patients' health-related information produced by healthcare systems (Belle, et al., 2015). Big data analytics in the healthcare domain is currently employed to aid the process of care delivery and disease exploration.

The enhancement of ICT in healthcare is now generating huge amount of medical data related to several aspects such as diagnosis, testing, monitoring, treatment and health management of patients, billing for healthcare services and asset-management of healthcare resources (Bock, et al., 2005). eHealth refers to the application of ICT to health, and a means of improving health services in terms of access, quality and efficiency. It is the health-related Internet applications delivering a range of content, connectivity, and clinical care (Maheu, Whitten, & Allen, 2001). eHealth applications are used by doctors, hospitals, insurance providers to record patient health information. These applications are the software and services that manage, transmit, store record information used in the healthcare treatment delivery, payment and record keeping. The eHealth field holds promise to support and enable health behaviour change and prevent from chronic diseases, it also contributes significantly in improving the healthcare services provided to patients in a more accurate manner. For example, wellness data generated by patients using wearable devices or smartphones can be a significant part of a Personal Health Record (PHR). It includes information from the electronic health record (EHR) such as health conditions of a patient, laboratory results and medical history. A PHR enables healthcare providers to obtain a much fuller and more reliable record of an individual's health and medical history. It serves as an evolving medical record of treatments provided and their effectiveness as information is added over time (Etzioni, 2010). The integration of patient-generated wellness data contributes significantly towards a better understanding of patients' health conditions by improving the communication between patients and clinicians (Grossman, Zayas-Cabán, & Kemper, 2009). Several researchers have demonstrated that utilizing patients' wellness data contributes significantly towards healthcare service betterment (Hibbard & Greene, 2013).

BACKGROUND

The healthcare industry has generated large amounts of information, driven by record keeping, compliance and regulatory requirements, and (of course) patient care. Information about patients' health generates special value when it is exchanged and collaboratively used among different parties involved in the healthcare area (Kitamura, et al., 2016). Several researchers and interviewed individuals consider immediate access to previously generated medical records during healthcare service delivery as highly important (Fabiana, Ermakovab, & Junghannsa, 2015). Healthcare information systems in healthcare organisations such as hospitals are required to collaborate with each other by exchanging information among medical staff and practitioners for medical care betterment purposes (Gaboury, Bujold, Boon, & Moher, 2009). The definition of the term "collaboration" in the field of healthcare includes the concept of sharing sensibility, a collective perspective that includes information, norms, social expectation, activity goals and meaning. It is the communication that occurs among healthcare practitioners when sharing information and skills regarding patient care (Weir, et al., 2011).

In the healthcare domain, patients usually acquire medical care from a wide range of caregivers based on their proximity, quality of care received, cultural attitudes and bedside manner. Medical care may be received from various caregivers such as hospitals, pharmacy, laboratory, physician group, nurses, school clinics, and public health places (Thompson & Brailer, 2004). This has led to fragmentation of patients' information in heterogeneous systems. The majority of this collected information is stored in heterogeneous distributed health information systems which are mainly proprietary (Kokkinaki, Chouvarda, & Maglaveras, 2006), and as a consequence, health-related information stored in these systems cannot be easily accessed to present a clear and complete picture of an individual patient when needed. For example, when a patient visits a healthcare provider such as general practitioner, he or she often requires additional medical services or attention over a period of time whether it is specialized medical examination such as magnetic resonance imaging scans, or routine medical examination such as cholesterol test and blood sugar checks.

A survey conducted by Software Advice found that 46 percent of patients want their doctors to directly exchange their health-related records while 21 percent preferred in-person delivery. When patients were asked about the way their medical records were shared among multiple healthcare providers, only 39 percent of patients said providers directly exchange records, and 25 percent had to deliver a physical document to other healthcare providers themselves. Such finding illustrates the challenge patients faced when they shared or obtain their medical records while using multiple healthcare providers (Pennic, 2015). A study in an outpatient clinic found that pertinent patient data were unavailable in 81% of cases; the entire medical record was unavailable 5% of the time with an average of four missing items per case (Walker, et al., 2004); these findings points to a need for having a certain mechanism to enable the sharing of patients' health information, and to achieve efficient collaboration among entities involved in the healthcare domain. The extensive information exchange in the healthcare domain takes place among primary and secondary healthcare providers in two flow directions as described in (Casola, Castiglione, Choo, & Esposito, 2016). The first communication flow takes place when secondary healthcare providers retrieve data about patients to provide the appropriate follow-up examination such as specialist medical services and examinations, while the second communication flow happens when primary healthcare providers are notified whenever new information such as medical records relating to a patient becomes available. Another flow of information that takes place at the administration level, for example, collecting relevant information for a range of administration-related functions such as billing. The concept of sharing information in the healthcare domain helps to better understand the health needs and therefore improve the quality of care provided to patients (Kitamura, et al., 2016). For that, the seamless exchange of multimedia clinical information is considered as a fundamental requirement. Different technological approaches can be adopted for enabling the communication and sharing of health records segments (Tsiknakis, Katehakis, & Orphanoudakis, 2002). Many efforts have been put towards facilitating the share of information in the healthcare sector in various countries, for example, the Public Health Information Network (PHIN) is an initiative developed by the Centre for Disease Control and Prevention (CDC) to establish and implement a framework for sharing public health information electronically (Rouse, Margaret, 2010). The main goal of the network is to facilitate communication among public health practitioners throughout the United States, to make information accessible, and make secure data exchange as swift and smooth as contemporary technology will allow. A virtual Health Information Network for New Zealand is another attempt that aims to create and sustain an environment that captures value from linking health data collections, through world leading health research, policy development and service planning (Olds, 2015). The European Health Information Initiative (EHII) is a World Health Organization (WHO) network committee to improving the information that underpins health policies in the European Region. The EHII network aims to foster international cooperation to support the exchange of expertise, build capacity and harmonize processes in data collection and reporting (World Health Organization, 2017).

The use of collected data is valuable source for analysis that benefit both medical research and practice. It leads to effective ways of preventing and managing illnesses, as well as the discovery of new drugs and therapies, however, there are a number of challenges that need to be overcome before obtaining the best of what sharing information in the healthcare can offer. For example, sharing healthcare information across different parties in the healthcare increases concerns related to security, privacy, integrity, and confidentiality of healthcare data. The information in the healthcare domain may contain commonly considered private information that may concern patients when sharing it with other parties. Patients require their information to remain always secure and private as a condition for granting the permission to share it among different parties. Several privacy-related laws and policies are enforced in almost every social setting to preserve the privacy of individuals' information. In fact, the share of healthcare information conflicts with two main ethical issues, which are privacy and security (Denecke, et al., 2015). In Deering (2013), the author briefly outlined a number of concerns that may arise among both providers and patients due to receiving data from patient about their health outside the clinical visit. The author also outlines a number of technical issues related to the capture, transmission, and integration of the data. For example, standardization is a challenge that is currently hindering the integration of data from the various health application systems. Information should not only be received but also understood. In fact, the utility of the current advancement of ICT in the healthcare domain is still in early stages, there is a number of challenges that require overcoming before obtaining the best of what such advancements can offer. This chapter will focus on two challenges that are currently hindering the feasibility of sharing patients' records in an effective manner namely: privacy and interoperability.

INFORMATION PRIVACY

In Whiddett, Hunter, Engelbrecht, & Handy (2006), widespread patient consultation, including NZ patients, found high levels of support for sharing their health-related information provided that such information remains secure. Personal information refers to the information that includes factual or subjective information about an identifiable individual. Information privacy refers to an aspect of information technology that deals with the ability that an organisation or individual has to determine what data in a computer system can be shared with third parties. It is the flow of information according to social norms, as governed by context (Nissenbaum, 2009). The privacy of information exists when the usage, release and circulation of personal information are controlled (Culnan, 1993).

The continuous advances in information technology have reduced the amount of control over personal data and opened up the possibility of a range of negative consequences as a result of access to personal information (Van-den Hoven, et al., 2016). Privacy related regulations are considered one of the biggest challenges to health data sharing; they prohibit the transmission and distribution of personal health information even among collaborating organisation impeding research and reducing the utility of the datasets (Ezea & Peyton, 2015). Due to privacy concerns and the lack of healthcare information sharing as a consequence of it, most of the facilities aim at building clinical decision support systems using a limited amount of patient data from their healthcare information systems to provide important diagnosis relation decisions. Moreover, it becomes infeasible for a newly established healthcare facility to build a robust decision-making system due to the lack of sufficient patient record required to train such decision-making models (Li, Bai, & Reddy, 2016). According to the Privacy Act 1993 (New Zealand), personal information should be collected directly from the individual, unless they have authorised another person to pass on their information, or if it is not reasonably practical in the circumstances.

Healthcare systems contain sensitive information that must be managed in a privacy-preserving way. For that, it is a mandatory step to adhere to legal frameworks such as the Health Insurance Portability and Accountability Act (HIPPA) (Public Law, 1996) and the Data Protection Act (Gunasekara & Dillon, 2008). Such frameworks clearly specify the responsibilities of organisations with regards to the privacy protection of personal health information. However, complying with these frameworks is both challenging and costly for healthcare organisations (Gkoulalas-Divanis & Loukides, 2015). Several attempts have been made by researchers to allow the exchange of medical information among medical practitioners / data analysts in a privacy preserving manner. The main privacy challenge remains in the management of this collected data which is still largely unaddressed (Weber, 2015). There are many policy-related issues such as privacy policies that must be addressed to realise the full potential of sharing healthcare information(Hripcsak et al, 2014; Gkoulas-Divanis & Loukides, 2015) .

In Rashid & Yasin (2015), the authors state that sharing healthcare information using healthcare information systems based on privacy preservation rarely handles healthcare information sharing among healthcare-related entities at different places; therefore, there is a need to address such collaboration based on privacy preservation. Due to the diversity and complexity of the existing healthcare structure, in which patients' health information are distributed to multiple entities such as hospitals, healthcare centres and cloud servers, an appropriate architecture is one of the most important design issues for sharing healthcare information in a privacy-preserving manner. A centralized architecture design would not be convenient due to the lack of interoperability of the vast majority of healthcare information systems. Interoperability is defined as the ability to share and use information across multiple systems seamlessly (Oude, Velsen, Huygens, & Hermens, 2015). Currently, it is determined that there is no existing single data standardization structure that can effectively share and interpret patient data within heterogeneous systems (Blackman, 2017). Therefore, considering the increasingly mobile nature of healthcare information, a non-centralized architecture would be most suitable option for the intended collaboration among healthcare-related entities.

Despite the use of information technology solutions in the healthcare industry, there are various challenges encountered such as the high infrastructure management costs, dynamic needs for computational resources, scalability multi-tenancy and increased demand for collaboration (Priyanga.P & MuthuKumar.V.P, 2015). The advancement in the healthcare industry requires modernizing healthcare information systems to facilitate collaboration and coordination among parties involved in the healthcare domain at lower costs. In healthcare, the availability of information regardless the location of patient and the clinician is a key driver towards patients' satisfaction and healthcare service betterment. For that, there is a stressing need for having a decentralized design of architecture for healthcare information systems that allows for asynchronous interactions among parties involved in the healthcare domain with respect to privacy regulation (Casola, Castiglione, Choo, & Esposito, 2016).

Cloud computing appears to be the dreamed vision of healthcare industry; it matches the need of healthcare information sharing directly to various healthcare-related parties over the internet, regardless their location and the amount of data being shared (Guo, Kuo, & Sahama, 2012). Health information exchanges enable healthcare organization to share data contained in largely proprietary information systems. Cloud computing technology is seen as a potential solution for enabling healthcare organizations to focus their efforts on clinically relevant services and improved patient outcomes (Kuo, 2011). Cloud Computing is an emerging new computing paradigm designed to deliver computing resources and services through networked media such as the Web (Sultan, 2014). It is a computing paradigm in which resources of the computing infrastructure are provided as a service over the internet (Yu, Wang, Ren, &

Lou, 2010). In the simplest terms, cloud computing refers to means of storing and accessing data and programs over the internet instead of computer's hard drive (Griffith, 2016).

The technology of cloud computing enables relatively new business models in the computing world. It offers functionality for managing information data in a distributed, ubiquitous and on-demand network access to a shared pool of configurable computing resources (Mell & Grance, 2011). Resources in cloud computing can be rapidly provisioned and released with minimal management effort supporting several platforms, systems, and applications (Doukas, Pliakas, & Maglogiannis, 2010). Cloud computing is an attractive paradigm of computing for the healthcare domain, due to the elasticity of resources and reduction of the operational costs. This allows for new ways of developing, delivering and using healthcare services (Griebel, et al., 2015). Cloud computing offers practical solutions in the healthcare domain and sharing information is one of them (Zhang & Liu, 2010). For example, the Collaboration Care Solution is a system developed by IBM and Active Health Management in 2010. The cloud-based system enabled medical and healthcare staff to easily access healthcare data and information from different sources. The system was beneficial for patients, who were suffering from chronic conditions, to connect with their physicians and follow up their prescribed medications and treatment (Aziz & Guled, 2016).

However, despite the advantages that cloud computing offers to the healthcare domain; privacy protection is a major challenge (Yüksel, Küpçü, & Özkasap, 2017). Such concerns are caused by the fact of having medical data and information, that are classified as confidential, stored in cloud servers, a virtual world where information can be easily hacked (Aziz & Guled, 2016). From the consumers' perspective, the privacy when storing and sharing health-related information on the cloud is a primary concern, because data is located in different places. Such concern prohibits the adoption of cloud computing in the healthcare domain (Chen & Zhao, 2012; Shariati, Abouzarjomehri, & Ahmadzadegan, 2015).

Information privacy is the desire of individuals to control or have some influence over data about themselves (Bélanger & Crossler, 2011). It is, in other words, the right of individuals to determine how and to what extent information they communicate to others is used. Healthcare data includes sensitive records that should not be made available to unauthorized people in order to protect the privacy of patients. Information privacy protection is very essential to build users' trust in order to reach the full potential of cloud computing in the healthcare domain. For that, an important characteristic in healthcare cloud-based information systems is the ability to assure patients that their data is protected in the cloud, and their private information will only be disclosed to responsible parties.

INTEROPERABILITY

With the advancement of the information and communication technologies (ICT), it has become feasible for healthcare providers to collect and make use of patients' information promptly. Such advances have created new methods to manage patients' information through the digitization of health-related information, and have contributed significantly towards improving the health care provided to patients at lower costs. Recently, the healthcare sector has shown a growing interest in information technologies. The amount of health-care records is rapidly growing in detail and diversity and it is increasingly collected outside traditional medical records such as within mobile devices, wearable sensors and home wireless networks (Mamlin & Tierney, 2016). The "internet of things" (IoT) is an example of such technology. IoT refers to any physical object embedded with technology capable of exchanging data and is pegged to create a more efficient healthcare system in terms of time, energy and cost (Christopher, 2016). It is fundamentally a network of networks with the Internet as a backbone. It associates diverse sensors, actuators, computing system to provide intelligent services to human society (Bandyopadhyay, Balamuralidhar, & Pal, 2013). The automatic exchange of information between two systems or two devices without any manual input is the main objective of the Internet of Things (Borgohain, Kumar, & Sanyal, 2015).

Collected health information generates special value when being shared and collaboratively used among different parties involved in the healthcare area (Kitamura, et al., 2016). Several researchers and interviewed individuals consider immediate access to previously generated medical records during healthcare service delivery as highly important (Fabiana, Ermakovab, & Junghannsa, 2015). However, despite the benefits of patient-generated data in the field of healthcare, the adoption of it in reality is still limited due to several barriers such as the interoperability of the systems involved.

The seamless exchange of vital information among healthcare practitioners played significant role in reducing medical errors and facilitated better integration of health related records (Iroju, Soriyan, Gambo, & Olaleke, 2013). Healthcare information systems in healthcare organizations such as hospitals are required to collaborate with each other by sharing information among medical staff and practitioners for medical care betterment purposes (Gaboury, Bujold, Boon, & Moher, 2009).

To realize the full potential of collected medical data, health-related IT systems and products are required to share information seamlessly among each other, but unfortunately, the vast majority of medical devices, electronic health records, and other IT systems lack interoperability. Interoperability is defined as the ability for two or more systems of components to exchange information and use the information that has been exchanged (Oude, Velsen, Huygens, & Hermens, 2015). It is the ability to share and use information across multiple system technologies seamlessly. Interoperability is a fundamental requirement for the health care system to derive the societal benefits promised by the adoption of electronic healthcare records (Brailer, 2005).

The authors in Whitman and Panetto (2006) defined four levels of interoperability namely; technical, syntactic, semantic and organizational; a similar definition was given by the European Telecommunication Standards Institute (ETSI) (Veer & Wiles, 2008). Technical interoperability refers to the ability of heterogeneous systems to exchange data without guaranteeing the ability of the receiving system to understand the data in a meaningful way. Syntactic interoperability is the preservation of the clinical purpose of the data during transmission among healthcare systems. Semantic interoperability refers to the ability of systems to interpret the information that has been exchanged in a similar way through predefined shared meaning of concepts while organizational interoperability refers to the ability to facilitate the integration of business processes and workflows beyond the boundaries of a single organization. In Diaz (2016), the author states that sharing data in a useful way in the healthcare domain is impossible without semantic interoperability among disparate healthcare IT systems. Semantic interoperability deals with the content of the message exchanged among health information technology systems. It is about the ability of systems to understand the meaning of the shared data. Interoperability is important because treatment and health care providers have increased and become more specialized, and patients have become mobile. Such large-scale adoption of electronic healthcare applications requires semantic interoperability (Sachdeva & Bhalla, 2010).

Patients' health records are often stored in a non-standard, non-coded, structured and non-structured form hindering the exchange of information among health information systems (Lau & Shakib, 2005). It is currently a major challenge in the healthcare industry to achieve interoperability among proprietary applications provided by different vendors (Cantwell & McDermott, 2016). For instance, a hospital may use one or more applications to share clinical and administrative information, and each application may support multiple communication interfaces and protocols that must be modified and maintained. Adopting common data structures within the healthcare organizations is a decision that has been met with reluctance due to financial concerns and other barriers related to changing the existing work flow and staff training costs (Gabriel, Furukawa, Jones, King, & Samy, 2014). One of the primary reasons for this reluctance is the inability of the electronic health records to interlink and communicate with each other due to the lack of comprehensive data standard that facilitates the exchange of data using a common data model (Bowles, et al., 2013). The inability of healthcare information systems (HISs) to interoperate on the national scale reaps the full benefits of e-health (ITU, 2011). In Iroju, Soriyan, Gambo, and Olaleke (2013), the authors aimed to upraise the concepts of interoperability in the context of healthcare, its benefits and its attendance challenges. The authors write: "However, as beneficial as data interoperability is to healthcare, at present, it is largely an unreached goal". This is primarily because electronic healthcare information systems used within healthcare organizations have been developed independently with diverse and heterogeneous ICT tools, methods, processes and procedures. This leads to generating a large number of heterogeneous and distributed proprietary models for representing and recording patients' information.

Heterogeneity is considered a major obstacle for healthcare information systems' interoperability. Healthcare information systems differ from application to another and from a country to another. This means that the structure of healthcare records and the methods used for exchanging their contents may significantly vary. Due to the existence of various independent data standards repositories such as LOINC (Logical Observation Identifiers, Names, and Codes), ICD (International classification diseases), and SNOWMED (Systematized Nomenclature of Medicine), it is not possible for healthcare facilities to successfully achieve interoperability. There is no unified standardization format that can act as a single comprehensive standard for data interpretation and translation of medical vocabulary and terminologies (Ogunyemi, Meeker, Kim, & Boxwala, 2013). For that, the solution is expected in the standardization of electronic health information structure, content and the way of exchanging them (Gross, 2005). Currently, it is determined that there is no existing single data standardization structure that can effectively share and interpret patient data within heterogeneous systems (Blackman, 2017).

The International Organization for Standardization (ISO) defines standards established by consensus and approved by a recognized body, that provides, for common and repeated use, rules, guidelines or characteristics for activities or their results, aimed at the achievement of the optimum degree of order in a given context (ISO, 2004). The concept of standardization grants a number of benefits including preventing from single vendor lock-in, promoting a healthy market competition with associate cost savings, reducing the risks of new technology development and removing the need for expensive customized solutions (Meingast, Roosta, & Sastry, 2006; Wager, Lee & Glaser, 2013). Standardization is an important aspect for enabling the use of networks to share and utilize medical and healthcare information. Healthcare-related information usually comes in various forms; not only names of diseases, drugs, and treatments, but also other data forms such as images, numerical values of examination results, graphs and text. Therefore, assuring the connection of different systems among institutions, regions, and nations requires integration to details such as terminology, encoding, protocol, and security (Ishigure, 2017).

Standards in general fall into two broad groups; proprietary standards and open standards (Adebesin, Foster, Kotz, & Greunen, 2013). Proprietary standards are developed for private use by profit-driven industry organizations. The specifications of such standards remain unrevealed and are subject for copyright law. Open standards are open for use by all interested stakeholders. They can be developed by for profit and non-profit organizations. The standard specifications and necessary documentations are made available for public use; either free of charge or at a nominal fee. There are various efforts that organizations globally have made to develop interoperability standards for healthcare systems. For example, the International Organization for Standardization (IOS) which is the world's largest developer of the standard has developed 162 national standards bodies globally (ISO, 2017). The ISO standards are developed by various group members in different technical committees that are made up of national member bodies. The ISO memberships options are: full, correspondent, and subscriber (ISO, 2017). Each membership category has different accessibility levels to the ISO's standards, to participation in working groups and to their development work. E-health Standards are developed by ISO's health informatics technical committee, ISO/TC 215 and those standards are meant to support the growth in the use of information and communication technology in the healthcare domain to facilitate the secure and seamless exchange of health-related information that is accessible to authorized users when required (ISO, 2013).

The World Health Organization (WHO) publishes and maintains the codes of International Classification of Diseases (ICD) for classification of diseases, health conditions and causes of death (WHO, 2017), the Anatomical Therapeutic Chemical Classification Systems with Defined Daily Doses (ATC/DDD) provides codes for the classification of medicines (WHO, 2017), and the Statistical Data and Metadata Exchange Health Domain (SDMX-HD), a standard for the exchange of health indicators (SDMX-HD, 2016) among others. The World Health Organization also collaborates with the International Health Terminology Standards Development Organization (IHTSDO) to enable cross mapping of the Systemized Nomenclature of Medicine Clinical Terms (SNOMED-CT) terminologies with ICD codes (WHO, 2017).

The European Committee for Standardization (CEN) is another non-profit organization that aims to develop standards to remove trade barriers across European countries through the coordination of the development of European standards (CEN, 2012). CEN comprises the national standard bodies of 27 European Union countries in which these standards are adopted at the national level. There is also a cooperation agreement between ISO and CEN that aims to prevent the development of conflicting or parallel standards. In this agreement, the ISO standards can be adopted as CEN standards and vice versa. The e-health standards of CEN are developed by the health informatics technical committee, CEN/TC 251 (CEN, 2009) and their goal is to facilitate the adoption of standards that can potentially enable organizations in Europe to optimally use their health informatics systems, via the development and adoption of international standards. The CEN/TC 251 also collaborates with other standards development organizations such as ISO/TC 215, the Clinical Data Interchange Standard Consortium (CDISD), Health Level Seven (HL7), and the IHTSDO. The Clinical Data Interchange Standard Consortium (CDISD) is a non-profit organization that is open, and multidisciplinary (CDISC, 2013). The major goal of CDISD is to develop standards to support the acquisition, exchange, submission, and archiving of clinical research data and metadata. CDISD aims at developing platform-independent standards that facilitate interoperability of information systems to improve research in the healthcare field. CDISD collaborates with HL7 via an agreement with the latter to facilitate harmonization of their clinical research standards (CDISC, 2013). Health Level Seven (HL7) is an American non-profit organization accredited by American National Standards Institute (ANSI) that develops standards for exchanging clinical and administrative data among heterogeneous healthcare applications (HL7, 2017). HL7 has a variety of membership categories such as individual, organizational, caregiver, students and supporter. Each membership category offers a range of different benefits. The standards of HL7 are developed by volunteers who work in various working groups, under the stewardship of a technical steering committee (Benson, 2012). HL7 also collaborates with other standard developing organizations including CEN, ASTM International, ISO and IHTSDO (HL7, 2017). The Institute of Electrical and Electronics Engineers (IEEE), which is known as the largest professional association in the world, also develops standards for IT healthcare to facilitate the interoperability of medical devices (IEEE, 2017). The IEEE also cooperates with other standards developing organizations such as ISO, the international electrotechnical commission (IEC), on joint development of international standards (IEEE, 2017).

There are many other organizations who are involved in the development of interoperability standards in the healthcare domain such as National Electrical Manufacturers (DICOM, 2011), ASTM International (ASTM, 2012), and Integrating the Health Enterprise (IHE) (IHE, 2016). Each of these organizations focuses on developing standards for healthcare information exchange for the goal of achieving interoperability between healthcare information systems. However, interoperability of electronic information remains a tremendous challenge especially with over 100 electronic healthcare information standards that currently exist and are being used (Ogunyemi, Meeker, Kim, & Boxwala, 2013).

As the need to exchange healthcare information continues to grow rapidly, the sharing and communicating of health-related information across healthcare information systems becomes increasingly challenging due to the variety of data standardization models employed by the healthcare information systems which can only ensure interoperability within its open operational domain. Currently, there is no single source data standardization model to achieve semantic health data interoperability between heterogeneous systems (Sinaci & Erturkmen, 2013; Blackman, 2017). In Khan et al. (2014), the authors write "Data interoperability is also impossible to accomplish in the current state due to the lack of a relationship between healthcare data and the different health information systems, a growing concern for healthcare practitioners and facilities since it prevents the provision of better patient care". Currently, there is no existing model that is implemented to support the different vocabularies, data interpretation algorithms, and mapping tools in a single source environment; they are all stand-alone applications that hinder interoperability among heterogeneous systems (Sinaci & Erturkmen, 2013).

FHIR Standard

In response to the issue of interoperability, or lack of, of healthcare information systems, Health Level Seven (HL7) has provided a series of frameworks for the exchange, integration, and search of medical health information and the group has developed standards to resolve interoperability between systems. CDA, V2 Message, and V3 Rim are the main standards developed and proposed by HL7 (Begoyan, 2007). CDA (Clinical Document Architecture) is an XML-based mark-up standard intended to specify the encoding, structure and semantics of clinical documents for exchange (Rouse, 2015). The HL7 V2 standard was firstly developed in the early 1990s and it is widely used nowadays. It is a messaging standard that allows the exchange of clinical data between systems. It was designed to support a central patient care system as well as a more distributed environment where data resides in departmental systems. However, the drawback of HL7 V2 standard is that it takes a long time to develop various services based on HL7 V2. It also lacks an information transfer that ensures semantic interoperability. Therefore, applications participating in communication using HL7 V2 must have mutual agreements to achieve interoperability (Begoyan, 2007).

HL7 V3 Rim is another standard that was developed in 2005 to overcome the drawbacks of the previous version (V2). It ensured interoperability and used XML technology and object-oriented approaches. However, the development using this standard was not easy due to the complexity of medical information and the difficulties associated with the modelling of complete services by engineers who lacked application-domain knowledge (West, 2015).

To overcome the drawbacks of the previously mentioned versions, HL7 introduced Fast Healthcare Interoperability Resources (FHIR) as the next-generation standard for sharing healthcare records. It is a new standard framework that is based on previous data format standards and utilizes the beneficial elements of HL7-Version 2 and HL7-Version 3 (HL7, 2016). FHIR is a standard that is based on a Representational State Transfer (REST) architecture style that enables it to be extended to mobile and other light-weight devices. As a result, the interface provides services that can be accessible to various healthcare-related practitioners such as pharmacists, doctors and patients (HL7, 2015). The authors in Lee, Kim, and Lee (n.d.) list a number of improved functions in the FIHR compared with the existing standards which include strong focus on implementation, multiple implementation libraries, specification is free to use with no restrictions, interoperability out-of-the-box base resources can be used as is with adaptability for local requirements, evolutionary development path from HL7 Version 2 and CDA standards, strong foundation in web standards such as XML, JSON, HTTP and OAuth, RESTful architectures support, seamless exchange of information using messages or documents, concise and easily understood specifications, human-readable wire format for ease of use, and finally solid ontology-based analysis with rigorous formal mapping for correctness. More information about FHIR's improved functions can be found in (HL7, 2016).

FHIR is gaining widespread attention for its potential to foster innovative approaches to sharing clinical data using very modern web technology-based ideas. It is attractive due to its relatively easy implementation; it comprises a set of modular components called resources that can easily and incrementally be assembled into working systems (Alterovitz & Yao, 2015). In Ahier (2015), the author writes "FHIR is not simply adding additional standards to an already overflowing kettle, but rather the next step in the evolution of standards that will truly promote interoperability". In HIMSS (2016), Russel Leftwich who serves on the HL7 board believes FHIR-based applications will spread rapidly as the standard matures. He likens the standard's maturity journey to the evolution of the iPhone, where capabilities and use will increase with each successive version. "The potential for what it will be able to support over the next few years is tremendous," said Leftwich, a senior clinical advisor for interoperability at InterSystems, and serves as an adjunct assistant professor of Biomedical Informatics and Vanderbilt University School of Medicine.

Several efforts have been started by researchers who aim to adopt FHIR standards integration in various healthcare related information systems; for example in Alterovitz et al. (2015), the researchers aim to link genome and phenome variants to patient's electronic health records to eventually support clinical decision support systems. The main intention of the research was to unify how genomic variant data are accessed from different sequencing systems. The scope of the research aimed to develop a specification for the basis of a clinic-genomic standard that builds upon FHIR. The research resulted in a successful design, deployment, and use of the Application Programming Interface and was demonstrated and adopted by HL7 Clinical Genomics Workgroup; the feasibility of their approach was demonstrated through the development of three apps targeted at various types of users. The research concluded that an entirely data (and web) standards-based approach could prove both effective and efficient for advancing personalized medicine. In Khalilia et al. (2015), the authors demonstrated a software architecture for developing and deploying clinical predictive models using web services via the FHIR standard. The resulting predictive models were deployed as FHIR resources that receive requests of patient information, perform prediction against the deployed model and respond with prediction scores. The response and prediction time of the FHIR modelling web services were evaluated to assess the practicality of the approach. The research found that the system was reasonably fast with one second total response time per patient prediction. Another research conducted in Franz, Schuler, and Krauss (2015) aimed to show an integrated monitoring solution based on Continua and Integrating the Healthcare Enterprise, which was tested by more than 130 patients and 14 healthcare institutions. The low battery life of smartphones, due to high data traffic, was the trigger to conduct the research. The research found that there was a significant decrease in data traffic when relying on a RESTful architecture in combination with FHIR, due to the efficient resource handling of web service connections that FHIR offers.

Utilizing information from various systems and environments in the healthcare industry adds significant value to the field of healthcare. Information is today collected from different sources and heterogonous systems, which require aggregation to make use of it. For this aggregation to happen, it is important to make sure that patients have permitted to share their health-related information. Information privacy is a key reason behind the patients' rejection towards sharing their health information. On the other hand, the aggregation of information from various systems require transmitting information from a source to another however, due to the lack of standardization and therefore poor interoperability, it becomes not possible to automatically transmit information from a system to another. Privacy and interoperability can drive the healthcare sector to better position in terms of information utility.

CONCLUSION

Healthcare information systems play a vital role in the quality of care provided to patients; however, the utility of such systems in terms of sharing information is hindered and considered a bleeding edge in the information technology field. Privacy is a major challenge towards gaining the trust of patients when sharing their records among responsible parties. To gain patients' trust and acceptance to share their health-related information, there is a stressing need to design privacy mechanisms that enable the share of healthcare information in privacy-preserving manner. A potential research direction can be answering the question of how can information be shared to responsible parties without breaching the privacy of patients. Categorizing the need of using data in for a particular patient can be another research direction; the less access to information will lead to less privacy breach. Designing a cloud-based architecture seems to be a potential solution if confidentiality is enforced on the information stored on it. Sharing healthcare information through giving access to responsible parties can facilitate using such information in a privacy-preserving manner; however, this requires privacy mechanisms to protect the privacy of information stored on the cloud and to ensure responsible persons are using the information. Mechanisms to protect the privacy of information in terms of its access is also a future direction of research. Interoperability is considered another major challenge. Healthcare data are being collected by various systems that lack interoperability with each other. This requires designing a common adapter that can be used to aggregate information from these heterogeneous systems and effectively use them. FHIR seems to be a potential solution to the interoperability challenge; nevertheless, it remains a research challenge to achieve intelligent mapping techniques to employ in universal adapters to aggregate with other information that is stored on other heterogeneous systems.

REFERENCES

Adebesin, F., Foster, R., Kotz, P., & Greunen, D. V. (2013). A review of interoperability standards in e-Health and imperatives for their adoption in Africa. *South African Computer Journal*, 55-72.

Ahier, B. (2015, January 6). *FHIR and the future of interoperability*. Retrieved March 01, 2017, from HealthcareITNews: http://www.healthcareitnews.com/news/fhir-and-future-interoperability

Alterovitz, G., Warner, J., Zhang, P., Chen, Y., Ullman-Cullere, M., Isaac, D. K., & Kohane, S. (2015). SMART on FHIR Genomics: facilitating standardized clinico-genomic apps. American Medical Informatics Association.

Alterovitz, G., & Yao, H. (2015). A Genomics Plan for FHIR. *FHIR Genomics for January 2016 Connectathon*, 1-43.

ASTM. (2012). *ASTM International Standards for Healthcare Services, Products and Technology*. ASTM International.

Aziz, H., & Guled, A. (2016). Cloud Computing and Healthcare Services. *Journal of Biosensors & Bioelectronics*.

Bandyopadhyay, S., Balamuralidhar, P., & Pal, A. (2013, August). Interoperation among IoT Standards. *Journal of ICT Standardization*, 253–270. doi:10.13052

Begoyan, A. (2007). An Overview of Interoperability Standards for Electronic Health Records. *Integrated Design and Process Technology*, 1-8.

Bélanger, F., & Crossler, R. E. (2011, December). Privacy in the digital age: A review of information privacy research in information systems. *Management Information Systems Quarterly*, *35*(4), 1017–1042. doi:10.2307/41409971

Benson, T. (2012). *Principles of health interoperability HL7 and SNOMED*. Springer. doi:10.1007/978-1-4471-2801-4

Blackman, S. M. (2017). Towards a Conceptual Framework for Persistent Use: A Technical Plan to Achieve Semantic Interoperability within Electronic Health Record Systems. *Proceedings of the 50th Hawaii International Conference on System Sciences*, 4653-4662. 10.24251/HICSS.2017.566

Bock, C. E., Carnahan, L. J., Fenves, S. J., Gruninger, M., Kashyap, V., Lide, B. B., . . . Sriram, R. D. (2005). Healthcare Strategic Focus Area: Clinical Informatics. National Institute of Standards and Technology, Technology Administration, 1-33.

Borgohain, T., Kumar, U., & Sanyal, S. (2015). Survey of Security and Privacy Issues of Internet of Things. *International Journal of Advanced Networking and Applications*, *6*(4), 2372–2379.

Bowles, K. H., Potashnik, S., Ratcliffe, S. J., Rosenberg, M., Shih, N.-W., Topaz, M., ... Naylor, M. D. (2013). Conducting research using the electronic health record across multi-hospital systems: Semantic harmonization implications for administrators. *The Journal of Nursing Administration*, *43*(6), 355–360. doi:10.1097/NNA.0b013e3182942c3c PMID:23708504

Brailer, D. J. (2005). Interoperability: The Key To The Future Health Care System. *Health Affairs.* doi:10.1377/hlthaff.w5.19 PMID:15659454

Cantwell, E., & McDermott, K. (2016). Making technology talk: How interoperability can improve care, drive efficiency, and reduce waste. *Healthcare Financial Management, 70.* PMID:27382711

Casola, V., Castiglione, A., Choo, K.-K. R., & Esposito, C. (2016). *Healthcare-Related Data in the Cloud: Challenges and Opportunities.* IEEE Cloud Computing.

CDISC. (2013). Retrieved February 23, 2017, from Clinical Data Interchange Standards Consortium.: http://goo.gl/Wt7HN

CDISC. (2013). *CDISC: FAQ.* Retrieved February 23, 2017, from Clinical Data Interchange Standards Consortium: http://goo.gl/yWkkz

CEN. (2009). *Health Informatics, Published Standards.* Retrieved February 23, 2017, from European Committee for Standardization: http://goo.gl/MMXY3

CEN. (2012, December). *Hands on Standardization, A starter Guide to Standardization For Experts in CEN Technical Bodies.* Retrieved February 23, 2017, from European Committee for Standardization: ftp://ftp.cen.eu/CEN/Services/Education/Handsonguides/Handsonstandards.pdf

Chen, D., & Zhao, H. (2012). Data Security and Privacy Protection Issues in Cloud Computing. In *International Conference on Computer Science and Electronics Engineering (ICCSEE).* IEEE. 10.1109/ICCSEE.2012.193

Christopher, G. (2016, July 19). *Internet of Things Features.* Retrieved February 13, 2017, from ComputerWorldUk: http://www.computerworlduk.com/iot/iot-centred-healthcare-system-3643726/

Compton, M., & Mickelberg, K. (2014, October). *Connecting Cybersecurity with the Internet of Things.* PricewaterhouseCoopers.

Culnan, M. (1993). *How Did They Get My Name? An Exploratory Investigation of Consumer Attitudes Towards Secondary Information Use.* Academic Press.

Denecke, K., Bamidis, P., Bond, C., Gabarron, E., Househ, M., Lau, A. Y., ... Hansen, M. (2015, August). Ethical Issues of Social Media Usage in Healthcare. *Yearbook of Medical Informatics, 10*(1), 137–147. doi:10.15265/IY-2015-001 PMID:26293861

Diaz, B. (2016, December 10). *Health Language Blog: What is Semantic Interoperability?* Retrieved February 25, 2017, from Health Language: http://blog.healthlanguage.com/what-is-semantic-interoperability

DICOM. (2011). *Part 1: Introduction and Overview. Digital Imaging and Communications in Medicine (DICOM).* Retrieved from Digital Imaging and Communications in Medicine.

Doukas, C., Pliakas, T., & Maglogiannis, I. (2010). Mobile healthcare information management utilizing Cloud Computing and Android OS. In *Engineering in Medicine and Biology Society (EMBC), 2010 Annual International Conference of the IEEE.* IEEE. 10.1109/IEMBS.2010.5628061

Etzioni, A. (2010). Personal Health Records Why Good Ideas Sometimes Languish. *Issues in Science and Technology,* 59–66.

Ezea, B., & Peyton, L. (2015). Systematic Literature Review on the Anonymization of High Dimensional Streaming Datasets for Health Data Sharing. *Procedia Computer Science, 63,* 348–355. doi:10.1016/j.procs.2015.08.353

Fabiana, B., Ermakovab, T., & Junghannsa, P. (2015, March). Collaborative and secure sharing of healthcare data in multi-clouds. *Information Systems, 48,* 132–150. doi:10.1016/j.is.2014.05.004

Franz, B., Schuler, A., & Krauss, O. (2015). Applying FHIR in an Integrated Health Monitoring System. *European Journal for Biomedical Informatics, 11*(2).

Gaboury, I., Bujold, M., Boon, H., & Moher, D. (2009). Interprofessional collaboration within Canadian integrative healthcare clinics: Key components. *Social Science & Medicine, 69*(5), 707–715. doi:10.1016/j.socscimed.2009.05.048 PMID:19608320

Gabriel, M. H., Furukawa, M. F., Jones, E. B., King, J., & Samy, L. K. (2014). Progress and challenges: Implementation and use of Electronic Health Records among Critical Access Hospitals. *Health Affairs,* 1262–1270. doi:10.1377/hlthaff.2014.0279 PMID:25006155

Gkoulalas-Divanis, A., & Loukides, G. (2015). Introduction to Medical Data Privacy. In *Medical Data Privacy Handbook* (pp. 1–14). Springer International Publishing. doi:10.1007/978-3-319-23633-9_1

Griebel, L., Prokosch, H.-U., Köpcke, F., Toddenroth, D., Christoph, J., Ines Leb, I. E., & Sedlmayr, M. (2015). A scoping review of cloud computing in healthcare. *BMC Medical Informatics and Decision Making,* 1–16. PMID:25888747

Griffith, E. (2016, May 3). *What Is Cloud Computing?* Retrieved March 21, 2017, from PCMag: http://au.pcmag.com/networking-communications-software-products/29902/feature/what-is-cloud-computing

Gross, G. (2005, January 10). *Lack of standards hinders electronic health records. Interoperability concerns loom large.* Retrieved February 12, 2017, from IDGNS: http://www.infoworld.com/article/2668312/security/lack-of-standards-hinders-electronic-health-records.html

Grossman, J. M., Zayas-Cabán, T., & Kemper, N. (2009). Information Gap: Can Health Insurer Personal Health Records Meet Patients' And Physicians' Needs? *Health Affairs, 28*(2), 377–389. doi:10.1377/hlthaff.28.2.377 PMID:19275993

Gunasekara, G., & Dillon, E. (2008). Data Protection Litigation in New Zealand: Processes and Outcomes. *Victoria University of Wellington Law Review (VUWLR), 39.*

Guo, Y., Kuo, M.-H., & Sahama, T. (2012). Cloud computing for healthcare research information sharing. In *IEEE 4th International Conference on Cloud Computing Technology and Science (CloudCom).* IEEE. 10.1109/CloudCom.2012.6427561

HL7. (2015). *Introduction to HL7 Standards.* Retrieved February 26, 2017, from Health Level Seven: Health Level Seven, http://hl7.org/

HL7. (2016). *Health Level Seven Fast Healthcare Interoperability Resources.* Retrieved February 26, 2017, from Health Level Seven Fast Healthcare Interoperability: http://www.hl7.org/implement/standards/fhir/

HL7. (2016). *Home.* Retrieved February 26, 2017, from FHIR: http://www.hl7.org/implement/standards/fhir/

HL7. (2017). *HL7 Backgrounder Brief.* Retrieved February 23, 2017, from Health Level Seven: http://www.hl7.org/newsroom/HL7backgrounderbrief.cfm

HL7. (2017). *Home Page.* Retrieved February 23, 2017, from Health Level Seven: http://www.hl7.org/

Hibbard, J. H., & Greene, J. (2013). What The Evidence Shows About Patient Activation: Better Health Outcomes And Care Experiences; Fewer Data On Costs. *Health Affairs, 32*(2), 207–214. doi:10.1377/hlthaff.2012.1061 PMID:23381511

HIMSS. (2016). *Playing with FHIR.* InterSystems.

Hripcsak, G., Bloomrosen, M., FlatelyBrennan, P., Chute, C. G., Cimino, J., Detmer, D. E., ... Wilcox, A. B. (2014). Health data use, stewardship, and governance: ongoing gaps and challenges: a report from AMIA's 2012 Health Policy Meeting. *Journal of the American Medical Informatics Association, 21*(2), 204–211. doi:10.1136/amiajnl-2013-002117 PMID:24169275

IEEE. (2017a). *About IEEE.* Retrieved February 23, 2017, from http://www.ieee.org/about/index.html

IEEE. (2017b). *Formal Liaisons.* Retrieved February 23, 2017, from http://goo.gl/DLZl8

IEEE. (2017c). *Healthcare IT standards.* Retrieved February 23, 2017, from http://goo.gl/ahz3u

IHE. (2016). *About IHE.* Retrieved February 23, 2017, from http://www.ihe.net/About_IHE/

Iroju, O., Soriyan, A., Gambo, I., & Olaleke, J. (2013). Interoperability in Healthcare: Benefits, Challenges and Resolutions. *International Journal of Innovation and Applied Studies*, 262-270.

Ishigure, Y. (2017). *Trends, Standardization, and Interoperability of Healthcare Information.* Retrieved February 20, 2017, from NTT Technical Review: https://www.ntt-review.jp/archive/ntttechnical.php?contents=ntr201104gls.html

Islam, S. M., Kwak, D., Kabir, M. H., Hossain, M., & Kwak, K.-S. (2015). The Internet of Things for Health Care: A Comprehensive Survey. *IEEE Access: Practical Innovations, Open Solutions, 3*, 678–708. doi:10.1109/ACCESS.2015.2437951

ISO. (2004). *Standardization and Related Activities - General Vocabulary.* ISO/IEC Guide 2.

ISO. (2013). *Business Plan.* Retrieved February 21, 2017, from Business Plan: ISO/TC 215 Health Informatics: http://isotc.iso.org/livelink/livelink/fetch/2000/2122/687806/ISO_TC_215__Health_informatics_.pdf?nodeid=1001750&vernum=-2

ISO. (2017a). *About ISO.* Retrieved February 21, 2017, from ISO: http://www.iso.org/iso/home/about.htm

ISO. (2017b). *ISO Membership Manual.* Retrieved February 22, 2017, from ISO: http://www.iso.org/iso/iso_membership_manual.pdf

ITU. (2011). *Standards and eHealth.* Retrieved February 15, 2017, from https://www.itu.int/dms_pub/itu-t/oth/23/01/T23010000120003PDFE.pdf

Jiang, S., Cao, Y., Iyengar, S., Kuryloski, P., Jafari, R., Xue, Y., . . . Wicker, S. (2008). CareNet: an integrated wireless sensor networking environment for remote healthcare. *BodyNets '08 Proceedings of the ICST 3rd international conference on Body area networks.* 10.4108/ICST.BODYNETS2008.2965

Karla Felix Navarro, E. L., & Lim, B. (2009). Medical MoteCare: A Distributed Personal Healthcare Monitoring System. In *International Conference on eHealth, Telemedicine, and Social Medicine* (pp. 25 - 30). Cancun: IEEE. doi:10.1109/eTELEMED.2009.19

Khalilia, M., Choi, M., Henderson, A., Iyengar, S., Braunstein, M., & Sun, J. (2015). Clinical Predictive Modeling Development and Deployment through FHIR Web Services. American Medical Informatics Association.

Khan, W. A., Khattak, A. M., Hussain, M., Amin, M. B., Afzal, M., Nugent, C., & Lee, S. (2014). An Adaptive Semantic based Mediation System for Data Interoperability among Health Information Systems. *Journal of Medical Systems*, *38*(8), 28. doi:10.100710916-014-0028-y PMID:24964780

Kitamura, T., Kiyohara, K., Matsuyama, T., Hatakeyama, T., Shimamoto, T., Izawa, J., ... Iwami, T. (2016, March 5). Is Survival After Out-of-Hospital Cardiac Arrests Worse During Days of National Academic Meetings in Japan? A Population-Based Study. *Journal of Epidemiology*, *26*(3), 155–162. doi:10.2188/jea.JE20150100 PMID:26639754

Kokkinaki, A., Chouvarda, I., & Maglaveras, N. (2006). *Integrating SCP-ECG files and patient records: an ontology based approach.* University of Thessaloniki.

Kumar, P., & Lee, H.-J. (2012). Security Issues in Healthcare Applications Using Wireless Medical Sensor Networks: A Survey. *Sensors (Basel)*, *12*(1), 55–91. Retrieved from http://www.mdpi.com/1424-8220/12/1/55/htm PMID:22368458

Kuo, A. M.-H. (2011). Opportunities and Challenges of Cloud Computing to Improve Health Care Services. *Journal of Medical Internet Research*, *13*(3), e67. doi:10.2196/jmir.1867 PMID:21937354

Lau, L. M., & Shakib, S. (2005). Towards Data Interoperability: Practical Issues in Terminology Implementation and Mapping. *77th AHIMA Convention and Exhibit.*

Lee, C. H., Kim, Y. S., & Lee, Y. H. (n.d.). *Implementation of SMART APP Service Using HL7_FHIR.* Academic Press.

Li, Y., Bai, C., & Reddy, C. K. (2016, February 10). A distributed ensemble approach for mining healthcare data under privacy constraints. *Information Sciences*, *330*, 245–259. doi:10.1016/j.ins.2015.10.011 PMID:26681811

Mamlin, B. W., & Tierney, W. M. (2016, January). The Promise of Information and Communication Technology in Healthcare: Extracting Value From the Chaos. *The American Journal of the Medical Sciences*, *351*(1), 59–68. doi:10.1016/j.amjms.2015.10.015 PMID:26802759

Meingast, M., Roosta, T., & Sastry, S. (2006). Security and privacy issues with health care information technology. In *Engineering in Medicine and Biology Society. 28th Annual International Conference of the IEEE* (pp. 5453-5458). IEEE. 10.1109/IEMBS.2006.260060

Mell, P., & Grance, T. (2011). *The NIST Definition of Cloud Computing. National Institute of Standards and Technology*. NIST.

Montgomery, K., Mundt, C., Thonier, G., Tellier, A., Udoh, U., Barker, V., & Kovacs, G. (2004). *Lifeguard - a personal physiological monitor for extreme environments. Engineering in Medicine and Biology Society, 2004. IEMBS '04. 26th Annual International Conference of the IEEE. 1*. San Francisco: IEEE. Retrieved from http://ieeexplore.ieee.org/stamp/stamp.jsp?tp=&arnumber=1403640

Nissenbaum, H. (2009). *Privacy in Context: Technology, Policy, and the Integrity of Social Life*. Stanford University Press.

Ogunyemi, O., Meeker, D., Kim, H., & Boxwala, A. (2013). Identifying Appropriate Reference Data Models for Comparative Effectiveness Research (CER) Studies Based on Data from Clinical Information Systems. *Medical Care, 51*, 45–52. doi:10.1097/MLR.0b013e31829b1e0b PMID:23774519

Oude, W., Velsen, L. v., Huygens, M., & Hermens, H. (2015). Requirements for and Barriers towards Interoperable eHealth Technology in Primary Care. *IEEE Internet Computing*, 10–19.

Pais, S., Parry, D., & Huang, Y. (2017). Suitability of Fast Healthcare Interoperability Resources (FHIR) for Wellness Data. In *Proceedings of the 50th Hawaii International Conference on System Sciences* (pp. 3499-3505). HICSS. 10.24251/HICSS.2017.423

Pennic, F. (2015, February 2). *4 Challenges of Establishing EHR Interoperability*. Retrieved February 15, 2017, from HIT Consultant: http://hitconsultant.net/2015/10/02/4-challenges-of-establishing-ehr-interoperability/

Priyanga, P., & MuthuKumar, V.P. (2015). Cloud computing for healthcare organisation. *International Journal of Multidisciplinary Research and Development*, 487-493.

Public Law. (1996). Health insurance portability and accountability act of 1996. Public Law 104-191, 104th Congress.

Rashid, A. H., & Yasin, N. B. (2015, March). Sharing healthcare information based on privacy preservation. *Scientific Research and Essays, 10*(5), 184–195. doi:10.5897/SRE11.862

Rghioui, A., L'aarje, A., Elouaai, F., & Bouhorma, M. (2014). *The Internet of Things for Healthcare Monitoring: Security Review and Proposed Solution. In 2014 Third IEEE International Colloquium in Information Science and Technology* (pp. 384–389). CIST. Retrieved from http://ieeexplore.ieee.org.ezproxy.aut.ac.nz/stamp/stamp.jsp?tp=&arnumber=7016651

Rouse, M. (2015, June). *SearchHealthIT*. Retrieved February 25, 2017, from TechTarget: http://searchhealthit.techtarget.com/definition/Clinical-Document-Architecture-CDA

Sachdeva, S., & Bhalla, S. (2010). Semantic Interoperability in Healthcare Information for EHR Databases. Graduate Department of Computer and Information Systems. doi:10.1007/978-3-642-12038-1_11

SDMX-HD. (2016). Statistical Data and Metadata Exchange-Health Domain Standard Specification.

Shariati, S. M., Abouzarjomehri, & Ahmadzadegan, M. H. (2015). Challenges and security issues in cloud computing from two perspectives: Data security and privacy protection. In *2nd International Conference on Knowledge-Based Engineering and Innovation (KBEI)*. IEEE. 10.1109/KBEI.2015.7436196

Sinaci, A., & Erturkmen, G. B. (2013). A federated semantic metadata registry framework for enabling interoperability across clinical research and care domains. *Journal of Biomedical Informatics, 46*(5), 784–794. doi:10.1016/j.jbi.2013.05.009 PMID:23751263

Sultan, N. (2014). Making use of cloud computing for healthcare provision: Opportunities and challenges. *International Journal of Information Management, 34*(2), 177–184. doi:10.1016/j.ijinfomgt.2013.12.011

Sung, M., & Pentland, A. (2004). Health and Lifestyle Networking through Distributed Mobile Devices. In *WAMES 2004* (pp. 15-17). Retrieved from http://lcawww.epfl.ch/luo/WAMES%202004_files/WAMESproceedings.pdf#page=15

Thompson, T. G., & Brailer, D. J. (2004). *The Decade of Health Information Technology: Delivering Consumer-centric and Information-rich Health Care: Framework for Strategic Action*. Department of Health & Human Services.

Van-den Hoven, Blaauw, Martijn, Pieters, Wolter, Warnier, & Martijn. (2016). Privacy and Information Technology. In The Stanford Encyclopedia of Philosophy. Academic Press.

Veer, H. v., & Wiles, A. (2008). *Achieving Technical Interoperability - the ETSI Approach*. European Telecommunications Standards Institute.

Vo, M.-T., Nghi, T. T., Tran, V.-S., Mai, L., & Le, C.-T. (2015). Wireless Sensor Network for Real Time Healthcare Monitoring: Network Design and Performance Evaluation Simulation. *5th International Conference on Biomedical Engineering in Vietnam, 46*, 87-91. 10.1007/978-3-319-11776-8_22

Wager, K. A., Lee, F. W., & Glaser, J. P. (2013). *Health Care Information Systems: A Practical Approach for Health Care Management* (3rd ed.). Jossey-Bass.

Walker, J., Pan, E., Johnston, D., Adler-Milstein, J., Bates, D. W., & Middleton, B. (2004). The Value Of Health Care Information Exchange And Interoperability. Center for Information Technology Leadership.

Weber, R. H. (2015). Internet of things: Privacy issues revisited. *Computer Law & Security Review, 31*, 618–627.

Weir, C. R., Hammond, K. W., Embi, P. J., Efthimiadis, E. N., Thielke, S. M., & Hedeen, A. N. (2011, August). An exploration of the impact of computerized patient documentation on clinical collaboration. *International Journal of Medical Informatics, 80*(8), 62–71. doi:10.1016/j.ijmedinf.2011.01.003 PMID:21300565

West, M. (2015). *A Comparative Analysis of HL7 and NIEM: Enabling Justice-Health Data Exchange*. Technical Brief.

Whiddett, R., Hunter, I., Engelbrecht, J., & Handy, J. (2006, July). Patients' attitudes towards sharing their health information. *International Journal of Medical Informatics, 75*(7), 530–541. doi:10.1016/j.ijmedinf.2005.08.009 PMID:16198142

Whitman, L. E., & Panetto, H. (2006). The missing link: Culture and language barriers to interoperability. *Annual Reviews in Control*, *30*(2), 233–241. doi:10.1016/j.arcontrol.2006.09.008

WHO. (2017). *Classifications*. Retrieved February 22, 2017, from World Health Organization: http://www.who.int/classifications/icd/en/

WHO. (2017). *SNOMED CT to ICD-10 Cross-Map Technology Preview Release*. Retrieved February 22, 2017, from World Health Organization: http://goo.gl/o0d8s

WHO. (2017). *Structure and principles*. Retrieved February 22, 2017, from Who Collaborating Centre for Drug Statistics Methodology: https://www.whocc.no/atc/structure_and_principles/

Yang, G., Li, X., Mantysalo, M., Zhou, X., Pang, Z., Xu, L. D., ... Zheng, L. (2014). Technologies and architectures of the Internet-of-Things (IoT). *IEEE Transactions on Industrial Informatics*, *10*(4), 2180–2191. doi:10.1109/TII.2014.2307795

Yu, S., Wang, C., Ren, K., & Lou, W. (2010). Achieving Secure, Scalable, and Fine-grained Data Access Control in Cloud Computing. In *INFOCOM, 2010 Proceedings IEEE*. IEEE.

Yüksel, B., Küpçü, A., & Özkasap, Ö. (2017). Research issues for privacy and security of electronic health services. *Future Generation Computer Systems*, *68*, 1–17. doi:10.1016/j.future.2016.08.011

Zhang, R., & Liu, L. (2010). Security Models and Requirements for Healthcare Application Clouds. In *IEEE 3rd International Conference on Cloud Computing (CLOUD)*. IEEE. 10.1109/CLOUD.2010.62

This research was previously published in Advances in Data Communications and Networking for Digital Business Transformation edited by Debashis Saha, pages 245-271, copyright year 2018 by Business Science Reference (an imprint of IGI Global).

Chapter 85

Cloud Computing in the 21st Century:
A Managerial Perspective for Policies and Practices

Mahesh Raisinghani
Texas Woman's University, USA

Efosa Carroll Idemudia
Arkansas Tech University, USA

Meghana Chekuri
Texas Woman's University, USA

Kendra Fisher
Texas Woman's University, USA

Jennifer Hanna
Texas Woman's University, USA

ABSTRACT

The constant changes in technology has posed serious challenges to top management teams, employees, and customers on how to collect, store, and process data for competitive advantage and to make better decisions. In this chapter, to address this issue, we present the managerial perspective of cloud computing that provides the infrastructure and/or tools for decision making in the 21st century. Since the year 2000, the interest in cloud computing has had a steady increase. (Mason, 2002) Not only has cloud computing substantially lowered computing costs for corporations, it continues to increase their abilities for market offerings and to access customers' information with ease. Cloud computing has allowed managers to focus more on their business plans and bottom line to enhance competitive advantage.

DOI: 10.4018/978-1-5225-8176-5.ch085

INTRODUCTION

The constant changes in technology has posed serious challenges to top management teams, employees, and customers on how to collect, store, and process data for competitive advantage and to make better decisions. To address this issue, we present the managerial perspective of cloud computing that provides the infrastructure and/or tools for decision making in the 21st century. Since the year 2000, the interest in cloud computing has had a steady increase. (Mason, 2002) Not only has cloud computing substantially lowered computing costs for corporations, it continues to increase their abilities for market offerings and to access customers' information with ease. Cloud computing has allowed managers to focus more on their business plans and bottom line to enhance competitive advantage.

Imagining the Internet, we often think of a big cloud connected to network maps. Prior to the popularity of cloud computing, these network maps occupy physical spaces and would show routers, servers, users, mainframes, etc., connected to the Internet, which was represented by the big cloud. The cloud was also a representation of "everything else" that was on the Internet, outside of the corporate network. Essentially, cloud computing can employ processing power, storage, applications, cost efficient, almost unlimited storage space, easy access to information, and various services over the Internet. Cloud computing has become the way of organizing the "everything else" (i.e., data collection, data use, data storage, data processing, and so forth) on the Internet.

For cloud computing, the data storage and processing is done on a remote server. This means that the users don't have to install any software, store any data, or run programs, allowing for applications to be ran on a web browser. Thus, allowing users to access the information with ease from any part of the world. Most people using the Internet have likely used cloud computing. For example, most popular email providers like Gmail, Hotmail or Yahoo mail are all examples of cloud computing. This is also referred to as Software as a service (SaaS), or on-demand software that allows users to access applications over the Internet through automatic software integration. Hence, as long as the user has access to the Internet, they can connect to their applications and online data.

History and Evolution

The history of cloud computing can be dated back almost as early as computers themselves, when the ability for computers to connect through a mainframe was first introduced in academia and business corporations during the 1950s. At this time these terminal computers, or "static terminal" were only able to communicate, but did not possess any processing abilities relating to data collection, data storage, and data use for competitive advantage. These large-scale mainframes were very costly, occupies lot of space, produce lot of heat, and to improve cost efficiency and space availability users shared devices as well as time on the CPU-Central Processing Unit- so the devices were constantly being used. This practice became known in the industry as time-sharing, but in the 1970s was known as RJE-Remote Job Entry (Weik, 1961).

It was in the 1960s that John McCarthy stated that computation would be available to public someday to improve data collection and usage (Simson, 2011). It wasn't until the 1990s that telecommunication companies began offering Virtual Private Network (VPN) services to save cost. A VPN allows users to send private information and data across a public network, through means like encryption that would protect the information as though it were on a private network. However, it would have the benefit of superior functionality and services of a public network (Mason, 2002).

It was not until the year 2000 that cloud computing began gaining popularity because of cost efficiency, unlimited storage, and easy access to information. More and more corporations began utilizing cloud computing. Amazon was one of the first in the industry to implement cloud computing for competitive advantage. Like most other corporate computer networks, they were using a small fraction of their capacity to allow any jumps in activity. Amazon innovated their data centers, which allowed for less physical space needed and a smaller operating staff. They were able to extend cloud computing to their customers in 2006 with their launch of Amazon Web Services (AWS) (Hof, 2006). The AWS helps Amazon to improve customers' loyalty and satisfaction because Amazon is able to address customers' immediate needs and wants.

IMPACT OF CLOUD COMPUTING

In less than twenty years cloud computing has revolutionized the way that not only large corporations utilize the Internet, but individual users as well. The impact of cloud computing in technology stretches from individual users to small and large businesses. Many are using cloud computing in our day-to-day lives, without even knowing the just how much. Mac users especially are using cloud computing for much of their data storage, use, and processes. All of our online collaboration is based in cloud computing going back to the early days of social networking on MySpace. Cloud Computing can also be found when routing our destinations in using the average day GPS system (Mather, Kumarasawmy & Latif, 2009). As we become more and more dependent on our mobile and smart devices, the more we utilize the impact of cloud computing to access information with ease and have unlimited space.

Cloud Computing Service Models

Many of the IT services accessible through cloud computing can be categorized into three main service models as shown in Figure 1; which are described as follows:

- **Infrastructure as a Service (IaaS):** In this model, cloud service providers (CSPs) host consumers' infrastructure. It provides fundamental building blocks such as hardware and storage so customers can create their own platform or individual services using the cloud infrastructure (Zissis & Lekkas, 2012). Customers possess complete responsibility for securing their applications deployed in the IaaS cloud and cannot expect any security assistance from CSPs other than firewall protection (Mather, Kumaraswamy & Latif, 2009).
- **Platform as a Service (PaaS):** In this service model, CSPs offer a platform that encompasses generic software modules, so consumers can build their own software programs or services. The consumers have no control over the underlying cloud infrastructure such as operating systems, network, and storage components. However, they do have control over the deployed applications and configurations of application hosting environment (Zissis & Lekkas, 2012).
- **Software as a Service (SaaS):** Within this service model, a cloud service provider offers application software with specific service features so consumers can host their software services on the cloud, and it is the most popular offering in the industry today. The SaaS providers are mainly responsible for securing the applications they offer customers. However, consumers are account-

Figure 1. The cloud computing stack
(Source: Voorsluys et al. 2011)

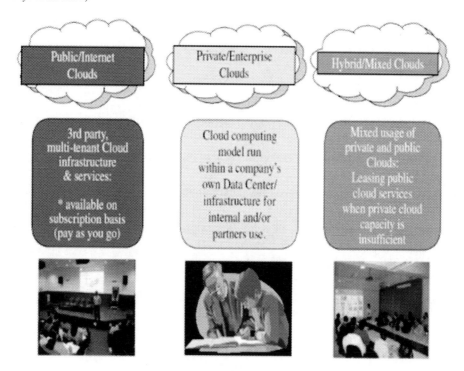

able for operational security functions. Similar to the PaaS service model, the consumer has no control over the underlying cloud infrastructure such as operating systems, networks, storage, and servers (Zissis & Lekkas, 2012).

Cloud Deployment Models

A cloud deployment model refers to a particular type of cloud environment, which can be differentiated by its size, proprietorship and access as shown in Figure 2. The four cloud deployment models that are identified within the cloud-computing infrastructure are described as follows:

- **Private Cloud:** This particular cloud infrastructure is designed for an individual organization. It can be managed by the organization or the cloud service provider and may exist on-site or at a location remote to the organization's premises (Zissis & Lekkas, 2012).
- **Community Cloud:** This type of infrastructure is shared by several organizations in the community that have specific shared interests. This form of cloud can be managed by various organizations or by a third party provider, and may be deployed either on-site or off-site (Zissis & Lekkas, 2012).
- **Public Cloud:** This cloud infrastructure is accessible by general public or a large organization. It is generally owned by an organization that offers cloud services to public (Zissis & Lekkas, 2012).

Figure 2. Types of clouds based on deployment models
(Source: Voorsluys et al. 2011)

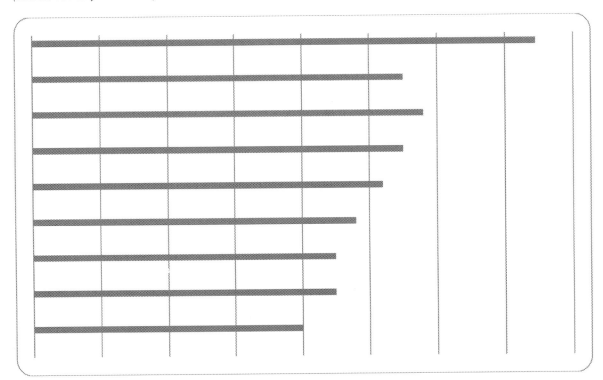

- **Hybrid Cloud:** The hybrid cloud infrastructure is a combination of two or more clouds such as public, private, and community cloud. The two clouds are united by standardized or exclusive technology to enable portability of data and applications between the clouds (Zissis & Lekkas, 2012).

Benefits of Cloud Computing

Cloud computing provides a great example of how the Information Technology (IT) evolution is playing a crucial role in changing the way businesses operate today for competitive advantage. Organizations are utilizing cloud computing to boost their productivity, cost efficient, unlimited storage space, easy access to information, and overall performance. The benefits of cloud computing are numerous and some of the main benefits are listed below.

- **Reduced Costs and Better Financial Management:** Cloud computing helps an organization by decreasing or eliminating its upfront IT investments such as hardware and software purchases (Erl, Mahmood & Puttini, 2013). The organizations avoid heavy investment in hardware as the payments depend on the amount of cloud usage. As the infrastructure for hardware and software is rented and not bought, the costs are controlled and minimized. This in turn helps companies to start with a small investment, but can expand their IT resource allocation based on their requirements. Cloud computing reduces operational costs by avoiding unnecessary maintenance and electricity costs (Shivakumar & Raju, 2010). The reduction of up-front financial commitments and operational costs allows organizations to redirect the capital for essential business requirements leading to increased efficiency (Velte, Velte & Elsenpeter, 2010). Thus, it should be noted that cloud computing is the most efficient method to use, maintain, and update software and hardware. Cloud computing lower companies IT expenses and investment relating to licensing fees for multiple users using the systems.

- **Increased Scalability and Flexibility:** Cloud computing makes it easier for businesses to scale their service offerings that are increasingly reliant on accurate information, and subject to client's demand thus increasing customers' loyalty and satisfaction. Since the computing resources are managed through software, they can be deployed quick and efficiently as and when new requirements emerge. In fact, the central element to cloud computing is the ability to scale resources up or down, by dynamically managing them through software APIs with minimal service provider interaction (Marston et al., 2011). With the availability of pools of IT resources, along with associated tools and technologies designed to leverage them collectively, it makes it possible for clouds to almost instantly and dynamically allocate IT resources to cloud consumers, on-demand or via the cloud consumer's direct configuration. This empowers cloud consumers to not only scale their cloud-based IT resources, but also offers flexibility in terms of accommodating processing fluctuations and demand peaks automatically or manually (Erl, Mahmood & Puttini, 2013). With easy to install technology and increased flexibility, such as adding resources on demand, turning them off and reassigning as per business requirements costs, it further increases value proposition for consumers and attracts more companies to move to cloud (Shivakumar & Raju, 2010). Thus, cloud computing encourages automatic software integration for easy use.
- **Automation and Increased Storage Capacity:** The cloud can store much more data than a personal computer and provides unlimited storage space (Erl, Mahmood & Puttini, 2013). The companies need not worry about the amount of storage space availability or computer hardware upgrades. Moreover, backing up and recovery of data is simplified as all the information is stored on the cloud versus a physical device (Erl, Mahmood & Puttini, 2013). Automation is one of the attractive features of cloud computing. Automation helps businesses by not requiring dedicated teams to manage system updates and back-ups which in turn allow businesses to utilize the freed resources for other priority tasks (Shivakumar & Raju, 2010).
- **Mobile Business and Location Independence:** With cloud computing system, the workload has shifted significantly where the local computers are not required to do all the work (Shivakumar & Raju, 2010). The cloud providers operate from various locations which allow businesses to go mobile and decrease dependency on a specific location. In addition to traditional computers, cloud services can be accessed from various devices such as tablets, smart phones and other devices. Hence, consumers have increased flexibility with device options and easy access to data from anywhere in the world where there is an Internet connection (Erl, Mahmood & Puttini, 2013).
- **Better Business Support:** Time is one of the vital factors for any successful business. Cloud computing helps IT react quicker to the changing dynamics of a business by decreasing the time and effort required to launch new applications (Shivakumar & Raju, 2010). For instance, a project that usually takes 4 months to complete can be accomplished immediately or in less than 5 weeks utilizing cloud services. The decreased project turnaround time results in competitive advantage, as it helps cut overall costs,SS and improves operational efficiency.

Risks and Challenges Associated With Cloud Computing

Although cloud computing offers several benefits to the consumers, businesses need to be aware of the risks and challenges that comes with adopting cloud services. Some of the critical challenges involved with cloud computing are addressed below.

- **Greater Security Vulnerabilities:** Security is one of the primary concerns when considering cloud computing. Traditionally, companies feared connecting to any system outside of one's organization as it provided access to company's sensitive information (Zissis & Lekkas, 2012). This conceptual boundary protected an organization's information resources. However, shifting of business data to the cloud implies that a company's private information is shared with the cloud provider. With increasing cloud services, the conceptual boundary is becoming fuzzier and is requiring cloud consumers to expand trust boundaries (Erl, Mahmood & Puttini, 2013). Establishing a secure architecture without introduction of vulnerabilities can be challenging as the trust boundaries overlap between the cloud consumer and cloud provider. In addition, cloud providers having access to cloud consumers data increases the chances of data exposure and makes it difficult to estimate the extent to which the data is secure. This overlapping of trust boundaries and increased chances of data exposure provide malicious users or hackers with greater opportunities to attack IT resources. Such malicious users can steal or destroy cloud consumer's personal data or a company's business data, thus increasing security threats (Erl, Mahmood & Puttini, 2013). A survey conducted by International Data Corporation (IDC) on cloud services showed that security is one of the main concerns. The following figure 3 illustrates the cloud concerns with security issue leading at 74.5percent (Velte, Velte & Elsenpeter, 2010). To address this issue relating to security in cloud, top management must be absolutely sure to choose the most reliable and reputable service providers that will help to keep company's information and data secure.
- **Decreased Administrative Control:** Cloud consumers are allowed a certain degree of governance control. However, it is lower than what consumers would enjoy with IT resources being on-premise (Erl, Mahmood & Puttini, 2013). This limited control can introduce risks depending on how a cloud provider operates one's cloud network. For example, if the geographic distance between the cloud provider and the cloud consumer is more, then it requires extra network hops, leading to delays in data transfer and eventually decreased efficiency. With cloud services being accessed remotely, certain features of the software might be inferior when compared to running it locally (Erl, Mahmood & Puttini, 2013).
- **Interoperability and Portability:** Migrating between different clouds, such as transferring of IT infrastructure resources from a private cloud to a public cloud, can be challenging (Mather, Kumarasawmy & Latif, 2009). In other words, the interoperability and portability of data from one cloud system to another plays a vital role in the adoption of cloud computing. Unfortunately, there are no mature standards for interoperability between different cloud systems. As a result, IT organizations fail to respond quickly to the dynamic business changes (Mather, Kumarasawmy & Latif, 2009).
- **Cloud Service Provider Dependency:** One of the main drawbacks of cloud computing is the dependency on a cloud service provider (Mather, Kumarasawmy & Latif, 2009). A cloud service provider (CSP) holds valuable information and may have certain business rules in place that makes it difficult or impossible for a cloud user to shift to a different cloud provider. When

Figure 3. Cloud concerns (in percent)

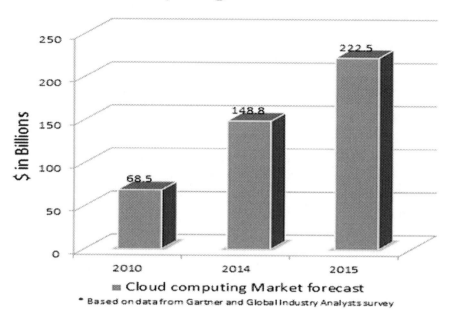

Cloud computing Market forecast

a particular CSP cannot match the changing needs of a business, then the cloud consumer might want to move to another cloud provider. However, this change can be problematic and cumbersome, as it requires transfer of huge data between the old and the new providers. This decreased flexibility can affect the overall business goals and decrease efficiency (Mather, Kumarasawmy & Latif, 2009).

- **Connectivity Dependency:** The complete potential of cloud computing is dependent on the availability of high-speed access to the Internet, which can be disadvantageous (Mather, Kumarasawmy & Latif, 2009). Cloud consumers have to be mindful of the fact that cloud service providers can experience cloud outage and downtime issues. If any connectivity or network problem arises then the whole system set up is worthless and ineffective (Velte, Velte & Elsenpeter, 2010).

- **Multi- Regional Compliance and Legal Issues:** Cloud service providers usually establish data centers in geographic locations that are inexpensive or convenient (Erl, Mahmood & Puttini, 2013). Cloud consumers are generally ignorant about where their IT resources and physical data actually resides. This variability in information can pose serious legal issues as organizations nowadays are expected to maintain privacy of personal data, such as HIPPA for the health care industry. Countries have certain laws in place that require selected data to be disclosed to the government. As a result of the US Patriot Act, the US governmental agencies can access a European cloud consumer's data positioned in the US cloud. On the contrary, European Union countries may not be able to access the US cloud consumer's data easily when hosted in the European Union. Although the information is held by the third party cloud provider, many regulatory frameworks require cloud consumer companies to safeguard personal data (Erl, Mahmood & Puttini, 2013). Hence organizations have to be knowledgeable about their accountability and mindful in considering cloud computing as an option.

Cloud Computing Security Best Practices

In an effort to counteract some of the security concerns within Cloud Computing, many strategies and best practices have come into play. Cloud providers and users alike are strongly encouraged to execute these best practices, as they present defense mechanisms against possible security and data breaches.

- **Policy:** Policy is a major best practice contributor to cloud security. Whether supplying the cloud or consuming it, ensuring there is a policy in place outlining the specific aspects of the cloud is a must. The policy should include the security information, and be assessable to the entire organization (Winkler, & Meine, 2011). This may sound like a common knowledge expectation, but ensuring all parties involved are aligned with the guidelines and regulations of the service play a vital role in securing the cloud. Once your policies are in place, a focus in risk management leadership should be established. Also, the policy should be updated regularly to address the constant changes in technology. It should be noted that most companies policy relating to BYOD or cloud computing are out of date because technology changes everyday/rapidly.
- **Risk Management:** The cloud is heavily used among many managers across many fields; however, one's ability to provide risk management is essential. To implement risk management as a best practice to securing the cloud is key to having a system in place, which reduces security risk in the cloud. Within risk management, one has to have a clear understanding of what types of security risk a particular cloud may present (Winkler, & Meine, 2011). This allows possible security measures to take place, which may counteract those risks. From this information, various types of securities are in place and then tested and monitored for their ability to secure (Winkler, & Meine, 2011). To emphasize how instrumental risk management is to securing the cloud, Winkler states that it is the "core activity around which your security practice revolves" (Winkler, & Meine, 2011). Also, companies should invest regularly on training relating to risk management associated with cloud computing.
- **Auditing:** Auditing is another type of best practice that is heavily used in the field. Auditing helps ensure the effects of current security systems are compliant. To ensure accurate auditing of the system, one should complete a series of specific steps. The first item within an audit includes a routine schedule check of any possible problems or weaknesses within the system (Winkler & Meine, 2011). With new risk arising daily, security controls should be checked to make sure they are up to date and current in their ability to control these risks. Policies in place as mentioned earlier should also go through audits to make sure they are still compliant (Winkler & Meine, 2011). To help identify any upgrades that should be made to the monitoring of security, system logs need to be audited occasionally by a manual review. There are many different auditing tools, which can be leveraged that include these best practices; yet, one should ensure they are choosing the right one. For example, those using platform as a service provider may find more challenges in using commercialized auditing programs due to their tenants having a bit less control (Winkler & Meine, 2011). Outside of this concern, commercialized audits allow a common interface and automation within the audit (Winkler & Meine, 2011).
- **Segregation of Duties:** Segregation of Duties is a best practice, which states the idea that privileges should not be given to individuals that are outside of their primary role (Winkler & Meine, 2011). Within this concept, privileges are only given and limited to what is needed for the completion of one's responsibilities and task. When one's access is limited only to their particular area,

this allows for specific monitoring to take place. Segregation of duties goes as far as to limit sensitive material and task to what is known as the two-person rule, where access is given only to two specific individuals (Winkler & Meine, 2011).

As an attempt to continue creating best practices, many have joined together to find continued resolutions in helping secure the cloud (Subashini & Kavitha 2011). The Cloud Security Alliance (CSA) has taken the initiative to partner with providers among many others in helping identify the most secure processes to incorporate into cloud computing. They have founded the Open Web Application Security Project (OWASP), which includes the top threats to cloud computing and is updated as security threats change in the field (Subashini & Kavitha 2011).

Changes to the Cloud

There are a few important aspects of the cloud that must also be taken into consideration outside of ensuring maximum security to the system. In an effort to overcome some of the challenges mentioned earlier, specific changes should be made to the cloud.

- **User Outage and Performance:** User outage and performance are two of the items which Cloud providers must take a closer look into making necessary alterations. Companies such as Amazon, and Google have already experienced such opportunities in their fields (Armbrust, et al., 2010). When consumers purchase or rent out their data within the cloud, they are expecting their information to be readily available at all times. It has been suggested to help avoid cloud outages; businesses should obtain their software stacks from multiple providers, as oppose to one or two (Armbrust, et al., 2010). The idea is that if one were to go down, it would not disrupt the flow of the entire entity. From here, the focus would be on the competition between the Cloud providers, their performance, and price, as businesses would look for the providers that would work best with their company's needs.
- **Data Lock-In:** Some companies have been hesitant to convert to cloud computing due to the fear in losing their data not only temporarily, but all together from data lock-in (Armbrust et al., 2010). Whether this is due to being locked into a company contract, or the inability to extract data from one provider to another, data lock-in can pose a major problem. A possible change to the current process could include incorporating service across multiple clouds, enabling users to pull their data as needed (Armbrust et al., 2010). Another advantage to this change includes the users ability to have their data at an alternate location, in the event that one provider looses their data permanently (Armbrust et al., 2010).

IMPLICATIONS FOR RESEARCH

The content within this paper in addition to other research on cloud computing can be used to help gain an understanding on cloud computing, and the technological advances it possesses. Although the information presented an overall framework on cloud computing, the research also offered ways to help compensate for some of its disadvantages. While conducting research on cloud computing, we found that when looking for scholarly or academic journals on the impact of cloud computing, the amount of research was not as extensive as first thought. Considering how fast cloud computing has grown within businesses and for private use, we would have liked to see a larger amount of academic resources supporting it.

There was also a major focus in research on the security concerns of the cloud. We were able to find other opportunities outside of security risk, but when looking for alternate solutions, the research was very limited. When one thinks of cloud computing concerns, their immediate thought may be security, yet as mentioned in our paper, there are several other opportunities that should equally be addressed. Going forward, further research should be obtained on the opportunities of cloud computing outside of security risk, and how those opportunities should be addressed, in addition to the positive impact of cloud computing obtained from academic sources. Also, future research are encourage to investigate the specific factors that influence security vulnerability, administrative control, and portability relating to cloud computing to enhance competitive advantage.

IMPLICATIONS FOR MANAGEMENT

Managers should expand their knowledge on cloud computing and consider using cloud computing for their business. With the ability to conserve on expenses, and re-allocate task and responsibilities from systems to projects and strategies, this alone can help produce tangible results for the company. Managers should look at the advantages of cloud computing, and see how they would be of benefit to their company. From here, they should look at the specific items needed for their business, and align those to a provider who can meet those expectations. From the research gathered, managers should also ensure they are aware of the opportunities in cloud computing, and set the best practices in place to help them reduce the risk of security breaches, and the loss of data. For managers looking for more flexibility, the ability to cut expenses, free resources, and technically advance, cloud computing could be a great resource for businesses and managers. Finally, top management teams should invest on training relating to cloud computing; and should also make sure that their organization's policies for cloud computing are current and updated to enhance their organization's competitive advantage.

RECOMMENDATION

Our recommendation is for businesses and individuals alike to strongly consider using cloud computing based on the managerial perspective presented in our paper.

By 2015, cloud computing is expected to grow to a 222.5 billion dollar industry (Jayaprakash 2011). With that large of an industry, companies will be competing to see who can be a part of cloud computing first, and we suggest that everyone take advantage of the benefits now. With the ability to start your own cloud, join a provider individually, or have your entire company convert to cloud computing, the advantages are extensive relating to competitive advantage and establishing customers' loyalty and satisfaction.

Figure 4. Cloud market forecast (in billions)

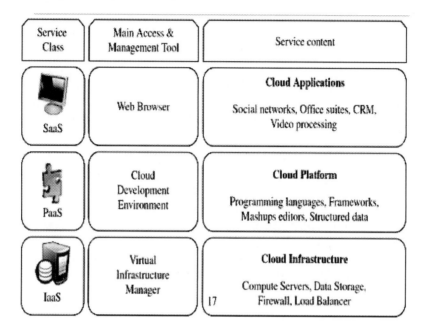

CONCLUSION

The constant and daily changes in technology has posed serious challenges to top managements, employees, and customers on how to collect, store, and process big data for competitive advantage and to make better decision. To address this issue, we present the managerial perspective of cloud computing in the 21st century. From the research conducted, one can see how cloud computing has become the leading service in how we use the Internet. With one of the greatest advantages being cost, companies who use cloud-computing can look forward to operational cost reduction, flexibility in time and scaling, and an unlimited amount of data storage. It should be noted that cloud computing offers easy access to customers' current information and data to improve customers' services, loyalty, and satisfaction. Although there are some challenges and opportunities in cloud computing; and our study presents different resources and best practices that should be set in place to help compensate for those opportunities so one can reap the benefits of cloud computing. Cloud computing continues to grow daily and can enhance one's business, work, and personal life.

REFERENCES

Armbrust, M., Armando, F., Griffith, R., Joseph, A. D., Katz, R., Konwinski, A., ... Zaharia, A. (2010). A view of cloud computing. *Communications of the ACM*, *53*(4), 50–58. doi:10.1145/1721654.1721672

Erl, T., Mahmood, Z., & Puttini, R. (2013). *Cloud computing: Concepts, technology & architecture*. Upper Saddle River, NJ: Prentice Hall.

Farber, D. (2008). *The new geek chic: Data centers*. CNET News.

Jayaprakash, G. (2011, September 15). Cloud computing security, is your seatbelt on? *Infosys*. Retrieved October 31, 2013, from http://www.infosysblogs.com/cloud/2011/09/

King, R. (2008). Cloud Computing: Small Companies Take Flight. *Business Week*.

Marston, S., Li, Z., Bandyopadhyay, S., Zhang, J., & Ghalsasi, A. (2011). Cloud computing- the business persepective. *Decision Support Systems*, *51*(1), 176–189. doi:10.1016/j.dss.2010.12.006

Mason, A. G. (2002) *Secure Virtual Private Network*. Cisco Press.

Mather, T., Kumarasawmy, S., & Latif, S. (2009). *Cloud security and privacy* (1st ed.). Sebastopol, CA: O'Reilly Media, Inc.

Shivakumar, B. L., & Raju, T. (August 2010). Emerging role of cloud computing in redefining business operations. *Global Management Review, 4*(4).

Simson, G. (2011). *"The Cloud Imperative"*. *Technology Review*. MIT.

Subashini, S., & Kavitha, V. (2011). A survey on security issues in service delivery models of cloud computing. *Journal of Network and Computer Applications*, *34*(01), 1–11. doi:10.1016/j.jnca.2010.07.006

Velte, A. T., Velte, T. J., & Elsenpeter, R. (2010). *Cloud computing: A practical approach*. New York, NY: McGraw-Hill.

Voorsluys, W., Broberg, J., & Buyya, R. (February 2011). Introduction to Cloud Computing. In R. Buyya, J. Broberg, & A. Goscinski (Eds.), *Cloud Computing: Principles and Paradigms* (pp. 1–44). New York: Wiley Press. doi:10.1002/9780470940105.ch1

Weik, M. H. (1961). *A Third Survey of Domestic Electronic Digital Computing Systems*. Ballistic Research Laboratories.

Winkler, J. R., & Meine, B. (2011). *Securing the cloud*. Waltham, MA: Syngress.

Zissis, D., & Lekkas, D. (2012). Addressing cloud computing security issues. *Future Generation Computer Systems*, *28*(3), 583–592. doi:10.1016/j.future.2010.12.006

KEY TERMS AND DEFINITIONS

Community Cloud: This type of cloud infrastructure is shared by several organizations in the community that have specific shared interests. It can be managed by various organizations or by a third party provider, and may be deployed either on-site or off-site.

Hybrid Cloud: The hybrid cloud infrastructure is a combination of two or more clouds such as public, private, and community cloud. The two clouds are united by standardized or exclusive technology to enable portability of data and applications between the clouds.

Platform as a Service (PaaS): In PaaS, cloud service provide offer a platform that encompasses generic software modules, so consumers can build their own software programs or services.

Private Cloud: A cloud infrastructure is designed for an individual organization. It can be managed by the organization or the cloud service provider and may exist on-site or at a location remote to the organization's premises.

Public Cloud: This cloud infrastructure is accessible by general public or a large organization. It is generally owned by an organization that offers cloud services to public.

Software as a Service (SaaS): In SaaS, a cloud service provider offers application software with specific service features so consumers can host their software services on the cloud.

Virtual Private Network (VPN): A VPN allows users to send private information across a public network, through means like encryption that would protect the information as though it were on a private network, albeit with the benefit of superior functionality and services of a public network.

This research was previously published in Advanced Research on Cloud Computing Design and Applications edited by Shadi Aljawarneh, pages 188-200, copyright year 2015 by Information Science Reference (an imprint of IGI Global).

Chapter 86
Security Risks of Biomedical Data Processing in Cloud Computing Environment

Babangida Zubairu
Jaipur National University, India

ABSTRACT

The emergence of new innovations in technology changes the rate of data generated in health-related institutions and the way data should be handled. As such, the amount of data generated is always on the increase, which demands the need of advanced, automated management systems and storage platforms for handling large biomedical data. Cloud computing has emerged as the promising technology for present and future that can handle large amount of data and enhance processing and management of the data remotely. One of the disturbance concerns of the technology is the security of the data. Data in the cloud is subject to security threats, and this has highlighted the need for exploring security measures against the threats. The chapter provides detailed analysis of cloud computing deployment strategies and risks associated with the technology and tips for biomedical data storage and processing through cloud computing services.

INTRODUCTION

Cloud computing environment enables sharing of computing resources and accessing services supported by the technology through the internet; the client of the technology can benefit from tremendous advantages offered by the technology such as boundary less accessibility of remotely stored data. The stored data can be accessed via any computing devices that can support internet connectivity such as PC and smart phone. The merits of this technology can benefit every sector of human endeavors, such as biomedical data handling, one of the challenging issues is the security of the data stored in the cloud environment, the threats can be from the malicious user behavior in the process of data accessing or other form of threat that disturb the functionality of the technology. Due to the sensitivity and concern about biomedical data in the cloud environment, a robust security measures are required for proper

DOI: 10.4018/978-1-5225-8176-5.ch086

storage, delivery and processing of the data. The chapter intends to highlight and digests the security threats that can hinder the processing of biomedical data in the cloud environment and presented the countermeasures against the threats. The chapter also presents details of the merits and demerits of the services supported technologies to the organization and individual that handles data, such as biomedical one and envisaging migrating to the cloud computing. Some vital tips were presented for enhancing the technology deployment, data storage, retrieval and integration for successful delivery of biomedical data processing in the cloud environment.

BACKGROUND

Computers are used in biomedical and health related fields to support data storage, analysis, and integration of biomedical and genetic information. Now a day more advanced technologies are being evolved, the sophistication and advancement of the high throughput technologies will significantly influence more biomedical data generation. This reveals that the ability to measure, store, manage and process precise data on individuals will surpass the capabilities of traditional datacenter of organizations. Enhanced quantitative evaluation and analysis of individual data and qualities become possible due to the advancement in technologies, thereby waiving limits and increases opportunity for advanced studies and evaluation of combined factors that can predict disease and care. As more advanced technologies become available, the demands of handling volumes of increasingly detailed data and analysis may lead to potential increases for drawing erroneous conclusions about the data. This shows the need of an advanced automated system for management, retrieval, and interpretation of biomedical and health related data such as cloud computing technology. Some online database system of nucleic acid exists such as European Molecular Biology Laboratory (EMBL), Gen Bank and DNA databank of Japan, but these databases are not enough to suit the demand of most organizations in biomedical data management. For instance, EMBL is managed by the European Bioinformatics Institute in the UK to support research in molecular biology; GenBank is maintained by the National Center for Biotechnology Information (NCBI) in the US for nucleotide sequences and their protein translations. The DNA Databank is maintained by the National Institutes in Genetics in Japan for the analysis of genetic diseases and genetic fingerprinting for criminology and genetic genealogy (Francesco, Giuliana, & Luigi, 2009). The mentioned online databases may only complement the need of some organizations not all. Therefore, the need for other research institutions and organization handling biomedical data to migrate to cloud technology becomes inevitable; this will provide the avenue for data sharing with other research community around the globe. Securing data is the paramount need of most organizations, peer to peer (P2P) novel technique was presented by (Mohammad, & Adnan, 2018), the approach integrates the P2P with the caching technique and dummies from real queries, this helps in preserving privacy and security of data, Cloudlets technologies were presented by (Panigrahi, Tiwary, Pati, & Das, 2016) as the solution to big data analysis for areas that face low internet connectivity and devices disruptions, the technologies can be useful if employed to manage and process big data in the cloud computing environment. However, watermarking technique was proposed using Odd-Even Method for insertion and extraction of watermark in a bio medical image with large data hiding capacity, security as well as high watermarked quality (Kumar, Nilanjan, Sourav, Achintya, & Sheli, 2014). Similarly, Interpolation and trigonometric techniques were proposed by (Sayan, Prasenjit, Arijit, Debalina, & Nilanjan, 2014) for insertion and extraction of watermark in digital image, this accomplish by embedding secrete bits key into the gray planes of color image.

CLOUD COMPUTING AND ITS ENVIRONMENT

According (Azure, 2017), cloud computing is the delivery of computing services which includes the servers, storage, databases, networking, software, analytics and more over the Internet. Hence, the technology is a solution that provides elastic, on-demand, and scalable computing infrastructure for many application needs (Elhossiny, Nirmeen, & Fatma, 2016). The technology is supported and maintained by the companies. The companies offering the technology are called cloud service providers. The resources and services of cloud computing are used by the client on demand basis and billing is based on the usage of the services, this provides scalability of the services to the client, a client has an option of upgrading or down scaling the services based on demands, the scalability and flexibility of the technology help the client in cutting the cost of computing expenses. The technology provides substantial relieve to clients from infrastructures investment in basic hardware and software, this will enable the clients to concentrate more on innovations and creativity on new ideas to improve their services (Kar, Parida, & Das, 2016). Hence, the technology offers the following:

- Application development environment
- Data storage, back up and recover
- Host websites and blogs
- Stream audio and video services
- Deliver software based on demand
- Data Analyses

Judith Hurwitz (2016) outlined three key players in cloud technology as follows:

1. The Cloud Technology Client (CTC)
2. The Technology Service Providers (TSP) and
3. The Cloud Technology Management (CTM).

The technology defends on resources sharing such as the storage, server, software and network for optimal economy of scale through internet.

Figure 1. Cloud Technology players

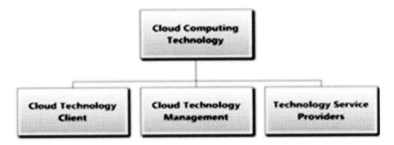

Technology Service Providers (TSP)

The infrastructure of cloud technology comprises the physical components that run applications and data storage. The physical entities enable the creation of the virtual environment for running virtual servers and virtual storage to hold application and data. Virtual abstraction is used for managing servers and storage as logical entities rather than physical. TSP is responsible for smooth running and functionality of the infrastructure as well as logical components and ensures an adequate guarantee of the services operations and security.

Cloud Technology Management (CTM)

In cloud computing, the data and application reside in the virtual environment, the virtual management and control of the data and applications are achieved through Cloud Technology Management. The goal of CTM is to ensure a smooth running of applications and services so that different applications can be used to access the same data. Accurate Information dissemination is the ultimate goal of cloud technology. For instance, a client can access stored data and run the application via the internet from far distances; the data may be stored in the US and be accessible in India. Therefore, CTM provides overall management of information dissemination, maintenance of the storage and smooth running of the cloud application services. It is the responsibility of CTM to provide 24/7 technical supports of the services to the clients, thus, CTM is the general overseer of the cloud services.

Cloud Technology Client (CTC)

This is the end-user that leases the services of cloud technology from the TSP on demand basis; the technical know-how on how the technology works, where the technology resides and how is being maintained, is of no business to the client, but only enjoy the services renders by the TSP and CTM. For example, from Figure 2, the biomedical data resides on cloud storage which is maintained by CTM,

Figure 2. Biomedical Cloud Technology representation

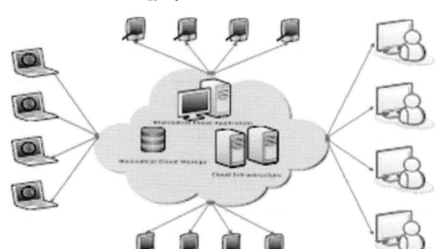

the application services for the data processing, storing and retrievals as well as application interface for accessing the data are provider responsibilities.

The client can access and run application services for biomedical data processing. The stored data can also be accessed and retrieved via the internet with the help of a web browser. The access of the application services and storage can be done with Personal Computer (PC), laptop, smart phone or any handheld devices that can be connected to the internet.

CLOUD TECHNOLOGY DEPLOYMENTS

Cloud computing technology has three different modes of deployments (Azure, 2017):

- Public clouds
- Private clouds
- Hybrid clouds

Public clouds are owned and operated by cloud service provider, which deliver their computing resources such as application, servers, and storage over the Internet to the public, the cloud services may be free or pay per usage, the technology is designed to use shared physical resources which are accessible over a public network. The provider owned and manages the hardware, software and supporting infrastructure. Microsoft Azure, Google and Amazon Elastic, IBM's Blue Cloud and Sun Cloud are examples of the public cloud.

Private cloud offers a separate and secure cloud based environment for only particular client, private cloud operates some advantages of the public such as scalability, on demand and self-service, but they differ in ownership, moreover, unlike public clouds, which deliver services to multiple organizations on shared basis, a private cloud is dedicated to a single organization for dedicated usage, which means the resources are exclusively dedicated for use by a single client, the services and infrastructure are maintained and manage on a private network. The private cloud can be tailored by the organization's networks since is only dedicated and accessible by a single organization. And this will make the technology to be easily managed and configured by an organization. Most private cloud is used by the financial organization, government agencies, and security organizations.

A Hybrid cloud is a cloud computing technology that employed the approaches of the public and the private cloud technology for the data and applications to be shared between the two technologies and use by a single organization. Hybrid cloud provides organizations with a better flexibility and more deployment options by allowing data and applications to be moved between private and public clouds, creating the hybrid cloud type. The hybrid cloud enables organizations to enjoy the benefits of the public cloud to store vital and protected data on public and also benefits from private cloud futures while maintaining the ability of the computational resource from the public cloud to run applications that rely on the data.

CLOUD SERVICES FOR BIOMEDICAL DATA PROCESSING

The cloud computing services provide tremendous benefits which are enjoyed by the client of the technology so as to ease and assist the client in executing task diligently and efficiently. The services can be rented by the client and use them on demand basis, that means the usage of the services can be upgraded whenever the need arises or downgraded when the client is not in-need of the services, this provides flexibility options (Hurwitz, Bloor, Kaufman, & Halper, 2016), this provide a great advantage for the client to scale-down or scale-up the services as the technology is being used.

The cloud services can be categorized into Platform as-a-Service (PaaS), Infrastructure as-a-Service (IaaS) and Software as-a-Service (SaaS), (Rani, 2014).

Platform as-a-Service (PaaS)

PaaS is the complete delivery platform that enables and provides a development environment for a software developer to develop an application or software that runs on cloud environment (Rani, 2014). The platform supports operating systems enable environment and needed services for particular software to run (Furht, & Escalante, 2010). A client need not to buzzer about the storage facility usage such as the server and the network, all these facilities are managed, control, maintain and supported by the technology providers. PaaS provides database management systems and development tools for complete web application life cycle ranging from building an application, testing, deploying, managing and updating of the application. PaaS supports the following for biomedical data processing:

- Development platform to develop and customize cloud-based applications to suit organization's need and demand.
- Platform environment to process and analyze data remotely.
- Virtual environment to store data, backup, and retrieval of data.
- Secured virtual environment for data sharing.

Advantages of PaaS in Biomedical Data Processing

- Database of biomedical data processing application can be developed for multiple platforms including mobile and PC.
- PaaS offers opportunities for organization to use sophisticated, advanced software and tools that are too expensive and costly for organization to afford.
- PaaS support distribution of biomedical data processing, since data and database are accessible remotely over the internet.

Figure 3. Cloud service

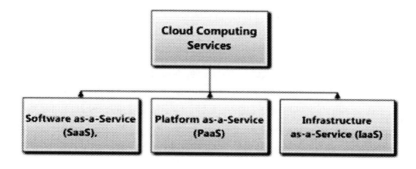

- The virtualization of storage environment supported by PaaS enhances data handling more securely.
- The PaaS capabilities enhance efficiency and easy of data management and application.

Infrastructure as-a-Service (IaaS)

IaaS offers a service to the client to rent a usage of cloud infrastructures such as the network resources, the storage facilities, the servers and other hardware resources of the cloud (Velte, Velt, & Elsenpeter, 2010), for example, a research laboratory may decide to rent a storage facility on the cloud to store biomedical data of its research or lab findings, rent a server space to host data processing applications, rent a network facility or any other cloud facility that may be needed, use them on demand basis and pay per resource usage. The basic services of IaaS as described by (Azure, 2017) are:

- IaaS offers benefits to the client of the services with the virtual development environment to develop new applications quickly; new application can be tested from the environment for ease of application deployment, the environment can be scaled up and down depends on the needs and demands of the client.
- With IaaS, organization's website can be hosted in the robust and secure platform. IaaS can handles big data Storage like biomedical data remotely; the services enable data backup and recovery for precaution against system failure and disaster.
- High-Performance Computing (HPC) for solving complex problems such as protein folding simulations and other biomedical data processing and analysis, the services enables mathematical and statistical operations on higher computing technology such as supercomputers, computer grids or computer clusters.

Advantages of IaaS in Bi-Medical Data Processing

- IaaS reduces the huge capital expense associated with establishing and managing an on-site (traditional) datacenter.
- IaaS improves availability and reliability of data processing, comparison to the traditional system of data processing. A client can access applications and data remotely even during a disaster or system outage.
- IaaS reduces cost of data processing and analysis.
- IaaS enhances the security of client applications and data than what is obtainable in traditional data center.

Software as-a-Service (SaaS)

In cloud computing, SaaS provides clients access to the applications directly for individual and enterprise users, including the content of the application, database and other infrastructure resources on demand. The accessibility of the services is via the internet, the user can use any internet based device to link to the internet and access cloud resources directly. In laboratory settings, SaaS can be rented from the service providers for storing data related to laboratory investigations, analysis, and other findings, the data stored is accessible remotely and can be accessed by multiple users concurrently from a different location. SaaS support the following services in biomedical data processing:

- Client can rent software service from service providers and tailored to suit the need and demand of an organization.
- SaaS provides web-based support so that data and database can be accessed via the internet.
- On-demand service usage metered on a pay--per usage basis.

Advantages of SaaS in Biomedical Data Processing

- The traditional system of software installation, management and debug fixing are completely eliminated compared to the on-site data center.
- SaaS service can be automatically scales up and down according to the need, demand, and level of usage.
- SaaS services provides clients with access to the advanced and sophisticated software that some organization may not afford.
- Remote service accessibility either with mobile or station PC via the internet.

BENEFITS OF BIOMEDICAL DATA PROCESSING IN CLOUD COMPUTING

- **Processing Speed:** Cloud computing facilitates provide smooth and fastest data processing since data can be processed in parallel and distributed mode regardless of location and distance.
- **Cost Effective:** To establish traditional datacenter, an organization needs to invest huge capital expenses ranging from hardware like the PCs, network facilities, servers and associated facilities. Expenses are also required for software such as OS and applications. Staffing the center with IT personnel that will take care of managing and maintenance of the center and also the provision of electricity for power and cooling of the center, all there when sum together will acquire very huge expenses to an organization. Cloud computing services can supplement the on-site data center with effective fewer expenses compare to the former.
- **Parallel Processing:** Data processing can be done from multiple terminals or systems concurrently.
- **Efficiency:** The efficiency of data processing is enhanced, for example, the rapidly increasing volume and complexity of the biomedical data from laboratories can range from hundreds of bytes to terabytes or even bigger (Anderson, 2007). The processing of such data can take a longer time with less accuracy under the traditional datacenter system, but processing of the data with cloud technology will take less time with better efficiency. However, the large size of data can be processed at a relatively less cost to the client.
- **Productivity Enhancement:** The daily task required in traditional data center consumes organization employees' time to manage the center like hardware setup and troubleshooting, cloud computing eliminates the need for these operations. The productivity of an organization can be enhanced by utilizing the time for other essential tasks.

RISKS IN BIOMEDICAL DATA PROCESSING OVER CLOUD ENVIRONMENT

Improper adequate planning when migrating to cloud computing can lead to unprecedented disappointment to the client. The client should ensure adequate security protection of the data; hence, inadequate planning when using cloud services could result in potential loss of organization's vital data and eliminating the prospective benefits of cloud computing technology. As the cloud computing popularity increases, the more serious security issues increases in deployment. In cloud technology, the facilities including the data and applications reside in the virtual environment created and maintained by the cloud services provider and the clients do not have control over the facilities but only use them as they are. The serious risk is when a provider is out of the business as a result of one reason or the other or a total failure due to natural or manmade disaster, the retrieval of the stored data and applications on the cloud may be difficult to the client. Some network devices may perform cheating during data transmission by sniffing sensitive and useful information and leak them to the malicious user (Suciu, 2013). The client must have a clear understanding of possible security risks and benefits associated with the technology when considering migration to cloud technology. The client needs to understand realistic expectations from the cloud provider, different services offered by the technology have different security requirement and approach; the client should take into consideration the security level supported by each service and capabilities of the service. However, it is important for the client to understand the regulations and the relevant obligations bounded on the provider and the client such as data retention, security provision and interoperability of client existing system with the provider's platform. These will enable the client to identify and understand the provider capabilities, legal issues and the possible legal risks before migrating data to a cloud environment. There are certain issues associated with cloud computing that an organization needs to scrutinize adequately before migration biomedical data to cloud environment, such as:

- **Reluctance of Commitment:** Migrating data to cloud environment means client's complete submission of data ownership and control, some issues that are out of service agreement may arise and the provider may be reluctant to address them in time and this will create security hitches of the data.
- **Responsibility Ambiguity:** Both the provider and client are liable to responsibilities of managing and control and security provision for data protection in the virtual cloud environment, both parties responsibilities should be clearly mentioned in the service agreement, the client and provider roles should be clearly stated to avoid ambiguities. Provider and client must understand the responsibilities and roles bounded on them and must strictly adhere to them for the successful deployment and implementation of the system.
- **Authorization:** Adequate complex authentication mechanism should be enforced since the cloud resources are accessible remotely from anywhere via the Internet, there is a need to establish a more complex verification mechanism for user identity, hence strong and adequate authentication mechanism is among the critical concern issues.
- **Failure Risk:** Client should understand that public cloud is a multi-tenancy system, the cloud resources are shared among the clients of the services and the risk of system failure is inevitable and cannot be predicted, thus adequate planning needs to be made from the client part before any happen.

- **Legal Risks:** Client should understand the legal risk carefully and must adhere to the responsibilities provided in the service agreement.
- **Apparent Maintenance**: Cloud technology provider should have proactive infrastructure maintenance capability to handle issues such as hardware failure and software updates; this will enhance reliability, availability and security of services.
- **Load Balancing:** A provider needs to support load balancing technology, this will help to reduce excess congestion by distributing incoming system's user requests across pools of instances for maximum performance of the services.

CLOUD SERVICE PROVIDER RESPONSIBILITIES

The provider of the cloud technology service should have certain obligations that are expected to be fulfilled, these include:

1. The provider is responsible for maintenance, workability, and availability of the services, the signed contract agreement between provider and client is expected to be adhered by both parties, all the agreed terms as providers responsibilities most to strictly adhere.
2. Security of the data and services must be maintained by the provider.
3. The provider is responsible for keeping transactions and system logs for system auditing.
4. Provider needs to have complete commitment for adequate delivery of the services; the services ought to remain available, operational and accessible to the client at any time.

CLOUD SERVICES CLIENT RESPONSIBILITIES

The client is expected to ensure maximum utilization of services throughout the period of the contract.

1. By agreeing to use the cloud services, the client has entered a contract and is expected to adhere to all its terms, including adherence to an upfront payment of services usage when needed.
2. It is the responsibility of the client to determine and assign who should use and access the services and data, as such, is oblige to assign the user(s) who should access and use the cloud services
3. The provider only provides space for setting and storing the data, but maintenance and updating the data is sole responsibilities of the client.

CLOUD TECHNOLOGY SECURITY TIPS

Before choosing a cloud provider an organization needs to ensure the following security guidelines are strictly abided by the service provider.

1. Confidentiality of data should be enforced to support technical and security tools such as encryption and decryption and access control, as well as data legal protections. There should be a set of

very strict rules that will limit access to certain types of information except for authorized access. This means keeping an organization's data secured and safe is the paramount and the information between the service provider and the client and should not be disclosed to an unauthorized person.

2. The service provider ought to be honest, and maintain integrity degree of confidence that the data in the cloud is what is supposed to be there and adhere to moral and ethical principles of data integrity. The data should be strictly save guided and protected against accidental, eventuality or deliberate alteration of data. The integrity should be supported by authorized and sophisticated audit system to ensure adequate adherence to rules of law.

3. Availability of data should be enforced so that the data and necessary tools and facilities subscribed by the client are available and accessible for 24x7 regardless of time and distance, theses means the client should be able to use the services as anticipated. This cannot be achieved without adequate facilities provision and capacity of the service provider.

4. The provider has clients' obligations to account for the activities and system logs of the services access and transactions for proper accountability and should be responsible for auditing the logs as well as providing secure system access control.

5. The provider has the responsibility to ensure the guarantee of the services, as well as the system workability and the system performance behaves as expected.

BIOMEDICAL DATA SCIENCE

Data science as explained by (Amos, 2017) it involves coordination and integration of disciplines such as Biomedical Informatics and Biostatistics for automated management, retrieval, and interpretation of extensive biomedical and health related information. Biomedical data science can be viewed as the scientific methods that provide conceptual integration of technologies and tools that enable the processing, retrievals, analysis, interpretation, and presentations of biomedical data in secured and understandable fashion for end-user consumption.

Data science as scientific method comprises fact findings and investigation for the purpose of acquiring new knowledge from the data and integrating previous knowledge from the data, this involves systematic observation, experiment, measurement, formulation, and testing of hypotheses with the aim of discovering new ideas and concepts. To achieve the success of this scientific method, techniques are required in the science of data, such as tools and theories drawn from many fields of knowledge within the broad areas of mathematics and statistics, software tools and applications, security and cloud computing from computer science (see Figure 4). The goal of biomedical data science is to turn data into actionable knowledge through vigorous analysis and interpretation of an idea from information generated based on data analysis and interpretations.

BIOMEDICAL BIG DATA IN CLOUD

Biomedical data are the type that deals with the life of a human being and such data can be generated from experiment or test carried out from collecting samples. The data may be much larger than the organization's facility's capacity to handle. Biomedical big data are data sets related to health issues

Figure 4. Data science in biomedical data processing

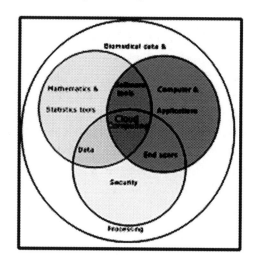

that can be analyzed to discover patterns and trends associated with the facts. The advancement of new technologies and innovations has increased the rate of data generation and its complexity and these have influenced the expansion of data such as biomedical one, as such, the intensity of the data complexity cannot be handled by a traditional application designed for data processing such as relational database (Sharvari, 2017).. These have demanded new technology like cloud computing as the alternative solution for data storage and processing. Cloud Technology like all other technologies has its possible bottleneck as expressed by (Marx, 2013). With the cloud technology, a client can harness both the computing power and the facilities needed online and use them on demand to carry out data processing online with the computing services supported by the technology. The technology therefore, provides an opportunity for data to be stored in the cloud environment regardless of size for future use; such data can also be retrieved at any time regardless of distance.

Choosing cloud technology means entrusting organization's vital data to a distant service provider; the services may be subject to obstructions due to one reason or the other such as hardware failure, system outage and security threats. However, issues may arise when data are stored in several clouds and need to be merged. Several questions need to come to the client's minds for this, such as where is the data stored? Is the data stored in the client's vicinity, is the data stored in a secure form, what will happen to the data when a client no longer needs the services of the cloud service provider and can the data be transferred to a new service provider in case of a change of service provider. Many forget to think and ask them self about these critical questions. However, a political phenomenon needs to be considered in deciding cloud providers, since the provider may not necessarily be from the host country of the client. For example, making inferences from the previous and current political and power struggles among different countries across the globe, either in the same or different region, choosing a cloud provider has to be critical within the domain of future occurrences. This will helps an organization to plan adequately and avoid being a victim of circumstances; failures to make curious choices may lead an organization to be a victim of worth dilemma. Therefore, it is important for organizations and individuals envisaging migrating to cloud computing technology to consider these factors.

DATA PROTECTION IN CLOUD

Virtualization of resources is the core of cloud computing technology; the technology allows the use of abstract logical interfaces for accessing cloud resources such as the servers, network, and storage. Security is becoming a serious issue of concern in the technology, many individuals, organizations, and government establishments are becoming victims of a cyber security breach due to inadequate enforcement of security policy, data protection policy is becoming a serious problem associated with cloud storage technology, the providers of this technology are trying their best to provide and maintain the security of the technology at some level of protections but still more needs to be done. The alternate option of system backup is required as precaution mechanism. Organization's hardware and software can be utilized for a backup system to supplement cloud technology and use both as needed to complement eventualities.

Data Backup

Data backup is a system that enables a duplicate copy of vital data to be stored in another means for retrievals in a case of natural disaster or system failure; this will help to reduce the effects of a catastrophic consequence of data loss. Today, there are many data backup systems and services that will be useful for enterprises and organizations to secure data such as a biomedical one; the backup mechanism will ensure that data and information are not lost due to disaster or system failure.

Data Backup Policy

In computing technology backup process is apply to critical databases to safeguard the data against eventualities accuracy. Backup should be scheduled for at least once a week, especially during weekends or off-time hours. To supplement weekly full backups, organizations can schedule a sequence of differential or incremental data backup that backup only data that has changed since the last full backup took place (Rouse, 2016). With a backup system, an organization can keep a copy of its vital data and database system on backup storage device

SECURITY IN CLOUD TECHNOLOGY

The goal of cloud technology is to acquire the clients' data to be completely migrated to the cloud provider without considering the security risk of doing that, though some cloud providers like Google and Amazon have the infrastructure that can deflect and survive a cyber attack but not every cloud provider has such capability (Lori, 2009). Cloud computing like other related computing technologies is featured with security threats that can affect the proper performances of the technology. Adequate measures are needed to save guard the vital data stored in the cloud; the measures should include effective policy, strategy, governance and holistic approach to the security related problems. However, there is a need for a standard universal security mechanism and policy to address the challenges at the global level, and enforcement of the policy and standard for abiding by all providers should be adopted for smooth running and technology challenges handling.

TIPS FOR SELECTING CLOUD STORAGE PROVIDER

Cloud storage environment is a virtual setting that allows data to be stored and access by the client remotely; the provider of the technology needs to ensure adequate safety of the storage system. It is also vital for the client to assess the reliability and capability of a service provider before entrusting organization's vital data to the provider. Some criteria were set to be the guidelines for choosing a cloud service provider (Azure, 2017) .

- **Financial Strength:** The provider should have a good track record of financial stability with sufficient capital strength to operate successfully over the long term.
- **Truest:** The provider should have a good reputation of trust.
- **Technical Know-How:** Provider should have the technical expertise and know-how for handling technical issues, user support and capability to understand client needs.
- **Resource Monitoring:** Provider should have a provision of resource monitoring and configuration management to track and monitor services provided to clients.
- **Billing System:** There should be automated billing and accounting system to monitor resources usage and cost.
- The provider should have mechanisms for easy deployment, management and upgrades of software and applications.
- **Application Interfaces:** The provider should have provision of standard Application Interfaces (APIs) for client to easily build connections to the cloud and integration support with the client existing infrastructure
- **Service Documentation:** The provider should have adequate documentation for operating the services.
- There should be comprehensive and adequate security mechanisms, policies and procedures in place for controlling access and client systems.
- **Backup and Restore:** Provision of policies and procedures for data backup and restore of client data.

CLOUD DATA STORAGE

Data is the key component for any organization that deals with biomedical facts, the success and failure the organization depend on how the data is handling, processed and stored. Cloud data Storage is a service that enables maintenance, management, and backup of data remotely. When data is stored in the cloud, the client of the cloud service can access the data remotely. The data storage services provided by the cloud providers reduce cost of handling the data through consolidation of all the data types in one single platform of storage, organizations can achieve full capacity utilization of its strength for maximum usage of the data, and with the services supported by cloud technology, the data can be managed, processed and delivered easily either in single or distribution form. However, availability of data is assured with the services since the data can be accessed remotely provided there is internet access. The centralized online backup and control can also be achieved with the technology and this will be useful in case of disaster and system failure.

Advantages of Cloud Data Storage

- **Accessibility**: With the data stored in the cloud, the client or the user(s) can access the data from any location regardless of distance provided there is an internet connection from the access location.
- **Data Safety and Assurance:** The cloud technology offers advantage of safety since data stored on PC can be corrupt due to faulty from the storage device or other hardware failures.
- **Security:** Cloud service providers provide better and enhance security than traditional data storage
- **Data Sharing:** Data can be shared easily from one user to another in more secure manner
- **Data Recovery:** Cloud providers provide quick recovery of data in case of failure, this makes the technology safer and secure than traditional data storage system.
- **Automatic Data Backup:** Client can benefit from services supported by the provider to schedule automatic backup of data.
- **Usability of Data:** The data stored in the cloud environment can be used by more than one user at the same time. However, the data used by one user also can be reused by another user for a different purpose.
- **Disaster Recovery:** Cloud storage can be used as a backup plan in case of emergency or disaster since the data are stored at a remote location and can be accessed via the internet.
- **Cost Savings:** Organizations subscribing the services of cloud technology can reduce operational costs of data handling; storage and processing since establishing a local datacenter within an organization require the cost of staffing the datacenter, software and hardware maintenance annually. When comparing to the cost of using cloud storage; the technology offers better cost effective than traditional datacenter.

Disadvantages of Cloud Data Storage

- **Breach of Security:** To access cloud service, the user or client need to be authenticated before login, the most common login mechanism are the user-id and password, if these are not handle safely, may fall in to the wrong hands. A cyber breach like user's credentials hacking can be a serious threat to the technology and can lead to unauthorized access of the data. It is recommended to remember the login access details and keep them safely, a user should avoid using several passwords that cannot remember; it is a good idea to adopt the habit of using unique credentials for most common online accesses. However, uses of complex and sophisticated credentials are recommended to secure login and the data access.
- **Technical Hitches:** Technical failures can be a setback for the service, for example, to access the data remotely, internet connection is required. If the connection is not available at a particular access location then the user will not have access to the data. Also when an internet access goes down due to a technical problem the user will not be able to access the data. However, provider's server can fail as results of unprecedented technical issues; when any one of these happened, can be a drawback of cloud technology.
- **Provider Option:** Many cloud storage providers exist online, some are free while some are not, and an organization has the option to choose one of its choices, on which the organization can

trust. It is important to take not in mind that the providers are meant for profit making due to one reason or the other, a provider may fall into a dilemma such bankruptcy which can make the provider exit from the business, when quitting the provider may not necessarily notify its' customers. It is recommended for any organization that deals with boil-medical data to avoid free online providers and go for reputable and esteem providers, hence the security of such data is crucial to any organization.

- **Data Security:** Even though an organization has submitted its vital data to cloud providers, the risk of losing confidentiality of the data is there. Recently, there are serious concerns about the safety and privacy of data across the globe. Some security agencies were accused of accessing private data stored in the cloud without the approval of the concerned data owners. An organization migrating to cloud computing should take note of serious risks associated with the technology and make adequate plan for deployment of the technology.
- **Bandwidth Issues:** Accessing data from cloud require the use of the internet, it could be a tedious task if an organization is having a bandwidth problem, though, some cloud storage provider unlimited bandwidth and some have a specific bandwidth allowance for clients. By surpassing the allowed bandwidth, additional charges are applied to the client. These are issues that organization should take into considerations when migrating to cloud technology.

CLOUD STORAGE CLASSES

Cloud computing enables scalable data and application storage that require durability and high availability. The technology supports various categories of storage and services. Some larger organizations require processing of hundreds of terabytes of data and larger storage space such as financial and scientific organizations. Some organization requires medium processing and medium storage space. Some small organizations need small processing and small storage space. The technology providers have support for various demands with payment options of pay per service usage basis. The levels of storage support and capabilities depend on the provider operational plan; some support multi-regional, regional and low-cost storage of hot and cool access depending on data usage frequencies.

For example, Google offers four storage classes of multi-regional storage, regional storage, nearline storage, and coldline Storage. All the classes offer the same throughput, low latency, and high durability. The classes differ by their availability, minimum storage durations, and pricing for storage and access (Coldline, 2017).

- **Multi-Regional Storage:** This class is best for storing data that is frequently accessed around the world to ensure maximum availability of client's data, the provider store client data in at least two regions separated by at least 100 miles, this helps to save guard the data against an event of disruptions, such as natural disasters.
- **Regional Storage:** This class enables storing frequently accesses data in the same region and enables the client to store data at lower cost, with the data being stored in a specific regional location, instead of having data distributed over a large geographic area. The advantage of this class over multi-regional is the reduction in network charges to the client.
- **Nearline Storage:** This class is ideal for the data which is less frequently accessible on an average of once a month and is Ideal for backup, disaster recovery, and archival. A client can continuously

add files to Cloud Storage and plan to access those files once a month for analysis. Hence, the plan is cost effective for less frequently uses data.

- **Coldline Storage:** This class is the ideal choice for data access at most once a year, the class offers very low cost plan compare to nearline storage and is good for data archive, online backup, and recovery.

The Microsoft azure cloud storage, on the other hand, provides four services of blob storage that support hot and cool access levels, table storage, queue storage, and file storage. The services are elastic and the client pay for the amount of data stored and the number of requests made against the data, that means client pay per usage basis (Azure, 2017).

- **Blob Storage:** Is designed for data storage of all kinds, the data can be text or binary, such as a document, media file, or application. Blob offers storage robustness, availability of data and services scalability for the client to upgrade or downgrade the services. The hot access level indicates that the data objects in the cloud storage will be more frequently accessed and this give cost benefits for the client. The Cool access level indicates that the data objects in the cloud storage will be less frequently accessed than hot access level, the plan provides lower data storage cost to the client.

- **Table Storage:** Provides support for the storage of structured datasets, the services offer storage availability at all time, the service is scalable for an upgrade and down grade, and the data from this service can be rapidly processed in a larger quantity and can be accessed easily. This type of storage class is mostly used by software developers to create agile applications since it supports fast and cost effective data access for all kinds of applications. Table storage supports flexible datasets storage, such as user data for web applications, and, biomedical data for processing via web and desktop applications.

- **Queue Storage:** Provides the client with a reliable storage facility that supports message workflow processing and asynchronous communication between various application components in the cloud services domain.

- **File Storage:** Is ideal for storing data that needs to be shared among applications, with Azure virtual machines, cloud services can share file data across application components via mounted shares, and on-premises applications can access file data in a shared mode.

Similarly, Amazon Web Services (AWS) provides on-demand cloud computing platforms such as data storage that can handle a large amount of biomedical data. AWS offers a complete range of cloud storage services to support both application and backup compliance requirements. An awesome future of AWS is support for innovations in healthcare and clinical analytics. AWS like other cloud providers provide supports for a range of storage classes (Amazon, 2017):

- **Amazon Elastic File System (Amazon EFS):** Provides scalable storage for use with Amazon EC2 instances in the AWS Cloud. EFS supports high availability and durability of the services, and provides support for storage in Big Data and analytics such as biomedical, media processing workflows, content management and web services.

- **Amazon Simple Storage Service (Amazon S3):** Is designed to support object storage and access of any type of data over the Internet. S3 is object storage built to store and retrieves any amount of data remotely; the data is accessible via web sites and mobile apps, corporate applications, and data from IoT sensors or devices. S3 can support backup and recovery, data archive and Big Data analytics.

- **Amazon Elastic Block Storage (Amazon EBS):** Is designed to support highly available, consistent, low-latency block storage for Elastic Compute Cloud (EC2) web services by enhancing client's applications storage capacity and performances.
- **Amazon Glacier:** Is a low-cost and highly durable object storage service for long-term backup and archive of any type of object data. The service is designed to support low cost cloud storage for frequently less accessed data.
- **AWS Storage Gateway:** Is a software platform services that seamlessly links client's on-premises environment to Amazon cloud storage. The gateway connects to AWS storage services such as Amazon S3, Amazon Glacier and Amazon EBS. The technology has support for local storage with a highly optimized data transfer mechanism and connectivity to AWS Cloud storage, and helps with migration and storage bursting capabilities of the client.
- **Data Transfer Services:** Amazon supports a platform for data transfer services for data migration into and out of the AWS cloud. The services help the client to explore more cloud benefits such as accelerating data transfers quickly and securely to cloud archives and capture continuous data streaming from multiple sources.

FUTURE RESEARCH DIRECTIONS

Security is one of the main challenging issues in the cloud data storage technology as discussed in the chapter; this reveals that, there is a need for more research to be done to design and develop automatic resource and sophisticated security management system for enhancing data storage technology. This includes concrete security policy measures and standard that should be adopted by all the players in the technology.

CONCLUSION

The emergence of cloud computing technology provides many opportunities and flexibility for handling large and complex data, the services supported technologies are scalable, the client can upscale or downscale the services base on demand, similarly, the client pays the service usage based on pay as you go plan, this can provide an organization or the client opportunity to save costs and increases organization's productivity. Organizations handling biomedical data can benefit from the services support by cloud computing technology as an automated platform for handling and processing large amount of data. Despite the benefits of the technology, data in the cloud environment is subjective to security threats. The chapter provides detailed analysis of cloud computing deployment strategies, services supported by the technology for biomedical data processing and security risks associated with the services. Tips were presented in the chapter that will be useful for organization and individual considering cloud computing deployment as an alternative option for biomedical data storage and processing. The chapter also discusses the benefits that can be driven from the cloud computing technology and the demerits of the technology, the challenges associated with the technology deployment and solution to the security intimidations in the data storage were also discussed. Cloud storage classes supported by some major players in the technology were presented with different features, benefits and supported technology with related to the cloud data storage. Therefore, for organization envisaging cloud computing technology should be aware about the tremendous benefits that can be driven from the technology, which can also promote the organization's standard, but curious and serious care should taken into consideration to safeguard the integrity of the data with optimum security measures and for the organization that had embraced the technology should take extra security measures to promote the validity and integrity of the entrusted data to the cloud.

REFERENCES

Amazon. (2017). *Healthcare Providers and Insurers in the Cloud.* Retrieved 7 13, 2017, from Amazon web services: https://aws.amazon.com/health/providers-and-insurers/

Amos, C. (2017). *Biomedical data science.* Retrieved June 29, 2017, from Geisel School of Medicine: https://bmds.dartmouth.edu/biomedical-data-science

Anderson, N. R.-H., Lee, E. S., Brockenbrough, J. S., Minie, M. E., Fuller, S., Brinkley, J., & Tarczy-Hornoch, P. (2007). Issues in Biomedical Research Data Management and Analysis: Needs and Barriers. *Journal of the American Medical Informatics Association*, *14*(4), 478–488. doi:10.1197/jamia.M2114 PMID:17460139

Anthony, T., & Velte, T. J. (2010). *Cloud Computing A practical Approach.* New Delhi: McGraw Hill.

Arijit Kumar, P., Nilanjan, D., & Sourav, S. (2014). A hybrid reversible watermarking technique for color biomedical images. In Computational Intelligence and Computing Research. New Delhi: IEEE.

Azure, M. (2017). *What is cloud computing?* Retrieved 7 2, 2017, from Micrososft Azure: https://azure.microsoft.com/en-in/overview/what-is-cloud-computing/

Borko Furht, A. E. (2010). *Hand Book on Cloud Computing.* London: Springer. doi:10.1007/978-1-4419-6524-0

Dimpi Rani, R. K. (2014, June). A Comparative Study of SaaS, PaaS and IaaS in Cloud Computing. *International Journal of Advanced Research in Computer Science and Software Engineering*, *4*(6), 458–461.

Elhossiny, I., Nirmeen, A. E., & Fatma, A. O. (2016). *Task Scheduling Algorithm in Cloud Computing Environment Based on Cloud Pricing Models. In Computer Applications & Research.* Cairo, Egypt: IEEE.

Francesco, E., Giuliana, D., & Luigi, P. (2009). A Summary of Genomic Databases: Overview and Discussion. In Bioinformatice Data and Applications (pp. 37-59). Springer-Verlag Berlin.

George Suciu, S. H. (2013). Cloud Computing as Evolution of Distributed Computing – A Case Study. *Informações Econômicas*, *7*(4), 109–122. doi:10.12948/issn14531305/17.4.2013.10

Google. (2017, June 29). *Archival Cloud Storage: Nearline & Coldline.* Retrieved July 12, 2017, from Google Cloud Platform: https://cloud.google.com/storage/archival/

Ipsita Kar, I., Parida, R. N. R., & Das, H. (2016). *Energy aware scheduling using genetic algorithm in cloud data centers. In Electrical, Electronics, and Optimization Techniques.* IEEE.

Judith Hurwitz, R. B. (2016). cloud Computing for dummies (J. Jensen, Ed.). Delhi, India: A Wiley Brand.

Lori, M. K. A. (2009). Data Security in the World of Cloud Computing. *IEEE Security & Privacy, 7*(4), 1-64.

Marx, V. (2013, June). Biology: The big challenges of big data. *Nature, 498*(7453), 255–260. doi:10.1038/498255a PMID:23765498

Mohammad, Y., & Adnan, A. A. (2018). Improving Privacy and Security of User Data in Location Based Services. *Ambient Computing and Intelligence, 9*(1), 24.

Panigrahi, C. R., Tiwary, M., Pati, B., & Das, H. (2016). Big Data and Cyber Foraging: Future Scope and Challenges. In B. Mishra, S. Dehuri, E. Kim, & G. N. Wang (Eds.), *Techniques and Environments for Big Data Analysis. Studies in Big Data* (Vol. 17). Cham: Springer. doi:10.1007/978-3-319-27520-8_5

Rouse, M. (2016, September). *What is your strategy for selectively performing data backup?* Retrieved 06 20, 2017, from TechTerget: http://searchdatabackup.techtarget.com/definition/backup

Sayan, C., Prasenjit, M., Arijit, K. P., Debalina, B., & Nilanjan, D. (2014) Reversible Color Image Watermarking Using Trigonometric Functions. Electronic Systems Signal Processing and Computing Technologies.

Sharvari, C. T., Vijender, K. S., Pati, B., & Madhuri, S. J. (2017). The Basics of Big Data and Security Concerns. In *Privacy and Security Policies in Big Data.* IGI Global.

KEY TERMS AND DEFINITIONS

Biomedical Big Data: A large and complex data related to the health status.

Biomedical Data: Row facts related to the health status that can be processed to get information.

Biomedical Data Science: A scientific method that provides conceptual integration of technologies and tools that enables processing, retrievals, analysis, interpretation, and presentations of biomedical data in secured and understandable fashion for end-user consumption.

Cloud Computing: The delivery of computing services and resources such as the servers, storage, databases, networking, software, and analytic through the internet.

Cloud Environment: An accessible virtual environment for computing resources and services that holds data and applications remotely.

Cloud Technology Client: The end-user that leases the services of cloud computing technology and uses them on demand basis.

Cloud Technology Management: The virtual management and control of the data and applications over cloud environment.

Data Processing: The act of data manipulation through integration of mathematical tools, statistics, and computer application to generate information.

Data Science: A knowledge acquisition from data through scientific method that comprises systematic observation, experiment, measurement, formulation, and hypotheses testing with the aim of discovering new ideas and concepts.

This research was previously published in the Handbook of Research on Information Security in Biomedical Signal Processing edited by Chittaranjan Pradhan, Himansu Das, Bighnaraj Naik, and Nilanjan Dey, pages 177-197, copyright year 2018 by Information Science Reference (an imprint of IGI Global).

Chapter 87
Meeting Compliance Requirements While Using Cloud Services

S. Srinivasan
Texas Southern University, USA

ABSTRACT

Compliance with government and industry regulations is an essential part of conducting business in several sectors. Many of the requirements revolve around financial, privacy, or security aspects. Most of the requirements are due to federal regulations in USA while some are industry requirements that are applicable globally. Even some of the federal regulations in USA apply to service providers abroad when they are providing service to entities in USA. In that sense, all of the compliance requirements discussed here apply to a global audience. In this chapter, the authors discuss in detail the scope of the Health Insurance Portability and Accountability Act, Sarbanes-Oxley Act, Federal Information Security Management Act, Gramm-Leach-Bliley Act, Payment Card Industry Requirements, and the Statement on Auditing Standards 70. These compliance requirements concern protecting the customer data stored in the cloud with respect to confidentiality and integrity. Several of these requirements have significant enforcement powers associated with them, and businesses need to take these requirements seriously and comply. The compliance aspect involves gathering and reporting appropriate information on a regular basis. The authors present details on all these aspects in this chapter.

1. INTRODUCTION

Many businesses are required to meet certain compliance requirements either by the government or by the industry in which they operate. For many years businesses were able to gather the necessary data for compliance because they owned their IT system. With the popularity of cloud computing many businesses, both large and small which use cloud services, have to gather the necessary data in order to meet the compliance requirements. In this chapter we will identify the necessary compliance requirements and how businesses could meet those requirements with respect to some of the major laws and

DOI: 10.4018/978-1-5225-8176-5.ch087

industry requirements. These are: Health Insurance and Portability Act (HIPAA), Sarbanes-Oxley Act (SOX), Gramm-Leach-Bliley Act (GLBA), Federal Information Security Management Act (FISMA), Payment Card Industry (PCI), and Statement on Auditing Standards 70 (SAS 70). These requirements are put in place to provide adequate security and privacy for the data related to financial transactions, health care records, and credit cards. Some of these laws were enacted to address the abuse of trust placed in businesses. All the requirements specified in this chapter relate to laws and requirements in USA. Because of the worldwide reach of many multinational corporations in USA many of these laws and requirements extend beyond USA and are applicable in other countries as well when they relate to businesses in USA. Thus the implications of the use of the cloud services globally have implications when it is related to an American business.

Use of cloud services by its very design leaves the control of the computing infrastructure outside the control of the business using the cloud service. Many surveys have confirmed that this lack of control is a major concern for businesses when it comes to data security. Some technologies are better suited to protecting confidential information than others. Antonopoulos and Gillam discuss many of the fundamental issues associated with cloud computing in their book (Antonopoulos, 2010). Their book provides further amplification on many of the topics discussed in this book. Information Technology is a necessary conduit to facilitate business transactions of all kinds. Today businesses gather vast amounts of data effortlessly from every type of action an individual performs with a business. Some of these data may contain confidential information related to a person's health or financial standing. The various laws and industry requirements that we will discuss in this chapter address aspects related to privacy and security of such data. In many cases the requirements involve processes and data flow aspects that businesses follow. For the cloud computing industry there is an international organization called Cloud Security Alliance (CSA) that offers guidelines and forums (Cloud Security Alliance, 2013). CSA is the leading industry supported group that provides guidelines to service providers and customers worldwide. Major corporations and government agencies that participate in CSA activities are: Amazon Web Services, Google, Microsoft, HP, Cisco, RSA, Rackspace, Oracle, US Department of Defense, and Salesforce.

Before analyzing the compliance aspects that we set out to discuss in this chapter, we discuss some of the important literature on this topic first. The growth of cloud computing is discussed in detail by Armbrust, et al in their View of Cloud Computing (Armbrust, 2010). One of the main contributions of this work is that cloud computing takes advantage of economies of scale in locating their data centers. Furthermore, many cloud providers depend on open source software since licensing models for commercial software are often a handicap for growth of cloud computing. In the influential paper "Hey, You, Get Off of My Cloud" the authors Ristenpart, Tromer, Schacham and Savage argue that the major risk in cloud computing is data co-location for multiple users. These authors recommend two ways to mitigate this risk by blocking network-based co-residence checks or a customer using all the virtual machines on a physical server irrespective of how much computing resource they need on a single server (Ristenpart, 2009). Since the growth of cloud computing is rapid, Sengupta, Kalgud and Sharma examine the security aspects in the cloud and the future research directions. Their analysis discusses the major concerns in cloud computing such as the physical security of the cloud providers' system, the way the cloud provider handles data in their servers and in backup systems, access control for the various cloud resources for the customer, and how the providers support compliance aspects (Sengupta, 2011). We conclude this brief review of current literature with the work of Yang and Tate in which they categorize the contributions of nearly 150 research articles (Yang, 2012).

Our goal in this chapter is to present details on compliance required by federal laws and industry standards. We will discuss how a business must design its business processes in order to gather the necessary data for compliance requirements. In some cases the cloud service user must enter into a specific agreement with the cloud service provider in order to gather the necessary data. We will give examples of processes and technological approaches that will support meeting these compliance requirements. In the next several sections we will describe the major laws and industry requirements first and then follow it up in the last section about how to meet many of the compliance requirements when using a cloud based solution.

2. HIPAA

Health Insurance Portability and Accountability Act (HIPAA) was enacted in 1996 to address the health care challenges people face when they switch or lose jobs (HIPAA, 2013). In many instances the insurers were excluding people for a set period of time from coverage under the pre-existing clause for any type of medical condition. HIPAA was enacted to address this problem whereby the insurers were required to continue medical coverage for people for a set period of time under the same terms they were in when they switched or lost jobs. Thus, HIPAA facilitated mobility of people from one job to another as well as movement from one place to another without fear of job lock. Simultaneously, HIPAA added data security and privacy aspects when it came to dealing with a person's health data. First, HIPAA clearly delineated that the individual about whom the health data has been gathered must consent when the data is shared with others. Second, the organizations such as hospitals that gather health data of individuals must have verifiable processes to protect the data from being exposed to unauthorized people. Third, anyone collecting health care data about an individual must have a clear purpose for such collection. Any individual or organization violating these principles is subject to severe penalties. Even though HIPAA mandated that patients must consent to sharing their health data for any purpose, the USA PATRIOT Act that was enacted in the aftermath of the September 11, 2001 terrorist attacks exempted law enforcement from notifying or seeking permission of the patient when their health data was required for any investigative purposes. This Act, commonly referred to as the Patriot Act, stands for Uniting and Strengthening America by Providing Appropriate Tools Required to Intercept and Obstruct Terrorism. It was reauthorized in 2005 with some minor changes.

As discussed above, the principal scope of HIPAA is to protect and secure patient data. For this reason HIPAA violations are seriously prosecuted. Consequently, people dealing with HIPAA are adequately trained in handling sensitive data. One of the HIPAA requirements is that organizations that collect health care data about individuals must have a process to protect the data, its storage must be encrypted and any transmission of data to other parties must follow strict security protocols. Today many health care providers such as hospitals, pharmacies, laboratories and insurers are required to comply with HIPAA requirements and prove to their licensing bodies that they are compliant. In order to meet the compliance requirements organizations must gather data. When health care data is prepared for creating policies and procedures the data must de-identify the individual. When data is owned by the organization they will be in a better position to comply with these requirements. However when the data is stored in the cloud and transmitted over the internet, then meeting the compliance requirements are more challenging.

A major modification to the HIPAA rules were announced on January 25, 2013 in light of the introduction of electronic medical records and use of cloud services in health care. The changes proposed to the HIPAA rules under this revision are intended to enhance the Health Information Technology and is known as the HITECH Act. This stands for Health Information Technology for Economic and Clinical Health and was enacted in 2009 to take advantage of the technological capabilities to ensure sharing of health records as well as protecting the security and privacy of such data. These new rules clarify the responsible party for any HIPAA violation. A health care organization such as a hospital, pharmacy, laboratory or a health insurance company is known as the 'covered entity' under this rule. Organizations such as IT vendors who provide services to facilitate transmission and storage of electronic health data are known as 'business associates.' Under the 1996 HIPAA requirements only the covered entities were responsible for data security, privacy and protection unless they had an explicit arrangement with a vendor for these purposes. An analysis of the data breaches related to health data reveals that many of them happened with the loss of mobile devices such as laptops, flash drives and PDAs that were used by the business associates. Since the use of these types of devices is only growing more, the responsibility for data protection had to be identified clearly. With the advent of cloud computing, the modified rules hold the business associates responsible for protection of health data because they deal with much of the data processing. As mentioned before there is a severe penalty for any violation. For example, a business associate will be fined $1.5 million per violation under the modified rule as part of the HITECH Act. Moreover, the HITECH Act removes the exemption provided under the original HIPAA rules which allowed for revocation of penalties if the violations were corrected within a 30 day period. Given the severity of the penalties that many businesses would face, they have to take adequate protective measures to guard against any violation.

HIPAA rules require each covered entity to have written plans for:

1. Disaster recovery
2. Data backup
3. Emergency mode operation

Besides these requirements, each covered entity should also take prudent steps to encrypt all protected health information both in transit and at rest, have access controls in place and an audit process to verify that these requirements are met. The audit results will be used in providing evidence for compliance requirements. These are considered prudent measures and assume that the covered entity has control over the information system infrastructure and storage. Given today's widespread use of cloud services organizations that use cloud services must have adequate measures to verify the compliance aspects related to these three expectations. We will address this aspect in greater detail later in this chapter in section 8.

The Electronic Medical Record (EMR) provision of HIPAA was intended to facilitate sharing of medical information among the various entities involved in providing health care to individuals (Federal Register, 2013). Often health records of individuals were held by the providers for their exclusive use. This practice prevented providing quality health care whereby certain parties in the health care loop needed additional information about the patients but were unable to obtain them in a timely manner. The availability of EMR facilitates storing the data related to a patient in a shareable database that other providers could access under proper access control. Cloud Computing is a natural conduit for this purpose. By using the cloud all providers will be able to load their data for a patient in a shareable database without having to have the necessary computing infrastructure to manage the complex computing system. In Europe such a centralized system exists for many years because each individual has a health identification card that has basic information about the individual and the use of this card enables health care providers around Europe to transfer health data for the patient to the central storage which then becomes available for other providers to use. In Europe's model the individual's health identification card serves the authentication purpose for accessing the confidential health data. In Europe such a model works well because of nationalized health care. For USA, the suitable method to share necessary health data is facilitated by the cloud services but the authentication part is still the responsibility of the customer who provides access to selected individuals.

When multiple providers start loading EMR data for individuals the volume of data stored in the database grows very rapidly. In order to process such volumes of data rapidly Google developed the MapReduce process. An open source implementation of MapReduce is Hadoop by Apache software. Many of the cloud solution providers in the medical field implement the Hadoop technology to handle large volumes of data. One of the major EMR providers is GE Health Care's Centricity program. MedCloud, in partnership with GE Health Care, provides a cloud based solution to physicians to implement EMR in their practices. The major benefits of this cloud based approach is the ability to get a robust service implemented quickly at a lower cost and not have the need to have an IT specialist on staff to manage the system. This Software as a Service (SaaS) solution provides the physicians with the necessary HIPAA certified system that is scalable. Other comparable high-end cloud based solutions for EMR are AdvancedMD, AthenaHealth and MedPlus.

3. SARBANES-OXLEY ACT (SOX)

Sarbanes-Oxley Act (SOX) was enacted in 2002 as a direct result of the financial abuses of companies like Enron, WorldCom, Tyco, and Xerox as well as external auditors like the Arthur Anderson Company. All these companies, other than Xerox, went out of business because of direct financial fraud or abetting such action. SOX mandated strict compliance requirements for internal controls and accountability for all publicly traded companies. These compliance requirements have created a new set of businesses that specialize in helping organizations comply with SOX requirements. Businesses find the SOX compliance an expensive proposition. SOX compliance requires extensive record keeping and performing periodic audits. The general expectation for data retention for SOX compliance is five years. Because of the stringent requirements for compliance, financial frauds in publicly traded companies are going down. It is attributed that SOX compliance has cost businesses, especially small and medium sized business, significant sums of money without adequate return.

One of the requirements of SOX was the creation of Public Company Accounting Oversight Board responsible for developing audit report standards and rules and overseeing the audit of public companies. This was incorporated in the Act as a watchdog for potential false reporting by external auditors of publicly traded companies (SOX, 2002). In order to comply with SOX, companies had to gather data periodically to include in their reports. Gathering such data based on inventory, attempted breach of computing resources, possible loss of data, etc requires automated processes. For example, a Radio Frequency Identification (RFID) based inventory management system will be able to provide the necessary data quickly. Aspects related to attempted data breaches are gathered from log information. Since the SOX compliance requirements are multi-faceted there is need for plenty of different forms of data. So, a business should have the necessary processes to gather such data periodically. Collecting such data becomes somewhat easier if the organization controls the computing infrastructure. Since all aspects of SOX reporting are tied to extensive computerized record keeping, computer logs play an important role.

When a business with a SOX compliance requirement uses a cloud based service for their computing services then they have to work with their service provider to obtain the necessary data for reporting purposes. We will address this aspect in detail in section 8 of this chapter.

Gathering the necessary data for SOX compliance is expensive for many businesses. Many new businesses that specialize in helping organizations with SOX compliance have developed systems and processes to gather the required data. This level of diversity in data gathering is a cause for concern as many businesses do not have the necessary financial resources to invest in the integration of multiple tools available. Thus the proposed solution to fix financial fraud in the form of SOX Act has the unintended consequence of affecting business growth as businesses are consumed by the compliance requirements. For this reason the Act was amended multiple times since its enactment to exempt certain types of businesses from the compliance requirements.

SOX Act applies to businesses in USA. Many of the businesses in USA also have subsidiaries or partners in other countries. Since the compliance requirements apply to all businesses in USA they are obligated to collect the necessary financial and other data from their overseas subsidiaries and partners. In this sense the scope of SOX Act extends beyond USA even though the enforcement powers and penalties are limited to USA. Like HIPAA discussed earlier, enforcement of SOX compliance requirements are very strict in order to maintain the public's trust in publicly traded companies. The significance of the Act lies in the fact that many other countries have also adopted compliance requirements similar to SOX to overcome the financial problems faced by many European countries.

4. GRAMM-LEACH-BLILEY ACT (GLBA)

Gramm-Leach-Bliley Act (GLBA) was enacted in 1999 as a result of large banks, financial services companies and insurance companies lobbying to repeal the prohibition of Glass-Steagall Act from mergers among these three entities. With the passage of GLBA banks and financial services companies were allowed to merge and develop new financial products. It is also known as the Financial Services Modernization Act. This Act was aimed at financial services companies that provided consumer loans, insurance products, or financial/investment advice to consumers to inform their customers of their data sharing practices, safeguarding of sensitive data and privacy protection policies. The three main sections of the Act are the Financial Privacy Rule, the Safeguards Rule and the Pretexting provisions (GLBA, 2006). All three of these sections are governed by compliance requirements. The Financial Privacy Rule places restrictions on what types of financial information an organization can collect and disseminate. The Safeguards Rule requires the financial institutions to have policies and procedures to protect the financial information of individuals that they collect. The Pretexting Rule prohibits an organization to collect information under false pretenses. Most organizations are required to provide compliance reports with regard to the Safeguards Rule.

The more visible implementation of Gramm-Leach-Bliley Act is the requirement that every organization disclose their privacy policies with regard to protection of any sensitive information that they collect and how they share it with other organizations. The scope of this bill was deregulatory in nature and so large financial houses were able to develop risky and creative financial products in the mid-2000s which resulted in the global financial meltdown in late 2008.

As a result, the Dodd-Frank Act was passed in 2010 to regulate the financial industry and set up oversight councils. Another important aspect of GLBA is section 501(b) which requires all financial institutions to adequately protect and secure all non-public personal information of their customers. Today, organizations find it easy to collect lot of non-public personal information about their customers based on their electronic footprint. Some of this information is gathered from Voice-over-IP (VoIP) transactions. This results in volumes of data being gathered about each customer. Both VoIP and Cloud Computing are two rapidly evolving fields that businesses see beneficial to them from a cost perspective. As part of GLBA compliance requirements businesses should carefully evaluate the risks posed by these new technologies since the laws often lag behind technological capabilities. As an example, consider the customer expectation to deposit a physical check with an electronic image of the check sent over the internet to the financial institution. This process is known as Remote Deposit Capture (RDC) and it deals with sensitive information in the form of images which contain confidential data such as customer bank account number. As part of the GLBA compliance the bank would be expected to show the types of internal controls it has in place to protect the RDC transaction. The type of controls developed for this process would come from the risk assessment that the bank conducts noting the ways in which the images are transferred to the banking center. This risk assessment is different from the organizational risk assessment of its data center which would be required as part of SOX compliance discussed earlier. Thus the main thrust of GLBA compliance would be to know that organizations should focus on information protection for each of its processes rather than counting on the capabilities of the technology.

5. FEDERAL INFORMATION SECURITY MANAGEMENT ACT (FISMA)

The Federal Information Security Management Act (FISMA) was enacted in 2002 with the aim of protecting all federal information systems. This Act applies only to federal systems. Since the federal government is a major player as a regulator in various areas such as transportation, banking and finance, utilities, commerce, etc the scope of this Act extends far and wide. This Act recognizes the significance of information security to economic and national security matters (FISMA, 2010). In order to strengthen the federal information security requirements, the National Institute of Standards and Technology (NIST) has been given the responsibility to develop the necessary procedures and policies to reduce the risks. NIST has developed extensive guidelines for federal information security, which would also apply to the private sector for information protection. We will discuss next the NIST information security guidelines.

NIST SP800-18 is a significant set of guidelines (NIST, 2006) for protecting federal information systems. As the first step, NIST requires all federal agencies to have an inventory of their information systems. Maintaining this inventory will enable the agency to identify the level of security and access restrictions each system must have in order to protect the overall security. As part of meeting the FISMA compliance requirements the Department of Homeland Security and the Department of Justice have developed the tool called CyberScope. This tool helps gather data in manual and automated manner related to IT Asset Inventory, System Configuration and Vulnerability Management. These are all essential to protecting all federal information systems. As a result of FISMA, in 2011 all Cabinet Departments provided automatic feed to CyberScope. It is worth noting that the US Congress is monitoring FISMA compliance as shown in the chart below (Figure 1) (OMB, 2012). This chart shows the level to which each Cabinet Department is able to provide data feed to CyberScope in each of the three areas identified.

This analysis shows that because of FISMA the Treasury Department is able to note that their system is not able to generate the necessary data to verify compliance. So they need to devote the necessary resources and people to comply.

Figure 1. FISMA compliance by all cabinet departments in 2011
Note: Developed from Office of Management and Budget, FISMA Compliance Report 2011

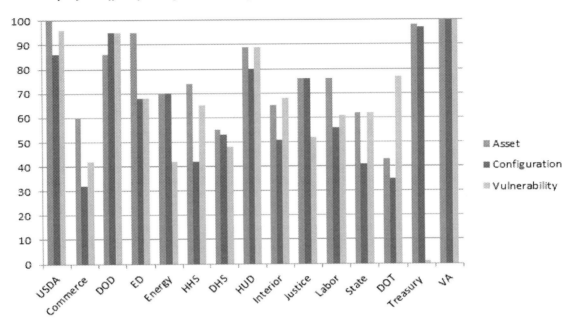

*For a more accurate representation see the electronic version.

6. PAYMENT CARD INDUSTRY (PCI)

Payment Card Industry (PCI) standards are developed for the benefit of protecting consumer credit card data generated by thousands of businesses globally. This industry-led effort is managed by the PCI Security Standards Council, a global consortium of the five major credit card brands – Master Card, Visa, American Express, Discover, JCB (Japan Credit Bureau) International. The primary goal is to set compliance standards that must be followed by all merchants participating in the credit card network. PCI compliance requirements apply to all members who accept credit cards either online or offline. The Data Security Standard (DSS) is the chief guideline from PCI to protect customer data (PCI, 2013). The type of compliance varies by size of business and the compliance requirements and penalties are administered by the individual payment brand such as MasterCard and Visa. The three main components of PCI DSS are Assess, Remediate and Report. The Assessment part involves knowing the systems used in processing credit card data. This assessment includes knowing the vulnerabilities of the system. The Remediate aspect requires the business to fix the vulnerabilities and at the same time take steps to collect only the required data. The Report feature is the compliance part and it involves submission of the periodic reports to the associated banks and card brands.

The main goal of PCI DSS is to prevent, detect and react to security incidents involving credit card processing. Most of the highly publicized violations such as the one involving the Heartland Payment Credit Card system occurred due to technical and process failures. In the case of Heartland Systems, which deals with over 175,000 merchants and 100 million credit card transactions per month, the breach occurred in 2008. This is not an isolated case. According to PrivacyRights.Org more than 510 million records have been breached since 2005. That is why PCI-DSS implementation is critical to businesses and monitoring compliance of the PCI requirements is essential. In order to address the vulnerabilities the merchants should take steps to secure the point-of-sale system, store data securely and allow only encrypted communications from their hotspots. The last one may pose a problem to customers but they should be required to have the suitable API in order to use the hotspot. For example, if the hotspot is from Starbucks then the hotspot user should have the necessary API with encryption enabled. At present the hotspot recommendation above is not mandated by PCI and as such is a potential vulnerability in the payment processing system.

PCI security involves building a firewall that restricts all traffic from untrusted nodes and networks. Another requirement is the prohibition of direct access from the Internet and any system that holds card holder data. In spite of the recommendation from PCI to store only the necessary data, a survey by Forrester Consulting shows that businesses hold a variety of data as follows:

- Credit card numbers 81%
- Credit card expiration dates 73%
- Card verification codes 71%
- Customer data 57%

Businesses store such data to facilitate customer ease of use of their system. Unfortunately this practice opens up the possibility for hackers to steal sensitive information about credit cards. Businesses that follow any of these practices should be required to encrypt all stored data. Given the periodic breach of credit card data, the enforcement of PCI DSS standards compliance appears to be inadequate.

PCI DSS contains 12 requirements. Even though each of these requirements is significant in offering the necessary protection to the credit card transaction, Requirement 9 especially requires the business to restrict access to customer data that they store. This is a very basic requirement in any asset that is being protected. When the business loses control over the storage of that asset because of choice of technology such as cloud computing, then the business should have adequate measures to validate that such data is being protected by the cloud service provider. There is not enough case law to know where the liability would rest. Just as we emphasized in the GLBA section, the business should assess the risks in each of their processes when it comes to capturing and storing sensitive data. Another expectation from PCI DSS is that each business must change the default password provided by the equipment vendor in order to access the internal system or to communicate data to the transaction authorization system. Every business using a PCI system must have a data retention policy that is consistent with legal requirements and purge unwanted data periodically. Table 1 shows which data could be stored and which data should be encrypted when stored.

Table 1. PCI data storage guideline

Type of Data	Data Storage Permitted	Encryption Required
Credit card number	Yes	Yes
Cardholder Name	Yes	No
Expiration Date	Yes	No
Card Verification Value	No	n/a
Full magstripe data	No	n/a
PIN	No	n/a

We discussed above some of the data storage restrictions associated with PCI DSS compliance. In addition to the above requirements, PCI compliance requires the business to restrict physical access to data storage devices, logical access to data content and have an audit trail to track data access. Further, the business organization must have policies for secure data backup, data breach notification and incident response plan.

7. STATEMENT ON AUDITING STANDARDS 70 (SAS 70)

Statement on Auditing Standards 70 (SAS 70) was developed by the American Institute of Certified Public Accountants (AICPA) in 1993. It is a comprehensive audit of the procedures and controls used by an organization and this audit is widely recognized. There are two types of SAS 70 audits – Type I and Type II. Type I Audit is performed for a specific point in time and is usually a precursor to a Type II audit which is more exhaustive (SAS, 2013). Type II audit closely follows many of the Internal Control requirements mentioned in the Sarbanes-Oxley Act. This audit also meets the compliance requirements associated with Health Insurance Portability and Accountability Act and Gramm-Leach-Bliley Act. The SAS 70 Audit does not follow a checklist for audit; instead it relies on the AICPA's standards for field work, quality control and reporting requirements. The audit report is the considered opinion of the auditor on processes as well as financial controls in place in the organization. Because of this type of freedom that the auditor has the SAS 70 Audit reports have wide variance in their reporting. The mere fact that a service provider underwent a SAS 70 Type II Audit does not mean anything in particular with respect to the sufficiency or reliability of the controls the organization has. The onus is on the business planning to use the services of the provider by examining the audit report for conclusions and recommendations of the auditor.

Type I Audit is limited in scope and less expensive for the organization. However, its results are not sufficient to meet the compliance requirements of SOX, HIPAA and GLBA. An organization that has not had an external audit about their internal financial controls will benefit from a Type I Audit. Type II Audit is more exhaustive and expensive for an organization. The Auditor would benefit from a Type I Audit report as it would have helped the organization prepare all the necessary internal compliance reports that would form part of the Type II Audit report. In Type II Audit the Auditor tests and reports on the operating effectiveness based on tests done over a six month period. This exhaustive report is widely accepted and its findings support the organization's claims on meeting the necessary compliance requirements.

When some service providers, be it on the cloud or VoIP or something similar, follow the path of SAS 70 Type II Audit for compliance, it only means that the provider meets many of the auditing standards for compliance which are widely recognized. This vendor compliance would not absolve any client of their responsibility in meeting the specific compliance requirements that are expected for their line of business. We will discuss this in greater detail relative to cloud computing in the next section.

8. SUPPORT FOR COMPLIANCE REQUIREMENTS IN CLOUD SERVICES

Cloud services are becoming popular because of the flexibility it offers. It is especially attractive for small and medium sized businesses because of the cost savings it offers and the high level of computing service that they would be able to afford. Simultaneously businesses are expected to meet certain compliance requirements depending on their line of business. As we discussed in the previous sections there are federal laws that mandate certain levels of compliance with regard to protecting customer information, affording customer privacy for the data that they collect and meeting certain industry standards. In this section we will explore in detail the benefits and drawbacks relative to meeting the necessary compliance requirements.

In this section we highlight the compliance provisions supported by the major cloud service providers. Amazon Web Services (AWS) is the largest cloud service provider globally and they support the computing requirements for small, medium and large businesses (Amazon Web Services, 2013). They offer all three types of cloud services – SaaS, PaaS and IaaS. For compliance purposes our focus would be on AWS' ability to provide the cloud customers the necessary means to gather the required compliance data in an automated manner for their public cloud offerings. As a first step, AWS is SAS 70 Type II compliant. This helps organizations in meeting their HIPAA and SOX compliance. Other major providers such as Google, Microsoft and Salesforce are also SAS 70 Type II audit compliant. All these providers enable the customers to gather the necessary compliance data in an automated manner, which is key to meeting the compliance requirements. Moreover, this frees up the cloud service providers from devoting their time and effort to gather the necessary compliance data for their customers.

HIPAA compliance requirements apply to all organizations that provide health related services. Both HIPAA and HITECH Acts support electronic storage, access and retrieval of patients' health data. Because of the sensitive nature of the information being handled all users that come in contact with health data are expected to be HIPAA certified so that they understand the requirements of the law and the penalties that apply when the law is violated. The law's requirements, when enacted, assumed that the organization had the ability to control the resources in order to comply with the requirements. Over the past decade newer technologies have evolved that are changing the way people access their personal data and where organizations keep the data. In this context cloud computing and mobile devices have added many layers of complexity in meeting the HIPAA requirements. We will now explore the benefits and constraints that cloud computing presents in meeting the HIPAA compliance requirements.

Hospitals, health clinics, laboratories, pharmacies, insurance companies, and physicians are all expected to comply with HIPAA requirements as part of their business license. All these entities note the benefits that a cloud service provider offers, especially with regard to system availability, remote accessibility, demand elasticity and usage based cost. Depending on the size of the business entity the cloud service chosen varies. The simplest of these services is Software as a Service (SaaS) where the cloud service provider provides all infrastructure and software applications. In this type of service the client simply focuses on their core strengths and benefits from the service provided by the cloud service provider. The total control on hardware, storage of data, backup and security of software applications rests with the service provider. The customer is responsible for providing the necessary access credentials to their users and the service provider is responsible only to validate the access credentials for authentication. The service provider will have no knowledge of the sensitivity of the data being stored and so will not be able to provide any differentiated data protection. So the service provider would not feel responsible for any compliance requirements with regard to the data generated, stored and transmitted through their systems. Given this type of different expectations from the customer and service provider with regard to security, it is important to spell out appropriate responsibilities in the contract for service. In cloud contracts, customer is the "data controller" and the service provider is the "data processor." So, the obligations of the data processor are less compared to the data controller. This understanding is reflected in the Ponemon Institute study. The 2013 Ponemon Institute Study reported that majority of cloud service providers felt that it is not their responsibility to protect customer data (Ponemon, 2013).

We discussed above the SaaS service where the customer would lack control on many of the infrastructure aspects with regard to compliance. There are two other types of services – Platform as a Service (PaaS) and Infrastructure as a Service (IaaS). In PaaS the customer has slightly more control over the system they choose for cloud service and in IaaS the customer has lot more control over the system. In order for meeting the compliance requirements the customer must have plenty of visibility on the controls that the cloud service provider has in place. The importance of compliance for the customer is reinforced by a Cloud Security Alliance survey about the leading constraints on cloud adoption. In this survey, based on a scale of 1 to 5, customers ranked the significance of their ability to meet regulatory compliance at 4.01, which had the ranking of 4 out of 11(Cloud Security Alliance, 2013). Also, the customer must have trust in the ability of the service provider to offer privacy and security. It takes time to build this trust. Cloud customers must evaluate the risks to their clients before deciding to use cloud services. One way to protect client data would be to encrypt all transactions and store the keys locally while storing the encrypted data on the cloud for the flexibility it offers. This bifurcated approach requires additional processing capabilities before accessing the stored data. Often customers are attracted to the cloud by the benefits and flexibility it offers. Customers should also evaluate the security aspects prior to making a commitment to use cloud services. This can be accomplished by evaluating third party reports such as SAS 70 Type II Audit report and ISO 27001 certification achieved by the cloud provider.

One of the large companies that has been very successful in providing cloud service is Salesforce. It specializes in Customer Relations Management (CRM) over the cloud. Since its introduction nearly 15 years ago it has grown into a very mature organization that provides its customers several ways to meet their compliance requirements. To start with, Salesforce is SAS 70 Type II certified. The privacy protection provisions for customer data that Salesforce offers supports compliance requirements of GLBA and HIPAA. Many businesses try to leverage their social media presence and it adds another layer of requirement for compliance especially with respect to data protection. Salesforce has a service similar to LinkedIn called Chatter that is integrated with its main CRM product offering in the cloud (Salesforce, 2013). The significance of Chatter is that it enables the users to capture and archive all customer communications automatically in order to meet their compliance requirements. Salesforce partners with other third party providers so that their encryption service is available to their customers in order to meet the compliance requirements of FISMA, PCI, GLBA and HITECH.

Compliance with laws and industry standards strengthens a company's information processing capabilities and offers protection under liability claims. In this regard the compliance requirements extend beyond the country or region for which the compliance requirements apply. We have already identified the impact of SOX beyond USA. In a similar manner, the US-EU Safe Harbor agreements and the International Safe Harbor Privacy Principles extend the scope of the compliance requirements beyond these regions. It is worth noting that many of these compliance aspects are discussed in detail by Chaput and Ringwood in their article on Cloud Compliance (Chaput, 2010).

Often compliance expectations assume that the organization that owns the data is responsible for protecting the data. In the traditional computing models organizations controlled the location where they stored the data. In cloud computing, be it SaaS, PaaS, or IaaS, the cloud service provider may not be able to provide the physical location of the data since they have their data centers distributed around the world, with backup systems equally spread out. For this reason it will be very difficult for the cloud customer needing data location information for compliance purposes to certify about physical security of data storage and backup systems. So, the cloud customer must obtain this information prior to finalizing a cloud service provider for their needs. During this phase of the evaluation the customer should try to obtain peer assessments of the service provider's ability to provider compliance data. This might also require the service provider to identify potential references. Even though this might be helpful, lack of an external reference should not be considered as negative as many businesses may not be willing to take time to answer questions from other businesses. What is more important for a customer to know is what happens to their data at the end of the contract and what type of Service Level Agreement (SLA) that they could expect from the service provider regarding data availability. The customer should be told when their data would be purged from the provider's storage at the end of their contract and how the provider will facilitate transfer of all data to another service provider chosen by the customer. This transfer aspect should spell out any costs associated with the data transfer and the bandwidth that the service provider would be able to dedicate. Many businesses fail to work out the details at the beginning of their contract on these aspects as the customers accumulate large volumes of data, often in peta bytes, over a period of time. The following hypothetical scenario is worth noting as an example in this respect. Company AllForAll contracts with a major cloud service provider for SaaS service and stores all data generated over one year with the provider. During the period of the one year contract AllForAll's data storage has reached one peta byte. At the end of the contract AllForAll plans to move to a different service provider and asks the service provider to transfer all their data. Service provider offers a rate plan with three different tiered pricing as follows:

Based on this hypothetical data transfer rate availability and cost by the service provider, the time and money it will take AllForAll to move their data to a new service provider would be as follows:

The analysis shown in Tables 2 and 3 are intended to show that there is a significant cost and time involved when a customer decides to move from one provider to another. Providers do not make it easy for customers to move by using proprietary storage solutions for storage. This aspect is known as *stickiness* in spite of touting the fact that the cloud service is pay-as-you-go model and there is no requirement for any long term contract for the service or the level of service. The primary reason for stickiness being a potential problem is the lack of universal standards for data storage in the cloud.

Table 2. Hypothetical data transfer rate and cost

Tier Level	Data Transfer Rate	Transfer Cost
1	10 GB/s	$0.15 / GB
2	100 GB/s	$3 / 100GB
3	500 GB/s	$25 / 500GB

Table 3. AllForAll Company estimated time and cost for 1 petabyte data transfer

Tier Level	Time Required to Transfer all Data	Cost of Data Transfer
1	≈ 1 day + 4 hrs.	$15,000
2	≈ 2 hrs. + 50 mts.	$30,000
3	≈ 34 mts.	$50,000

In our analysis of cloud services relative to compliance requirements we have identified some key issues that a cloud customer must be aware of prior to switching to cloud service. In this regard another important question to be answered by the service provider is the access to customer data in case the service provider goes out of business. This is achieved by having access to data backup systems for the customer. Cloud computing is evolving rapidly and there is no standard yet that customers could rely on for meeting their compliance requirements. Since cloud computing uses distributed resources there is even more uncertainty and lack of control for cloud customers regarding the physical security of the system. From the service provider perspective any time that they have to perform a manual operation to gather the necessary data for the customer, it is expensive.

Cloud service providers would benefit from having a lot of automation in their systems so that they can provide log data in an automated manner to the customer. The internal control processes that the service provider has initiated should be transparent to the customers. Cloud service providers have built-in automated processes for acquiring and releasing additional computing or storage resource on demand. They have to leverage the expertise gained from this process to provide enough transparency in systems processing so that the customers can meet their varying compliance requirements. In this context it is worth noting the dilemma faced by service providers with regard to knowing the value of any data stored by the customers. Given the level of automation expected by the customers, it will be impossible for the service provider to know which data needs higher level of protection. This is one reason why many service providers think that they are not responsible for security and privacy of customer data.

Small and medium sized organizations may use cloud services in a big way but their resource requirements are much less when compared to enterprise level organizations. In many large organizations, given the nature of budgeting, internal controls and approval processes, many units within the organization find it easy to subscribe to cloud services for specialized needs. Since cloud computing is still an evolving technology, enterprises do not have a centralized approval process for subscribing to cloud services by individual units within the organization. At present the practice in many organizations is such there is a mushrooming of subscriptions to cloud services because it is easy to subscribe to specialized SaaS applications that the business unit needs. This practice has resulted in disparate data that does not integrate well between applications. This problem has been identified as the result of Cloud Identity Management (CIM). CIM has become a focus in many large enterprises because the security offered by the enterprise firewall is no longer available when people in the enterprise use cloud services as needed without getting clearance from a central group in the enterprise. Many large organizations have noticed this problem and are instituting centralized approval processes for all cloud services. As a result of this effort large organizations have noticed that many of the specialized requests for cloud services could be met internally. A related effort in this regard is discussed later as a standardization process initiated by the Internet Engineering Task Force.

Another important cloud service is data backup. Cloud backup requires an automated process. Furthermore, the customer should have automated validation that the backup succeeded. Users also have the ability to require on-demand backup of sensitive data. Companies providing the backup service to customers should provide the end user to have access to log data that is compiled at the end of the backup process. Federal regulations require record maintenance for a certain period of time based on the type of data being stored. Cloud service provides the ability to maintain a large amount of such information as needed. One of the compliance requirements involves proof of data archival which the customer should be able to obtain from the cloud provider as part of their general archival process. Backup is only a part of the backup and recovery system that is required under HIPAA. As mentioned earlier the backup process is automated. The recovery process on the other hand is on-demand and it does not require any manual handling by the cloud service provider. The end user should be able to select the file or folder for recovery and they will be decrypted and restored to the location of choice.

Some of the compliance requirements involve the type of documentation that the cloud service provider would be able to provide. This involves the cloud service provider providing a successful completion of SAS 70 Type II Audit for their system. Another type of audit information that would be useful for the customer is the OCR (Office of Civil Rights) Audit result that the service provider could provide their customers in order to show evidence of privacy protection. The customer could then use this information in their compliance reporting requirement.

Next, we look at some of the major applications that many organizations, both large and small, use. One such is Google Apps. It is a SaaS application that many businesses use. As we pointed out earlier SaaS, in general, lacks support for many compliance requirements. Noting the importance to customers of the ability to capture the relevant data for compliance, the CloudLock feature in Google Apps provides the ability to documenting SOX compliance with information protection. Google Docs is one component of Google Apps and is used by approximately 20% of users according to an IDC Study. This application provides the tools to gather usage statistics relative to the Disclosure Controls (Section 302) and Internal Controls (Section 404) of SOX. In Table 4 we show the ways in which Section 302 and Section 404 reporting requirements of SOX are met by Google Docs.

The discussion so far in this section points to the fact that compliance standards require all components in the system support one or more aspects of compliance. Taking a holistic approach to compliance, the methods discussed so far are focused on each component in a larger system being compliant and the burden of proof resting with the system provider. Microsoft Corporation is trying a new approach to compliance in the cloud whereby the compliance is demonstrated at the platform level and each user who uses an application on the platform validates their application for compliance. This way the platform provider is able to provide a master compliance document and all applications are individually able to provide their fit with the platform for compliance (Microsoft, 2012). At a practical level, Microsoft Azure cloud service provides strict compliance data for clinical trials of new drugs. This is achieved by providing access to various databases developed by National Institutes of Health (NIH) using the Azure platform whereby the cloud customer could test their innovative solutions for drug discovery. Since the Azure platform is SAS 70 Type II Audit, FISMA, HIPAA and ISO 27001 certified, any application that uses the Azure platform has to provide compliance data for the application specific activities only, which the customer should be able to gather based on their use of the application. Thus, shifting the compliance requirement from the building blocks to the platform level facilitates compliance aspects on the cloud.

Table 4. Google Docs support for SOX reporting requirements

SOX Section	Google Docs Support
302	CloudLock Access Management System provides file access privileges for all files in the domain for all users in an automated manner. Also, there is additional alert capability to approve access to sensitive data. IT can set access control and file sharing policies in Google Docs usage. Any deviation from the policies will result in an alert being sent to IT.
404	CloudLock Security Policy Engine will alert IT based on deviation from Acceptable Use Policies. This data will be useful in security audit reporting.

In many parts of the discussion on cloud computing so far we have alluded to the concern of customers about security in the cloud. This is a natural concern because the customer does not have control over the infrastructure or storage of data in the cloud. Depending on the type of service they choose such as SaaS, PaaS, or IaaS, the customer has varying levels of control on the applications that they deploy in the cloud. For this reason we raised the issue of who is liable to protect the customer data – the service provider or the customer. Earlier in this section we identified the reasoning of the provider, based on the Ponemon Institute study, that the provider does not have the necessary information to know the level of protection to be afforded different data that are stored in the cloud. This is one piece of information that the customer would need for meeting compliance requirements. However, the service provider is at an advantage when it comes to protecting centralized hardware and software since the customer may not be able to afford the level of protection that a cloud service provider could afford based on the economies of scale. In this context we highlight the role of Simple Customer Identity Management (SCIM) which is being discussed by the Internet Engineering Task Force (IETF), the agency responsible for internet standards. SCIM is focused towards large enterprises. SCIM would help a lot in meeting compliance requirements of HIPAA, SOX, GLBA, FISMA, PCI and SAS 70 in that the organization that allows access to their data controls who would get that access. The SCIM model has three important components:

1. Service provider holds the identity information for allowing access to resources
2. Customer using SCIM protocol manages the identity data used by service provider
3. Resources are service provider managed entities that have attributes

It is clear from this model that the service provider's role is limited to managing access to resources on the cloud for users that the customer authorizes and manages. This division of responsibility is enforceable and attributable in audit. In Table 5 we summarize the actions allowed for each resource.

We have discussed several compliance aspects in this section. One of the compliance requirements deals with how secure the data would be in the cloud for any customer. Al-Aqrabi et al studied this aspect and found out the availability of Unified Threat Management (UTM) approach to protect systems and facilitate compliance. From a theoretical perspective this concept works well but in practice UTM is found to degrade service quality. Also, UTM at times becomes a bottleneck for organizations (Al-Aqrabi, 2012). Consequently UTM approach may not the right solution for businesses to meet the compliance requirements for security.

We conclude this section with the observation that in order to meet the compliance requirements for services on the cloud each customer must understand what the service provider could provide. For example, the cloud service provider would be responsible for the physical security of the cloud system and would manage the customer access restrictions set by the customer. The cloud service provider must have the ability to provide in an automated manner access to service logs and compliance audit data for

Table 5. Summary of allowed actions for resources in SCIM

Resource	Allowed Action
User	Retrieve, Add, Modify users
Group	Retrieve, Add, Modify groups
Service Provider	Retrieve the service provider's configuration

each customer that requires it. The customer should work with the application vendors as to the level of compliance that is expected of the application in order to meet their own compliance requirements either for the federal laws in effect or the industry standards.

9. SUMMARY

In this chapter we have examined the compliance requirements for using cloud services by businesses both with respect to federal laws as well as industry standards. In particular, we described the main aspects of each of the federal laws related to Health Care (HIPAA and HITECH), financial services (SOX, GLBA), federal information security (FISMA) and industry standards (SAS 70 and PCI). Then we discussed in greater detail the various issues associated with compliance for services on the cloud and highlighted how sometimes the old paradigm of a party responsible for data is responsible for its protection from abuse may not be applicable when it comes to cloud services. In this context we were able to bring to the discussion the different view points from different stakeholders. Overall, compliance is important and both the federal laws and industry standards should keep up with the changes in technology in order to identify the responsible party for security and privacy of customer data.

REFERENCES

Al-Aqrabi, H., et al. (2012). Investigation of IT security and compliance challenges in security-as-a-service for cloud computing. In *Proceedings of IEEE 15th International Symposium on OCS Workshops*, (pp. 124-129). IEEE.

Amazon Web Services. (2013). Retrieved from http://aws.amazon.com/

Antonopoulos, N., & Gillam, L. (2010). *Cloud computing: Principles, systems and applications*. London: Springer. doi:10.1007/978-1-84996-241-4

Armbrust, M., & ... (2010). A view of cloud computing. *Communications of the ACM, 53*(4), 50–58. doi:10.1145/1721654.1721672

Chaput, S. R., & Ringwood, K. (2010). Cloud compliance: A framework for using cloud computing in a regulated world. In *Cloud computing* (pp. 241–256). London: Springer. doi:10.1007/978-1-84996-241-4_14

Cloud Security Alliance. (2013). Retrieved from http://www.cloudsecurityalliance.org

Federal Register. (2013, January 25). *HIPAA Privacy, Security, Enforcement and Breach Notification Rules, 78*(17), 5566-5702.

FISMA. (2010). Retrieved from http://www.dhs.gov/federal-information-security-management-act-fisma

GLBA. (2006). Retrieved from http://business.ftc.gov/privacy-and-security/gramm-leach-bliley-act

Goolge Apps. (2013). Retrieved from http://www.google.com/intl/en/enterprise/apps/business/

HIPAA. (2013). Retrieved from http://www.hhs.gov/ocr/privacy/

Microsoft. (2012). *Guiding principles and architecture for addressing life science compliance in the cloud*. Redmond, WA: Microsoft.

NIST. (2006). *Guide for developing security plans for federal information systems*. Gaithersburg, MD: National Institute for Standards and Technology.

OMB. (2012). *FISMA compliance report to US congress for 2011*. Washington, DC: Office of Management and Budget.

PCI. (2013). Retrieved from https://www.pcisecuritystandards.org/security_standards

Ponemon. (2013). *Security of cloud computing users*. Ponemon Institute Study.

Ristenpart, T., Tromer, E., Schacham, H., & Savage, S. (2009). Hey, you, get off of my cloud: Exploring information leakage in third-party compute clouds. In *Proceedings of the 16th ACM Conference on Computer and Communications Security*, (pp. 199-212). ACM.

Salesforce. (2013). Retrieved from http://www.salesforce.com

SAS. (2013). Retrieved from http://sas70.com

Sengupta, S., Kaulgud, V., & Sharma, V. S. (2011). Cloud computing security – Trends and research directions. In *Proceedings of IEEE World Congress on Services*, (pp. 524-531). IEEE.

SOX. (2002). Retrieved from http://www.soxlaw.com

Yang, H., & Tate, M. (2012). A descriptive literature review and classification of cloud computing research. *Communications of AIS*, *31*(2), 35–60.

This research was previously published in Security, Trust, and Regulatory Aspects of Cloud Computing in Business Environments edited by S. Srinivasan, pages 127-144, copyright year 2014 by Information Science Reference (an imprint of IGI Global).

Chapter 88

Legal Issues Surrounding Connected Government Services:
A Closer Look at G-Clouds

Mariam Kiran
University of Bradford, UK

ABSTRACT

Recent technological advances have led to a knowledge-driven economy, where we expect and need information accessible from anywhere. Connected Government (c-government) enables governments to communicate through technology with their citizens and other governments. The use of ICT and emerging technologies has made this relationship much more effective. Although, most research is focused towards infrastructures and flexible services provision, form, there is a need for a layer of legal regulations to be followed. Legal issues can further aid in the provision of transparency, data confidentiality and encryption techniques. This is where Cloud Computing infrastructures can play an important role. This chapter looks into the Cloud infrastructure and discusses how Clouds are being used for connected government services, while further extending the discussion by looking at the legal issues surrounding the use of Clouds, particularly focusing on the UK G-Cloud as a case study.

INTRODUCTION

C-Government (Connected government) extends the concept of e-government (electronic government) and describes the services and interactions that take place between the government and its citizens using digital connection and socially connected media. These digital connections can influence businesses and government agencies, where information is communicated through technologies. Traditionally, operations of the government were mostly paper-based and involved understanding their citizens, with finding new manual ways to engage with their citizens. Recent technology advances, as a result of smart phones and M2M connected devices, have led government services to now being used as smart applications which

DOI: 10.4018/978-1-5225-8176-5.ch088

can be accessed through any mediums such as mobile phones or tablet devices. This change in trend has led to a knowledge-led economy where information is constantly needed to be available every second and on-the-go in any location.

With this current push led by technology, there is an additional trend that the governments are pursuing and that is towards *Smart Cities*. The drive towards fast innovations in the digital world has raised a number of concerns from the user's perspective in terms of safety, security and manageability, particularly through the available infrastructures. In addition to these, there are major legal and ethical issues, which are still playing catch up, to encompass the various changes being brought about by technology. This chapter discusses these various legal concerns which have become the focus of much user and end user usage when they use the c-government services. The chapter highlights the need for a holistic framework which provides an effective governance procedure aiming for a citizen-centred vision of a government with increased transparency, improved management and efficient use of services through the Internet and ICT.

Figure 1 presents the various delivery models the governments use to connect to the public. These involve various layers of interaction such as connecting with other governments, citizens, businesses and the government employees. Information can be communicated through mechanisms such as 'push notifications' for regulatory services or through 'two-way' communications such as through city councils for localised interaction. Further services such as health, taxation, military services, all form examples of services which the government needs to offer. Governance laws such as encouraging voting, consultation and localised aid is all part of government activities which need to keep a proper functioning of the system.

Although, Figure 1 highlights the complicated architecture in which the government functions, due to the number and complexity, some of these tasks have to be automated for the services being offered. C-government services do this, by making some of these processes and information available online. However, this method of communication is plagued by various controversies of incorrect information,

Figure 1. C-Government delivery models

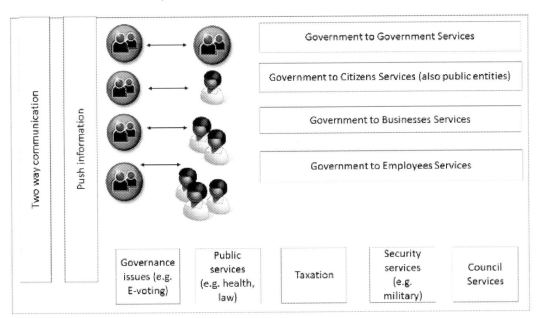

surveillance and some loss of privacy and file security issues. Inaccessibility is another hurdle for common citizens, where internet access in not available to all parts of the country, raising concerns of costs and dependency on devices for up-to-date infrastructures. However, still, there is a higher demand for the government to have a more connected tiered system with more synergies between all the departments for sustainable development. This has led to increasing the current scope of c-government for cohesive, coordinated and integrative processes (OECD, 2012).

The structure of this chapter is organised in the following way. We first present the concepts and role of ICT infrastructures such as cloud computing and connected devices for their use in c-government services. We then present the literature background which discusses current work in this area of legal issues in government services. Various architectures, such as the SOA-based framework, for Web applications development and the current use of Cloud to enable this are discussed. The chapter then focuses on the legal risks related to these, looking at them from a contractual perspectives. This leads to the discussion of using the current UK G-Cloud for government services and the current Service Level agreements drawn up which describe how these services are made available to the public. Finally, the chapter concludes by presenting a discussion on a solution on how legal risks should be managed, monitored and made transparent for citizens to be able to use C-Government services more effectively.

LITERATURE BACKGROUND

Cloud Computing for Connected Government

The cloud environment can allow various governmental departments and other agencies to be integrated together. Refer to Figure 2. In todays' technology driven lives, all services are being moved to mobile devices and online resources. The advent and popularity of cloud computing has been an enabler technology to make most of this possible. However, with an industry attraction, to saving costs and ease of use, having services online raises a number of legal issues which have to be clarified for end-users and service providers which are more important when governments are involved. The Australian government defines cloud computing as *an ICT sourcing and delivery model for enabling convenient, on-demand network access to a shared pool of configurable computing resources (e.g. networks, servers, storage, applications and services) that can be rapidly provisioned and released with minimal management effort or service provider interaction* (Australian Government, 2011). This definition highlights how Clouds are automatically adopted as a shared resource which needs to be provisioned quickly and with minimum effort.

The cloud computing platform offers a range of services from software to infrastructure which can then be exploited as needed by the users and developers. These are as follows:

- Software as a service (SaaS): This provides software as a service through applications which are accessible via the web, such as a web-based email.
- Platform as a service (PaaS): This variety offers the platform for developers as a service so that they can develop applications, such as programming languages and tools.
- Infrastructure as a service (IaaS): This leval offers the infrastructure such as operating systems or storage servers as services, where consumers can deploy and run their software such as Amazon EC2 cloud services.

Figure 2. Cloud-base e-governance

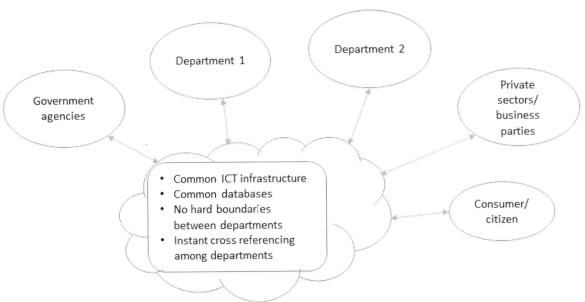

Cloud computing also exists in different ecosystem forms such as being either private cloud, with a single provider for internal hosting of services, or as a public cloud, which can essentially be outsourced to multiple users have access to the services, or a combination of hybrid clouds, which mixes both private and public clouds depending on what is needed by the end users. Figure 3 describes the cloud ecosystems in detail as to how the computers are connected and how this would influence how data is distributed.

From Figure 3, it is evident that the data will be more secure in the private cloud scenario as the hosts and the users will all be maintained locally. Issues are raised when public or external clouds are accessed through bursting or multiple clouds coming to work together for providing the services. Which cloud ecosystem is used will influence the legal issues surrounding government use.

Legal Issues Surrounding C-Government Services

The report by Snooks (2013) highlights the general points and concerns that need to be legally considered for government services:

- How information is protected – there is a need to take contractual measures to keep information secure, and ensure all agreements are met. The document can also highlight if there will be any compensation for any data loss.
- Liability – this discusses if there are any limitations or personal injuries raised due to loss of any data.
- Performance management – this relates to the service levels being maintained by the infrastructure providers - this includes data on response times, service flexibility or any disaster recovery measures.

Figure 3. Cloud computing ecosystems. Adapted from Kiran (2014).

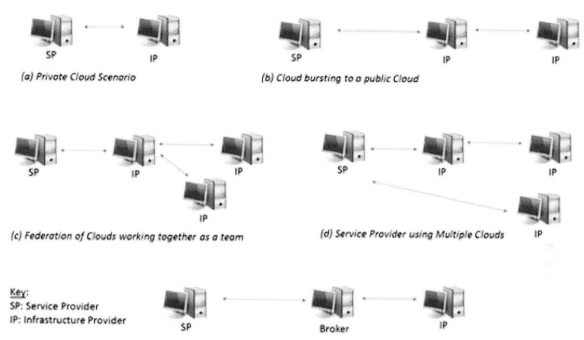

- Terminating the contract – refers to determining if there is a termination fee, defaults or legal advice on termination which citizens have to made aware of, if using these services.
- Dispute resolution guidelines – this suggests if there any forums for handling disputes.
- Other legal issues – this includes introduction of harmful code, change of control to certain software.

Even though the report by Snook (2013) highlights most of the main features of legal issues which need to be covered and resolved by governments, there are still a number of issues such as the legal licenses for some of the software being distributed through these services and how they are handling the data which passes through them which is not discussed. This is probably because issues surrounding the technicalities of how these services work is an extremely complex issue which needs further technical analysis.

Various researches now focus on how regulations can be set out to maintain the issues of data transfer within and outside borders. Eecke (2014) argues that the European Union rules are substantially more restrictive than other countries like the America. The author discusses the concepts of the data controller and processors who are responsible for the different activities in handling data. It is crucial to know who is responsible for which part of the ecosystem associated with the protection measures placed at each stage. However currently the cloud platforms used by EU governments are not physically located within the EU boundaries. Eecke (2014) also proposes to have applications in place which ask for transfer of data with permissions whenever data is moved. The U.S. uses the laws set out by the safe harbor to cater to the digital needs of any services hosting online (Swire, 1993).

Using Clouds for Government Services

Gray (2013) discusses the Force majeure clauses ("Acts of God") as unforeseen circumstances that would prevent the data provider from delivering on their promised services. These scenarios can be natural disasters or communication link breakdowns, or more, and are thus extremely unclearly defined in the legal agreements with the providers. This is an issue that governments need to look at if they start using Clouds for their services. (Al-Soud, 2013) presents a case for the Jordanian government cloud as a single pool for twelve governorates with benefits in terms of four dimensions, such as interaction and accessibility, location and distance, time and availability, and finally products and services. Being a developing country, the lack of resources can allow Clouds to be useful for being used for government resources. With a potential of reduction in computing resources needed, the Jordanian services do not need to procure, maintain or monitor the IT resources, as these are the responsibility of the cloud provider. The case of the cloud in developing countries for government services is also made in (Kumar et al, 2013), saying that it would transform the Indian nation. The authors present a SWOT analysis outlining the strengths, weakness, opportunity and threats associated with the model. Figure 4 describes how government services can be mapped to the cloud models. In Figure 4, G2G, G2E and G2C refer to government to government; government to enterprise; and government o citizens, respectively. The characteristics are briefly listed below:

- **Strengths:** All connected government projects involve utilizing internet technologies, which is made accessible through mobile phones today. Cloud also allows services to be scaled up depending on the demand at different times of the day. Reduction costs of maintenance, time to upgrade and data management is also a plus point.
- **Weaknesses:** One of the major hurdles is the literacy for cloud services construction and deployment. There is a shortage in skills which can cater to this field.
- **Opportunities:** There is a lot of scope for setting up hardware and media for public and private relations, which is also good for developing countries to use this.
- **Threats:** There are a number of basic threats which include loss of jobs, support legislators, and unclear guidelines.

Further challenges for adopting cloud based software are also highlighted by Janssen (2013) as difficulties to control the IT function. Apart from the issues surrounding quality, privacy, security and business continuity, delivering software through the cloud requires a complete restructure of the organization to make this possible. There is also a lack of resources which will standardize software which is needed to be accessible from anywhere at any time. The author suggests that there are more risks associated with it rather than the advantages as a trade-off between the two. Further challenges and achievements are also summarized in Table 1 which briefly mention the key benefits of clouds for the US government.

Further research is needed individually in the areas of software for secure signatures, tax storage requirements and data retention issues. Singh et al. (2013) have summarized that e-governance capabilities are good, but citizens need to have trust in their own government for the benefits the technologies provide and are used.

Figure 4. Layers of cloud for connected government. Adapted from Kumar et al. (2013)

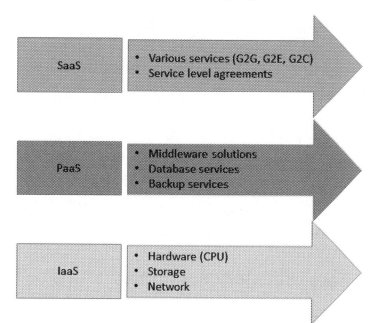

Table 1. Before and after cloud implementation in US and UK government scenarios (Oleg, 2014)

Before Cloud Implementation	After Cloud Implementation
Lack of flexibility and agility. Process took 6 months to complete	Improved elasticity, agility and flexibility: process take 1 day to complete
Underutilized massive IT infrastructure: Average utilization in the UK was 10%.	Reduced IT infrastructure needs: Most services are now involved in the UK G-Cloud
Impact on Environment	Reduced environment footprint: Comparing the carbon footprint on the environment.
Energy Inefficiency	Energy efficient: Several group can now share computing resources with fewer servers and less energy consumption

ROLE OF ICT IN C-GOVERNMENT

The current trends of internet of things has driven the availability of skills and easy connected devices, allowing different age ranges to get connected through social media e.g. facebook, twitter. Some ICT infrastructures such as cloud platforms provide service-oriented access, keeping issues like security and connectivity in check. Figure 5 describes the architecture being used for C-Government services describing the layers of workflow components (hosts services), the business process and business logics being used. This architecture displays how multi-tenancy services can be hosted on the same process and logic being applied. These services can be made scalable and interconnected for communication between them. The workflows applications components show the various applications the government can outsource as services to the citizens. The overall principle of business logic and process would be the same across all of them.

Figure 5. Architecture for c-government

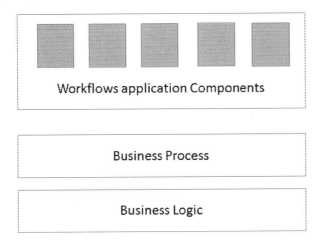

Government Services as a Service (GSaaS)

Figure 6 describes the main key elements of the government services being offered. The Internet is a suitable medium through which various devices such as phones, mobiles and computers can connect and have access to middleware and databases. Service-oriented architectures can be easily mapped to these layers of communications. These services can be of three kinds:

- **Process Services:** For actual workflows combining composed and basic services.
- **Composed Services:** For services which can be combined to present a more complex composed service.
- **Basic Services:** For basic functionality of services.

Figure 6. Key elements of c-government services. Adapted from OECD (2012).

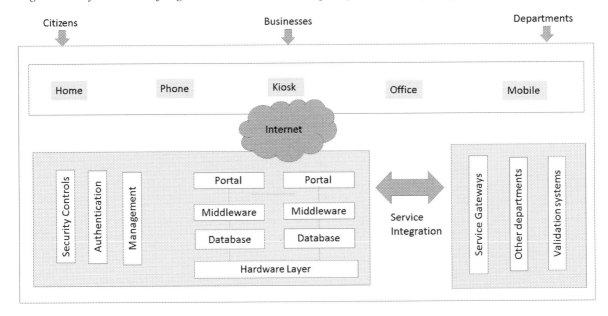

Services can process data and logic. Data services can be read from or written to various backend systems providing minimal business functionality. Logic services represent the business rules with corresponding inputs and minimal functionalities. Examples of such services include the Belgium eDepot online platform which allows companies to register and deposit forms. This is a form of public administration, with end-users and businesses needing to register and in the process offering a high level of reusability by public and private actors. A few other examples are discussed by Wauters et al. (2011) when they describe the shift in the perception of ICT participation:

- Replacing existing administrative processes, towards process re-engineering and reorganisation of institutional boundaries;
- Interest in technologies (e.g. eIDM, eSignature, eAuthentication) that allow for better integration of administrative processes and for delivery of personalised services.
- Technologies that integrate internal/external processes (back/front office).
- Need to harmonise rules and procedures to give more priority to interoperability and exploiting the use of 'open' environments (e.g. open standards and source).

Figure 7 describes the conceptual cloud on how various c-government applications are hosted and accessed through an online application. Recent studies have shown a growth in this manner of use and a growth in the sectors using collaborative productions of public services and also turning to third parties for available infrastructures showing a sustainable growth (Europe, 2010).

Cloud Computing as an Enabler

Cloud is increasingly becoming one of the key driving force in c-government initiatives and applications as it provides the necessary architecture and platforms needed. OECD (2012) has repoted how well ICT has been applied to c-government with a full range of functions through cloud infrastructures. Based on this report, UK rated 3rd on the connected index for connected government readiness, highlighting that the UK is in a good position for connected government services. Table 2 depicts the applicability of cloud computing to c-government services.

Figure 7. Cloud model of public services. Adapted from Wauters (2011).

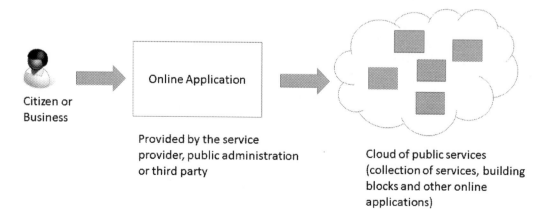

Citizen or Business

Online Application

Provided by the service provider, public administration or third party

Cloud of public services (collection of services, building blocks and other online applications)

Table 2. Applicability of cloud computing to c-government services. Adapted from OECD (2012)

Model	Characteristics	Services Offered	Applicability to C-Government	Relevance
Software as a service (SaaS)	• software application is offered as an application (as a service) • prebuilt applications deployed on demand. • Service virtualisation.	• E-governances services (government to government, government to citizen. • Value added services. • Gateway services (e.g. payment gateway).	• Actual government services offered to end customers accessible through internet. • Easy to deploy and rollout. • Similar application for different department can be provisioned faster. • Reduces TCO as application is available off the shelf.	High
Platform as a Service (PaaS)	• Provides required platform to develop and customise applications. • Exposes services components and APIs. • Integration platform. • Choice of different platforms.	• Plain or pre-configures application stack. • Work flow and message queues services. • Application instances (middleware containers). • Application clustering.	• Preconfigured stack and middleware elements available facilitating faster application development and rollout. • Consistency and repeatability helps redeploy multiple instances quicker. • End customer does not have to buy the software licences. • Reduces maintenance and management overheads.	Low
Infrastructure as a Service (IaaS)	• Provides hardware infrastructure (servers, OS). • Virtualised environments highly scalable. • high availability • Choice of different platforms.	• Slices of hardware (server, storage). • Data backup and restore services. • Clustering solutions. • Disaster recovery. • Visualised containers.	• Preconfigured hardware instances that can be provisioned faster. • Resource augmentation easier to support scaling. • Uniformity of the environment configuration to ensure consistency. • End customer does not have to buy hardware and OS licenses.	Medium

Cloud computing is an ideal environment for c-government services and has advanced to encompass most of current business architectures and ICT related activities to it, as discussed earlier in Table 1. Clouds by definition are a large pool of resources which are virtual and easily usable and can be reconfigured for dynamic variable load. It follows a pay-per-use model so that the infrastructure providers guarantee their availability to the end-users.

A successful cloud infrastructure is underpinned by delivering the optimum Quality of Service (QoS) such that users minimise risk and maintain a cost-effective and energy efferent operation. Users can understand and deploy the QoS requirements when they use the cloud resources. Some key characteristics identified by Vijaykumar (2011) have made it very attractive for c-government approaches. These being:

- Accessibility using passwords from anywhere.
- Scalability depending on demand using the virtualisation factor of Clouds.
- Service oriented architecture for services.
- Interoperability and multi-tenancy of services for different end-users.
- Information security looking at confidentiality, availability and integrity.
- Costs of running the infrastructure.
- Less time to market

Legal Issues With Respect to ICT

Das et al. (2011) describes that the building blocks for cloud computing for c-government resources can reduce the cost of infrastructure and the software involved. Due to the distributed nature of c-government services, cloud computing offers the suitable model to deploy these services. But however, this often blurs the location of and security measures associated with the data held in the services. This situation particularly collides with legal data protection requirements especially if sensitive citizen data is held. Citizens and businesses must be familiar with the regulations that govern their data in order to assess the risk levels of communicating through c-government services.

From the legal perspective, among the realities that citizens and governments have to realise are the following:

- Their data, applications and infrastructure are stored and managed by others in remote locations.
- Their proprietary data can be stored with the data of other tenants (some of whom may even be competitors) on shared infrastructure (at least in the public cloud or infrastructures).
- Data is provisioned dynamically which brings along a loss of control for personal data processed online.
- Their current architecture providers often subcontract and outsource the provisioning of their services to unknown third parties in unknown locations.
- Data and databases can be easily reproduced on the internet.
- Can potentially generate new information, derived from the data made available from users (either individuals or companies).

Therefore, the most important aspects to consider are: data protection, data security and ownership rights.

LEGAL DEFINITIONS USING SLAS IN C-GOVERNMENT

Service Level Agreements (SLAs) can define all QoS variables for the users when they use services. These include performance, availability, security measures and legal issues as well. This document serves as a legal binding contract between the end user and the infrastructures of the cloud services. In a case, where some of the QoS requirements are not being satisfied, these can be identified as *legal* issues and would thus need mitigation strategies from a legal point of view.

There are several legal issues connected with the use of clouds, especially with regard to data protection and data security (ENISA, 2009) including:

- Destruction of data
- Loss of data
- Loss of ownership rights of data
- Alteration of data
- Disclosure of data

- Unauthorized access by third parties or authorities outside EU/EEA
- Appropriate measures
- Uncertain regulatory compliance
- Other risks (e.g. unknown risks)

Legal Risk Model

Legal risk is often viewed as a function of fourteen critical variable presented (Jackson, 2002). A rudimentary risk model can be constructed by viewing legal risk in the context of a regression model. This is as follows:

$$LR = f(D,R,P,C,Lo,J,Ch,I,T,E,Cr,St,L,S)$$

where, LR=legal risk, D=documentation, R=regulation, P=type of products, C=type of counterparties, Lo=location of counterparties, J=judicial decisions, Ch=choice of law/legal environment, I=initial mark-to-market, T=technology, E=exposure to counterparties, Cr=credit rating, St=corporate structure, L=lawyers, S=staff.

The legal risk model is just a starting point to quantity the legal risk, but the goal is to recognise it and minimise it in the operations of the government. Various aspects recognised are as follows:

- Data protection and data security:
  - Trust and Control of the data. This is commonly the key inhibitor for using Cloud Computing by consumers.
  - Data security builds trust.
- Intellectual property rights:
  - Who owns the data in the Cloud?
  - Cloud computing has the technology to create new data e.g. data mining tools.
  - The concept of ownership implies that the owner exerts control.
- Green legislation:
- Compliance with laws and standards.
  - Anticipate Carbon Laws.

G-CLOUDS: USING CLOUD AS ENABLING ARCHITECTURE

Hashemi et al, (2013) have highlighted green computing, disaster recovery as some of the advantages of using Clouds for c-government services to ensure connectivity at all times. Most governments around the world have implemented using clouds for their services. Singapore has implemented their own G-cloud with three zones to meet the different levels of security and governance requirements of the people:

- High Assurance Zone – for a physically dedicated computing resource pool, only used by Government to serve its high assurance needs.
- Medium Assurance Zone – a computing resource pool which will be shared with non-government cloud users to lower cost of computing resources for Government.

- Basic Assurance Zone – a computing resource pool which is shared with public cloud users for basic functionality.

The USA has an official web portal (www.usa.gov) which is one of the busiest website portals in the world receiving approximately 342,000 visits daily (Wyld, 2009). It is called the best site to visit when the US government services are required, designed to aid the citizens of the US to interact with the government departments efficiently. However, users can still frequently suffer long delays and downtimes during high traffic periods, such as during voting seasons, monthly unemployment statistics release days, and natural disasters.

The UK government has introduced the 'G-cloud', which is designed to be a government-wide cloud computing network, a strategic priority (Glick, 2013). The goal of using G-cloud was to improve IT use in government and allow for more services to online migration. To support this action, the UK's IT procurement efforts have been focused on enabling government to become a leading force in the use of cloud computing. The report states that: "The Government's impact on the digital economy goes way beyond its role as policy maker. In delivering public services, as a large customer of ICT products and services and as the owner of data systems, the public sector has enormous influence on the market. In many areas, such as education, health and defence, Government can use its position as the leading procurer of services, to drive up standards (in some cases to set standards) and to provide an investment framework for research and development". Further information is available at the Digital Britain team at http://digitalbritainforum.org.uk/.

In Japan, the national government is undertaking a major cloud computing initiative, called the 'Kasumigaseki Cloud'. The government wants to develop a private cloud environment that would host all of the Japanese government's computing. According to Japan's Ministry of Internal Affairs and Communications (MIC) (Wyld, 2010), the Kasumigaseki Cloud will provide greater information and resource sharing and, in addition, promote more standardization and consolidation in the IT resources of government. Further similar initiatives are being undertaken by the Thailand government (Segkhoonthod, 2012).

Use Case Example 1: eDepot

Sweden, Italy and Belgium have used an example of electronic public services called the eDepot project. This project is a collaboration between the Royal Federation of Belgian Notaries, the Belgian Federal Institution for Communication and Technology (FEDICT) and the Agency for Administrative Simplification, It offers notaries a quick and easy way to create a company in all administrative databases, with via the eDepot, companies can sign deeds deposited electronically using a 'REAL card' system to serve as e-ID card. This can be used to identify the companies activities.

This example shows that through collaboration of the involved parties and the SOA-based implementation for reusable services the process of starting a company in Belgium has been substantially simplified and made more efficient. Instead of taking 56 days to complete it now takes no more than 3 days (Wauter, 2012).

Use Case Example 2: UK G-CLOUD

In October 2011, the UK government piloted a six-month framework for public sector use of cloud computing, developing the CloudStore, an online catalogue of accepted cloud services (CloudStore,

2013). CloudStore, itself cloud-based, was hosted on Windows Azure PaaS. This led to another mini project called Cloud Legal Project at the University of London, which analysed the procurement process, purchasing (call-off) process and contractual structures for government services on the Cloud. It used the G-Cloud as a case study to illustrate key issues arising on cloud contracts and discusses some lessons learned, particularly regarding contractual and public procurement issues.

This project looked at issues of applying supplier contract terms, such as SLAs, payment terms and intellectual property rights, and specified mandatory 'overlay' terms. The initial draft documentation omitted liability provisions, which meant that supplier liability provisions (such as total liability exclusions) were being governed. The government concluded that an additional liability was needed to protect the suppliers to change their terms, materials or even amend the contract terms.

Security accreditation of the services accepted onto the G-Cloud framework is work still in progress (Hon et al, 2012), but meanwhile customers were allowed to use services which had low impacts and needed low security. For example, a SaaS provider may build or 'layer' its services on the services of an IaaS or PaaS provider, but have little control over the IaaS or PaaS provider. Various rights of Cloud audits need to be investigated in this context especially if sensitive citizen data is hosted. The CloudStore provided an online marketplace for suppliers to offer their services to the public sector via the G-Cloud framework. Public sector bodies can review and buy these services. This can allow avoiding long contracts, buying the exact computing resources needed and saving on money on maintenance and physical storage. It offered 1200 suppliers with 13,000 services under the terms in Table 3 and prices in Table 4.

Table 3. SLA definitions and standards used by Azure

Capability	Details
Assurance	Complies with G-Cloud definitions (https://www.gov.uk/government/publications/g-cloud-service-definitions)
Security classifications	There are 3 government security classifications for information (OFFICIAL, SECRET, TOP SECRET). Most CloudStore services are classified OFFICIAL, based on the government's cloud Security Principles. When suppliers submit a new service to the G-Cloud framework, they need to: (1) select from a list of statements that show how they meet the cloud Security Principles (2) provide evidence and documents to support their answers (3) continuously update their security details, ensuring buyers always have the latest information
Information assurance	ISO-27001 certification which is scheduled be within the life of this framework.
Safe Harbour Framework	Microsoft abides by the Safe Harbour framework as set forth by the U.S. Department of Commerce regarding the collection, use, and retention of data from the European Union, the European Economic Area, and Switzerland. See: http://www.microsoft.com/online/legal/en-us/Azure_privacy_statement.htm
Data Centre Locations	The Windows Azure Platform (compute and storage) is hosted within 6 Microsoft data centres as follows: (Dublin, Ireland),(Amsterdam, Netherlands),(Chicago, IL),(San Antonio, TX), (Hong Kong, China),(Singapore)
Environmental Focus	By using sensor and monitoring equipment, new high-efficiency container-based data centre designs and air cooling systems can reduce the need for mechanical chillers, Microsoft's new data centres consume 50 per cent less energy for the same level of output than data centres built just three years ago.
Compliance	In addition to basic rules, Microsoft has also implemented its own version of compliances to abide by. These include: • ISO/IEC 27001:2005 Audit and Certification • SOC 1 and SOC 2 SSAE 16/ISAE 3402 Attestations • Cloud Security Alliance Cloud Controls Matrix • Federal Risk and Authorization Management Program (FedRAMP) • Payment Card Industry (PCI) Data Security Standards (DSS) Level 1 • United Kingdom G-Cloud Impact Level 2 Accreditation • HIPAA Business Associate Agreement (BAA) • Family Educational Rights and Privacy Act (FERPA)

Table 4. Pricing plan for g-Cloud services (Hon et al, 2012; http://azure.microsoft.com/en-us/support/trust-center/compliance/)

Windows Azure Service Components	Most Common Configuration	G-Cloud Price (British Pounds)	Categories
Windows Azure computer service	Azure Small Instance	0.0641 per hour	Lot 1 – compute
Windows Azure VM role	Azure Small Instance	0.0641 per hour	Lot 1 – Other
Windows Azure Storage service	Azure Storage	0.0747 Per GB per month	Lot 1 – Storage
SQL Azure	Business Edition	53.3315 per month per 10 GB of database	Lot 1 – Other
Windows Azure Service Bus	Per 10k Messages	0.0088 per 10k msgs	Lot 1 – Other
Windows Azure Access Control Service	Per 100k Transactions	1.0615 per 100k tx	Lot 1 – Other
Windows Azure Caching service	128MB Cache	24.0016 per month	Lot 1 – Other
Windows Azure Market place	50 GB Gov Open Data	0.0000 up to 50 GB	Lot 1 – Other
Windows Azure Content delivery Network	Azure CDN Zone 1	0.0801 per GB per month	Lot 1 – CDN

G-Cloud Framework was designed with agreements with suppliers that set out terms and conditions under which purchases (or call-offs) can be made throughout the term of the agreement. The difference between G-Cloud and the other frameworks was that it allowed the customer to pay for services as they used them, rather than being tied to inflexible, long-term contracts through CloudStore. Windows Azure was employed for use with G-cloud (Windows Azure SLA, 2013), as presented in Figure 8.

TOWARDS A LEGAL MONITORING SYSTEMS FOR C-GOVERNMENT SERVICES

Refer to Figure 9. It describes the span of services of e-government services with a closer look at security and cost. The use of private cloud is more costly and more secure; therefore services which need these two aspects would be outsourced on private clouds rather than public clouds. Most of public commu-

Figure 8. Azure Control services. Adapted from SLA (2013).

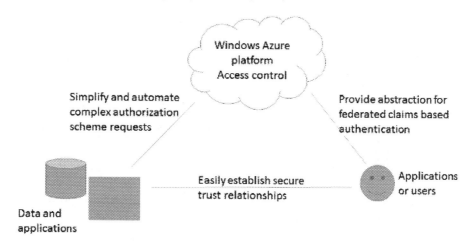

Figure 9. Four dimensions of e-government implementation strategy. Adapted from Hashemi (2013).

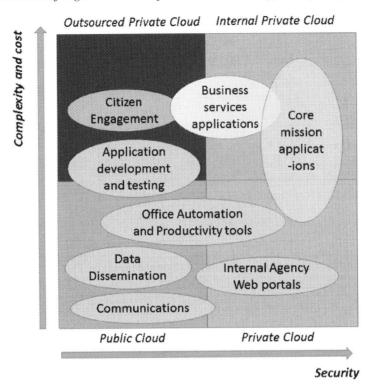

nication activities can take place via public clouds but internal business matters need to be secure and are often placed on private clouds.

Table 5 describes how ENISA rationalised a security risk in their documentation. Legal risk can be rationalised in a similar manner. Table 5 lists the requirements collected in the legal perspective of government services with the related assets and the threats against each service offered.

Figure 10 describes the model of how each requirement established in Table 6 can be analysed in detail. The stakeholders can be citizens, government or businesses using the services. Then each requirement can be mapped to the assets and how measure can be taken to mitigate their risk of being leaked.

Table 5. Abstract from ENISA (ENISA, 2009)

Probability	Very high
Impact	High
Vulnerability	V30. Lack of information on jurisdictions. V29. Storage of data in multiple jurisdictions and lack of transparency about this.
Affect assets	A1. Company reputation A2. Customer trust A5. Personal trust A6. Personal data A10. Service delivery
Risk	High

Table 6. Analysing the legal threats in order to quantify the legal requirements

Legal Requirement Number	Description (Threat Scenario)	Asset	Threat Agent	Rule to Be Checked
LR1	Show the data controllers in government infrastructure	Data, Government infrastructure		This is a simple requirement which the government can choose to disclose or not.
LR2	Monitoring of all current processing operations in the data manager, particularly with regard to the location of processing includes Data transfer to third world countries.	Data	Data manager	Government can place checks on where data is hosted geographically.
LR3	No externalization of resources to data centres in countries without an adequate level of protection includes data transfer to third world countries.	data	Data manager	Government can place checks on where data is hosted geographically.
LR4	Externalisation to third countries only if there are additional legal safeguards in place (e.g. standard contractual clauses) includes Data transfer to third world countries.	Data	Data manager	Government can place checks on where data is hosted geographically.
LR5	Ensure monitoring of data processing at processors	Data Controller	SLA management	Government can place checks on how data is processed, whether any movement is involved.
LR6	Processors must process data only on instructions from the controller	Data Controller	SLA management	Government can place checks on how data is processed, whether any movement is involved.
LR7	Further subcontracting (with sub-processors) must require consent of cloud customer	Data Controller	SLA management	Any legal obligations to subcontracting
LR8	Provide means to conclude controller-to-processor contracts in electronic form	Data Controller	SLA management	How services are being delivered is monitored.
LR9	Data manager must ensure that personal data is protected against accidental or unlawful destruction	Data	Security agents	The use of secure algorithms and encryption methods for security measures
LR10	The Data Manager must not allow any unauthorised modifications applied to existing data which results in a difference compared to the time before the modification came into effect	Data	Security agents	The use of secure algorithms and encryption methods for security measures
LR11	Create logs concerning any alteration made to the data	Data	Security agents	Monitoring security logs
LR12	Personal data must be protected against unauthorised disclosure in order to guarantee the safe and uninterrupted transfer of data by using encryption	Data	Security agents	The use of secure algorithms and encryption methods for security measures
LR13	Personal data must be protected against unauthorised access by implementing an Identity and Access Management	Data	Security agents	The use of secure algorithms and encryption methods for security measures
LR14	Government security framework Follows particular standards such as ISO 27000 standards	Government infrastructure	Security agents	The use of secure algorithms and encryption methods for security measures
LR15	Ownership rights in cloud of data	Government infrastructure	SLA management	No rule
LR16	Green legislation, energy monitoring	Government infrastructure	Energy monitoring	Monitoring of service usage
LR18	Legal issues for contract law	Government infrastructure	SLA management	No rule

Figure 10. Modelling legal risk to quantify all possible legal issues

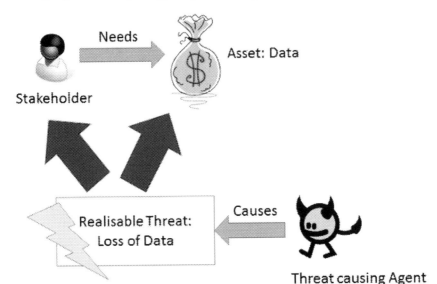

Although, there are a number of ethical issues surrounding c-government services, this chapter attempts to technically provide answers to some of them. These issues can be related to security, data integrity and privacy (Ahmadu, 2012). These issues are extremely crucial for both the development and the correct operations of e-government structures. These decisions can be automated in the following ways:

- **Security:** Using technology to ensure security mechanisms are in place for transactions, data being sent across the web and e-identification systems.
- **Signature Authentication:** Using authenticated digital signatures is crucial to e-government operations. Authentication methods use private and public keys to encode electronic documents as a means of safeguarding the integrity of online transactions and business deals.
- **Data Integrity:** There are other problems associated managing the electronic databases for public or private sector use. A fundamental issue is to make sure the database is accurate and up-to-date to prevent fraud and unauthorised access or misuse. This is because e-government structures aggregate and process enormous amount of data from different sources, maintain their integrity is a complex task for reliable online government systems and services.
- **Certification Authority:** The Government can think of establishing and managing a national certification authority to process digital signatures for validating automated public decisions.

FUTURE DIRECTIONS AND RECOMMENDATIONS

E-government is not a complete systems but an abstract of many services which the governments can use and make available to citizens. The vision is to identify a holistic framework by which all of them can be monitored through one system and one business logic to ensure collective governance over them. The following steps can be followed for legal issues for government:

Step 1: Identify each service that needs to be outsourced, identify all the government services that need to be made into electronic versions for c-government service.

Step 2: Identify and recognise each asset of the services to identify the affected data and citizens in the service such as in Table 4.

Step 3: Identify the potential of threats for each scenario for each c-government service such as in Figure 8.

Step 4: Identify the possible mitigation strategies for the services for each of the identified threat.

Step 5: Identify each threat and mitigation strategy with legal laws corresponding to the government laws and issues.

Step 6: Perform a parameter break down. This will help identify what is being measured and if are clearly defined. This will aid in the monitoring process.

Step 7: Create a profile for each parameter in relation to the threat scenarios and services online. This can help identify which can be ignored and which parameters are at a higher priority to monitor.

CONCLUSION

This chapter suggests that there is a need for further measures that can be taken by the governments to ensure monitoring and test methodologies so that all services are compliance with the government services. The governments can also consider independent third parties to ensure trustworthy measurements are met in terms of the legal requirements of each of the c-government services being offered. However, there are a number of issues which need considerable research that is still lacking,

- Vendor lock in which prevents from discontinues the service.
- Involvement of multiple parties which is not clear to the citizens.
- Auditing requirements, needed on cases of bankruptcy which could influence the citizens personal data to be at risk.
- Special protection to storage of data, in case of data loss due to unforeseen reasons.

The issue is that the cloud computing has brought about a complex working environment for software and many of the current legal laws are not resolving most of the inherent issues. Some of the problems need a multi- and inter- disciplinary approach working with software engineers, technology providers and lawyers to set out the correct legal issues and checklist before governments start using clouds for deploying their services. Problems such as who owns the software, how can data be transferred across countries, who monitors and who is liable if the personal and private citizens' data goes missing. Considerable amount of laws still need to be drawn out to clearly understand which laws are applicable to which cases and how they comply with both local government laws and global laws across the EU and the entire world.

REFERENCES

Ahmadu, M.L. (2012). *The Legal Aspects of Electronic Government in Pacific Island Countries: A Reflection*. Academic Press.

Al-Soud, A. R. (2013). *Towards Adoption Of Cloud Computing For Boosting The Jordanian E-Government*. Paper presented at the European, Mediterranean & Middle Eastern Conference on Information Systems.

Australian Government. (2011). *Department of Finance and Deregulation, Cloud Computing Strategic Direction Paper: Opportunities and applicability for use by the Australian Government, April 2011*. Available Online: http://www.finance.gov.au/files/2012/04/final_cloud_computing_strategy_version_1.pdf

CloudStore. (2013). *Cabinet Office*. Retrieved from https://www.gov.uk/how-to-use-cloudstore

Das, R. K., Patnaik, S., & Misro, A. K. (2011). Advanced Computing. *Communications in Computer and Information Science, 133*, 161–172. doi:10.1007/978-3-642-17881-8_16

Eecke, P. V. (2014). *DLA Piper Brussels, Cloud Computing Legal issues*. Retrieved from http://www.isaca.org/Groups/Professional-English/cloud-computing/GroupDocuments/DLA_Cloud%20computing%20legal%20issues.pdf

ENISA. (2009). *Cloud Computing: Benefits, Risks and Recommendations for Information Security, Nov 2009*. Available online: https://www.enisa.europa.eu/activities/risk-management/files/deliverables/cloud-computing-risk-assessment

Europe 2020. (2010). *A Strategy for smart, sustainable and inclusive growth*. European Commission COM (2010) 2020 final, March 2010.

Glick, B. (2009). Digital Britain commits government to cloud computing. *Computing*. Retrieved from http://www.computing.co.uk/computing/news/ 2244229/digital-britain-commits

Gray, P. (2013). Legal issues to consider with cloud computing. *Tech Decision Maker*. Available at http://www.techrepublic.com/blog/tech-decision-maker/legal-issues-to-consider-with-cloud-computing/

Hashemi, S., Monfaredi, K., & Masdari, M. (2013). Using Cloud Computing for E-Government: Challenges and Benefits, World Academy of Science, Eng and Tech. *Int. Journal of Computer, Information Systems, and Control Engineering, 7*(9).

Hon, K., Millard, C., & Walden, I. (2012). *UK G-Cloud v1 and the Impact on Cloud Contracts*. Retrieved from http://www.scl.org/site.aspx?i=ne26144

Jackson, C. (2002). Legal Risk Optimisation. *Risk Magazine*. Retrieved from http://www.risk.net/risk-magazine/feature/1506604/legal-risk-optimisation

Janssen, M., & Joha, A. (2013). *Challenges for adopting Cloud-based software as a service in the public sector*. Academic Press.

Kiran, M. (2014). *A Methodology for Cloud Security Risks Management, Cloud computing*. Springer International publishing.

Kumar, M., Shukla, M., Agarwal, S., & Pandey, G.N. (2015). *An E Governance model using cloud computing technology for Developing Countries, 2013*. Academic Press.

OECD. (2012). *United Nations E-Government Survey 2012*. United Nations Department of Economic and Social Affairs. Retrieved from http://stats.oecd.org

Oleg M. (2014), Next generation e-government: G-Cloud and beyond, Evolving E-Governance through Cloud Computing based environment. *Int Journal of Advanced Research in Computer and Communication Engineering, 3*(4).

Segkhoonthod, S. (2012). *Adopting Cloud Computing as an e-Government Platform.* Electronic Government Agency (Public Organization). Retrieved from http://csathailand.cio16.org/portals/4/AdoptingCloud.pdf

Singh, V. J., & Chandel, A. (2013). Cloud Based E-Government: Benefits and Challenges. *Int Journal of Multi-Disciplinary Sciences and Engineering, 4*(6).

Snooks, A. (2013). *Negotiating the cloud – legal issues in cloud computing agreements.* Australian Government. Available Online: http://www.finance.gov.au/files/2013/02/negotiating-the-cloud-legal-issues-in-cloud-computing-agreements-v1.1.pdf

Swire, P. (1993). Safe Harbors and a Proposal to Improve the Community Reinvestment Act. *Virginia Law Review, 79*(349), 1993.

Vijaykumar, N. (2011). Role of ICT in e-governance: Impact of Cloud computing in Driving new initiatives. *SETLABS Briefings, 9*(2). Retrieved from www.infosys.com/infosys-labs/publications/Documents/e-governance/ict-e-governance.pdf

Wauters, P., Declercq, K., vander Peijl, S., & Davie, P. (2012). *Study on cloud and service oriented architectures for e-government.* Ref. Ares (2012) 149022 - 09/02/2012 Deloitte 05-12-2011 Framework Contract no: DI/06691-00.

Windows AzureS. L. A. (2013). Retrieved from http://assets-production.govstore.service.gov.uk/G4/Phoenix_Software_Ltd-0386/52396e3f354067cf477de18d/QD2/Windows-Azure-Platform-Service-Definition-FA1.pdf

Wyld, D. C. (2009). Moving to the cloud: An introduction to cloud computing in government. Washington, DC: IBM Center for the Business of Government.

Wyld, D. C. (2010, January). The Cloudy Future of Government IT: Cloud Computing and the Public Sector around the World. *Int Journal of Web & Semantic Technology, 1*(1), 1–20.

ADDITIONAL READING

Adams, R. (2013). *The emergence of cloud storage and the need for a new digital forensic process model.* Murdoch University. doi:10.4018/978-1-4666-2662-1.ch004

Mather, T., Kumaraswamy, S., & Latif, S. (2009). *Cloud Security and Privacy: An Enterprise Perspective on Risks and Compliance.* O'Reilly Media, Inc.

Mowbray, M. (2009). The Fog over the Grimpen Mire: Cloud Computing and the Law. *SCRIPTed, 6*(1), 129. doi:10.2966crip.060109.132

Ottenheimer, D. (2012). *Securing the Virtual Environment: How to Defend the Enterprise Against Attack.* Wiley.

Rouse, M. (2012). G-cloud (government cloud), *Search Cloud Computing*. Retrieved 26 September 2013 from http://searchcloudcomputing.techtarget.com

Srinavasin, M. (2012). *State-of-the-art cloud computing security taxonomies: a classification of security challenges in the present cloud computing environment.* ACM ICACCI. doi:10.1145/2345396.2345474

KEY TERMS AND DEFINITIONS

Complexity: This is a characteristic of the system which implies too many units working together in a complex manner which is hard to test and track for data movement across them.

Cost: It is a characteristic which refers to the cost either in terms of money or loss of infrastructure associated with the use of resources.

Data Integrity: This refers to the validity of data. Since, data can be compromised in a number of ways, various authentication and security mechanisms have been devised to minimize the threats to data integrity.

E-Government: This refers to the provisioning of a government's functionality and its services using the web and communications technologies including the latest software development and deployment paradigms and related methodologies such as Web 2.0 and mobile technologies.

Risk: This refers to a situation which measures the probability of danger to the infrastructure. It measure the chance of harmful effects to the asset that is being protected and the impact it will have to the current Cloud ecosystem.

Security: Sometimes a basic requirement of the system which insures the availability, integrity and confidentiality of the data is kept secure and up to date.

Service Level Agreements (SLAs): This refers to the legal agreement between the cloud providers and user which specifies the terms of conditions of using the services. This can contain details of what to do in situations of outages and data loss.

Service Oriented Architecture (SOA): This is an architectural style for developing and integrating large applications. The basic building block is a service that is independent and self-contained. The application system is a collection of such services linked in the correct way.

This research was previously published in Cloud Computing Technologies for Connected Government edited by Zaigham Mahmood, pages 322-344, copyright year 2016 by Information Science Reference (an imprint of IGI Global).

Chapter 89
Investigating the Determinants of Decision-Making on Adoption of Public Cloud Computing in E-Government

Juhua Wu
Guangdong University of Technology, China

Fang Ding
State Information Centre of China, China

Meng Xu
Guangdong University of Technology, China

Zan Mo
Guangdong University of Technology, China

Anran Jin
The University of Hong Kong, Hong Kong

ABSTRACT

This article analyzed decision-making in terms of the adoption of public cloud computing and its determinants in the context of e-government. The authors proposed a theoretical model and related hypotheses after reviewing the literature and combining technology adoption theory with IT decision-making authority theory. Then, they collected samples from 227 public sectors and tested hypotheses using structural equation modeling. The results show that the determinants of the three modes (IaaS, SaaS, and PaaS) of decision-making on adoption are different. The significant determinants of IaaS adoption include technical factors and business factors, those of PaaS adoption include technical factors and management factors, whereas those of SaaS include technical factors, business factors and management factors. The authors also find managerial/controlling power, which characterizes the special nature of Chinese culture, only have a significant influence on the decision-making on adoption of PaaS mode and SaaS mode.

DOI: 10.4018/978-1-5225-8176-5.ch089

INTRODUCTION

E-government, which adopts new information and communication technologies, is being increasingly recognized as an important means for transforming all facets of government operations and services (Tan et al., 2013). In China, the public continuously introduces new demands for e-government, such as providing open resource sharing services while casting off time and space limits, which has brought whole-new technological and managerial challenges to its development (Ding & Wu, 2012). However, a relatively small number of all e-government initiatives in China have been successful in attaining their major goals of information sharing and reducing the cost of infrastructure (Wang & Ding, 2015). To promote in-depth sharing of information resources, and improve the intensive level of e-government, the Chinese government is actively considering adopting public cloud computing in a way that can facilitate the management of information resources, and the innovation and creativity of operation modes (Qu et al., 2015). Cloud computing is not a new technical product, but rather a new mode of distributed shared pooling of IT infrastructure linked together to provide centralized IT services on demand. The cloud-based solutions providing various services can be divided into three types: public, private, and hybrid clouds (Harris, 2011). Public clouds, which are open network infrastructure, are designed to provide software access through web-based portals, whereas private clouds, which are proprietary infrastructure with encryption and security measures, are wholly operated for an organization, restricting access to shared resources only for authorized customers, and offer secure computing services either on the organization's premises or operated by a third party vendor offsite (Harris, 2011). The hybrid cloud is a combination of public and private delivery of IT services. The application of public cloud service can realize resource aggregation and virtualization, application service sharing and on-demand supply, and provide a lot of public sectors with computing and data services that are efficient and cost-effective and power-effective (Armbrust et al., 2010). In particular, compared with private and hybrid cloud computing, public cloud computing is more open and highly shared, rendering great risks of adoption (Paquette et al. 2010). Therefore, a proper decision-making on public cloud adoption is a challenge being faced by most public sectors and has been indispensable during the process of shifting e-government applications towards the cloud mode. Predicated by this challenge, in this study, we focus on the factors influencing decision-making on the adoption of public cloud computing in e-government rather than that of private and hybrid clouds.

Public clouds in e-government are a technical innovation (Armbrust et al., 2010). This implies that the technical characteristics of a public cloud may affect decision-maker adoption. The synthesis of this literature review suggests that cloud computing's technical ability to provide distributed systems consisting of virtualized resources that are used for dynamic provisioning on demand is arguably the main factor to influence its adoption (Mustafee, 2010). Other studies seek to provide empirical evidence from the perspective of financial features enabled by cloud computing, i.e., the financial ability for the firm to eliminate the fixed cost of IT infrastructure and only incur usage-based pricing for IT services from the external cloud vendor (Dorsch & Häckel, 2014).

In addition, public clouds are much more than information technology (IT) products, but rather the new managerial modes of government services and operations (Armbrust et al., 2010). Specifically, the power distance is greater in China (Liao et al., 2010); decision-making on public cloud adoption is very difficult because managerial/controlling power of information resources and applications in e-government will be very unclear when the e-government system is transferred to a public cloud platform and the ownership and storage location of information resources and applications are out of the control of the original public sectors (Winkler & Brown, 2013). Under such circumstances, data and applications will be stored and run on a remote resource platform of several cloud service providers in several places and even several countries; the complexity of IT decision-making authority allocation in public cloud services is thus immeasurable. In the absence of sufficient managerial/controlling power in the public cloud mode, government officials worry that the reliance on the IT infrastructure, integrated platform, and application of cloud service providers may weaken their power, so they are strongly opposed to adopt public cloud computing. Additionally, regulators of information systems also need to have the control over data resources for the purpose of auditing (Winkler & Brown, 2013). Therefore, managerial/controlling power is a vital key for adopting public clouds.

Current studies mainly focus on public cloud technical ability and financial performance, and there is lack of empirical studies on its adoption decision from the perspective of decision-makers in three aspects, i.e., technology, business and management. Specifically, the managerial perspective, such as management/controlling power, which shows the characteristics of Chinese culture, is neglected in current research. In addition, relatively little is known about the difference of determinants among the IaaS, SaaS, and PaaS modes of adoption of public clouds (See Table 1). To address this research gap, this study specifically discusses the following two issues based on relevant research results. First, an empirical examination is conducted of the three modes of adoption decisions in e-government, including IaaS, PaaS, and SaaS, from the three perspectives, i.e., technology, business, and management. Second, a comparison is made of significant influencing factors of decision-making on adopting the different modes of public cloud computing.

This study attempts to answer these two questions by integrating the literature on IT decision-making authority theory (Weill & Ross, 2004) and IT adoption theory (Venkatesh, et al., 2003). There are three significant contributions of this research. First, this study provides a comprehensive understanding of adoption of public cloud computing in e-government from the perspectives of three aspects, which include technical factors, business factors, and management factors. Second, this research facilitates our understanding of public cloud computing adoption in Chinese public sectors. Although developing e-government cloud computing has currently become a global trend, the mechanisms pertaining to the ways in which management-related factors affect government adoption still remain largely unclear. By addressing the factors of management/controlling power, the current study extends our understanding of public cloud computing adoption in the context of China. Furthermore, examining technology adoption theory and IT decision-making authority theory in e-government different from past studies helps us gauge the consistency of the various factors affecting the three modes adoption (IaaS, SaaS, and PaaS) of public cloud computing.

THEORETICAL FRAMEWORK AND HYPOTHESES

Cloud computing has been characterized into three building layers: infrastructure as a service (IaaS), platform as a service (PaaS), and Software as a Service (SaaS) modes, enabling millions of users to enjoy the service during peak times (Mell & Grance, 2011; Shin et al., 2014). IaaS provides cloud infrastructure, including a virtual machine, virtual storage, disk image library, virtual infrastructure, raw block storage, file or object storage, load balancer, IP addresses, firewalls, virtual local area networks, and cloud service providers supply these resources on demand from their large pools installed in data center bundles. Such a mode has the advantage of cost effectiveness by cutting back on user costs in building

Table 1. Cloud computing adoption studies published in peer reviewed journals

Adoption (Dependent Variable)	Theory Basis	Determinants (Independent Variable)	Resources
Cloud Computing	SWOT analysis	strengths; weaknesses; opportunities; threats	Marston et al. (2011)
Intention to Increase the Level of SaaS Adoption	theory of reasoned action	perceived risk (performance; economic; strategic; security; managerial); perceived opportunities (cost advantages; strategic flexibility; focus on core competencies; access to specialized resources; quality improvements)	Benlian & Hess (2011)
SaaS Satisfaction	dedication-constraint mechanism	competence-based trust; openness-based trust	Chou & Chiang (2013)
The Evaluation of SaaS	the balanced scorecard	learning and growth; Internal business processes	Lee et al. (2013)
The Economies of Scale of SaaS	a stochastic frontier approach	the output elasticity of capital; the output elasticity of labor	Ge & Huang (2014)
The Competition between SaaS Vendors	competition with heterogeneous products and switching costs	productivity; cost	Ma et al. (2014)
Consumer Adoption Behavior for Cloud Computing		service fee; storage capacity; stability	Shin et al. (2014)
Cloud Computing Adoption	diffusion of innovation theory; technology-organization-environment theory	(indirect) security and privacy concerns; cost savings; (direct) relative advantage; complexity; compatibility; technological readiness; top management support; firm size; competitive pressure; regulatory support	Oliveira et al. (2014)
Market Reaction to Cloud Computing Announcements	an extended resource based view	firm-specific factor (firm size; prior experience); resource-specific factor (service types; implementation types; realization of benefits); vendor-specific factor (vendor reputation)	Son et al. (2014)
Pricing Strategy for Cloud Computing	traditional damaged goods strategy		Huang et al. (2015)
SaaS Satisfaction		(indirect) service quality; responsiveness; security; (direct) trust; perceived value	Goode et al. (2015)
Behavioral Intention to Use Cloud Computing	unified six well-known theories,	attitude; compatibility; computer self-efficacy; service quality; perceived behavior control; perceived ease of use; perceived playfulness; perceived usefulness; result demonstration; subjective norm; trialability; visibility; voluntariness	Shiau & Chau (2016)
The Competition of Cloud Computing Services		cloud computing security; client-side security; IT security	Liu et al. (2015)
The Migration to Cloud Storage		disk capacity; storage costs; migration risk	Naldi & Mastroeni (2016)
Move to the Cloud	migration theory	(direct) users' intention; (indirect) relative usefulness; expected omnipresence; user dissatisfaction; users' switching costs; users' security concerns; (moderator) switching costs; security concerns	Bhattacherjee & Park (2014)
Usage Continuance of Cloud		rapport; responsiveness; reliability; flexibility; features; security	Benlian & Hess (2011)
SaaS Coordination		economic performance; information sharing	Demirkan et al. (2010)
Horizontal Allocation of Decision Rights for SaaS	agency theory, transaction cost economics, knowledge-based view	origin of the application initiative, scope of application use, business knowledge of the IT unit	Winkler & Brown (2013)
Governmental Use of Cloud Computing		tangible/known risks (access; availability; infrastructure; integrity); intangible/unknown risks	Paquette et al. (2010)

IT infrastructure for the first time and is also conductive for cloud service providers to generate scale economies. In PaaS mode, cloud service providers offer platform-level, integrated application solutions and tools. This includes a programming language execution environment, operating system, database, and web server. PaaS mode meets the requirement for cost effectiveness, which can reduce the time of organizations in developing new applications and reduce development and maintenance cost. Under SaaS layer, software applications are delivered as a service over the Internet, which enables consumers to use each type of software through online payments to the cloud service provider. Customers do not need to install software on the desktop, laptop or any other client devices, thereby reducing maintenance costs and realizing on-demand pricing and purchases.

Research Hypotheses

The term 'decision-making on adoption' is defined as the initial decision regarding whether to use a new technology made by the top management team of an organization (Thong et al., 2011). Before adopting the technology, those who make the decision need to forecast whether the application of the technology will elevate the business value based on sufficient evidence. The research model is established by combining technology adoption theory and IT decision-making authority theory. The widely referenced technology adoption theory studied whether the decision made by individuals or organizational leaders integrates certain IT into the application activities within organizations. Applying technology adoption theory to the study of factors influencing cloud computing adoption is considered applicable for this study in revealing the acceptance process and predicting the influence of leaders' behavior and perceptions to a new technology. The objective of adoption theory is to provide technology adopters with sufficient evidence to predict whether a new technology will in fact enhance service delivery and improve business performance (Goode et al., 2015). Therefore, the use of adoption theory is relevant to highlight the individual decision-making process of corporate managers based on their perceptions. The characteristics of technology and business, such as ease of use, usefulness, security, and cost effectiveness, were the main reasons for decision-makers' adoption (Shiau & Chau, 2016).

Similarly, Weill and Ross (2004) proposed that when IT decision-making on adoption involves the business strategy, a certain department shall not independently assume all of the obligations and responsibilities and the decision on adoption shall be jointly made by the senior management, business and IT functions. As the application of cloud computing has not reached a level of maturity, there are only a few successful cases in China (Qu et al., 2015). In particular, the application of public cloud computing in public sectors will bring destructive transformation to the government resource management mode, which is related to business and organizational strategies (Paquette et al., 2010). However, most studies on IT decision-making authority, such as managerial/controlling power, have been conducted in the context of business and identified as one of the crucial enablers of organizational benefits (Winkler & Brown, 2013; Ding et al., 2014), and we still know very little about the role of managerial/controlling power in the public sector delivery of e-services in public cloud mode. Our study explores this vital but relatively unaddressed aspect of managerial/controlling power using IT decision-making authority theory as the theoretical framework.

The decision-making on the adoption of public cloud computing is an organizational strategic decision-making and suitable for decisions by technical, business and management functions collectively. When making decisions, the technical manager mainly considers the technical factors of public clouds, i.e., exploring the technical features; the business manager mainly focuses on the business factors, i.e., investigating the impact of adoption on business; the management function concentrates on the management factors, i.e., whether it has irreconcilable contradictions with the existing management mode. Hence, this study investigated the determinants focused by the three departments, i.e., technical, business and management functions, to study the decision-making of adopting public cloud computing. The research model is shown in Figure 1.

Technology Perspective

When making decisions on whether to adopt public cloud computing, the IT function of public sectors should initially take into consideration whether it meets the demand for public services and operations (Marston et al., 2011). Because the focus is on the strategic level of the organization, we define the technical alignment of public clouds as the degree of fit between e-government strategy, cloud strategy, e-government infrastructure, and cloud infrastructure (Benlian & Hess, 2011). Compared with the traditional mode, the public cloud mode, based on pay-per-view, promotes the development of the lease operation of idle computing power of cloud service providers, and facilitates public cloud users to benefit from the cloud computing mode delivered through the service by running the application on a shared virtual machine (Demirkan & Delen, 2013). Therefore, we can conclude that if there is a strong degree of fit between the public cloud computing and the resource integration and sharing strategies of the e-government, they are more inclined to adopt public cloud computing (Oliveira et al., 2014). Marketers can conveniently obtain and share information resources at any time and in any place through the cloud service (Chou & Chiang, 2013). Some researchers believed that public cloud adoption is effective and useful for meeting special business functions and resource sharing demands (Lee et al., 2013). This ability enables an alignment between public cloud computing and government strategies for effective financial support and resource sharing that leads to efficient support for public services (Naldi & Mastroeni, 2016).

Adaptation to an e-government public cloud is the process by which users including governmental employees and citizens learn, negotiate, enact, and maintain the behaviors appropriate to the given e-government applications in the public cloud mode (Bruque et al., 2008). Appropriate adaptation to the cloud environment indicates some degree of fit between the user behaviors demanded by the cloud

Figure 1. Research model

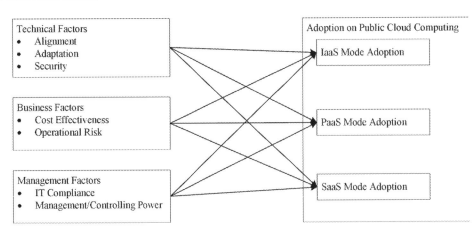

environment and those produced by the users of cloud applications, such that the users are able to achieve valued work goals (Bruque et al., 2008). The existing e-government structure of is complex. If being moved to the public cloud platform, transportability becomes a difficult issue (Naldi & Mastroeni, 2016). Often the reasons for user resistance to cloud-related changes in e-government are related with perceived loss of a desirable aspect of the "old" organization or perceiving a threat for losing some individual assets, such as power, influence, and security (Bhattacherjee & Park, 2014). Likewise, IT-induced changes in public cloud mode may fail to succeed due to members' resistance to change, which may be related to task mismatches and dysfunctional individual adaptation to a cloud-related change (Shiau & Chau, 2016). User adaptation to public cloud computing is particularly important when a cloud-enabled change has to be assimilated by all users (Giakoumis et al., 2015). Users subjected to such cloud-related changes, however, have the discretion to use the public cloud platform more or less effectively, to vary in the degree to which they take advantage of the possibilities offered by public cloud computing, and, consequently, determining the degree to which the technological capacity indeed translates into effective behaviors in their workplace (Oliveira et al., 2014). Hence, whether users of e-government systems can adapt to the public cloud platform cannot be ignored in the process of decision-making on adoption of cloud computing in e-government.

Security is always associated with prevention and detection of unauthorized activities in the networks or systems, and requires business to institute relevant strategic policies (Moreira et al., 2013). Technical security is defined as the degree to which the data, platform, and applications are secure against threats in the public cloud mode (Athens, 2010). Cloud computing's ability to disperse data across multiple data centers might introduce exploitation in countries that lack privacy laws (Oliveira et al., 2014). The flexibility of a cloud's pay per service is a cost motivation for adoption, but the movement of application from one network to another endangers security and trust in the confidentiality and integrity of data (Bhattacherjee & Park, 2014). Hacker and internet-based attack are more likely to make cloud service providers a target. The design of shared components in public clouds, such as CPU of infrastructure, buffer memory and storage device, is unsuitable for providing security isolation for multiple tenants (Benlian & Hess, 2011). Specifically, the executives in public sectors release the IT resource control to cloud service providers, creating a security defense gap. Most of the cloud service providers host the data of many users. Once the internal memory, storage and network route are 'attacked', this will lead to severe data loss. The applications of the e-government are run by the remote data center; however, the leaders of public sectors do not trust the security of SaaS mode, suggesting that placing all applications in external service providers other than a traditional internal IT team may lead to some unexpected threats (Goode et al., 2015). Battleson et al. (2016) also believed that when adopting public cloud computing, we need to first consider whether the technology has taken effective information security safeguard measures. Hence, we propose:

H1a: The higher the alignment of public cloud computing, the more likely for public sectors to adopt public cloud computing: (1) IaaS mode, (2) PaaS mode, and (3) SaaS mode.

H1b: The higher the adaptation of public cloud computing, the more likely for public sectors to adopt public cloud computing: (1) IaaS mode, (2) PaaS mode, and (3) SaaS mode.

H1c: The higher the security of public cloud computing, the more likely for public sectors to adopt public cloud computing: (1) IaaS mode, (2) PaaS mode, and (3) SaaS mode.

Business Perspective

Cost effectiveness has already been considered in relevant IT adoption studies, which explains how decision-makers change adoption decisions based on costs (Davis, 1989). Cost effectiveness is the ability of public cloud computing, which can remove the cost of purchasing infrastructure and improve the efficiency of operation (Truong, 2010). Oliveira et al. (2014) believed that the value of cloud computing lies in the fact that there are no upfront costs. For instance, there are no cost requirements for hardware, software, Internet, personnel, training, and other traditional network infrastructure. Choudhary and Vithayathil (2013) discovered that the integration of cloud computing infrastructure contributes to the cost reduction, i.e., cloud computing has brought on-demand access while eliminating prophase cost. Cloud adoption can reduce the costs of clients in purchasing software end-user licenses and relevant maintenance costs. Some researchers noted that public cloud computing realized cost effectiveness also through reducing IT operation, maintenance and fault correcting costs (Marston et al., 2011). The cost effectiveness of public technology is also reflected in the scale economies effect on cloud service providers. The shared resource pool offered by the providers has reduced the delivery cost, as a server can serve hundreds of users. The sharing of computing resources allows multiple users to jointly share software and hardware costs (Shiau & Chau, 2016), but cloud service providers must be able to deploy sufficient computing resources to realize the advantage of the scale economies. With the given resources, cloud suppliers reduce hardware cost through the multi-tenants method, whereas cloud users can benefit from low-priced and rapid resource access. Therefore, the advantages of public cloud computing include reducing the costs of users, while simultaneously cloud suppliers can realize scale economies. Cloud adoption can also reduce additional costs, such as the network hardware cost of the data center, electric power costs of the cooling system and labor costs. Yet the application of public cloud computing will save huge operating and maintenance costs for cloud users, thus stimulating the strong interest of decision-makers in public sectors for adoption.

When considering the cost effectiveness of public cloud computing, decision-makers also pay attention to the operational risk. Operational risk is defined as the potential for loss in the pursuit of a desired outcome when adopting public cloud computing in e-government (Benlian & Hess, 2011). Some researchers believe the design of the public cloud has definitely led to the risk of exposing sensitive information of unauthorized users (Marston et al., 2011). Information owners cannot control the hardware resources that carry information, so it is necessary to consider the risk when relying on virtualization to ensure information security (Benlian & Hess, 2011). E-government administrators suggest the development of authorization software to control the operational risk arising from the application of the public cloud and to define a normative operational standard for public cloud suppliers (Liu et al., 2015). These risk and authorization programs include such functions as verifiable governance, auditing and risk assessment (Maitner, 2011). Some e-government administrators believe that the risk related to cloud computing is not new, but a risk common in IT outsourcing services. As public cloud computing expands over time, the outsourcing storage of e-data and the existence of security risk make operational risk a paramount consideration in cloud technology adoption. In addition, because of the shortage of public cloud computing-based standards (Paquette et al., 2010), IT managers have no method of finding an effective reference to avoid operational risk. Therefore, the likelihood of the existence of operational risk increases significantly in public clouds. For most of the senior e-government managers, cost effectiveness is the major driving force for cloud adoption. However, the accompanied operational risk with the changes in service mode is the main factor impeding decision-makers from adopting public cloud computing. We thus propose:

H2a: The higher the cost effectiveness of public cloud computing, the more likely for public sectors to adopt public cloud computing: (1) IaaS mode, (2) PaaS mode, and (3) SaaS mode.
H2b: The lower the operational risk of public cloud computing, the more likely for public sectors to adopt public cloud computing: (1) IaaS mode, (2) PaaS mode, and (3) SaaS mode.

Management Perspective

IT compliance is composed of policies and regulations of organizations that are compulsory for cloud service providers to abide by. Any violation may lead to punishment based on measurement of the penalty (Cannoy & Salam, 2010). The punishment may range from penalty to imprisonment or both (Luthy & Forcht, 2006). Generally speaking, to minimize the occurrence of violations, senior e-government managers review the compliance on a regulator basis and compliance regulators act upon these policies and regulations to promote relevant organizations to take responsible actions. As many users are using the same resource when accessing data, it prevents the execution of compliance procedures (Chakraborty et al., 2010). The outcome of cloud adoption makes the privacy of organizations' data more vulnerable to infringement, and thus affects some compliance requirements (Cannoy & Salam, 2010). Cloud users expect cloud computing service providers can comply with specific national laws and regulations to protect data privacy and avoid unauthorized disclosure. Cloud service providers should provide their own compliance for potential clients. The providers offer individual resources based on the mode of multiple tenants, so cloud users care about data security, privacy protection and other trust issues. To meet the supervision requirements, the providers must ensure the physical security of internal IT procedures of clouds, such as system logs, log analysis, authentication, authorization, filing, backups, and the physical security of servers. The IT compliance of public clouds includes complying with organizations' internal IT procedures, data filing and backup, record, filing, and physical security of cloud services, among other requirements. As cloud computing triggers the privacy and confidentiality risk of cloud computing resources of users, the legal operation departments of many countries have established relevant civil and criminal punishment laws for data protection. Whether public cloud computing providers comply with these policies, laws, regulations, and rules is also an important issue to which decision-makers in public sectors pay great attention.

Managerial/controlling power means that governmental executives' authority to manage and control the data, application, and other resources in the public cloud (Winkler & Brown, 2013). Walz and Grier (2010) argued that when adopting public cloud computing, the managerial/controlling power of data resources, software and business application, among other IT resources shall be transferred to cloud service providers, which may undermine the managerial/controlling power of the top manage team in public sectors. Some researchers proposed that public cloud adoption undermining the control rights of IT resources, such as possession, utilization, upgrading and management, is the most crucial factor limiting cloud computing adoption (Winkler & Brown, 2013). In addition, when entrusting and authorizing the information security governance right to a third party organization, it comes as a huge challenge for internal management to adopt public cloud computing (Khoo et al., 2011). The resource sharing features of cloud computing and user priority make the IT decision-making authority of the management of e-government more complex (Khan & Malluhi, 2010). Data and applications may be stored and run on the remote resource platform of several cloud service providers in several places and even several countries. The regulators of information systems also need to have the control over data resources for the purpose of auditing. Gilbert (2011) found that the providers need to enhance communication and cooperation with cloud users to ensure that the cloud users' control mode concerning IT resources is not subject to impact or changes; in particular, they shall develop corresponding operation specifications so that cloud users can review the IT resources stored at the cloud service providers at any time. Thus, we propose the following hypotheses:

H3a: The higher the IT compliance of public cloud computing, the more likely for public sectors to adopt public cloud computing: (1) IaaS mode, (2) PaaS mode, and (3) SaaS mode.

H3b: The stronger the managerial/controlling power of public sectors over IT resources in public cloud mode, the more likely for public sectors to adopt public cloud computing: (1) IaaS mode, (2) PaaS mode, and (3) SaaS mode.

Control Variables

To test the hypotheses that the adoption of public cloud computing in e-government, we need to control for organizational variables, such as IT budget and geographical location, which have been previously found to influence it (Choudhary & Vithayathil, 2013). Geographical location is based on statistical yearbook data, whereas the IT budget is based on e-government budget in 2013.

RESEARCH METHOD AND RESULTS

Measurement Development and Assessment

Table 2 provides our conceptual definition and measurement items of the constructs and a summary of the sources from which the items for the scales were drawn. The research group launched pretest, technical verification and field survey to improve the reliability and validity of the scale. The pretest included three parts: an open-ended interview, a semi-structured interview and a highly structured questionnaire inspection. The research group initially conducted an open-ended interview with six public sectors of prefecture-level cities in Jiangsu province and the questionnaire was readjusted based on the suggestions of the respondents. With regard to the semi-structured interview, the discussion focused on the dependent variable—decision-making on adopting public cloud computing. We accepted the suggestions of the interviewees and revised some items. Based on the qualitative data of the interview and the exploratory factor analysis of the survey data, we removed some items so that the scale reached higher convergent validity and discriminant validity.

Then we did a pilot test of MBA students from a university in China. 100 revised questionnaires were distributed and 77 effective questionnaires were received. The Cronbach's alpha, indicator loadings, and average variance extracted are shown in Table 3. In terms of reliability, all indicators had loadings greater than .700, suggesting that more than 50% of the variance in the construct was explained. All of the constructs demonstrated strong convergent validity, as indicated by the inter-factor loadings being higher than the intra-factor loadings.

Table 2. Scale development of variables

Variables	Definition	Survey Questions	Resources
Decision-making on Adoption of Public Cloud Computing in E-government (IaaS, PaaS, and SaaS)	the subjective willingness of decision-makers in public sectors regarding whether to initially use the public cloud computing in e-government	I am willing to use public cloud computing technology (IaaS, PaaS, and SaaS). I feel that my organization's computational needs can be met by public cloud computing (IaaS, PaaS, and SaaS). I would feel comfortable recommending public cloud computing approaches in my organization (IaaS, PaaS, and SaaS). I feel that public cloud computing uses proven technology (IaaS, PaaS, and SaaS).	Venkatesh et al. (2003)
Technical Alignment	the degree of fit between e-government strategy, cloud strategy, e-government infrastructure, and cloud infrastructure	I feel that public cloud computing technology is fit with business strategy of our organization. I am concerned about the alignment of the technology used in public cloud computing services with management strategy of our organization. I feel that public cloud computing technology is more fit our usefulness than traditional enterprise networks methods.	Kearns & Lederer (2003)
Technical Adaptation	the degree of fit between the users' behaviors demanded by the cloud environment and those produced by the users of cloud applications such that the users of cloud applications is able to achieve valued work goals	I feel that the user will skillfully use the tools and applications the public cloud computing platform provides. I feel that the user will meet formal performance requirements of the job at the public cloud platform. I think it was not difficult for the user to adjust him- or herself to the new technology platform provided by cloud computing platform.	Bruque et al. (2008)
Technical Security	the degree to which the data, platform, and applications are secure against threats in the public cloud mode	I feel the degree of company's concern with data security on the public cloud computing is high. I feel the degree of concern for customers with data security in public cloud computing is high. I feel the degree of concern about privacy in public cloud computing is high.	Oliveira el al. (2014)
Cost Effectiveness	the ability of public cloud computing, which can remove the cost of purchasing infrastructure and improve the efficiency of operation	The cost of maintenance is lower with public cloud computing than with traditional IT methods. Public cloud computing provide a good value for their costs. I would consider public cloud computing to have considerable cost savings over traditional IT methods. The cost of acquiring public cloud computing is considerably cheaper than traditional computing methods.	Truong (2010); Oliveira el al. (2014)
Operational Risk	the potential for loss in the pursuit of a desired outcome when adopting public cloud computing in e-government	Adopting public cloud computing is associated with a high level of risk. There is a high level of risk that the expected benefits of adopting public cloud computing will not materialize Overall, I consider the adoption of public cloud computing to be risky.	Benlian & Hess (2011)
IT Compliance	it is composed of policies and regulations of organizations, which is compulsory that the e-government requires cloud service providers to abide by	Public cloud computing technology does/will significantly improve IT compliance. Public cloud computing is inherently reliable and meets IT compliance requirement. Public cloud computing is reliable than traditional computing methods and improves IT Sarbanes-Oxley compliance expectations. Public cloud computing systems are reliable and increase HIPAA compliance awareness.	Cannoy & Salam (2010); Luthy & Forcht (2006)
Managerial/ Controlling Power	the governmental executives' authority to manage/control the data, application, and other resources in the public cloud	I think e-government in public cloud computing mode does/will not significantly weaken organizational managerial/controlling power of IT resources. I think e-government in public cloud computing mode does/will not weaken organizational managerial/controlling power of data. I think e-government in public cloud computing mode does/will not weaken organizational managerial/controlling power of application and other resources.	Weill & Ross (2004); Ding et al. (2014)

Note: All items were measured on a 7-point Likert scale (1=strongly disagree; 7=strongly agree).

Table 3. Testing results of discriminant validity and convergent validity

Item	Cronch α	F1	F2	F3	F4	F5	F6	F7	F8	F9	F10
IaaS Adoption	.766										
IAAS1		.167	.272	**.717**	.095	.205	.501	.370	.517	.336	.063
IAAS2		.246	.336	**.704**	.074	.304	.028	.179	.438	.095	.410
IAAS3		.320	.013	**.903**	.512	.277	.180	.006	.074	.217	.162
IAAS4		.001	.248	**.929**	.006	.121	.005	.300	.209	.459	.333
SaaS Adoption	.791										
SAAS1		.103	.051	.350	.312	**.798**	.231	.093	.471	.307	.471
SAAS2		.171	.302	.232	.245	**.723**	.145	.271	.069	.229	.503
SAAS3		.008	.009	.108	.304	**.834**	.198	.077	.189	.024	.361
SAAS4		.115	.277	.446	.365	**.716**	.005	.326	.297	.438	.021
PaaS Adoption	.813										
PAAS1		.127	.512	.472	.211	.209	**.702**	.153	.443	.035	.051
PAAS2		.101	.37	.359	.189	.303	**.810**	.378	.126	.557	.228
PAAS3		.054	.007	.087	.301	.240	**.792**	.221	.519	.333	.317
PAAS4		.003	.021	.313	.404	.009	**.862**	.037	.471	.265	.019
Alignment	.921										
ST1		.304	.308	.257	**.844**	.306	.521	.055	.571	.335	.049
ST2		.002	.227	.089	**.789**	.278	.308	.347	.113	.292	.173
ST3		.090	.087	.476	**.683**	.165	.456	.291	.261	.560	.472
Adaptation	.825										
DE1		.022	**.698**	.058	.202	.387	.465	.497	.033	.079	.541
DE2		.569	**.791**	.231	.291	.432	.309	.002	.323	.134	.211
DE3		.047	**.669**	.509	.332	.354	.398	.017	.074	.041	.226
Security	.767										
CE1		**.673**	.273	.275	.356	.231	.478	.153	.258	.372	.243
CE2		**.721**	.409	.315	.273	.502	.190	.037	.391	.019	.471
CE3		**.926**	.007	.354	.209	.487	.276	.024	.527	.474	.365
Cost Effectiveness	.911										
YW1		.092	.079	.172	.329	.559	.409	**.774**	.502	.392	.394
YW2		.117	.408	.284	.271	.571	.115	**.697**	.447	.183	.119
YW3		.259	.591	.424	.036	.197	.397	**.680**	.140	.259	.004
Operational Risk	.774										
YY1		.170	.139	.049	.414	.031	.079	.098	**.812**	.561	.447
YY2		.082	.507	.072	.159	.297	.321	.327	**.709**	.371	.184
YY3		.291	.327	.391	.071	.576	.505	.119	**.798**	.093	.226

continued on following page

Table 3. Continued

Item	Cronch α	F1	F2	F3	F4	F5	F6	F7	F8	F9	F10
IT Compliance	.782										
HG1		.209	.307	.443	.273	.233	.149	.228	.338	**.829**	.617
HG2		.047	.017	.512	.326	.012	.317	.304	.009	**.781**	.307
HG3		.510	.196	.017	.002	.176	.071	.111	.124	**.745**	.073
HG4		.191	.271	.184	.479	.607	.503	.319	.003	**.731**	.153
Managerial/Controlling Power	.806										
KZH1		.098	.449	.089	.338	.117	.128	.440	.337	.287	**.901**
KZH2		.329	.007	.322	.440	.009	.007	.019	.221	.091	**.779**
KZH3		.220	.563	.415	.071	.557	.112	.207	.005	.587	**.837**
Variance Explained (%)		43.002	8.770	6.443	5.776	5.512	4.998	4.320	3.779	3.003	2.551
Cumulative Variance Explained (%) 88.151											

Sample and Data Collection

This research used a random sampling framework for the officers at various levels of China's public sectors, which can reduce external variation to some degree. Our research group conducted the investigation of public sectors in China from August 1, 2012 to December 15, 2012. We field-interviewed six CIOs of public sectors and gained a better understanding about the decision-making process of officers to adopt public cloud. Then, we summarized each sample's interview data and refined the questionnaires. In the first stage, 1000 surveys were sent to a list of CIOs from public sectors of 30 provinces, municipalities and autonomous regions in China. A total of 460 CIO surveys were returned for a total response rate of 46.0 percent for the first-stage survey. In the second stage, 460 surveys were sent to the selected top business executives of each public sector, for which we received a completed CIO questionnaire. A total of 306 of the 460 public sectors returned at least one business executive survey, yielding an organizational response rate of 66.5 percent for the second-stage survey. In the third stage, 306 surveys were sent to the selected HR managers of each public sector, for which we received a completed CIO and business executive questionnaire. A total of 230 of the 306 public sectors returned one HR manager survey, yielding a response rate of 63.9 percent for the third-stage survey. After removing incomplete and invalid questionnaires, we finally obtained 227 effective ones, with a response rate of 22.7%. For each questionnaire, the public sector had three responses. We then computed an aggregated average score for the constructs. Judging from the summarized results of the characteristics of the samples, we found that the distribution of the characteristics can comprehensively reflect the characteristics of China's public sectors, in accordance with the research purpose of this study. In addition, using the variance analysis technique, we did not find response bias with this questionnaire.

The correlation matrix of dependent variables and independent variables are shown in Table 4. The square root of the average variance extracted for a construct was larger than its correlations with other constructs, suggesting adequate discriminant validity. Furthermore, the results of the factor analyses showed that the loadings of items on their corresponding factors were much higher than cross-loadings on other factors.

Table 4. Correlation matrix

Variable	1	2	3	4	5	6	7	8	9	10
1 IaaS Mode Adoption	(.732)									
2 PaaS Mode Adoption	.306	(.810)								
3 SaaS Mode Adoption	.006	.085	(.746)							
4 Alignment	.412	.291	.293	(.721)						
5 Adaptation	.333	.323	.406	.435	(.852)					
6 Security	.254	.067	.009	.177	.306	(.772)				
7 Cost Effectiveness	.079	.003	.104	.092	.055	.002	(.750)			
8 Operational Risk	.425	.240	.151	.256	.194	.389	.079	(.809)		
9 IT Compliance	.002	.313	.331	.117	.409	.246	.212	.095	(.901)	
10 Managerial/Controlling Power	.017	.189	.010	.491	.385	.293	.309	.217	.032	(.761)

Assessing the Structural Model

Structural equation modeling (SEM) was used to test our hypotheses, and we conducted all statistical tests at a 5% level of significance, as implemented in Amos Graph 20.0. Given that existing literature had examined the impact of geographical distribution, IT budget, etc. as control variables, we first adopted one-way analysis of variance to verify control variable differences in affecting the adoption decision-making modes. The findings showed that there was no significant difference among the measurements of adoption decision-making in the samples with different geographical distribution and IT budget, indicating that the impact of two control variables on adoption was not significant. Thus, when conducting structural equation modeling and hypothesis testing, we did not consider the influencing effect of control variables, i.e., geographical distribution and IT budget, on dependent variables.

H1a, H1b, and H1c are fully supported. Thus, technical factors (alignment, adaptability, and security) have a significant impact on adoption decision-making of the IaaS, PaaS, and SaaS modes. H2a and H2b are partially supported, with business factors (cost effectiveness and operational risk) having a significant impact on adoption decision-making of the IaaS and SaaS modes, but the impact on the PaaS mode is not significant. H3a and H3b are also partially supported, with management factors (IT compliance and managerial/controlling power) imposing a significant impact on adoption decision-making of the PaaS and SaaS modes, but the impact on IaaS mode is not significant (see Figure 2).

CONCLUSION AND DISCUSSION

Little empirical research has examined the determinants of decision-making on adoption of public cloud computing based on the unique nature of Chinese culture, such as the IT decision-making authority and the system of group collective decision-making. To help fill the gaps in the cloud computing literature based on IT decision-making theory and technology adoption theory, this study provided insights into the determinants affecting public cloud adoption from technical, business and management perspectives.

Figure 2. SEM results

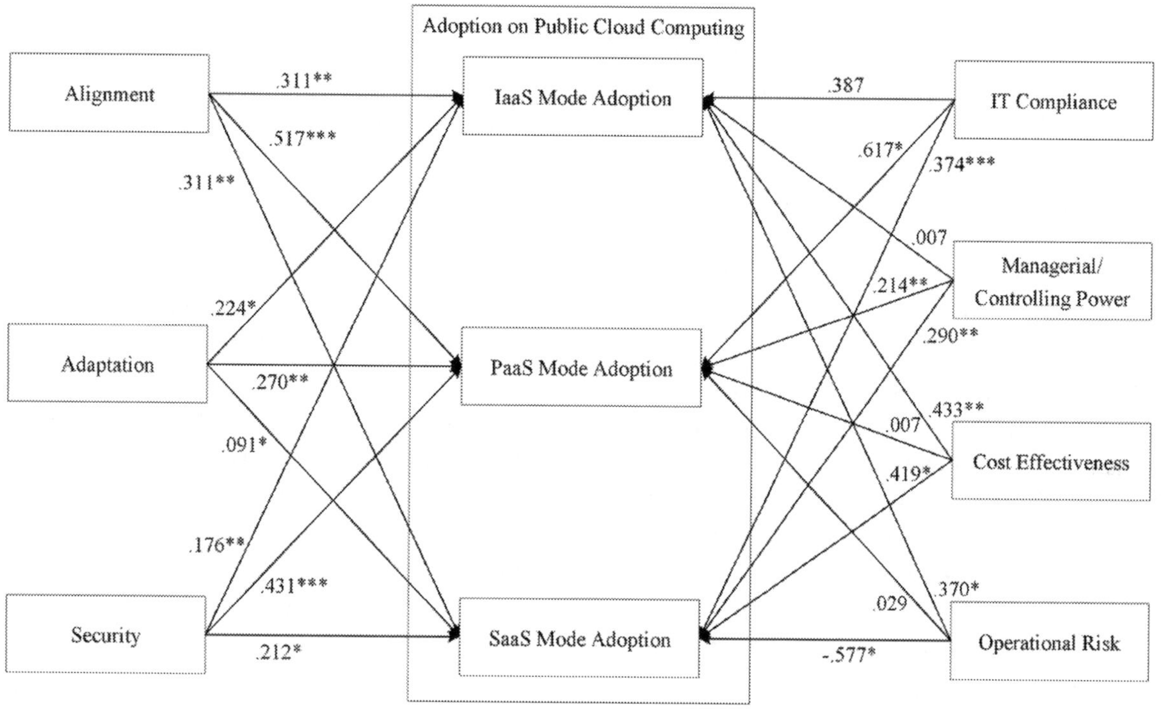

Note: * p< .05, ** p< .01, *** p< .001.

Findings and Limitations

The results revealed two findings. First, technical, business, and management factors have different effects on three types of decision-making modes on adopting public cloud computing, i.e., the SaaS, IaaS, and PaaS mode. Technical factors and business factors have a significant impact on the adoption decision-making on IaaS mode; business factors and management factors have a significant impact on the adoption decision-making on PaaS mode; technical factors, business factors and management factors have a significant impact on the adoption of SaaS mode. Second, managerial/controlling power, which characterized the nature of Chinese culture, only have a significant influence on the decision-making on adoption of PaaS mode and SaaS mode.

This study also has some limitations. First, the sample size of the research is relatively small, and so more samples need to be collected to further verify the hypotheses. Second, we only investigated data within a year, however, organizations have different life cycles, and so their technical, business and management factors may have different impacts on adoption decision-making. Therefore, some measurement items of this study may not reflect changes of variables with time. Future studies need to collect empirical data of different time intervals, more industries and organizational types to verify whether the research results in this study are robust for different time intervals, industries and organizational types. In addition, this research lacks a comprehensive consideration of other factors, such as characteristics of decision-makers and organizations. Future studies may analyze the determinants of adoption from more perspectives.

Implications for Theory and Practice

Despite the many factors that affect decision-making on adoption of public cloud computing, the comprehensive effect of technical, business, and management factors on three types of decision-making on adoption (IaaS, PaaS, and SaaS) is still debated in the existing literature. First, this is one of the first studies to extend the technology adoption theory by integrating IT decision-making theory as an overall antecedent of decision-making on adoption from the three perspectives of technology, business, and management factors.

Second, this study broadens our understanding of decision-making on adoption in the e-government context by hypothesizing the different antecedents of "IaaS mode adoption", "PaaS mode adoption", and "PaaS mode adoption". This study further reveals that technical factors will significantly affect different categories of decision-making on adoption, i.e., IaaS, PaaS, and SaaS mode. Hence, cloud providers should realize the technical ability of their cloud products is the most important factor. Business factors have significant effects on IaaS and SaaS mode adoption. Decision-makers should consider the IaaS and PaaS modes, which require a large amount of investment and have considerable risk. We also find management factors have significant effects on the PaaS and SaaS modes. In the process of decision-making on adoption of the PaaS and SaaS modes, management executives should participate in the decision-making, and then the IT compliance and managerial/controlling power will be considered.

Third, although prior descriptive studies proposed that technical and business factors could influence decision-making on adoption, the special attributes of Chinese culture, such as managerial/controlling power, were neglected. We provided insight into the effects of the two management factors on decision-making on adoption. As such, the current study uses the new lens of IT decision-making authority to examine the special nature of Chinese culture.

Finally, this study has important implications. First, this study revealed the decision-making process of adopting public clouds and explained the risk and benefits of public cloud adoption, which is enlightening for both decision-makers and public cloud service providers. For public sectors in China, there are some problems, including scattered resources, information islands, business divisions, etc. They can improve the efficiency and effectiveness of decision-making based on the technical features, business value and the administrative requirements of the organizations. Second, China's government should redesign the power system, such as the managerial/controlling power, when moving to PaaS and SaaS mode. Third, our theoretical model indicates cloud service providers need to improve the cloud service from technical, business, and management factors to meet the requirements of decision-makers in public sectors. Obviously, the executives in most of China's public sectors are still hesitant to adopt public cloud computing technology. Therefore, it is important to analyze the causes of those public sectors hesitance to adopt cloud computing from technical, business, and management perspectives.

REFERENCES

Armbrust, M., Stoica, I., Zaharia, M., Fox, A., Griffith, R., Joseph, A. D., ... Rabkin, A. (2010). A view of cloud computing. *Communications of the ACM*, *53*(4), 50–58. doi:10.1145/1721654.1721672

Athens, G. (2010). Security in the cloud. *Communications of the ACM*, *53*(11), 16–18. doi:10.1145/1839676.1839683

Battleson, D. A., West, B. C., Kim, J., Ramesh, B., & Robinson, P. S. (2016). Achieving dynamic capabilities with cloud computing: An empirical investigation. *European Journal of Information Systems*, *25*(3), 209–230. doi:10.1057/ejis.2015.12

Benlian, A., & Hess, T. (2011). Opportunities and risks of software-as-a-service: Findings from a survey of IT executives. *Decision Support Systems*, *52*(1), 232–246. doi:10.1016/j.dss.2011.07.007

Bhattacherjee, A., & Park, S. C. (2014). Why end-users move to the cloud: A migration-theoretic analysis. *European Journal of Information Systems*, *23*(3), 357–372. doi:10.1057/ejis.2013.1

Bruque, S., Moyano, J., & Eisenberg, J. (2008). Individual adaptation to IT-induced change: The role of social networks. *Journal of Management Information Systems*, *25*(3), 177–206. doi:10.2753/MIS0742-1222250305

Cannoy, S. D., & Salam, A. F. (2010). A framework for health care information assurance policy and compliance. *Communications of the ACM*, *53*(3), 126–131. doi:10.1145/1666420.1666453

Chakraborty, R., Ramireddy, S., Raghu, T. S., & Rao, H. R. (2010). The information assurance practices of cloud computing vendors. *IT Professional Magazine*, *12*(4), 29–37. doi:10.1109/MITP.2010.44

Chou, S. W., & Chiang, C. H. (2013). Understanding the formation of software-as-a-service (SaaS) satisfaction from the perspective of service quality. *Decision Support Systems*, *56*, 148–155. doi:10.1016/j.dss.2013.05.013

Choudhary, V., & Vithayathil, J. (2013). The impact of cloud computing: Should the IT department be organized as a cost center or a profit center? *Journal of Management Information Systems*, *30*(2), 67–100. doi:10.2753/MIS0742-1222300203

Davis, F. D. (1989). Perceived usefulness, perceived ease of use, and user acceptance of information technology. *Management Information Systems Quarterly*, *13*(3), 319–340. doi:10.2307/249008

Demirkan, H., Cheng, H. K., & Bandyopadhyay, S. (2010). Coordination strategies in an SaaS supply chain. *Journal of Management Information Systems*, *26*(4), 119–143. doi:10.2753/MIS0742-1222260405

Demirkan, H., & Delen, D. (2013). Leveraging the capabilities of service-oriented decision support systems: Putting analytics and big data in cloud. *Decision Support Systems*, *55*(1), 412–421. doi:10.1016/j.dss.2012.05.048

Ding, F., Li, D., & George, J. F. (2014). Investigating the effects of IS strategic leadership on organizational benefits from the perspective of CIO strategic roles. *Information & Management*, *51*(7), 865–879. doi:10.1016/j.im.2014.08.004

Ding, F., & Wu, J. H. (2012). Analysis on adopting on cloud computing in E-government. *China Economic & Trade Herald*, *31*, 75–77.

Dorsch, C., & Häckel, B. (2014). Combining models of capacity supply to handle volatile demand: The economic impact of surplus capacity in cloud service environments. *Decision Support Systems*, *58*, 3–14. doi:10.1016/j.dss.2013.01.011

Ge, C., & Huang, K. W. (2014). Analyzing the economies of scale of software as a service software firms: A stochastic frontier approach. *IEEE Transactions on* Engineering Management, *61*(4), 610–622.

Giakoumis, D., Mavridou, E., Votis, K., Giannoutakis, K., Tzovaras, D., & Hassapis, G. (2015). A semantic framework to support the management of cloud-based service provision within a global public inclusive infrastructure. *International Journal of Electronic Commerce, 20*(1), 142–173. doi:10.1080/10864415.2016.1061794

Gilbert, F. (2011). Cloud service providers as joint-data controllers. *Journal of Internet Law, 15*(2), 3–13.

Goode, S., Lin, C., Tsai, J. C., & Jiang, J. J. (2015). Rethinking the role of security in client satisfaction with Software-as-a-Service (SaaS) providers. *Decision Support Systems, 70*, 73–85. doi:10.1016/j.dss.2014.12.005

Harris, W. (2011). Cloud computing - based IT solutions for organizations with multiregional branch offices. *Proceedings of the European Conference on Information Management & Evaluation, 5*(6), 435-440.

Huang, J., Kauffman, R. J., & Ma, D. (2015). Pricing strategy for cloud computing: A damaged services perspective. *Decision Support Systems, 78*, 80–92. doi:10.1016/j.dss.2014.11.001

Kearns, G. S., & Lederer, A. L. (2003). A resource-based view of strategic IT alignment: How knowledge sharing creates competitive advantage. *Decision Sciences, 34*(1), 1–29. doi:10.1111/1540-5915.02289

Khan, K. M., & Malluhi, Q. (2010). Establishing trust in cloud computing. *IT Professional Magazine, 12*(5), 20–27. doi:10.1109/MITP.2010.128

Khoo, B., Harris, P., & Hartman, S. (2011). Information security governance of enterprise information systems: An approach to legislative compliant. *International Journal of Management and Information Systems, 14*(3), 49–55.

Lee, S., Park, S. B., & Lim, G. G. (2013). Using balanced scorecards for the evaluation of "Software-as-a-service". *Information & Management, 50*(7), 553–561. doi:10.1016/j.im.2013.07.006

Liao, J. Q., Zhao, J., & Zhang, Y. J. (2010). The influence of power distance on the Chinese leadership behavior research. *Chinese Journal of Management, 7*(7), 988–992.

Liu, Y., Sheng, X., & Marston, S. R. (2015). The impact of client-side security restrictions on the competition of cloud computing services. *International Journal of Electronic Commerce, 19*(3), 90–117. doi:10.1080/10864415.2015.1000224

Luthy, D., & Forcht, K. (2006). Laws and regulations affecting information management and frameworks for assessing compliance. *Information Management & Computer Security, 14*(2), 155–166. doi:10.1108/09685220610655898

Ma, D., & Kauffman, R. J. (2014). Competition between software-as-a-service vendors. *IEEE Transactions on Engineering Management, 61*(4), 717–729. doi:10.1109/TEM.2014.2332633

Maitner, R. E. (2011). Moving to the cloud: Is federal financial management fair game? *The Journal of Government Financial Management, 60*(3), 52–57.

Marston, S., Li, Z., Bandyopadhyay, S., Zhang, J., & Ghalsasi, A. (2011). Cloud computing-The business perspective. *Decision Support Systems*, *51*(1), 176–189. doi:10.1016/j.dss.2010.12.006

Mell, P., & Grance, T. (2011, September). The NIST definition of cloud computing. *National Institute of Standards and Technology*. Retrieved from http://nvlpubs.nist.gov/nistpubs/Legacy/SP/nistspecial-publication800-145.pdf

Moreira, E. D., Martimiano, L. A., Brandao, A. J., & Bernardes, M. C. (2013). Ontologies for information security management and governance. *Information Management & Computer Security*, *16*(2), 150–165. doi:10.1108/09685220810879627

Mustafee, N. (2010). Exploiting grid computing, desktop grids and cloud computing for e-Science: future directions. *Transforming Government: People. Process and Policy*, *4*(4), 288–298.

Naldi, M., & Mastroeni, L. (2016). Economic decision criteria for the migration to cloud storage. *European Journal of Information Systems*, *25*(1), 16–28. doi:10.1057/ejis.2014.34

Oliveira, T., Thomas, M., & Espadanal, M. (2014). Assessing the determinants of cloud computing adoption: An analysis of the manufacturing and services sectors. *Information & Management*, *51*(5), 497–510. doi:10.1016/j.im.2014.03.006

Paquette, S., Jaeger, P. T., & Wilson, S. C. (2010). Identifying the security risks associated with governmental use of cloud computing. *Government Information Quarterly*, *27*(3), 245–253. doi:10.1016/j.giq.2010.01.002

Qu, X. L., Xiao, P., & Bai, Q. (2015). Virtual resources supply strategy based on Elastic reserve mechanism in cloud environment. *Systems Engineering-Theory & Practice*, *35*(6), 1573–1581.

Shiau, W. L., & Chau, P. Y. (2016). Understanding behavioral intention to use a cloud computing classroom: A multiple model-comparison approach. *Information & Management*, *53*(3), 355–365. doi:10.1016/j.im.2015.10.004

Shin, J., Jo, M., Lee, J., & Lee, D. (2014). Strategic management of cloud computing services: Focusing on consumer adoption behavior. *IEEE Transactions on Engineering Management*, *61*(3), 419–427. doi:10.1109/TEM.2013.2295829

Son, I., Lee, D., Lee, J. N., & Chang, Y. B. (2014). Market perception on cloud computing initiatives in organizations: An extended resource-based view. *Information & Management*, *51*(6), 653–669. doi:10.1016/j.im.2014.05.006

Tan, C. W., Benbasat, I., & Cenfetelli, R. T. (2013). IT-mediated customer service content and delivery in electronic governments: An empirical investigation of the antecedents of service quality. *Management Information Systems Quarterly*, *37*(1), 77–109.

Thong, J., Venkatesh, V., Xu, X., Hong, S., & Tam, Y. K. (2011). Consumer acceptance of personal information and communication technology services. *IEEE Transactions on Engineering Management*, *58*(4), 613–625. doi:10.1109/TEM.2010.2058851

Truong, D. (2010). How cloud computing enhances competitive advantages: A research model for small businesses. *The Business Review, Cambridge*, *15*(1), 59–65.

Venkatesh, V., Morris, M. G., Davis, G. B., & Davis, F. D. (2003). User acceptance of information technology: Toward a unified view. *Management Information Systems Quarterly, 27*(3), 425–478.

Walz, J., & Grier, D. A. (2010). Time to push the cloud. *IT Professional Magazine, 12*(5), 14–16. doi:10.1109/MITP.2010.137

Wang, H. L., & Ding, F. (2015). Policies of data resources by applying big data technology. *China Economic & Trade Herald, 31*, 59–60.

Weill, P., & Ross, J. W. (2004). *IT Governance: How Top Performers Manage IT Decision Rights for Superior Results*. Harvard Business School Press.

Winkler, T. J., & Brown, C. V. (2013). Horizontal allocation of decision rights for on-premise applications and software-as-a-service. *Journal of Management Information Systems, 30*(3), 13–48. doi:10.2753/MIS0742-1222300302

This research was previously published in the Journal of Global Information Management (JGIM), 24(3); edited by Zuopeng (Justin) Zhang, pages 71-89, copyright year 2016 by IGI Publishing (an imprint of IGI Global).

Chapter 90
Communication Privacy Management and Mobile Phone Use

Debra L. Worthington
Auburn University, USA

Margaret Fitch-Hauser
Auburn University, USA

ABSTRACT

The introduction of new technologies effects rapid social change and challenges social norms. A major challenge with the advent of mobile phones is how the technology tests traditional notions of personal privacy and interaction involvement, particularly in public settings. Communication privacy management (CPM) theory provides a means of explaining the tensions between mobile phone users and proximate others. In this article, components of communication privacy management theory are outlined and its application to mobile communication is discussed. Next, privacy issues associated with specific mobile technology are reviewed and cultural differences in mobile communication privacy needs are examined. In light of the limited research in this area, suggestions for future research are also presented.

INTRODUCTION AND DEFINITION OF KEY CONCEPTS

The International Telecommunication Union estimates that the number of in-use mobile phones exceeds the number of earth's population (Pramis, 2013). The social interactions resulting from the use of the six billion active cell phones have altered both public space and behavior (Katz, 2007; Ling, 2008), and a significant body of research suggests that mobile technology impacts our social networks and interactions (Banjo, Hu, & Sundar, 2008; Campbell, 2007, 2008; Geser, 2006, Inbar, Joost, Hemmert, Porat, & Tractinsky, 2014; Poutiainen, 2007).

Mobile phone use challenges traditional notions of personal privacy and interaction involvement. Communication privacy management addresses how individuals control and reveal private information (Petronio, 2007). At the heart of their social interactions is how mobile phone users balance obligations to

DOI: 10.4018/978-1-5225-8176-5.ch090

absent others (i.e., the caller) against their responsibilities to proximate or co-present others (i.e., people around them), while at the same time managing privacy concerns of all parties (Banjo et al., 2008).

The theory of communication privacy management was first introduced by Sandra Petronio (1991). A Professor of Communication Studies at Indiana University-Purdue University Indianapolis, she has authored and co-authored numerous books and articles on CPM. More recent publications provide summaries of the theory (Petronio, 2008; Serewicz & Petronio, 2007), outline the development of CPM (2004), expand on the role of confidants (Petronio & Reierson, 2009) and secrecy (Petronio, 2000), and apply CPM to a variety of contexts (see, for example, Duggan & Petronio, 2009; Greene, Derlega, Yep, & Petronio, 2003).

Rich Ling, Ph.D., of IT University of Copenhagen, is a leading researcher in the area of the social consequences of mobile communication. He has authored and co-authored multiple books and articles in this area, including *New Tech, New Ties*: *How Mobile Communication is Reshaping Social Cohesion* (2010), *Mobile Phones and Mobile Communication (Polity)* (with Jonathan Donner) (2009), and *Taken for Grantedness: The Embedding of Mobile Communication into Society* (2012). A frequent co-author with Ling, Dr. Scott W. Campbell of the University of Michigan, has also made significant contributions to our understanding of normative mobile phone behaviors (e.g., *Mobile Communication: Bringing us Together and Tearing us Apart,* 2011; *The Reconstruction of Space and Time: Mobile Communication Practices,* 2009). His research in mobile telephony emphasizes the social implications of the medium. To date, only one study has applied the principles of CPM to mobile telephony (see Worthington, Fitch-Hauser, Valikoski, Imhof, & Kim, 2011).

In the following pages, we define privacy, outline components of communication privacy management theory, examine its application to mobile communication, and outline areas of future research.

SOCIAL NORMS AND MANAGING PRIVACY

The introduction of new technologies effects rapid social change and challenges social norms. Rapid change can result in differing expectations of what is appropriate behavior when using the technology. As rules that guide behavior, social norms provide a framework for individuals to assess which behaviors are acceptable and which are not (McLaughlin & Vitak, 2011). Social norms vary by gender, age, relationships and culture (Axelsson, 2010; Hall, Baym, & Miltner, 2014; Johar, 2005), and may or may not be followed at any given moment (Kallgren, Reno, & Cialdini, 2000). Despite this variability, social norms are the ties that bind social and relational order.

Privacy is a multi-faceted concept. Both a dynamic and dialectic process, the notion of privacy suggests that individuals regulate boundaries of disclosure, personal identity, and temporality (Palen & Dourish, 2003). More specifically, it refers to our ability to manage when, how, and the extent to which our personal information is revealed to others (Westin, 1967). Mobile phone norms have reached the point where particular behaviors can be seen as violations of others' rights, as insensitive, or as abusive (Ling & McEwen, 2010).

When discussing the intersection of technology and privacy, people often focus on technical issues associated with technology use (see, for example, Boyles, Smith, & Madden, 2012). In reality, individuals focus greater attention on managing privacy in their interpersonal lives. Only recently has attention been paid to matters of privacy and mobile communication.

REVIEW OF COMMUNICATION PRIVACY MANAGEMENT THEORY

Because CPM was originally developed for and applied to interpersonal relationships, much of the initial research focused on interpersonal contexts (e.g., family, health, etc.) (see, for example, Petronio, 2006; Petronio & Caughlin, 2005; Petronio, Jones, Morr, 2003;). However, since its introduction, CPM has been applied to a variety of mediated settings (e.g., short-message service, computer-mediated technology, and social media to explain disclosure in alternative contexts (see, for example, Child, Haridakis, & Petronio, 2012; Cho & Hung, 2011; Frampton & Child, 2013; Metzger, 2007; Waters & Ackerman, 2011).

Petronio (2007) describes CPM theory as "an evidenced-based, applied theory construct to be translatable into practices" (p. 219). The theory addresses the tension we experience when choosing what personal information will be revealed and what will remain private in our interactions with others (Petronio (2002). Underlying this tension is the assessment of the risks and benefits of disclosing to others and balancing desires for privacy against need for disclosure. Risks arise with disclosure, because once information is shared with another it moves from private ownership to shared or co-ownership.

Because of the threat of risks, we create boundaries around what we consider to be public information and private information. The purpose of these boundaries is to govern who has control of and access to information as well as how to protect that information (Petronio, Sargent, Andea, Reganis, & Cichocki, 2004). We manage or coordinate privacy boundaries based on negotiation of privacy rules related to linkages, boundary permeability, and information ownership (Petronio, 2002).

Linkages address the mutually agreed-upon privacy rules used to identify those who may share knowledge of the collectively held information (Petronio, 2002). Privacy rules regulate when and under what circumstances information is revealed. These rules are developed over time and become established through repeated use. At the same time, they are situational, and can be modified as conditions change or evolve. Privacy rules are affected by a number of factors, including cultural expectations, individual motivations, risk-benefit assessments, gender, and the needs of the situation (Petronio, 2009). Importantly, we utilize multiple rules during the boundary management process to determine to whom, as well as what and when, we disclose to others.

At times, these rules are broken. Petronio and Reierson (2009) describe confidentiality breaches as a type of boundary turbulence which occurs when the privacy expectations of the original owner of information are not met. Violations of confidentially have the potential to affect trust between individuals and to negatively affect the relationships of those involved. The authors describe three types of violations: discrepancy breaches of privacy, privacy ownership violations, and preemptive privacy control. Discrepancies in breaches of privacy occur when the original owner's expectations of privacy are not met by co-owners. We not only negotiate privacy rules with the conversation partners, but we also have established rules for what we do if our confidences are violated

Petronio and Reierson (2009) describe boundary permeability in terms of thickness and thinness. Thicker boundaries suggest that the coordinated rules of those collectively holding private information are relatively closed. The original owner of the information and the confidant negotiate the level of access third parties may have, including the scope and extent of private information that can be shared. Thinner boundaries result in more permeable walls, making information more easily accessible and open to third parties.

Ownership of information is also bound by privacy rules. Ownership rights are associated with both the original owner of the information as well as those who become co-owners once the information is shared. As Petronio (2002) notes, ownership rights can be difficult to ascertain because individuals must manage multiple privacy boundaries, many of which may be inter-related (e.g., can information revealed by a friend be shared with another mutual friend). Deliberate confidants purposely ask for information (e.g., college advisor and advisee), while reluctant confidants receive unwanted private information, which typically comes with feelings of obligation and responsibility. If the parties can reach agreement about privacy rules, and accept the means by which they became confidants, then the confidant relationship can be effectively regulated (Petronio & Reierson, 2009).

In summary, CPM is based on several principles (Petronio, 2007). The first principle is that we own our private information. Second, we feel we have the right to control the access of that private information. Third, we use privacy rules to establish boundaries around what information is and is not appropriate to reveal. After we exchange private information with others, we become co-owners of the information and are expected to follow shared privacy rules. Finally, when privacy rules are violated, co-owners may experience personal and interpersonal problems.

APPLYING CPM TO MOBILE PHONE COMMUNICATION

The ubiquitous nature of mobile phones and the constant technological changes mean that what we consider appropriate and inappropriate mobile phone usage continues to be evaluated. Thus, issues of privacy, privacy boundaries, and their relationship to mobile phone privacy behavior continue to develop and be negotiated. In this section, we discuss communication privacy management and mobile phone use as related to the principles of CPM, introduce privacy issues associated with specific mobile technology, and review cultural differences in mobile phone privacy management behaviors.

The first principle of CPM asserts that individuals own their private information. Mobile phone technology has, in several ways, further emphasized the ownership of private information. Historically, telephones had to be answered in place; they were location specific. Responding to a ringing phone was a dominant, socially expected norm. As a result, a ringing phone was "public" and could be answered by anyone in the immediate vicinity.

Observational studies of mobile phone use suggest that this norm remains as strong, if not stronger, than in times past (Hopper 1992; Bergvik 2004). However, one significant change has occurred. Mobile phone technology has moved the locus of a phone call from place to person. Reflecting this change, phones are seen as personal property and, as a result incoming calls are viewed as private communication between the caller and the owner of the phone. Both researchers and social commentators recognize this transformation arguing that today mobile phones are perceived as private and personal devices (Rosen, 2004; Häkkilä & Chatfield, 2005). Consequently, it is not unusual for individuals to allow another's cell phone to ring without answering it (or checking to determine who the sender is), in recognition that calls and texts are private belonging to the owner of the phone.

The notion of phones being tied to individuals has other implications for mobile phone use and the second principle of CPM (the belief that people feel they have the right to control the access of that private information). Traditional norms of interpersonal and social interactions require individuals both to be aware of and to engage in communication with those around them. The introduction of mobile communication tests this notion. During mobile phone interactions, users participate in both interproximate (with co-present others) and interkinesic (with the caller) communication (Ling, 2002). Mobile phone interactions allow individuals to be physically present, but psychologically distant (May & Hearn, 2005). As a result, they are less attentive to proximate others (Hampton, Livio, & Sessons, 2010). This occurs, despite, as Ling & McEwen (2010) write, that proximate others have an "entrenched right of way when compared to talking on a phone" (p. 19). In fact, the mere presence of a phone is a signal of a potential disturbance to the interaction (Ling & McEwen, 2010; Turkle, 2011). In their studies of public mobile phone use, both Humphreys (2005) and Ling & McEwen (2010) note that when a receiver ignores the proximate other in preference to the call (or text), the receiver may be viewed as transgressive because the proximate other believes face-to-face interactions should be favored over interaction with the caller. This negative view of receiving mobile phone calls while in conversation with someone is common across cultures. (Baron & Hård af Segerstad, 2010; Baron & Campbell, 2012).

One major reason that receivers preference callers over co-present others is that mobile phone users experience caller hegemony (Hopper, 1992; Bergvik, 2004). When this hegemonic state arises, individuals are less concerned with those who are physically proximate to them, giving the incoming caller (i.e., the absent other) higher priority, and leaving those around them in an asymmetric situation, vicariously participating in the interaction. Studies have found that receivers will ignore those around them, even friends, to attend to incoming calls or texts (Ling, 2008; Turkles, 2011).

Hence, the introduction and accessibility of mobile technology is leading to changes in what constitutes "public space" and what constitutes appropriate public behaviors (Sundar, Dou, & Lee, 2013). In earlier times, public space was a place of interaction with others in that space. Sundar et al. (2013) observe that when individuals access their phones in a public space, they react as though they are in a private space. Subsequently, users may reveal private information publically, resulting in privacy breaches or boundary turbulence. Thus, the changing view of public space increases boundary turbulence, which arises with conflicts between privacy rules and expected privacy boundaries (Petronio & Durham, 2008).

As noted previously, rules of privacy are used to establish boundaries around what is and what is not appropriate to reveal (Petronio, 2002). The third rule of CPM is that once an individual reveals information, the receiver becomes a co-owner of that information and is expected to follow shared privacy rules. In the context of mobile phone use, there are multiple discourse partners (i.e., proximate others and the absent other). Proximate others represent potential breaches of confidentiality, a type of boundary turbulence that mobile phone users face with great frequency. A caller's expectations for how private information should be treated may be compromised. This is even more significant with the realization that mobile communication favors interactions between individuals with close ties (e.g., family, friends, colleagues) (Ling, 2008). Arguably, it is with these relationships that receivers will have heightened interest in privacy management.

Importantly, proximate others typically have little or no input into negotiating the rules and boundaries of the information to which they are exposed. They often, however, attempt to provide callers with privacy, or at least the illusion of privacy (Ling, 2008). Co-present others frequently engage in behaviors that "remove" them from the space. For example, they may physically give the receiver greater physical space (e.g., step out of the office, move to another side of the store, etc.), or they may give the illusion of privacy by focusing on some other object, event, etc. (e.g., checking their texts, reviewing a menu, etc.) (Ling, 2008). Thus, co-present others find themselves attending to the receiver's privacy needs in an interaction that was once jointly owned.

In many cases, however, individuals become co-owners and assume ownership rights of information that they have not personally negotiated with the caller, and may have only tangentially negotiated with the receiver (e.g., nonverbal, oblique references). Again, mobile phones challenge traditional notions of privacy and heighten the risk that private information will become public.

Ordinarily, confidants negotiate the parameters of privacy management with the owner of the information and agree on the obligations that accompany the knowledge (Petronio & Reierson (2009). In this context, absent others and receivers are more likely to be deliberate confidants, and are in the traditional position of the ownership and co-ownership of shared information. However, the receiver and proximate others must manage the implications of further shared ownership or co-ownership of overheard information, which requires extending the premise of information ownership rights and reluctant confidants (Petronio, Jones, & Morr, 2003; Petronio & Reierson, 2009).

One predictive factor of CPM is the impact of context. Westerman, Van Der Heide, Klein, & Walther (2008) suggest that context can also lead individuals to change personal or collective privacy rules, particularly when driven by the need to achieve a goal. Related to the final principle of CPM, the public context leaves message receivers at greater risk, since they bear greater responsibility for managing privacy as they negotiate the interaction between the absent other and proximate others. Receivers also face an increased possibility of personal and interpersonal problems resulting from the violation of privacy rules.

Mobile phone technology makes it possible to contact others about anything anywhere. This ability adds new elements to decisions about what information to consider private and what information should be shared. Mobile phone users, however, can be strategic when managing privacy concerns (Worthington, et al., 2011). One obvious way of managing privacy in a mobile world is the means of communication (e.g., IM, SMS, calling, etc.). Each means of communicating comes with its own set of privacy concerns with some communication mediums implying greater ownership and having thicker boundaries than others. For example, in their study of short message communication, user perceived privacy, and social practices, Häkkilä and Chatfield (2005) found that mobile phones are perceived as private and personal devices, and that short message service (SMS) messages are assigned greater privacy, and are seen as more confidential, than voice calls.

A closely related method of communication to mobile phone texting is Instant Messaging (IM). IM allows people to connect instantly. In contrast to SMS, IM has thinner boundaries. IM was originally used to maintain social ties with friends (Grinter & Palen, 2002), but has since become a work tool (Kobsa & Meyer, 2009). With the advent of professional use, concerns of privacy breaches grew (e.g., saving and forwarding messages without consent, etc.) (Kobsa, Patil, & Meyer, 2009; Patil & Kobsa, 2004; 2005). Reflecting these concerns, Kobsa et al. (2009, p. 4) report that IM users employ a variety of tactics to manage their privacy, among them switching to another medium to relay sensitive information, imposing self-censorship when communicating via IM, blocking IM contacts, and negotiating an appropriate etiquette for sharing information with others.

Finally, mobile phone use differs across cultures and countries. Many studies, however, focused on normative use of the technology (see for example, Baron & Hård af Segerstad, 2010; Baron & Campbell, 2012; Campbell, 2007). Campbell found a number of differences in when and where individuals can use mobile phones in public settings. For example, Taiwanese respondents were more accepting of classroom use of mobile phones than those from Sweden. Other studies in related mediated contexts suggest that the sharing of private information is influenced by culture (Bellman, Johnson, Kobrin, & Lohse, 2004; Cho, Rivera, & Lim, 2009; Hofstede & Hofstede, 2005; VanLear 1991; Virtanen 2009; Werner, Altman, & Brown, 1992; Wilkins & Gareis, 2006). Young adults from individualistic cultures are more likely to reveal personal information on a range of topics, especially topics that are self-focused. However, these respondents were also less willing to disclose to the same depth as those from collectivist cultures, who expressed greater willingness to disclose more intimate information (see, for example, Hastings, 2000; Hofstede, 2001; Kito, 2005; Schwartz, Galliher, & Domenech Rodriguez, 2011).

Cultural differences have also been noted in privacy rules and boundaries. In a study of the effect of cultural differences on mobile phone usage, Worthington et al. (2011) found significant differences in user privacy concerns across the four countries they studied (Finland, Germany, South Korea, and the U.S.). For example, rules regarding what topics are appropriate for discussion in public locations differed, with Finnish and U.S. respondents being more sensitive to the interaction between conversational topics and location than South Korean and German participants were. These researchers also found cultural differences in the perception of the sensitivity of the topics discussed. For example, Koreans, Finns, and U.S. participants were sensitive to topics associated with interpersonal relationships, while Germans were less so. These findings suggest there are privacy concerns when phone conversations occur in the vicinity of others and that these concerns are influenced by one's culture.

Because individuals feel a greater sense of ownership for information related to sensitive topics, they may also have a greater awareness of their immediate surroundings and proximate others. When in a communication environment perceived as too public, most participants in the Worthington et al. (2011) study indicated they would tell the caller they needed to delay the conversation to a later time. This direct tactic was frequently reported by U.S. and German respondents. However, not everyone is willing to be direct. Some people still strive to meet privacy rules, but do so through a variety of indirect techniques. For example, Worthington et al. reported that Koreans were more likely to indicate they would change the topic of conversation, while Finns and U.S. Americans alter how they communicated (e.g., moving to texting, indicating they would call back later, etc.).

Privacy rules also extend to proximate others, and previous research suggests some rules are common across cultures. As noted previously, Ling & McEwen (2010) found that receiving mobile phone calls while in conversation with someone was viewed negatively by co-present others, while Worthington et al. (2011) found that eavesdropping on mobile phone conversations in public settings is interpreted as violating social norms and crossing privacy boundaries. Thus, when mobile phone conversations do occur in the presence of others, proximate others recognize privacy rules associated with the ownership of private information.

FUTURE RESEARCH

Applying the theoretical framework of Communication Privacy Management to mobile phone use provides insight into communication behaviors of both mobile phone users and proximate others. Although limited, research in this context suggests a number of fruitful avenues for future research. For instance, receivers make choices on what to disclose and what will remain private when taking a call in the presence of others. Decision criteria aid in the development and employment of underlying privacy rules (Durham, 2008; Petronio, 2002). A better understanding of the criteria used will enable researchers to better predict mobile phone behaviors. Cultural differences in decision criteria should also be explored.

A better understanding of underlying factors associated with boundary permeability and turbulence is also needed. Specific areas of research include the effect of privacy breakdowns on social relationships, self-disclosure, and privacy management practice; the influence of self-consciousness, self-monitoring and related psycho-social constructs on privacy management decisions and rule development; and the impact of caller hegemony on CPM choices.

Previous research has found that individuals will switch to alternative methods of communicating when privacy concerns arise (Cho & Hung, 2011; Worthington et al., 2011). It is unclear, however, how the thickness or thinness of privacy boundaries may affect strategic choices in mobile phone use. Callers with thicker privacy boundaries may be more concerned with potential privacy breaches. As a result, they may listen more closely for location cues, ask receivers about their location, inquire about the presence of others, or choose alternative means of communication (e.g., texting, short messaging services, etc.).

Three final areas of research include the role of deception, technology, and sex differences. For example, under what circumstances do users suggest a greater degree of privacy than actually exists? Can users employ applications to help navigate the tensions between being in public locations during private mobile conversations and managing privacy concerns? Previous research suggests that in dyadic relationships women disclose more information than men (Petronio, 2002). Do women and men differ in their mobile phone CPM strategies?

As social norms surrounding mobile phone use normalize, theory development in mobile phone use can and should be developed. Communication privacy management theory provides a foundation to begin explaining individual behavior in the context of mobile communication.

REFERENCES

Axelsson, A. (2010). Perpetual and personal: Swedish young adults and their use of mobile phones. *New Media & Society*, *12*(1), 35–54. doi:10.1177/1461444809355110

Banjo, O., Hu, Y., & Sundar, S. S. (2008). Cell phone usage and social interaction with proximate others: Ringing in a theoretical model. *The Open Communication Journal*, *2*(1), 127–135. doi:10.2174/1874916X00802010127

Baron, N. S., & af Segerstad, Y. H. (2010). Cross-cultural patterns in mobile-phone use: Public space and reachability in Sweden, the USA and Japan. *New Media & Society*, *12*(1), 13–34. doi:10.1177/1461444809355111

Baron, N. S., & Campbell, E. M. (2012). Gender and mobile phones in cross-national context. *Language Sciences*, *34*(1), 13–27. doi:10.1016/j.langsci.2011.06.018

Bellman, S., Johnson, E., Kobrin, S., & Lohse, G. (2004). International differences in information privacy concerns: A global survey of consumers. *The Information Society*, *20*(5), 313–324. doi:10.1080/01972240490507956

Bergvik, S. (2004). *Disturbing cell phone behavior – A psychological perspective. Implications for mobile technology in tourism.* (Report No. R 46/2004). Telenor R&D. Retrieved July 21, 2014 from https://blog.itu.dk/DMKS-E2008/files/2008/11/bergvik-disturbance-paper.pdf

Boyles, J. L., Smith, A., & Madden, M. (2012). *Privacy and data management on mobile devices.* Pew Research Internet Project. Retrieved July 15, 2014 from http://pewinternet.org/Reports/2012/Mobile-Privacy.aspx

Campbell, S., & Russo, T. C. (2003). The social construction of mobile telephony: An application of the social influence model to perceptions and uses of mobile phones within personal communication networks. *Communication Monographs*, *70*(4), 317–334. doi:10.1080/0363775032000179124

Campbell, S. W. (2007). Perceptions of mobile phone use in public settings: A cross-cultural comparison. *International Journal of Communication, 1,* 738–757. Retrieved from http://ijoc.org/index.php/ijoc/article/view/169/112

Campbell, S. W. (2008). Mobile technology and the body: Apparatgeist, fashion, and function. In J. E. Katz (Ed.), *Handbook of mobile communication studies* (pp. 153–164). Cambridge, MA: MIT. doi:10.7551/mitpress/9780262113120.003.0012

Child, J. T., Haridakis, P. M., & Petronio, S. (2012). Blogging privacy rule orientations, privacy management, and content deletion practices: The variability of online privacy management activity at different stages of social media use. *Computers in Human Behavior, 28*(5), 1859–1872. doi:10.1016/j.chb.2012.05.004

Cho, H., Rivera, M., & Lim, S. S. (2009). A multinational study on online privacy concerns and local response. *New Media & Society, 11,* 409–431. doi:10.1177/1461444808101618

Cho, V., & Hung, H. (2011). The effectiveness of short message service for communication with concerns of privacy protection and conflict avoidance. *Journal of Computer-Mediated Communication, 16*(2), 250–270. doi:10.1111/j.1083-6101.2011.01538.x

Duggan, A., & Petronio, S. (2009). When your child is in crisis: Navigating medical needs with issues of privacy management. In T. J. Socha (Ed.), Parent and children communicating with society (pp. 117–132). New York: Routledge.

Durham, W. T. (2008). The rules-based process of revealing/concealing the family-planning decisions of voluntarily child-free couples a communication privacy management perspective. *Communication Studies, 59,* 132–147. doi:10.1080/10510970802062451

Frampton, B. D., & Child, J. T. (2013). Friend or not to friend: Coworker Facebook friend requests as an application of communication privacy management theory. *Computers in Human Behavior, 29*(6), 2257–2264. doi:10.1016/j.chb.2013.05.006

Geser, H. (2006). Is the cell phone undermining the social order? Understanding mobile technology from a sociological perspective. *Knowledge, Technology & Policy, 19*(1), 8–18. doi:10.100712130-006-1010-x

Greene, K., Derlega, V., Yep, G., & Petronio, S. (2003). *Privacy and disclosure of HIV in interpersonal relationships: A sourcebook for researchers and practitioners.* Mahwah, NJ: LEA.

Grinter, R. E., & Palen, L. (2002). Instant messaging in teenage life. In *Proceedings of ACM Conference on Computer-Supported Cooperative Work (CSCW)* (pp. 21–30) New York: ACM.

Häkkilä, J., & Chatfield, C. (2005). "It's like if you opened someone else's letter": User perceived privacy and social practices with SMS communication. In M. Tscheligi, R. Bernhaupt, & K. Mihalic (Eds.), *Proceedings of the 7th International Conference on Human Computer Interaction with Mobile Devices & Services* (pp. 219-222). ACM. 10.1145/1085777.1085814

Hall, J. A., Baym, N. K., & Miltner, K. M. (2014). Put down that phone and talk to me: Understanding the roles of mobile phone norm adherence and similarity in relationships. *Mobile Media & Communication, 2,* 134-153. doi:10.1177/2050157913517684

Hampton, K. N., Livio, O., & Sessions Goulet, L. (2010). The social life of wireless urban spaces: Internet use, social networks, and the public realm. *Journal of Communication, 60*(4), 701–722. doi:10.1111/j.1460-2466.2010.01510.x

Hastings, S. O. (2000). Asian Indian "self-suppression" and self-disclosure: Enactment and adaptation of cultural identity. *Journal of Language and Social Psychology, 19*(1), 85–109. doi:10.1177/0261927X00019001005

Hofstede, G. (2001). *Culture's consequences: Comparing values, behaviors, institutions, and organizations across nations* (2nd ed.). Thousand Oaks, CA: Sage.

Hofstede, G., & Hofstede, G. J. (2005). Cultures and organizations. In *Software of the mind: Intercultural cooperation and its importance for survival* (2nd ed.). New York: McGraw-Hill.

Hopper, R. (1992). *Telephone conversation.* Indian University Press.

Humphreys, L. (2005). Cellphones in public: Social interactions in a wireless era. *New Media & Society, 7*(6), 810–833. doi:10.1177/1461444805058164

Inbar, O., Joost, G., Hemmert, F., Porat, T., & Tractinsky, N. (2014). Tactful calling: Investigating asymmetric social dilemmas in mobile communications. *Behaviour & Information Technology, 34*, 1–46. doi:10.1080/0144929X.2014.928743

Johar, G. V. (2005). The price of friendship: When, why, and how relational norms guide social exchange behavior. *Journal of Consumer Psychology, 15*(1), 22–27. doi:10.120715327663jcp1501_4

Kallgren, C. A., Reno, R. R., & Cialdini, R. B. (2000). A focus theory of normative conduct: When norms do and do not affect behavior. *Personality and Social Psychology Bulletin, 26*(8), 1002–1012. doi:10.1177/01461672002610009

Katz, J. (2007). Mobile media and communication: Some important questions. *Communication Monographs, 74*(3), 389–394. doi:10.1080/03637750701543519

Kito, M. (2005). Self-disclosure in romantic relationships and friendships among American and Japanese college students. *The Journal of Social Psychology, 145*(2), 127–140. doi:10.3200/SOCP.145.2.127-140 PMID:15816343

Kobsa, A., Patil, S., & Meyer, B. (2012). Privacy in instant messaging: An impression management model. *Behaviour & Information Technology, 31*(4), 355–370. doi:10.1080/01449291003611326

Ling, R. (2002). *The social juxtaposition of mobile telephone conversations and public spaces.* Paper presented at the conference on Social Consequences of Mobile Telephones, Chunchon, Korea. Retrieved July 14, 2014 from https://www.academia.edu/1048257/The_social_juxtaposition_of_mobile_telephone_conversations_and_public_spaces

Ling, R. (2008). *New tech, new ties: How mobile communication is reshaping social cohesion.* Cambridge, MA: MIT Press.

Ling, R., & Campbell, S. W. (Eds.). (2009). *The reconstruction of space and time: Mobile communication practices.* New Brunswick, NJ: Transaction Publishers.

Ling, R., & Campbell, S. W. (Eds.). (2011). *Mobile communication: Bringing us together and tearing us apart*. New Brunswick, NJ: Transaction Publishers.

Ling, R., & McEwen, R. (2010). Mobile communication and ethics: Implications of everyday actions on social order. *Nordic Journal of Applied Ethics, 4*(2). Retrieved July 25, 2014, from http://individual. utoronto.ca/rmcewen/publications.html

May, H., & Hearn, G. (2005). The mobile phone as media. *International Journal of Cultural Studies, 8*(2), 195–211. doi:10.1177/1367877905052417

McLaughlin, C., & Vitak, J. (2011). Norm evolution and violation on Facebook. *New Media & Society, 14*(2), 299–315. doi:10.1177/1461444811412712

Metzger, M. J. (2007). Communication privacy management in electronic commerce. *Journal of Computer-Mediated Communication, 12*(2), 335–361. doi:10.1111/j.1083-6101.2007.00328.x

Nardi, B. A., Whittaker, S., & Bradner, E. (2000). Interaction and outeraction: Instant messaging in action. In *Proceedings of the 2000 ACM Conference on Computer Supported Cooperative Work* (pp. 79-88). New York: ACM Press. 10.1145/358916.358975

Palen, L., & Dourish, P. (2003). Unpacking "privacy" for a networked world. In *Proceedings of the SIGCHI Conference on Human Factors in Computing Systems* (129-136). New York: ACM Press.

Patil, S., & Kobsa, A. (2004). Instant messaging and privacy. In *People and computers XVIII: Design for life: Proceedings of HCI 2004* (pp. 85-88). London: Springer-Verlag.

Patil, S., & Kobsa, A. (2005). Privacy in collaboration: Managing impression. In A. A. Ozok & P. Zaphiris (Eds.), *Proceedings of the 1ˢᵗ International Conference on Online Communities and Social Computing*. Las Vegas: ACM. Retrieved July 28, 2014 from https://www.ics.uci.edu/~kobsa/papers/2005-ICOCSC-kobsa.pdf

Patil, S., & Kobsa, A. (2009). Privacy considerations in awareness systems: Designing with privacy in mind. In P. Markopoulos, B. de Ruyter, & W. Mackay (Eds.), *Awareness systems: Advances in theory, methodology and design* (pp. 187–206). New York: Springer-Verlag. doi:10.1007/978-1-84882-477-5_8

Petronio, S. (1991). Communication boundary management: A theoretical model of managing disclosure of private information between married couples. *Communication Theory, 1*(4), 311–335. doi:10.1111/j.1468-2885.1991.tb00023.x

Petronio, S. (Ed.). (2000). *Balancing the secrets of private disclosure*. Mahwah, NJ: LEA.

Petronio, S. (2002). *Boundaries of privacy: Dialectics of disclosure*. Albany, NY: SUNY Press.

Petronio, S. (2004). Road to developing communication privacy management theory: Narrative in process, please stand by. *Journal of Family Communication, 4*(3-4), 193–207. doi:10.1080/15267431.200 4.9670131

Petronio, S. (2006). Impact of medical mistakes: Negotiating work-family boundaries for physicians. *Communication Monographs, 73*, 462–467. doi:10.1080/03637750601061174

Petronio, S. (2007). Translational research endeavors and the practices of communication privacy management. *Journal of Applied Communication Research, 35*(3), 218–222. doi:10.1080/00909880701422443

Petronio, S. (2008). Communication privacy management theory. In L. A. Baxter & D. O. Braithwaite (Eds.), *Engaging theories in interpersonal communication: Multiple perspectives* (pp. 309–322). Thousand Oaks, CA: Sage. doi:10.4135/9781483329529.n23

Petronio, S. (2009). Privacy management theory. In S. Littlejohn & K. Foss (Eds.), *Encyclopedia of communication theory* (pp. 797–799). Thousand Oaks, CA: Sage. doi:10.4135/9781412959384.n302

Petronio, S., & Caughlin, J. P. (2005). Communication privacy management theory: Understanding families. In D. Braithwaite & L. Baxter (Eds.), *Engaging theories in family communication: Multiple perspectives* (pp. 35–49). Thousand Oaks, CA: Sage.

Petronio, S., & Durham, W. T. (2008). Communication privacy management theory. In L. A. Baxter & D. O. Braithwaite (Eds.), *Engaging theories in interpersonal communication: Multiple perspectives* (pp. 309–322). Thousand Oaks, CA: Sage. doi:10.4135/9781483329529.n23

Petronio, S., Jones, S. M., & Morr, M. C. (2003). Family privacy dilemmas: Managing communication boundaries within family groups. In L. Frey (Ed.), *Group communication in context: Studies of bona fide groups* (pp. 23–56). Mahwah, NJ: LEA.

Petronio, S., & Reierson, J. (2009). Privacy of confidentiality: Grasping the complexities through communication privacy management. In T. Afifi & W. Afifi (Eds.), *Uncertainty, information regulation, and disclosure decisions: Theories and applications* (pp. 365–383). New York: Routledge.

Petronio, S., Sargent, J., Andea, L., Reganis, P., & Cichocki, D. (2004). Family and friends as healthcare advocates: Dilemmas of confidentiality and privacy. *Journal of Social and Personal Relationships, 21*(1), 33–52. doi:10.1177/0265407504039838

Poutiainen, S. (2007). *Finnish cultural discourse about mobile phone communication.* (Ph.D. thesis). University of Massachusetts, Amherst, MA.

Pramis, J. (2013, February 28). Number of mobile phones to exceed population by 2014. *Digital Trends.* Retrieved July 21, 2014, from http://www.digitaltrends.com/mobile/mobile-phone-world-population-2014/#!263I1

Rosen, C. (2004, Summer). Our cell phones, ourselves. *New Atlantis, 6,* 26–45. Retrieved from http://www.thenewatlantis.com/publications/our-cell-phones-ourselves

Schwartz, A. L., Galliher, R. V., & Domenech Rodriguez, M. M. (2011). Self-disclosure in Latinos' intercultural and intracultural friendships and acquaintanceships: Links with collectivism, ethnic identity, and acculturation. *Cultural Diversity & Ethnic Minority Psychology, 17*(1), 116–121. doi:10.1037/a0021824 PMID:21341904

Serewicz, M. C. M., & Petronio, S. (2007). Communication privacy management theory. In B. Whaley & W. Samter (Eds.), *Explaining communication: Contemporary theories and exemplars* (pp. 257–273). Mahwah, NJ: LEA.

Sundar, S. S., Dou, X., & Lee, S. (2013). Communicating in a Ubicomp world: Interaction rules for guiding design of mobile interfaces. In P. Kotzé, G. Marsden, G. Lindgaard, J. Wesson, & M. Winckler (Eds.), *Proceedings of INTERACT 2013, 8118* (vol. 2, pp. 730-747). Springer. 10.1007/978-3-642-40480-1_51

Turkle, S. (2011). *Alone together*. New York, NY: Basic Books.

Vanlear, A. (1991). Testing a cyclical model of communicative openness in relationship development: Two longitudinal studies. *Communication Monographs*, *58*(4), 337–361. doi:10.1080/03637759109376235

Virtanen, I. (2009). Finnish supportive communication: A qualitative study on middle-aged singles support seeking. In R. Wilkins & P. Isotalus (Eds.), *Speech culture in Finland* (pp. 117–139). Lanham, MD: University Press of America.

Waters, S., & Ackerman, J. (2011). Exploring privacy management on Facebook: Motivations and perceived consequences of voluntary disclosure. *Journal of Computer-Mediated Communication*, *17*(1), 101–115. doi:10.1111/j.1083-6101.2011.01559.x

Werner, C., Altman, I., & Brown, B. (1992). A transactional approach to interpersonal relations: Physical environment, social context and temporal qualities. *Journal of Social and Personal Relationships*, *9*(2), 297–323. doi:10.1177/0265407592092008

Westerman, D., Van Der Heide, B., Klein, K. A., & Walther, J. B. (2008). How do people really seek information about others? Information seeking across Internet and traditional communication sources. *Journal of Computer-Mediated Communication*, *13*(3), 751–767. doi:10.1111/j.1083-6101.2008.00418.x

Westin, A. F. (1967). *Privacy and freedom*. New York: Atheneum.

Wilkins, R., & Gareis, E. (2006). Emotion expression and the locution "I love you": A cross-cultural study. *International Journal of Intercultural Relations*, *30*(1), 51–75. doi:10.1016/j.ijintrel.2005.07.003

Worthington, D. L., Valikoski, T., Fitch-Hauser, M., Imhof, M., & Kim, S. (2012). Listening and privacy management in cell phone conversations among young adults: A cross cultural comparison of Finnish, German, Korean, & U.S. American Students. *Empedocles*: *European Journal for the Philosophy of Communication*, *3*, 43–60. doi:10.1386/ejpc.3.1.43_1

ADDITIONAL READING

Banjo, O., Hu, Y., & Sundar, S. S. (2008). Cell phone usage and social interaction with proximate others: Ringing in a theoretical model. *The Open Communication Journal*, *2*(1), 127–135. doi:10.2174/1874916X00802010127

Hopper, R. (1992). *Telephone conversation. Bloomington*. Indian University Press.

Katz, J. (2007). Mobile media and communication: Some important questions. *Communication Monographs*, *74*(3), 389–394. doi:10.1080/03637750701543519

Katz, J. E. (Ed.). (2008). *Handbook of mobile communication studies.* Cambridge, MA: MIT Press. doi:10.7551/mitpress/9780262113120.001.0001

Kobsa, A., Patil, S., & Meyer, B. (2012). Privacy in instant messaging: An impression management model. *Behaviour & Information Technology, 31*(4), 355–370. doi:10.1080/01449291003611326

Ling, R. (2002). The social juxtaposition of mobile telephone conversations and public spaces. Paper presented at the conference on Social Consequences of Mobile Telephones. Chunchon, Korea. Retrieved July 14, 2014 from https://www.academia.edu/1048257/The_social_juxtaposition_of_mobile_telephone_conversations_and_public_spaces

Ling, R. (2008). *New tech, new ties: How mobile communication is reshaping social cohesion.* Cambridge, MA: MIT Press.

Ling, R., & Campbell, S. W. (Eds.). (2011). *Mobile communication: Bringing us together and tearing us apart.* New Brunswick, NJ: Transaction Publishers.

Patil, S., & Kobsa, A. (2005). Privacy in collaboration: Managing impression. In A. A. Ozok, & P. Zaphiris (Eds.), *Proceedings of the 4th International conference on online communities and social computing.* New York: ACM.

Petronio, S. (2002). *Boundaries of privacy: Dialectics of disclosure.* Albany, NY: SUNY Press.

Petronio, S., & Reierson, J. (2009). Privacy of confidentiality: Grasping the complexities through communication privacy management. In T. Afifi & W. Afifi (Eds.), *Uncertainty, information regulation, and disclosure decisions: Theories and applications* (pp. 365–383). New York: Routledge.

Turkle, S. (2011). *Alone together.* New York, NY: Basic Books.

Worthington, D. L., Valikoski, T., Fitch-Hauser, M., Imhof, M., & Kim, S. (2012). Listening and privacy management in cell phone conversations among young adults: A cross cultural comparison of Finnish, German, Korean, & U.S. American Students *Empedocles. European Journal for the Philosophy of Communication, 3*, 43–60. doi:10.1386/ejpc.3.1.43_1

KEY TERMS AND DEFINITIONS

Absent Other: The caller making a mobile phone call to an individual.

Boundary Permeability: The level of access, scope, and extent of private information an individual is willing to share with third parties.

Boundary Turbulence: Occurs when privacy expectations of the original owner of information are not met and a confidentiality breach occurs.

Caller Hegemony: Occurs when receivers give an incoming mobile phone caller higher priority than individuals in the immediate vicinity.

Communication Privacy Management Theory: A theory addressing the tension people experience when choosing what personal information to reveal and what will remain private when interacting with others.

Co-Present Others: Individuals in the vicinity of the receiver of mobile phone call.

Privacy Boundaries: Personal boundaries separating public and private information in order to govern who has control of and access to information.

Proximate Other: Individuals in the vicinity of the receiver of mobile phone call.

This research was previously published in the Encyclopedia of Mobile Phone Behavior edited by Zheng Yan, pages 924-936, copyright year 2015 by Information Science Reference (an imprint of IGI Global).

Chapter 91

Benefits and Challenges for BPM in the Cloud

Ute Riemann

SAP Deutschland AG & Co. KG, Germany

ABSTRACT

Business processes are not only variable, they are dynamic as well. A key benefit of BPM is the ability to adjust processes accordingly in response to changing market requirements. In parallel to BPM, enterprise cloud computing technology has emerged to provide a more cost effective solution to businesses and services while making use of inexpensive computing solutions, which combines pervasive, internet, and virtualization technologies (Chang, Ramachandran, 2014). Despite the slow start the business benefits of cloud computing are as such that the transition of BPM to the cloud is now underway. Cloud services refer to the operation of a virtualized, automated, and service-oriented IT landscape that allows the flexible provision and usage-based invoicing of resources, services, and applications via a network or the Internet. The generic term "X-as-a-Service" summarized the business models delivering almost everything as a service. BPM in the cloud is often regarded as a SaaS application. More recently, BPM is being regarded as a PaaS as it facilitates the creation and deployment of applications, in this case business process solutions. The PaaS landscape is the least developed of the four cloud based software delivery models previously discussed. PaaS vendors, such as IBM, Oracle, Microsoft delivered an application platform with managed cloud infrastructure services however more recently the PaaS market has begun to evolve to include other middleware capabilities including process management. BPM PaaS is the delivery of BPM technology as a service via a cloud service provider. In order to be classified as a PaaS a BPM suite requires the following capabilities: the architecture should be multi-tenant, it should be hosted off premise and it should offer elasticity and metering by use capabilities. When we refer to BPM in the cloud what we are really referring to is a combination of BPM PaaS and BPaaS (Business Process as a Service). Business Process as a Service (BPaaS) is a set of pre-defined business processes that allows the execution of customized business processes in the cloud. BPaaS is a complete pre-integrated BPM platform hosted in the cloud and delivered as a service, for the development and

DOI: 10.4018/978-1-5225-8176-5.ch091

execution of general-purpose business process application. Although such a service harbors an economic potential, questions that need to be answered are as follows: Can an individual and company-specific business process supported by a standardized cloud solution, or should we protect process creativity and competitive differentiation by allowing the company to design the processes individually and solely support basic data flows and structures? Does it make sense to take a software solution "out of the box" that handles both data and process in a cloud environment, or would this hinder the creativity of business (process) development leading to a lower quality of processes and consequently to a decrease in the competitive positioning of a company? How to manage the inherent compliance and security topic. Within a completely integrated business application system, all required security aspects can be implemented as safeguards with just enough money. Within the cloud, however, advanced standards and identity prove is required to monitor and measure information exchange across the federation. Thereby there seems to be no need for developing new protocols, but a standardized way to collect and evaluate the collected information.

INTRODUCTION

To survive in a competitive business world, a company needs as much help as it can get. Collaboration is nothing new. Cloud Computing transforms the way many organizations work and offers benefit for operation management and service computing (Chang, V. 2013). The encouragement of process improvement and the assurance that processes do meet all compliance and risk regulations is of core business interest. In addition, customers increasingly want to get their products and services sooner, better, cheaper and in a more innovative and up-to-date way. The demands and expectations continually change so that the need to be dynamic in provisioning their products and services in the most efficient and effective manner through continuously improving processes rises. Process improvement is one of the ways addressing the challenges of increasing in regards to effectiveness, efficiency, capacity, flexibility and responsiveness (Chang, V., Walters, R. Wills, G, 2014).

More recently, a new generation of collaborative tools has evolved which support coordination of activities via a web based service. What is relatively new is the use of software systems to support the collaboration of business processes to facilitate new forms of collaboration. One major product emergence is the entire cloud service model as innovation and collaboration will frame the future of the cloud agenda. (Forrester, 2012) Due to this technological evolution, it becomes increasingly easier for companies to cultivate and orchestrate collaborative ecosystems around the cloud services. Whereas previously the data in IT systems largely stayed locked up behind corporate firewalls, more and more of that data is now flying in and out of a cloud. This digitization is transformative, driving business processes to ever-greater power and efficiency. Standardization is still and even more a key success factors that allows the digitization of business networks to expand and flourish. The business processes and related business parties, such as suppliers, distributors, customers, partners, and employees becomes increasingly complex and dynamic and stays as the most important factor of any competitive advantage.

Business processes are paramount for the success of a company towards its competitors in the market. Companies have always been working on improving processes for millennia. One can say that the systematic efforts at business process improvement started with Michael Hammer and James Champy in 1993 where they argued, among other things, that IT had often been used to automate bad processes and proposed that the proper combination of process redesign and IT could revolutionize the way companies worked.

Companies in almost every industry and of any size face similar questions how to handle their processes – no matter from which business area they are, no matter how standardized they are, no matter how important they are for the company. The need to improve their business processes continuously with an increasing level of creativity in regards to the design of the process itself and the collaboration of various processes with different partners is a mantra in today's business. In parallel the idea of supporting business processes by IT systems flies around since ages – even before we have thought about cloud and BPaaS. Mostly this has been done by standardization, documentation and with the help of ERP systems. Successful companies need to face this challenge with implementing a continuous and substantial change of the entire business processes. (Zahn & Schmidt, 1997) Companies all over the world have invest time and effort to standardized their processes, increase quality and support these processes as much as possible by IT systems. However, in by far too many cases, these systems have been installed in ways that are difficult to maintain or even to support the business process adequately. The current business environment is characterized by an ever-changing market environment with an aggressive. (Knyphausen, 1993) Consequently, the new design of a complex and flexible business process landscape need to cover this complexity together with another degree of interoperability to even further increase efficiency and flexibility. In this context the concept of agile business processes and cloud services gets more and more important since both concepts addresses the same process targets as they offer an interoperability to enable business partners distributed across an on-demand business process landscape to coordinate their functioning based on a shared understanding of the meaning of the data that flows among them.

The question is now, what additional value can be added with the use of BPaaS? Can such a pre-defined environment support the process dynamics and process creativity or will lead to an "over-standardization" to hinder agility and with little regard of the specifics such a process should have or support the focusing on the "agility-driven processes"?

In addition, we have to analyze the compliance risk while getting the benefits of these new services. New technology approaches such as cloud services are necessary to address these challenges and put pressure to reduce costs but makes the governance even more difficult: the need to assure that all tasks and all actions – independent of the IT infrastructure – are fully aligned with the business outlines how important it is for a governance model to exist within the organization while using cloud services. Process Governance is analyzed in various contexts by various authors. Summarizing their findings: Governance acts to guide Process Management, in which it is aided by an overarching goal and by roles and instruments aligned with that goal. It becomes an important tool supporting business management. Following the current discussion of „cloudification" of business processes all processes are considered similar in regards to their usability within the cloud. The truth is, that neither all processes have the same usability for cloud services not do they have the same importance for a specific company. In general, the role of process governance is to provide a framework for business processes and polices.

Since the goal of governance is to define rules of engagement, mitigate risk and ensure that the investment in IT provides value to the business, we need to define a governance model that ensures the coverage cloud-specific measures. Moreover, it is important to continuously measure and quantify the results of measures, in order to control and further improve the policies.

The assumption is that while identifying the modules of a business process the use of BPaaS will help companies to invest time, money and creativity in the design of process modules to enable a much higher degree of innovation and flexibility. Or in other words: An over-use of BPaaS will lead to a level of variety of process modules to allow a significant increase of process creativity and agility still with an inherent level of risk due to the cloud environment which does not make sense.

CLOUD SERVICES

Definition and Key Characteristics

The following definitions will help to structure the number of cloud services available. One very comprehensive definition is by Brendl (2010) who defined cloud computing as "collections of IT resources (servers, databases, and applications) which are available on an on-demand basis, provided by a service company, available through the internet, and provide resource pooling among multiple users." (Bisong, A. & Rahman, S.M., 2011) Another definition has been set by Mett, P. & Timothy, G. (2011): "Cloud computing is a model for enabling ubiquitous, convenient, on-demand network access to a shared pool of configurable computing resources (e.g. networks, servers, storage, applications, and services) that can be rapidly provisioned and released with minimal management effort or service provider interaction.." (Mett, P. & Timothy, G. 2011) The National Institute of Standards and Technology defines cloud computing as a model for enabling convenient, on-demand network access to a shared pool of configurable computing resources (e.g. networks, servers, storage, applications, and services) that can be rapidly provisioned and released with minimal management effort or service provider interaction. (Mell, P. & Grance, T., 2009) Leimeister et al. (2010) defines cloud services as "an IT deployment model, based on virtualization, where resources, in terms of infrastructure, applications and data are deployed via the internet as a distributed service by one or several service providers....services are scalable on demand and can be priced on a pay-per-use basis". Marston et al. (2011) provide a definition from a business perspective that encompasses key benefits for business as well as its technological features, i.e. IT services "are delivered on-demand to customers over a network in a self-service fashion, independent of device and location....users pay for the service as an operating expense without incurring any significant initial capital expenditure, with the cloud services employing a metering system. From a business perspective, the cloud service model is a model for providing and sourcing information technology services on a pay-per-use basis through web-based tools and applications. Cloud services are elastic, allowing them to be highly configurable, adaptable, and scalable, and requiring less up-front investment and ongoing operating expenditure than traditional IT models.

Structuring the Cloud Services

As guidance toward the cloud market two dimensions shall be used to define the cloud service market segments (Forrester, 2010): What resources are shared? and with whom resources are shared? For this chapter the slightly simplifying assumption that clouds are commonly classified into Public Clouds, Private Clouds and Hybrid Clouds will be used (Chang, V., Walters, R., Wills, G., (2014). Cloud com-

Figure 1. Cloud service levels (Adopted cloud global view, PAC SITSI® Horizontals | Cloud Services Overview | Global View, 2011)

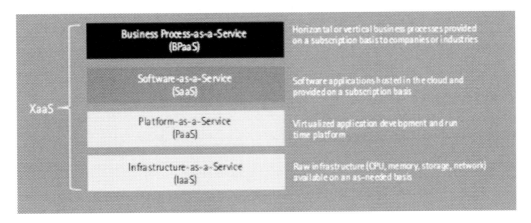

puting consists of a wide array of new business models, the most prominent of which are Software as a Service (SaaS), Platform as a Service (PaaS), and Infrastructure as a Service (IaaS). According to various documentations. (e.g. PAC, 2011, TBR Cloud Program, 2013)

Infrastructure as a Service (IaaS)

IaaS is the basis of the cloud architecture; and constitutes the dynamic provisioning of computing, storage, and network resources. IaaS users, in particular system administrators, IT architects, and developers (the latter for testing purposes), can access these infrastructure resources as required. IaaS provides linkage between different types of services which in turn leads to efficiency improvement and time reduction in business processes (Chang, V. 2013). With IaaS, the cloud offers platform virtualization to the customer. Instead of buying servers and other network equipment, users just rent these resources. In addition, whereas public cloud services are dominated by SaaS, "outsourced Private Cloud" services (managed/ hosted) are dominated by IaaS.

Platform as a Service (PaaS)

PaaS is on top of the IaaS architecture and comprises the middleware and/or development platform, that enables PaaS users, in particular application developers and IT designs, to develop applications within the Cloud and/or operate them. PaaS is the offering of a computing platform as a service. Users are able to deploy their applications on such a platform. The platform offers auxiliary functionality such as a web server, databases, load balancing and more.

Software as a Service (SaaS)

SaaS contains the uppermost layer of the Cloud architecture, the actual business application: e.g., CRM, ERP, collaboration, etc. SaaS users are generally "traditional" end-users within business units. SaaS is the basic cloud service models are well known. (Chandramouli & Mell, 2010). It is a model in which software is offered as a service to the user. The software is hosted on a server and users access the software by using a web browser.

Market Forces Driving Cloud Services

Three major market forces both enable cloud computing and drive its adoption by computing user organizations (i.e., subscribers to cloud services) and by service providers:

- IT becomes embedded in the business. As enterprises have awakened to the increasing interdependence of business and IT issues, they are building IT capabilities within a broader business context. The internet has driven a gradual migration of functionality from applications designed for single departments or processes toward resources that are shared and interconnected between people, departments, and companies. Buyers are more likely to measure technology investments in business terms, measuring technology value in terms of improved business outcomes, not traditional measures like the scope or speed or size of technology infrastructure. Forrester refers to this evolution as the shift from information technology (IT) to business technology (BT).
- Shared service architectures mature. The simultaneous shift toward shared IT resources reinforces the preference for one-to-many service architectures that leverage homogeneous platforms for more economical delivery of a broad portfolio of business services and solutions. Internal consolidation and virtualization of data centers is just the beginning for many companies. The quest for higher utilization of IT resources then leads users to try out shared platforms operated by external service providers, which have significantly higher levels of resource sharing and therefore lower per-unit costs.
- Technology Populism spreads. As the overall population becomes more Internet-literate, consumers, and digital natives in particular, are using technology to manage and integrate their private and business lives.5 Increasingly, digital devices and services will combine to create the personal cloud, an integrated resource for organizing, preserving, sharing, and orchestrating personal information and media.6 The rapid evolution of the personal cloud on the consumer side raises business users' expectations for immediate, universal access and unlimited scale of technology resources.

Business Benefit of Cloud Services

The idea of "the cloud" represents a paradigm shift in the way systems will be deployed. Cloud services may serve as a vital improvement to the business by acting as a potential disruptive innovation for its employees. However, these businesses should be mindful of the uses of cloud computing, as well as which services provide suitable public or private clouds. Cloud service is intended to enable companies of all size to quickly procure and use a wide range of enterprise services on a pay-per-use basis. It will also help companies to scale up or down their IT infrastructure. Cloud computing offers financial, technological & operational benefits to the user and it takes the technology, services, and applications that are similar to those on internet and turns them into a self-service utility. With the advent of cloud computing, the software service model would change from being an on premise model to an on-demand model.

The goal of cloud computing is to reduce upfront cost, on-going costs, and take complexity out of an application's lifecycle. The business benefits of moving IT applications to a cloud based infrastructure have been articulated at length elsewhere. Cloud service promises economic benefits. The combination of these various trends with the potential economic and functional superiority of external cloud infrastructures vis-à-vis internal enterprise IT will continue to drive company decisions to out-task the planning, building, and managing of technology assets and processes (Forrester Research, 2010):

- **Abstraction:** Cloud computing abstracts the details of the system implementation from the users and developers. Applications run on physical systems that are not specified, data is stored in locations that are unknown, administration of systems is outsourced to others, and access by users is ubiquitous.
- **Virtualization:** Cloud computing virtualizes systems by pooling and sharing resources. Systems and storage can be provisioned as needed from a centralized infrastructure, costs are assessed on a metered basis, multi-tenancy is enabled, and resources are scalable with agility.
- **Time-to-Value with Lower Start-Up Costs:** Cloud services reduce the upfront costs for both IT infrastructure as well as software. Beyond tactical cost reduction, companies are beginning to value the nearly immediate availability of cloud computing services without capital commitments. As cloud computing converts fixed costs into variable costs, it releases capital for investment in other areas of the business and allows companies to adjust their spending to changing business needs. In some instances, cloud computing can also enhance the balance sheet strength and credit rating of a company because the business will be able to direct more capital into revenue generating activities.
- **Capex to Opex - Business Flexibility:** From a strategic perspective, companies are trying to achieve IT flexibility. Cloud deployment replaces the risks associated with large capital investment with smoother predictable operational expenditure. Large one-off software upgrade costs are also eliminated.
- Companies need to move swiftly to adapt to change, seize new opportunities, and meet the demands for increased productivity and reduced costs. Similarly, as business workloads and requirements expand and contract, IT organizations must quickly match their computing resources to current business needs. As cloud computing provides flexible access to information system operations, it helps companies continue to change while maintaining a competitive advantage.

CLOUD SERVICE PLAYERS AND MARKET DEVELOPMENT

Revenues with Public Clouds represent the smallest segment so far; revenues generated with public storage and computing Clouds are still very small but promise significant growth during the coming years. Nevertheless, IaaS will not only partly replace conventional infrastructure outsourcing services; it is also growing at the expense of the hardware products market as manufacturers are increasingly offering their products (storage, computing, etc.) "as a service". Thus, IaaS will cannibalize existing business as opposed to just expanding new markets. Moreover, price pressure, already very high in the highly competitive area of infrastructure outsourcing, hosting as well as hardware markets, will remain immense and will negatively affect future growth of the IaaS market. This is not least enforced by competition from Public Cloud offerings that do not provide the same degree of guaranteed availability and security as Private Clouds or traditional outsourcing, but that increasingly set price benchmarks. As scale effects are so essential in the cloud business, and especially in the IaaS area, a further consolidation process on the provider side can be expected.

PaaS provides computational resources via a platform upon which applications and services can be developed and hosted. PaaS typically makes use of dedicated APIs to control the behavior of a server-hosting engine that executes and replicates the execution according to user requests (e.g. access rate). As each provider exposes their own API according to the respective key capabilities, applications developed for one specific Cloud provider cannot be moved to another Cloud host – there are however attempts to extend generic programming models with Cloud capabilities

SaaS provides applications/ services using a Cloud infrastructure or platform. After the ASP (application service providing) hype of 1999-2001, the original business model, the term "ASP", and many pure ASP suppliers virtually disappeared. Obviously, suppliers' and investors' short-term expectations for ASP were far too high. In the meantime, the model "survived" in ASP-friendly environments ("community Clouds"), in niche segments like travel administration, and as a basis for diverse BPO offerings, e.g. in the payroll processing and HR environment. Driven by success stories like Salesforce.com, the SaaS model – in many aspects similar to ASP – significantly gained importance. Today the decision in favor of or against an SaaS offering has become a pragmatic make-or-buy decision, often made by business units, not (mainly) by the IT unit. However, when considering Public Cloud offerings on their own, only few topics, such as eBusiness or niche solutions like travel expense management for SMBs, are approaching a certain maturity level. These niche solutions aside, the first wave of Cloud-based services fell broadly into the areas of CRM, human resources, and financial management (addressing mainly SMBs). Today, application Clouds span all major enterprise solution areas, from procurement to enterprise resource planning and content management. The degree of adoption, however, varies significantly from one solution to the other and between SMBs and large enterprises.

Generally, SMBs were early adopters of SaaS solutions. Especially in the areas of email and HCM, small and medium-sized businesses today use SaaS solutions, whereas large enterprises have been reluctant, preferring on-premise or hosted (or Private Cloud) solutions. However, in the large enterprise segment we expect a slower adoption than in the mid-market. Especially in "sensitive" areas such as finance, and email, where security and availability are of major importance, large companies are still very reluctant towards Public Cloud offerings. In these areas, we expect Private Cloud to remain predominant in the near future. Conversely, the mid-market is probably the most resistant to moving to the SaaS (and more generally to the Cloud) model: they have more complex legacy issues to deal with than small businesses, and are without the resources and motivation for large transformation programs as compared to large enterprises.

BUSINESS PROCESS AS A SERVICE (BPAAS) AS AN EMERGING CLOUD SERVICE MODEL

Cloud services will emerge over time, based on a combination of human-resource-based services with cloud-style delivery models. BPaaS goes beyond the traditional "IT Cloud" architecture, and also known as platform-based business process outsourcing (BPO), as it offers an externally provisioned service for managing an entire business process, such as claims processing, expense management, or procurement (Internet-enabled). "Process Cloud" uses a standardized platform (common to many customers) to automate highly standardized processes. It differs from SaaS in that it provides end-to-end process support, covering not just software but also processes supported by people, such as contact centers. These processes are typically priced on a per-transaction rather than per-seat basis.

Business Process as a Service (BPaaS) is the most mature "Cloud" market an represents a service in the public cloud – albeit rarely considered as part of the traditional "IT Cloud architecture", as it is part of the BPO and processing services market and thus often operated by process specialists or niche players. BPaaS is not covering just software but also processes supported by people, such as contact centers.

Traditional BPO services will gradually shift to dynamic BPO services. Similar to traditional application outsourcing, which will shift gradually to dynamic application services, Forrester predicts an evolution from traditional BPO services into dynamic BPO services. (Forrester, 2010) While still keeping some customer intimacy, the dynamic BPO service will differentiate itself with cloud style characteristics. Future shared services centers will embrace internal private cloud engagement models. The in-house alternative to BPO is also not new. It is a shared service center that consolidates, for example, all HR departments of all business units of a larger corporation into one corporate facility. This type of shared services center used to be one physical location in many cases, but it can also be a virtual shared services center. The important differentiator is the way the shared business services are charged to the business units. If, in addition to the people centric efforts, the total cost of IT systems are charged in a transparent pay-per-use model (with the shared services center basically making the same evolutionary step into a business process virtualization), than the pure data center has transformed from a virtualized hardware landscape into an internal private cloud approach. (Ried, Ph.D & Kisker, H. & Marzke, P. 2010)

Not only will conventional BPO services be increasingly transformed into BPaaS offerings: the emerging overall Cloud trend is also expected to bring with it new business models such as partnership models ha between IT platform/ SaaS providers and process specialists that combine forces in order to offer full business processes "as a service".

SUMMARY BPAAS AS THE NEW EMERGENCE IN CLOUD SERVICE MODELS

Cloud services model combines the efficient use of multitenant (shared) resources, radically simplified "solution" packaging, self-service provisioning, highly elastic and granular scaling, flexible pricing, and broad leverage of Internet standard technologies (Tapper & Kolding, 2012). Cloud services are a model for enabling ubiquitous, convenient, on-demand network access to a shared pool of configurable computing resources that can be rapidly provisioned and released with minimal management or service provider interaction (Mell & Grance, 2009). The cloud service models transforms the very many organizations work and offers benefits for operation management and service computing. Researchers have demonstrated the positive impacts it can offer for business engineering and service level management. In addition, Cloud Computing offers a variety of other benefits including agility, resource consolidation, and business opportunities and green IT. Integrating different business activities together into the same environment can improve efficiency, reduce costs and improve collaboration rather than using a number of standalone services. (Chang, V, 2012)

The Cloud concept means a way of provisioning and using technology, not a technology itself, i.e. it does not generally refer to a specific technology, but rather to a set of combined technologies and concepts. That is why there are still many different definitions of cloud services in the market. Moreover, the Cloud concept is not entirely new. Rather, it combines a number of IT trends of the past years, such as automation, centralization, shared services, service orientation (SOA), virtualization, and externalization (outsourcing, managed services). However, Cloud computing has particular characteristics that distinguish it from classic IT resource and service provisioning – or that are at least commonly associated with Cloud services, even if most of the following characteristics are only 100% true for a few public cloud offerings.

The business benefits that may be gained due to the use of a cloud-based infrastructure can be summarized as such: in general the costs for the star-up and the maintenance is reduced. The deployment is easier associated with a lower capital investment and a more predictable outcome; one-off software upgrade costs are significantly reduced. Cloud give an additional flexibility to the business as it is more elastic and scalable to be adapted to the business development and needs. In addition, it provides a higher performance with a continuous availability. The cloud services give the business several benefits:

- **Elasticity:** Instead of having to buy additional machines, computing resources can be reserved and released as needed. This means that there is no under- or over-provisioning of hardware by the cloud user.
- **Pay-Per-Use:** Cloud users are only billed for the resources they use.
- **No Maintenance:** the IT resources are maintained by the cloud provider. Any operational issues such as data redundancy and hardware maintenance are attended by the cloud provider instead of the cloud user.
- **Availability:** Clouds are accessible over the Internet. This enables the usage of data and processes over the internet and thus mainly everywhere.

By contrast there challenges in using cloud services are:

- **Security:** Data are stored within the cloud and accessible through the Internet. This may raise the question of confidentiality and compliance. The relevance of this security topic depends on the valuation of each business process. (Paulus & Riemann, 2013)
- **Data Transfer:** Large amounts of data transferred within the various business parties in order to collaborate within the entire business process landscape may increase the pricing since not only the storage bur as well the data transferred is measured and billed.

The objective is to allow two or more activities/services at any level (IaaS, PaaS, or SaaS) that are traditionally separate services to be integrated as a single service. This saves costs, improves efficiency, serves more purposes and provides more added values for businesses.

As an emerging service model Business Process as a Service (BPaaS) is an application delivered "as a Service" that is used by business process service provider personnel that perform activities on behalf of the service recipient. This service combines Business Process Outsourcing. BPaaS is the most sophisticated model that goes beyond pure technology, with companies increasingly considering ways to consume and offer Business Processes as a Service (BPaaS) as a horizontal or vertical business processes provisioning on a subscription basis to companies or industries. It is the BPO Services Move to the cloud. Overall, SaaS will continue to grow widely at the expense of the traditional software business. However, the SaaS model also addresses "new markets" – especially smaller companies that were not able to implement and run a complex software suite on their own.

The market leader is IBM as it holds dominance over cloud professional services vendors, but must fight to keep its customer base as software and niche vendors target existing cloud users as their own customers. SAP's cloud professional services customers are the most likely to purchase again, with 80% indicating they'd do repeat business with SAP, compared to just 63% of IBM customers, further posing challenges for current leader IBM. Implementation and support are the most important sales-specific attributes, giving the SIs a slight advantage. Customers rated expertise around cloud and knowledge of industry-specific idiosyncrasies as the most important vendor-specific attributes, providing more opportunity for Deloitte, Accenture and other consulting firms. According to a cloud professional service study, (2013) IBM remains the vendor of choice among cloud professional services purchasers. Microsoft, SAP, HP, and Oracle and Accenture (tied) round off the five vendors chosen most often. India-based vendors, however, are gaining traction — particularly among customers seeking vertical-specific solutions. These vendors typically catch up to market trends quickly, a movement already seen in cloud.

REQUIREMENTS TOWARDS BUSINESS PROCESS MANAGEMENT

In a world where the company's environment is driven by an ever-faster dynamics, the requirement to define rules, activities and processes to structure an integrative flow of data and information is mandatory. However, we are all well aware of the fact that full control of processes is an illusion. Old-fashioned business process management and too much process standardization need to be substituted by a new approach. However, doesn't the (strategic) interest to establish a company-wide flexibility contradict with the (tactical) interest for standardization? On the other hand, is it possible to seamlessly link both targets into one common concept? Traditional process modelling is only useful for highly structured and predictable approaches such as legally binding processes. Nevertheless, if processes require a certain level of agility to adapt to changing requirements? Adaptive processes – in contrast to structured processes – include a certain level of dynamic activities that are coordinated with the overall corporate targets to fulfil the market- and customer demands, but do not need stringent process governance. The approach to identify and successfully manage a process landscape is driven by the balance between defining the right level of process standardization and allowing the right level of process variability. The implementation of future-oriented, dynamic processes is mandatory to link the process targets to the corporate strategy in order to derive seamless processes to fulfil the market and customer demands, in line with the corporate strategy. This requires a step-wise approach to set up a modern, efficient and dynamic process management.

Efficiency and effectiveness of core processes that support the entire company value-chain are the key factors for sustainable corporate success. Consequently, business excellence depends on a powerful corporate process model that overcomes the traditional functional orientation of processes. Flexible processes are a key success factor in today's ever-changing economic environment. How to develop a process landscape that balances standardized and flexible processes? What is the methodology to de-couple and modularize processes in order to allow a maximum of adaptability without losing the efficiency advantages of integrated processes?

Process Standardization vs. Process Agility

Process standardization can undermine the very performance it is meant to optimize. Process standardization also has permeated nearly every service industry, generating impressive gains. However, if there is an over-dose of process, standardization that might neither fit to the process not to the process environment the required variability for the process is simply blindly reduced and though the value generated for the customer is no longer possible. If a process value is due to meet a demand uniqueness or needs to be flexible it is necessary design a process that has the capability of being highly flexible and dynamic in itself to accomplish the process targets and to deliver processes and services that standardized business processes cannot mimic.

According to Hall and Johnson we need to therefore differentiate the processes according to their requirement of creativity and agility. (Hall & Johnson, 2009) Adapting the suggested process matrix, which in its original form was driven from the value the process, adds helps to categorize processes and consider how they should be managed even in the light of the usage of BPaaS:

- Mass processes are processes with a high potential of standardization that are geared to eliminate variations in output. The process goal is always a consistent output for a narrow range of products or services. In such cases, standardization is a key value driver and any variance needs to be avoided
- Mass customization processes need to have a certain level of "controlled variance in their output. While the number of possible combinations might be, enormous output variability is limited to combinations of predefined components. Mass customization might represent the best of both worlds: control and variation
- Nascent or broken processes cannot produce a consistent output since the product or process uses radically new materials, technology, or designs. In these situations, we have to consider that output controlling might not be feasible or desirable. If variation cannot be controlled but is persuaded to value it, a highly agile process needs to be in place. If the variations are not tolerated the focus should be on understanding its causes and creating a standard process.
- An agile process leverage variability in the environment to create variations of products or services that customer's value.

Process Decomposition From a Business Process Management Perspective

Flexibility has always been a key business success factor, not only for business process management; it is the ability to effectively adapt to changing requirements and can therefore be interpreted as "transformation ability".

Consequently, we need to understand how to apply this principle to process management. Traditionally, process landscapes include processes, sub processes and variations thereof according to defined rules. In this framework, process alternatives are pre-defined within a given scope, and this is the critical limitation: agility-required variations and adaptations are not allowed since they are out of scope. Nevertheless, how should a concept look like that is able to flexibly adapt to even unforeseen changes in a truly agile way? Let us assume that flexibility within a company is generated by modularization of structures and processes as well as by de-coupling. De-coupled modules help to configure structures and processes based on new requirements – both internal and external – to increase organizational flexibility and process agility.

In this sense, modularization is defined as the development of processes based on modules with a kernel and interfaces, where the kernel consists of the core functionality. By de-coupling, flexibility is added to processes by defining process modules with standardized interfaces; this allows the flexible linkage of process modules. The Modularization and de-coupling will lead to a process inter- and intra-flexibility either within the process modules as the process modules can be individually combined and/ or between process modules as the process modules can be linked to individual end-to-end processes.

The process modules consists of a process kernel with the customizable functionality and the interfaces that allow a dynamic linkage to other processes and thus to generate dynamically the entire process landscape.

Summary: Cloudification of Agile Business Process Management

Business processes are of core value of each company in their successful acting on today's aggressive markets. However, the business processes are not a homogeneous group but need to be considered from their perceived outcome that is valuated by the customers. This leads to business process categories that need to be handled individually. For doing this the concept of an agile business process management that meets today's business requirements requires overcoming the traditional-hierarchical approach towards business processes needs to be applied. (Aier & Schönherr, 2004) In many cases the true value of a business processes is its flexibility, thus the decomposition into process modules is important. This de-composition leads to a process module inter flexibility (= the module in itself is standardized within the functionality and the interface but customizable) and process intra flexibility (= the flexibility to combine the various process modules while using the process interfaces).

Cloud services have been around for quite a while before it starts rapidly growing with the offering of various cloud service models. It is now the time that business process management and the supporting IT technology makes its transition "to the cloud". In the same way the business processes have been transformed to process modules the cloud services represents an opportunity to bring the process improvement to a new level covering the new challenges of managing an entire and complex process landscape. To reflect the required process flexibility in non-stable and dynamic environments the traditional hierarchic approach to process management gets obsolete. Business processes must be segmented into process modules, leading to the needed process flexibility. This enables the organization to shift certain process modules into other organizations service landscapes. Those modules consist of a process core, carrying all the major functionality of the process, and well defined interfaces, enabling the process to interconnect with other process modules. This dynamic connection of process modules further enables the generation of various business processes. The challenges an organization has to face is when it adjusts the processes to meet the new potential of cloud services, the organization must ensure that the processes are federated in such a way that they still meet the compliance requirements whilst at the same time prioritize the flexibility as a major benefit of using cloud services to be a competitive leader in the longer term. With the introduction of cloud services we have consider, that we cannot directly evaluate the processing system directly to achieve compliance even though the processing environment becomes an increasing integral part of the business process analysis.

BUSINESS PROCESS MANAGEMENT AS A SERVICE (BPAAS)

Business processes are not only variable, they are unpredictable as well. They need to be rapidly adjusted in response to changing market requirements. Still of now BPM software in the cloud is seen as a service application (SaaS): software is delivered remotely, on demand or via a "pay-as-you-go" model. More recently, BPM is being regarded as a PaaS as it facilitates the creation and deployment of applications, in this case business process solutions. The PaaS landscape is the least developed of the four cloud based software delivery models previously discussed. BPM PaaS is the delivery of BPM technology as a service via a cloud service provider. In order to be classified as a PaaS a BPM suite requires the following capabilities: the architecture should be multi-tenant, it should be hosted off premise and it should offer elasticity and metering by use capabilities. A special service model has been recently derived out of the SaaS model to be relevant, to provide business processes as a service (BPaaS). The expression (business) "process as a service" (BPaaS) was coined by Wang et al. (Wang & Bandara & Pahl, 2010) Meant thereby is the process level collaboration and outsourcing process steps.

In this chapter the following definition of BPaaS underlie: BPaaS is a is a special SaaS provisioning model in which enterprise cloud offers provide methods for the modeling, utilization, customization, and (distributed) execution of business processes. According to (Smith & Fingar, 2003), a business process is a collection of related, structured activities or tasks that produce a specific service or product (serve a particular goal) for a particular customer or customers. In the BPaaS model, pre-defined process modules are available which can be customized according to their needs, and remotely execute in the cloud. The pre-defined process modules can be put together, customized, and optimized, thereby leading to multi-tenancy. Finally, the resultant processes can be executed in the cloud; provided the necessary data is made available. In such sense, BPaaS provides a complete outsourcing (the whole process is managed in the cloud) or a partial outsourcing (only parts the process are managed in the cloud). The extension from SaaS to BPaaS is that within BPaaS a set of cloud-based best practice processes comes with a process tailoring to efficiently, flexible adapt these processes to the business and organizational need "as a Service". Businesses can achieve long-term sustainability by using Business Process as a Service (BPaaS) to improve business connectivity and streamline the essential process.

With this model-based approach process, integration efforts and system barriers are irrelevant so that the processes can immediately be used. Examples for providers on the market are SAP's Business ByDesign and IBM's CloudBurst which are two examples for the provision of BPaaS. BPaaS represents an evolution of this trend of process outsourcing, with the market moving towards the industrialization of business processes and the delivery of high volume, automatically scalable, highly standardized on-demand processes. The business benefits drawing organizations to BPO organizations apply equally to BPaaS. BPaaS allows organizations to outsource non-strategic back office functionality like payroll and expense management and focus on their core competencies and areas of differentiation. Organizations can benefit from reduced upfront costs and obtain increased organizational agility through the availability of process on demand. Companies undergoing new regulations can quickly achieve compliance by reaching into the cloud for a standardized BPaaS solution. For more complex business processes, such as case management processes organizations can use BPaaS to deliver process fragments during the execution of a case for example credit checks during a loan approval process. In return for these benefits, in the short term, customers must be willing to accept generic, good enough style processes. Longer term as the BPaaS market matures and the diversity of on demand process solutions increases customers will be able to move up the value chain from "good enough" to process solutions more tailored to their needs. In effect, BPaaS and the distribution of on demand business process solutions in the cloud represent the pinnacle of the move of BPM suites to the cloud.

Transformation of the Business With BPaaS

The key success factor of cloud services is when cloud services evolve from a hosting service for web applications, to catering for full outsourcing scenarios. This is where the business started referring to as 'BPaaS' – Business Process as a Service, adding an extension to the already existing layers IaaS, PaaS and SaaS. BPaaS is similar to what we understand as SaaS but is focused on business processes rather than business applications. BPaaS is the distribution of highly standardized end-to-end business processes delivered similar to SaaS via a pay-per-use, self-service consumption model. The cloud has created a whole new oligarchy of monster application providers such as Salesforce, NetSuite and Workday. It seems like these companies have grown overnight in producing multibillion dollar revenue streams by stealing enterprise clients from IBM, SAP and Oracle. Continued advances in software-as-a-service (SaaS), business-process-as-a-service (BPaaS) and infrastructure-as-a-service (IaaS) have created a shift towards configurable, cloud-based delivery models where services are enacted directly within technology platforms. These standardized platform-based services will gradually replace traditional labor-intensive transactional models and expensive, waterfall projects. Legacy application service providers have been slow to react and jump on the cloud bandwagon. However, cloud applications will increasingly dominate and overtake enterprise legacy applications because they offer accelerated time-to-value and superior return on investment.

Business Process as a Service (BPaaS) and Cloud BPM refers to a business process layer on top of cloud services such as Software as a Service (SaaS), Platform as a Service (PaaS) and Infrastructure as a Service (IaaS). It encompasses business process services for horizontal as well as vertical business processes through a feature-rich platform for delivering automated business outcomes. These solutions provide enterprises with several advantages including increased transparency in the business processes, virtualized workplaces, flexibility, informed decisions, and accelerated performance along with simplified operations. Service providers will focus on transforming businesses and business processes through technologies like cloud and applying analytics across the end-to-end services platform to deliver insights and create new value. Power has shifted away from IT to consumers and business executives, allowing operating executives to reach their clients and employees in new and exciting ways. Currently there are various providers on the market that offers BPaaS solutions.

To increase the cost effectiveness of a process execution and to avoid vendor locking, the Business Process as a Service and Cloud BPM solutions are being adopted to create a network amongst employees, partners, distributors, suppliers and others in the business ecosphere to deliver high value process outcomes. While enterprises across the globe are looking forward to breed the business process services into their current work scenarios, BPaaS and Cloud BPM providers look forward to gain better competitive advantage in the emerging market by creating multi-process platform that provides a complete solution for all business processes.

The need for increasing the agility of a business process, along with cost control measures is playing a cardinal role in shaping the future of Business Process as a Service and Cloud BPM market. Although the adoption of these solutions is relatively slow due to cautious approach of the top management and compliance concerns; these solutions are expected to enjoy enduring growth and have a pervasive existence across all major verticals, owing to the growing demand for automation and virtualization of workplace. These solutions are well positioned to provide solution for globally spread businesses, despite different organizational structures and business process needs. Markets and Markets further expects that the integration of Business Process as a Service and Cloud BPM solutions within the existing organizational framework will further amplify the growth of businesses, while ensuring the compliance and regulatory standards.

Summary: Business Benefits and Challenges of BPM in the Cloud

The main target is to combine the disciplines of business process management with a cloud-based enabling technology to facilitate the tool support of the designed business processes at is best. With BPaaS, cloud is not only an application and solution delivery infrastructure. BPaaS is the delivery of a business process management technology as a service via a cloud service provider. BPaaS will be used by many organizations to develop and execute their own business process landscape. What is used to be a benefit can of course turn out to be a challenge because many companies – even the competitor – might use the same cloud provider with the same best practice business processes. As seen the particular design of a business process, e.g., of supply-chain and customer management processes is considered as the DNA of a company keeping the business secrets – what happens when such a process is applied to pre-defined process models with its data in the cloud?

Benefits

BPM in the cloud represents an opportunity to transform the business case for BPM and process improvement. Today many BPM applications are largely limited to large and multinational enterprises. Deployment of BPM in the cloud presents the opportunity to extend the market reach of BPM applications into the SME (small and medium enterprise) market. Low start off costs and the ability to only pay for what you need with the reassurance of elasticity and scalability on demand has the potential to transform the business case for BPM for many organizations. BPaaS takes this a step further giving SMEs the opportunity to access business process solutions and industry best practice that they would have been unable to develop in house. Additionally BPM in the cloud also creates a BPO opportunity for organizations with a specific area of process expertise. Organizations with specific domain expertise in for example financial services, healthcare or legal services can now not only deploy cloud-based process solutions within their own enterprises but rapidly enter the BPO market and resell their intellectual property (IP) through the development of BPaaS process applications.

The deployment of business process solutions is de-risked through the opportunity for clients to carry out rapid prototyping and testing of BPM solutions in the cloud. For organizations, still developing their cloud strategy business process solutions can be incubated in the cloud before bringing on premise.

Extending Business Process to Mobile Devices Most BPM vendors offer applications across a variety of mobile devices and form factors. Cloud computing extends the mobile capabilities of BPM suites through access to cloud based storage and processing. Cloud based BPM further facilitates collaborative process design and execution on any device, anywhere.

Business Process Management Platform as a Service - BPM PaaS BPM suites combine the disciplines for managing processes e.g. business rules, SLAs, data, resources with the enabling technology to facilitate their design and delivery e.g. process modeling, process execution engine, connectivity and web forms. BPM platforms are today deployed globally to address the following common business challenges:

- Achieve continuous process improvement
- Deliver organizational transformation to achieve competitive advantage and differentiation
- Reduce the delivery cost associated with standardized and repetitive business processes
- Support the efficient delivery of non-standardized or unpredictable business processes
- Ensure compliance to industry regulations e.g. SOX and HIPAA o Reduce errors and improve exception handling
- Deliver improved visibility of operational performance down to an individual process and task level
- Deliver increased business agility through increased ability to respond to changing organizational and market conditions.

BPM PaaS is the delivery of BPM technology as a service via a cloud service provider. In order to be classified as a PaaS a BPM suite requires the following capabilities: the architecture should be multi-tenant, it should be hosted off premise and it should offer elasticity and metering by use capabilities.

BPM PaaS will be used by many organizations to develop and execute their own in house business processes. For multinationals it offers the ability to develop for example a human resources process or a sales process and roll it out rapidly and consistently across multiple jurisdictions. The cloud is, however, first and foremost an application and solutions delivery infrastructure. In the short term many organizations will develop and deploy their own in house processes, however, in the longer term BPM PaaS will also underpin the delivery of high volume, generic business processes (BPaaS) that will be able to leverage the agility benefits of a BPM suite and can also be offered to multiple clients.

The deployment of BPM in the cloud or BPaaS delivers value to the entire business process landscape and its management. BPaaS represents an opportunity to transform the business process management into an agile and flexible business process landscape improvement. Since business processes are somehow more or less static managed and stuck wither in their process documentation or in their IT system limitations cloud services offers an opportunity to adopt the new visionary ideas of the digitalization megatrends to the own process landscape and IT system landscape management. BPaaS however takes the benefits of clouds further as it offers business process solutions and industry best practices out of the box.

Challenges

Management of processes in the cloud needs to be available anytime and from anywhere. Process optimization choices need to be as rich in the cloud as they are in the enterprise. Integration and security require greater attention with distributed systems that cross the public domain.

BPM in the Cloud – The Challenges Some challenges which are common across all cloud based applications still remain, as do some that are specific to BPM in the cloud. Data Security o Many of the initial concerns about data security in the cloud have diminished over time. In 2009 the US government announced its cloud computing initiative aimed at slashing $76 billion in spending on IT services. In 2012 the UK government launched the G- Cloud Program signaling their intention to move away from traditional IT procurement models. These announcements indicate that the battle to articulate the business benefits of moving business applications and address concerns about data security in the cloud has largely been won.2 o Concerns in Europe about the USA Patriot Act, giving federal authorities access to customer data hosted in U.S. clouds, still have to be resolved. Failure to resolve this issue may lead to requests from European customers to host BPM solutions with EU cloud providers. o Application Integration o BPM solutions act as a process layer within organizations, in many cases cutting horizontally across departments and business applications. BPM tools must be able to integrate with business data where ever it resides in an organization e.g. in ECM, CRM, email or in legacy databases and put that information to work on behalf of the process. Many businesses may be reluctant to use a cloud delivered BPM platform until they migrate this data to the cloud thus slowing adoption. The Future - Process on Any Device Anywhere

The point at which business processes originate is changing. Today BPM applications exist in the front office through integration with CRM. Increasingly process participation is taking place on mobile devices. The transition of BPM to the cloud and the development of the first BPaaS services represent the next phase of a journey which will eventually deliver process on any device, anywhere. Today we are seeing the first phase in the development of what is known as the "internet of things." Over the next few years our homes and our cities will become smart through the deployment of radio frequency identification tags (RFID) on almost every type of consumer item. Our homes televisions and cars will contain RFID tags allowing them to be connected to the internet. This is happening already. For example smart pill bottles can be attached to a wireless system that can alert patients and can notify care providers if the bottle isn't opened.3Insurers are now offering 'pay as you drive car' insurance using in car telematics devices which monitor driver behavior and adjusts the price of car cover accordingly.4 Once web-enabled, the next step will see the extension of process to smart devices in the same way as mobile devices today. Cloud based storage and processing will facilitate the extension of business process from today's tablet, mobile or laptop devices to our homes and consumer goods such as televisions, cars and medicine bottles. Processes such as repair requests, prescription reordering, customer support, warranty registration will automatically be triggered by consumer devices attached wirelessly to the web. Cloud, mobile and the "internet of things" will coalesce with BPM to extend process to any device, anywhere.5,6,7 Summary The cloud has the potential to transform the business case for BPM. New BPM business models delivering low start-up costs, try before you buy, the ability to only pay for what you need with the promise of rapid scalability will drive BPM adoption in SME and non-traditional BPM markets. The emergence of BPaaS and the delivery of business process solutions on demand will enable new revenue models for organizations with process area expertize. Business Process Management technologies are today moving towards the edge of the organization. The transition of BPM to the cloud represents the next phase of a journey which will eventually deliver process on any device, anywhere.

The challenges of BPM in the cloud are mostly common to all cloud service models. Even though BPaaS as an Orchestration as a Service Infrastructure, BPaaS is process dependent and focused on a particular process at a time, and does not always connect different business activities. (Chang, V. 2012) Mostly they are concerned about compliance and security. By outsourcing the execution of business processes, cloud consumers lose control over their data and executions. (Chow & Golle & Jakobsson & Shi & Staddon & Masuoka & Molina, 2009)

Cloud services are a model for enabling ubiquitous, convenient, on-demand network access to a shared pool of configurable computing resources that can be rapidly provisioned and released with minimal management or service provider interaction. (Mell & Grance, 2009) The idea of cloud computing is any IT system resources are provided in a pay-per-use manner that are perceived as being unlimited. The cloud service models transforms the way many organizations work and offers added values for operation management and service computing. Researchers have demonstrated the positive impacts it can offer for business engineering and service level management. In addition, Cloud Computing offers a variety of other benefits including agility, resource consolidation, and business opportunities and green IT. Integrating different business activities together into the same environment can improve efficiency, reduce costs and improve collaboration rather than using a number of standalone services (Chang, V, 2012).

One goal of cloud services is to increase flexibility and adaptability at the same time when costs got to be reduced and complexity – even though it is increasing - is managed with less effort. One complexity driver is the frequency how often the process needs to be adapted. Within a traditional view on business processes and within a traditional IT system environment this volatility increases the effort and costs dramatically. This is where cloud services offer the capability to change business processes more easily. As we are getting more complex while moving towards dynamic process networks we have the benefit to break the business process down into process modules just to make it easier to construct new business processes and get a higher degree of variation simply because of the amount of potential combinations of the process flexibility.

REFERENCES

Accenture. (n.d.) (2014). *Cloud Image Map [Web Site]*. From Our cloud strategy approach: http://www.accenture.com/Microsites/cloudstrategy/documents/cloud_diagram/index.html

Accorsi, R. (2008): *Automated privacy audits to complement the notion of control for identity management.* Policies and Research in Identity Management, ser. IFIP Conference Proceedings, E. de Leeuw, S. Fischer-Hübner, J. Tseng, and J. Borking, Eds. Springer, 2008, vol. 261, pp. 39–48.

Accorsi, R., Lowis, L., & Sato, Y. (2011). Automated certification for compliant cloud-based business processes. *Wirtschaftsinformatik*.

Accorsi, R., & Stocker, T. (2008). Automated privacy audits based on pruning of log data,*" in Proceedings of the EDOC International Workshop on Security and Privacy in Enterprise Computing*. IEEE. 10.1109/EDOCW.2008.18

Accorsi, R., & Wonnemann, C. (2009). Detective information flow analysis for business processes. Business Processes, Services Computing and Intelligent Service Management, ser. Lecture Notes in Informatics, W. Abramowicz, L. Macaszek, R. Kowalczyk, and A. Speck, Eds. Springer, 2009, vol. 147, pp. 223–224

ACM. (2011). *Strong non-leak guarantees for workflow models. ACM Symposium on Applied Computing*, pp. 308–314

Agrawal, R., Johnson, C., Kiernan, J., & Leymann, F. (2006). *Taming compliance with sarbanes-oxley internal controls using database technology. Proceedings of the 22nd International Conference on Data Engineering*. IEEE Computer Society Press, pp. 92–101. 10.1109/ICDE.2006.155

Aier, S., & Schönherr, M. (2004). Enterprise Application Integration als Enabler flexibler Unternehmensarchitekturen. In M. Reichert (Ed.), *EAI 2004 – Enterprise Application Integration. Tagungsband des GI-/GMDS-Workshops EAI'04, OFFIS, Oldenburg, 12. – 13.Februar 2004*. Hasselbring, W.

Anstett, T., Leymann, F., Mietzner, R., & Strauch, S. (2009). *Towards bpel in the cloud: Exploiting different delivery models for the execution of business processes.* In Proceedings of the 2009 Congress on Services - I, pages 670 - 677, Washington, DC, USA, 2009. IEEE Computer Society. 10.1109/SERVICES-I.2009.32

Appian (2011). *BPM in the Cloud Its Time, Its Safe... Its Smart.* Oct. 2011.

Appian (2011). *Cloud, Mobile and Social BPM,* Mar. 2011.

Armbrust, M., Fox, A., Griffith, R., Joseph, A., Katz, R., Konwinski, A., . . . Zaharia, M. (2009). *Above the clouds: A Berkeley view of cloud computing.* EECS Department, University of California, Berkeley, Tech. Rep. EECS-2009-28, 2009.

Atluri, V., Chun, S. A., & Mazzoleni, P. (2001). A Chinese Wall security model for decentralized workflow systems. *ACM Conference on Computer and Communications Security.* ACM, pp. 48–57. 10.1145/501983.501991

Atluri, V., & Warner, J. (2008). Security for workflow systems. In M. Gertz & S. Jajodia (Eds.), *Handbook of Database Security* (pp. 213–230). Springer. doi:10.1007/978-0-387-48533-1_9

Bace, J., & Rozwell, C. (2006). *Understanding the components of compliance.* Gartner Research Paper.

Barry, W. J., & Chau, S. V. (2010). *Strategic Management: Principles and Practice* [Book]. London: Cengage Learning Emea.

Batini, C., Ceri, S., & Navathe, S. B. (1992). *Conceptual Database Design. An Entity-Relationship.* Redwood City, California: Approach. Benjamin Cummings.

Batini, C., Furlani, L., & Nardelli, E. *What is a good diagram? A pragmatic approach.* In: Chen, P. P.-S. (ed.): Proceedings of the 4th International Conference on the Entity- Relationship Approach: The Use of ER Concept in Knowledge Representation. Elsevier, North-Holland, 312-319

Bisong, A. & Rahman, S. (2011). *An overview of the security concerns in enterprises.* International Journal of Network Security & Its Applications (IJNSA), Vol.3, No.1.

Brewer, E. (2012). CAP twelve years later: How the »Rules« have changed. *Computer, 45*(2), 23–29. doi:10.1109/MC.2012.37

Chandramouli, R., & Mell, P. (2010). State of security readiness. *ACM Crossroads, 16*(3), 23–25. doi:10.1145/1734160.1734168

Chandramouli, R., & Mell, P. (2010). State of security readiness. *ACM Crossroads, 16*(3), 23–25. doi:10.1145/1734160.1734168

Chang, F., Dean, J., Ghemawat, S., Hsieh, W. C., Wallach, D. A., Burrows, M., . . . Gruber, R. E. (2006). *Bigtable: A distributed storage system for structured data.* In proceedings of the 7th conference on usenix symposium on operating systems design and implementation - volume 7, pages 205-218. 10.1145/1365815.1365816

Chang, V. (2013). Case Study for Business Integration as a Service. Business Integration as a Service: Computational risk analysis for small and medium enterprises adopting SAP. School of Computing and creative technologies, metropolitan university, Leeds, UK

Chang, V. (2013). Business Integration as a Service: Computational risk analysis for small and medium enterprises adopting SAP, INTERNATIONAL JOURNAL OF NEXT-GENERATION COMPUTING, Vol 4, No 3 (2013)

Chang, V. (2014). The Business Intelligence as a Service in the Cloud, in: Future Generation Computer Systems, Elsevier, Volume 37, July 2014, Pages 512–534 doi:10.1016/j.future.2013.12.028

Chang, V. (2014). An Introductory Approach to Risk Visualization as a Service [OJCC]. *Open Journal of Cloud Computing*, *1*(1), 2014.

Chang, V., & Ramachandran, M. (2014). Recommendations and Best Practices for Cloud Enterprise Security. In, *The first international workshop on Enterprise Security 2014 with CloudCom 2014, Singapore, Singapore, 15 - 18 Dec 2014.* (In Press).

Chang, V., Walters, R., & Wills, G. (2014). Review of Cloud Computing and existing Frameworks for Cloud adoption. In *Advances in Cloud Computing Research*. Nova Publishers.

Chang, V., Walters, R. J., & Wills, G. B. (2012). Business Integration as a Service. *International Journal of Cloud Applications and Computing*, *2*(1), 2012. doi:10.4018/ijcac.2012010102

Chow, R., Golle, P., Jakobsson, M., Shi, E., Staddon, J., Masuoka, R., & Molina, J. (2009). *Controlling data in the cloud: Outsourcing computation without outsourcing control. Proceedings of the ACM Workshop on Cloud Computing Security*. ACM, pp. 85–90. 10.1145/1655008.1655020

Cloud Computing Interoperability Forum (CCIF). http://cloudforum.org/

Cloud Computing Use Cases Group. http://cloudusecases.org/

Cloud Security Alliance. (2011): *Whitepaper Security Guidance for Critical Areas of Focus*. In Cloud Computing V3.0. https://cloudsecurityalliance.org/guidance/csaguide.v3.0.pdf

Curbera, F., Doganata, Y. N., Martens, A., Mukhi, N., & Slominski, A. (2008). *Business provenance - A technology to increase traceability of end-to-end operations*. On the Move to Meaningful Internet Systems Conferences, ser. Lecture Notes in Computer Science, R. Meersman and Z. Tari, Eds., vol. 5331. Springer, pp. 100–119.

Dean, J., Ghemawat, S., & Mapreduce, G. Inc. (2004): *Simplified data processing on large clusters*. In *OSDI04: Proceedings of the 6th conference on Symposium on Operating Systems Design and Implementation*. USENIX Association.

Debreceny, R., Lee, S.-L., Neo, W., & To, J. S. (2005). Employing generalized audit software in the financial services sector. *Managerial Auditing Journal*, *20*(6), 605–618. doi:10.1108/02686900510606092

Deelman, E., Singh, G., Livny, M., Berriman, B., & Good, J. (2008). *The cost of doing science on the cloud: the montage example*. In Proceedings of the 2008 ACM/IEEE conference on Supercomputing, SC '08, pages 50:1- 50:12, Piscataway, NJ, USA, 2008. IEEE Press. 10.1109/SC.2008.5217932

Drake, J., Jacob, A., Simpson, N., & Thompson, S. *Open Data Center Alliance: Developing Cloud-Capable Applications*. White Paper.

Eriksson, H.-E., & Penker, M. (1998). *UML Toolkit*. Wiley & Sons.

Eriksson, H. E., Penker, M. agnus: *"Business Modeling with UML: Business Patterns at work"*, Wiley & Sons, Fall 1999

Forrester report (2012). *The Changing Cloud Agenda*. April 24, 2012.

Ghose, A., & Koliadis, G. (2007). *Auditing business process compliance*. Proceedings of the Conference on Service-Oriented Computing, ser. Lecture Notes in Computer Science, B. J. Kr¨amer, K.-J. Lin, and P. Narasimhan, Eds., vol. 4749. Springer, pp. 169–180. 10.1007/978-3-540-74974-5_14

Goossens, B., & Schouten, N. (1981). Using the computer for audit. *Information & Management, 4*(1), 3–10. doi:10.1016/0378-7206(81)90019-7

Governatori, G. (2008). *Business Process Compliance*. Queensland Research Laboratory.

Group, O. M. (2002). *BPMN 2.0 by Example Version 1.0 (non-normative)*. http://www.omg.org/spec/BPMN/2.0/examples/PDF, Jan. 2002.

Group, O. M. Business Process Model and Notation (BPMN) Version 2.0. http://www.omg.org/spec/BPMN/2.0/PDF, Jan. 2011.

Gunestas, M., Wijesekera, D., & Singhal, A. (2008). *Forensic web services*. IFIP Conference on Digital Forensics, ser. IFIP, I. Ray and S. Shenoi, Eds., vol. 285. Springer, pp. 163–176. 10.1007/978-0-387-84927-0_14

Guo, Z., Song, M., & Song, J. (2010): *A Governance Model for Cloud Computing*. Paper presented at the Management and Service Science (MASS). Linthicum, D. S. (2009). Cloud Computing and SOA Convergence in Your Enterprise 10.1109/ICMSS.2010.5576281

Haeberlen, A. (2010). A case for the accountable cloud. *Operating Systems Review, 44*(2), 52–57. doi:10.1145/1773912.1773926

Hall, J. M., & Johnson, M. E. (2009). Process Be Art. *Harvard Business Review*, (March): 2009.

Han, Y.-B., Sun, J.-Y., Wang, G.-L., & Li, H.-F. (2010). A cloud-based bpm architecture with user-end distribution of non-compute-intensive activities and sensitive data. *J. Comput. Sci. Technol., 25*(6), 1115–1167. doi:10.100711390-010-9396-z

Jin, H., Ibrahim, S., Bell, T., Gao, W., Huang, D., & Wu, S. (2010). Cloud types and services. In B. Furht & A. Escalante (Eds.), *Handbook of Cloud Computing* (pp. 335–355). Springer, US. doi:10.1007/978-1-4419-6524-0_14

Katz, R. N., Goldstein, Ph. J., & Yanosky, R. (2009). *Demystifiying Cloud Computing for Higher Education*. In EDUCAUSE Center for Applied Reserach. *Research Bulletin (Sun Chiwawitthaya Thang Thale Phuket), 2009*(19).

Kavantzas, N. & Burdett, D. & Ritzinger, G. & Fletcher, T. & Lafon, Y. & Barreto. C. (2005). *Web Services Choreography Description Language Version 47 1.0.* World Wide Web Consortium, Candidate Recommendation CRws- cdl-10-20051109.

Kelly, R. (2003). *A survey of trusted computing specifications and related technologies.* SANS Publication Series.

Knuplesch, D., Ly, L. T., Rinderle-Ma, S., Pfeifer, H., & Dadam, P. (2010). *On enabling data-aware compliance checking of business process models.* Conference on Conceptual Modeling, ser. Lecture Notes in Computer Science, J. Parsons, M. Saeki, P. Shoval, C. C. Woo, and Y. Wand, Eds., vol. 6412. Springer, pp. 332–346. 10.1007/978-3-642-16373-9_24

Leymann, F., & Roller, D. (1999). *Production Workflow: Concepts and Techniques.* Prentice Hall.

Lu, R., Lin, X., Liang, X., & Shen, X. (2010). Secure provenance: The essential of bread and butter of data forensics in cloud computing. *ACM Symposium on Information, Computer and Communications Security*, D. Feng, D. A. Basin, & P. Liu, Eds. ACM, pp. 282–292. 10.1145/1755688.1755723

Mell, P., & Grance, T. (2009). *The NIST Definition of Cloud Computing.* National Institute of Standards and Technology.

Mell, P. & Grance, T (2011). *The NIST definition of cloud computing (draft).* NIST special publication 800, 145.

Mett, P., & Tomothy, G. (2011). *The NIST Definition of Cloud Computing [Document From Web Site].* from http://www.csrc.nist.gov/publications/nistpubs/800-145/SP800-145.pdf

Moddy, D. L. Shanks, G.: *Improving the Quality of Entity Relationship Models:* An Action Research Programme. In: B. Edmundson, & D. Wilson (eds.): *Proceedings of the 9th Australiasian Conference on Information Systems.* Vol. II, Sydney (1998), 433-448

Moody, D. L.; Shanks, G. G.: *What makes a Good Data Model? A Framework for Evaluating and Improving the Quality of Entity Relationship Models.* The Australian Computer Journal, 30 (1998) 3, 97-110.

Ohtaki, Y., Kamada, M., & Kurosawa, K. (2005). A scheme for partial disclosure of transaction log. *IEICE Transactions Fundamentals*, 88-A(1), 222–229. doi:10.1093/ietfec/E88-A.1.222

PAC, 2011. *Cloud Services Overview. Global View. Cloud Computing, Overview Concept, Pros & Cons, Business Models.* SITSI® Horizontals.

Papazoglou, M. P. (2008). *Web Services - Principles and Technology.* Prentice Hall.

Paulus, S. & Riemann, U. (2013). *Value-chain oriented identification of ERP-system supported End-to-End processes in the light of the use of Cloud Services.* Inderscience, 2013.

Report, F. (2010). *The Evolution Of Cloud Computing Markets For Vendor Strategy Professionals.* Forrester Research, Inc.

Ried, St. & Kisker,H. & Matzke, P. (2010). *The Evolution Of Cloud Computing Markets for Vendor Strategy Professionals.*

Rinderle-Ma, S., Ly, L. T., & Dadam, P. (2008). *Business process compliance.* EMISA Forum, vol. 28, no. 2, pp. 24–29.

Roscoe, B. (1966). *Intensional specifications of security protocols. Proceedings of the 9th IEEE Computer Security Foundations Workshop.* IEEE Computer Society Press, pp. 28–38.

Santos, N., Gummadi, K., & Rodrigues, R. (2009). *Towards trusted cloud computing. Conference on Hot topics in Cloud Computing.* USENIX Association, pp. 3–3.

SAP AG. (2013). *SAP HANA Cloud Platform.* from SAP HANA Cloud Documentation: https://help.hana.ondemand.com/help/frameset.htm?e7c9982cbb571014a97a8a675cf28c15.html

Sayana, A. (1997). *Using CAATs to support is audit.* Information B. Schneier and J. Kelsey, "Remote auditing of software outputs using a trusted coprocessor. *Future Generation Computer Systems, 13*(1), 9–18. doi:10.1016/S0167-739X(97)00004-6

Schmidt, R., & Nurcan, S. (2008). Bpm and social software. In Business Process Management Workshops. pages 649-658.

Shvachko, K. & Kuang, H. & Radia, S. & Chansler, R. (2010). *The Hadoop Distributed File System.*

Smith, H., & Fingar, P. (2003). *Business Process Management.* MK Press.

Sosonsky, B. (2011). *Cloud Computing Bible* [Book]. Indianapolis: Wiley Publishing.

Stevenson, A., & Vaite, M. (2011). *Concise Oxford English Dictionary.* New York: Oxford University Press.

Tabaki, H., Joshi, J., & Ahn, G.-J. (2010, November-December). Security and privacy challenges in cloud computing environments. *IEEE Security and Privacy, 8*(6), 24–31. doi:10.1109/MSP.2010.186

Tapper, D., & Kolding, M. (2012). *Industry Development Models. From traditional to cloud services. A Market Framework.* IDC.

TBR Cloud Program (2013). *Cloud Professional Services Customer Report.*

The Open Group Cloud Computing Work Group. (2011). *The Security for the Cloud & SOA Project of The Open Group Cloud Computing Work Group Security Principles for Cloud and SOA.* A White Paper.

van der Aalst, W., van Hee, K., van der Werf, M., & Verdonk, M. (2010). Auditing 2.0: Using process mining to support tomorrow's auditor. *IEEE Computer, 43*(3), 90–93. doi:10.1109/MC.2010.61

van der Aalst, W. M. P., & ter Hofstede, A. H. M. (2000). Verification of workflow task structures: A petri-net-baset approach. *Information Systems, 25*(1), 43–69. doi:10.1016/S0306-4379(00)00008-9

Vries, P. (2013). *Escaping poverty: The origins of modern economic growth.* Goettingen: Vandenhoeck & Ruprecht. doi:10.14220/9783737001687

Wang, M., Bandara, K. Y., & Pahl, C. (2010). *Process as a service. IEEE International Conference on Services Computing.* IEEE Computer Society, pp. 578–585.

Wei, Y., & Blake, M. B. (2010). Service-oriented computing and cloud computing: Challenges and opportunities. *IEEE Internet Computing*, *14*(6), 72–75. doi:10.1109/MIC.2010.147

Weske, M. (2007). *Business Process Management: Concepts, Languages, Architectures*. Springer.

White, S. (2004). *Introduction to BPMN*. http://www.bpmn.org/Documents/Introduction%20to%20BPMN.pdf, 2004.

Zahn, E. (1996). Strategische Erneuerung für den globalen Wettbewerb. In Zahn, E. (1996, Hrsg.): Strategische Erneuerungen für den globalen Wettbewerb. Stuttgart,1996. - Tagungsband des Stuttgarter Strategieforum 1996, S. 1-30.

Zamperoni, A., & Löhr-Richter, P. *Enhancing the Quality of Conceptual Database Specifications through Validation*. In: Elmasri, R. A., Kouramajian, V., Thalheim, B. (eds.): Proceedings of the 12th International Conference on the Entity-Relationship Approach – ER `93. Springer-Verlag, Berlin et al. (1993), 85-98

Zhang, Q. & Cheng, L. & Boutaba. R. (2010). *Cloud computing: state-of-theart and research challenges*. *Journal of Internet Services and Application*. 1:7, 18, 2010. doi:10.100713174-010-0007-6

zu Knyphausen, D. (1993). Überleben in turbulenten Umwelten: Zur Behandlung der Zeitproblematik im Strategischen Management. *Zeitschrift für Planung*, *4*, 143–162.

This research was previously published in the International Journal of Organizational and Collective Intelligence (IJOCI), 5(1); edited by Victor Chang and Dickson K.W. Chiu, pages 32-61, copyright year 2015 by IGI Publishing (an imprint of IGI Global).

Chapter 92
Security and Privacy Issues in Cloud–Based E–Government

Heru Susanto
Universiti Brunei Darussalam, Brunei & The Indonesian Institute of Science, Indonesia

Mohammad Nabil Almunawar
Universiti Brunei Darussalam, Brunei

ABSTRACT

Cloud computing services have grown rapidly over the years. Government agencies are also interested in cloud-based provision for their E-government processes. Despite the advantages of cloud-related technologies, there are many security issues as well that fall into several categories of breaches with serious impacts. All these breaches have serious legal and reputational implications. Therefore, governments need to ensure that inherent security threats can be neutralized to ensure that data or information stored in the cloud are well protected. It is imperative for cloud-based e-government (CB-eGov) to use an information security management system (ISMS) to effectively manage CB-eGov. The purpose of this chapter is to discuss how cloud computing can be incorporated in an e-government implementation to improve its efficiency without compromising information security. As such, the government needs to take special care in ensuring security, privacy, and confidentiality of information stored in the cloud.

INTRODUCTION

Information security is important in any information system. It becomes crucial if the system is accessible through a computer network, especially a public network such as the Internet. Most e-government systems nowadays are accessible through the Internet; hence, their existence is highly influenced by their securities. If an e-government system is attacked, say, by website defacement, it will create many problems, including downgrading of the credibility of the entire e-government system. As a result, the users (citizens and the business sector) will hesitate to use the system as they lose their trust in the system and then the transactions using the system will suffer. One example of a security attack is denial of service (DoS), which can make a system inaccessible through the Internet.

DOI: 10.4018/978-1-5225-8176-5.ch092

Before we discuss security issues in e-government, especially cloud-based e-government, here is what we mean by e-government. An e-government system can be seen as a concept of using information and communication technology (ICT) to not only organize and manage information but also facilitate administrative processes in government, transactional and interactive processes between government and public. In general, an e-government system has two main subsystems, the front-end system that interacts with users and the back-end system that performs all necessary processes to fulfil requests from the users through the front-end system (Lambrinoudakis et al., 2003). The back-end system is normally composed of web server(s), database server(s) and other necessary software. The back-end system normally resides on government premises, managed and maintained by the government. The front-end systems are users' devices (desktops, laptops, tablets, and smart phones) equipped with client programs that can access the back-end system through the Internet.

The government can outsource the back-end system to a cloud provider, creating a cloud-based e-government system (CB-eGov). As servers and related software are outsourced to a cloud provider, the problem of server maintenance and software update can be avoided. Cloud-based e-government (CB-eGov) is an interesting idea as it can provide quality service delivery to the public with many benefits compared to the old way. Cloud computing is flexible, scalable and relatively inexpensive as compared to the conventional approach of computing (Chen & Almunawar, 2015). However, despite many benefits offered by cloud computing in implementing e-government, there are security issues and risks that need to be understood and addressed properly. In fact, one of the main obstacles to adoption of cloud computing for e-government is the perception of lost control as the back-end system no longer resides in a location under the government control. This perception creates hesitancy concerning the security of CB-eGov.

Numerous possible security breaches can happen in any CB-eGov. In general, security breaches associated with CB-eGov or any information system can be divided into three categories. Firstly, breaches with serious criminal intent (fraud, theft of commercially sensitive or financial information). Secondly, breaches caused by 'casual hackers' (defacement of web sites or 'denial of service' which cause web sites to crash). Thirdly, the flaws in systems design and/or set up leading to security breaches (genuine users seeing/being able to transact on other users' accounts). All of these threats have serious potential for legal and reputations implications. All possible security breaches need to be addressed comprehensively and systematically as security involves both technical and non-technical aspects. An information security standard can be adopted to address all possible security issues. A compliance to an information security standard can help to boost confidence on security of an information system, including CB-eGov.

This chapter is organized as follows. The following section discusses CB-eGov. The next section discusses information security awareness within CB-eGov, followed by a discussion on potential security attack on CB-eGov. In order to protect information system resources, this chapter also looks at several information systems security standards and provides a comparison between them. Next, we discuss potential security attacks in CB-eGov followed by a discussion on how to monitor such attacks. The chapter ends with a conclusion making recommendations for future research directions.

UTILIZING CLOUD COMPUTING FOR E-GOVERNMENT

Cloud computing is a computing model where the computing resources are provided by cloud providers and used by the consumers on demand. The National Institute of Standards and Technology (NIST) at the U.S. Department of Commerce provides the following definition of cloud computing (Mell & Grance, 2011): *Cloud computing is a model for enabling ubiquitous, convenient, on-demand network access to a shared pool of configurable computing resources (e.g. networks, servers, storage, applications and services) that can be rapidly provisioned and released with minimal management effort or service provider interaction.* Cloud computing is predicted to be the next revolution in computing and everybody will be influenced it, changing the way people interact, manage and utilize with computing resources (Wyld, 2009).

E-government provides computing resources, in the form of e-services owned by the government. The resources are normally located in government premises (such as data centres) and used exclusively for e-government related systems. Recently the adoption of cloud computing by government is increasing and some high ranking government officers in the US such as the first chief technology officer (CTO), Anees Chopra and the first federal chief information officer (CIO), Vivek Kundra, highly support the utilization of cloud computing for public sector (Wyld, 2009). US government spending for cloud computing has recently increased. For example, there was more than 70% increase in spending for cloud computing by seven agencies in the US: from $307 million in 2012 to $529 million in 2014.

Kundra (2010) published a document on cloud computing for public sector containing federal cloud computing studies as well state and local computing case studies. He states that "Cloud computing has the potential to greatly reduce waste, increase data center efficiency and utilization rates, and lower operating costs."

Cloud computing offers the government a new way to implement e-government. CB-eGov can be launched and delivered much faster as the government does not need to have data centres and maintain the traffic of websites. Cloud computing creates a new way of processing and organizing data, as universal access to data and applications can be done through a uniform front-end system that can be accessed through the Internet. There are many benefits of cloud computing such as cost savings, flexibility, reliability and scalability. Of course, there are some challenges, including security issues. Further details of benefit and cost of e-government implementation in cloud computing can be found in (Chen & Almunawar, 2015).

Paquette, Jaeger and Wilson (2010) identify several security risks of cloud computing utilization in the public sector. They classify security risks into tangible and intangible security risks. Tangible security risks include access, availability, infrastructure, and integrity. Intangible security risks sac as law and policy issues.

INFORMATION SECURITY AWARENESS

Information Security Awareness (ISA) is the knowledge and attitude of members of any organization or government agency relating to the protection of tangible and intangible assets (Furnell, 2010), especially for CB-eGov information assets. According to the European Network and Information Security Agency (enisa.europa.eu), ISA is an awareness of the risks and available safeguards in the first line of defence for the security of information systems. The goal of security awareness is to achieve long-term change of employees' attitudes through a cultural and behavioural change within agencies towards information security.

ISA have highlighted a number of important topics that are highly related to CB-eGov. These include:

- Information security effectiveness (Kankanhalli et al. 2003; Straub, 1990; Woon & Kankanhalli 2003)
- Security planning and risk management (Straub, 1998; Straub & Welke, 1998)
- Economics of information security and evaluation of information security investments (Cavusoglu, Cavusoglu, and Raghunathan 2004; Cavusoglu, Mishra, and Raghunathan 2004a, 2004b) and
- The design, development and the alignment of the ICT (Doherty & Fulford, 2006; Siponen & Livari, 2006).

While these studies have expanded the understanding of information security from various perspectives, ISA research is particularly underrepresented in the leading information security journals (Willison & Siponen, 2007). An emerging research stream on the human perspective of information security focuses on end-user (insider) behaviours and attempts to identify the factors that lead to compliance behaviour on information security. The current literature recognises that insiders, a term that refers to employees who are authorised to use a particular system or facility (Neumann, 1999), may pose a challenge to an organisation because any ignorance, mistakes, and deliberate acts can jeopardize information security (Durgin, 2007; Lee & Lee, 2002).

ISA should be viewed as a key enabler and an integral part of a government business process, not as a series of rules restricting the efficient working of business processes. Pipkin (2000) and Sherwood et al. (2005) unveil ISA from the business standpoint and argue the need for information security to become a business enabler and an integral part of a business, and that ISA may help to raise trust of an agency by stakeholders and to allow an agency to effectively use newly emerging technologies for greater service success. Therefore, it would be prudent to support the information assets by trying to stop information breaches and overcome several issues associated with ISA. Furnell (2005) indicates several items related to ISA as follows:

- The important and sensitive information and physical assets, such as trade secrets and privacy.
- Concerns and confidential classified information.
- Responsibilities of employees and contractors in handling sensitive information.
- Requirements for proper handling of sensitive material in physical form.
- Proper methods for protecting sensitive information in ICT systems; password policy and use of factor authentication.
- Other computer security concerns: malware, phishing, social engineering.
- Workplace security: building access, wearing of security badges, reporting of incidents, forbidden articles, etc.
- Consequences of failure to properly protect information: potential loss of employment, economic consequences to the firm, damage to individuals whose private records are divulged, and possible civil and criminal.

Boss & Kirsch (2007) introduce the concept of mandatories, which have been shown to motivate individuals to take security precautions. Despite the importance of ISA, there is a paucity of empirical studies that assess the impact of ISA on information security. Siponen (2000, 2001) conceptually analyzed ISA and suggested methods to enhance awareness. D'Arcy et al. (2009) suggest that organisations can use three security countermeasures - user awareness of security policies; security education, training, and awareness programs; and computer monitoring - to reduce user's misuse. Beyond showing the direct influence of ISA on an employee's attitude towards compliance, the countermeasures aim to understand the antecedents of compliance by disentangling the relationships between ISA and an employee's outcome beliefs about compliance and noncompliance.

However, ISA implementation should be viewed as an agency's serious efforts to improve an organization,s selling point to users (Kotler & Amstrong., 2013) and organization imaging and branding (Dwyer, 1987), as one of the marketing tools (Kotler, 2002), to win the competitive edge within its related service area (Morrison, 1998), to increase e-government organization' trust (Brown et.al., 2000) and also to create loyal users through trust (Brown et al., 2005). Kottler et al. (2001) state, "It is obvious that the business organisations or government agencies as service provider are interdependent with their users for the service sustainability". In terms of e-government, customer loyalty is all about attracting the right users, winning their trust and providing convenience, getting them to use various services, and bring even more users (Patell, 1976).

CB-eGov Security Breaches Issues

Cherdantseva & Hilton (2013) adopt a multidimensional and enterprise-wide approach to information security and propose inclusion of a wider scope of information security that covers various aspects of business such as marketing and customer service. Information security is no longer considered purely from a technical perspective, but also from a managerial, system architects' and designers' perspectives, which may enable businesses to increase their competitiveness economic investment (Tsiakis & Stephanides, 2005; Anderson, 2001; Gordon & Loeb, 2002), products or services to world markets transparently and in compliance with prevalent standards, such as ISO 27001 (Theoharidou et al., 2005).

It is obvious that information security needs to be managed properly as related issues are quite complex. In terms of CB-eGov, several information security management standards are available to assist government agencies in managing the security of their information system assets. It is important to adopt an Information Security Management System (ISMS) standard to manage the security of an agency's information assets effectively. The following list provides some of the security challenges of CB-eGov.

- Privacy. In Cloud Computing, data or information is not stored and processed locally. Data is normally stored and processed at the cloud provider system.
- Lack of user control. As data is stored at a third party or cloud provider, the government cannot guarantee total control of data and the third party can access the data without the government's knowledge. This can be quite serious if the data is sensitive or confidential.
- Data leakage. Data leakage affects the trust of citizens in CB-eGov. CB-eGov system contains sensitive data and information about users and businesses, therefore security of the sensitive data is important. Data leakage can also seriously affect the adoption of CB-eGov.
- System failure. Service failure affects users' trust. Government services should be available to citizens 24/7. Here, back-up scenario is one solution to handle system failure issues.
- Security. CB-eGov security concerns the "confidentiality, availability and integrity of information". Security plays an important role in establishing the trust of the users in CB-eGov.

INFORMATION SECURITY STANDARDS

There are several standards within ICT Governance which are also applicable to govern information security in CB-eGov. Some of these are: PRINCE2, OPM3, CMMI, P-CMM, PMMM, ISO27001, BS7799, PCIDSS, COSO, SOA, ITIL and COBIT (Solmn, 2005; Susanto et al., 2011). Unfortunately, some of these standards are not widely adopted by the organizations, with a variety of reasons. From those standards mentioned above, based on global adoption, there are five main information system management security (ISMS) standards: ISO27001, BS 7799, PCIDSS, ITIL, and COBIT. The review of each standard and comparative study to determine their respective strengths, focus, main components and their adoption and implementation was conducted by Susanto et al. (2011). Any e-government system, including CB-eGov, should adopt an information system security standard in order to protect all information system resources in a comprehensive and systematic manner.

Key Benefits of Information Security Implementation for CB-eGov

By adopting security standard for CB-eGov, the government has the opportunity to prove high credibility to users and other stakeholders that they protect information resources according to the recognized best practices. Kosutic (2012) states several benefits of adoption of information security standards including the following four important benefits:

- **Compliance:** It often shows the quickest "return on investment" – if an organization must comply with various regulations regarding data protection, privacy and IT, then security standards can bring a methodology, which enables it to be done in the most efficient way.
- **Marketing Edge:** In a competitive market, it is sometimes very difficult to find something with a unique selling point to customers. Security standards can contribute a unique selling point, especially if an organization handles clients' sensitive information.
- **Lowering the Expenses:** Information security is usually considered as a cost with no obvious financial gain. However, there is financial gain if an organization can minimize expenses caused by incidents. It always sounds good if an organization brings such cases to customer's attention.
- **Putting a Business in Order:** A growing organization may face some management problems such as who has to decide what, who is responsible for certain information assets, who has to authorize access to information systems, etc. An Information security standard is particularly good in sorting these things out – it will force an organization to define very precisely both the responsibilities and duties, and therefore strengthen internal organization information security.

Below, we present brief summaries of the five ISMS mentioned in the previous section.

ISO 27001

ISO 27001 was designed to ensure the selection of adequate and proportionate security controls to protect information assets. This standard is usually applicable to all types of organizations (*e.g.* commercial enterprises, government agencies, and non-profit organizations) and all sizes from micro-businesses to huge multinationals (Calder & Watkins, 2010; Bakry & Al-Ghamdi, 2008).

ISO 27001 was also intended to be suitable for several different functionalities and usabilities, including:

- Usage within organizations to formulate security requirements and objectives;
- Usage within organizations as a way to ensure that security risks are cost-effectively managed;
- Usage within organizations to ensure compliance with laws and regulations;
- Usage within an organization for the implementation and management of controls to ensure that the specific security objectives of an organization are meet with the requirement of standard (Bakry & Al-Ghamdi, 2008);
- The definition of new information security management processes;
- Identification and clarification of existing information security management processes;
- Usage by the management of organizations to determine the status of information security management activities;
- Usage by the internal and external auditors of organisations to demonstrate the information security policies, directives and standards adopted by an organisation and determine the degree of compliance with those policies, directives and standards;
- Usage by organisations to provide relevant information about information security policies, directives, standards and procedures to trading partners and other organisations that they interact with for operational or commercial reasons (Furnell, 2010);
- Implementation of a business enabling information security; and
- Use by organisations to provide relevant information about information security to customers (Calder & Watkins, 2010).

Refer to Figure 1.

BS 7799

The British Standard 7799 (BS 7799) consists of two parts. The first part contains *the best practices (code of practice) of information technology* for information security management. The second part is *information security management systems specification guidance*. BS 7799 introduced the Plan Do

Figure 1. The three levels of security controls

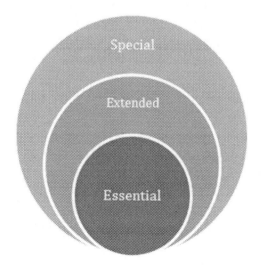

Check Action (PDCA), the Deming's quality assurance model. BS 7799 has 10 controls, which address key areas of information security management. The controls are as follows (Calder and Watkins, 2005):

- Information security policy for the organization. This activity involves a thorough understanding of the organization business goals and its dependency on information security.
- Creation of information security infrastructure. A management framework has to be established to initiate, implement, and control information security within the organization. This needs proper procedures for approval of the information security policy, assigning of the security roles and coordination of security across the organization.
- Asset classification and control. One of the most laborious but essential tasks is to manage inventory of all the IT assets, which could be information assets, software assets, physical assets or other similar services. These information assets need to be classified to indicate the degree of protection.
- Personnel security. Human errors, negligence and greed are responsible for most thefts, frauds or misuse of facilities. Various proactive measures should be taken to make personnel screening policies, confidentiality agreements, terms, and conditions of employment, and information security education and training.
- Physical and environmental security. Designing a secure physical environment to prevent unauthorized access, damage and interference to business premises and information is usually the beginning point of any security plan.
- Communications and operations management. Proper documentation of procedures for the management and operation of all information processing facilities should be established. This includes detailed operating instructions and incident response procedures.
- Access control. Access to information and business processes should be controlled by the business and security requirements. This will include defining access control policy and rules, user access management, user registration, privilege management, user password use and management, review of user access rights, network access controls, enforcing path from user terminal to computer, user authentication, node authentication, segregation of networks, network connection control, network routing control, operating system access control, user identification and authentication, use of system utilities, application access control, monitoring system access and use and ensuring information security when using mobile computing and tile-working facilities.
- System development and maintenance. Security should ideally be built at the time of inception of a system. Hence, security requirements should be identified and agreed prior to the development of information systems.
- Business Continuity Management. A business continuity management process should be designed, implemented, and periodically tested to reduce the disruption caused by disasters and security failures.
- Compliance. It is essential that strict adherence is observed to the provision of national and international IT laws, pertaining to Intellectual Property Rights (IPR), software copyrights, safeguarding of organizational records, data protection, and privacy of personal information, prevention of misuse of information processing facilities, regulation of cryptographic controls and collection of evidence.

PCIDSS

PCIDSS is a set of policies and procedures intended to optimize the information security of credit, debit and cash card transactions and protect cardholders against misuse of their personal information (Morse & Raval, 2008; Bonner 2011). The PCIDSS specifies and elaborates six major objectives (Laredo, 2008; Rowlingson and Winsborrow, 2006).

- First, a secure network must be maintained in which transactions can be conducted. This requirement involves the use of firewalls that is robust enough to be effective without causing undue inconvenience to cardholders or vendors.
- Second, cardholder information must be protected wherever it is stored. Repositories with vital data such as dates of birth, mothers' maiden names, social security numbers, phone numbers, and mailing addresses should be secured against hacking.
- Third, systems should be protected against the activities of malicious hackers by using frequently updated anti-virus software, anti-spyware programs, and other anti-malware solutions.
- Fourth, access to system information and operations should be restricted and controlled. Cardholders should not have to provide information to businesses unless those businesses must know that information to protect them and effectively carry out a transaction.
- Fifth, networks must be constantly monitored and regularly tested to ensure that all security measures and processes are put in place, are functioning properly, and kept up-to-date.
- Sixth, a formal information security policy must be defined, maintained, and followed at all times and by all participating entities. Enforcement measures such as audits and penalties for non-compliance may be necessary

ITIL

ITIL describes procedures, tasks and checklists, used by an organization for establishing a level of competency. It allows the organization to create a baseline from which it can plan, implement, and measure. It is used to demonstrate compliance and to measure improvement. It consists of a number of core controls as follows (ITGI, 2008) and as presented in Figure 2.

- Service strategy. It provides advice on clarification and prioritization of service-provider investments in services. More generally, service strategy focuses on helping IT organizations improve and develop over the long term. In both cases, service strategy relies largely upon a market-driven approach. Key topics covered include service value definition, business-case development, service assets, market analysis, and service provider types.
- Service design. It provides good-practice guidance on the design of IT services, processes, and other aspects of the service management effort. Within ITIL, design work for an IT service is aggregated into a single service design package (SDP). Service design packages, along with additional information about services, are managed within the service catalogues. One of the covered processes is information security management system. ITIL-process security management

Figure 2. The three levels of security controls

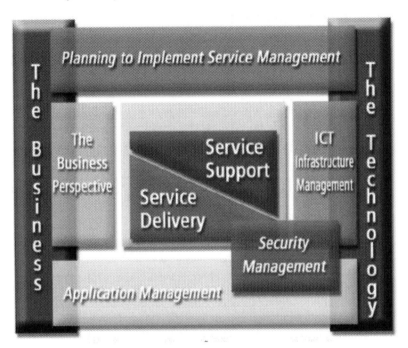

describes the structured fitting of information security in the management organization. ITIL security management is based on the code of practice for ISO 27001. The basic goal of security management is to ensure adequate information security. The primary goal of information security is to protect information assets against risks, and thus to maintain their values to the organization. This is commonly expressed in terms of ensuring their confidentiality, integrity, and availability, along with related properties or goals such as authenticity, accountability, non-repudiation, and reliability.

- Service transition. It relates to the delivery of services required by a business into live/operational use, and often encompasses the "project" side of IT rather than business as usual (BAU). This area also covers topics such as managing changes to the BAU environment.
- Service operation. It is aimed at providing the best practice for achieving the delivery of agreed levels of services to both end-users and customers. Service operation is part of the lifecycle where the services and values are actually delivered. The functions include technical management, application management, operations management and service desk as well as, responsibilities for staff engaging in service operation.

COBIT

Control Objectives for Information and related Technology (COBIT) is an IT governance standard and supporting toolset that allows managers to bridge the gap between control requirements, technical issues, business risks, and security issues (ITGI, 2007; 2008). Moreover, COBIT has five IT Governance areas of concentration (Solms, 2005) as presented in Figure 3.

Figure 3. COBIT components

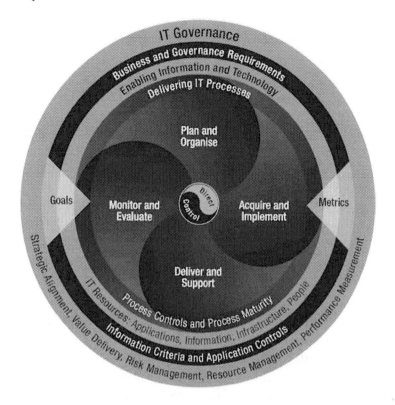

- Strategic alignment focuses on ensuring the linkage of business and IT plans; defining, maintaining and validating the IT value proposition; and aligning IT operations with enterprise operations.
- Value delivery is about executing the value proposition throughout the delivery cycle, ensuring that IT delivers the promised benefits against the strategy, concentrating on optimizing costs and proving the intrinsic value of IT.
- Resource management is about the optimal investment and the proper management of critical IT resources: applications, information, infrastructure and people.
- Risk management is a clear understanding of the enterprise's appetite for risk, understanding of compliance requirements, and transparency into the organization.
- Performance measurement tracks and monitors the strategy of implementation, project completion, resource usage, process performance and service delivery, for example, balanced scorecards that translate strategy into action to achieve goals measurable beyond conventional accounting.

The business orientation of COBIT consists of linking business goals to IT goals, providing metrics and maturity models to measure their achievement, and identifying the associated responsibilities of business and IT processes. The focus of COBIT is illustrated by a process model that subdivides IT into four domains (Plan and Organize, Acquire and Implement, Deliver and Support, and Monitor and Evaluate) in line with the responsibility areas of plan, build, run and monitor (ITGI, 2007). It is positioned at a high level and has been aligned and harmonized with others, such as IT standards and good practices such as ITIL, ISO 27001, The Open Group Architecture Framework (TOGAF), and Project Management Body of Knowledge (PMBOK).

The Big Five: A Summary of Facts

Alfantookh (2009), Bakry & Al-Ghamdi, and Calder (2006) have indicated mandatory requisition controls that should be implemented by an organization, as critical requirements of the information security criteria, due to features as basis of parameters for fulfillment of standards (Neubauer et al., 2008; Freeman, 2007). Details of those mandatory requisition controls are as follows:

- **Information Security Policy:** It is how an institution expresses its intent with emphasis on information security, i.e. the policy by which an institution's governing body expresses its intent to secure information, gives direction to management and staff and informs the other stakeholders of the primacy of efforts.
- **Communications and Operations Management:** It is a defined security policy on security in the organization, in reducing security risk and ensuring correct computing, including operational procedures, controls, and well-defined responsibilities.
- **Access Control:** It is a system, which enables an authority to control access to areas and resources in a given physical facility or computer-based information system.
- **Information System Acquisition, Development and Maintenance:** An integrated process that defines boundaries and technical information systems, beginning with the acquisition, and development and maintenance of information systems.
- **Organization of Information Security:** A structure owned by an organization in implementing information security, which consists of; management commitment to information security, information security co-ordination, authorization process for information processing facilities. There are two major directions: internal organization, and external parties.
- **Asset Management:** It is based on the idea that it is important to identify, track, classify, and assign ownership for the most important assets to ensure they are adequately protected.
- **Information Security Incident Management:** A suite of programs prepared for possible incidents. From a management perspective, it involves identification of resources needed for incident handling. Effective incident management will also help with the prevention of future incidents.
- **Business Continuity Management:** It is to ensure continuity of operations under abnormal conditions. Plans promote the readiness of institutions for rapid recovery in the face of adverse events or conditions, minimize the impact of such circumstances, and provide means to facilitate functioning during and after emergencies.
- **Human Resources Security:** It is to ensure that all employees (including contractors and user of sensitive data) are qualified for and understand their roles and responsibilities of their job duties and that access is removed once employment is terminated.
- **Physical and Environmental Security:** It is to measures taken to safeguard systems, buildings, and related supporting infrastructure against threats associated with their physical environment, buildings and rooms that house information and information technology systems must be afforded appropriate protection to avoid damage or unauthorized access to information and systems.
- **Compliance:** Compliance issues are divided into two areas: the first area involves compliance with the myriad laws, regulations, or even contractual requirements, which are part of the fabric of every institution. The second area is compliance with information security policies, standards and processes.

Table 1 shows a comparison on the big five ISMS standards concerning mandatory requisition controls of information security. Positions of each standard can be seen in Figure 4. It shows that ISO is more applicable and appropriate than the four other security standards. Referring to mandatory requisition controls of information security, ISO 27001 covered 11 controls, BS 7799 10 controls, PCIDSS 10 controls, ITIL 7 controls, and COBIT 10 controls.

The main focus of ISO27001 and BS7799 is information security governance, while ITIL and COBIT are focused on project management that leads to information security. PCIDSS emphasized on information security aspect of smart card for electronic devices.

Table 1. Features of big five of isms standard

		ISO 27001	BS 7799	PCIDSS V2.0	ITIL V4.0	COBIT V4.1
12.	Information Security Policy	√	√	√	√	√
13.	Communications and Operations Management	√	√	√	●	√
14.	Access Control	√	√	√	√	√
15.	Information Systems Acquisition, Development and Maintenance	√	√	√	●	√
16.	Organization of Information Security	√	√	√	√	√
17.	Asset Management	√	√	●	√	√
18.	Information Security Incident Management	√	●	√	√	√
19.	Business Continuity Management	√	√	√	√	√
20.	Human Resources Security	√	√	√	●	●
21.	Physical and Environmental Security	√	√	√	●	√
22.	Compliance	√	√	√	√	√

Figure 4. Position of each standard

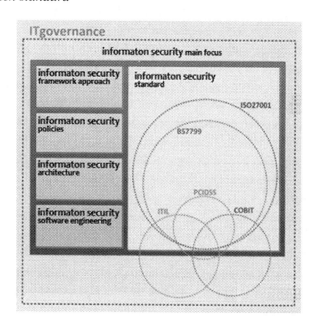

POTENTIAL SECURITY ATTACKS ON CB-eGov

Furnell and Karweni (1999) examined the general requirement for information security technologies in order to provide a basis for trust in the ICT domain. In a modern business environment, ICT is strongly recognized and in fact, modern businesses hardly operate without ICT (Solis, 2012). As a result, modern business organisations are highly dependent on ICT either as a support in their operations or as a business enabler (Sherwood et al, 2005; Pipkin, 2000). The dependency of business organisations in ICT makes the issue of information security very important to address (Baraghani 2007); as this issue has become a main concern for customers. Therefore, an organisation needs to assure that information resources, electronic services and transactions are well protected at the acceptable level of the information security risk through risk management (dealing with information security) or information risk management (IRM) (D'Arcy and Brogan, 2001).

Information risk management is one of the points in Information Security Awareness (ISA). It is mentioned in the clause of *business continuity management*, and falls under the item *information security in the business continuity process and business continuity risk management / assessment*. Information risk management is a recurrent activity that deals with the analysis, planning, implementation, control, and monitoring of measurements and the enforced security policy, procedures and practices to reduce the effects of risk to an acceptable level (Blakley et al, 2001; Lichtenstein & Williamson, 2006).

Information risk management consists of methods and processes used by government organisations to manage risks and to seize opportunities related to the achievement of their objectives. By identifying and proactively addressing risks and opportunities, an organisation protects and creates value for their stakeholders, including owners, employees, customers, regulators, and society overall. Information risk management has gained considerable importance in organisations because of the increased regulatory demands and a growing awareness of its importance in preventing systemic failure. In other words, government agencies must demonstrate that they actually use information risk management as a key component of business processes (Sumner, 2000).

A major threat and challenge to agencies information security are the rising number of incidents caused by social engineering attacks. Social engineering is defined as the use of social disguises, cultural ploys, and psychological tricks toward computer users for the purpose of information gathering, fraud, or gaining computer system access (Goodchild & Glennon, 2010; Anderson, 2008). Despite the continued efforts of organisations to improve user awareness about information security, social engineering malware has been successfully spread across the Internet and have infected many computers (Bailey et al., 2007).

Botnet (robot network)[1] leverages on a wide range of malicious software (malware) to infect network-accessible devices, with the majority of the devices being personal computers in homes, businesses, schools, and governments. Once infected, these devices (or nodes) form botnets and are remotely controlled by the botmasters for illicit activities such as sending e-mail spam and extortion by threats of launching distributed denial-of-service (DDoS) attacks (Dietrich et al., 2013; Khosroshahy et al., 2013). To succeed, social engineering activity such as malware needs to be activated and run on the cloud-network of e-government. Identifying attack strategies is vital to develop countermeasures that can be incorporated into preventive mechanisms like e-mail filtering and end-user security. Information on the behaviour of the malware during propagation helps in the creation of early warning systems (Rahim & Muhaya, 2010). When computer malware is activated, it makes various changes in the computer by opening backdoors that enable it to spread to other machines. It also executes defensive strategies in order to remain undetected. Identification for malware activation is helpful in discovering malware activity in its early stages on end-user machines, and blocking it from being executed completely and propagating further (Rahim & Muhaya, 2010).

There has been an explosion of malware appearance on computing systems over the last decade, whose goal is to compromise the confidentiality, integrity and availability (CIA-triad) of infected computing systems (Fredrikson et al., 2010). The exponential growth in malware population is articulated by pertinent encyclopaedias: for example, by March 2009, there were 340,246 specimens of malware listed in TrendMicro; of which, only 37,950 species were collected before 2000 and 123,802 breeds were compiled in 2006.

Malware often locates victim systems using an array of mechanisms including host scanning, hit-list gleaning, and network snooping. In the process, affected systems are bombarded by voluminous network traffic and a large amount of their computational resources is consumed, thus decreasing their productivity (Weaver et al., 2003). When successful, the malware frequently implants in infected machines extra pieces of code, termed "payloads", that typically lead to information leakage, distributed denial-of-service attacks, and security degradation (Skoudis & Zeltser, 2003). To extend its life span, malware not only covers its codes with cryptographic techniques, but also resorts to polymorphism and metamorphism (Kawakoya et al., 2010; Leder et al., 2009). In this regard, each of the produced clones diversifies in terms of coding sequence and functionality, defeating anti-malware products that exclusively rely on pattern matching for malware detection (Walenstein et al., 2010; Costa et al., 2005).

Malicious software is an extreme threat to the network ecosystem as it can irreparably damage cloud-network system. The essential challenge in identifying malware species is to capture the characteristics that distinguish them. Malware traces left on infected machines include modifications to the file system, manipulations on registry databases, or network activities, which are typically obtained by static analysis of malicious binaries (Moser et al., 2007).

MONITORING POTENTIAL SECURITY ATTACKS

In this section, we introduce a prototype to monitor potential security attacks within CB-eGov as implementation of CB-eGov security awareness. Security monitoring management (SMM) of CB-eGov monitors real-time system activity, firewall and network management to provide security monitoring and potential security breaches. SMM tools collect event data in real time to enable immediate analysis and response for further attack analysis of e-government through cloud computing Refer to Figure 5.

Firewall Management

Firewall Management (FM) is a module-based cloud security system that controls the incoming and outgoing cloud-network traffic by analysing the data packets based on a set of rules and subsequently determines whether they are allowed to pass through or not. A firewall establishes a barrier between a trusted secure internal network and another network, which are assumed insecure and not trusted.

FM is frequently used to prevent unauthorised Internet users from accessing private networks connected to the Internet, especially intranets. All messages entering or leaving the network passes through the firewall, which examines each message and blocks those that do not comply with the specified security criteria (Figure 6).

Figure 5. Security monitoring management of CB-eGov

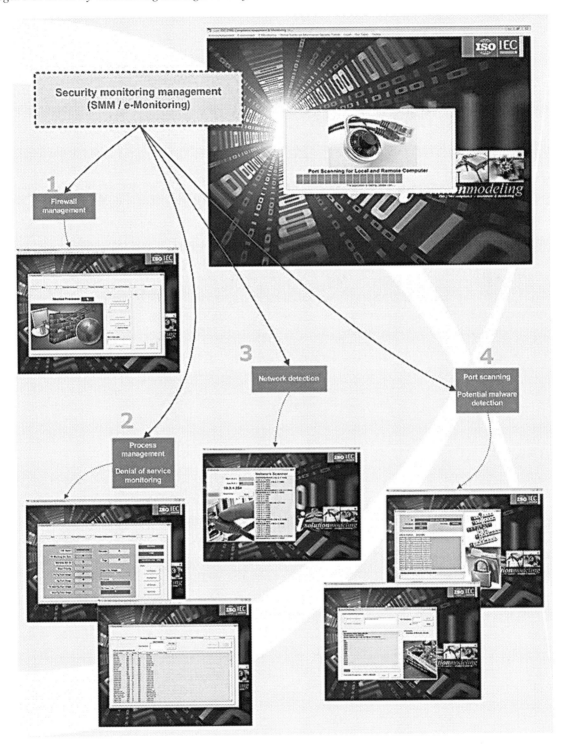

Figure 6. Firewall Management

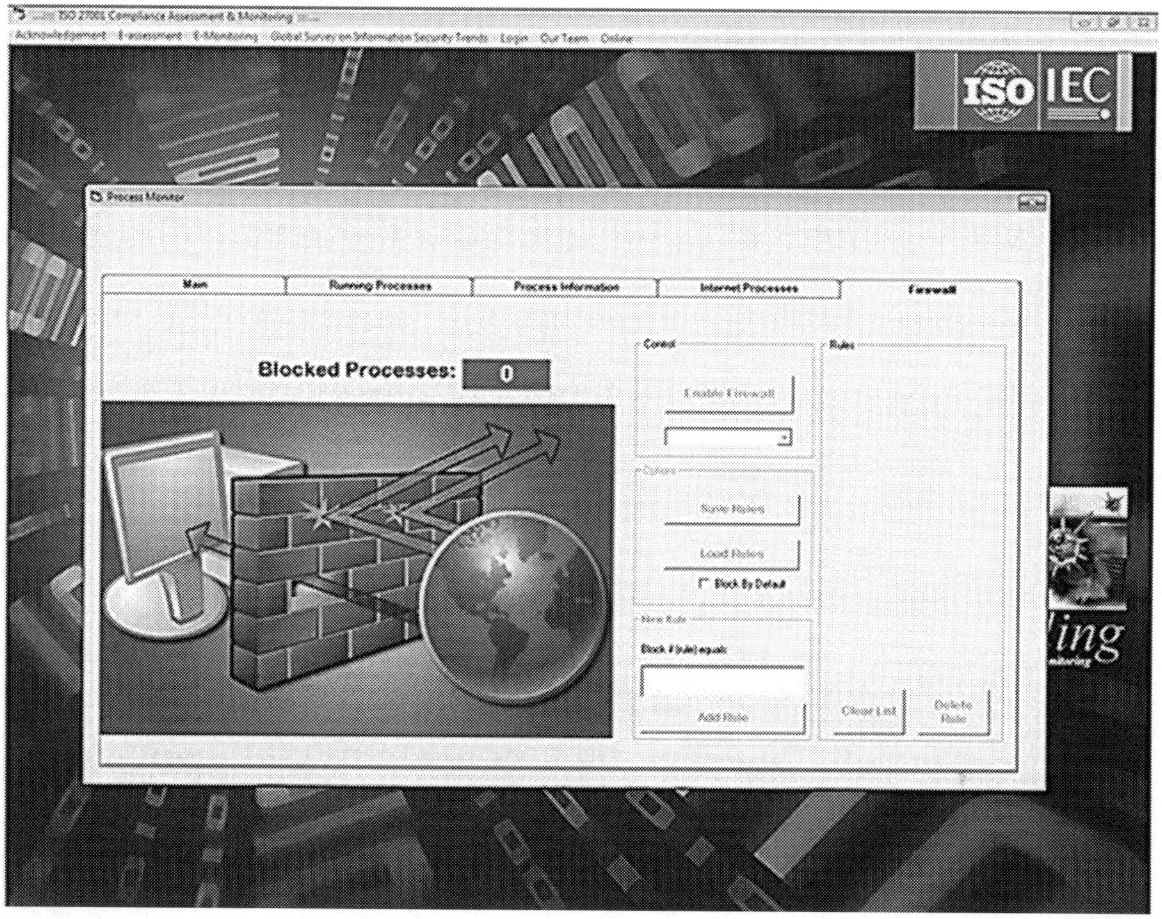

Firewall management can also be used as a tool to maintain network activity, to follow procedures and guidance of information security scenarios. Moreover, FM manages files that are executed by a computer machine either coming out or coming in to the cloud-network and the respective workstation. If it is considered suspicious, such as iteration and traffic process to access a file or application in a network or machine for instance that exceeds 100Mb.secon^{-1} or more than 1000 access.secon^{-1}, this would indicate a traffic anomaly, the system then gives an indication signal showing "blocked processes" as a preventive scenario to assure security of the cloud computing network.

The early system indicator is needed to ensure that the cloud-network traffic is under control, to prevent viruses, worms, or hackers getting into the system.

Process Information

To further analyse malicious software detected by the firewall, more detail is needed about the cloud-network activity to find out suspected security breaches such as malware, botnet, and denial of service.

The module "process information" allows users to learn more about the potential suspect processes. In this module, each suspect is monitored in more detail with information such as: file name accessed, set size, threads, file type (service / program / port), process ID and the parent process (Figure 7).

By looking at the file's properties and details, it becomes easier for users to further analyse the suspected file, by analysing the traffic processes and file repetition accesses by malicious software. This module also comes with some additional features, such as: set priority process and kill process. "Kill process" aims to stop a running process if it is suspected to endanger the system, called denial of service (DoS).

A DoS attack is an attempt to make a machine or network resource unavailable to its intended users. Although the means to carry out, motives for, and targets of a DoS attack may vary, it generally consists of efforts to temporarily or indefinitely interrupt or suspend services of a host connected to the network. One common method of attack involves saturating the target machine with external communications requests. In general, DoS attacks are implemented by either forcing the targeted computer(s) to reset, or consuming their resources so that they can no longer provide their intended services, or obstructing the communication media between the intended users and the victims can no longer communicate adequately.

Figure 7. Running processes

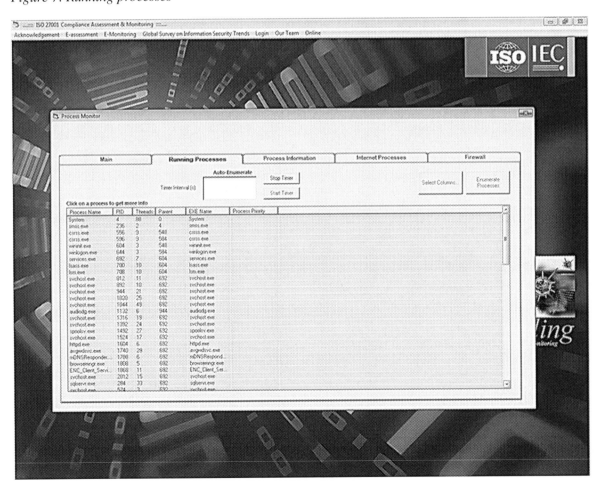

Network Detection

Network detection functions as workstation monitoring that connects to the entire cloud-network, be it wired or wireless. Various types of hardware might be connected to the network such as a personal computers, tablets, or smart mobile devices (smart phones). For instance, if a system administrator would like to know who is currently on the network within the IP range of 10.2.1.1 to 10.2.1.255, the monitor will show a list of names of network-connected machines with their IP addresses. If there is a machine that is unrecognisable as a network member, then the system administrator perpetrates preventive action to protect related network, data, and information. Refer to Figure 8.

If an intruder penetrates into an organisation's network, it may lead to information scrounging and will adversely influence the customers' trust, as it indicates that the CB-eGov is vulnerable.

Port Scanning for Cloud Network

A port is an application-specific or process-specific software construction serving as a communications endpoint in a computer's host operating system. A port is associated with an IP address of the host, as well as the type of protocol used for communication. The purpose of ports is to uniquely identify different applications or processes running on a single computer and thereby enable them to share a single physical connection to a packet-switched network like the Internet. Ports are also used by hackers to

Figure 8. Process information

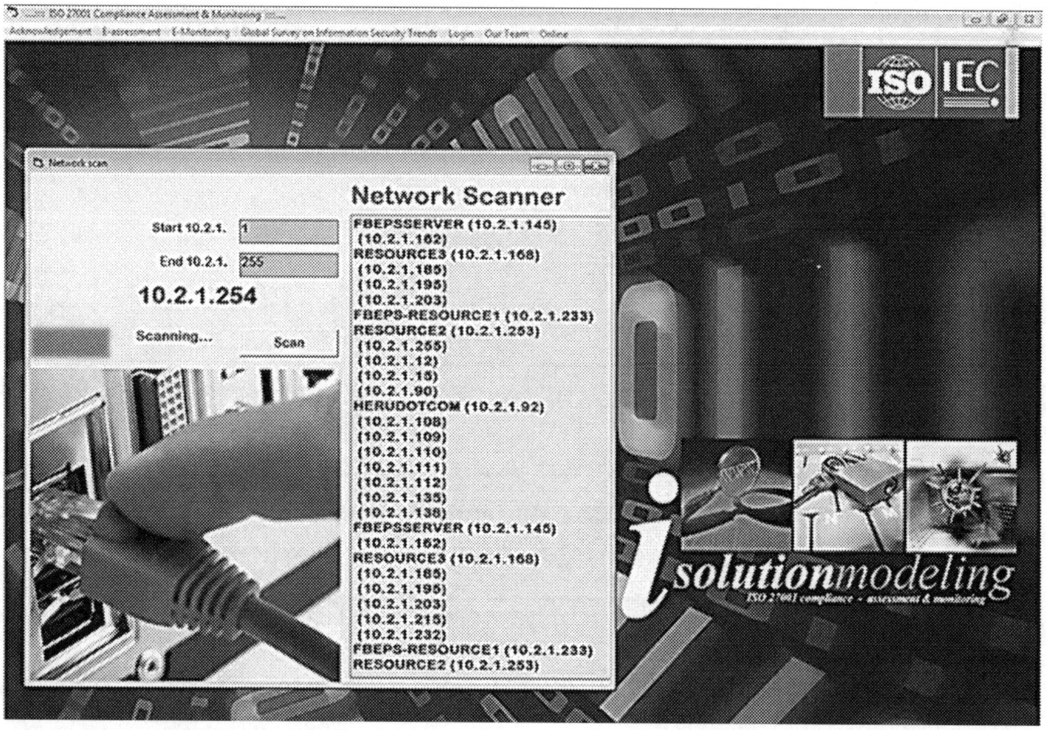

destruct cloud-network components, information and data. Therefore monitoring of ports is required, particularly to prevent the things that are not desired as stated. Securing the port does not mean closing all the ports, because it will instead hinder the flow of traffic and data communication in the network (Figure 9).

There is an abundance of available ports, from port "1" to port number "65535", which is a permutation of 216 (2^{216}) (Table 2). Port 21 is commonly used for broadband Internet and data communications traffic, which is very common and always open. Moreover, this module provides a tool to detect which ports are open and used for such service. If it is deemed dangerous and threatens the security of information, the user can close the port.

The protocols that primarily use ports are the Transport Layer protocols, such as the Transmission Control Protocol (TCP) and the User Datagram Protocol (UDP) of the Internet protocol suite. A port is identified for each address and protocol by a 16-bit number, commonly known as the port number. The port number, added to a computer's internet protocol (IP) address, completes the destination address for a communications session. Data packets are routed across the network to a specific destination IP address, and then, upon reaching the destination computer, are further routed to the specific process bound to the destination port number.

Figure 9. Port scanning for remote computer

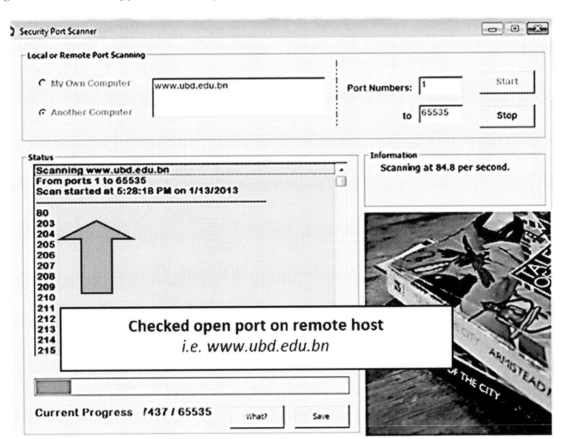

Table 2. Port number and function

Number	Function
20 & 21	File Transfer Protocol (FTP)
22	Secure Shell (SSH)
23	Telnet remote login service
25	Simple Mail Transfer Protocol (SMTP)
53	Domain Name System (DNS) service
80	Hypertext Transfer Protocol (HTTP) used in the World Wide Web
110	Post Office Protocol (POP3)
119	Network News Transfer Protocol (NNTP)
143	Internet Message Access Protocol (IMAP)
161	Simple Network Management Protocol (SNMP)
443	HTTP Secure (HTTPS)

Note that it is the combination of IP address and port number together that must be globally unique. Thus, different IP addresses or protocols may use the same port number for communication, e.g., on a given host or interface UDP and TCP may use the same port number, or on a host with two interfaces, both addresses may be associated with a port having the same number.

Applications implementing common services often use specifically reserved, well-known port numbers for receiving service requests from client hosts. This process is known as listening and involves the receipt of a request to the well-known port and establishing on one-to-one server-client connection, using the same local port number; other clients may continue to connect to the listening port. The core network services, such as the World Wide Web, typically use small port numbers less than 1024. In many operating systems, special privileges are required for applications to bind to these ports because these are often deemed critical to the operation of IP networks. Conversely, the client end of a connection typically uses a high port number allocated for short term use, therefore called an ephemeral port.

The port numbers are encoded in the transport protocol packet header, and they can be readily interpreted not only by the sending and receiving computers, but also by other components of the networking infrastructure. In particular, firewalls are commonly configured to differentiate between packets based on their source or destination port numbers. Port forwarding is an example application of this.

The practice of attempting to connect to a range of ports in sequence on a single computer is commonly known as port scanning. This is usually associated either with malicious cracking attempts or with network administrators looking for possible vulnerabilities to help prevent such attacks. Port connection attempts are frequently monitored and logged by computers. The technique of port knocking uses a series of port connections (knocks) from a client computer to enable a server connection.

CONCLUSION: RECOMMENDATIONS AND FUTURE DIRECTIONS

Users' trust is one of the key success factors for any information system, including CB-eGov to be adopted. Users normally hesitate to use a system if they are not sure about the security of the system. One of the main issues of CB-eGov is information security as data and information are normally stored in the cloud, not government premises. However, securing data and information in the cloud can be made using the existing methods. If users as well as government officers can be convinced that data and information stored in the cloud as well transactions conducted in the cloud are secure, then CB-eGov is a very viable alternative in delivering government services.

The main aim of information security in e-government is to protect government's information system assets and support the achievement of goals. Security of information provides advantages such as improved efficiency of government. As information security is very important, it has to be managed properly through an information security management system (ISMS).

Securing information system assets from unauthorised access is important to maintain e-government operations, whether it is to protect assets or used as a marketing tool. Information security needs to be managed in a proper and systematic manner as it is quite complex. One of the effective ways to manage information security is to comply with an ISMS. There are many ISMS, however the most widely adopted are ISO 27001, BS 7799, ITIL, COBIT, and PCIDSS. One of these standards needs to be selected (such as ISO 27001) to help manage information system security on CB-eGov. Compliance with a standard (such as compliance with ISO 27001) will definitely help convince users that the system is secure and encourage them to use the system to access government services or to transact with government electronically.

Besides compliance with an ISMS standard such as ISO 27001, an information security monitoring tool can help to detect potential security threats, so that the system is always alert, hence the threats can be neutralized as early as possible.

There are many opportunities to study information security in CB-eGov system. The study can be focused on enhancing government agencies security, change management associated with the implementation of security cultures, incident management dealing with the impact and escalation of disaster, software release management, IT service continuity management and configuration management to handle security incidents in CB-eGov systems.

A robust security monitoring tool in CB-eGov system must be developed to help monitor security threats which can be further developed into an information security decision support system, an expert system and a security pattern recognition system, complemented with a knowledge inference and learning system to emulate the decision-making ability of a human expert. This software ability could create an early warning system for suspected security breaches and help enhance strategic planning of information security.

REFERENCES

Alfantookh, A. (2009). *An Approach for the Assessment of The Application of ISO 27001 Essential Information Security Controls*. King Saud University.

Anderson, R. (2001). Why information security is hard - an economic perspective. In *Proceedings of the 17th Annual Computer Security Applications Conference (ACSAC '01)* (pp. 358-365). Washington, DC: IEEE Computer Society. 10.1109/ACSAC.2001.991552

Anderson, R. (2008). Information security economics - and beyond. In *Deontic Logic in Computer Science* (pp. 49–49). Berlin: Springer. doi:10.1007/978-3-540-70525-3_5

Bailey, M., Oberheide, J., Andersen, J., Mao, Z. M., Jahanian, F., & Nazario, J. (2007). Automated classification and analysis of internet malware. In *Recent Advances in Intrusion Detection* (pp. 178–197). Berlin: Springer. doi:10.1007/978-3-540-74320-0_10

Bakry, S. H., & Al-Ghamdi, A. (2008). A framework for the knowledge society ecosystem: A tool for development. In *The Open Knowlege Society. A Computer Science and Information Systems Manifesto* (pp. 32–44). Berlin: Springer. doi:10.1007/978-3-540-87783-7_5

Baraghani, S. N. (2008). *Factors influencing the adoption of internet banking*. Lulea University of Technology.

Blakley, B., McDermott, E., & Geer, D. (2001). Information security is information risk management. In *Proceedings of the 2001 Workshop on New security paradigms* (pp. 97-104). New York: ACM. 10.1145/508171.508187

Bonner, E., O' Raw, J., & Curran, K. (2011). Implementing the Payment Card Industry (PCI) Data Security Standard (DSS). *Telkomnika*, *9*(2), 365–376. doi:10.12928/telkomnika.v9i2.709

Boss, S. R., & Kirsch, L. J. (2007). The last line of defense: motivating employees to follow corporate security guidelines. In *Proceedings of the 28th International Conference on Information Systems*. Academic Press.

Brown, J. R., Dev, C. S., & Lee, D. J. (2000). Managing marketing channel opportunism: The efficacy of alternative governance mechanisms. *Journal of Marketing*, *64*(2), 51–65. doi:10.1509/jmkg.64.2.51.17995

Calder, A. (2006). Information Security Based on ISO 27001/ISO 17799: A Management Guide. Zaltbommel: Van Haren Publishing.

Calder, A., & Watkins, S. (2005). *IT governance: A manager's guide to data security and BS 7799/ISO 17799*. Kogan Page Publishers.

Calder, A., & Watkins, S. G. (2010). *Information Security Risk Management for ISO27001/ISO27002*. It Governance Ltd.

Cavusoglu, H., Cavusoglu, H., & Raghunathan, S. (2004). Economics of IT Security Management: Four Improvements to Current Security Practices. *Communications of the Association for Information Systems*, *14*(1), 37.

Cavusoglu, H., Mishra, B., & Raghunathan, S. (2004a). A model for evaluating IT security investments. *Communications of the ACM*, *47*(7), 87–92. doi:10.1145/1005817.1005828

Cavusoglu, H., Mishra, B., & Raghunathan, S. (2004b). The effect of internet security breach announcements on market value: Capital market reactions for breached firms and internet security developers. *International Journal of Electronic Commerce*, *9*(1), 70–104.

Chen, C. C., & Almunawar, M. N. (2015). Cost-benefit of cloud computing for connected government. In Mahmood (Ed.), *Cloud computing technologies for connected government*. Hershey, PA: IGI Global.

Cherdantseva, Y., & Hilton, J. (2013). Information Security and Information Assurance: Discussion about the Meaning. *Organizational, Legal, and Technological Dimensions of Information System Administration*, 167.

Costa, M., Crowcroft, J., Castro, M., Rowstron, A., Zhou, L., Zhang, L., & Barham, P. (2005, October). Vigilante: End-to-end containment of internet worms. *Operating Systems Review*, *39*(5), 133–147. doi:10.1145/1095809.1095824

D'Arcy, J., Hovav, A., & Galletta, D. (2009). User awareness of security countermeasures and its impact on information systems misuse: A deterrence approach. *Information Systems Research*, *20*(1), 79–98. doi:10.1287/isre.1070.0160

D'Arcy, S. P., & Brogan, J. C. (2001). Enterprise risk management. *Journal of Risk Management of Korea*, *12*(1), 207–228.

Dietrich, C. J., Rossow, C., & Pohlmann, N. (2013). CoCoSpot: Clustering and recognizing botnet command and control channels using traffic analysis. *Computer Networks*, *57*(2), 475–486. doi:10.1016/j.comnet.2012.06.019

Doherty, N. F., & Fulford, H. (2006). Aligning the information security policy with the strategic information systems plan. *Computers & Security*, *25*(1), 55–63. doi:10.1016/j.cose.2005.09.009

Durgin, N., Mitchell, J., & Pavlovic, D. (2003). A compositional logic for proving security properties of protocols. *Journal of Computer Security*, *11*(4), 677–721.

Dwyer, F. R., Schurr, P. H., & Oh, S. (1987). Developing buyer-seller relationships. *Journal of Marketing*, *51*(2), 11–27. doi:10.2307/1251126

Fredrikson, M., Jha, S., Christodorescu, M., Sailer, R., & Yan, X. (2010, May). Synthesizing near-optimal malware specifications from suspicious behaviors. In *Proceedings of Security and Privacy (SP)* (pp. 45-60). IEEE. 10.1109/SP.2010.11

Freeman, E. H. (2007). Holistic information security: ISO 27001 and due care. *Information Systems Security*, *16*(5), 291–294. doi:10.1080/10658980701746478

Furnell, S. (2005). Why users cannot use security. *Computers & Security*, *24*(4), 274–279. doi:10.1016/j.cose.2005.04.003

Furnell, S. (2010). Jumping security hurdles. *Computer Fraud & Security*, *2010*(6), 10–14. doi:10.1016/S1361-3723(10)70067-1

Furnell, S. M., & Karweni, T. (1999). Security implications of electronic commerce: A survey of consumers and businesses. *Internet Research*, *9*(5), 372–382. doi:10.1108/10662249910297778

Goodchild, M. F., & Glennon, J. A. (2010). Crowdsourcing geographic information for disaster response: A research frontier. *International Journal of Digital Earth*, *3*(3), 231–241. doi:10.1080/17538941003759255

Gordon, L. A., & Loeb, M. P. (2002). The economics of information security investment. *ACM Transactions on Information and System Security*, *5*(4), 438–4. doi:10.1145/581271.581274

IT Governance Institute (ITGI). (2007). *COBIT 4.1. Excerpt*. Author.

IT Governance Institute (ITGI). (2008). *Aligning CobiT® 4. 1, ITIL® V3 and ISO/IEC 27002 for Business Benefit A Management Briefing From ITGI and OGC*. ITGI Rolling Meadows.

Kankanhalli, A., Teo, H. H., Tan, B. C., & Wei, K. K. (2003). An integrative study of information systems security effectiveness. *International Journal of Information Management, 23*(2), 139–154. doi:10.1016/S0268-4012(02)00105-6

Kawakoya, Y., Iwamura, M., & Itoh, M. (2010, October). Memory behavior-based automatic malware unpacking in stealth debugging environment. In *Proceedings of Malicious and Unwanted Software (MALWARE)* (pp. 39-46). IEEE. 10.1109/MALWARE.2010.5665794

Khosroshahy, M., Mehmet Ali, M. K., & Qiu, D. (2013). The SIC botnet lifecycle model: A step beyond traditional epidemiological models. *Computer Networks, 57*(2), 404–421. doi:10.1016/j.comnet.2012.07.020

Kosutic, D. (2012). *Risk assessment of ISO 27001*. Retrieved November 10, 2013, from http://blog.iso27001standard.com/

Kotler, P. (2002). *Marketing places*. Simon and Schuster.

Kotler, P., & Armstrong, G. (2013). *Principles of Marketing* (15th ed.). Upper Saddle, NJ: Prentice Hall.

Kundra, V. (2010). *State of public sector cloud computing*. Washington, DC: CIO Council.

Lambrinoudakis, C., Gritzalis, S., Dridi, F., & Pernul, G. (2003). Security requirements for e-government services: A methodological approach for developing a common PKI-based security policy. *Computer Communications, 26*(16), 1873–1883. doi:10.1016/S0140-3664(03)00082-3

Laredo, V. G. (2008). PCI DSS compliance: A matter of strategy. *Card Technology Today, 20*(4), 9. doi:10.1016/S0965-2590(08)70094-X

Leder, F., Werner, T., & Martini, P. (2009). Proactive botnet countermeasures: An offensive approach. *The Virtual Battlefield: Perspectives on Cyber Warfare, 3*, 211–225.

Lee, J., & Lee, Y. (2002). A holistic model of computer abuse within organizations. *Information Management & Computer Security, 10*(2), 57–63. doi:10.1108/09685220210424104

Lichtenstein, S., & Williamson, K. (2006). Understanding consumer adoption of internet banking: An interpretive study in the Australian banking context. *Journal of Electronic Commerce Research, 7*(2), 50–66.

Mell, P., & Grance, T. (2009). The NIST definition of cloud computing. *National Institute of Standards and Technology, 53*(6), 50.

Morrison, A. (1998). Small firm co-operative marketing in a peripheral tourism region. International. *Journal of Contemporary Hospitality Management, 10*(5), 191–197. doi:10.1108/09596119810227802

Morse, E. A., & Raval, V. (2008). PCI DSS: Payment card industry data security standards in context. *Computer Law & Security Report, 24*(6), 540–554. doi:10.1016/j.clsr.2008.07.001

Moser, A., Kruegel, C., & Kirda, E. (2007, December). Limits of static analysis for malware detection. In *Proceedings of Computer Security Applications Conference* (pp. 421-430). IEEE. 10.1109/ACSAC.2007.21

Neubauer, T., Ekelhart, A., & Fenz, S. (2008). Interactive Selection of ISO 27001 Controls under Multiple Objectives. In S. Jajodia, P. Samarati, & S. Cimato (Eds.), *Proceedings of The Ifip Tc 11 23rd International Information Security Conference* (pp. 477–492). Springer US. 10.1007/978-0-387-09699-5_31

Neumann, P. G., & Porras, P. A. (1999). Experience with EMERALD to Date. In *Proceedings of 1st USENIX Workshop on Intrusion Detection and Network Monitoring* (pp. 73–80). USENIX.

Paquette, S., Jaeger, P. T., & Wilson, S. C. (2010). Identifying the security risks associated with governmental use of cloud computing. *Government Information Quarterly*, *27*(3), 245–253. doi:10.1016/j.giq.2010.01.002

Patell, J. M. (1976). Corporate Forecasts of Earnings Per Share and Stock Price Behavior: Empirical Test. *Journal of Accounting Research*, *14*(2), 246–276. doi:10.2307/2490543

Pipkin, D. L. (2000). *Information security*. Prentice Hall PTR.

Rahim, A., & Bin Muhaya, F. T. (2010). Discovering the botnet detection techniques. In *Security Technology, Disaster Recovery and Business Continuity* (pp. 231–235). Berlin: Springer. doi:10.1007/978-3-642-17610-4_26

Rowlingson, R., & Winsborrow, R. (2006). A comparison of the Payment Card Industry data security standard with ISO17799. *Computer Fraud & Security*, *2006*(3), 16–19. doi:10.1016/S1361-3723(06)70323-2

Sherwood, J., Clark, A., & Lynas, D. (2005). Enterprise security architecture. *Computer Security Journal*, *21*(4), 24.

Siponen, M. (2000). A conceptual foundation for organizational information security awareness. *Information Management & Computer Security*, *8*(1), 31–41. doi:10.1108/09685220010371394

Siponen, M. (2001). Five dimensions of information security awareness. *Computers & Society*, *31*(2), 24–29. doi:10.1145/503345.503348

Siponen, M., & Livari, J. (2006). Six design theories for is security policies and guidelines. *Journal of the Association for Information Systems*, *7*(7), 445–472.

Skoudis, E., & Zeltser, L. (2003). *Malware: Fighting malicious code*. Upper Saddle River, NJ: Prentice Hall.

Solis, B. (2012). *The end of business as usual: rewire the way you work to succeed in the consumer revolution*. Hoboken, NJ: Wiley.

Solms, S. H. (2005). Information security governance–compliance management vs operational management. *Computers & Security*, *24*(6), 443–447. doi:10.1016/j.cose.2005.07.003

Straub, D. W. Jr. (1990). Effective IS security: An empirical study. *Information Systems Research*, *1*(3), 255–276. doi:10.1287/isre.1.3.255

Straub, D. W., & Welke, R. J. (1998). Coping with systems risk: Security planning models for management decision making. *Management Information Systems Quarterly, 22*(4), 441–469. doi:10.2307/249551

Sumner, M. (2000). Risk factors in enterprise-wide/ERP projects. *Journal of Information Technology, 15*(4), 317–327. doi:10.1080/02683960010009079

Susanto, H., Almunawar, M. N., & Tuan, Y. C. (2011). Information security management system standards: A comparative study of the big five. *International Journal of Electrical & Computer Sciences, 11*(5), 21–27.

Theoharidou, M., Kokolakis, S., Karyda, M., & Kiountouzis, E. (2005). The insider threat to information systems and the effectiveness of ISO17799. *Computers & Security, 24*(6), 472–484. doi:10.1016/j.cose.2005.05.002

Tsiakis, T., & Stephanides, G. (2005). The economic approach of information security. *Computers & Security, 24*(2), 105–108. doi:10.1016/j.cose.2005.02.001

Walenstein, A., Mathur, R., Chouchane, M. R., & Lakhotia, A. (2006, September). Normalizing metamorphic malware using term rewriting. In *Proceedings of Source Code Analysis and Manipulation* (pp. 75-84). IEEE. 10.1109/SCAM.2006.20

Weaver, N., Paxson, V., Staniford, S., & Cunningham, R. (2003, October). A taxonomy of computer worms. In *Proceedings of the 2003 ACM workshop on Rapid malcode* (pp. 11-18). ACM. 10.1145/948187.948190

Willison, R., & Siponen, M. (2007). A critical assessment of IS security research between 1990-2004. In *Proceedings of 15th European Conference on ISs*. St. Gallen, Switzerland: Academic Press.

Woon, I. M., & Kankanhalli, A. (2007). Investigation of IS professionals' intention to practise secure development of applications. *International Journal of Human-Computer Studies, 65*(1), 29–41. doi:10.1016/j.ijhcs.2006.08.003

Wyld, D. C. (2009). *Moving to the cloud: An introduction to cloud computing in government*. IBM Center for the Business of Government.

ADDITIONAL READING

Baker, S. (2007). Google and the wisdom of clouds. *Business Week, 14*.

Bertot, J. C., Jaeger, P. T., & Grimes, J. M. (2010, May). Crowd-sourcing transparency: ICTs, social media, and government transparency initiatives. In*Proceedings of the 11th Annual International Digital Government Research Conference on Public Administration Online: Challenges and Opportunities* (pp. 51-58). Digital Government Society of North America.

Burroughs, J. M. (2009). What users want: Assessing government information preferences to drive information services. *Government Information Quarterly, 26*(1), 203–218. doi:10.1016/j.giq.2008.06.003

Buyya, R., Yeo, C. S., & Venugol, S. (2008). Market-oriented cloud computing: vision, hype, and reality for delivering IT services as computing utilities. Paper presented at the 10th IEEE International Conference on High Performance Computing and Communications. 10.1109/HPCC.2008.172

Chen, Y.-C., & Perry, J. (2003). Outsourcing for e-Government: Managing for success. *Public Performance and Management Review, 26*(4), 404–421. doi:10.1177/1530957603026004007

Crandall, R., & Waverman, L. (2000). *Who pays for universal service?* Washington, D.C.: Brookings Institute.

Crouhy, M., Galai, D., & Mark, R. (2006). *The essentials of risk management.* Toronto, ON: McGraw-Hill.

Dibbern, J., Goles, T., Hirschhiem, R., & Jayatilaka, B. (2004). Information systems outsourcing: A survey of analysis of the literature. *The Data Base for Advances in Information Systems, 35*(4), 1–97. doi:10.1145/1035233.1035236

Hand, E. (2007). Head in the clouds. *Nature, 449*(7165), 963. doi:10.1038/449963a PMID:17960208

Jaeger, P. T., Bertot, J., McClure, C. R., & Rodriguez, M. (2007). Public libraries and Internet access across the United States: A comparison by state from 2004 to 2006. *Information Technology and Libraries, 26*(2), 4–14.

Jaeger, P. T., Lin, J., & Grimes, J. M. (2008). Cloud computing and information policy: computing in the policy cloud? *Journal of Information Technology & Politics, 5*(3), 269–283. doi:10.1080/19331680802425479

Jaeger, P. T., Lin, J., & Grimes, J. M. (2008). Cloud computing and information policy: Computing in a policy cloud? *Journal of Information Technology & Politics, 5*(3), 269–283. doi:10.1080/19331680802425479

Jaeger, P. T., Lin, J., Grimes, J. M., & Simmons, S. N. (2009). Where is the cloud? Geography, economics, environment, and jurisdiction in cloud computing. *First Monday, 14*(5). doi:10.5210/fm.v14i5.2456

Jaeger, P. T., McClure, C. R., & Bertot, J. (2005). The e-rate program and libraries and library consortia. Information technology and libraries, 24(2), 57–67.

Kubicek, H. (2008). Next generation FoI between information management and Web 2.0. Paper presented at the 2008 International Conference on Digital Government Research, Montreal, QC.

Mack, E. A., & Grubesic, T. H. (2009). Forecasting broadband provision. *Information Economics and Policy, 21*(4), 57–67. doi:10.1016/j.infoecopol.2009.08.001

Managing business risks in the information age. (1998). New York, NY: The Economist Intelligence Unit.

Pokharel, M., & Park, J. S. (2009, November). Cloud computing: future solution for e-governance. In *Proceedings of the 3rd international conference on Theory and practice of electronic governance* (pp. 409-410). ACM. 10.1145/1693042.1693134

Quinn, A. C. (2003). Keeping the citizenry informed: Early congressional printing and 21st century information policy. *Government Information Quarterly, 20*(3), 281–295. doi:10.1016/S0740-624X(03)00055-8

Vijaykumar, N. (2011). Role of ICT in e-Governance: Impact of Cloud Computing in Driving New Initiatives. Infosys Technologies Limited, SetLabs Briefings, 9(2).

Washington, D. C., Paquette, S., Jaeger, P. T., & Wilson, S. C. (2010). Identifying the security risks associated with governmental use of cloud computing. *Government Information Quarterly, 27*(3), 245–253. doi:10.1016/j.giq.2010.01.002

Zissis, D., & Lekkas, D. (2011). Securing e-Government and e-Voting with an open cloud computing architecture. *Government Information Quarterly, 28*(2), 239–251. doi:10.1016/j.giq.2010.05.010

KEY TERMS AND DEFINITIONS

Cloud Computing: Cloud computing is a computing model that enables access to a shared pool of computing resource through the Internet. The resource can be rapidly provisioned utilizing pay-per-used method.

Denial of Service: (DoS): DoS is an attempt to make a machine or network resource unavailable to its intended users.

E-Government: E-government can be seen as a concept of using information and communication technology (ICT) to not only organizing and managing information but also facilitating administrative processes in government, transactional and interactive processes between government and public.

Firewall: A network security system that controls the incoming and outgoing network traffic based on applied rule set. A firewall establishes a barrier between a trusted, secure internal network and another network (e.g., the Internet) that are assumed not to be secure and trusted.

Information Security Management System (ISMS): It is a collection of policies concerned with information security management or IT related risks.

Information Security Monitoring System: Information security monitoring system performs real-time security monitoring to detect potential security breaches. Security Monitoring Management (SMM) tool collects event data in real time to enable immediate analysis and response to further attack.

Information Security: Information security is the practice of defending information from unauthorized access, use, disclosure, disruption, modification, perusal, inspection, recording or destruction. It is a general term that can be used regardless of the form the data may take (electronic, physical, etc.).

Network Detection: An intrusion detection system that seeks to discover unauthorized access to a computer network by analyzing traffic on the network for signs of malicious activity.

ENDNOTES

[1] *Botnet* is a collection of Internet connected programs communicating with other similar programs in order to perform tasks. This can be as mundane as keeping control of an Internet Relay Chat (IRC) channel, or it could be used to send spam email or participate in distributed denial-of-service attacks. The word botnet is a stand for *robot* and *network*.

This research was previously published in Cloud Computing Technologies for Connected Government edited by Zaigham Mahmood, pages 292-321, copyright year 2016 by Information Science Reference (an imprint of IGI Global).

Chapter 93
Smart Healthcare Administration Over Cloud

Govinda K.
VIT University, India

S. Ramasubbareddy
VIT University, India

ABSTRACT

Cloud computing is an emerging technology that is expected to support internet-scale critical applications, which could be essential to the healthcare sector. Its scalability, resilience, adaptability, connectivity, cost reduction, and high-performance features have high potential to lift the efficiency and quality of healthcare. With the widespread application of healthcare information and communication technology, constructing a stable and sustainable data sharing circumstance has attracted rapidly growing attention in both academic research area and the healthcare industry. Cloud computing is one of long dreamed visions of healthcare cloud (HC), which matches the need of healthcare workers, information sharing directly to various health providers over the internet, regardless of their location and the amount of data. This chapter proposes a cloud model for health information sharing and integration in HC and looks into the arising challenges in healthcare.

INTRODUCTION

With the development in healthcare and economic fields, more number of medical records are generated. There is an urgent need and demand to improve the levels and standards of modern health-care records management by using innovative technology. The objective of this paper is to introduce the concept of Cloud Computing and discuss the challenges of applying Healthcare Cloud (HC) to improve the Health Information Science research. With the new concept of Cloud Computing emerging in recent years, more and more interests have been sparked from a variety organizations and individual users, as they increasingly intend to take advantage of web applications to share a huge amount of public and private data and information in a more affordable way and reliable IT architecture.

DOI: 10.4018/978-1-5225-8176-5.ch093

More specifically, the medical and health information system based on the cloud computing is desired, in order to realize the sharing of medical data and health information, coordination of clinical service, along with the effective and cost-containment clinical information system infrastructure via the implementation of a distributed and high-integrated platform.

Mobile devices are growing in terms of utilization in our daily life to voice conversations and video chatting with others. Especially the smart phones became an important tool in our daily activities in e-commerce, IT industries. Even though mobile device is capable of enough to handle high end applications but still suffering with limited resources such as short battery lifetime, storage and processor. These changes help users to make environment where all devices share resources to run application efficiently.

The conventional computing only deals with the compute and process computation tasks. The modern technologies got birth to satisfy user requirements; Big data, networking, cloud computing, fog computing, mobile cloud computing, IOT, the user will always require modern infrastructure to achieve increasing demand on both mobility and connectivity (Goswami, 2013). Among many technologies mobile cloud computing became a popular model (Zimmerman, 1999). Mobile computing allows many devices interacting with other mobile devices through network technologies (Wi-Fi and 4G). The mobile devices have many advantages like portability and mobility features. The mobile computing is integrated with cloud computing technology in order to form new technology called as MCC (Bahwaireth, Lo'ai, Tawalbeh, Benkhelifa, Jararweh, & Tawalbeh, 2016). The MCC can overcome the limitations of mobile device. In the case of implementing real MCC model, we have to take into account few challenges which cause troubles while establishing MCC environment. Mobile devices are limited by storage, battery lifetime, processing, and video streaming, augmented reality application. We should consider another important challenge in the mobility of device are moving from one network environment to another network environment. This affects quality of performance and connectivity with remote cloud (Qi, & Gani, 2012). The MCC can avoid limitations of mobile device by offloading computational task into remote cloud which requires more processing power locally. In result the remote cloud will process it with less power consumption (Benkhelifa, Welsh, Tawalbeh, Jaraweh, & Basalamah, 2015). MCC is considered as new trend among many new technologies in coming years. Generally the mobile devices connecting to cloud computing via various network technologies such as 3G and 4G. These technologies cause high cost, limited bandwidth and connectivity problems as shown in Figure 1. The important issue is nothing but security. Providing security to data from attackers over wire or wireless channel (Moh'd, Aslam, Marzi, & Tawalbeh, 2010) is a big challenge in both cloud and mobile cloud computing. The user always expects his data need to be safe and not to be affected by attackers (Tawalbeh, & Eardley, 2010]. There are many encryption techniques to protect data from attackers (Tawalbeh, Jararweh, & Mohammad, 2012; Tawalbeh, Tenca, Park, & Koc, 2004].

Since health informatics seek new ways of driving health information science research forward, for example, international research collaboration, growing demands are now placed on computer networks to provide hardware and software resources and pave a new avenue to share sensitive and private medical data from different geographic locations. This new model of service (Cloud Computing) offers tremendous opportunities for the collaborative health information science research purpose; unfortunately, it has also introduced a set of new and unfamiliar challenges, such as lack of interoperability, standardization, privacy, network security and culture resistance. In this paper, we will identify the challenges of applying healthcare cloud in the health information research and discuss potential approaches to conquer those barriers, such as audit, disaster recovery, legal, regulatory and compliance.

Figure 1. Overview of HFMS

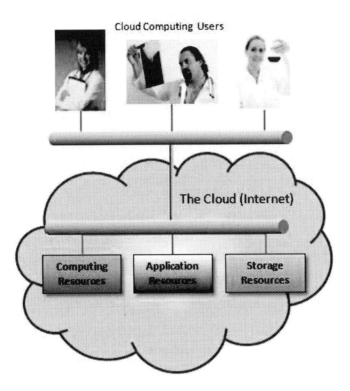

Finally, the paper will focus on the security of Cloud Computing applied in the health information science research. Research on the various security issues surrounding healthcare information systems has been heated over the last few years.

LITERATURE REVIEW

The advent of cloud computing in recent years has increased a lot of interests from different stakeholders, business organizations, institutions and government agencies. The growing interest is fueled by the promised new economic model of cloud computing which brings a change from heavy IT infrastructure invest for limiting resources that are internally managed and owned to pay per use for IT service owned by a service provider. Cloud computing paves a new avenue to deliver enterprise IT. As all major disruptive changes in technology and Internet revolution, it represents an innovative democratized of Web computing. Cloud computing not only upgrade the business models and the way IT infrastructure is being consumed, but also the underlying architecture of how we develop, deploy, run and deliver applications.

The researches have been putting lot of efforts across the world for improving Mobile cloud computing. The users require numerous application in mobile device, each of these application require data exchange and receive as well as require lot of processing power. This paper (D. Huang, 2011), describes how the mobile computing is formed from both mobile computing and cloud computing. The author also discussed about challenges, scope of MCC and development. The sensors in network technology inspired lot of researchers in world to collect data from different useful aspects of life in clouding military, hospital, IT organization, education institutions, and crowd management (Lo'ai, & Bakhader, 2016). The huge amount of data will be generated every day that data need to be stored efficiently all that data has to be stored in cloud server for storage and processing (Lo'ai, & Bakhader, 2016) . In paper (Miettinen, & Nurminen, 2010), the author has analyzed main factors which cause more power consumption in mobile devices while using remote cloud. This provided an example on how to save energy between mobile device and remote cloud. They have discussed main characteristics of modern mobile device. The jobs from users can be schedule among VMs inside cloudlet was discussed in (Shiraz& Gani, 2012). The key metrics are overhead of VM life cycle, scheduling of VM, job allocation to VM. The author in (Lo'ai, & Bakhader, 2016) has discussed importance of scheduling of VMs in cloud environment in order to reduce execution time by using Cloudsim cloud environment tool. This paper proposes architecture was fine grained cloudlet to manage all applications inside cloudlet. The cloudlet can be chosen dynamically not like previous model. The cloudlet is fixed near wireless access point. In this paper (Jararweh, Ababneh, Khreishah, & Dosari, 2014], the author had proposed mobile cloud computing model which is different from other previous published model in terms of scalability features. These paper experimental results have covered intended numbers of cloudlets available in covered area. The mobile device is known to acquire more power while running excessive applications. The author is motivated by the fact that optimizing power is important in MCC. In this paper (Al-Ayyoub, Jararweh, Lo'ai, Tawalbeh, Benkhelifa & Basalamah, 2015), the author had produced mathematical model to optimize power consumption in MCC. The author in (Tawalbeh, & Eardley, 2016), had conducted experiment on mobile device by analyzing each and every component and cloudlet each component participation in total power consumption.

Definition of Cloud Computing

Mell and Grance (2010) give a definition of cloud computing that is a model for enabling convenient, on-demand network access to a shared pool of configurable computing resource that can be rapidly provisioned and released with minimal management effort or service-provider interaction. We have already seen similar more limited applications for years, such as Google Docs or Gmail. Nevertheless, cloud computing is different from traditional systems (Mell, & Grance, 2010). Armbrust et al. introduce that cloud computing offers a wide range of computing sources on demand anywhere and anytime; eliminates an up-front commitment by cloud users; allows users to pay for use of computing resources on a short-term basis as needed and has higher utilization by multiplexing of workloads from various organizations. Cloud computing includes three models: (1) Software as a Service (SaaS): the applications (e.g. EHRs) are hosted by a cloud service provider and made available to customers over a network, typically the Internet;

(2) Platform as a Service (PaaS): the development tools (such as OS system) are hosted in the cloud and accessed through a browser (e.g. Microsoft Azure); (3) Infrastructure as a Service (IaaS): the cloud user outsources the equipment used to support operations, including storage, hardware, servers and networking components. The cloud service provider owns the equipment and is responsible for housing, running and maintaining it (Armbrust, Fox, Griffith, Joseph, Katz, Konwinski, ... & Zaharia, 2010). In the clinical environment, healthcare providers are able to remotely access the corporate Intranet via a local Internet service provider, since they have the option to have an ISDN line installed to their home or hospital linking with Cloud.

Application of Cloud Computing in Healthcare

The majority of physicians in healthcare do not always have the information they require when they need to rapidly make patient-care decisions, and patients often have to carry a paper record of their health history information with them from visit to visit. To address the problems, IBM and Active Health Management collaborate to create a cloud computing technology-based Collaborative Care solution that gives physicians and patients access to the information they need to improve the overall quality of care, without the need to invest in new infrastructure (Guo, Kuo, & Sahama, 2012). IBM facilitated American Occupational Network and HyGen Pharmaceuticals to improve patient care by digitizing health records and streamlining their business operations using cloud-based software from IBM MedTrak systems, Inc. and The System House, Inc. Their technology handles various tasks as a cloud service through the internet instead of developing, purchasing and maintaining technology onsite (Guo, Kuo, & Sahama, 2012). Acumen solution's cloud computing CRM and project management system were selected by the U.S. Department of Health & Human Services' office of the National.

Coordinator for Health IT to manage the selection and implementation of EHR systems across the country. The software will enable regional extension centers to manage interactions with medical providers related to the selection and implementation of an EHR system. Sharp Community Medical Group in San Diego will be using the collaborative.

Care solution to change the way physicians and nurse's access information throughout the hospital group's multiple electronic medical record systems to apply advanced analytical and clinical decision support to help give doctors better insight and work more closely with patient care teams (Guo, Kuo, & Sahama, 2012). One of similar example of applying cloud service in the healthcare area is the architecture of the hospital file management system (HFMS). A HFMS cluster contains a master server and multiple blocks of servers by multiple client access.

PROPOSED METHOD

I have presented an overview of the security challenges in the healthcare information sharing, and Different security concerns related to threats and vulnerabilities are analyzed. Here, we propose ways of alleviating these barriers. There are steps we can take to reduce the risk that an EHR system will be hacked:

- Keep the EHR on a segregated network, if possible. Shelter the EHR from the rest of the network infrastructure. Otherwise it's very easy for a provider's practice management system or mobile or medical device to pass on a virus or other infiltration to the EHR system.
- Check for vulnerabilities. Run risk assessments and conduct audits. Correct weaknesses discovered.
- Consider buying and running a data loss prevention software program, which runs on the perimeter server.
- Apply security patches to internet applications that are connected to the EHR systems, such as internet explorer, java and adobe acrobat.
- Make sure that the firewalls are installed properly, and that the antivirus programs are operational. Hackers are looking for easy access into computer networks. Don't make the EHR system that easy a target.

Figure 2. Proposed architecture of smart healthcare over cloud

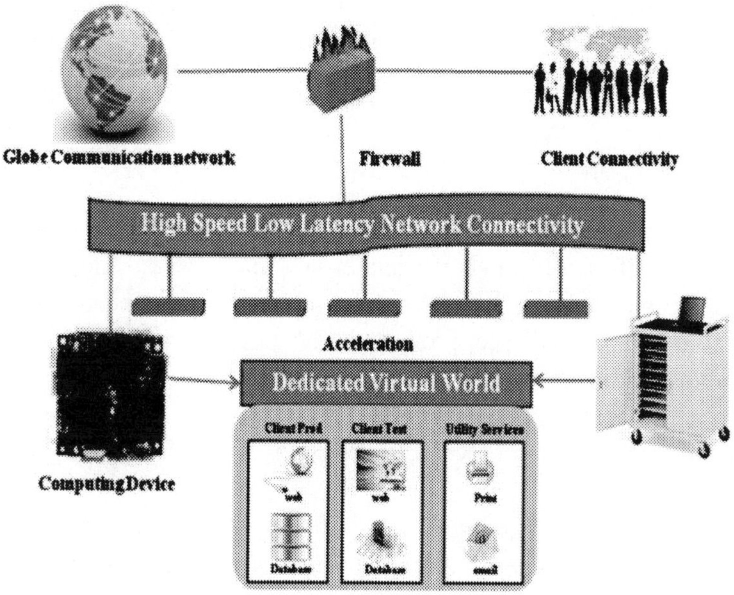

- Comply with objective, specific measures, such as those recommended by the National Institute of Standards and Technology or HITRUST, so you can defend the adequacy of the safeguards you took to protect patient information.
- Make sure that the EHR and health IT vendor contracts support off-the-shelf antivirus software.
- Designate who within the organization is responsible for maintaining the integrity of the system.
- Clearly delineate with the EHR/Health IT vendor who will be responsible for security patches. Don't assume that the vendor will do it; many vendors don't.
- Make sure that any medical software you're working with runs without "super user" rights. This makes it harder for a hacker to gain access to the records.

SECURITY MEASURES

Cloud security architecture is effective only if the correct defensive implementations are in place. An efficient cloud security architecture should recognize the issues that will arise with security management. The security management addresses these issues with security controls. These controls are put in place to safeguard any weaknesses in the system and reduce the effect of an attack. While there are many types of controls behind a cloud security architecture, they can usually be found in one of the following categories:

- **Deterrent Controls:** These controls are intended to reduce attacks on a cloud system. Much like a warning sign on a fence or a property, deterrent controls typically reduce the threat level by informing potential attackers that there will be adverse consequences for them if they proceed. (Some consider them a subset of preventive controls.)

- **Preventive Controls:** Preventive controls strengthen the system against incidents, generally by reducing if not actually eliminating vulnerabilities. Strong authentication of cloud users, for instance, makes it less likely that unauthorized users can access cloud systems, and more likely that cloud users are positively identified.

Physical Security

Cloud service providers physically secure the IT hardware (servers, routers, cables etc.) against unauthorized access, interference, theft, fires, floods etc. and ensure that essential supplies (such as electricity) are sufficiently robust to minimize the possibility of disruption. This is normally achieved by serving cloud applications from 'world-class' (i.e. professionally specified, designed, constructed, managed, monitored and maintained) data centers.

Personnel Security

Various information security concerns relating to the IT and other professionals associated with cloud services are typically handled through pre-, para- and post-employment activities such as security screening potential recruits, security awareness and training programs, proactive

Privacy

Providers ensure that all critical data (credit card numbers, for example) are masked or encrypted and that only authorized users have access to data in its entirety. Moreover, digital identities and credentials must be protected as should any data that the provider collects or produces about customer activity in the cloud.

ENCRYPTION MEASURES

Attribute-Based Encryption Algorithm

Cipher Text-Policy ABE (CP-ABE)

In the CP-ABE, the encryptor controls access strategy, as the strategy gets more complex, the design of system public key becomes more complex, and the security of the system is proved to be more difficult. The main research work of CP-ABE is focused on the design of the access structure.

In the KP-ABE, attribute sets are used to explain the encrypted texts and the private keys with the specified encrypted texts that users will have the left to decrypt.

Fully Homomorphic Encryption (FHE)

Fully Homomorphic encryption allows straightforward computations on encrypted information, and also allows computing sum and product for the encrypted data without decryption.

Searchable Encryption (SE)

Searchable Encryption is a cryptographic primitive which offers secure search functions over encrypted data. In order to improve search efficiency, an SE solution generally builds keyword indexes to securely perform user queries. Existing SE schemes can be classified into two categories: SE based on secret-key cryptography and SE based on public-key cryptography.

THE CLOUDLET USES IN E-HEALTH SYATEMS

In E-healthcare systems, the cloud computing and cloudlet technologies are required. The cloudlet technology is available to analyze patient records and also process, extract recommended features from patient database. In this system, we discussed the state of art on healthcare systems in cloud computing the application growth on healthcare is growing day by day. Also this application requires lot of computation and communication resources. The application requires access huge amount of data from organizations within and outside of the boundaries. The data pattern is typically dynamic. It is only support granularity interaction. In cloud environment (Mehmood, Faisal, & Altowaijri, 2015), the future application will have to support heterogeneous platform inside (or) outside organization (Macias, & Thomas, 2011). There is no wonder to say that the advantages of cloud computing can be helpful for the organization including healthcare systems. The healthcare organization depends on cloud environment for processing and storage of huge amount of data. Another important challenge is risk management. The cost of maintained health data is stored in cloud (Lo'ai, Bakhader, Mehmood, & Song, 2016) because of sensitivity of health data. The cost of health maintained data and also provide privacy and security laws is gradually growing. Taking decision for storing of data of healthcare and other organizations into cloud required lot of confidence. In this paper (Mehmood, Faisal, & Altowaijri, 2015), the author had proposed transport load and capacity sharing. The healthcare systems in smart city meeting demands by adapting cloud computing. The cloud computing is beneficial because distribution of cloudlet across world. The study on grid computing shared poor accessing remotely. How it useful in healthcare applications deployment is presented (Altowaijri, Mehmood, & Williams, 2010). Though the paper is focused on grid computing, it also suits for cloud computing technology. Multiple organizations and application scenarios for deployment of grid computing based on different classes of organization as well as various types of applications. The requirements of healthcare system is identified and analyzed based on result of iteration in terms of throughput. This platform identifies the computational and communicational requirements of healthcare system application. This analysis is important because the network traffic connecting health care system is dominated by analytical applications which require zero network latencies. The individual request is not heavy in terms of data but causes heavy traffic in feature communication. The cloudlet concept can be applied on this communication and computation concept in order to analyze the performance of cloud computing health care application. In this paper (Council, 2016), the author had discussed adaption of cloud solutions in healthcare systems in order to make health service provider move forward. Also, discussed privacy, security, risk management and work flow challenges. There are many papers in cloud computing focused on health care applications including foundation for health care (IBM, 2016), impact of cloud computing on healthcare (Council, 2016).

RESULTS

Comparison Between Full Homomorphic and Attribute Based Encryption

See Figures 3-5.

Figure 3. Comparison is based on time. Here the dark line refers to ABE method and light line belongs to FULL Homomorphic method. Hence ABE method is better.

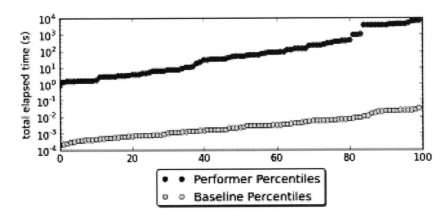

Figure 4. Comparison based on efficiency (of computation); light line represents Full homomorphic and dark line ABE method. Hence ABE method is better.

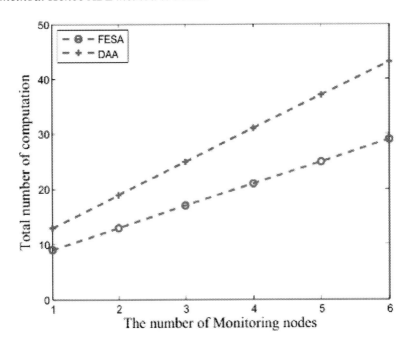

Figure 5. Comparative Strength of ABE and RSA. Hence ABE method is better.

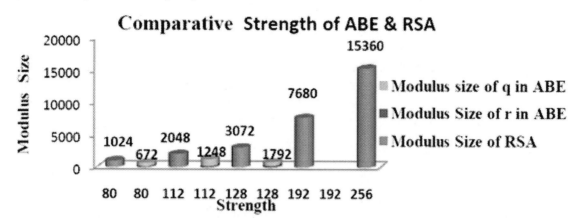

For a more accurate representation see the electronic version.

CONCLUSION

Little literature in the health information science research addresses the critical challenges and solutions of applying Cloud Computing. While the use of Cloud Computing continues to increase, legal concerns are also increasing. Although Cloud Computing providers may run afoul of the obstacles, we believe that over the long run providers will successfully navigate these challenges. By using Cloud Computing security framework, the collaborative parties can answer questions related to governance and best practice and determine whether the organization is capable of IT governance in the Cloud Computing applications.

REFERENCES

Al-Ayyoub, M., Jararweh, Y., Lo'ai, A., Tawalbeh, E., Benkhelifa & Basalamah. (2015). Power Optimization of Large Scale Mobile Cloud Computing Systems. In *Proceedings of the 3rd IEEE International conference on Future Internet of things and Cloud (Fi- Cloud)*. Rome, Italy: IEEE.

Altowaijri, S., Mehmood, R., & Williams, J. (2010, January). A quantitative model of grid systems performance in healthcare organisations. In *Intelligent Systems, Modelling and Simulation (ISMS), 2010 International Conference on* (pp. 431-436). IEEE. 10.1109/ISMS.2010.84

Ansi, I. (2003). TS 18308 health informatics-requirements for an electronic health record architecture. ISO.

Armbrust, M., Fox, A., Griffith, R., Joseph, A. D., Katz, R., Konwinski, A., ... Zaharia, M. (2010). A view of cloud computing. *Communications of the ACM, 53*(4), 50–58. doi:10.1145/1721654.1721672

Bahwaireth. (2016, June). Experimental Comparison of Simulation Tools for Efficient Cloud and Mobile Cloud Computing Applications. *EURASIP Journal on Information Security., 15*. doi:10.118613635-016-0039-y

Benkhelifa, E., Welsh, T., Tawalbeh, L., Jararweh, Y., & Basalamah, A. (2015). User profiling for energy optimisation in mobile cloud computing. *Procedia Computer Science*, *52*, 1159–1165. doi:10.1016/j.procs.2015.05.151

Benkhelifa, E., Welsh, T., Tawalbeh, L., Khreishah, A., Jararweh, Y., & Al-Ayyoub, M. (2016, March). GA-Based Resource Augmentation Negotation for Energy-Optimised Mobile Ad-hoc Cloud. In *Mobile Cloud Computing, Services, and Engineering (MobileCloud), 2016 4th IEEE International Conference on* (pp. 110-116). IEEE. 10.1109/MobileCloud.2016.25

Council, C. S. C. (2012). *Impact of cloud computing on healthcare. Technical report*. Cloud Standards Customer Council.

Fox, A., Griffith, R., Joseph, A., Katz, R., Konwinski, A., Lee, G., . . . Stoica, I. (2009). Above the clouds: A Berkeley view of cloud computing. Dept. Electrical Eng. and Comput. Sciences, University of California, Berkeley, Rep. UCB/EECS, 28(13), 2009.

Goswami. (2013). Mobile Computing. *Int. J. Adv. Res. Comput. Sci. Softw. Eng.*, 846–855.

Guo, Y., Kuo, M. H., & Sahama, T. (2012, December). Cloud computing for healthcare research information sharing. In *Cloud Computing Technology and Science (CloudCom), 2012 IEEE 4th International Conference on* (pp. 889-894). IEEE. 10.1109/CloudCom.2012.6427561

Huang, D., & ... (2011). Mobile cloud computing. *IEEE COMSOC Multimed. Commun. Tech. Comm. MMTC E-Lett.*, *6*(10), 27–31.

IBM. (2011). *Cloud Computing: Building a New Foundation for Healthcare*. IBM Corporation. Available: https://www-05.ibm.com/de/healthcare/literature/cloud-newfoundation- for-hv.pdf

Jararweh, Y., Ababneh, F., Khreishah, A., & Dosari, F. (2014). Scalable cloudlet-based mobile computing model. *Procedia Computer Science*, *34*, 434–441. doi:10.1016/j.procs.2014.07.051

Lo'ai, A. T., & Bakhader, W. (2016, August). A Mobile Cloud System for Different Useful Applications. In *Future Internet of Things and Cloud Workshops (FiCloudW), IEEE International Conference on* (pp. 295-298). IEEE.

Lo'ai, A. T., Bakhader, W., Mehmood, R., & Song, H. (2016, December). Cloudlet-based Mobile Cloud Computing for Healthcare Applications. In *Global Communications Conference (GLOBECOM)* (pp. 1-6). IEEE.

Lo'ai, A. T., Bakhader, W., Mehmood, R., & Song, H. (2016, December). Cloudlet-based Mobile Cloud Computing for Healthcare Applications. In *Global Communications Conference (GLOBECOM)* (pp. 1-6). IEEE.

Lo'ai, A. T., Bakheder, W., & Song, H. (2016, June). A mobile cloud computing model using the cloudlet scheme for big data applications. In *Connected Health: Applications, Systems and Engineering Technologies (CHASE), 2016 IEEE First International Conference on* (pp. 73-77). IEEE.

Macias, F., & Thomas, G. (2011). *Cloud Computing Advantages in the Public Sector: How Today's Government, Education, and Healthcare Organizations Are Benefiting from Cloud Computing Environments*. Retrieved from Cisco website: http://www.cisco.com/web/strategy/docs/c11-687784_cloud_omputing_wp. pdf

Mehmood, R., Faisal, M. A., & Altowaijri, S. (n.d.). Future Networked Healthcare Systems: A Review and Case Study. In *Handbook Res. Redesigning Future Internet Archit.* (pp. 564–590). Academic Press.

Mehmood, R., & Graham, G. (2015). Big data logistics: A health-care transport capacity sharing model. *Procedia Computer Science, 64*, 1107–1114. doi:10.1016/j.procs.2015.08.566

Mell, P., & Grance, T. (2010). *The NIST definition of cloud computing.* NIST.

Miettinen, A. P., & Nurminen, J. K. (2010). Energy Efficiency of Mobile Clients in Cloud Computing. *HotCloud, 10*, 4–4.

Moh'd, A., Aslam, N., Marzi, H., & Tawalbeh, L. A. (2010, July). Hardware implementations of secure hashing functions on FPGAs for WSNs. *Proceedings of the 3rd International Conference on the Applications of Digital Information and Web Technologies (ICADIWT.*

Mohammad, A., & Gutub, A. A. A. (2010). Efficient FPGA implementation of a programmable architecture for GF (p) elliptic curve crypto computations. *Journal of Signal Processing Systems for Signal, Image, and Video Technology, 59*(3), 233–244. doi:10.100711265-009-0376-x

Qi, H., & Gani, A. (2012, May). Research on mobile cloud computing: Review, trend and perspectives. In *Digital Information and Communication Technology and it's Applications (DICTAP), 2012 Second International Conference on* (pp. 195-202). IEEE.

Shiraz, M., & Gani, A. (2012, February). Mobile cloud computing: Critical analysis of application deployment in virtual machines. In *Proc. Int'l Conf. Information and Computer Networks (ICICN'12)* (*Vol. 27*). Academic Press.

Tawalbeh, L. A., Alassaf, N., Bakheder, W., & Tawalbeh, A. (2015, October). Resilience Mobile Cloud Computing: Features, Applications and Challenges. In *e-Learning (econf), 2015 Fifth International Conference on* (pp. 280-284). IEEE.

Tawalbeh, L. A., Jararweh, Y., & Mohammad, A. (2012). An integrated radix-4 modular divider/multiplier hardware architecture for cryptographic applications. *The International Arab Journal of Information Technology, 9*(3).

Tawalbeh, L. A., Tenca, A. F., Park, S., & Koc, C. K. (2004). A dualfield modular division algorithm and architecture for application specific hardware. In *Thirty-Eighth Asilomar Conference on Signals, Systems, and Computers* (pp. 483-487). IEEE Press.

Tawalbeh, M., Eardley, A., & Tawalbeh, L. (2016). Studying the energy consumption in mobile devices. *Procedia Computer Science, 94*, 183–189. doi:10.1016/j.procs.2016.08.028

Zimmerman, J. B. (1999). Mobile computing: Characteristics, business benefits, and the mobile framework. *University of Maryland European Division-Bowie State, 10*, 12.

This research was previously published in Contemporary Applications of Mobile Computing in Healthcare Settings edited by R. Rajkumar, pages 34-50, copyright year 2018 by Medical Information Science Reference (an imprint of IGI Global).

Section 7
Critical Issues and Challenges

Chapter 94
A Comparative Study of Privacy Protection Practices in the US, Europe, and Asia

Noushin Ashrafi
University of Massachusetts Boston, USA

Jean-Pierre Kuilboer
University of Massachusetts Boston, USA

ABSTRACT

This article describes how national and international companies in the US and Europe, as well as newly industrialized countries such as China and India, are striving to gain consumer trust by offering visible and meaningful Privacy Protection Policies (PPP) on their websites. This article deploys large sets of data and descriptive indicators to compare and contrast the extent of the visibility, specificity, and lucidity of privacy policies posted by interactive companies on the Internet. Examining about 2000 Interactive companies in the USA, Europe, and Asia provides a measure of divergent responses to the growing demand for privacy protection. The results of this comparative study should help interested readers from the business world, academics, and administrations get a grasp of the extent of efforts by international corporations to protect personal information privacy in an increasingly global economy.

INTRODUCTION

The combined effect of a global economy and the propagation of e-commerce has elevated the privacy and security issues to a worldwide platform. Online commercial transactions create and deploy an unprecedented amount of information about individuals. While the flow of information is essential for the growth of international commerce, its side effect; increased level of vulnerability and threats of breaching personal privacy, poses a real concern for individuals, the business community, and society (Birnhack, 2008).

DOI: 10.4018/978-1-5225-8176-5.ch094

From a practical point of view when the business world is in constant transition and almost every business is going online; to stay competitive, it is increasingly important to gather data related to personal information including users' demographics, habits, preferences, and tastes. Businesses believe they can provide better services if they access personal information for better target prospects. But, as personal data become electronically available, the idea of who collects and crunches the most amounts of data becomes more critical. Personal information is collected, shared, exchanged, and often sold. The improper disclosure of critical personal information could have alarming consequences, the least of which is selling the information to the highest bidder in the market for marketing and selling purposes.

The purpose of this study is to build on the existing research while taking into account the practical side of privacy protection practices. The study is exploratory and offers a descriptive analysis allowing to compare and contrast the extent of fair treatment of consumers' personal information in the US, Europe, and Asia by interactive companies. To make a reasonable assessment of privacy protection practices in the target countries, it is essential that readers have a sense of the basic laws, regulations, directives, as well as the specific issues regarding how privacy is perceived and dealt with by different nations.

The study includes the United States. Since European countries within the EU have their own directives, it would have been impossible to investigate each and every country, hence three countries were used as examples. France, Britain, and Germany were chosen not only because they are important members of EU, but also due to the capabilities of the authors of this study to speak the languages. The two Asian countries; China and India were chosen because these two nations are becoming major players in the global economy. The authors were also interested to investigate the impact of company size, measured by the annual revenue, on the visibility and the extent of compliance with privacy policies.

The objectives of this study are threefold (1) to provide insight into how privacy policies are practiced in different parts of the world, (2) help constituencies from the business world, academics, and administrations view the differences regarding privacy protection policies and practices in a global economy, and (3) get a grasp of underlying issues in proper contexts. The organization of the paper is as follows: Next section provides background information, followed by an overview of information privacy protection from a global point of view. Definition and details of Fair Information Practice Principles (FIPPs) are described. The methodology, findings of this study and conclusions are presented. The article is concluded with citing of the limitation and suggestions for future research.

BACKGROUND

Assessing advantages and disadvantages of personal data collection and how different countries perceive and deal with information privacy have been topics of interest for researchers as well as e-commerce practitioners (Greenberg, Wong-On-Wing, & Lui, 2008; Schmidt et al., 2008; Susanto et al., 2013; Treiblmaier & Chong, 2011; Reay et al., 2009; Sumeeth et al., 2010; Totterdale, 2010; White et al., 2011; Srinivasan & Barker, 2012). Numerous studies have investigated privacy protection practices in the US (Caudill & Murphy, 2000; Milne & Culnan, 2002; Pavlou, 2003; Milne & Culnan, 2004; Ashrafi & Kuilboer, 2005). Fewer studies have examined European regulatory practices (Armstrong, 2004; Massa-Mias, Ashrafi, Koehler, & Kuilboer, 2007; Singh & Hill, 2003; Warren & Dearnley, 2005).

Most recently, India and China have become significant players in the arena of global e-commerce. The rapid growth of the economy along with outsourcing and the development and expansion of international companies promise progress and prosperity in India and China. To maintain and expand their roles as viable players in the networked market economy, both countries are making efforts to embark on implementing policies to protect the personal privacy of individuals. Yet, privacy protection research in India has been limited and is primarily focused on consumer behavior and their interpretation of the notion of privacy (Basu, 2010; Gupta, Iyer, & Weisskirch, 2010; Brahmbhatt, 2010; Bajaj, 2012; Ardhapurkar, 2010.) Similarly, the amount of research on exploring developments in privacy protection practices in China has been restricted to cultural aspects and the explanation of privacy law and regulations (Xue, 2010; Wu et al., 2011; Medlin & Chen, 2010; Greenleaf, 2009).

Multinational companies that rely on the transnational market as a substantial source of revenue find it necessary to adhere to the cross-border data flow laws of the European Union and consequently Fair Information Privacy Practice Principles of the U.S.A. (Wright, 2012). The effectiveness of privacy protection practices and the commitment of the companies to online privacy should be of major interest to academics and practitioners. Existing literature, however, has mostly focused on the concept of privacy as perceived in each of these regions and the relevant privacy regulations. The focus of this paper is on actual practices and the extent of the compliance and the implementation process. Statistical analysis, missing from most of the existing literature, is used to uncover the trends and changes in privacy practices supporting the objectives of this study.

CONTRASTING VIEWS OF PRIVACY PROTECTION

Due to the globalization of e-commerce, the threat of breach of privacy and the necessity to protect personal information are on the rise. The United States and European Union (EU) have been the pioneers in initiating privacy protection and setting up guidelines that represent concepts concerning fair information practice in an electronic marketplace. In recent years, the U.S.A. has continued to lead the inquiry into ways that online entities collect and use personal information and EU has been updating the Directives (95/46/EC) to protect the privacy of all EU citizens, especially as it relates to processing, using or exchanging personal data (Hustinx, 2013). In the meantime, developing countries like India and China are playing more important roles in the global e-commerce environment. Although the underlying principles are based on Fair Information Practice Principles (FIPPs), each nation interprets and reacts to privacy-related issues differently. This differentiation stems from how privacy is perceived and defined in developed and developing countries. A brief explanation of the perception of privacy and implementation process in the targeted countries lays the ground for better interpretation of data analysis.

Privacy Protection Policies in U.S.A. and Europe

The US and EU are the largest trade partners and have several sets of international cross-border business rules. But, for decades trans-Atlantic privacy policies have been at odds with each other. Europe treats data protection as an element of public law, which puts the citizen in control of the collection and use of personal information. The latest attempt to reinforce and unify data protection for all individuals within the European Union (EU) is the requirement that all organizations that collect, store or process data on residents of the EU must demonstrate full compliance with the European General Data Protection Regulation (GDPR) (Hyland, 2017). The US, however, relies on industry self-regulation and technological mechanism for fair information practices. The concept of personal information privacy initiated in Europe when the council of Europe began the study of effects of technology on human rights in 1968. In 1995 the European Union introduced the Data Protection Directive for its member states. As a result, many organizations doing business within the EU began to draft policies to comply with this Directive. In the same year, the U.S. Federal Trade Commission (FTC) published the Fair Information Practice Principles (FIPPs), which provided a set of non-binding governing principles for the commercial use of personal information. The bill of rights in the United States does provide some guidance for the privacy policy but lacks the reach and the uniformity to apply it in today's global environment. Whereas in the U.S., markets and self-regulation, but not law, shape information privacy, in Europe it is the responsibility of the government to protect citizens 'right to privacy.'

To sum up, in Europe, privacy is seen as a fundamental human right, in the U.S., privacy is seen as a commodity subject to market and is cast in economic terms. In July 2000, the US and the European Union signed the "Safe Harbor Agreement" to allow safe trans-border flow of data (Smith, 2001). The Safe Harbor agreement guided U.S. companies to respect European privacy laws in their business dealings with the EU or face prosecution by European authorities. However, the Safe Harbor Agreement was annulled by the Court of Justice of the EU. While the GDPR prohibits companies from transferring personal data outside of the European Economic Area, the EU-US Privacy Shield agreement (EU-US Privacy Shield 2017) allows European companies to continue to keep the data in the cloud using US-based companies such as Google, Dropbox, and Amazon (Weiss, 2016).

Privacy Protection Policies in China

China, like many other countries, continues to grapple with the issue of whether and how to protect personal information in light of new technologies and services designed to collect and use personal information in new and different ways. However, the privacy protection and solution take a different profile from those in the United States and Europe; it is more capacious and murkier in content (Greenberg, Wong-On-Wing, & Lui, 2008; Schmidt et al., 2008). As the population of Chinese netizens had reached 564 million, and the number of mobile phone users is approaching 1.1 billion, turning China into the biggest media sharing country, according to a survey conducted by China Youth Daily in 2002, more than 55% of the interviewees believe it was harder and harder to protect privacy. By November 2015, the number of cell phones reached 1.3 billion.

In response to the nationwide concern, the Chinese government passed the Decision of the Standing Committee of the National People's Congress on Strengthening Information Protection on Networks in 2012. The "Decision" mainly emphasizes three criteria: (1) Protecting Personal Digital Information, (2) Standardizing the Collection and Application of Digital Information, and (3) Assuring Online Identity. One of the more far-reaching legislative efforts in recent years was a new regulation issued by the Ministry of Industry and Information Technology ("MIIT") governing the collection, storage and use of personal information by Internet companies. This regulation was put into effect on March 15th, 2012. Internet Regulations provided a definition of personal information for the first time as 'information relating to a user that, alone or in conjunction with other information, is sufficient for a third party to identify the user.' While the 2012 Internet Regulations obviously fall short of all international standards because of its lack of access and correction rights, and its limited scope to Internet information providers, it meets the basic standards of the principles in the OECD Guidelines in many other respects. The other significant place at which it falls short is that the limitations on disclosure, which only applies to user-provided personal data, excluding those that have been collected from third parties or generated from transactions. Yet 2012 Internet Regulations is a very significant step for China, even if it would be considered quite limited in other countries.

Privacy Protection Policies in India

As India becomes a leader in Business Process Outsourcing (BPO), increasing amounts of personal information from other countries are flowing into India, raising questions about the ability of Indian companies to adequately protect this wealth of information (Kumaraguru, Cranor & Newton, 2005). International companies are major clients of Indian outsourcing and businesses rely on Indian companies to protect their personal information leading to an increasing concern about India's privacy laws. Whether the Indian outsourcing industry can properly protect personal data has become an issue to the point that a research conducted by scholars at Carnegie Mellon has suggested that the Indian high-tech workforce may not be sufficiently aware of privacy issues and that the outsourcing industry and international businesses may need to provide privacy training to their employees (Kumaraguru & Cranor, 2006; Kumaraguru, Cranor & Newton, 2005).

To address these concerns, government officials, organizations, and lawmakers are discussing the creation of privacy laws in India that would mandate privacy protections for data from other countries handled by India's outsourcing industry (Kumaraguru, Cranor & Newton, 2005). The Data Security Council of India (DSCI) was established in 2008 as a not-for-profit, independent entity. The service providers in India faced with a major challenge of demonstrating compliance with laws of countries where the data originates and led by National Association of Software and Services Companies (NASSCOM), established DSCI as a Self-Regulatory Organizations (SRO.) DSCI has established a privacy framework that is composed of nine privacy principles that are as follows: notice, choice and consent, collection limitation, use limitation, access and correction, security, disclosure to third parties, openness, and accountability. The implementation of these privacy principles in IT/BPO companies is ensured through the DSCI Privacy Framework, which focuses on information visibility of cross-border data flows from a client in any country to the service provider in India. At each stage of data flow, risks associated with privacy and security of data are identified and mitigated through the best practices of DSIC. For further effectiveness, DSCI is in the process of creating the infrastructure to foster awareness of privacy protection requirements while training IT/BPO companies to develop privacy policies and carry out privacy impact assessment.

FAIR INFORMATION PRACTICES PRINCIPLES

With all the discrepancies on the perception of the concept of privacy and the protection of personal information, Fair Information Practices Principles (FIPPs) provide a set of reliable and consistent principles that lay the ground for most privacy protection practices. FIPPs are defined as a set of "procedures that provide individuals with control over the disclosure and subsequent use of their personal information and govern the interpersonal treatment that consumers receive" Culnan and Bies (2003, page 330). The growth of information technologies and globalization, coupled with several well-publicized breaches of consumer privacy protection (Desai, 2009), has led to the realization that personal data require more effective safeguards. Fair Information Practice Principles (FIPPs), a self-regulatory enforcement initiative, is the result of such awareness. The FIPPs are designed so that the organization implementing the FIPPs will abide by a set of ethics and values that are widely accepted by most consumers (Folger & Bies, 1989).

FIPPs was initiated by the United States' Federal Trade Commission, but the concept of privacy protection was soon spread to other countries in Europe. The Organization for Economic Cooperation and Development (OECD) Guidelines, Council of Europe Convention, and European Union Data Protection Directive relied on FIPPs as core principles. The prevalent privacy protection practices in the United States follow these self-regulatory guidelines. These guiding principles are primarily concerned about the manner in which personal information is collected and used. They are formulated to assure that the practice is fair and provides adequate information privacy protection.

No single law in the US provides a more comprehensive treatment to the issue than FIPPs. While not mandated, these principles provide guidance on how to draft privacy policies.

Publishing Privacy policies on a company's website are the first and necessary step for information privacy protection (Culnan, 2000). Privacy policy principles are guidelines to give the consumer the right to know what information is being collected, object when information is utilized for purposes other than those authorized, view their information and correct any erroneous information. FIP provides a definition of the building blocks of each principle to avoid any misinterpretation of the principles. In what follows, a brief description of each of these principles including their building blocks is provided.

Notice

Privacy notices represent the manner in which the collector acquires, uses, shares, protects and provides access to an individual's personal information. The rest of the information practices become meaningful when the consumer has the notice of an entity's policies and his/her rights with respect to their personal information. Notice can be further defined by its building blocks as listed below:

- **Personal Information:** The organization posting the privacy policy should clearly state why information is collected, what information is collected, how it will be used, and the information retention policy.
- **Cookies:** Cookies are instruments through which the browsing and buying habits of consumers can be tracked (Rogers, 2004; Wang, Lee & Wang, 1998). The user should be notified that when visiting a site, information might be fed to a "cookie" file, either as a session cookie to track visits or as a permanent cookie on the user's computer for future reference (King, 2003.)
- **Privacy Policy Amendment:** The user should be notified of any changes to existing policies. An amendment should clarify the changes and specify the date they are to be implemented.
- **Public Forum:** Marketers or others can get e-mail addresses or identify visitors from bulletin boards and newsgroups. Visitors should be warned to this effect, so they can use available anonymizing technology in order to keep their privacy.

Choice

This guideline also referred to as Consent gives the consumer control over how personal data may be used and allows them to remove their names from existing marketing lists before such lists are shared with third parties. The building blocks of this principle are:

- **Opt-out/Opt-In:** Users should be able to Opt-Out not only from the collection of personal, unnecessary data but also from direct communications about additional products and services. In "Opt-In" the client chooses what to share and with whom.
- **Third-Party Privacy Policy:** When a company contains links to other sites, it should not share users' personal information with those websites.
- **IP Address:** When the website records the referrer and destination of a visitor, the data should not be personalized in order to complete the profile of the clients.
- **Children:** An organization should not contact children under age 13 about special offers for marketing purposes without a parents' permission.
- **Survey and Questionnaire:** The information collected via surveys and questionnaires online should be aggregated. No personally identifiable information may then be shared with the third parties without hampering personal privacy.

Access

This guideline refers to the individual's ability to access personal information collected by a company. This Principle includes consumers' ability to verify and contest its accuracy. Furthermore, the access must be inexpensive and timely in order to be useful to the consumer. The building blocks are:

- **Contact Information:** The organization should offer means to remediate potential errors in the data collection, retention, or use. Convenient points of contact should be available so that the user can review, change, and/or correct his/her information.
- **Registration:** When a user is registered and has an account with a firm, he/she should be able to review their personal information and request the deletion of their account, or any of their personal information held by the company in an easy and convenient way.
- **Correction to Personal Information:** The user should be given the opportunity to examine his or her personal information and be able to correct it in a convenient and inexpensive manner.

Security

FIP requires websites to take reasonable measures to protect the security of customer personal information. The data collector is obligated to protect personal data against unauthorized use as well as loss or destruction. Although security requirements vary depending on the nature and sensitivity of collected data, the firm must maintain security programs to minimize threats as well as inform customers about companies' security practices. In other words, the companies are required not only to have a security program but also to disclose their security practices in order to enhance consumer confidence. While no security system is absolutely impenetrable, software systems and security procedures should be constantly reviewed, refined, and upgraded to reflect new tools, laws, and information as they become available. To this effect, encryption and authentication should be used when appropriate.

METHODOLOGY

To compare and contrast the privacy protection practices, data were collected on posted policies by the top 500 interactive companies in each country. All together close to 2000 websites were visited and four spreadsheets, one for each country were created. The three European countries; Germany, Great Britain, and France were lumped together and are referred to as EU henceforward. Each spreadsheet contained the names, website of each company, and the four basic principles of FIPPs namely Notice, Choice, Access, and Security. To get more detailed information the basic principles were drilled down into their pre-defined parameters such as cookies to trace electronic "footprints" that consumers leave behind. These were labeled as pre-defined to distinguish them from parameters that were discovered while examining the websites of the interactive companies. After ensuring that the selected companies actually have an interactive website, the authors investigated the percentage of interactive companies that had published privacy policies on their websites and drilled further down to examine the depth of their pledge to privacy protection.

All parameters were coded into 0's and 1's, 1 indicating the presence of the said parameter and 0 indicating the lack of it. Descriptive indicators were drawn from these spreadsheets and were calculated to find out the extent of compliance (in percentage) of each country to FIPPs and furthermore to investigate each country idiosyncrasies as they see information privacy and deal with them.

The data source for the top 500 US companies was from the list of fortune 500 published by CNN Money. For EU two websites were used; List of largest European Companies and Best Companies-Europe. For India, the Economic Times 500 list (ET 500) was used for reference. Economic Times is the world's second-biggest Financial Daily, after the Wall Street Journal. The list is one of India's most awaited lists as it presents the Top 500 Indian companies in the order of decreasing Market Capital. For 500 interactive companies in China, China.org.cn which lists the top 500 enterprises of China was referenced.

FINDINGS

The first task was to find out the percentage of companies that actually have posted PPP on their websites. Table 1 shows the percentages of Companies having Privacy Policy posted on their website.

Table 1. % of companies with PPP posted on their websites

Country	% of Companies Having Privacy Policy Posted on Their Website
US	82%
EU	71%
India	40%
China	29%

Table 2 illustrates the differences among nations to respond to the most fundamental element of compliance with PPP; informing the users that they indeed have a mechanism in place to allow some control of personal information. Posting of PPP on company websites does not necessarily mean that compliance is being carried on. For example, a company may indicate on its website that there is a privacy protection policy in place, but when looked into it, there may be no content or just a partial explanation of privacy policies such as notice, choice, access, and security. Further analysis is required to reveal to what extent our targeted regions detailed the pre-defined parameters (Notice, Choice, Access, and Security).

As expected, the highest percentages of US companies have the four major principles as part of their privacy protection policies, followed by the aggregate of three European countries. India takes the third place and is ahead of Chinese companies. It is interesting to observe that the EU companies lag behind the US although they are governed by the EU law with an even stricter set of rules. Similarly, India leads China with its self- regulatory policies as compared to China's government-imposed regulation of privacy protection.

Next step was to drill down to examine the extent of the commitment of the business to the details of privacy protection policies. For such investigation, FIP principles were selected as benchmarks. While Table 2 shows the percentages of companies in each country to include the major four principles as part of their privacy protection policies, Table 3 goes further to show the components of each principle

Table 2. % of companies that posted the four policies

	US	EU	China	India
Notice	79%	71%	17%	27%
Choice	65%	55%	21%	16%
Access	68%	44%	6%	21%
Security	64%	46%	18%	26%

Table 3. % of companies that have mentioned pre-defined parameters

Notice	**US**	**EU**	**India**	**China**
Personal Information	85%	32%	32%	19%
Cookies	78%	57%	26%	8%
Privacy Policy Amendment	80%	11%	23%	5%
Public Forum	77%	NA	NA	NA
Choice				
Third Party Privacy Policy	80%	22%	33%	21%
IP-Address	67%	NA	NA	NA
Children	48%	10%	5%	4%
Contact Info.	75%	39%	23%	7%
Access				
Registration	63%	NA	NA	NA
Correction to personal info	78%	NA	22%	6%

and the percentage of companies that have mentioned clearly those components as their posted privacy protection policies.

One finding worth mentioning is that while the majority of US companies comply with all components of four principles, companies in EU, India, and China don't necessarily comply with all components. Examples are a public forum, IP-address, and registration. As mentioned above, FIP principles are used as the benchmark, thus it makes sense for US companies to comply thoroughly with FIPPs, where, for example, EU members with their specific directives would have different priorities, one of which is the retention of information for a given period of time.

Correlation between revenue and compliance was another interesting question. Revenue for US companies was available and was classified in groups of 100 (in millions) from the most revenue and profit generating company to the least revenue and profit generating ones on the list of 500 interactive companies in the US. Table 4 shows no significant difference leading to the conclusion that companies in a different range of revenue respond to users' concern about privacy almost equally.

A number of pre-defined metrics were selected to investigate the possible variations among US companies separated by the range of revenue. It is interesting to note that the range of variation is almost negligible; from 2% for personal information to 7% for IP address as indicated in Table 5.

In the course of research, the authors came across some metrics that did not gel with the other pre-defined parameters and they were particular to the financial sector rather than the holistic ones that apply across the sample size. As the global e-commerce grows, these additional parameters may become standard parameters. While analyzing the data for US 500, a trend was observed in three categories from US companies; fraud alert, privacy and online safety tips and mobile application privacy.

Table 4. % of companies in various range of revenue that have posted PPP on their website

US Top 500 Visibility						
Rank	1-11	101-200	201-300	301-400	401-500	n/a
Privacy Policy Visibility	18%	17%	15%	16%	14%	18%

Table 5. % of companies that have included pre-defined metrics on their ppp

US TOP 500 Pre-Defined Metrics						
	1-100	101-200	201-300	301-400	401-500	Range of Variation
Cookies	17%	17%	15%	14%	14%	17%-14%=3%
IP Address	16%	17%	14%	10%	10%	7%
Children Policy	12%	10%	10%	9%	8%	4%
Conditions of Use	17%	18%	15%	15%	16%	3%
Notices & Revisions	18%	17%	15%	14%	14%	4%
Contact Info	18%	16%	12%	14%	14%	6%
Personal info	18%	18%	17%	16%	16%	2%
Communication Policy	10%	15%	12%	13%	12%	5%
Third Party Notice	19%	17%	15%	14%	14%	4%

As technology advances and access to technology becomes more mobile, need for metrics to cover and safeguard the personal information on these devices is on the rise. Figure 1 shows a low percentage for the emerging categories. This, however, is expected to rise at a faster rate in near future due to shifting of some basic tasks such as checking the bank balance, news, and online payments through the mobile phones.

DISCUSSION

In the international landscape of an economic system, in which investment in and the ownership of means of production and distribution has crossed national boundaries, privacy policies by one nation affect the others. Competition to attract customers intensifies the efforts by the service providers to gain their trust by complying with privacy protection policies. Overall as the anxiety of customer over the breach of their personal information rises, the free market responses accordingly by putting in place mechanism to reassure the customers that they will keep some control over their personal data. It is also evident that as long as there is no serious penalty when it comes to non-compliance with the policies mandated by the government, self-regulation based on the free market competition works the best. The major hurdle for implementation of a single privacy practice has been the absence of standardization among nations. Also, certain landscapes require the policies to be more stringent or less intrusive for the service provider.

This empirical study reveals that basically, nations around the world have responded to the notion of privacy protection in similar ways, but with different emphasis. The widely accepted FIPPs are the basis for privacy protection practices in the United States, Canada, Europe and other parts of the world. Publishing these principles help a consumer choose whether to disclose personal information to the company as well as helping them decide whether to transact with the company in question (Culnan & Milberg, 1998). The discrepancies of the degree of privacy protection practices among the nations chosen

Figure 1. % of top three emerging parameters in the US

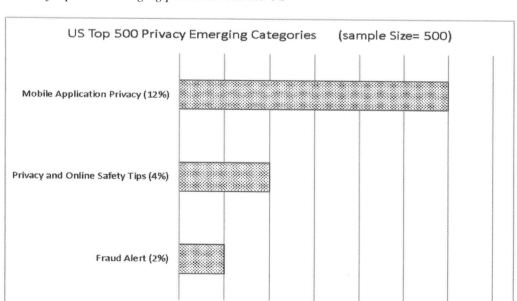

for this research are interesting, but not surprising; the United States self-regulatory practices yield the best results, followed by regulated practices of Europe. India and China are lagging behind as they are at the beginning of entering the international market.

Comparing the findings of this study to our previous work helps determine the impact of globalization on the development, process, and implementation of privacy protection policies. Table 6 illustrates the trend of compliance in the last decade.

As Table 6 shows, in 2003 India and China had no interest in PPP whereas their participation in privacy protection of personal information rose to 40% and 29% respectively in a decade of intense globalization.

Because of directives tailored for each country, it was difficult to focus on uniform parameters that were used across the European countries and not all categories and metrics analyzed for the US applied to the EU companies. While comparing the basic principles such as notice, choice, access, and security was possible, there was not exactly a common platform on which to further compare the US and EU results. The same problem existed for comparing the US with India and China, but that was expected. An upward trend shows efforts by all companies to gain customers' trust by publishing the PPP on their websites. India and China show rapid improvement where the State shows the least upward trend.

Comparing the extent of compliance with privacy policies in developed countries such as US and EU with developing countries such as India and China, the Table 7 shows that the latter two are lagging behind.

By any means of calculation (range of values, median, and mean) it is evident that developed countries are in a better shape than developing countries.

The third interesting finding was the effectiveness of self- regulatory versus government-imposed privacy protection policies. Comparing US and India where practices are self-regulated to China and EU where the compliance is mandatory reveals another interesting outcome that self –regulation is more effective than government-imposed regulations. This is depicted in Table 8.

Table 6. A comparison of compliance with FIP for 2003, 2009, and 2013

Compliance With PPP			
	2003	**2009**	**2013**
The United States of America	73%	81%	82%
European Union	65%*	67%*	71%*
India	NA	27.6%	40%
China	NA	18.4%	29%

*Average of UK, Germany, and France

Table 7. % of companies in developed versus developing countries that have posted four policies

Country	Notice		Choice		Access		Security		3 Modes of Calculation		
Developed	US	EU	US	EU	US	EU	US	EU	Range	median	Mean
	79%	71%	65%	55%	68%	44%	64%	46%	44%-79%	64.5%	61.5%
Developing	India	China	India	China	India	China	India	China	Range	Median	Mean
	27%	17%	16%	21%	21%	6%	26%	18%	6%-27%	29.5%	19%

Table 8. % of companies in self-regulated versus government imposed

Policy	Notice		Choice		Access		Security		3 Modes of Calculation		
Regulated	China	EU	China	EU	China	EU	China	EU	Range	Median	Mean
	17%	71%	21%	55%	6%	44%	18%	46%	6%-71%	32.5%	34.75%
Non-Regulated	India	US	India	US	India	US	India	US	Range	Median	Mean
	27%	79%	16%	65%	21%	68%	26%	64%	16%-79%	45.5%	53.88%

Interestingly, mandatory regulations do not prompt higher compliance as it is evidenced in Table 8.

CONCLUSION

Global growth and infiltration of e-commerce have changed the boundaries of transaction processing allowing a large quantity of personal information to move across national borders hence increasing the possibility of data trailing and information trafficking. Countries around the world have established their own privacy protection policies, with some common threads, however, the implementation remains a problem as efforts for lobbying and delaying prohibit passing of regulations that are comprehensive and effective. As a result, a great deal of guessing game is on the display.

This research is exploratory and descriptive in nature. A large set of data and descriptive analysis are used to discover some interesting trends in privacy protection practices by interactive companies. With the day to day increase in e-commerce activity and customers shifting from the traditional brick and mortar model of doing business the need to cater to the personal service and preferences of the customers has become the priority of e-commerce business to sustain their online business. This study was designed to gauge the global response to the issue of protecting information privacy. Large sets of data told us the story of compliance for different settings; US, EU, India, and China. The future research should include South America specifically pivotal countries such as Brazil and its 2014 Brazilian Internet Act and the 2015 draft of Personal Data Privacy Bill. It would also be interesting to look again in a few years to see how international companies in China and India are catching up with western hemisphere. There is no uniformity in the specifics of privacy policies among countries, but as globalization becomes stronger and more profound in years to come, it might be different.

REFERENCES

Ardhapurkar, S., Srivastava, T., & Sharma, S. (2010). Privacy and data protection in cyberspace in Indian environment. *International Journal of Engineering Science and Technology*, 2(5), 942–951.

Armstrong, J. (2004). Privacy in Europe: The new agenda. *Journal of Internet Law*, 8(5), 3–7.

Ashrafi, N., & Kuilboer, J.-P. (2005). Online privacy policies: An empirical perspective on self-regulatory practices. *Journal of E-Commerce in Organizations*, 3(4), 61–74. doi:10.4018/jeco.2005100104

Bajaj, K. (2012). Promoting data protection standards through contracts: The Case of the Data Security Council of India. *The Review of Policy Research*, *29*(1), 131–139. doi:10.1111/j.1541-1338.2011.00541.x

Basu, S. (2010). Policy-making, technology and privacy in India. *Indian Journal of Law and Technology*, *6*(1), 65–88.

Birnhack, M. D. (2008). The EU Data Protection Directive: An engine of a global regime. *Elsevier. Computer Law & Security Report*, *24*(6), 508–520. doi:10.1016/j.clsr.2008.09.001

Brahmbhatt, B. J. (2010). Position and perspective of privacy laws in India. In *AAAI Spring Symposium: Intelligent Information Privacy Management* (pp. 29-33).

Caudill, E. M., & Murphy, P. E. (2000). Consumer online privacy: Legal and ethical issues. *Journal of Public Policy & Marketing*, *19*(1), 7–19. doi:10.1509/jppm.19.1.7.16951

Culnan, M. J. (2000). Protecting privacy online: Is self-regulation working? *Journal of Public Policy & Marketing*, *19*(1), 20–26. doi:10.1509/jppm.19.1.20.16944

Culnan, M. J., & Bies, R. J. (2003). Consumer privacy: Balancing economic and justice considerations. *The Journal of Social Issues*, *59*(2), 323–342. doi:10.1111/1540-4560.00067

Folger, R., & Bies, R. J. (1989). Managerial responsibilities and procedural justice. *Employee Responsibilities and Rights Journal*, *2*(2), 79–90. doi:10.1007/BF01384939

Greenberg, R., Wong-On-Wing, B., & Lui, G. (2008). Culture and consumer trust in online businesses. *Journal of Global Information Management*, *16*(3), 26–44. doi:10.4018/jgim.2008070102

Greenleaf, G. (2009). Five years of the APEC Privacy Framework: Failure or promise? *Computer Law & Security Review*, *25*(1), 28–43. doi:10.1016/j.clsr.2008.12.002

Gupta, B., Iyer, L. S., & Weisskirch, R. S. (2010). Facilitating global e-commerce: A comparison of consumers' willingness to disclose personal information online in the US and in India. *Journal of Electronic Commerce Research*, *11*(1), 41–52.

Hustinx, P. (2013). EU data protection law: The review of Directive 95/46/EC and the proposed general data protection regulation. Collected courses of the European University Institute's Academy of European Law, 24th Session on European Union Law.

Hyland, J. (2017). Data Protection in EU Businesses: An Introduction to GDPR. *DBS Business Review*, *1*, 146–148. doi:10.22375/dbsbr.v1.12

King, I. (2003). Online privacy in Europe: New regulation for cookies. *Information & Communications Technology Law*, *12*(3), 225–236. doi:10.1080/1360083032000198745

Kumaraguru, P., & Cranor, L. (2006, January). Privacy in India: Attitudes and awareness. In *Privacy Enhancing Technologies* (pp. 243–258). Berlin, Heidelberg: Springer. doi:10.1007/11767831_16

Kumaraguru, P., Cranor, L. F., & Newton, E. (2005, September). Privacy perceptions in India and the United States: An interview study. In *Proceedings of the 33rd Research Conference on Communication, Information and Internet Policy (TPRC)* (pp. 23-25).

Massa-Mias, G., Ashrafi, N., Koehler, W., & Kuilboer, J.-P. (2007). Privacy policy regulations- An empirical investigation. In *Proceedings of the 38th Annual Meeting Decision Sciences Institute*, Phoenix, AZ, November 17-20.

Medlin, B. D., & Chen, C. C. (2010). *A global perspective of laws and regulations dealing with information security and privacy. In Information Communication Technology Law, Protection, and Access Rights* (pp. 136–150). Hershey, PA: IGI Global.

Milne, G. R., & Culnan, M. J. (2002). Using the content of online privacy notice to inform public policy: A longitudinal analysis of the 1998-2001 U.S web surveys. *The Information Society*, *18*(5), 345–359. doi:10.1080/01972240290108168

Milne, G. R., & Culnan, M. J. (2004). Strategies for reducing online privacy risks. Why consumers read (or don't read) online privacy notices. *Journal of Interactive Marketing*, *18*(3), 15–29. doi:10.1002/dir.20009

Pavlou, P. A. (2003). Integrating trust and risk with the consumer acceptance of electronic commerce: Technology Acceptance Model. *International Journal of Electronic Commerce*, *7*(3), 69–103.

Reay, I., Beatty, P., Dick, S., & Miller, J. (2009). Do you know where your data is? A study of the effect of enforcement strategies on Privacy Policies. *International Journal of Information Security and Privacy*, *3*(4), 68–95. doi:10.4018/jisp.2009100105

Rogers, K. M. (2004). The Privacy Directive and resultant regulations? The Effect on spam and cookies, part I. *Business Law Review*, *25*(10), 271–274.

Schmidt, M. B., Johnston, A. C., Arnett, K. P., Chen, J. Q., & Li, S. (2008). A cross-cultural comparison of US and Chinese computer security awareness. *Journal of Global Information Management*, *16*(2), 91–103. doi:10.4018/jgim.2008040106

Singh, T., & Hill, M. E. (2003). Consumer privacy and the internet in Europe: A view from Germany. *Journal of Consumer Marketing*, *20*(7), 634–651. doi:10.1108/07363760310506175

Smith, J. H. (2001). Information Privacy and Marketing: What the U.S should (and shouldn't) learn from Europe. *California Management Review*, *43*(2), 8–33. doi:10.2307/41166073

Srinivasan, S., & Barker, R. (2012). Global analysis of security and trust perceptions in web design for e-commerce. *International Journal of Information Security and Privacy*, *6*(1), 1–13. doi:10.4018/jisp.2012010101

Sumeeth, M., Singh, R. I., & Miller, J. (2010). Are online privacy policies readable? *International Journal of Information Security and Privacy*, *4*(1), 93–116. doi:10.4018/jisp.2010010105

Susanto, A., Lee, H., Zo, H., & Ciganek, A. P. (2013). Factors affecting internet banking success: A comparative investigation between Indonesia and South Korea. *Journal of Global Information Management*, *21*(2), 72–95. doi:10.4018/jgim.2013040104

Totterdale, R. L. (2010). Globalization and data privacy: An exploratory study. *International Journal of Information Security and Privacy*, *4*(2), 19–35. doi:10.4018/jisp.2010040102

Treiblmaier, H., & Chong, S. (2011). Trust and perceived risk of personal information as antecedents of online information disclosure: Results from three countries. *Journal of Global Information Management*, *19*(4), 76–94. doi:10.4018/jgim.2011100104

Wang, H., Lee, M. K., & Wang, C. (1998). Consumer privacy concerns about Internet marketing. *Communications of the ACM*, *41*(3), 63–70. doi:10.1145/272287.272299

Warren, A., & Dearnley, J. (2005). Data protection legislation in the United Kingdom: From development to Statute, 1969–84. *Information Communication and Society*, *8*(2), 238–263. doi:10.1080/13691180500146383

Weiss, M. A., & Archick, K. (2016). *US-EU data privacy: from safe harbor to privacy shield*. Congressional Research Service.

White, G. L., Mediavilla, F. A. M., & Shah, J. R. (2011). Information Privacy: Implementation and Perception of Laws and Corporate Policies by CEOs and Managers. *International Journal of Information Security and Privacy*, *5*(1), 50–66. doi:10.4018/jisp.2011010104

Wright, D. (2012). The state of the art in privacy impact assessment. *Computer Law & Security Review*, *28*(1), 54–61. doi:10.1016/j.clsr.2011.11.007

Wu, Y., Lau, T., Atkin, D. J., & Lin, C. A. (2011). A comparative study of online privacy regulations in the US and China. *Telecommunications Policy*, *35*(7), 603–616. doi:10.1016/j.telpol.2011.05.002

Xue, H. (2010). Privacy and personal data protection in China: An update for the year end 2009. *Computer Law & Security Review*, *26*(3), 284–289. doi:10.1016/j.clsr.2010.01.004

This research was previously published in the International Journal of Information Security and Privacy (IJISP), 12(3); edited by Mehdi Khosrow-Pour, D.B.A., pages 1-15, copyright year 2018 by IGI Publishing (an imprint of IGI Global).

Chapter 95

Survey on DDoS Attacks and Defense Mechanisms in Cloud and Fog Computing

Deepali Chaudhary
National Institute of Technology Kurukshetra, India

Kriti Bhushan
National Institute of Technology Kurukshetra, India

B.B. Gupta
National Institute of Technology Kurukshetra, India

ABSTRACT

This article describes how cloud computing has emerged as a strong competitor against traditional IT platforms by offering low-cost and "pay-as-you-go" computing potential and on-demand provisioning of services. Governments, as well as organizations, have migrated their entire or most of the IT infrastructure to the cloud. With the emergence of IoT devices and big data, the amount of data forwarded to the cloud has increased to a huge extent. Therefore, the paradigm of cloud computing is no longer sufficient. Furthermore, with the growth of demand for IoT solutions in organizations, it has become essential to process data quickly, substantially and on-site. Hence, Fog computing is introduced to overcome these drawbacks of cloud computing by bringing intelligence to the edge of the network using smart devices. One major security issue related to the cloud is the DDoS attack. This article discusses in detail about the DDoS attack, cloud computing, fog computing, how DDoS affect cloud environment and how fog computing can be used in a cloud environment to solve a variety of problems.

1. INTRODUCTION

The long-held dream of computing as a utility was achieved with Cloud Computing (Gupta & Badve, 2017; Ahuja & Kaja, 2015) that provides the potential of transforming a large part of the IT industry. Organizations which are at the early stage no longer need to invest large capital in buying hardware to deploy their service or large human expense to operate it. There is no need to be concerned about

DOI: 10.4018/978-1-5225-8176-5.ch095

under-utilization of expensive resources for a service which did not meet the expected predictions or exhaustion of the available resources by the service that becomes wildly popular, which may lead to missing potential customers and revenue. Moreover, organizations with large batch-oriented work load can get quick results alongside the scaling of their program, since the cost of accessing 1,000 servers for one hour is almost as much as accessing one server for 1,000 hours. Hence, these features like the elasticity of resources, pay-as-you-go, resource provisioning, on-demand service and much more have made cloud computing very popular (Gupta & Kumar, 2013). However, as all the services in the cloud are hosted over the Internet making cloud prone to many security issues and one such issue is addressed in this paper i.e. the DDoS attack.

DDoS attack or Distributed DoS attack (Gupta et al., 2012; Douligeris & Mitrokosta, 2004) is an attack performed on the victim with the help of a large number of machines which are known as zombie machines or bot that are infected by some malicious code or compromised by an attacker. These machines are centrally controlled and coordinated by an attacker to initiate the attack on the victim machine. The DDoS attack is mainly an attack on availability i.e. victim machine becomes unavailable to the legitimate users trying to establish a connection with it. But when a DDoS attack occurs in a cloud environment (Bhusan & Gupta, 2017; Somani et al., 2016), it exhausts all the resources of the target VM and over-burdens it. This situation can be handled by cloud with the allocation of more resources to the victim VM to process all the requests made to it. But the further allocation of additional resources can go on to an extent where either cloud provider runs out of idle resources or the owner of VM cannot pay for the increasing demand of resources anymore.

Fog computing can also be described as an extension to cloud computing which removes several limitations of cloud computing like need of huge amount of data to be forwarded to a cloud server, the high latency for real-time problems, high transportation cost and much more (Lee et al., 2015; Chuck, 2015). Fog computing introduces a new paradigm for cloud computing that includes performing necessary analysis and computation at the edge of the cloud to provide many benefits like less bandwidth consumption and networking strain, decreased costs, reduced latency, faster access, security, and accountability (Stolfo et al., 2012). Fog computing connects machines, sensors, and devices directly to each other enabling real-time decision making without transmitting a vast amount of data through the cloud (Bonomi et al., 2012; Chow et al., 2009). Therefore, fog computing concept can be beneficial for efficient DDoS attack detection and mitigation in future.

Several features of cloud computing including pay-as-you-go pricing model, on-demand services, rapid elasticity, etc. make it more vulnerable to the variety of DDoS attacks. As ensuring availability of cloud services is still a challenge for the service providers, this paper presents various security issues faced by cloud environment, and different DDoS defence mechanisms in the literature are also discussed in this paper. Further, as fog computing overcomes various limitations of cloud computing; therefore, it could be helpful in DDoS attack detection and mitigation. Hence, we have presented the basic concepts of fog computing, its architecture, and its role in DDoS attack defence in cloud computing. We have also discussed various recent approaches in the direction of DDoS attack defence in the cloud using fog computing. Moreover, we have discussed some use cases to help us understand how and where fog computing can be used in order to make our lives easier and safer.

This paper is mainly divided into five sections, section 2 presents the DDoS attack model and statistics. Section 3 elucidates cloud computing environment with its service model and deployment model along with various cloud security challenges. This section also explains how the DDoS attack is carried out in a cloud environment and discusses some recently proposed techniques for defense from DDoS attack in the cloud environment. Section 4 introduces fog computing along with its architecture. It also highlights some security challenges faced in fog computing environment and some recent techniques that use fog computing to provide security in a cloud environment. Finally, section 5 concludes the paper.

2. DDOS ATTACK STRATEGY AND STATISTICS

To perform a DDoS attack, an attacker performs the following steps (Geng & Whinston, 2000; Badve et al., 2015) as shown in Figure 1:

1.   The attacker tries to compromise internet's weekly secure channels i.e. it searches for machines with very less security and compromises them to create zombie machines.
2.   Generates a large amount of traffic with the help of zombie machines and use them as weapons for attacking the victim machine to exhaust its resources.
3.   Completely defeat the victim's security defense rendering it unavailable to the legitimate users.
4.   Hide attacker machine's identity by using the hierarchical structure of zombies.

According to Akamai's Q2 report, it was observed that during Q2 2016 there was 129% rise in the total DDoS attacks as compared to Q2 2015. Furthermore, infrastructure layer attacks were increased by 151% and there was 70% rise in UDP flood attack. Additionally, there was a total of 9% rise in DDoS attack from first to second quarter of 2016 with 10% rise in infrastructure layer attack and UDP attack increased to 47%. It was reported that 98.36% DDoS attack took place in infrastructure layer, whereas only 1.64% attack was on application layer which is further represented in Figure 2.

Figure 1. DDoS attack strategy; Source: Authors' work

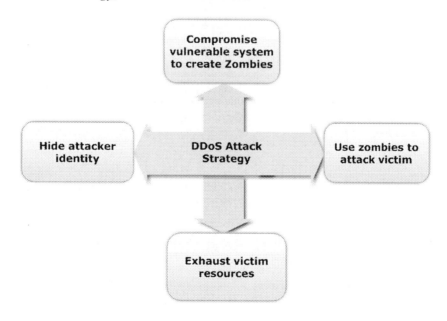

Figure 2. DDoS attack vector frequency for (a) Infrastructure layer attacks (b) Application layer attacks; Source: Authors' work

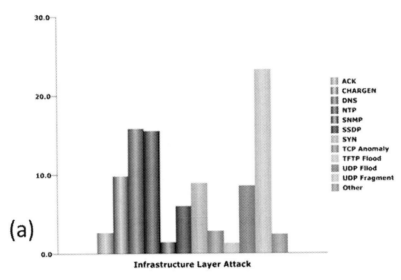

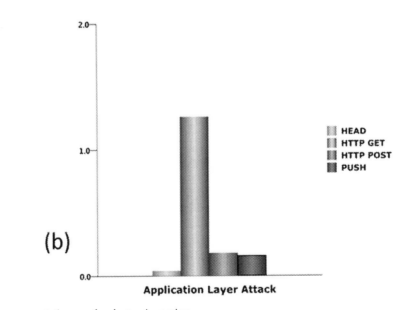

*For a more accurate representation see the electronic version.

Figure 3 shows how the attack size of DDoS attack has increased in the last decade (Marchette, 2001). The growth in the size of attack has been quite significant over the last few years and hence become one of the main concerns. Whereas, Figure 4 represents the most recent statistics for the DDoS attack in different industrial sectors. It is evident from the graph that gaming sector is the biggest victim of DDoS attack followed by media and entertainment sector, whereas education sector experience lowest number of DDoS attacks.

Attacker's objective to perform DDoS attack can be anything from extortion for financial gain, espionage to gain information about rival company, protesting to catch victim's attention, to cause nuisance i.e.

Figure 3. Attack size over the years; Source: Authors' work

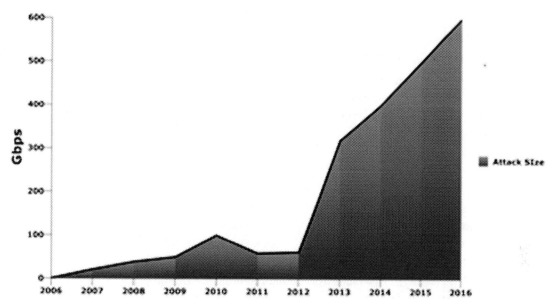

Figure 4. DDoS attack frequency by Industry 2016; Source: Authors' work

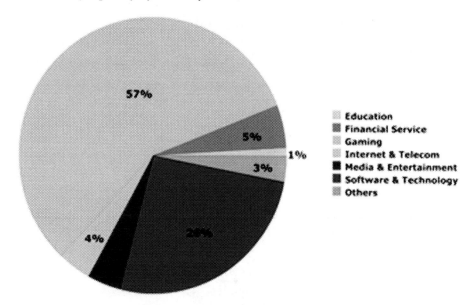

For a more accurate representation see the electronic version.

causing inconvenience in network or in machine or it could also be defamation i.e. to harm company's image that may lead to customer loss to the company ultimately causing huge financial loss. Various other reports (Shruthi & Nijagunarya, 2016) also suggests that the existing DDoS defence mechanisms are still vulnerable.

3. CLOUD COMPUTING

Cloud offers several benefits like pay-for-use, resource provisioning, rapid elasticity, fast deployment, scalability, lower costs, rapid provisioning, ubiquitous network access, multi-tenancy, rapid elasticity, greater resiliency, lower cost disaster recovery and data storage solution (Jouini et al., 2016; Bhushan & Gupta, 2017) and much more as shown in Figure 5. But it has several security issues which require immediate attention because a large amount of sensitive data is stored in the cloud. Harm to the data can occur due to leakage, loss, unavailability, vulnerability attacks, etc., can cause a lot of damage in terms of money and business continuity.

As we can see in Figure 6, cloud computing has four deployment models and a service model with three layers. The most commonly used deployment model in the cloud is a public cloud (IBM Blue Mix Cloud, Amazon EC2) which is accessible to or can be used by anybody be it individual user or an organization. Whereas private cloud is an on-premise cloud, it is accessible to only the users inside the boundaries or premise of the private cloud. An organization can have their own private cloud which is only accessible to the employees of the organization inside the premise of the cloud. One such example is Amazon VPC. Whereas, hybrid cloud is a combination of the public and private cloud. Lastly, a community cloud is a public cloud which is only accessible to a community with similar ideologies, goals, beliefs, etc.

Cloud service model has three layers (Goy et al., 2014), the bottom-most layer is IaaS (Infrastructure as a Service) which provides with hardware components to users like storage, processing power, network or any other capability required by the user for running their applications like Amazon EC2. Whereas, Paas (Platform as a Service) provides the user an environment where they can develop and deploy their application like Google App Engine. The top layer is SaaS (Software as a Service) which is used by the user to access the application running on a cloud like Microsoft Office 356 where users make changes in settings according to their requirement.

Figure 5. Cloud Computing Features; Source: Authors' work

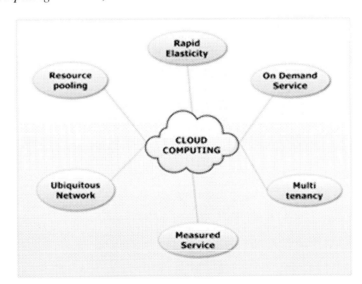

Figure 6. Cloud Models; Source: Authors' work

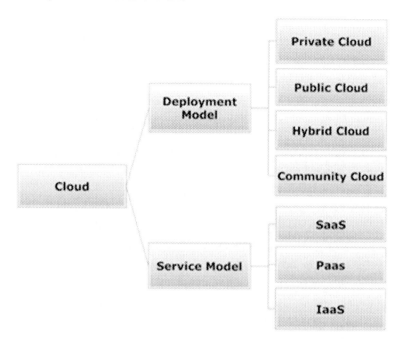

3.1. Cloud Security Challenges

Determining all the cloud challenges is a challenge in itself. However, this section addresses some of these challenges with their countermeasures. Cloud security challenges that are addressed in this chapter are shown in Figure 7.

Figure 7. Cloud Security Challenges; Source: Authors' work

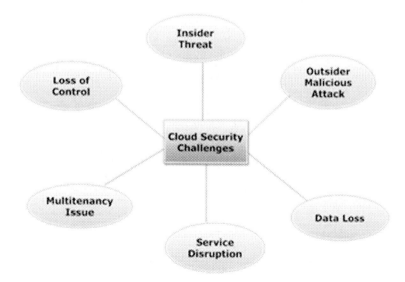

3.1.1. Insider Threat

The problem due to insider threat (Behl, 2011; Kandias et al., 2011) is not properly addressed as much as other issues. Therefore, not much research has been done on this issue. Insider threats are the threats from some malicious insider. This insider can exist in the cloud as well as client side. The damage caused by insider attack can be way more than the damage caused by outside malicious attack. Insider on the provider side and client side due to their business roles on their respective sides can use his or her authorization to access sensitive data.

Countermeasures: It is the responsibility of both client and provider to ensure security. Hence, both should take appropriate measures to ensure security in the cloud. Countermeasures need to be implemented on both client-side and provider side for protection from insider threats. On the client side, cryptographic techniques can be used to maintain confidentiality and integrity of the data stored in the cloud. Data can be saved in multiple data center so that if one of the data centers is compromised our data can still be accessed. Log auditing on client side along with host-based IDS/IPS can also be implemented. Whereas, on the provider side, the measures that can be taken include separation of duties on provider as well as client side, using multifactor authentication, legally binding the employee, anomaly detection, and logging mechanism.

3.1.2. Outsider Malicious Attack

Outside threats are one of the most important challenges in the cloud as it leads to release of all the secret or confidential information. Therefore, it affects the reputation of an organization. These attacks can be performed on six attack surfaces as shown in Figure 8. The summary of the cloud security issues is presented in Table 1.

Different attacks are performed on each surface. There are six attack surfaces (Gruschka & Jensen, 2010) (a) Service-to-User: attacks performed are buffer overflow, Privilege escalation or SQL injections, (b) User-to-Service: attacks performed are SSL certificate spoofing, browser caches attacks or Phishing attacks on client emails, (c) Cloud-to-Service: attacks include resource exhaustion attacks, Denial-of-

Figure 8. The Six attack surfaces of Cloud Triangle; Source: Authors' work

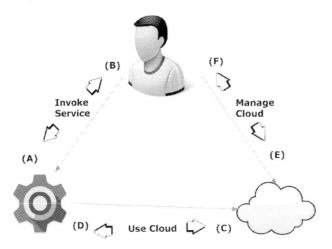

Table 1. Cloud Security Challenges; Source: Authors' work

Challenge	Description	Countermeasure
Insider Threat	Threat from malicious insider at cloud provider or cloud outsourcer side	• Cryptographic techniques • Use of proper Logging mechanism • Legal bindings • Anomaly Detection
Outsider Malicious Attack	Attacks performed by an outsider on cloud services like XSS, DDoS, SQL injection, etc., on any of the six attack surfaces (Gruschka & Jensen, 2010).	• Firewalls • ACL's and IPS • Honeypots • Virtual machine isolation
Data Loss	Loss of data on cloud due to various factors like insufficient authentication, operational failures, accounting controls, etc. (Vitti et al., 2014).	• Having a proper DPL strategy • Identify data flow source and destination
Service Disruption	Unavailability of cloud services due to factors like DDoS attack, fraud, exploiting vulnerabilities etc (Ren et al., 2012).	• Prohibiting sharing of credential between VM users • Validating each VM or sessions • Two-factor authentication • Proactive monitoring to prevent unauthorized access
Multi-tenancy Issue	When multiple users are using the same application on the same physical hardware hosting their VMs (Subashini & Kavita, 2011).	• Use of authorization models like RBAS and hRBAC (Calero et al., 2010). • Proper isolation of VMs • Defense-in-depth approach
Loss of Control	As the cloud is hosted off-premise and the user has no idea as to where their data is stored or their service is hosted, the user feels that they have no control over their data plus this also leads to jurisdiction problem.	• Private cloud • Proper SLA's • Caas • Proper laws for inter boundary disputes in cloud • Transparency between user and cloud provider

Service attack, Triggering provider for more resources or attack on the cloud system hypervisor, (d) Service-to-Cloud: attacks performed are availability reduction i.e. shutting down service instances, malicious interference, privacy related attacks and many more (e) Cloud-to-User: this surface is a little hard to explain as both cloud and user do not have an actual touching point, user always uses a service to access cloud and (f) User-to-Cloud: includes every attack that targets a user and originates at the cloud machine.

Countermeasures: Firewall can be used to provide perimeter protection, ACL's and IPS is absolute and honeypots must be used along with AAA systems. This will make it a challenging task for hackers or attackers to break into the machines. Furthermore, Virtual machines (VM) must be isolated from each other for every customer. A context-based firewall must use for every VM so that even if one machine gets compromised it cannot be used as an attack base by the attacker to launch further attacks on other VMs.

3.1.3. Data Loss

Factors responsible for data losses are insufficient authentication, data center reliability, accounting controls, authorization, inconsistent use of encryption and encryption keys, political issues and operational failures. Data loss and leakage cause reputation damage, financial loss, and customer count loss for an organization.

Countermeasures: Steps to tackle the problem of data loss (Ouf & Nasr, 2015) are: Identify the data source, flow, and destination, security should be enforced as everybody's responsibility, choose the right tool according to the requirement and tuning the DLP strategies. It is necessary to convince the management and the stakeholders to view and understand the results that are obtained after the implementation of the DLP process and tools. So that DLP strategy can be supported.

3.1.4. Service Disruption

Service disruption (Behl, 2011) can lead organizations into deep water because their resources become unavailable to users and will result in customer dissatisfaction and demotivate the employees. It is caused by attacks such as phishing, exploitation of software vulnerabilities, fraud, and even an attacker can launch a DoS or DDoS attack by leveraging botnets and auto dialers. Compromised machines can become launch bases for attackers. Service disruptions can lead to loss of valuable customer base to competitors and businesses to halt.

Countermeasures: Sharing account credentials amongst tenants should be prohibited by all means. Services should be validated for each VM or session. Strong two-factor authentication technique should be implemented by providers, rigid initial customer registration and validation processes can be useful to deter any attacks even before occurring. Furthermore, proactive monitoring to detect unauthorized activity in a session or in VM can be implemented.

3.1.5. Multi-Tenancy Issues

Multitenancy in cloud environment means that multiple users use the same application on their respective VMs that run on same physical hardware. This can cause exploitation, information leakage, and increased attack surface. The risk of VM-to-VM attack increases and compromised VM can also be used as a launch base for further attacks (Nagar & Suman, 2016). Furthermore, traditional authorization framework cannot deal with multiple cloud resources and integrate security for cloud data in their security matrices and policies.

Countermeasures: An Authorization model (Calero et al., 2010) was designed to facilitate access control of information and services for various cloud services using the cloud infrastructure. This model was defined by using 5-tuple to define RBAC (Role Based Access Control) and hRBAC (hierarchical RBAC). Defence-in-depth approach can also be used; it includes defending the cloud's virtual infrastructure with different protection mechanisms at different layers as per the layer requirements and characteristics. Furthermore, proper VM isolation should be implemented so that no two VMs can have intentional or unintentional access to each other

3.1.6. Loss of Control

One of the main reasons that make companies reluctant to adopt cloud is it's off-premise data storage and losing control over their sensitive data. Knowledge about data security implementation provided by the provider is not known to clients. Furthermore, many developing countries do not have internal cloud providers and hence their only option is foreign cloud providers. But some countries don't allow their data to cross their national boundaries (Gupta & Kumar, 2013; Bhushan & Gupta, 2017) and hence many potential cloud users cannot switch to cloud.

Countermeasures: Government should provide assistance in the countries with no cloud providers so that they can switch to cloud without worrying about their data crossing national boundaries. It is the responsibility of the companies to carefully read the SLAs (Avram, 2014) before taking any decision and understand provider's security policies. Both parties must sit and discuss for making an agreement on some metrics that can benefit them both. Providers should be willing to allow the customers to port their security processes to customer's virtual domain. Customers should specify what they want and ask for desired changes in SLAs and process policies. CaaS (control as a service) can also be implemented. The alternative for access control problem is always mentioned as switching to a private cloud or proper SLA. But no proper method is defined to provide transparency between the provider and user.

3.2. DDoS Attack in Cloud Environment

There are many DDoS defense mechanisms for the traditional environment but for a cloud environment, these defense mechanisms do not work due to the following three reasons (Aazam & Huh, 2014) (shown in Figure 9).

1. In the normal environment, the computation and network resources are controlled by the user but in a cloud environment, these resources are controlled by the cloud provider. Hence, the application server is not in control of the defender network.
2. According to the defender, topology changes due to virtual machine migration and resource allocation are very fast and hence to defend the network the defender should be able to maintain prompt reaction capability and high detection rate while trying to adapt to topological changes.
3. In the cloud, many users use the same network infrastructure. Hence, the defender should ensure that the DDoS defense mechanism does not impact another cloud user or vice versa.

Over the years several defense techniques have been proposed to defend cloud from DDoS attack, some of them used anomaly-based detection, some used signature based while others used both. Bakshi et al. (2010) proposed a signature based intrusion detection system located in VMs to detect the DDoS attack. SNORT is used in IDS sensors to detect the IP of the source of the attack packets. Furthermore, packets from blacklisted IPs are dropped. Lo et al. (2010) proposed a distributed IDS based mechanism located inside cloud environment. Whenever an attack is detected by IDS, it sent an alert to other IDS

Figure 9. DDoS attack issues in Cloud; Source: Authors' work

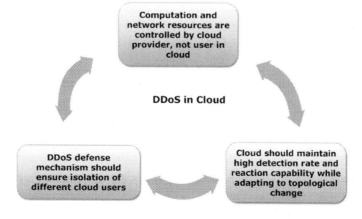

distributed inside the Cloud. This approach is useful for IDS to mitigate the attacks which are detected and reported by other IDS. Whereas, Gul et al. (2011) used NIDS to detect malicious attack traffic using multiple threads. NIDS has three modules: capture and queuing, analysis/processing and reporting. Whenever an attack is detected by NIDS it raises an alarm to the third party which further reports to cloud management system. Moreover, Karnwal et al. (2012, 2013) used the filter tree approach to detect DDoS attack due to SOAP messages. Its Cloud defender having five modules is used to filter attack: Sensor filter, Hop Count filter, IP Frequency Divergence filter, Confirm Legitimate User IP filter and lastly Double Signature filter. First four filters detect HTTP DDoS attack while last filter detects XML DDoS attack. Negi et al (2013) proposed a modified form of confidence Based Filtering method (CBF) which for cloud computing environment examined correlation pattern for mitigation of DDoS attacks on the Cloud. This modification in CBF introduces a nominally increased bandwidth and tries to improve the processing speed of the victim server.

While most of the researchers used signature-based detection there were many who used anomaly-based detection for the DDoS attack in the cloud. Kwon et al. (2011) used IDS based on self-similarity feature as it was known that behavior of legitimate traffic was similar while the behavior of attack traffic (i.e. outlier) was similar. Cosine similarity at optimal time interval is used to determine self-similarity index in the proposed model. In the case of nonvalid self-similarity index, an alert is generated and the report is sent to the system administrator. Bedi et al. (2012) proposed a system to provide security to cloud infrastructure from coexisting DDoS attack with the help of game theory. A game inspired defense of firewall was implemented to provide security against co-resident malicious and legitimate VM behavior on the same physical machine. Huang et al. (2013) used artificial intelligence to propose a model to detect HTTP base flooding attack with multi-stage detection and text-based turning test. Traffic behavior of each virtual cluster was retrieved and recorded using DDoS attack detection module while text-based turning test module generates a randomly selected question to be answered by the requestor of redirected blocked packets. Access was granted only when the correct answer was provided by the requestor. Iyengar et al. (2014) proposed a multilevel thrust filtration model with four prevention and detection modules to protect attacker from entering the cloud environment. The four modules are traffic analysis, abnormality detection, abnormality classification and attack prevention. Both host and router based techniques are used to detect the attack at an early stage before it reaches the data centers by using intermediate look-up web server located in the cloud. Furthermore, an authentication token based defense strategy was proposed by Michelin et al. (2014). This approach works in two modes, first is monitoring mode in which overloading of the system is carried out using stress test. Token from every user is verified in this module, in case of invalid token the user is put in the grey list. Whenever overloading is detected, monitoring mode is switched to filtering mode and the grey list becomes black list. REST (Representational State Transfer) of all the users in the blacklist is dropped. Filter mode is changed back to monitoring mode once the system is decongested. In another related work from Choi et al. (2014) presented a data mining approach for the situation arising due to a significant increase in internet traffic. HTTP GET DDoS attack is mitigated using a map reduce model. This approach had three modules: Packet and Log collection, Pattern Analysis, and a Detection module. The proposed approach produces better results than Snort by identifying latest attack profiles and takes lesser processing time.

Some of the recent anomaly based techniques include a Cloud DDoS Attack defense models DaMask proposed by Wang et al. (2015), which contains two modules: DaMask-D and DaMask-M. Firstly, an alert is raised whenever an attack is detected by DaMask-D module. DaMask-M receives forwarded alert and packet information, it makes an entry in the log if it does not already exist and decides on the desired countermeasure for that attack. If the packet is legitimate, it is simply forwarded to the destination. Moreover, Marnerides et al. (2015) proposed a model which carries out statistical depiction and decomposition of measured signals. This model is named as E-EMD (Ensemble Empirical Mode Decomposition). This model is based on the fact that non-linear and non-stationary behavior is exhibited by the majority of monitored traffic. This model can be deployed on hypervisor level by function through analyzing network information of every VM. Whereas, Alqahtani et al. (2015) introduced an approach which can detect DDoS attack not only at cloud level but at tenant, service and application level as well. Somani et al. (2017) proposed a novel framework which provides performance isolation by using the affinity-based victim-service resizing algorithm, and a TCP tuning technique to rapid attack disconnections, therefore reducing the attack cooling down time to minimal. This framework provides a significant reduction in service downtime to 50%, thus providing faster attack mitigation and hence shows major improvement the efficiency of DDoS mitigation service.

Over the past few years, many approaches have been proposed to defend cloud from DDoS attack using both anomalies based and signature-based DDoS detection. Kwon et al. (2011) proposed a model with three level anomaly detection. First is the monitoring level which uses known attack patterns to detect the DDoS attack, the second level uses lightweight anomaly detection and Bayesian technique for analyzing DDoS attack candidates. While the last level uses unsupervised learning to detect both known and unknown DDoS attack patterns. Modi et al (2012) proposed a hybrid NIDS which used Snort tool that contains known attack patterns information and a Bayesian classifier which statistically predicts the probability of a networking event for classifying it into malicious or legitimate class with high accuracy. Whereas, Somani et al. (2016) shows how DDoS attack on cloud affects the stakeholders as shown in Figure 10.

Figure 10. DDoS effect on Cloud Stakeholders; Source: Authors' work

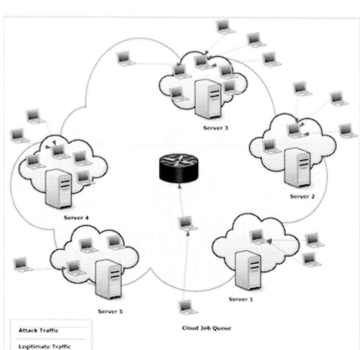

In this paper, DDoS attack scenario in a cloud infrastructure with many high capacity physical servers with multiple VMs running on them is considered. Whenever a VM is attacked and all its resources including the idle resources available for expansion are exhausted then auto-scaling algorithm automatically start another VM instance on the same or some other server in the same cloud infrastructure. If this new VM instance is also exhausted the more instances are created until the whole cloud is exhausted or the user's allowed limit is reached. This paper suggests various solutions to deal with the issue. Sharma et al. (2016) proposed a defensive scheme with a triple filter. Whereas, He et al. (2017) proposed a machine learning approach deployed at the cloud side for defending from DDoS attack generated from cloud VMs. This approach uses statistically obtained information from the cloud VMs and hypervisor to control the outbound traffic of cloud. This model was tested with nine different kinds of machine learning algorithms from which it obtained 99.7% accuracy for four types of DoS attack. Some DDoS attack defense mechanism in cloud computing are shown in Table 2.

Table 2. DDoS attack defense mechanism in cloud computing; Source: Authors' work

Year	Reference	Detection Technique	Deployment Location	DDoS attack type
2010	Bakshi & Yogesh, 2010	Signature-Based	Access point	Infrastructural level
	Lo et al., 2010	Signature-Based	Access point	Infrastructural level
2011	Kwon and Kim	Hybrid	Access point	Infrastructural level
	Gul & Hussain, 2011	Signature-based	Access point	Not Stated
	Kwon et al., 2011	Anomaly-Based	Access point	Not Stated
2012	Modi et al., 2012	Hybrid	Access point	Not Stated
	Bedi & Shiva, 2012	Anomaly-Based	Access point	Not Stated
	Chonka & Abawajy, 2012	Hybrid	Not Stated	Application level
	Karnwal et al., 2012	Signature-Based	Distributed	Application level
2013	Karnwal et al., 2013	Signature-Based	Distributed	Application level
	Gupta & Kumar, 2013	Signature-Based	Access point	Infrastructural level
	Huang et al.,2013	Anomaly-Based	Access point	Infrastructural level
	Negi et al., 2013	Signature-Based	Not Stated	Infrastructure level
2014	Michelin et al., 2014	Anomaly-Based	Access point	Application level
	Iyengar et al., 2014	Anomaly-Based	Distributed	Not Stated
	Choi et al.	Anomaly-Based	Distributed	Infrastructural level
2015	Wang et al.	Anomaly-Based	Access point	Not Stated
	Alqahtani & Gamble, 2015	Anomaly-Based	Access point	Infrastructural level
	Mernerides et al., 2015	Anomaly-Based	Access point	Not Stated
2016	Somani et al., 2016	Hybrid	Access point	Infrastructural level
	Sharma & Singh et al., 2016	Anomaly-Based	Not Stated	Not Stated
2017	Somani et al., 2017	Anomaly-Based	Access point	Infrastructural level
	He & Zang et al., 2017	Anomaly-Based	Source-end	Infrastructure level

4. FOG COMPUTING

Fog Computing is an extension to cloud computing where fog devices are the devices that sit between the end devices and the cloud (Vaquero & Radero, 2014; Dastjerdi et al., 2016). They allow machines to communicate directly to each other without going through the cloud. Fog connects machines, sensors, and devices directly to each other enabling real-time decisions to be made without transmitting a vast amount of data through the cloud (Dastjerdi & Bhuya, 2016; Aazam & Huh, 2014). It connects all devices to cloud with open communication standards resulting in a smart network of devices that provide smart decision making and react in real time to a changing environment.

Internet of things as we all know is a term used for devices connected to the internet through routers and switches producing a vast amount of data every second and every minute (Stergiou et al., 2016). Cisco has further extended this term to IoE (Internet of Everything) as shown in Figure 11, it comprises of people, processes, data, and things. Processes are needed to make the internet flow smoothly and avoid problems whereas, it is necessary to deliver the right information to the right person at the right time. Data is the currency of internet of everything as a lot of data is continuously flowing through the network at all times. Hence, proper techniques should be used to keep this flow of data under control. Lastly, the things i.e. the routers, switches, devices, actuators, etc., are the most important part of IoE.

4.1. Fog Architecture

In fog architecture (Bonomi et al., 2012) as shown in Figure 12 there are 4 layers from which the center two layers are the fog layers, whereas the topmost layer i.e. layer 1 consists of cloud and layer 4 are sensor nodes or end devices. Layer 4 consists of end devices or sensors that are geospatially distributed, highly reliable, non-invasive and low cost. These sensors generate a large amount of data stream that needs to be processed as a coherent whole.

Figure 11. Internet of Everything (IOE) (Source: Authors' work)

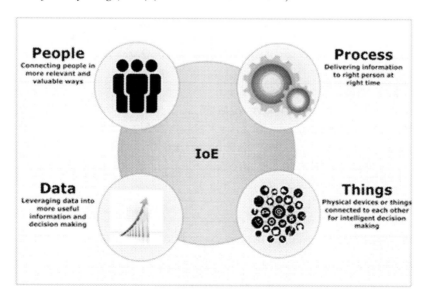

Figure 12. Fog Architecture; Source: Authors' work

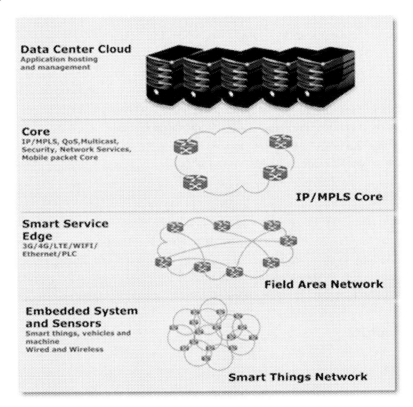

Raw data from this layer is forwarded to next layer i.e. layer 3 that consists of high performance and low-power computing nodes or edge devices. Each of these edge devices is responsible for a local group of sensors. The output generated by these edge devices has two parts: first is the report of analysis of intermediate node to upper layer i.e. layer 2 and second is the quick feedback to the intermediate node after processing the data obtained from them.

Layer 2 consists of intermediate computing nodes each of which is connected to a number of edge devices at layer 3 and uses the report sent by them to predict potential hazardous events. This layer also provides quick response mechanism when such hazardous events are detected. Hence, this quick feedback mechanism provided by layer 2 and 3 provides localized "reflex" decisions to avoid potential damage.

The topmost layer i.e. the cloud computing data center consists of data analysis results that are used for long-term and large-scale behavioral analysis and conditional monitoring. This layer is mainly used for long-term or citywide behavior analysis, pattern recognition etc for dynamic decision making.

Layer 2 and 3 can also be called as fog layers as fog technology is applied at these two layers to perform analysis and convert raw data into valuable one, and only this valuable data is further sent to cloud thereby reducing the amount of data.

In (Aazam & Huh, 2014) architecture was proposed for Smart Gateway with Fog Computing. This paper addresses the need for trimming the data generated by IoT devices and then forwarding only that use data to the cloud. Smart gateway is introduced in the communication channel between IoT devices and cloud. The smart gateway acts as fog layer in this scenario and trims the data coming from IoT devices before forwarding it to cloud.

4.2. Use Cases

In this section, we will see a few use cases which will help us understand how and where fog computing can be used in order to make our lives easier and safer.

4.2.1. Smart Traffic Light System (STLS)

STLS (Bonomi et al., 2014) is a system that consists of smart connected vehicles, smart traffic lights (STL) and advanced transportation system. In an STLS, STL equipped with sensors are deployed at every intersection and these sensors can measure the speed and distance of the approaching vehicles from every direction. These sensors can also detect any cyclist or pedestrian on the street. It also helps in sending a slow down warning to the vehicles at risk of crossing the red light and STL may also sometimes modify their own cycle to prevent collisions. STLS mainly have three goals that prevent accidents, maintain a steady flow of traffic and collect relevant data over time to evaluate and improve the system.

4.2.2. Wind Farm

Large wind farms (Bonomi et al., 2012) mostly have hundreds of wind turbines spread over hundreds of square miles and each wind turbine is equipped with a closed control loop that aims to improve power quality, wind power capture and reduce structural loading. In wind farms there are typically four operating regions: first, when speed is low, say less than 6m/sec which is not economical to run the wind turbines. Second is normal operating conditions i.e. between 6 and 12m/sec then the blades are positioned so as to produce maximum electrical power from wind power conversion. The third is the region where wind speed increases a certain threshold then the power of turbines is limited to avoid exceeding safe load limit electrically and mechanically. Fourth is the case with very high wind speed say above 25 m/s where turbines are powered down to avoid excessive operating load. Hence sensors in these wind turbines are used to detect the speed of the wind to operate turbines accordingly to increase efficiency and prevent damage.

4.2.3. Smart City

The smart city consists of large-scale management of smart lighting, smart houses, video surveillance, smart grid, electric bus, wind farm etc. The use cases mentioned above are also part of the smart city and the example taken in STLS can be further extended to demonstrate fog utilization in smart cities. The STL or smart vehicles can be used to inform hospital about the approaching ambulance so that they can stay ready in advance. Or the ambulance could be informed about the nearby hospital etc.

4.3. Fog Computing in DDoS Attack Defense

Fog computing that is located at an intermediate layer between the user side and the cloud environment as discussed in this paper provides same resources as cloud, faster response time, locality and some more features. When a DDoS attack is directed to cloud it causes exhaustion of valuable resources, huge billing (can also be referred as EDoS attack) and usage of huge computational power. DDoS defense mechanism, when applied to the Cloud, is effective but it consumes lots of computational power and resources which is quite costly (Badve et al., 2015). Moreover, the attack had already reached the cloud. Therefore, to remove these challenges Fog Computing can be used to defend Cloud from the DDoS attack at the edge of the network before it reaches cloud at a much lower cost (Agarwal et al., 2016).

Recently, a framework was proposed (Deepali & Bhushan, 2017) in which DDoS attack Detection and mitigation for Cloud was implemented using the intermediate fog layer. The framework was implemented in real time using different attack tools performing an attack from different Linux and Windows VMs on an ownCloud Cloud server. An intermediate fog defender machine was set up through which all the traffic from user passed through to reach the cloud server. It was observed that when no defense rules are applied on fog defender DDoS attack traffic is simply allowed to pass through to Cloud server, the cloud server becomes unavailable to the legitimate user machine. Whereas, when defense rules are applied on fog defender machine DDoS attack is successfully detected and attack packets are dropped. Hence, cloud server availability is not affected.

Furthermore, another work proposed (Deepali & Bhushan, 2017) an approach to perform load balancing in fog servers which perform the analyses near the user at a lower cost without going to Cloud. The traffic is forwarded to cloud only when all the fog servers were unavailable. This approach has two modules: fog defender module whose working is explained in (Deepali & Bhushan, 2017) and second is resource provisioning module which performs load balancing according to the proposed modified optimal response time service broker policy. Therefore, in this approach first, the DDoS traffic passes through the fog defender where it is detected and filtered, while legitimate traffic is forwarded to further fog servers. In resource provisioning module request is served according to proposed algorithm. But when load increases significantly then the limited fog server resources get exhausted and the traffic is forwarded to cloud to ensure availability of service to users. It was observed that cost was significantly reduced using this approach and hence this approach proved to be a good solution for EDoS attack problem in Cloud Computing.

Similar to these existing approaches more research work can be done on Fog Computing to use it to provide security for Cloud Environment. Better defense techniques can be implemented using intermediate fog devices to defend the DDoS attack. But while using fog computing to provide security for Cloud, it is important to ensure the security of fog devices. Some of the security issues related to fog computing are explained in next section.

4.4. Challenges in Fog Computing

Security is very important in fog computing, as the intelligence is pushed to the edge of the network. Hence, security should also be increased on the edge. IOT fog adoption has introduced some security threats as shown in Figure 13.

4.4.1. Authentication

Authentication is a very important security concern and it is required at different levels of gateway for example in smart meters at home. All the smart meters or appliances have unique IP addresses which can be spoofed and meter readings can be tampered with. IDS can be used to detect intrusion in the machine by using signature-based or anomaly-based detection. In (Stojmenovic & Wen, 2014) an example of man-in-the-middle attack was demonstrated through an experiment where a 3G user sends a video call to WLAN user and the gateway between them is compromised using MITM attack. Hook program was

Figure 13. Fog Challenges; Source: Authors' work

used to redirect the received data to the attacker. But in this MITM attack, there were less fog device resources i.e. the memory and CPU consumption during the attack and therefore anomaly-based detection was not useful in detecting this attack.

4.4.2. Malicious Detection Technique in Fog Computing Environment

Hybrid detection techniques are useful when it comes to detection of malicious code in compromised fog nodes. The hybrid technique is a combination of both signatures based and behavior-based detection technique. But behavior based technique causes more overhead and hence signature-based technique is more efficient. Some behavior-based techniques that are running in the cloud can be distributed to fog nodes and whenever a suspected malware file is found in fog it is reported to the cloud. Cloud further checks the existence of pattern in its signature database, if the pattern does not exist in database it is updated in it and further sent to fog node for updating fog database.

4.4.3. Malicious Fog Node Problem

Fog nodes process data received from IoT devices and as this data is large, it is distributed amongst several fog nodes for analysis. But if some fog nodes are compromised by a malicious person then it is difficult to ensure the integrity of the data. Therefore, before the computation begins the fog nodes must be trusted by each other and then by cloud and thus a proper authentication mechanism is required, where only the nodes authenticated by the cloud are allowed in fog environment.

4.4.4. Data Protection

A large volume of data is produced by IoT devices and it is divided and sent to several fog nodes to process it. The data is required to be analyzed without exposing it. When this distributed data is merged after analysis its integrity should be maintained. Light Weight encryption algorithm and masking techniques are required to solve this problem.

4.4.5. Data Management Issue

Sensor nodes in fog are geographically distributed and these nodes located at different places may or may not provide same services. Whereas, some fog nodes may contain duplicate files causing wastage of resources. Therefore, security problems related to personal information has occurred in fog nodes by the wrong approach used by users.

5. CONCLUSION

In this paper, we have provided a survey of DDoS attack in Cloud and Fog Computing environment. First, we have explained cloud computing including its services, deployment models, and security challenges faced in a cloud environment. After that, the significant impact of the DDoS attack on cloud environment along with the various recent DDoS defence techniques proposed in the literature is explained. Various research has been done on the security of cloud computing and the DDoS attack. However, fog computing is a recent concept which can be explored to provide a solution to various problems. Hence, we have discussed the concept of fog computing with IoE that further helps in the understanding of fog computing architecture.

Moreover, how fog can provide a solution to DDoS attacks is explained with the help of some recent work. As per the best of our knowledge, this is the first review that discusses the utility of fog computing in DDoS attack mitigation and we believe that this review will shape the future research direction in the field of DDoS attack mitigation in cloud computing using fog computing.

For future work, we will work on experimental analysis and validation of various work in the literature to mitigate DDoS attacks in cloud computing using fog computing. This will provide a more accurate illustration of the problem and the presented solutions.

ACKNOWLEDGMENT

This research work is being supported by Project grant (SB/FTP/ETA-131/2014) from SERB, DST, Government of India.

REFERENCES

Aazam, M., & Huh, E. N. (2014). Fog computing and smart gateway based communication for cloud of things. In *2014 International Conference on Future Internet of Things and Cloud (FiCloud)* (pp. 464-470). IEEE.

Agarwal, S., Yadav, S., & Yadav, A. K. (2016). An efficient architecture and algorithm for resource provisioning in fog computing. *International Journal of Information Engineering and Electronic Business*, *8*(1), 48–61. doi:10.5815/ijieeb.2016.01.06

Ahuja, S. P., & Kaza, B. (2015). Performance evaluation of data intensive computing in the cloud. In *Cloud Technology: Concepts, Methodologies, Tools, and Applications* (pp. 1901-1914). Hershey, PA: IGI Global. doi:10.4018/978-1-4666-6539-2.ch088

Alqahtani, S., & Gamble, R. F. (2015,). DDoS attacks in service clouds. In *2015 48th Hawaii International Conference on System Sciences (HICSS)* (pp. 5331-5340). IEEE. 10.1109/HICSS.2015.627

Avram, M. G. (2014). Advantages and challenges of adopting cloud computing from an enterprise perspective. *Procedia Technology, 12*, 529–534. doi:10.1016/j.protcy.2013.12.525

Badve, O. P., Gupta, B. B., Yamaguchi, S., & Gou, Z. (2015). DDoS detection and filtering technique in cloud environment using GARCH model. In *2015 IEEE 4th Global Conference on Consumer Electronics (GCCE)* (pp. 584-586). IEEE. 10.1109/GCCE.2015.7398603

Bakshi, A., & Dujodwala, Y. B. (2010). Securing cloud from ddos attacks using intrusion detection system in virtual machine. In *Proceedings of the Second International Conference on Communication Software and Networks ICCSN'10* (pp. 260-264). IEEE. 10.1109/ICCSN.2010.56

Bedi, H. S., & Shiva, S. (2012, August). Securing cloud infrastructure against co-resident DoS attacks using game theoretic defense mechanisms. In *Proceedings of the International Conference on Advances in Computing, Communications and Informatics* (pp. 463-469). ACM. 10.1145/2345396.2345473

Behl, A. (2011). Emerging security challenges in cloud computing: An insight to cloud security challenges and their mitigation. In 2011 world congress on Information and communication technologies (WICT) (pp. 217-222). IEEE.

Bhushan, K., & Gupta, B. B. (2017). A novel approach to defend multimedia flash crowd in cloud environment. *Multimedia Tools and Applications.*

Bhushan, K., & Gupta, B. B. (2017). Security challenges in cloud computing: State-of-art. *International Journal of Big Data Intelligence, 4*(2), 81–107. doi:10.1504/IJBDI.2017.083116

Bhushan, K., & Gupta, B. B. (2017). Network flow analysis for detection and mitigation of Fraudulent Resource Consumption (FRC) attacks in multimedia cloud computing. *Multimedia Tools and Applications.*

Bonomi, F., Milito, R., Natarajan, P., & Zhu, J. (2014). Fog computing: A platform for internet of things and analytics. In *Big Data and Internet of Things: A Roadmap for Smart Environments* (pp. 169–186). Springer International Publishing. doi:10.1007/978-3-319-05029-4_7

Bonomi, F., Milito, R., Zhu, J., & Addepalli, S. (2012). Fog computing and its role in the internet of things. In *Proceedings of the first edition of the MCC workshop on Mobile cloud computing* (pp. 13-16). ACM. 10.1145/2342509.2342513

Calero, J. M. A., Edwards, N., Kirschnick, J., Wilcock, L., & Wray, M. (2010). Toward a multi-tenancy authorization system for cloud services. *IEEE Security and Privacy, 8*(6), 48–55. doi:10.1109/MSP.2010.194

Choi, J., Choi, C., Ko, B., & Kim, P. (2014). A method of DDoS attack detection using HTTP packet pattern and rule engine in cloud computing environment. *Soft Computing, 18*(9), 1697–1703. doi:10.100700500-014-1250-8

Chonka, A., & Abawajy, J. (2012, September). Detecting and mitigating HX-DoS attacks against cloud web services. In *Network-Based Information Systems (NBiS), 2012 15th International Conference on* (pp. 429-434). IEEE. 10.1109/NBiS.2012.146

Chow, R., Golle, P., Jakobsson, M., Shi, E., Staddon, J., Masuoka, R., & Molina, J. (2009). Controlling data in the cloud: outsourcing computation without outsourcing control. In *Proceedings of the 2009 ACM workshop on Cloud computing security* (pp. 85-90). ACM. 10.1145/1655008.1655020

Dastjerdi, A. V., & Buyya, R. (2016). Fog computing: Helping the Internet of Things realize its potential. *Computer*, *49*(8), 112–116. doi:10.1109/MC.2016.245

Dastjerdi, A. V., Gupta, H., Calheiros, R. N., Ghosh, S. K., & Buyya, R. (2016). Fog computing: Principles, architectures, and applications. *arXiv:1601.02752*.

Deepali, B., K. (2017). DDoS attack mitigation and Resource provisioning in Cloud using Fog Computing. In *Proceedings of International Conference On Smart Technologies For Smart Nation (SmartTechCon2017)*. IEEE

Deepali, B., K. (2017). DDoS attack Defense Framework for Cloud using Fog Computing, in *Proceedings of 2nd IEEE International Conference on Recent Trends in Electronics, Information & Communication Technology*. IEEE 10.1109/RTEICT.2017.8256654

Douligeris, C., & Mitrokotsa, A. (2004). DDoS attacks and defense mechanisms: Classification and state-of-the-art. *Computer Networks*, *44*(5), 643–666. doi:10.1016/j.comnet.2003.10.003

Geng, X., & Whinston, A. B. (2000). Defeating distributed denial of service attacks. *IT Professional*, *2*(4), 36–42. doi:10.1109/6294.869381

Goy, A., Petrone, G., & Segnan, M. (2014). A cloud-based environment for collaborative resources management. *International Journal of Cloud Applications and Computing*, *4*(4), 7–31. doi:10.4018/ijcac.2014100102

Gruschka, N., & Jensen, M. (2010). Attack surfaces: A taxonomy for attacks on cloud services. In *2010 IEEE 3rd International Conference on Cloud Computing (CLOUD)* (pp. 276-279). IEEE. 10.1109/CLOUD.2010.23

Gul, I., & Hussain, M. (2011). Distributed cloud intrusion detection model. *International Journal of Advanced Science and Technology*, *34*(38), 135.

Gupta, B. B., & Badve, O. P. (2017). Taxonomy of DoS and DDoS attacks and desirable defense mechanism in a cloud computing environment. *Neural Computing & Applications*, *28*(12), 3655–3682. doi:10.100700521-016-2317-5

Gupta, B. B., Joshi, R. C., & Misra, M. (2012). Distributed denial of service prevention techniques. arXiv:1208.3557

Gupta, S., & Kumar, P. (2013, August). Vm profile based optimized network attack pattern detection scheme for ddos attacks in cloud. In *International Symposium on Security in Computing and Communication* (pp. 255-261). Springer, Berlin, Heidelberg. 10.1007/978-3-642-40576-1_25

He, Z., Zhang, T., & Lee, R. B. (2017, June). Machine Learning Based DDoS Attack Detection from Source Side in Cloud. In *Cyber Security and Cloud Computing (CSCloud), 2017 IEEE 4th International Conference on* (pp. 114-120). IEEE. 10.1109/CSCloud.2017.58

Huang, V. S. M., Huang, R., & Chiang, M. (2013, March). A DDoS mitigation system with multi-stage detection and text-based turing testing in cloud computing. In *2013 27th International Conference on Advanced Information Networking and Applications Workshops (WAINA),* (pp. 655-662). IEEE. 10.1109/WAINA.2013.94

Iyengar, N. C. S. N., Ganapathy, G., Mogan Kumar, P. C., & Abraham, A. (2014). A multilevel thrust filtration defending mechanism against DDoS attacks in cloud computing environment. *International Journal of Grid and Utility Computing, 5*(4), 236–248. doi:10.1504/IJGUC.2014.065384

Jouini, M., & Rabai, L. B. A. (2016). A Security Framework for Secure Cloud Computing Environments. *International Journal of Cloud Applications and Computing, 6*(3), 32–44. doi:10.4018/IJCAC.2016070103

Kandias, M., Virvilis, N., & Gritzalis, D. (2011). The insider threat in cloud computing. In *International Workshop on Critical Information Infrastructures Security* (pp. 93-103). Springer, Berlin, Heidelberg.

Karnwal, T., Sivakumar, T., & Aghila, G. (2012, March). A comber approach to protect cloud computing against XML DDoS and HTTP DDoS attack. In *2012 IEEE Students' Conference on Electrical, Electronics and Computer Science (SCEECS).* IEEE. 10.1109/SCEECS.2012.6184829

Karnwal, T., Thandapanii, S., & Gnanasekaran, A. (2013). A filter tree approach to protect cloud computing against xml ddos and http ddos attack. In *Intelligent Informatics* (pp. 459–469). Berlin, Heidelberg: Springer. doi:10.1007/978-3-642-32063-7_49

Kwon, H., Kim, T., Yu, S. J., & Kim, H. K. (2011). Self-similarity based lightweight intrusion detection method for cloud computing. In *Asian Conference on Intelligent Information and Database Systems* (pp. 353-362). Springer, Berlin, Heidelberg. 10.1007/978-3-642-20042-7_36

Lee, K., Kim, D., Ha, D., Rajput, U., & Oh, H. (20). On security and privacy issues of fog computing supported Internet of Things environment. In *2015 6th International Conference on the Network of the Future (NOF).* IEEE.

Lo, C. C., Huang, C. C., & Ku, J. (2010). A cooperative intrusion detection system framework for cloud computing networks. In *2010 39th international conference on Parallel processing workshops (ICPPW),* (pp. 280-284). IEEE. 10.1109/ICPPW.2010.46

Marchette, D. J. (2001). *Computer intrusion detection and network monitoring: a statistical viewpoint.* Springer Science & Business Media. doi:10.1007/978-1-4757-3458-4

Marnerides, A., Spachos, P., Chatzimisios, P., & Mauthe, A. Malware detection in the cloud under ensemble empirical mode decomposition. In *Proceedings of IEEE International conference on computing, networking and communications (ICNC) and information security symposium* (pp. 82–88). Garden Grove, CA; 2015. 10.1109/ICCNC.2015.7069320

Marnerides, A. K., Spachos, P., Chatzimisios, P., & Mauthe, A. U. (2015). Malware detection in the cloud under Ensemble Empirical Mode Decomposition. In *2015 International Conference on Computing, Networking and Communications (ICNC)* (pp. 82-88). IEEE. 10.1109/ICCNC.2015.7069320

Michelin, R. A., Zorzo, A. F., & De Rose, C. A. (2014, December). Mitigating DoS to authenticated cloud REST APIs. In *2014 9th International Conference for Internet Technology and Secured Transactions (ICITST)* (pp. 106-111). IEEE. 10.1109/ICITST.2014.7038787

Modi, C. N., Patel, D. R., Patel, A., & Muttukrishnan, R. (2012, July). Bayesian Classifier and Snort based network intrusion detection system in cloud computing. In *2012 Third International Conference on Computing Communication & Networking Technologies (ICCCNT)*. IEEE. 10.1109/ICCCNT.2012.6396086

Nagar, N., & Suman, U. (2016). Analyzing Virtualization Vulnerabilities and Design a Secure Cloud Environment to Prevent from XSS Attack. *International Journal of Cloud Applications and Computing*, 6(1), 1–14. doi:10.4018/IJCAC.2016010101

Negi, P., Mishra, A., & Gupta, B. B. (2013). Enhanced CBF packet filtering method to detect DDoS attack in cloud computing environment. arXiv:1304.7073

Ouf, S., & Nasr, M. (2015). Cloud Computing: The Future of Big Data Management. *International Journal of Cloud Applications and Computing*, 5(2), 53–61. doi:10.4018/IJCAC.2015040104

Ren, K., Wang, C., & Wang, Q. (2012). Security challenges for the public cloud. *IEEE Internet Computing*, 16(1), 69–73. doi:10.1109/MIC.2012.14

Sharma, N., Singh, M., & Misra, A. (2016, March). Prevention against DDOS attack on cloud systems using triple filter: An algorithmic approach. In *Computing for Sustainable Global Development (INDIACom), 2016 3rd International Conference on* (pp. 560-565). IEEE.

Shruthi, B. T., & Nijagunarya, Y. S. (2016). X-DoS (XML Denial of Service) Attack Strategy on Cloud Computing. *Imperial Journal of Interdisciplinary Research, 2*(12).

Somani, G., Gaur, M. S., Sanghi, D., Conti, M., & Buyya, R. (2017). Service resizing for quick DDoS mitigation in cloud computing environment. *Annales des Télécommunications*, 72(5-6), 237–252. doi:10.100712243-016-0552-5

Stergiou, C., Psannis, K. E., Kim, B. G., & Gupta, B. (2016). Secure integration of IoT and cloud computing. *Future Generation Computer Systems*.

Stojmenovic, I., & Wen, S. (2014). The fog computing paradigm: Scenarios and security issues. In *2014 Federated Conference on Computer Science and Information Systems (FedCSIS)*. IEEE.

Stolfo, S. J., Salem, M. B., & Keromytis, A. D. (2012). Fog computing: Mitigating insider data theft attacks in the cloud. In *2012 IEEE Symposium on Security and Privacy Workshops (SPW)* (pp. 125-128). IEEE.

Subashini, S., & Kavitha, V. (2011). A survey on security issues in service delivery models of cloud computing. *Journal of Network and Computer Applications, 34*(1), 1–11. doi:10.1016/j.jnca.2010.07.006

Vaquero, L. M., & Rodero-Merino, L. (2014). Finding your way in the fog: Towards a comprehensive definition of fog computing. *Computer Communication Review*, *44*(5), 27–32. doi:10.1145/2677046.2677052

Vitti, P. A. F., dos Santos, D. R., Westphall, C. B., Westphall, C. M., & Vieira, K. M. M. (2014). Current issues in cloud computing security and management. In *SECURWARE 2014* (p. 47).

Wang, B., Zheng, Y., Lou, W., & Hou, Y. T. (2015). DDoS attack protection in the era of cloud computing and software-defined networking. *Computer Networks*, *81*, 308–319. doi:10.1016/j.comnet.2015.02.026

This research was previously published in the International Journal of E-Services and Mobile Applications (IJESMA), 10(3); edited by Mirjana Pejic-Bach, pages 61-83, copyright year 2018 by IGI Publishing (an imprint of IGI Global).

Chapter 96

Multi–Aspect DDOS Detection System for Securing Cloud Network

Pourya Shamsolmoali
Advanced Scientific Computing, CMCC, Italy

Masoumeh Zareapoor
Shanghai Jiao Tong University, China

M.Afshar Alam
Jamia Hamdard University, India

ABSTRACT

Distributed Denial of Service (DDoS) attacks have become a serious attack for internet security and Cloud Computing environment. This kind of attacks is the most complex form of DoS (Denial of Service) attacks. This type of attack can simply duplicate its source address, such as spoofing attack, which defending methods do not able to disguises the real location of the attack. Therefore, DDoS attack is the most significant challenge for network. In this chapter we present different aspect of security in Cloud Computing, mostly we concentrated on DDOS Attacks. The Authors illustrated all types of Dos Attacks and discussed the most effective detection methods.

INTRODUCTION

Cloud computing according to National Institute of Standards and Technology (NIST) is "a service that is provided in two forms. Computing power and data storage, remotely over the internet with negligible efforts for resource allocation, management, and release" (Mell and Grance, 2011). The US National Institute of Standards and Technology (NIST) have captured five essential cloud characteristics which are (Mell & Grance, 2011). "Ubiquitous network access, Rapid elasticity, Resource pooling, on-demand self-service, measured service".

DOI: 10.4018/978-1-5225-8176-5.ch096

With Cloud Computing, users use a range of devices, including PCs, laptops, smartphones and PDAs to access programs, storage, and application development platforms over the Internet, via services offered by cloud computing providers Cloud computing provides three major services to its users at various layers of computing. These include as follow: "software as a service, platform as a service and infrastructure as a service". Advantages of the cloud computing technology consist of cost savings, high availability and easy scalability (Man & Huh, 2011). Cloud computing has three basic abstraction layers i.e. "system layer (which is a virtual machine abstraction of a server), the platform layer (a virtualized operating system of a server) and application layer (that includes web applications)" (Shelke et al., 2012).

While switching from traditional local computing paradigm to the cloud computing paradigm, new security and privacy challenges come out because of the distributed nature of cloud computing. A number of these security vulnerabilities leave open doors, which stem from the existing computing models; and some of them, inherent from cloud-based models. Therefore, Attacker force these doors to attack the system, and they attack end-users' private data; processing power, bandwidth or storage capacity of the cloud network.

Armbrust et al. (2010), noted, the cloud has the ability to change a large part of the IT industry. Currently, it is rising as a computing key platform for distributing infrastructure resources, software resources and application resources (Doua et al., 2013). "DDOS attacks prevents the legitimate access the server, exhaust their resources and accrues large financial loss and have become one of the most important security threats to the Net". It is simple to start an attack with few tools but at the victim side, it is not easy to stop it (Du and Nakao, 2010; Doua et al., 2013). Therefore, these critical services need some advanced protection system. "Network Performance degradation, revenue loss, and service unavailability is an issue that motivated us to offer protection for these collaborative applications.

Since Cloud infrastructure has massive network traffic, the traditional Intrusion Detection Systems are not competent enough to handle such a large data flow. Most known Intrusion Detection Systems are single threaded and due to prosperous dataset flow, there is a need of multi-threaded Intrusion Detection Systems in Cloud computing environment.

In this chapter, it is aimed to offer definitions and properties of several attack types in cloud network and to introduce DDOS detection and prevention models to resist these types of attacks. The Proposed model has a high accuracy, very simple to set up and requires very small storage.

BACKGROUND

The increased incidences of security threats and increased harm by DDoS attacks have motivated the development of multiple types of attack detection mechanisms. These approaches differ depending on the purpose of detection and set of rules required for operation. Most of these methods are based on identifying anomalies in network traffic.

Specht and Lee (2004), Shamsolmoali et al. (2014) mentioned "DDOS attack is generally classified into bandwidth depletion and resource depletion attack. In bandwidth depletion attack, attackers flood the target with huge packet traffic that avoids the legitimate traffic and intensifies the attack by sending messages to broadcast IP address." In resources reduction attack, attackers aim to tie up the significant resources (processor and memory) then trying to enable the victim to process the services.

Karimazad and Faraahi (2011) introduced an anomaly based DDoS detection system based on features of attack packets. For evaluation, the author used Radial Basis Function (RBF) neural networks. Vectors with seven features are used to activate an RBF neural network and classify traffic into normal or DDoS attack traffic. They evaluated the approach by using UCLA Datasets. Their system can be classified either normal or attack, but the system can't classify and identified which form of attacks has been targeted the network. Dou et al. (2013) "proposed a method for filtering a DDOS attack called CBF. This system calculates the score of a particular packet at the attack time and decides whether to discard it or not."

In Basheer Nayef (2005), the correlation between the outgoing and incoming traffic of a network is discussed and the changes in the correlation are the metrics to detect DDoS attack. Fuzzy classification is used in order to guarantee the accuracy. Their method is evaluated by using DARPA datasets.

In Chen et al. (2006), "a multiple data mining approaches is used to classify the traffic pattern and diverse attacks. Decision Tree has been used in this model to select important attributes and neural networks are exploited to analyze the selected attributes".

Oktay and Sahingoz (2013) presented a "review on the different attack types, which affect the availability, confidentiality and integrity of resources and services in cloud computing environment. Additionally, the chapter also introduces related intrusion detection models to identify and prevent these types of attacks".

Raj Kumar and Selvakumar (2012) have done research work on DDOS attack detection systems. "They evaluate the performance of a comprehensive set of machine learning algorithms for choosing the best classifier. They note that single classifier creates an error on different training samples. So, by creating an ensemble of classifiers and combination of their outputs, the total error can be much reduced and the detection accuracy can be significantly improved".

Limwiwatkul and Rungsawang (2006) proposed a model to discover DDoS attack against well-defined rules and conditions, and distinguishing the difference between legitimate and attack traffic. The authors significantly focus on ICMP, TCP, and UDP flooding attacks. In (Thwe and Phyu, 2013), this approach is a statistical approach based on multiple features values. The proposed system only showed features extraction module and saved these features into the database to identify normal and attack packets.

(Varalakshmi and Selvi, 2013), proposed "a multiple level DDOS defense mechanisms by using an information divergence method that detects the attacker and rejects the packets in a fixed amount of time in an organized way". Du and Nakao (2010), Shamsolmoali et al. (2014) "proposed architecture to mitigate DDOS attacks by introducing a credit-based accounting mechanism, where a machine can send packets based on its credit points".

In Thwe and Thandar (2013) the proposed system has a combination of data mining technique to detect protocol anomaly against DDoS attack. In this work, traffic features are extracted from network traffic and then it clustered into legal and attack traffic by using a data mining classification algorithm. Chonka et al. (2011) noted "HTTP Denial of service and XML Denial of service attacks are the most serious threats to cloud computing. They offer a scheme called as Cloud Trace Back (CTB) to locate the source of these attacks". Li and Li (2010) introduced an adaptive system, which is used for defending against DDOS attacks. Lu et al. (2007) "proposed a novel framework to robustly detect DDOS attacks and recognizes attack packets." Kim and Reddy (2008) "Proposed a traffic detector, which can be worked in real time by monitoring the packet headers".

Man and Huh (2011), proposed a model called as Collaborative Intrusion Detection System. "The proposed system could reduce the impact of these kinds of attacks through providing timely notifications about new intrusions to Cloud users' systems. To provide such ability, IDSs in the cloud computing regions both correlate alerts from multiple elementary detectors and exchange knowledge of interconnected Clouds with each other".

CLOUD COMPUTING SECURITY

Cloud Computing

Cloud Computing is getting extensive in the worldwide business and IT industry. Clouds computing can be distinct as an Internet-based computing which Virtual shared servers provide all the required resources to the Cloud customer (CAIDA, 2007). The most advantage of Cloud Computing is that the customers can able to select what they want at any location. It also aims to diminish the maintenance and operational cost. The third party provider commonly known as Cloud provider provides any kind of physical infrastructure for rent. Hence, Cloud customers do not need to own the physical infrastructure, therefore, reduces the cost of physical infrastructure. There are three layers in the Cloud computing these three layers are discussed as follow:

1. **Cloud Application:** This is the first layer of the Cloud. The remote clients get access to all applications and data provided by a web browser. So it is not required to install the applications on customer's computer and thereby it decline the maintenance cost and operational cost of a Companies.
2. **Cloud Platform:** This is the second layer in the Cloud. The computational service is supplied by this layer to the customer. This Computational service enables customers to make modification in the server's configuration and settings according to the demand of a customer.
3. **Cloud Infrastructure:** The last layer of the Cloud provides a Cloud Infrastructure. The conception of Virtualization is provided by this Cloud layer. Virtualization enables customers to share a range of software and hardware components and supply platform by means of splitting a single piece of hardware and independent components. Virtualization is the establishment of a near version of software and hardware components. These are then interconnected with others for flexibility and additional storage (CAIDA, 2007).

The cloud computing layers are described in architecture diagram as following (see Figure 1).

The main benefits for all the small scale and large scale organizations using Cloud Computing are mentioned below:

1. **Cost Reduction:** By shifting to Cloud environment Customers avoid the heavy expenditure of spending a large amount of cost for establishing set-up. This also decreases the operational cost. The customers may pay for only what they use.
2. **Scalable and Flexible:** Companies are able to start a business from the simpler model and can create the complex model and if required can again get back to the previous model. Verity enables Customers to use more resources at peak time in order to satisfy the requirements of clients.
3. **Quick and Easy Implementation:** A Company can get the Cloud service in a short period and easy to implement without any software licenses or implementation services.
4. **Reduced Maintenance Cost:** The Cloud service provider provides any maintenance to the customer and maintenance of application is done by APIs, thus reducing maintenance cost.
5. **Quality of Service:** Cloud service provider provides 24*7 support and immediate service in case of faults.
6. **Mobility:** Cloud customer can able to access the data and application from any location at any time by just having an internet connection. So it is idle for increasing productivity by a mobile user.

Figure 1. Cloud architecture

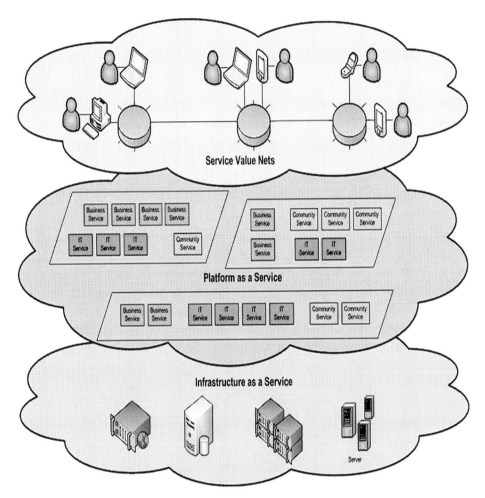

Virtual Machines

Virtualization is a vital component in cloud computing. "It is a key element which simplifies the service delivery of a set of animatedly scalable resources such as storage, software, processing power and other computing resources to the cloud users which can be accessed over the Internet on demand. A user needs only a browser and an Internet connection to use these resources. Virtual machines (VMs) are created within a virtualization layer" (Jin et al., 2011). A cloud is built upon numerous host machines these physical machines then run multiple virtual machines, which is accessible to the end-users. Moreover, virtualization software existing that can imitate entire computer, for an instant, a single computer can perform as though it were actually 50 computers. With the use of such kind of software, one might be able to migrate from a datacenter with thousands of servers to very few numbers.

"Virtual machines are only limited in the way that their stipulation cannot exceed their host machine."

A virtual machine is a software execution of a computing environment in which an operating system (OS) or program can be installed and run. "The virtual machine normally emulates a physical computing environment but asks for CPU, memory, hard disk, network and other hardware resources from the host machine that is handled by a virtualization layer which translates these requests to the underlying physical hardware. Researchers have the right to test applications, their deployments, and upgrades more efficiently by using VMs." They do not need several OS and installation configurations.

Cloud Security Issues

Cloud computing security is one significant issue in the practice of cloud services. Cyber-attacks to the large internet ventures keep on rising and they directly affect the cloud users. Cloud customers (organizations) are questioning the security of moving their computational resources to the cloud. "These improper operations are generally conducted due to a number of reasons. Financial gain also can motivate to steal valuable information from sensitive organizations such banking sector. Cyber surveillance operations in general conducted to compile the information about financial or industrial adversaries are some of the new trends over the internet". Current network security mechanisms encounter new challenges in the cloud such as DDOS attacks (Monowar et al., 2013), "virtual machine intrusion attacks and malicious user activities. Thus, new security methods" (Chuan et al., 2012), (Subashini and Kavitha, 2011) are required to raise users' level of trust to cloud computing.

At the present era, cloud service providers implement data encryption for the data centers, virtual firewalls, and access control lists. (Cloud Security Alliance, 2010) identify the following threats in the initial document:

- Abuse and Nefarious Use of Cloud Computing,
- Insecure Application Programming Interfaces,
- Malicious Insiders,
- Shared Technology Vulnerabilities,
- Data Loss/Leakage, and
- Account, Service & Traffic Hijacking.

DDOS Attack

A DDOS attack is a malicious effort to do not let the resources (a server or a network resource) be available for the end users, usually by blocking or interrupting the services of a host machine. DDOS attack took place by using a number of computers and Internet connections often distributed globally. Figure 2 shows a simple DDOS attack scenario (Weiler, 2002), (Bhadauria et al., 2011) in which multiple attacker computers are sending streams of malicious packets to the victim machine.

DDoS Attacks in Past

DDoS attacks are commenced by a network of remotely controlled, well structured, and widely dispersed nodes called Zombies. The attacker launches the attack with the help of zombies. These zombies are called as secondary victims. "The recent attacks in 2013 take in the attack in China's websites, Bitcoin, largest cyber-attack by Cyber Bunker, NASDAQ trading market, Iranian Cyber-attacks on FBI and so. From the above survey, most of the victims of DDoS attacks are distributed and shared. Apart from the list illustrated there are numerous anonymous tools emerging day by day".

Figure 2. Distributed denial-of-service attack scenario

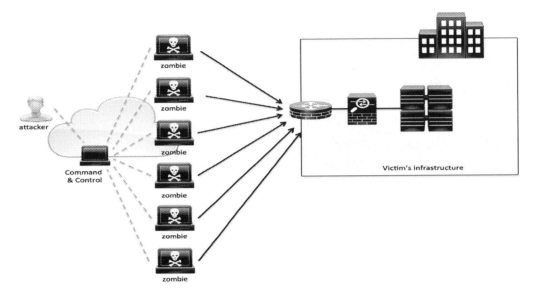

Table 1 lists the DDoS attacks occurred over years and how it evolved (DDOS attack tool, 2000; History of ddos, 2012; Denial of service, 2012).

DDOS attacks try to carry out the following malicious operations:

1. Control legitimate network traffic by flooding the network with malicious traffic.
2. Deny access to a service by way of disrupting communication between legitimate sender and receiver,
3. Block the right to use a particular service or an individual.

DDOS attacks guide to interruption of services in the cloud and is considered as one of the significant intrusions in cloud computing. Intrusion detection and prevention systems taxonomy attacks are classified as outside and inside attacks (Specht and Lee, 2004), (Vasanthi and Chandrasekar, 2011). The attacks that enter from external origins are called outsider attacks. Insider attacks involve unauthorized internal users attempting to expand and misuse non-authorized access privileges. Intrusion detection is the mechanism of monitoring computers or networks for unauthorized entry, activity or file variation. Attacks may be treated as incidents. "Although many incidents are malicious naturally, many others are not; for example, a person might mistype the IP address of a computer and by coincidence attempt to connect to a different system without authorization.

There is an established underground cybercriminal economy which works to attain their private individual goals best known for their keen interest in spying or for competitive monetary gains, motives that are possible by the use of disruptive technologies like DDOS attack". Thus creating the science of DDOS attacks ever evolving and growing in the current context in such a method that a continuous monitoring with sophisticated watchdog capabilities is required as these attacks continue to generate online outrages, "customer inconvenience and reputation damages across all industries and geographies". The best-known victims of recent moves of these DDOS attacks (Udhayan and Anitha, 2009), (Chuiyi

Table 1. DDoS attacks in past

Year	Details
1998	First, DDoS tools were discovered. These tools were not used widely but point-to-point DoS attacks and Smurf amplification attacks continued.
1999	Trinoo network was used to flood a single system at the University of Minnesota, which made the network unusable for more than 2 days. And massive attack using Shaft was detected. The Data gathered during the attack was then analyzed in early 2000 by Sven Dietrich and presented in a paper at the USENIX LISA 2000 conference.
2000	• 15 year old boy Michael Calce (Mafiaboy) launched attack on Yahoo's website. He was then sentenced in juvenile detention center for 8 months. He also went forward to degrade the servers of CNN, eBay, Dell, and Amazon, showing how easy it was to damage such major websites. • One of the first major DDOS flooding on Yahoo
2001	• The attack size grows from Mbps to Gbps. Efnet was affected by a 3 Gbps DDoS attack. • DNS servers attack as reflectors. DOS attack on Irish Government's Department of Finance server. The target was Register.com
2002	• It was reported that 9 of the 13 root internet servers were under serious threat of DDoS attack. Congestion due to attack made few rootname servers were not reachable from many parts of the global Internet, which made many valid queries unanswered. • DDOS flooding attack thru Domain Name System (DNS) service.
2003	• Mydoom was used to shut down the service of SCO group's website. Thousands of PC's were infected to send the data to target server. • Attack on SCO and Microsoft.
2004	• Authorize-IT and 2Checkout were Online payment processing firms attacked by DDoS in April targeted. It was later known that the attackers extorted and threatened to shut down there sites. • Attack on SCO Group website to make it inaccessible to valid users.
2005	In August of 2005, jaxx.de, a gambling site was under DDoS attack and to stop this attack, the attacker demanded 40,000 euros.
2006	• A number of DDoS attacks targeted the blog of Michelle Malkin. The attacks started on Feb. 15, and continued till Feb. 23. • Target US Banks for financial gain.
2007	• In December 2007 during the riots in Russia, government sites suffered severe DDoS attacks. Access to IP addresses outside Estonia was removed by many of them for several days. • Estonia Cyber Attack
2008	• In November 2008, the Conficker worm used vulnerabilities found in Microsoft OS. It uses vulnerable machine and other machines are unwillingly connected to it, to make a large botnet. • DDOS Attack on BBC, Amazon.com and eBuy.
2009	• On 4th July (Independence Day in the US) 27 websites of White House, Federal Trade Commission, Department of Transportation, and the Department of the Treasury were attacked. On 1st august, Blogging pages of many social networking sites (Twitter, Facebook etc.) were affected by DDoS attack, aimed at "Cyxymu" Georgian blogger. • DDOS flooding attacks on South Korea and the United States in July 2009 against government news media and financial websites.
2010	• Operation Payback: DDoS attacks launched on websites of MasterCard, PayPal and Visa, as they decide to stop giving service to WikiLeaks.
2011	• LulzSec hacktivist group attacked website of CIA (cia.gov). • DDOS attack on Sony.
2012	• Many attacks at us banks involve use of itsoknoproblembro DDoS tool. Many such do-it-yourself toolkits are available. • DDOS Attack on Canadian Political Party Elections and on US and UK Government Sites
2013	• DDOS attack on stock exchange websites in London. • 150 Gbps DDoS attacks are increasing.
2014	114 percent increase in average peak bandwidth of DDOS attacks in Q1 vs. Q4 2013. The Media and Entertainment industry was the target of the majority of malicious attacks. (Retrieved December 05, 2014 from http://www.akamai.com/html/about/press/releases/2014/press-041714.html)

et al., 2011) and "those who have been successfully being able to mitigate such attacks can never get a sound sleep as it is apparent from current incidences of this attack globally".

Types of DDOS Attacks

Distributed Denial of Service (DDoS attack) is a customized form of DoS attack. DoS attack is triggered to make unavailable the targeted system to its intended users by flooding the targeted system with malicious traffic using a single node. While DDoS attack is initiated by gaining illegal remote access to some compromised machine known as Zombies.

"DDOS attacks uses zombies, to send infinite requests to a target system on command from the attacker. generally DOS attacks involve spoofing of the attackers' IP addresses as the victims' IP addresses, making it complex to recognize the attackers" (Chonka et al., 2012), (Kim et al., 2011), (Shamsolmoali et al., 2014) "have done systematic review on the dark side of the internet. The authors summarized the most important type of DOS attacks". The main forms of DOS attacks are as follow.

1. **Network Depletion Attack:** In network depletion attack, the attacker tried to consume all the targeted network bandwidth by flooding targeted network with malicious traffic which will eventually avoid the legitimate traffic from approaching the targeted network. Network depletion attack can further classify into two types.
    a.   Flood Attack.
    b.   Amplification Attack.
2. **Ping Flood:** "A ping flood is the basic form of DOS attack. In this type of attack, the attacker simply sends a large number of ping packets to the victim node. If the target sends replies, the effect is amplified".
3. **Smurf Attack:** "It is very similar to the ping flood attack; a smurf attack uses ping packets. The attacker sends ping packets, with the spoofed source IP address to be the victim's IP address, in the direction of computers that keep a broadcast address. All computers in the broadcast address that get the ping packet send responds to the victims' IP address. A packet that sent to the broadcast address is amplified by the number of computers that send reply packets".
4. **UDP Flood:** "In a UDP flood attack, the attacker sends a large number of UDP packets to random ports to the target. As the UDP does not have a congestion control system, the attacker can potentially send infinitive packets. This attack is generally used with IP address spoofing so that the attacker can stay away from detection".
5. **Mail Bomb Attack:** "In a mail bomb attack, the attacker sends a lot of e-mails to a target e-mail address to overflow the victim's mailbox or slow down the mail server. The attacker may command zombies to send e-mails to the victim e-mail address simultaneously. An attacker may create each e-mail with a different message to pass the spam filters".
6. **Resource Depletion Attack:** In this kind of attack, attacker goal is to exhaust server's processing capabilities or memory. two types of attack which target Server resources are as follows:
    a.   **Protocol Exploit Attack:** "The idea behind this kind of attack is to find an exploit in a specific feature of the protocol used by the victim and then consume the excess amount of resources from it" (Mell and Grance, 2011). The best example of this kind of attack is TCP SYN attacks.

b. **Malformed Packet Attack:** Data Packet is wrapped with the malicious information. "This kind of packet is sent to the victim's server by an attacker to crash it. IP Address attack and IP Packet options attack are the best example for this kind of attack" (Mell and Grance, 2011).

7. **TCP SYN Flood:** "TCP SYN flood is a type of attack which the attacker sends a large number of SYN packets (connection requests) to the target, and fills up the connection queues on the target, so the victim cannot launch connections for legitimate clients".

8. **Peer-to-Peer Attack:** "Conventional DDOS attacks use zombie computers to send a large number of requests to the victim.P2P attacks to use clients linked to P2P file sharing hubs".

9. **Application Attack:** In this kind of attack, the attacker finds an exploit in the application protocol. An attacker can target any of the application protocol such as HTTP, HTTPS, DNS, SMTP, FTP, VOIP, and other application protocols which hold exploitable weakness.

10. **Protocol Attacks:** Protocol Attacks take advantage of a specific feature or implementation bug of some protocol installed at the victim for the function of consuming the maximum amount of its resources to take benefit of protocol intrinsic design. "All these attacks require a lot of attackers (zombies) and are mitigated by changing the protocol features. Some examples of popular protocol attacks Smurf Attack, UDP Attack, ICMP Attack, SYN attack, Attack using DNS systems", CGI request attack, Attack using spoofed address in ping, Authentication server attack etc.

Figure 3. Taxonomy of DDoS attacks

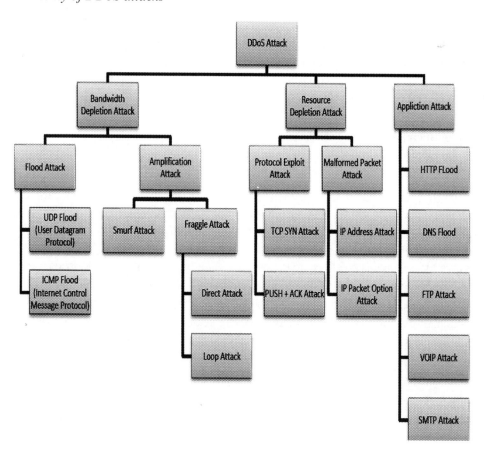

11. **Software Vulnerability Attacks:** Software Vulnerability Attacks allows an attacker to take advantage of a software program design flaw that may be a Land attack, Ping of Death or Fragmentation etc. Vulnerability in software means a weakness which permits an attacker to lessen a system's information assurance.

DDOS Attack Statistics

Attackers are getting complicated. "They are changing their tools and techniques to intrude into the network of others and attack intentionally". Following are the factors that show light on attack sophistication of the intruders:

- Intruders are doing their best to apply multi-vulnerability attack mechanism to target all layers of the victim's IT infrastructure. The layers namely the network, servers, and application layers.
- Intruders are more concentrating on DDoS tools to focus on applications rather than distributed denial of service (DDoS) attack tools that focused on networks.
- Intruders are using "low & slow" attack mechanism keeping in mind to misuse the application resource rather than resources in the network stacks.
- Intruders are more focusing on evasion techniques to avoid detection and mitigation including SSL based attacks, changing the page request in a HTTP page flood attacks etc.

Following components/processes are "required to ensure high availability of services for the cloud customers that means appropriate scrubbing centers are required for this purpose either at cloud service provider end or user end which is not an easy task."

- Detection and Monitoring System.
- Threat correlation services.Threat alert system.
- Threat identification service with false positives recognition.
- Threat rate of change.
- Threat severity analysis.
- Threat heuristics at every layer.

Hence, when a centralized data cleansing stations are organized having all achievable capabilities as mentioned above where traffic is scrutinized and mischievous traffic (DDOS, known susceptibilities and exploits) are moved or absorbed. There is normally an assumption that volumetric attack bandwidth consumption can be defeat by adding more and more bandwidth, and swallow all data traffic thereby continuing the services. Since "the target of the any DDOS attackers is normal to block or oversubscribe resources in such a way that it leads to degraded service performance time, long response time matching the demand of processing the incoming workload remains a constant headache." Many methods have been evolved over a considerable time now and all these methods or technologies that claim to safeguard us from DDOS attacks also consider the various possible correlations which might be working for the advantage of the attackers.

Existing Techniques for Detecting DDoS Attacks

In this part, we present a review of existing literature on DDoS attack detection methods. These methods are based on the structural design discussed above namely, victim-end, source-end, and in-network. We discuss these schemes without taking into consideration their practical deploys ability in real networks. Current trends illustrate that soft computing approaches have been used heavily for DDoS attack detection:

1. **Statistical Methods:** In Muda et al. (2011) authors proposed "network detection solution by combining supervised learning technique and unsupervised learning technique. They used K-Means algorithm for unsupervised learning and Naive Bayes algorithm for supervised learning". The first step of the algorithm is "using K-Means algorithm to group data to normal or attack. Then, use Naïve Bayes algorithm to classify the obtained result into attack type. The KDD 99 dataset was used to evaluate the performance of this algorithm. The detection rate was improved to 99.6 percent. However, this solution is not practical for the real network because K-Means algorithm requires" other time to process vast data in real networks which could lead to bottleneck trouble and system crash.

2. **Intrusion Detection System:** The majority standard feature of IDS is that it consistent for each virtual machine in a cloud environment. This is the method is used for detecting the DDoS attacks in (Lonea and Popescu, 2013). In IDS system, the IDS are used at the cluster controller. And it is "applied to each virtual machine and in this way cloud computing platform avoids the overloading problem that could be caused by DDoS attack. And the furthermore advantage of this strategy as described by Roschke et al. (2009)" is the advantage of decreasing the impact of the probable attacks by the IDS Sensor VMs.

3. **IDS Based DempsterShafer Theory:** This technique generally focuses on detecting and analyzing the Distributed Denial of Service (DDoS) attacks in cloud computing environments. The DDoS attacks mostly target on cloud service disruptions. The "solution is imposed to combine the previous work of Intrusion Detection Systems (IDSs) deployed in the virtual machines of the cloud environment along with a data fusion methodology in the front-end. So when the attacker attacks cloud system, the VM-based IDS will get a warning, which will be stored in the Mysql database" or any database that is joined to the cloud system placed within the (CFU) i.e. Cloud Fusion Unit of the front-end server. "A quantitative solution is proposed for analyzing alerts generated by the IDSs, using the Dempster-Shafer theory (DST) operations in 3-valued logic and the fault-tree analysis (FTA) for the mentioned flooding attacks". At the final step, the solution uses the Dempsters combination rule to fuse evidence from several independent sources.

4. **Packet Information Gathering and Pre-Processing:** DDOS attacks have various categories like Zombie Cloud Client, correlated to virtual machines like hypervisor attack of the virtual machine. In (Modi et al., 2013) authors concentrated on distinguishing the hypervisor attack. While this attack took place it causes the resource imbalance and data loss. "The detection procedure is done with packet analysis that consists a packet loader and packet collector. Packet loader stores the files about collected packets using packet capture tool in HDFS". Packet collector performs packet information gathering through Libcap and Jpcap module from the live interface.

5. **Host Based Intrusion Detection Systems:** In (Modi et al., 2013) author explained a "host-based intrusion detection system i.e. HIDS which monitors and analyzes the information collected from a host machine. And the detection procedure follows in which the different type of the informa-

tion such as system files used, calls of system, type of data etc". Afterward, this detection system observes the modification in the host kernel and moreover checks for program's behavior. If any deviation is observed from the default behavior then the report of the attack is generated.

6. **Network-Based Detection System:** In (Muda et al., 2011) author proposed "network detection solution by combining supervised learning technique and unsupervised learning technique. They used K-Means algorithm for unsupervised learning and Naive Bayes algorithm for supervised learning". The first step of the algorithm is "using K-Means algorithm to group data to normal or attack. Then, use Naïve Bayes algorithm to classify the obtained result into attack type. The KDD 99 dataset was used to evaluate the performance of this algorithm. The detection rate was improved to 99.6 percent. However, this solution is not practical for the real network because K-Means algorithm requires" other time to process vast data in real networks which could lead to bottleneck trouble and system crash.

7. **Real-Time Detection System:** In (Komviriyavut et al., 2009) authors proposed a real-time detection approach. "They used a packet sniffer to sniff network packets in every 2 seconds and pre-processed it into 12 features and used decision tree algorithm to classify the network data. The output can be categorized into 3 types which are DDoS, Probe and normal. The result shows that this algorithm as 97.5 percent of detection rate. This technique is fast and able to use in the real network. However, it was not designed to detect unknown attacks".

Although there are many techniques are developed so far to detect and mitigate the DDoS attacks in the cloud environment but none an ideal technique has been developed yet.

DDOS Attack in Cloud Environment

Recently cloud computing has been greatly increased equally in academic research and industry technology. DDoS are one of the security threats that challenge the availability. According to Cloud Security

Figure 4. DDoS defense mechanisms

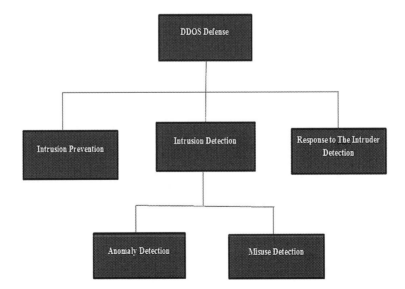

Table 2. Comparative analysis of different DDoS detection techniques

Name of Techniques	Throughput	Fault Tolerance	Performance	Overheads	Response Time	Detection Rate (%)
Statistical Method	NO	NO	YES	NO	NO	NA
Ids	YES	NO	YES	YES	YES	NA
Ids based dempster-Shafer theory	NO	YES	YES	NO	NO	NA
Packet information gathering and pre-processing	NO	NO	NO	NO	NO	NA
Host-based Intrusion Detection Systems	NO	NO	YES	NO	YES	NA
Network Detection System	NO	YES	NO	NO	NO	99.6
Real-time Detection System	YES	NO	YES	YES	YES	97.5

Alliance, DDoS is one of the main nine threats to cloud computing environment. Out of many attacks in cloud environment 14% are DoS attacks. Many recognized websites like yahoo were affected by DDoS in early 2000. Website of grc.com was hit by huge DDoS in May 2001 (Ferguson and Senie, 2001). The company was dependent on the internet for their creation work and business was seriously impacted. Forrester Consulting was contracted by VeriSign in March 2009 to carry out a study on DDoS threats and protection. The survey was performed among 400 respondents from the US and Europe (Cert advisory, 1998). 74% had experienced one or more DDoS attacks in their organizations. Out of this 74%, according to 31%, the attacks caused service disruption, according to 43% attacks does not result in services disruption. The survey of DoS attacks in cloud says that as the use of cloud increases the rate of DDoS attacks will also grow at a fast pace. In Cloud environment when the workload increases on a service, it will start providing computational power to endure the extra load. Which means Cloud system works not in favor of the attacker, but to some extent it supports the attacker by enabling him to do most possible harm to the availability of service, starting from single attack entry point.

Cloud service consists of other services provided on the same hardware servers, which may suffer by workload caused by flooding. Thus, if a service tries to run on the same server with another flooded service, this can affect its own accessibility. Another effect of a flooding is raising the bills for Cloud usage drastically. The problem is that there is no "upper limit" to the usage (Jensen et al., 2009). And one of the potential attacks to a cloud environment is neighbor attacks i.e. VM can attack its neighbor in same physical infrastructures and thus avoid it from providing its services. These attacks can affect cloud performance and can cause financial losses and can cause a destructive effect on other servers in same cloud infrastructure.

Impact of Cloud Computing on DDoS Attack Defense

Currently, attackers can launch a range of DDoS attacks including resource-focused ones (e.g. network bandwidth, memory, and CPU) and application-focused ones (e.g. web applications, database service) from approximately everywhere.

To be realistic, 'we have to assume attackers can reside either in a private network, in a public network, or in both. To this end, we find the following properties of cloud computing affect DDoS attack defense".

1. Instead of users, cloud providers control network and computation resources, i.e., physical servers. This property differs from the system model in the usual DDoS attack defense, where the protected application servers are within the defender prohibited network.
2. Resource allocation and virtual machine migration are new sources of network topological changes from the defender's view. "Moreover, the resource allocation and virtual machine migrations processes are fast-paced.

The DDoS attack defense must be able to adapt to a dynamic network with frequent topological modifies and still maintain high detection rate and prompt reaction capability".

All cloud users distribute the same network infrastructure of the cloud. "This raises a reliable network separation requirement, which has not been considered in traditional DDoS attack defense. The enterprise must make certain its DDoS attack detection/defense operations neither affect nor be affected by other cloud users".

HOW CLOUD COMPUTING CAN IMPROVE EXISTING DDOS SECURITY TECHNIQUES

DDoS attacks can probably affect every layer of the OSI model, but the mitigation of large-scale DDoS attacks take place over layers 3, 4 and 7. Our discussion focuses on attacks performed over layer 4 and 7, because of their current rise in reputation and complexity at defending and mitigating their effects. A DDoS attack originating from malware infected SG devices that are executed over these layers could have major impacts on the operations of the SG (Goel, 2015).

There are several different techniques to defend against DDoS attacks (Darwish et al., 2013), but our analysis is limited to the DDoS defense techniques that can be enhanced by operating the inherent attributes of CC. "We are also accepting that CC is a fully included component of SG, to the extent that CC is not just being used for data storage, but also data processing, virtualizing software for energy suppliers, utility companies, consumers, and integrating corporate networks and industrial control systems." (Peng et al., 2007) DDoS defense techniques categorized into four major types:

*   Attack prevention,
*   Attack detection,
*   Attack source identification, and
*   Attack reaction.

Attack Prevention Defense Mechanisms

Attack prevention mechanisms try to stop DDoS attacks earlier than they can approach their target, typically through the use of a variety of packet filtering techniques (Mirkovic & Reiher, 2004; Park & Lee, 2001). "Methods such as ingress/egress filtering and router-based packet filtering are effective for small scale attacks, but in large, commonly distributed DDoS attacks; they are ineffective even when the source of the attack is known" (Swaprava et al., 2012). As the efficiency of filtering techniques is questionable, particularly for OSI layer 7 attacks, energy suppliers, and utility companies could utilize honey pots and honeynets to gain intelligence of potential DDoS attacks. Honeypots are systems configured with partial security to trick would-be attackers to target them as an alternative to the actual system (Spitzner, 2002). Honeypots could take benefit of CCs ability to virtualize servers and duplicate services (Biedermann et al., 2012).

Traditionally, high-interaction honeypots have been costly to maintain, "Especially when virtualization is unavailable. The design of an array of honeypots with different configurations, to detect vulnerabilities from malware, replication vectors, and databases could be implemented economically, be less resource intensive, and be restored more quickly if compromised". In combination with a robust network intrusion detection system (IDS), honeypots could be dynamically distributed across VMs to moderate computational overload, and play an integral role in a coordinated DDoS defense strategy (Biedermann et al., 2012; Bakshi & Yogesh, 2010).

Attack Detection

Attack detection techniques should be able to detect attacks in real-time plus post incident. Detection of DoS attacks is largely based on network data analysis (e.g. connection requests, packet headers, etc.) to distinguish anomalies in traffic patterns and imbalances in traffic rates (Carl et al., 2006). The detection system must be able to differentiate between legitimate and malicious traffic, keeping false positives outcome low down so that genuine users are not affected. Furthermore, these systems must have good system coverage and a short recognition time (Mahajan et al., 2002). Moreover, if verification schemes for SG attached devices are cooperation, attack source identification schemes may verify very useful at detecting malicious action (Fadlullah et al., 2011).

DoS-Attack-Specific Detection is used to identify attacks that "utilize the Transmission Control Protocol (TCP) over OSI layer 4 (e.g., SYN Flooding). DoS-Attack-Specific detection methods try to identify when incoming traffic is not proportional to outgoing traffic, the traffic is statistically unstable, or the attack flow does not have periodic behavior" (Gil and Poletto, 2001). These forms of detection techniques have had limited success against DDoS attacks (Peng et al., 2007), as each compromised host can closely mimic a legal user since there is no need to control the traffic pattern of a single host. Pretentious that the natural features of the attack are able to be detected early, elastic computing resources could make stronger SYN flood defense methods (Ghanti & Naik, 2014), and hypothetically be used to initiate an intentional increase in attack strength. "The geographic diversity of cloud resources could be leveraged, use of data from both the first mile and last mile routers throughout a CSPs network to pinpoint the attack source and aid ingress or egress filtering. This, coupled with redundant resources able to execute packet state investigation, would decrease the amount of time needed to shut out illegitimate traffic" (Choi et al., 2012).

Anomaly-Based Detection plans at detecting irregularities in traffic patterns on OSI layer 7 that do not match common traffic patterns collected from training data. This detection method has seen partial success against DDoS attacks because of the size and perceived legitimacy of BOTNETs. "Anomalies are not detected when traffic seems to observe with normal traffic patterns. This technique may only be effective if irregularities can be detected concerning the geographical location of IP addresses or percentage of new IP addresses seen by the victim (Peng et al., 2007). Historical data from across geographic diverse CSP resources may make anomaly detection techniques more effective by providing a more robust data set for analysis". The agile and elastic concert capabilities of CC may permit more resilient mitigation algorithms, such as an adaptive system for detecting XML and HTTP application layer attacks (Vissers et al., 2014), and SOTA (Chonka et al., 2011) to further mitigate X-DoS and DX-DoS attacks.

Attack Source Identification

Attack source recognition attempts to place where DDoS attacks are originating from. These techniques are extremely reliant on the Internet router infrastructure, and because DDoS attacks begin from the different geographical locality, many Traceback schemes are not successful against DDoS attacks. The hash-based IP Traceback system is worth mentioning as it has been shown to be successful against DDoS attacks, with some caveats (Snoeren et al., 2001). The network topology promise offered by SG and CC (Hahn et al., 2013) may possible new attack source identification schemes that succeed where usual Traceback schemes have fallen short (Park and Lee, 2001). "For hash-based IP Traceback to be effective there needs to be a wide geographic sharing of modern Traceback routers and an abundance of computing overhead to analyze packet data, especially over long periods of time (Snoeren et al., 2001). Assuming that CSPs have a large distribution of Traceback routers throughout their network and that cloud resources are spread out geographically, IP Traceback could take advantage of the agile and redundant resources available in CC. The agile and redundant computational capabilities could be leveraged for packet filtering techniques working in conjunction with other DDoS defense mechanisms" (Vasanthi & Chandrasekar, 2011), to maintain SG services, and achieve data analysis from Traceback routers on the CSP network to aid ingress and egress filtering.

Attack Reaction

Attack reaction techniques try to mitigate or eliminate the effects of a DDoS attack. For the prospect SG, this is an essential feature to avoid the SG from being completely paralyzed by an attack (Hahn et al., 2013). "Techniques consist of but are not limited to filtering out bad traffic, duplicating network resources, or even assigning costs to certain processes or transactions to limit the abuse of computational resources. CC offers many opportunities to enhance these capabilities, increasing their capacity and endurance."

History-based IP filtering (HIP) is a mechanism where routers permit arriving packets when they are verified against a pre-populated IP address database (Mitrokosa & Douligeris, 2007). "This defensive process is deemed meaningless if devices with a rightful reason on the SG are compromised and being used as part of a BOTNET (Mitrokotsa & Douligeris, 2007). "HIP filtering defense could leverage the geographic diversity, agility, and elastic performance of CC, but additional detail would be needed about how CSPs would implement the authentication process for IPs to know how and when this would be a benefit."

Load balancing is come to picture when there is a need to amplify the available server functions for vital systems to avoid them from shutting down in the event of a DDoS attack (Mitrokotsa and Douligeris, 2007). Load balancing has the ability to utilize computational resources across distributed networks (Randles et al., 2010), readily utilizing inherent abilities of CC, such as agility and redundancy, real-time response and elastic act, and virtualization and automation services (Randles et al., 2010; Begum & Prashanth, 2013). There are challenges to defeat, such as the cost of the distributed computational load (Khiyaita et al., 2012), latency, and computational bottlenecks (Hu et al., 2010), but if accurately implemented, the benefits of load balancing could be used by CSPs to help mitigate the effects of a DDoS attack made in opposition to the SG.

Discriminating pushback attempts to filter the data stream close to the DDoS attack source by finding the source of the attack and transfer the location data to all upstream routers (Mahajan et al., 2002). When attack traffic is normally distributed, or the attack basis IP is spoofed, tries of filtering attack traffic become difficult (Peng et al., 2007). Regardless of the exact technique used to monitor network congestion and packets legitimacy, the goal of the pushback technique is to filter the bad traffic as near to the source of the attack as possible. CC would be deployed indirectly, much like with DoS-Attack-Specific Detection and IP Traceback, taking benefit of agility, geographic diversity, and elastic performance to enhance the effectiveness of pushback schemes such as the cooperative pushback mechanism proposed by (Mahajan et al., 2002).

Source-end response schemes, such as D-WARD, attempt to catalog data flow statistics by continually monitoring the two-way traffic between the source network and the rest of the Internet (Mirkovic et al., 2002). "Statistics are collected such as the ratio of in-traffic and out traffic, and a number of connections per destination. The system periodically compares collected data against normal flow data models for each type of traffic that the source network receives, and if a mismatch occurs, traffic is either filtered or rate-limited" (Mirkovic et al., 2002). with the exception of privacy issues, the ability of CC could be leveraged with virtualization and automation services to catalog the traffic between SG infrastructure, CSP resources, utility companies, and infrastructure control networks, managing a robust dataset that could be used to look after the SG infrastructure. Furthermore, the elastic concert of CC could be leveraged to swiftly and efficiently compare historically and new data to detect irregularities and create quicker attack responses.

Fault Tolerance methods believe that it is impossible to prevent or stop DDoS attacks fully and to a certain extent focus on mitigating the effects of attacks so the affected network can remain operational. The line of attack is based on duplicating network services and diversifying points of the right of entry to the network. In the event of an attack, the blocking caused by attack traffic will not take down the entire affected network.

Similar to that of load balancing, "fault tolerance methods could leverage CC attributes, such as agility and redundancy, real-time response and elastic performance, and virtualization and automation services to duplicate services and keep the SG network responsive for legitimate traffic."

Resource Pricing is a mitigation move toward that utilizes a distributed gateway architecture and payment protocol to set up a dynamically changing cost, or computational burden, for initiating different forms of network services (Cert Advisory, 1998). "This technique favors users who perform well and discriminates against users who abuse system resources, by partitioning services into pricing tiers to avoid malicious users from flooding the system with false requests to attempt price operation. The high agility and elastic performance inherent in CC would alleviate the computational burden of Resource Pricing techniques" (Lonea and Popescu, 2013).

As the order of assigning prices to users grows, the computational demand would be simply mitigated by the ability of CSPs to insert extra computing resources. Expenditure levels could easily be allotted to put users into a cost hierarchy, and virtualization capabilities could be used to duplicate network resources and infrastructure capabilities, partitioning users spending dissimilar cost levels into separate processing areas. Unlawful traffic would be sectioned off from the lawful traffic, sinking the impact of an attack, and if desirable, be geographically independent.

Response to Detection

In the case when DDoS attack is detected, the next issue to do is the attack should be blocked and attacker should be traced for discovery out attacker's identity and location. This can be done in two days, firstly manually using ACL or automatically. Certain schemes used for tracing and identifying the attacker as shown in Table 4. Besides various techniques used to stop DDoS attacks but not all of the can be detected and prevented. All that can be done is to decrease the impact of the attack.

Table 3. Defense techniques and beneficial cloud computing attribute

Type of Defense	Type of Attack	Defense Technique	Beneficial CC Attributes*
Attack Prevention	SYN Flood (TCP), Smurf Attack, PDF GET, HTTP GET, HTTP POST	Honeypots	AR, SH, V
Attack Detection	SYN Flood, Smurf Attack	DoS-Attack-Specific Detection	AR, DLI, RPP
	PDF GET, HTTP GET, HTTP POST	Anomaly-Based Detection	AR, DLI, RPP
Attack Source Identification	SYN Flood, Smurf Attack; PDF GET, HTTP GET, HTTP POST	Hash-Based IP Traceback	AR, DLI
Attack Reaction	SYN Flood, Smurf Attack; PDF GET, HTTP GET, HTTP POST	HIP Filtering	AR, DLI, RPP
		Load Balancing	AR, RPP
		Selective Pushback	AR, DLI, RPP
		Source-End Reaction	AR, RPP
		Analysis of Traffic Data	AR, RPP, SH, V
		Fault Tolerance	AR, DLI, RPP, SH, V
		Resource Pricing	AR, DLI, RPP, V

*AR: Agility & Redundancy, SH: Self-healing, V: Virtualization, DLI: Device & Location Independence, RPP: Real-time Response & Elastic Performance

Table 4. Traceback Methods

Method	Description
ICMP traceback	The mechanism deals with forwarding low probability packets to each router and also sends an ICMP traceback message to the destination. With major no of ICMP messages which used to identify the attacker, faces issues like additional traffic, also the validation of these packets is difficult and moreover path detection overhead of information from route map.
IP traceback	This method traces back the attacker's path to find the origin of the attack. In this technique, the path of the attacker is followed back to find its source. But this becomes difficult if source accountability in TCP/IP protocol is disabled and also internet is stateless.
Link-testing traceback	This mechanism tests each of incoming links to check the probability of it being an attack. This is done by flooding large traffic and testing if it causes any network disruption. But the precondition to do this would be a system that will be able to flood traffic and information about the topology of the network.
Probabilistic packet marking	This technique overcomes drawbacks of link-testing traceback as it does not require previous knowledge of network topology, large traffic etc. This advantage also overheads the systems but there are many methods to avoid this overhead as proposed in.

Architecture of Proposed System

We have proposed a novel architecture for securing cloud towards network based attacks based on the previous research gaps that we have identified. Our proposed DDOS detection system is a novel architecture for detecting and mitigating DDOS from virtual machines and external entities on a cloud network. Our work focuses on offering robust security to cloud with reasonable cost. This section describes proposed model. The overall architecture of proposed model showed in Figure 5.

The proposed model consists of three main phrases as follow:

Firstly, the most important features are extracted from packets. Most effective features are extracted from the packet. Detection system extract features such as source IP, TTL, destination IP, ports and protocol flags as basic features. Karimazad et al. (2011) declared some parameters to identify the DDoS attack packets in traffic data. We also use these features because the analysis of traffic based on these features can improve the detection accuracy (Reyhaneh & Ahmad, 2011). Seven traffic features are used to detect the packets as legitimate or attack traffic. In the proposed model, only the Source port, Destina-

Figure 5. Overall architecture of proposed model

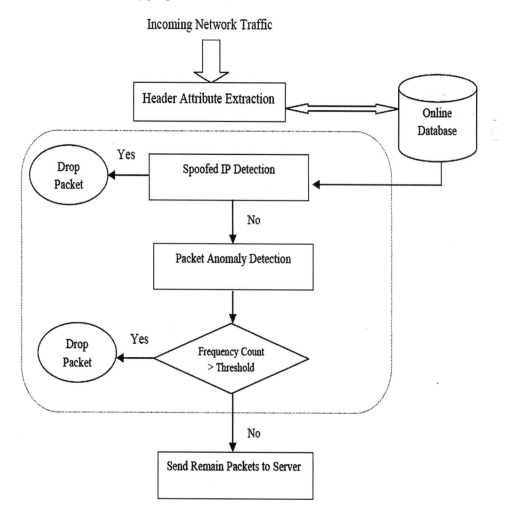

tion port, TTL, Total length, Protocol type, Window size and Flag of the packet are extracted. Secondly, the system "extracts the TTL value for all incoming packet and calculate the number of hops the packet has traveled. The attacker is able to spoof the packet header but cannot manipulate the number of Hop that each packet traveled to reach the destination count" (Varalakshmi & Thamarai, 2013). By comparing TTL's value with IP to hop count value. If exact matches do not found, so the packet is spoofed and the system discards it directly (Swaprava et al., 2012). The rest of the packets are passed to the next level.

At the end, the system clusters the traffics into ordinary or attack traffics by using deviation or anomaly behavior detection. In modern level the header information compares with the profile information which is previously trained in the database, to determine the information divergence between the two profiles. The packets are considered at this point for any anomaly behavior in the Header of the packets. The extracted attributes and their possibility for each field are considered for a certain time span. The trained profile of each attribute updates regularly to ensure negligible changes in the behavior of genuine users. We used the concept of Jensen-Shannon Divergence. The following Equations were used to compute Information Divergence (D).

By comparing the profile of already trained traffic with the new incoming traffic, the system can distinguish the legitimate traffic from the attack traffic. Information divergence is a non-commutative measure of the difference between two probability distributions P and Q. P typically represents the True distribution of data, or a precise calculation theoretical distribution. The measure Q usually represents a theory, model, or approximation of P. By referring to (1) this system firstly compute divergence for (P $\parallel$ M) and (Q $\parallel$ M) then by using (2) we can get the total divergence for the (ith) IP. If for the (ith) IP Information Divergence is more than learned profile (D$i \succ \gamma$) so the two probabilities have divergence. Therefore, P and Q denote the behavior of different entities. But if Di is equal to 0.0 then it indicates that there is a possibility of attack.

We analyze the packets which are stored in an intermediate buffer for attack use the frequency counter. The system, campers each packet with the blacklisted IP for similarity. If an exact match identified the frequency count of the packet is incremented by 1. There is a very high possibility that the attacker sends similar packet continuously which almost happens in a flooding attack. The frequency count of each packet is checked. If it exceeds the threshold value for a particular IP, the system indicates the packet as an attack and that IP is identified as the attacker. Then the system discards the packet and adds the attacker IP to the blacklist.

$$Di = \sum P(i) \times \log \frac{P(i)}{Q(i)} \tag{1}$$

$$Di = \frac{1}{2} D(Pi \parallel Mi) + \frac{1}{2} D(Qi \parallel Mi) \tag{2}$$

$$M = \frac{1}{2} - (P + Q) \tag{3}$$

In the proposed model, two algorithms are developed; Hope-count Algorithm and deviation or anomaly detector algorithm to distinguish attack packets from legitimate packets.

Algorithm 1. Hope-count

```
Algorithm Input: Network
Packet
 Output: Detect spoofed packets
  Start
   For each packet:
    Extract the TTL and the source IP address; Retrieve
    the initial TTL (Tij);
    Estimate the hope-count Hci=Tij-Tfi;
     Obtain the stored hope-count (Hsi)
            for the indexed Si; If
            (Hci≠Hsi)
          Packet is manipulated, "so it
             spoofed" drop it;
          Else
          The packet is
           legitimate to pass
           it;
          End If
        End
  For
  End
```

Algorithm 2. Packet Anomaly Detection

```
Algorithm Input: packet Header
Attributes
Output: Detect Attack Packet
Start
  For each section (t)
  If learning period
   classify probabilities of each
 value for header Attributes;
   Else
        identify probabilities of each
        value for the header Attributes for
        every IP;
        Define the Di
for IPi; If Di
≈0.0
```

```
chance of flooding
attack Use
frequency counter;
   If flooding attack "(frequency
   counter > threshold)" DDOS attack
   detected
   Drop matching
  packets;
      Else
  Pass the
 packet; End
 If
      Else
  Add the Attacker IP to
 Blacklist; End If
End
If End
For
End
```

Evaluation of the System

An effective detection system should be able to overcome all the existing issues of cloud computing to could detect all the known and unknown DDOS attack to the cloud environment.

The proposed model is evaluated with respect to implementation. For generating network traffic and DOS attack we created a cloud Lab. We have chosen a HP proliant DL 180 Gen9 server with following features: Intel Xeon E5606, 8 GB RAM, 2×500 GB SCSI Hard Drives, we also selected VMware ESXI 5.0.0 Hypervisor as virtual machine manager (VMM) and windows 7 as guest operating system. We also have 5 clients with following features: Intel core 2 duo (2.53 GHZ), 2GB RAM.

On each client machine, we installed virtual machines with the random IP addresses for generating traffic. Three client machines are generating Normal traffic consist of FTP access, Web page access, e-mail access and UDP traffic. 2 of the client machines generate attack traffic. The performance of server at the time of attack traffic is shown in Figure 6.

This work used Netwag tool to generate DDOS attacks. "For capturing the packets and access to header information, a packet capturing tool JPCap is used. JPCap is an open source java Library tool for capturing network packets And devolve applications to capture packets from a network interface and explore them in java" (Varalakshmi & Thamarai, 2013). In the beginning, all non-spoofed packets are allowed in the training period and once profiled are trained, the deviation can recognize the result in rules being framed and therefore DDOS attack packets which match the rules are discarded. Once an attack is detected, rules are framed in order to stop similar packets from entering the system" (Varalakshmi & Thamarai, 2013). This might decline the number of false positive to a small extent. In our first experiment, we used 2000 data points randomly from our lab dataset to check the detection rate and the false alarm rate of proposed system.

Figure 6. Server Performance

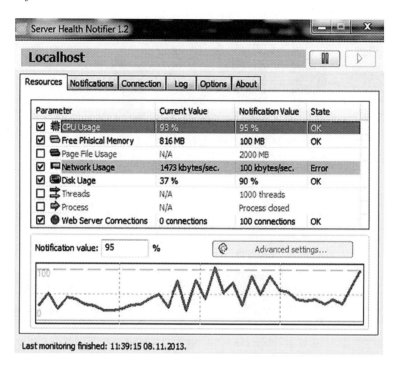

For evaluation of proposed system, we compared our proposed model with the Some Classifiers. From the presented list we have selected PART, Random Forester, Ripper and NaiveBayes to classify attack type. We used two datasets to ensure the performance of our model against the existing algorithms. Our synthetic Lab dataset and CAIDA dataset "DDoS Attack 2007". On the other hand to check the performance of proposed system with the balance and imbalance dataset as well. The dataset contains approximately one hour of anonymized traffic traces from a DDoS attack on August 4, 2007. The details of performances are showed in Figure 7, 8 and 9. "The classification accuracy shows the amount of attacks which are classified correctly, the number of unclassified instances measures the technique's limitations, which means failures in classifying a number of attacks" (Khorshed et al., 2012).

Figure 7. Detection accuracy

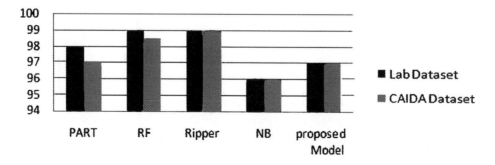

Figure 8. False alarm rate

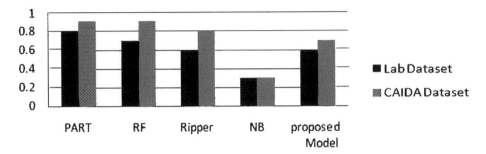

Figure 9. Detection processing time

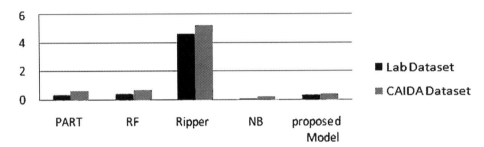

As it is evident in Figure 3 and 4 the detection accuracy of proposed model by used of Lab dataset is above 97% and the false alarm rate is 0.6%. On the other hand, Random Forester detection rate and False Alarm rate are 98% and 0.7% respectively. Furthermore, Ripper classification algorithm has more than 99% of detection nevertheless the false alarm rate is 0.7%. NaiveBayes has above 96% of detection and the false alarm rate is around 0.5%. The part algorithm has the detection rate of 97%; moreover, the false alarm rate is 0.8%. By this comparison, there is no doubt that PART, Ripper and Random Forester Classifiers in detection accuracy and False Alarm Rate have negligible better performance in comparison with our proposed model. The results show that our proposed system has an insignificant problem in the detection rate of attack traffic. This indicates that the DDOS defense system setting required to be adjusted for improving the efficiency. In Figure 5 the time processing of different classifiers showed. By comparing the time processing of different classifiers we observed. Ripper, PART, and Random Forester have significant consumption time than the proposed model. From the overall result, it is evident that the proposed model has better performance in compare to the State of Art Classifiers.

CONCLUSION

DDoS attack is one of the most significant security threats on the Internet. Detection of DDoS attack is considered to be one of the main phases in overcoming the DDoS problem. In this system, the packet features which exhibit the DDoS attack in traffic are discussed and we proposed two level of filtering to detect the attack. At the beginning, the proposed system extracts the header fields of the incoming packet to the system. In the next level, the system compares the value of TTL with the stored value of IP2HC. If there be no exact matching, the packet is spoofed and the system drops the packet. At the end, we used the concept of Jensen-Shannon Divergence. The incoming packets header information compare with the profile information that already stored in the database, to figure out the information divergence among the profiles. The core of our work is to present a system with an efficient reduce the false alarm rate and processing time. From the simulation experiments, it is evident that the proposed model in the overall has better performance in comparison to the state of art classifiers.

REFERENCES

Advisory, C. E. R. T. CA-1998-01, Smurf IP Denial-of-Service Attacks. (1998). Available: http://www.cert.org/advisories/CA-1998-01.html

Armbrust, Fox, Griffith, Joseph, Katz, Konwinski, Lee, Patterson ... Zaharia. (2010). A view of cloud computing. ACM, 53(4), 50–58.

Bakshi, A., & Yogesh, B. (2010). Securing cloud from ddos attacks using intrusion detection system in virtual machine, in Communication Software and Networks, 2010. ICCSN'10. Second International Conference on. IEEE.

Basheer Nayef, A. D. (2005). *Mitigation and traceback countermeasures for DDoS attacks*. Iowa State University.

Begum, S., & Prashanth, C. (2013). Review of load balancing in cloud computing. *International Journal of Computer Science Issues, 10*(1), 343–352.

Bellovin, S. (2000). The ICMP traceback message. Network Working Group, Internet Draft. Available at http://lasr.cs.ucla.edu/save/rfc/draft-bellovin-itrace-00.txt

Bhadauria, R. C. R., Chaki, N., & Sanyal, S. (2011). A survey on security issues in cloud computing. Retrieved from http://arxiv.org/abs/1109.5388

Bhuyan, K., Kashyap, H. J., Bhattacharyya, D. K., & Kalita, J. K. (2013). Detecting Distributed Denial of Service Attacks: Methods, Tools and Future Directions. *The Computer Journal, 57*(4), 537–556. doi:10.1093/comjnl/bxt031

Bhuyan, M. H., Kashyap, H. J., Bhattacharyya, D. K., & Kalita, J. K. (2014). Detecting distributed denial of service attacks: Methods, tools and future directions. *The Computer Journal, 57*(4), 537–556. doi:10.1093/comjnl/bxt031

Biedermann, S., Mink, M., & Katzenbeisser, S. (2012). Fast dynamic extracted honeypots in cloud computing. In *Proceedings of the ACM Workshop on Cloud computing security workshop*. 10.1145/2381913.2381916

Brody, A. (2013). History of DDoS. Retrieved from: http://www.timetoast.com/timelines/history-of-ddos

Brown, R. E. (2008). Impact of smart grid on distribution system design, in Power and Energy Society General Meeting-Conversion and Delivery of Electrical Energy. *2008 IEEE International conference.*

Burch, H., & Cheswick, H. (2000). Tracing anonymous packets to their approximate source. Proceedings of USENIX LISA (New Orleans) Conference.

Carl, G., Kesidis, G., Brooks, R. R., & Rai, S. (2006). Denial-of-service attack detection techniques. *IEEE Internet Computing, 10*(1), 82–89. doi:10.1109/MIC.2006.5

Chen, Y., Hwang, K., & Ku, W. S. (2006). Distributed change-point detection of DDoS attacks over multiple network domains. *Proceedings of the IEEE International Symposium on Collaborative Technologies and Systems*, (pp. 543–550). IEEE.

Choi, K., Chen, X., Li, S., Kim, M., Chae, K., & Na, J. (2012). Intrusion detection of nsm based dos attacks using data mining in smart grid. *Energies, 5*(10), 4091–4109. doi:10.3390/en5104091

Chonka, A., Xiang, Y., Zhou, W., & Bonti, A. (2011). Cloud security defense to protect cloud computing against HTTP-DOS and XML-DOS attacks. *Journal of Network and Computer Applications, 34*(4), 1097–1107. doi:10.1016/j.jnca.2010.06.004

Chonka, A., Xiang, Y., Zhou, W., & Bonti, A. (2011). Cloud security defence to protect cloud computing against http-dos and xml-dos attacks. *Journal of Network and Computer Applications, 34*(4), 1097–1107. doi:10.1016/j.jnca.2010.06.004

Chonka, A., Xiang, Y., Zhou, W., & Huang, X. (2012). Protecting Cloud Web Services from HX-DoS attacks using Decision Theory. IEEE International conference on communications in china: advanced internet and cloud (AIC). IEEE.

Cloud Security Alliance. (2010). Top Threats to Cloud Computing. Retrieved from http://www.cloudsecurityalliance.org/topthreats/csathreats.v1.0.pdf

Darwish, M., Ouda, A., & Capretz, L. F. (2013) Cloud-based ddos attacks and defenses. In Information Society (i-Society), IEEE International Conference. Retrieved from http://staff.washington.edu/dittrich/talks/sec2000/timeline.html

Doan, M. N., & Eui-Nam, H. (2011). A Collaborative Intrusion Detection System Framework for Cloud Computing. *Proceedings of the International Conference on IT Convergence and Security*, (pp. 91-109).

DoS and DDoS Evolution. (n.d.). Retrieved from http://users.atw.hu/denialofservice/ch03lev1sec3.html

Doua, W., Chen, Q., & Chen, J. (2013). A confidence-based filtering method for DDoS attack defence in cloud environment. *Future Generation Computer Systems, 29*(7), 1838–1850. doi:10.1016/j.future.2012.12.011

Douligeris, C., & Mitrokotsa, A. (2004). Ddos attacks and defense mechanisms: Classification and state-of-the-art. *Computer Networks, 44*(5), 643–666. doi:10.1016/j.comnet.2003.10.003

Du, P., & Nakao, A. (2010). OverCourt: DDoS mitigation through credit-based traffic segregation and path migration. *Computer Communications, 33*(18), 2164–2175. doi:10.1016/j.comcom.2010.09.009

Fadlullah, Z. M., Fouda, M. M., Kato, N., Shen, X., & Nozaki, Y. (2011). An early warning system against malicious activities for smart grid communications. *IEEE Network*, *25*(5), 50–55. doi:10.1109/MNET.2011.6033036

Feng, Y., Guo, R., Wang, D., & Zhang, B. (2009). *A comparative study of distributed denial of service attacks, intrusion tolerance and mitigation techniques, intrusion tolerance and mitigation techniques.* Academic Press.

Ferguson, P., & Senie, D. (2001). Network ingress filtering: defeating Denial of Service attacks which employ IP source address spoofing. RFC 2827.

Ghanti, S. R., & Naik, G. (2014). Protection of server from syn flood attack. *International Journal of Electronics and Communication Engineering & Technology*, *5*(11), 37–46.

Gibbens, R. J., & Kelly, F. P. (1999). Resource pricing and the evolution of congestion control. *Automatica*, *35*(12), 1969–1985. doi:10.1016/S0005-1098(99)00135-1

Gil, T. M., & Poletto, M. (2001). Multops: a data-structure for bandwidth attack detection. In *USENIX Security Symposium*.

Goel, S. (2015). Anonymity vs. security: The right balance for the smart grid. *Communications of the Association for Information Systems*, *36*(1).

Hahn, A., Ashok, A., Sridhar, S., & Govindarasu, M. (2013). Cyber-physical security testbeds: Architecture, application, and evaluation for smart grid. Smart Grid. *IEEE Transactions on*, *4*(2), 847–855.

Hu, J., Gu, J., Sun, G., & Zhao, T. (2010). A scheduling strategy on load balancing of virtual machine resources in cloud computing environment. *International Symposium on Parallel Architectures, Algorithms and Programming (PAAP)*.

Jin, H., Xiang, G., & Zou, D. (2011). A VMM-based intrusion prevention system in cloud computing environment. *The Journal of Supercomputing*, 1–19.

Karimazad, R., & Faraahi, A. (2011). An anomaly based method for DDoS attacks detection using rbf neural networks. In *Proceedings of the International Conference on Network and Electronics Engineering*.

Khiyaita, A., Zbakh, M., Bakkali, H., & Kettani, D. (2012). Load balancing cloud computing: state of art. In *Network Security and Systems (JNS2), National Days of*. IEEE. doi:10.1109/JNS2.2012.6249253

Khorshed, M., Ali, A. B. M. S., & Wasimi, S. A. (2012). A survey on gaps, threat remediation challenges and some thoughts for proactive attack detection in cloud computing. *Future Generation Computer Systems*, *6*(28), 833–851. doi:10.1016/j.future.2012.01.006

Kim, S., & Narasimha Reddy, A. L. (2008). Statistical techniques for detecting traffic anomalies through packet header data. *IEEE/ACM Transactions on Networking*, *16*(3), 562–575. doi:10.1109/TNET.2007.902685

Kim, W., Jeong, O.-R., Kim, C., & So, J. (2011). The dark side of the Internet: Attacks, costs and responses. *Information Systems*, *36*(3), 675–705. doi:10.1016/j.is.2010.11.003

Komviriyavut, T., Sangkatsanee, P., Wattanapongsakorn, N., & Charnsripinyo, C. (2009). Network intrusion detection and classification with decision tree and rule based approaches. *International Symposium on Communications and Information Technology (ISCIT)*, (pp. 1046-1050). 10.1109/ISCIT.2009.5341005

Li, M., & Li, M. (2010). An Adaptive Approach for Defending against DDoS Attacks. *Mathematical Problems in Engineering*, 1–15.

Limwiwatkul, L., & Rungsawang, A. (2006). Distributed denial of service detection using TCP/IP header and traffic measurement analysis. *Proceedings of the IEEE International Symposium Communications and Information Technology*, (pp. 605–610).

Lo, C. C., Huang, C. C., & Ku, J. (2010). A Cooperative Intrusion Detection System Framework for Cloud Computing Networks. In *39th International Conference on Parallel ProcessingWorkshops*, (pp. 280-284). 10.1109/ICPPW.2010.46

Lonea, A. M., & Popescu, D. E. (2013). TianfieldDetecting DDoS Attacks in Cloud Computing Environment. *Int J Comput Commun*, (1), 70-78.

Lu, K., Wu, D., Fan, J., Todorovic, S., & Nucci, A. (2007). Robust and efficient detection of DDoS attacks for large-scale internet. *Computer Networks*, *51*(18), 5036–5056. doi:10.1016/j.comnet.2007.08.008

Mahajan, R., Bellovin, S. M., Floyd, S., Ioannidis, J., Paxson, V., & Shenker, S. (2002). Controlling high bandwidth aggregates in the network. *Computer Communication Review*, *32*(3), 62–73. doi:10.1145/571697.571724

Meiko, J., Jorg, S., & Nil, G. (2009). On technical issues in cloud computing. *IEEE International Conference on Cloud Computing*. IEEE.

Mell, P., & Grance, T. (2009). *Effectively and Securely Using the Cloud Computing Paradigm*. US National Institute of Standards and Technology.

Mell, P., & Grance, T. (2011). The NIST Definition of cloud computing. National Institute of Standards and Technology Special Publication, 800-145. doi:10.6028/NIST.SP.800-145

Mihailescu, M., & Teo, Y. M. (2010). Dynamic resource pricing on federated clouds. In Cluster, Cloud and Grid Computing (CCGrid), IEEE/ACM International Conference, (pp. 513–517).

Mirkovic, J., Prier, G., & Reiher, P. (2002). Attacking ddos at the source. *IEEE International Conference*, (pp. 312–321). IEEE.

Mirkovic, J., & Reiher, P. (2004). A taxonomy of ddos attack and ddos defense mechanisms. *Computer Communication Review*, *34*(2), 39–53. doi:10.1145/997150.997156

Mitrokotsa, A., & Douligeris, C. (2007). Denial-of-service attacks. Network Security: Current Status and Future Directions, 117–134.

Modi, C., Patel, D., Borisaniya, B., Patel, H., Patel, A., Rajarajan, M., & Gujarat, N. S. (2013). A survey of intrusion detection techniques in Cloud. *Journal of Network and Computer Applications*, *36*(1), 42–57. doi:10.1016/j.jnca.2012.05.003

Muda, Z., Yassin, W., Sulaiman, M.N., & Udzir, N.I. (2011). Intrusion detection based on K-Means clustering and Naïve Bayes classification. Emerging Convergences and Singularity of Forms, 1-6.

Oktay, U., & Sahingoz, O. K. (2013). Attack types and intrusion detection systems in cloud computing. 6th international information security & cryptology conference, (pp. 71-76).

Parag, K., Shelke, S. S., & Gawande, A. D. (2012). Intrusion Detection System for Cloud Computing. *International Journal of Scientific & Technology Research, 1*(4), 67–71.

Park, K., & Lee, H. (2001). On the effectiveness of route-based packet filtering for distributed dos attack prevention in power-law internets. *Computer Communication Review, 31*(4), 15–26. doi:10.1145/964723.383061

Peng, T., Leckie, C., & Ramamohanarao, K. (2007). Survey of network-based defense mechanisms countering the dos and ddos problems. *ACM Computing Surveys, 39*(1), 1–42. doi:10.1145/1216370.1216373

Pourya, S. (2014). C2DF: High Rate DDOS filtering method in Cloud Computing. *Computer Network and Information Security, 6*(9), 43–50. doi:10.5815/ijcnis.2014.09.06

Raj Kumar, P. A., & Selvakumar, S. (2011). Distributed denial of service attack detection using an ensemble of neural classifier. *Computer Communications, 34*(11), 1328–1341. doi:10.1016/j.comcom.2011.01.012

Raj Kumar, P. A., & Selvakumar, S. (2012). M2KMIX: Identifying the Type of High Rate Flooding Attacks using a Mixture of Expert Systems. *Computer Network and Information Security, 1*, 1–16.

Raj Kumar, P. A., & Selvakumar, S. (2013). Detection of distributed denial of service attacks using an ensemble of adaptive and hybrid neuro-fuzzy systems. *Computer Communications, 36*(3), 303–319. doi:10.1016/j.comcom.2012.09.010

Randles, M., Lamb, D., & Taleb-Bendiab, A. (2010). A comparative study into distributed load balancing algorithms for cloud computing. In Advanced Information Networking and Applications Workshops (WAINA), IEEE International Conference on. 10.1109/WAINA.2010.85

Reyhaneh, K., & Ahmad, F. (2011). An Anomaly-Based Method for DDoS Attacks Detection using RBF Neural Networks. *International Conference on Network and Electronics Engineering IPCST*.

Roschke, S., Cheng, F., & Meinel, C. (2009). Intrusion Detection in the Cloud. In *Eighth IEEE International Conference on Dependable, Autonomic and Secure Computing*, (pp. 729-734).

Savage, S., Wetherall, D., Karlin, A., & Anderson, T. (2001). Network support for IP traceback. IEEE/ACM Transaction on Networking, 9(3), 226-237.

Snoeren, A. C., Partridge, C., Sanchez, L. A., Jones, C. E., Tchakountio, F., Kent, S. T., & Strayer, W. T. (2001). Hash-based ip traceback. *Computer Communication Review, 31*(4), 3–14. doi:10.1145/964723.383060

Specht, S. M., & Lee, R. B. (2004). Distributed Denial of Service: Taxonomies of Attacks, Tools, and Countermeasures. *Proceedings of the International Workshop on Security in Parallel and Distributed Systems*, (pp. 543-550).

Specht, S. M., & Lee, R. B. (2004). Distributed Denial of Service: Taxonomies of Attacks, Tools, and Countermeasures. International Conference on parallel and Distributed computing Systems, International Workshop on Security in Parallel and Distributed Systems, (pp. 543–550).

Spitzner, L. (2002). *Honeypots: tracking hackers* (Vol. 1). Addison-Wesley Reading.

Subashini, S., & Kavitha, V. (2011). A survey on security issues in service delivery models of cloud computing. *Journal of Network and Computer Applications, 34*(1), 1–11. doi:10.1016/j.jnca.2010.07.006

Swaprava, N., Ekambaram, V. N., Anurag, K., & Vijay, K. P. (2012). Theory and Algorithms for Hop-Count-Based Localization with Random Geometric Graph Models of Dense Sensor Networks. *ACM Transactions on Sensor Networks, 8*(4), 111–149.

The CAIDA UCSD. (2007). DDoS Attack 2007 Dataset. Retrieved from: http://www.caida.org/data/passive/ddos-20070804_dataset.xml

Thwe, O. T., & Thandar, P. (2013). A Statistical Approach to Classify and Identify DDoS Attacks using UCLA Dataset. *International Journal of Advanced Research in Computer Engineering & Technology, 2*(5), 1766–1770.

Thwe & Thandar. (2013). DDoS Detection System based on a Combined Data mining Approach. *4th International Conference on Science and Engineering.*

ToolN. (n.d.). Retrieved from: http://ntwag.sourceforge.net/

Udhayan, J., & Anitha, R. (2009). Demystifying and Rate Limiting ICMP hosted DoS/DDOS Flooding Attacks with Attack Productivity Analysis. *Advance Computing Conference. IACC 2009,* (pp. 558-564). 10.1109/IADCC.2009.4809072

Varalakshmi, P., & Thamarai Selvi, S. (2013). Thwarting DDoS attacks in grid using information divergence. *Future Generation Computer Systems, 29*(1), 429–441. doi:10.1016/j.future.2011.10.012

Vasanthi, S., & Chandrasekar, S. (2011). A study on network intrusion detection and prevention system current status and challenging issues. Advances in Recent Technologies in Communication and Computing, 181-183.

Vissers, T., Somasundaram, T. S., Pieters, L., Govindarajan, K., & Hellinckx, P. (2014). DDOS defense system for web services in a cloud environment. *Future Generation Computer Systems, 37,* 37–45. doi:10.1016/j.future.2014.03.003

Weiler. (2002). Honeypots for Distributed Denial of Service Attacks. International Workshops on Enabling Technologies: Infrastructure for Collaborative Enterprises (WETICE'02).

Xia, Du, Cao, & Chen. (2012). An Algorithm of Detecting and Defending CC Attack in Real Time. Industrial Control and Electronics Engineering (ICICEE), (pp. 1804-1806).

Xie, Zhang, Bai, Luo, & Xu. (2011). A Distributed Intrusion Detection System against flooding Denial of Services attacks. Advanced Communication Technology, 878-881.

KEY TERMS AND DEFINITIONS

DDoS: A distributed denial-of-service (DDoS) attack occurs when multiple systems flood the bandwidth or resources of a targeted system, usually one or more web servers.

Information Divergence: Is a measure of the difference between two probability distributions.

Virtualization: In computing, virtualization refers to the act of creating a virtual (rather than actual) version of something, including virtual computer hardware platforms, operating systems, storage devices, and computer network resources.

This research was previously published in the Handbook of Research on End-to-End Cloud Computing Architecture Design edited by Jianwen "Wendy" Chen, Yan Zhang, and Ron Gottschalk, pages 222-252, copyright year 2017 by Information Science Reference (an imprint of IGI Global).

Chapter 97
Session Hijacking Over Cloud Environment:
A Literature Survey

Thangavel M.
Thiagarajar College of Engineering, India

Pandiselvi K.
Thiagarajar College of Engineering, India

Sindhuja R.
Thiagarajar College of Engineering, India

ABSTRACT

Cloud computing is a technology that offers an enterprise model to provide resources made available to the client and network access to a shared pool of configurable computing resources and pay-for-peruse basis. Generally, a session is said to be the collective information of an ongoing transaction. This package is typically stored on the server as a temporary file and labeled with an ID, usually consisting of a random number, time and date the session was initiated. That session ID is sent to the client with the first response, and then presented back to the server with each subsequent request. This permits the server to access the stored data appropriate to that session. That, in turn allows each transaction to be logically related to the previous one. Session hijacking is the common problem that is experienced in the cloud environment in which the session id is gained and information is gathered using the session ID compromising its security. This chapter covers session hijacking and the countermeasures to prevent session hijacking.

INTRODUCTION

Cloud Computing is considered as a small or medium-sized data centers with computational power, as this technology equally rely on virtualization for management with large data or information processing requirements and it includes the combination of Software as a Service (SaaS) and utility computing.

DOI: 10.4018/978-1-5225-8176-5.ch097

Due to the innovative hacking techniques the risk in security has increased to a greater extent in the cloud environment. To safeguard security several security management and measures are followed such as Information Technology Infrastructure Library (ITIL) guidelines, ISO/IEC 27001/27002 standards and Open Virtualization Format (OVF) standards that focuses on security principles (Challa 2012). Despite having such measures researchers cannot promise cloud security is the dark side of this picture. Some of the hacking techniques are Heartbleed, ShellShock, Poodle, Rosetta Flash, Hacking PayPal Accounts with 1 Click, Google Two-Factor Authentication Bypass etc. There are two explanations in reality; 1) weaknesses in the security that is currently adopted all over the globe, 2) the innovative hacking techniques that are quickly becoming extraordinarily intelligent, sophisticated and hard to detect.

Clients are the user of the cloud where they store their valuable information and the communication between the clients are taken place. If the client can access the application from any location, then the privacy of the client could be compromised. Authentication techniques are used for securing privacy. While providing authentication the client should be aware of the assaults in cloud computing. The authentication attacks included in cloud computing are Eavesdropping, Man-in-the-Middle Attacks, Cookie Poisoning, Replay Attack, Session Hijacking, Shoulder Surfing, Cloud Malware Injection, Password Discovery Attacks, Reflection Attack, Customer Fraud Attack, Denial-of service Attack, Insider Attack, Wrapping Attack, Flooding Attack, Browser Attack, Impersonating Attack, SSL Attacks, Guessing Attack, Brute Force Attack, Dictionary Attack, Video Recording Attack, and Stolen Verifier Attack (Misbahuddin 2013).

The authentication attacks that are listed above are explained one after the other. Eavesdropping is the process of listening or monitoring the established communication between two authorized clients by which information are gathered. In Man in the middle attack, hacker impersonates as the authorized client and gains the information that is communicated between authorized users. Cookie poisoning is done where the attacker gains the access permission by modifying the credentials information of the authorized client that is stored in the cookies (Khare 2015). Replay Attack is an attack where the communication between the authorized users is intruded by the attacker, the message from the sender is received then modified by the attacker and it is modified and sent back to the receiver. Shoulder Surfing is to gain the sensitive information by observing the clients entry of data via keyboard by the attacker. Cloud Malware Injection aims to inject a malicious service or virtual machine instance, which appears as the valid service instance running on the cloud platform. Password Discovery is an attack where various techniques are involved to gain the password of the authorized client. Reflection Attack is processed on mutual authentication schemes in which the attacker tricks the victim by revealing the secret to its own challenge. Customer Fraud Attack is where the client deliberately compromises its authentication token. Denial-of-service is harassing in which the hacker sends the request to the target machines by which the legitimate clients request is not responded (Zunnurhain 2012; Dacosta 2012). Among these attacks the most powerful is the Session hijacking attack as the legitimate user is unaware of this attack that compromises his privacy and data security. In this chapter, author will discuss the methodology of session hijacking, its major risks and the countermeasures to prevent it from occurring in the cloud environment.

SESSION HIJACKING

Session hijacking is the process of knowing the session ID (SID) of an active client, so that his account can be impersonated or hijacked. The application tries to identify him based on his cookie value, which contains the SID (Clark 2005). SID value of any active client can be used and logged into the application by a victim. It is shown in Figure 1.

As Hyper Text Transfer Protocol (HTTP) 1.1 protocol is introduced the concern towards session hijacking became serious and in the former version 1.0 of HTTP protocol this kind of hijacking was not possible as these were inherently stateless. The connection exists between two entities for a limited amount of time in the prior versions of HTTP protocols. Only these connections are terminated as soon as the sender forwards the data packet and the receiver receives the packet.

According to the security perspective, it was a safer form of communication in which the illegitimate client cannot access or hack as the connection is no longer active. For example, when a client tries for online ticket booking first selects the destination, time and ticket category and further proceeds to the subsequent page to approve the ticket and then payment. An active session between the client and the server is required for such type of communication to display the output and activeness of the session was fulfilled with the introduction of session states to keep track of client's activities (sending, receiving) on the web. Session hijacking vulnerabilities are very simple to be exploited thus easily cause danger to the system. To overcome such vulnerability in most of the computers TCP/IP is used. By this TCP/IP the system can be protected against hijacking to a little extent unless another protocol is used to secure (Margaret 2014). Only when encryption is used the countermeasure that is explained in that section can be executed. Major dangers that are caused by hijacking are identity theft, information loss, fraud activities, etc.

Rather than to enter the system directly, the session hijacking process easily sneaks in as a genuine client. An established session is found by session hijacking process and that session can be taken over after a genuine client has accessed and authenticated. The attacker can stay connected for hours once the session has been hijacked. This session is the effective chance gained by the attacker to plant backdoors or to even gain an additional access privilege to a system. To identify an attacker who impersonates as a genuine client is difficult, thus it is one of the main reasons for which the session hijacking is complicated. All routed traffic sent to the client's IP address are redirected to the attacker's system (Chou 2013). The hijacking process can be broken down into three broad phases such as tracking the connection, desynchronizing the connection, injecting the attacker's packet. The Session hijacking techniques are brute force (attacker attempts different IDs until he succeeds), Stealing (attacker uses different techniques to

Figure 1. Session hijacking

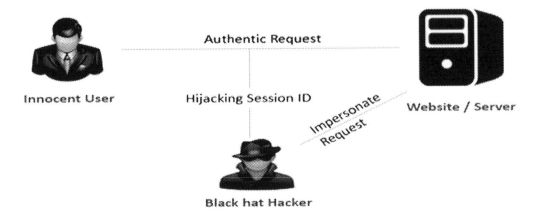

steal session IDs) and calculating (using non-randomly generated IDs, an attacker tries to calculate the session IDs).

This section highlights various types of session hijacking attacks and the techniques used to perform those attacks. And methods that are involved to hijack the session are also briefly explained with examples. Tools that are needed to perform session hijacking attacks are also listed with the uses and procedures to handle the tools respectively.

Types of Attacks

Various types of session hijacking attacks are explained here (Bhaturkar 2014).

Active Session Hijacking

An active attacker searches for an active session and utilizes the session for communicating between the client and server. Here the active attacker impersonates as a genuine client / client where the client is being manipulated and the server is being fooled by the active attacker.

Passive Session Hijacking

An attacker hijacks a session in the traffic that is being sent onwards but sits back, watches and records all the traffic in the network. In a passive attack the traffic or communication taking place between the client and the server is being monitored. In this situation where the traffic is monitored and captured while going across the wire Sniffing software is utilized.

Session Hijacking in OSI Model

Session hijacking attacks are classified based on the OSI model as application level session hijacking and network level session hijacking. The techniques that are involved for these attacks are explained in detail. It is shown in Figure 2.

Application-Level Session Hijacking

In the application level session hijacking attack, the unauthorized privileges to the web server is gained by forecasting a valid session token which is compromised to gain. Application-level hijacking is performed by gathering the information, which is provided through network-level hijacking. Therefore, in most of the cases network-level and application-level session hijacking occurs together. Application-level session hijacking involves either creating a new session using the stolen data or gaining control of an existing session. Application- level session hijacking transpires with HTTP sessions. By gaining the control of the respective session IDs and the unique identifiers of the HTTP sessions, HTTP sessions can be hijacked as it is defined by web application.

Various ways in which application-level session hijacking can be proficient by compromising the session tokens are mentioned below.

Figure 2. Session hijacking attacks

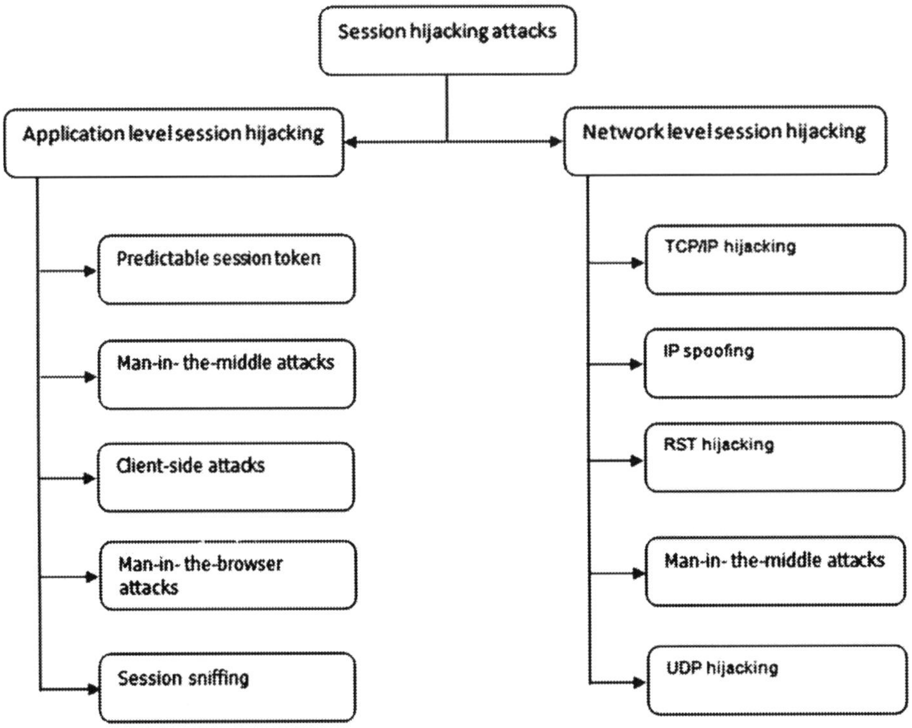

- Predictable session token,
- Man-in- the-middle attacks,
- Client-side attacks,
- Man-in- the-browser attacks, and
- Session sniffing.

Predictable Session Token

It is a method used for forecasting a session ID or impersonating a website client. Predicting or forecasting a session ID is also known as session hijacking. By negotiating the client's privileges, attacker gets the capability to ping the requests in website. The attacker accomplishes the attack, by forecasting the unique session value or guessing the session ID.

Session Fixation

The attacker tries with a known session ID to entice a client to authenticate himself and by the knowledge of the client session ID attacker hijacks the client-validated session. The vulnerability of a server which allows a client to use fixed Session ID is exploited by the attacker.

Network-Level Session Hijacking

Network-level session hijacking is implemented by the web applications through the data flow of the protocol which is shared. Critical information that is helpful to the attacker to attack the application - level sessions are provided by the attacks on network-level sessions.

Network-level session hijacking includes:

- TCP/IP hijacking,
- IP spoofing,
- RST hijacking,
- Blind hijacking,
- Man - in - the -middle, and
- UDP hijacking.

TCP/IP Hijacking

A TCP session hijacker tries to forge acceptable packets for both ends which acts as the real packets and creates a state where the client and server are unable to exchange data. Attacker is able to achieve control of the session. Wherein, the Server's Sequence Number (SSN) no longer matches the Client's Acknowledgement Number (ACK) and vice versa that is the reason why the client and server drop packets sent between them.

Blind Hijacking

Even if the source-routing is disabled, the attacker can introduce malevolent data or commands into the interrupted communication in the TCP session. The attacker has no access to see the response but can send the data or comments.

IP Spoofing

It is a host-file hijack or an IP address forgery, a hijacking technique which an attacker impersonates as a trusted host to obscure his distinctiveness, hijack browsers, spoof a website, or gain access to a network. The hijacker obtains the IP address of a genuine user and modifies the packet headers so that the genuine user appears to be the source.

Man in the Middle

It is one common method used to track what is being communicated using packet sniffing tools, between two systems.

RST Hijacking

Hijacker involves introducing an authentic-looking reset (RST) packet using spoofed source address and forecasting the acknowledgment number. By using a packet crafting tool such as Colasoft's Packet Builder and TCP/IP analysis tool such as tcpdump, RST Hijacking can be executed.

UDP Hijacking

UDP hijacker sends a counterfeit reply to the client´s UDP request before the server responds to it. To intercept server´s response to the client, attacker uses man-in-the-middle and sends its own forged reply. Managing sequence number and other TCP mechanisms is not yet needed to be worried by UDP attackers. As UDP are connectionless communications injecting data into session without being detected is extremely easy.

This network level hijacking process is done through three-way handshaking and sequence number.

Three-Way Handshake

A three -way handshake is performed by the two parties and thus the connection is established by using TCP. Once a three -way handshake starts the connection, it exchanges all the parameters needed for the communication between the two parties. Thus a new connection is established in TCP by using a three -way handshake. It is shown in Figure 3.

Initially client and server establish the connection. In which the connection is in the closed state on the client side and the connection is in the listening state on the server side. The Initial Sequence Number (ISN) is being sent initially by the client and setting the SYN flag. Now the state of the client is changed as the SYN-SENT state. The server acknowledges the client sequence number (ISN), and sends its own ISN with the SYN flag set on receipt of this packet. Now the state of the server is changed as SYN-RECEIVED state. The client acknowledges the server sequence number (ISN) by incrementing it and setting the ACK flag on receipt of this packet.

Now the client is in the established state. At this point, both the machines established a session or connection and can begin the communication. The server enters the established state and sends back the acknowledgment by incrementing the client's sequence number on receiving the client's acknowledgement. By either using the FIN or RST flag or by time out the connection can be closed or terminated.

Figure 3. Three-way handshake

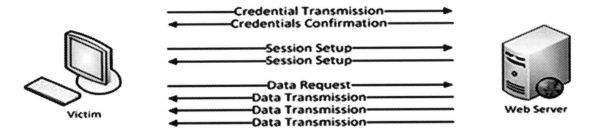

The receiving host enters the CLOSED state and frees all resources correlated with this occurrence of the connection if the RST flag of a packet is set. And any of the incoming packets which are additional for that connection will be dropped.

The receiving host closes the connection as it enters the CLOSE-WAIT mode if the packet is sent with the FIN flag turned on. If the sequence number is within the range and follows its predecessor, the packets sent by the client are accepted in an established connection. The packet is dropped and an ACK packet will be sent using the expected sequence number, if the sequence number is beyond the range of the acceptable sequence numbers.

The required things for the three parties to communicate are as follows:

- The IP address,
- The port numbers, and
- The sequence numbers.

The IP address and the port number are listed in the IP packets thus finding out is easy, as it does not change throughout the session. After discovering the addresses, the information exchanged stays the same for the remainder of the session that are communicating with the ports.

The attacker must successfully guess the sequence numbers for a blind hijack since the sequence numbers change. The attacker can successfully hijack the session if the attacker can fool the server to receive his or her spoofed packets and to execute them.

For example:

- By sending a packet to the server with the SYN bit set Bob initiates a connection with the server.
- The server replies Bob by sending a packet with the SYN/ACK bit as it receives this packet and sends an ISN (Initial Sequence Number) for the server.
- Bob increments the sequence number by 1 and to acknowledge the receipt of the packet, sets the ACK bit.
- A session is established successfully between the two machines.

Sequence Number

In TCP the three-way handshake has been already discussed. Full duplex reliable stream connection is provided between two end points by TCP. Four elements which is used to define a connection is IP address of the sender, IP address of the receiver, TCP port number of the sender, and TCP port number of the receiver. In the three-way handshaking protocol sequence number has incremented for each step. A particular sequence number is carried by each byte which is sent by a sender that is acknowledged by the receiver at its end. With the same sequence number, the receiver responds to the sender. The sequence number is different for different connections, and each session of a TCP connection has a different sequence number for security purposes (Cappelli 2012).

These sequence numbers are fundamental for security; which makes it very difficult to guess them since they are 32 bits, and thus there are more than 4 billion possible combinations. They are also significant for an attacker to hijack a session. When the initial sequence number is predictable an attacker can send packets that are forged to appear to come from a trusted computer. Attackers gaining access to unauthorized information can also perform session hijacking.

The next step is to introduce randomness in the ISN and tighten the OS implementation of TCP. Pseudo random number generators (PRNGs) are used carry out this. Using PRNGs, ISNs are randomized which is used in TCP connections. However, adding a series of numbers provides insufficient variance in the range of ISN values because of the implications of the central limit theorem, thereby against vulnerable TCP/IP stack implementations which allows an attacker to disrupt or hijack existing TCP connections or spoof future connections. The insinuation is that systems that rely on haphazard increments to generate ISNs are still susceptible to statistical attack. In other words, as the haphazardness is based on an internal algorithm that a particular operating system uses over time, even computers choosing haphazard numbers will repeat them. All the packets that follow will be the ISN_1 and a sequence number has been agreed. Thus injecting data into the communication stream is made possible.

The following are some of the terms that are used to refer to ISN numbers:

- **SVR_SEQ:** The next byte to be sent by the server's Sequence number.
- **SVR_ACK:** In server, the Next byte to be received (the sequence number plus one of the last byte received).
- **SVR_WIND:** Receiving window of the server.
- **CLT_SEQ:** The next byte to be sent by the client's Sequence number.
- **CLT_ACK:** In client, the Next byte to be received.
- **CLT_WIND:** Receiving window of the client.
- Initially, SVR_SEQ _ CLT_ACK and CLT_SEQ _SVR_ACK has no data to be replaced.
- When the connection is in a quiet state (i.e., no data is being sent on each side, these equations are also true.
- When data is sent, these equations are not true during fleeting states.

The following are the header fields of the TCP packet: Source port (SP), Destination port (DP), Sequence number (Sequence number of the first byte in this packet), and Acknowledgment number (AN) Expected sequence number of the next byte to be received).

The following are some of the control bits URG (Urgent pointer), ACK (Acknowledgment), PSH (Push function), RST (Reset the connection), SYN (Synchronize sequence numbers), FIN (No more data from sender), Window (Window size of the sender), Checksum (TCP checksum of the header and data), Urgent pointer (TCP urgent pointer), Options (TCP options), SEG_SEQ (Refers to the packet sequence number), SEG_ACK (Refers to the packet acknowledgment number), SEG_FLAG (Refers to the control bits).

On a characteristic packet sent by the client (no retransmission), SEG_SEQ is set to CLT_SEQ, and SEG_ACK is set to CLT_ACK.

The following actions will take place if a client initiates a connection with the server:

- On the client side the connection is in the CLOSED state.
- On the server side the connection is in the LISTEN state.
- Initially the client sends its ISN and sets the SYN bit:
  - SEG_SEQ =CLT_SEQ_0, SEG_FLAG = SYN.
- Now SYN-SENT is its state.
- The server acknowledges the client sequence number, sends its own ISN, and sets the SYN bit when it receives this packet:

- ○ SEG_SEQ_SVR_SEQ_0
- ○ SEQ_ACK _ CLT_SEQ_0_1
- ○ SEG_FLAG _ SY N
- And in turn sets:
  - ○ S V R _ A C K _C LT_S E Q_0_ 1
- Now SYN-RECEIVED is its state.
- The client acknowledges the server ISN on receipt of this packet:
  - ○ SEG_SEQ _ CLT_SEQ_0_1
  - ○ SEQ_ACK _ SVR_SEQ_0_1
- And in turn sets:
  - ○ CLT_ACK_SVR_SEQ_0_1
- Now ESTABLISHED is its state
- The server enters the ESTABLISHED state on receipt of this packet:
  - ○ C LT_S E Q_C LT_S E Q_0_ 1
  - ○ C LT_ A C K_S V R_S E Q_0_ 1
  - ○ SVR_SECLSVR_SEQ_0_1
  - ○ S V R_ A C K_C LT_S E Q_0_ 1
- The next steps in the process are shown in Figure 4.

Figure 4. Connection establishment

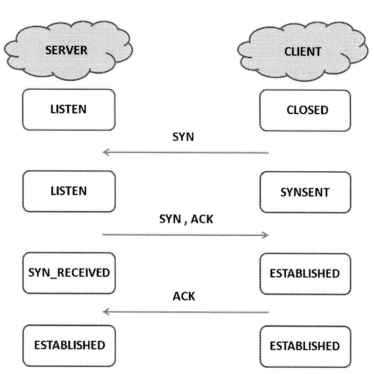

Any attacker can introduce data into the session stream if a sequence number within the receiving window is known, or if he or she knows the number of bytes, so far transmitted in the session (only applicable to a blind hijack) and terminate the connection.

With different sequence numbers that fall within the appropriate range the attacker sends out a number of packets and can guess a suitable range of sequence numbers into the network. To close a connection recalls that the FIN packet is used. It is likely that the server accepts at least one packet since the range is known. The attacker can resort to send an appropriate number of packets with sequence numbers a window size apart but does not send a packet for every sequence number.

The number of packets to be sent is known by the attacker by dividing the range of sequence numbers to be covered by the fraction of the window size used and increment, is obtained. This randomization is taken care by PRNG. The randomness of the ISNs is directly proportional to the difficulty of carrying out such attacks. To these attacks, the more random the ISN, the more difficult it is.

Sequence Number Prediction

The server responds (SYN/ACK) with a sequence number, once a client sends a connection request (SYN) packet to the server which then the client must acknowledge (ACK). The attacker connects to a service first with its own IP address, records the sequence number chosen, and then opens a second connection from the counterfeit IP address since sequence number is predictable. The attacker can guess the correct response though he does not see the SYN/ACK (or any other packet) from the server. The attacker can use one-sided communication to break into the server if the source IP address is used for authentication.

METHODS

Reverse-proxies, cross-site scripting, network sniffing and source-routed IP packet method are the methods which are currently in use to steal active sessions. By employing strong encryption algorithms, regeneration of cookies after successful login process and the use of long random session IDs are different measures used to reduce the likelihood of session hijacking.

Due to the various technical impurities it was also noticed that the problem still exists. For the whole client area, by using the Secure Socket Layer/Secure Hyper Text Transfer Protocol (SSL/HTTPS) communication mechanism this problem can be solved. Not all pages that are being sent to the cloud clients are protected by SSL. It is also an evident that it will sufficiently reduce the network speed, so to address this issue, HTTPS protocols can be used, if all pages are needed to be protected by SSL. In this case, the cookies will be sent to the client through a SSL link along with the regular cookies and the client will be logged into the system by using a page protected by HTTPS. Despite successful session hijacking, the adversary would not be able to, because once the client again tries to access the client area; the client browser needs to send the secure cookie along with the regular cookie. If it is not possible to protect the whole client area with SSL this remedy will work best. It will protect the cloud clients even if their valid session cookie has been hijacked by disallowing the multiple active sessions at the same time, but this will work only when the real client is still logged in. This problem can be solved to a great extent by checking the IP address of the cloud client for a safer way of communication and where the cloud clients have a static IP address, on every new HTTP request made by the client. From a remote location the possibility of session hijacking will rule out. Even in case of successful cookie theft, the cloud client can still remain secure since the encryption should also be applied on the session value itself (Cheng 2010).

One of the ways of session hijacking is source-routed IP packet method. To commence data transfer between the two victims through its machine an invader, which usually is an anonymous cloud client, places him between two clients X and Y. When the intruder comes into power to send any command to obtain control over the victim's machine, the connection is established. A network sniffing program of session hijacking is using to monitor the conversation between the two nodes is another famed approach where once it gets the packet and decrypts it the hacker can get the control over victim's machine. This type of attack is called middleman attack (Misbahuddin 2013). A HTTP request is modified and a client data is transmitted to a malicious code in which there are the methods of Reverse-proxies but this way of session hijacking is not an important worry for cloud security as clients of a cloud are not using the same local area network. An attacker uses a sniffing tool to sniff the communication between the nodes to steal cookies is yet another widespread technique of session hijacking called Session side-jacking. It is probable that not all the pages are supported with a secure form of communication though cloud providers use the protected way of communication such as SSL. A malicious code is run on the client system to obtain access to the cookies is still a threat to cloud security in which it is Cross-site scripting. Filtering techniques can play an essential role to filter-out the merely concerned data packets (i.e., packets containing the text login and afterward those packets can be analyzed though it is fairly impractical to inspect and examine each and every data packet (Larry 2009).

These techniques are in fact not a work of the cloud service providers and they have developed diverse solutions to undertake such attacks. A few examples of procedures in use to safeguard a cloud from such bots are the encryption algorithms, regeneration of cookies after successful login and the use of long haphazard session IDs to prevent the likelihood of session hijacking.

To safeguard their client's communication almost every major cloud enterprise is using the secure socket layers such as SSL or Transport Layer Security (TLS). Session state timeout has created outstanding results with the use of strong encryption/decryption algorithms. Session hijacking still has a lucid anxiety in 2013 as evidences of successful hijacking are constantly being reported in the IT news at present regardless of all the measures taken by the cloud vendors. Firesheep, extension of Mozilla Firefox exaggerated clients of Facebook and Twitter they were using it and Firesheep extension of Mozilla Firefox came under this type of attack in October 2010. A fresh attack is experimented on a Google mobile messaging application, WhatsApp in May 2012 in which clients connected to the same network were able to gain the right to enter and view the WhatsApp messages of each other (Al-Nemrat 2015).

SESSION HIJACKING TOOLS

Zaproxy Tool

Zed Attack Proxy is an open-source web application security scanner. It is planned to be used by both those who are new to professional penetration testing as well as application security. In OWASP projects ZAP is one of the most active projects that have been given Flagship status. It is being interpret into over 25 languages and is also completely internationalized. It permits the user to manipulate all of the traffic that passes through it, including traffic using https when it is used as a proxy server (Baishya 2014).

REST Application programming interface is used to control when ZAP tool run in a "daemon" mode. It is offered in all of the admired operating systems such as Microsoft Windows, Linux and Mac OS X This cross-platform tool is written in Java and in the Thought Works Technology Radar ZAP was added in May 2015 in the trial ring (Larry 2009).

Burp Suite Tool

In the web applications for performing security testing Burp Suite tool acts as an integrated platform. Its diverse tools work flawlessly together, from initial mapping and analysis of an application's attack surface, through which the security vulnerabilities are found and exploited. Burp provides the full control, hiring by the combination of highly developed manual techniques with state-of-the-art mechanisms, to create the work faster and more effectual (Baishya 2014).

J-Hijack Tool

A Java Hijacking tool is used for web application session security assessment. An easy Java Fuzzer that can mostly be used for parameter enumeration and numeric session hijacking.

In addition to Zaproxy, Burp Suite, and J-hijack, numerous other session hijacking tools exists. These session hijacking tools permit attacker to hijack a TCP session. These tools even hijack HTTP connections to steal cookies (Al-Nemrat 2015).

Hamster Tool

Hamster is a tool or it is "side-jacking". It replaces your cookies with session cookies stolen from somebody else, allowing you to hijack their sessions by acting as a proxy server. Using the Ferret program, the cookies are sniffed. The attacker only needs a copy of the cookies sniffed.

Surf Jack Tool

A Surf Jack tool is the tool which is used to permit the attacker to hijack HTTP connections to steal cookies and even on HTTPS sites. It works on both Ethernet and Wi-Fi (monitor mode). It requires Python 2.4 and Scapy (Baishya 2014).

Ettercap Tool

Ettercap is an open source network security tool which is used for man-in-the-middle attacks on LAN. It can also be used for security auditing and computer network protocol analysis. It works on a variety of Unix-like operating systems which includes Linux, Mac OS X, BSD and Solaris, and on Microsoft Windows. It is accomplished by interrupting the traffic on a network segment through active eavesdropping and capturing passwords (Long 2010).

Hunt Tool

Hunt tool is the hijacking software that has the following functionality features (Baishya 2014):

- **Connection Management:** Sets what are the connections that the users are interested in. Not alone the start of SYN, noticing all the continuing connection. The detection of the ACK storm is used to perform active hijacking. With the detection of successful ARP spoof, ARP spoofed/normal hijacking is performed. After hijacking, the true client is synchronized with the server thus the connection does not reset.
- **Daemons:** For automatic connection, reset the daemon. ARP spoof or relay daemon has the capability to transmit all packets from spoofed hosts for ARP spoofing of the hosts. For gathering the MAC addresses, MAC discovery daemon is used. Sniff daemon has the capability to investigate for a particular string for logging TCP traffic.
- **Host Resolving:** Delayed host is decided through DNS helper servers.
- **Packet Engine:** For watching ARP, TCP, UDP, and ICMP traffic, extensible packet engine is used. With sequence numbers and the ACK storm detection, TCP connections are gathered.

PerJack Tool

PerJack is a tool which is used to hijack the session in TCP and it is written in Perl language. It exhibits all active sessions, takes over the chosen TCP session and performs a man-in-the-middle attack (Baishya 2014).

Whatssup Gold Engineer's Toolkit

The Whatsup Gold Engineer's Toolkit was intended to make easy for the attacker to act as a network administrator. Three new tools are there for helping to increase the capability to manage the network quickly and easily. Syslog Server tool permits the attacker to collect, save, view and forward Syslog messages in the network. Interface Bandwidth tool affords with one interface from which they can read, gather and understand traffic information. TFTP Server is the service-based tool which can help to transfer system and configuration files such as operating system software, device configuration files securely through the network (Baishya 2014).

Juggernaut Tool

Juggernaut is fundamentally a network sniffer which can also be used in TCP sessions hijacking. It works on Linux as well as, has a Trinux module. Juggernaut tool can be made active to monitor all the network traffic on the local network, or can set to pay attention for an extraordinary token. For example, Juggernaut tool remains until the login prompt, and then collects evidence of the password.

It can be used for traditionally capturing certain types of network traffic by merely leaving the tool running for a few days, and then the attacker has to take the log file that has the recorded traffic. Comparing to regular network sniffers this tool is different which records all network traffic and makes a log file tremendously huge. But its capability to preserve a connection is the main feature of this tool. This means that an attacker can monitor the entire local network TCP based connection and probably "hijack" that session. Attacker can monitor the entire session only when the connection is made.

Cookie Cadger Tool

Cookie Cadger tool helps to recognize the information that leaked from application using HTTP GET requests, which is insecure.

Cookie Cadger is the first open-source pen-testing tool which is used for interrupting and repeating particular insecure HTTP GET requirements into a browser.

Compatibility and Use

Cookie Cadger operates on Windows, Linux, or Mac, and it needs Java 7. For using Cookie Cadger, it requires having "tshark" which has the utility to act as a part of the Wireshark that needs to be installed.

Capturing Wi-Fi traffic needs hardware proficient of monitor mode, and the information of placing the device into monitor mode.

SESSION HIJACKING USING WIRESHARK

- Wireshark is a packet sniffer in which cookies can also be captured.
- Open wireshark and click on interface list and select LAN and then start. Once it is started wireshark would capture all the packets as shown in Figure 5.
- The credential of the given website is captured using wireshark as shown in Figure 6.
- Cookie is tracked as shown in Figure 7.

Figure 5. Capturing the packets using wireshark

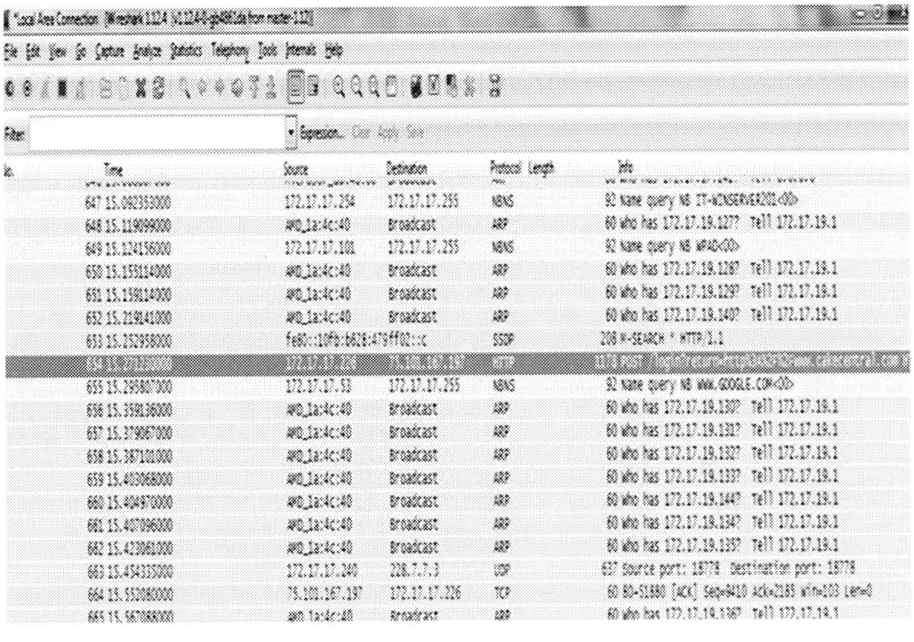

Figure 6. Capturing the credentials of the given site

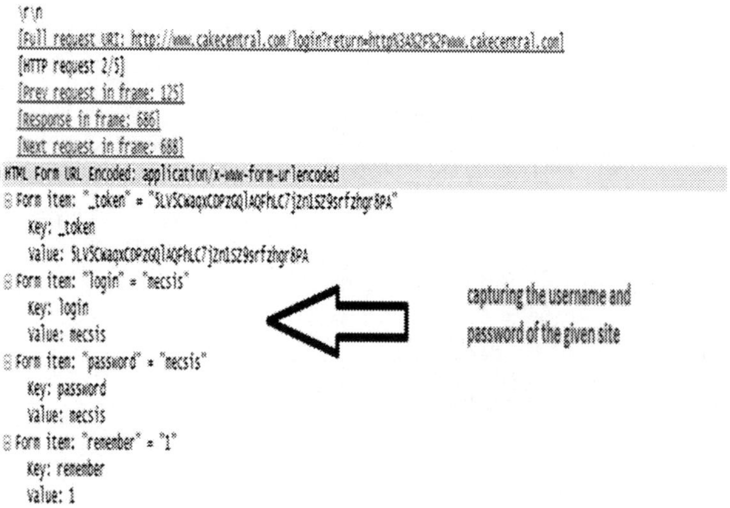

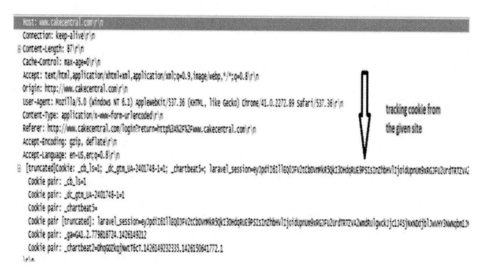

Figure 7. Tracking the cookies

- Now insert the session ID into our cookie field, so we can impersonate the user currently logged-in to his device. Open up Firefox, go to a cookie manager and find the session value. Replace this with the value copied from the step above and save it.
- In Chrome, edit cookie manager, as shown in Figure 8.
- When you hit the refresh button on the browser it will submit a request for the page but this time it will make the request using the new session ID you have just inserted. If every step is followed, you will now be logged in as a victim.

Figure 8. Cookie is replaced

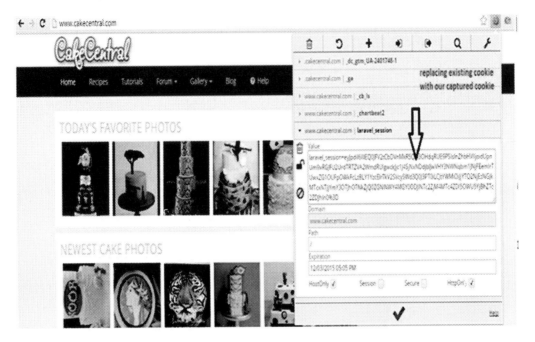

THREATS OF SESSION HIJACKING

Man-in-the-Middle Attack

It is used to interrupt the messages that are being replaced between the end users in a network. Attacker split the TCP connection into two connections (attacker-to-server and client-to-attacker) and uses different techniques.

An attacker can read, modify, and insert fraudulent data into the interrupted communication after the interception of TCP connection is successful. The TCP connection between the client and the server becomes the target in case of an http transaction (Zunnurhain 2012).

Client-Side Attack

The attacker can negotiate the session token by sending malicious activities such as malwares to the client-side programs (Cheng 2010).

Man-in-the-Browser Attack

In this attack the calls between the browser and its security mechanisms or libraries are intercepted by using Trojans. To cause financial dishonesties by influencing transactions of Internet banking systems is its main objective (Kavitha 2011).

Session Sniffing

In this attack, the attacker uses a sniffer tool to capture a valid or correct session token called session ID. Attacker then uses the session ID to get authenticated as a genuine user to the web server (Cappelli 2012).

SOLUTIONS FOR SESSION HIJACKING THREATS

Protecting Against Session Hijacking

The following are the ways that are used to protect against session hijacking (Nikiforakis 2011).

Use Secure Shell (SSL) to Create a Secure Communication Channel

Communication security over the internet is provided by SSL protocol. At the transport layer the SSL encrypts the segments of network connections. An attacker can send any confidential information such as credit card numbers, addresses, and other payment details through the internet with SSL configured on the attacker's network (Jayaram 2008).

Pass the Authenticated Cookies Over HTTPS Connection

On adding the security capabilities or SSL to the standard HTTP communication, it then results to HTTPS. HTTPS offers protection for cookies transferred over it similar to SSL.

Implement the Log-Out Functionality for Client to End the Session

To avoid session hijacking is to implement the log-out functionality as one of the most defensive steps. When a session is started, it forces to authenticate (Danish 2011).

Generate the Session ID After Successful Login

As the attacker will not be aware of the session ID generated after login, this prevents the session fixation attacks (Nikiforakis 2011).

Pass the Encrypted Data Between the Client and the Web Server

Before transmitting it over the Internet encrypts victim's data so that the attackers stealing the data are unable to understand the message or data.

Use String or Long Random Number as a Session Key

A very important factor in communication is session keys. A string or a long random number can be used as a session key to avoid risk.

Use Different Client Names and Passwords for Different Accounts

Longer passwords make it tricky for attackers to deduct or manipulate. When the attacker succeeds in compromising one account using different client names and passwords for different accounts avoids the risk of compromising all the accounts.

Minimize Remote Access

The injection by attackers in the communication session of the legitimate client with the remote server is avoided by minimizing remote access.

Educate Employees

The employees must be educated about the various kinds of session hijacking attacks, signs, and defenses against attacks, to prevent session hijacking attacks.

Do Not Transport Session ID in Query String

Through referrer, the Session IDs in query strings or form fields are being leaked. Session IDs in the query string is recommended not to transport.

Limit Incoming Connections

When the IP ranges are finite and predictable, the incoming connection works well. Example is an intranet of such an environment.

Use Switches Rather Than Hubs

In a network, hubs transfer data to all the systems connected which in turn makes the attacker's job easy to encroach. Switches send data only to the destined host. Hence, prefer switches over hubs to avoid session hijacking attacks.

Use Encrypted Protocols That are Available at OpenSSH Suite

Collection of SSH connectivity tools are known as OpenSSH. In OpenSSH all the encrypted protocols are available and the encrypted passwords would transmit across the Internet. The risk of connection hijacking, eavesdropping, and other attacks are eliminated by encrypting all the traffic in the internet by OpenSSH.

Configure the Appropriate Internal and External Spoof Rules on Gateways

On the border gateway suitable internal and external spoof rules are needed to be configured by the user to avoid blind spoofing or Remote Network Session Hijacking (RNSH). Similarly, ARP cache poisoning is monitored by using ARP watch or IDS products. It also uses peer- to-peer VPNs or strong authentication "like Kerberos" (Seltzer 2009).

To avert network intrusions a practice of using multiple security systems or technologies is called as Defense-in-depth. A comprehensive security plan's key component is the defense-in-depth and particularly the network is protected from session hijacking attacks. If one countermeasure fails to safeguard the network, there are additional levels of protection to provide security which is the central idea behind this concept. While the attacker tries to penetrate through abundant layers of security, performing an attack the speed is slowed down by defense-in-depth. Thus for the security administrators, it gives additional time to detect and defend against the attack. A good example of the defense-in-depth strategy is a new firewall configuration strategy. Highly secure networks are implemented by several types of firewall to achieve a defense-in-depth strategy (Larry 2009).

Web Developer's Countermeasures

By exploiting the vulnerabilities that are caused when the session is established session hijacking can be frequently performed, where security is focused often by Web developers (Nair 2013). The risk of session hijacking can be avoided to an extent if the web developers follow the below measures during the development process (Adi 2012):

- Generate session keys with random number or lengthy string in order that it is difficult for an attacker to detect a legitimate session key.
- Encrypt the session key and the data that is transmitted between the web server and the client.
- Prevent eavesdropping technique within the network.
- After a successful login regenerate the session ID to prevent from session fixation attack.
- As soon as the client logs out of the session, it has to be expired.
- A session's or a cookie's life span must be reduced.

Web Client's Countermeasures

Ensure that the attacker's applications are locked when attacker uses the Internet, and select only authorized sites for browsing. While browsing the Internet some of the measures to be followed are:

- Links that are received through emails should not be clicked.
- Prevent malevolent content from entering the network using firewalls.
- Restrict cookies by using firewall and browser settings.
- The websites are to be ensured for verified certificates.
- After every sensitive and confidential transaction from the browser make sure to clear all such as history, offline content, and cookies.
- Rather than using HTTP protocol for transmitting confidential and sensitive data, prefer a secure transmission protocol like HTTPS.
- Instead of closing the browser, logout from the browser by clicking on the Logout option.

Safeguarding Cloud From Session Hijacking

Prior to the HTTP 1.1 protocols, session hijacking was not an issue because the previous versions of HTTP protocols were intrinsically stateless. This problem is experienced by the cloud clients in various forms (Ahmed 2014). For example, reverse-proxy's method by using a HTTP request, network sniffing and cross-site scripting are the variants of account hijacking techniques. It can also be reduced by using Secure Socket Layer (SSL), antivirus, firewalls and code scanners (Larry 2009).

IPSec

IP Security is the expansion of IPSec. At the IP layer a collection of protocols is referred to support secure exchange of packets. It is the VPN technology which is deployed broadly to address confidentiality, integrity, authentication, and key management in the IP networks. IPSec with the help of security services in cryptography, it protects the communication.

Both the sending and receiving devices must share a public key for proper functionality of IPSec. Characteristically, by using Internet Security Association and Key Management Protocol /Oakley (ISAKMP/Oakley) it is achieved. The receiver is allowed to authenticate the sender based on the digital certificates and to obtain a public key by this protocol (Jayaram 2008).

The benefits that are offered by IPSec include:

- Replay protection,
- Data confidentiality,
- Data integrity,
- Data origin authentication, and
- Network-level peer authentication.

IPSec Architecture

At the network layer, IPSec offers its services as shown in Figure 9. This reduces the restrictions of selecting the necessary security protocols, for the services. The corresponding cryptographic keys are requested to make the available services based on its requirement. IPSec uses two traffic security protocols to such as Authentication Header (AH) and Encapsulating Security Payload (ESP) and cryptographic key management protocols and procedures to assure confidentiality, integrity and authenticity (Long 2010).

Encapsulating Security Payload (ESP)

It is essentially used for providing encryption and authentication services.

Authentication Header (AH)

Only datagram authentication service is provided in this mode and it does not provide encryption.

Figure 9. IPSec

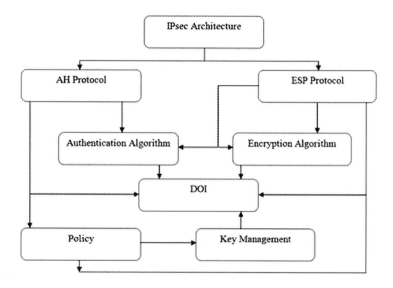

Domain of Interpretation (DOI)

For security information it characterizes the payload formats, types of exchange, and naming conventions such as security policies or cryptographic algorithms. The ISAKMP is intended to support security services at all layers in addition to the IP layer. Exactness of the DOI is needed for IP Security.

ISAKMP (Internet Security Association and Key Management Protocol)

In the IPSec architecture, ISAKMP is a key protocol. The required security is provided for a variety of internet communications by combining the security concepts of authentication, key management and security association, such as government, private and commercial.

Policy

Policy establishes whether the two entities can communicate with each other or not thus it is also the key element. If the entities can communicate, then the transformation is predicted. If the policy is not defined appropriately, then those entities may not be able to communicate with each other.

Modes of IPSec

IPSec modes are linked by the two core protocols namely, Authentication Header (AH) and Encapsulating Security Payload (ESP). By adding a datagram to the header, both these protocols offer protection. The difference between these two protocols is in terms of the parts of protected IP datagram and headers arrangement (Halton 2014). Two modes of encryption supported by IPSec are transport mode and the tunnel mode.

Transport Mode

In the transport mode, leaving the header untouched each packet of the payload is encrypted by IPSec. ESP authenticates two linked computers and also has an alternative to encrypt data transfer. It is compatible with NAT. So far, NAT can be used to make available VPN services.

Tunnel Mode

In tunnel mode, both the payload and the header are encrypted by using IPSec thus tunnel mode is highly secure. AH is also called in the Tunnel mode. By the IPSec-compliant device the encrypted data will be decrypted on the receiver's side. NAT is not capable of rewriting the encrypted IP header and it is not capable of providing VPN services as the tunnel mode encrypts the header of the IP packet.

IPSec Authentication and Confidentiality

In IPSec the data authentication includes two concepts, data integrity and data origin authentication. Even though origin authentication is reliant upon data integrity, data authentication refers either to integrity alone or to both of these concepts.

- Data integrity makes sure that the data has not been distorted.
- Data origin authentication makes sure that the data was sent only by the claimed sender.
- ESP affords confidentiality (encryption) in addition to integrity, authentication, and protection against replay attack. It can be used along with AH. On default setting, it protects only the payload of the IP data but otherwise, it protects both the IP header and the payload in tunnel mode.

Components of IPSec

IPSec consists of the components as follows,

- IPSec Driver is the software that achieves protocol-level function necessary to encrypt, decrypt, authenticate, and verify the packet (Halton 2014).
- Internet Key Exchange (IKE) is an IPSec protocol in which it fabricates the security keys for IPSec and other protocols.
- Internet Security Association Key Management Protocol (ISAKMP) is an IPSec protocol that permits encryption of data using frequent security settings to communicate between two computers. The exchange of keys is also secured.
- Oakley is an IPSec protocol that generates a master key and a key that is particular to each session in IPSec data transfer by using the Diffie-Hellman algorithm.
- IPSec Policy Agent is a windows 2000 series from Active Directory that gathers IPSec policy settings and then it sets the configuration.

IPSec Implementation

Based on the platform the IPSec implementation varies. Here platform-independent IPSec implementations are discussed. The main set of components in IPSec implementation is as follows:

- IPSec base protocols,
- SADB,
- SPD,
- Manual keying,
- ISAKMP/IKE,
- SA management, and
- Policy management.

IPSec base protocols implement both ESP and AH. By interacting with the SPD and SADB, it processes the headers and determines the security of the packet. Fragmentation and PMTU is also handled by it.

SADB maintains a list of active SAs for both inbound and outbound processing. Either manually or with the help of an automatic key management system such as IKE it supports the population of SAs.

SPD mainly determines the security of a packet. For both inbound and outbound processing of the packet it is referred. The IPSec base protocol component consults the SPD in order to check whether the security afforded to the packet meets the security configuration of the policy. The IPSec base protocol consults SPD to decide whether outbound packet needs any security which is similar for outbound processing.

Internet Key Exchange is considered as a client-level process in most of the operating systems but it does not support in embedded operating systems. In embedded operating systems with routers (example of node in a network), there is no difference between the client space and kernel space. The policy either mandates an SA or when the SA bundle is present, the policy engine invokes IKE but the SA is not established. Peer invokes IKE when the nodes are needed to be communicated securely.

PENETRATION TESTING

In Session hijacking, penetration testing involves the same steps as that of the session hijacking attack. First the penetration tester locates a session. Various possibilities to hijack a session are then checked by the penetration tester. Depending on the network and the mechanisms which are used for the communication, the possibilities may vary but still there exists standard procedures for session hijacking penetration testing (Whitaker 2005). See Figure 10.

Step 1: Locating a Session

As it is mentioned early, the first step of hijacking is to locate a target active session in order to take control over it through packet sniffing. Check whether the session ID is used in the URL after locating a session. If session ID is used in the URL, check whether the session is encrypted. If session ID is not used in the URL, sniff session traffic between two machines (Clark 2005).

Figure 10. Penetration testing

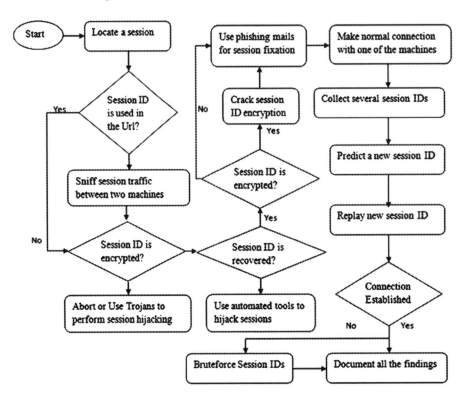

Step 2: Sniffing the Session Traffic Between Two Machines

Using various available tools such as CACE pilot, Wireshark, Capsa network analyzer, Win dump, etc. between two machines, the session traffic is sniffed. The victim's network traffic is watched and a session is grabbed. Next, the session is checked for whether it is encrypted or not. Recover the session ID if the session is not encrypted otherwise either abort or use Trojans to perform session hijacking.

Step 3: Recuperate the Session ID

Automated tools such as Paros proxy, Burp Suite, Web scarab, etc are used to hijack the session if the session IDs are unable to be recovered. The session hijacking process is made easy by using these tools. Using various algorithms, the Session IDs are created whereas if the attacker is able to predict the algorithm he can easily recover or regenerate the session IDs. The attacker can also perform session fixation by sending phishing mails to the victim in case of an encrypted Session ID .

Step 4: Crack Session ID's Encryption

Usually the client authentication process is carried out by using session IDs. If the URL is encoded such as, HTML encoded, Unicode encoded, Base64 encoded, or hex encoded, and then original session IDs of the victim is obtained by cracking the encrypted session IDs. If the attackers are able to recuperate the Session IDs of an authentic client, then the attacker can introduce a malicious activity in between the victim's machine and the remote machine as well as the unauthorized connection can be used for attacking purposes. Session fixation with the help of phishing mails later can be done by the attacker later, if he succeeds in cracking the encrypted Session ID.

Step 5: Make Normal Connection With One of the Machines in the Network

A normal connection can be executed with one of the machine targeted in the network traffic and can gain the entry to the remote machine by impersonating as the authorized client of the network after performing session attacks.

Step 6: Collection of Several Session IDs

Attacker can collect several session IDs of the machines that are connected in the network, once the attacker gets connected to one of its machines. For retrieving the session IDs there are two different techniques available. First technique is to retrieve the session ID from a cookie in the response headers, and next technique is to match a usual expression against the response body. Attacker must make sure that the "from message body" check box is not selected, while collecting session IDs from the cookies, thought the above option is selected while collecting the session IDs from the message body.

Step 7: Prediction of a New Session ID

To predict or guess the new session ID investigate the collected session IDs. To perform replay attack and in order to find the current session ID attacker should forecast a new session ID.

Step 8: Replay New Session ID

When an attacker copies a stream of messages (session IDs) between two parties in the network and repeat the stream to one or more of the parties replay attack occurs.

Now the connection establishment of the machine is checked and when the connection is established the penetration tester should document all the findings of the penetration testing. If the connection establishment is not done, then establish the connection by brute forcing technique to find the current valid session ID.

Step 9: Brute Force Session IDs

Brute forcing the session ID is the process in which all the possible range of values are tried for the session ID, until the correct session ID is obtained. SessionIDs are randomly generated and while brute forcing thousands of requests are involved by these session IDs. This is the most inclusive technique but still this process requires more time.

Step 10: Document All the Findings

The last step of penetration testing is to document all the findings that are obtained through each and every step that are tested for the analysis.

FUTURE RESEARCH

In the web application session hijacking is a severe issue and thus hijacker implements various methods to capture the cookies and to perform session hijacking in the web application. Because of the developing technology the need to access information from web application has its greater significance.

In WLAN, new intrusion detection techniques are needed to be developed to attain low false positive rate and misdetection ratio whereas the packet delivery ratio is to be increased. These detection techniques can also be developed to Mobile Ad-hoc Networks (MANET) and Wireless Sensor Network (WSN). The scope of wired networks execution lies on investigating the likelihood of executing intrusion detection techniques for diverse standards of IEEE 802.11X. Networks and applications must be monitored and tested to ensure that it is no more vulnerable to the tricks that are carried out by the hijacker.

The IN-Network approach can be executed with diverse and many more common approaches appropriate to numerous platforms. Some of the restrictions in executing these methods on a fabricated network are: The server value is not common. In the Windows machine, the detect ability rate can be enhanced. In the Out-Network approach the significant constraint used to distinguish and compose a resolution, is the IP address, but for the potential values to augment the security: User agent string, Session created time, and Session ID must be used always.

CONCLUSION

Cloud computing faces serious issues regarding account hijacking as the attackers can fortify secret information, infringe data integrity and can perform monetary transactions. The significant factor that security analysts should be apprehensive with this is that the interface and the authentication layer must not be combined into a single layer because it causes risk to the authentication system as the interface is already uncovered to the world. For helping the cloud users to protect the devices, login-aiding along with secret keys other than passwords can be used. This method can be additionally enhanced by executing a few rational security measures.

Thus the severe issues of session hijacking particularly after introducing HTTP 1.1 protocols are solved by using the SSL/HTTP communication mechanism. The optimal merge of HTTPS and SSL protocols can solve many problems of hijacking. The session hijacking can also be prevented from the attacker by using various tools in the cloud environment. Thus, the major issue of session hijacking can be handled effectively thereby protecting the information by following the countermeasures and penetration testing steps in the right sequence.

REFERENCES

Adi, P., Bhavesh, B., Chirag, M., Dhiren, P., & Muttukrishnan, R. (2012). *A survey on security issues and solutions at different layers of Cloud computing.* Springer.

Ahmed, M., & Ashraf Hossain, M. (2014). Cloud computing and security issues in the cloud. *International Journal of Network Security & Its Applications, 6*(1), 25–36. doi:10.5121/ijnsa.2014.6103

Al-Nemrat, Tawil, Mangut, & Benza. (2015). ARP Cache Poisoning Mitigation and Forensics Investigation. *IEEE Trustcom/BigDataSE/ISPA.*

Baishya, R. C., Bhattacharyya, D. K., Hoque, N., Kalita, J. K., & Monowar, H. (2014). Network attacks: Taxonomy, tools and systems. *Journal of Network and Computer Applications, 40,* 307–324. doi:10.1016/j.jnca.2013.08.001

Bhaturkar, K. P., & Bagde, K. G. (2014). Prevention of Session Hijacking and IP Spoofing With Sensor Nodes and Cryptographic Approach. *International Journal of Computer Science and Mobile Computing, 3*(Issue.5), 1198–1206.

Cappelli, D., Moore, A., & Trzeciak, R. (2012). *The CERT Guide to Insider Threats: How to prevent, Detect and Respond to Information Technology Crimes (Theft, Sabotage, and Fraud).* Addison-Wesley Professional.

Challa, K. A., & Meena, B. (2012). Cloud Computing Security Issues with possible solution. *International Journal of Computer Science and Technology, 2*(1).

Cheng, K., Gao, M., & Guo, R. (2010). Analysis and Research on HTTPS Hijacking Attacks. *Networks Security Wireless Communication and Trusted Computing (NSWCTC), 2010 Second International Conference,* 223-226.

Chou, T.-S. (2013). Security threats on Cloud Computing vulnerabilities. *International Journal of Computer Science & Information Technology, 5*(3), 79–88. doi:10.5121/ijcsit.2013.5306

Clark, Smith, Looi, & Gill. (2005). *Passive techniques for detecting session hijacking attacks in IEEE 802.11 wireless networks.* Academic Press.

Dacosta, I., Chakradeo, S., Ahamad, M., & Traynor, P. (2012). One-time cookies: Preventing session hijacking attacks with stateless authentication tokens. *ACM Transactions on Internet Technology, 12*(1), 1–24. doi:10.1145/2220352.2220353

Danish, J., & Hassan, Z. (2011). Security Measures in Cloud computing and Countermeasures. *International Journal of Engineering Science and Technology, 3*(4).

Halton, W. (2014). *Security Issues and Solutions in Cloud Computing.* Wolf Halton Open Source Security.

Jayaram, K. R., & Mathur. (2008). On the Adequacy of Statecharts as a Source of Tests for Cryptographic Protocols. *Annual IEEE International Computer Software and Applications Conference.* 10.1109/COMPSAC.2008.203

Kavitha, V., & Subashini, S. (2011). A Survey on Security Issues in Service Delivery Models of Cloud Computing. *Journal of Network and Computer Applications, 34*(1), 1–11. doi:10.1016/j.jnca.2010.07.006

Kazi, Z., & Vrbsky. (2012). Security Attacks and Solutions in Clouds. The University of Alabama.

Khare & Verma. (2015). A Strong Authentication Technique in Cloud Environment Using: SMTP OTP and MD5. *International Journal of Innovative Research in Computer and Communication Engineering, 3*(12).

Larry, S. (2009). *Spoofing Server-Server communication: How can you prevent it?* Retrieved from https://otalliance.org/resources/EV/SSLStrip_Whitepaper.pdf

Long, X. & Sikdar, B. (2010). A mechanism for detecting session hijacking in wireless networks. *Wireless Communication, IEEE Transactions*, 1380-1389.

Margaret, R. (2014). *Session Hijacking (TCP Session Hijacking). What is it?* Academic Press.

Misbahuddin, M., & Sumitra, B. (2013). A Survey of Traditional and Cloud Specific Security Issues, Security in Computing and Communications. *Communications in Computation and Information Science, Springer, 377*, 110–129. doi:10.1007/978-3-642-40576-1_12

Nair, S. (2013). *How to Avoid Session Hijacking in Web Applications*. TechNet. Microsoft.

Nikiforakis, Meert, Younan, Johns. & Joosen. (2011). Session Shield: Lightweight protection against session hijacking. In *Engineering Secure Software and Systems*. Springer Berlin Heidelberg.

Whitaker, A., & Newman, D. P. (2005). *Penetration testing and network defense*. Pearson Education.

KEY TERMS AND DEFINITIONS

Active Session Hijacking: An active attacker searches for an active session and utilizes the session for communicating between the client and server. Here the active attacker impersonates as a genuine client where the client is being manipulated and the server is being fooled by the active attacker.

Application-Level Session Hijacking: It is performed by gathering the information, which is provided through network-level hijacking.

Client-Side Attack: The attacker can negotiate the session token by sending malicious activities such as malwares to the client-side programs.

IPSec: At the IP layer a collection of protocols is referred to support secure exchange of packets.

Man-in-the-Browser Attack: In this the calls between the browser and its security mechanisms or libraries are intercepted by using Trojans. To cause financial dishonesties by influencing transactions of Internet banking systems is its main objective.

Man-in-the-Middle attack: To interrupt the messages that is being transferred between the end users in a network. Attacker split the TCP connection into two connections (attacker-to-server and client-to-attacker) and uses different techniques to impersonate the users.

Network-Level Session Hijacking: It is implemented by the web applications through the data flow of the protocol which is shared. Critical information that is helpful to the attacker to attack the application - level sessions are provided by the attacks on network-level sessions.

Passive Session Hijacking: An attacker hijacks a session in the traffic that is being sent onwards but sits back, watches and records all the traffic in the network.

Session Hijacking: Session hijacking is the process of knowing the session ID (SID) of an active client, so that his account can be impersonated or hijacked.

Session Sniffing: In this the attacker uses a sniffer tool to capture a valid session token called session ID. Attacker then uses the session ID to get authenticated as a legitimate user to the web server.

This research was previously published in Advancing Cloud Database Systems and Capacity Planning With Dynamic Applications edited by Narendra Kumar Kamila, pages 363-391, copyright year 2017 by Information Science Reference (an imprint of IGI Global).

Chapter 98

Impact of Big Data on Security:
Big Data Security Issues and Defense Schemes

Kasarapu Ramani
Sree Vidyanikethan Engineering College, India

ABSTRACT

Big data has great commercial importance to major businesses, but security and privacy challenges are also daunting this storage, processing, and communication. Big data encapsulate organizations' most important and sensitive data with multi-level complex implementation. The challenge for any organization is securing access to the data while allowing end user to extract valuable insights. Unregulated access privileges to the big data leads to loss or theft of valuable and sensitive. Privilege escalation leads to insider threats. Also, the computing architecture of big data is not focusing on session recording; therefore, it is becoming a challenge to identify potential security issues and to take remedial and mitigation mechanisms. Therefore, various big data security issues and their defense mechanisms are discussed in this chapter.

INTRODUCTION

To harness the power of big data, one requires an infrastructure that can manage and process huge volumes of structured and unstructured data in real-time and can preserve data privacy and security.

Security management and data access are primary concerns for both persistent and moving data. Persistent data security is usually managed in layers: Physical, Network, Application, and at the database. Data moving between applications and organizations need additional security to protect the data in transit from unauthorized access.

The focus of this chapter is to high light the impact of security and privacy aspects on capacity and performance implications of big data solutions, which must be taken into account for such solutions to be viable. This chapter gives an overview of root causes for security and privacy challenges in big data and their consequences. It also describes the defense mechanism aspects that must be considered to make secured Big Data environment and suggests good practices to be followed for Big Data solutions, both now and in future.

DOI: 10.4018/978-1-5225-8176-5.ch098

BACKGROUND

What Is Big Data?

The Smartphones, Science facilities, Readers/ Scanners, Programs/ Software, Social media, and cameras are working as data generation points in Healthcare, Security Systems, Traffic Control, Manufacturing Sector, Sales, Sensors, Telecommunication, On-line gaming, Location-based services and Trading are leading to Big Data. The data generated and collected from different sources is doubling in every two years. The Big data become increasingly important in enterprises, government, and sciences. The process of capturing, storing, filtering, sharing, analyzing and visualizing this voluminous data itself is a challenge in Big Data. The purpose of Big Data is to generate value from stored large volumes of information by processing it using analytical techniques. The Big data helps in generating revenue, better services, strategic decisions, executive efficiency, specify needs, determine new trends, and flourish new products.

Characteristics of Big Data

Big data is characterized by 5 Vs: volume, velocity, variety, veracity and value. Volume represents huge data; velocity represents rapidity of data; variety indicates data collected from variety of sources with different data types; veracity defines consistency and trustworthiness of data; and value capture greater insights into data and supports in decision making from huge data sets. Defining characteristics of Big data will be helpful in obtaining hidden patterns available in data.

Big Data Types

Big Data includes structured, semi-structured and unstructured data.

- **Structured Data:** Represents the formal structure of data associated with relational databases or any other form of data tables and which can be generated by humans or software or computers. Structured data are often managed with SQL. Structured data are easy to input, query, store, and analyze. Examples of structured data include numbers, words, and dates.
- **Semi-Structured Data:** Also called self-describing structure, contain marks such as tags to separate semantic elements. Also, the records and fields of data can be arranged in hierarchies. XML, JSON, EDI, and SWIFT are few examples of this kind of data.
- **Unstructured Data:** Has no pre-defined data model. Now a day 80% of data accounts for unstructured data in any organization and which includes data from e-mails, video, social media websites and text streams.

Similar to structured data, this unstructured data can be generated by human or machine. Human-generated data includes text messages, e-mails, and social media data. Machine generated data includes radar and sonar data, satellite images, security, surveillance, traffic videos and atmospheric data. Often data are generated by a combination of these three groups.

Uses of Big Data

According to McKinsey Global Institute (2011), the proper management of Big Data will lead to many advantages, such as:

- Creates transparency by making relevant data readily accessible.
- Enables experimentation to expose variability, discover needs, and improve performance. i.e Data can be analyzed to identify variability in performance and to understand the root causes.
- Segments customers to customize their actions and tailors products and services to meet their specific needs.

Figure 1. Big Data value chain

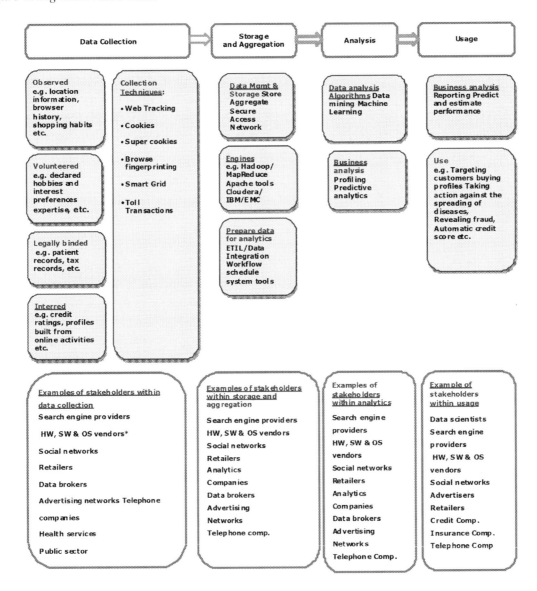

- Replaces/supports human decision-making with Machine Learning algorithms in order to minimize risk.
- Innovates new business models, products, and services.

Big Data Classification

Big data can be categorized into ten types based on data type, data source, content format, data usage, data consumer, data analysis, data frequency, data store, data processing propose, and data processing method and is shown in Figure 2.

Issues With Big Data

Need of Privacy and Security Implications and Analysis in Big Data

To a huge degree, Big Data includes reuse of information. But, it requires a sensible framework for its data access ensuring confidentiality due to the following reasons:

Lack of Transparency

Absence of openness and information on how data is compiled and used is resulted in no control over on our own data. For example, an average Internet user has almost no knowledge of how the web-based promoting market works and how their own information might be gathered and used by an extensive variety of business.

Data Compilation May Uncover Sensitive Information

Through the Big Data tools, it is possible to identify a person's inherent qualities related to politics, health etc.

Big Data also involves challenges in terms of data security which may likewise be significant for the protection of privacy. Cases of such security challenges incorporate utilization of several infrastruc-

Figure 2. Big Data classification

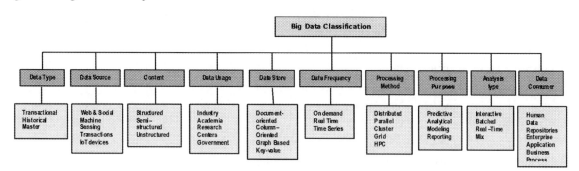

ture layers with a specific end goal to process Big Data, new sorts of the framework to deal with the tremendous stream of information and in addition non-versatile encryption of large data sets. Further, a data breach may have more severe consequences when enormous datasets are stored. According to McKinsey Global Institute (2014), enterprises that acquire and maintain large sets of personal data must be responsible stewards of that information.

VARIOUS SECURITY AND PRIVACY ISSUES IN BIG DATA

According to Yunling Wang (2016), the existing Big Data initiatives are focusing on Volume, Velocity, Veracity, Variety, Variability, and Value, but not on security and data privacy. According to Kalyani (2015), the existing IT security practices such as Access permissions, Encryption schemes, Transport layer security, Firewalls and their limitations are well-known, making the attackers perform malicious attacks on applications and operating systems in Big Data. Big Data need techniques to audit, protect data processes, and monitor in terms of data, application and infrastructure.

According to Abid Mehmood (2016), Data Privacy represents the privilege of having control over the way in which the personal data is collected and used. User's privacy may be breached under the following circumstances:

- Most of the business organizations are collecting buying preferences of users by gathering personal information such as healthcare records and location-based information etc. to improve their marketing.
- The sensitive data are stored and processed in a location not secured properly and data leakage may occur during storage and processing phases.
- The sensitive data are stored and processed in a location which is not secured properly and data leakages may occur during storage and processing phase.

According to Porambage (2016), one serious privacy issue to the personal data such as medical records, criminal records, political records, financial data, website data or business-related information is identification during transmission over the network. According to Jing (2014), Information Security is protecting data from malicious attacks and misusage of data for profit and ensuring integrity, confidentiality, and availability of data. Therefore, such information security mechanisms are to be extended to achieve Big Data Security.

According to Fei (2016) Cloud Secure Alliance categorized privacy and security issues of Big Data in four different groups as follows:

- Infrastructure Security Issues
  - Insecurity due to Distributed Processing of Data.
  - Insecurity due to Schema-free databases.
- Data Privacy Issues
  - Insecurity due to Data mining and Analytical mechanisms.
  - Insufficient Cryptographic mechanisms for Data Security.
  - Insufficient Access Control mechanisms.

- Data Management and Integrity Issues
  - Insecure Data Storage and Transaction Log Procedures.
  - Ineffective Granular Audits.
  - Data Provenance issues.
- Reactive Security Issues
  - Insufficient End-to-End Filtering & Validation mechanisms.
  - Ineffective Supervising Security monitoring mechanisms in Real-Time.

Infrastructure Security Issues

Impact of Distributed Data on Security

Now a day's data are distributed and new technologies are used for storage and process large volumes of data. For example, the Cloud Computing technologies such as Hadoop are explored for big data storage and processing.

The Big Data uses a distributed programming framework based on parallel programming for computations and storage mechanism to have massive amounts of data processing. One of the popular Big Data techniques is MapReduce framework, which divides an input file into multiple partitions in the initial phase of MapReduce, and then each partition of Mapper reads input data, do some computation activity, and provides a list of key/value pairs as output. In the second phase, the Reducer performs the summary operation based key/value pairs. Insecure Computation is due to distributed environment feature of Big Data, where parallel computation across multiple servers/workstations, lead to an opportunity for the security breach. Identifying a malicious node and securing the sensitive data from the unreliable node is a major challenge. Another issue of concern is sometimes the Mappers leak private records either intentionally or unintentionally. Also, the MapReduce computations may be subjected to replay attacks, the man in the middle attacks and denial of service attacks. According to Fei (2016), malicious data nodes may be added to a network, with an intention to receive replicated data and then to deliver modified MapReduce code. According to Fei (2016) creating the snapshots of corresponding legitimate nodes and re-introducing the concerned modified copies is an avoidable attack in the distributed environment. In healthcare, large volumes of Electronic Medical Records are creating Big Data. These kinds of data collected from networked hospitals are generally stored in a Cloud. A malicious user can make an intrusion attack by using a un-trusted computation program to leak sensitive information, or to perform data corruption and to launch DoS attack. Most of the distributed nodes' computations are having only a single level of protection mechanism, which is not sufficient and hence not recommendable also.

Hadoop and other Big Data technologies for instance: MongoDB, Accumulo does not communicate securely when it comes to inter-node communication where inter-node communication is not protected by using SSL and TLS.

There are several ways a malicious program to create big security risk:

1. Sensitive data such as credit cards, personal profile can be accessed by a malicious program, which can corrupt the data leading to incorrect results.
2. A malicious program can perform even Denial of Service attack into Big Data environment leading to financial loss.

Impact of Non-Relational Databases on Security

The big data storage has migrated from traditional relational database to unstructured NoSQL database. NoSQL database architecture is designed to be a multi-sourced data, hence leaves it vulnerable to attacks. The security in NoSQL databases is embedded in middleware and they are not supported by any dedicated security mechanism. Transactional integrity is not properly maintained in NoSQL databases. It is difficult to inculcate complex integrity constraints into NoSQL databases as it may hamper with functionality and it makes NoSQL databases not to be scalable and inefficient. The authentication techniques are not properly defined in NoSQL databases. There is no mechanism to store the password in NoSQL databases. They use Basic HTTP or Message Digest based authentication schemes and which are subjected to man in the middle attack. The HTTP protocol based on Representational State Transfer (REST) is leading to cross-site scripting, request forgery and injection attacks such as array injection, JSON injection, REST injection, view injection, schema injection, Generalized Query Language (GQL) injection, and others. NoSQL has no support of blocking with the help of the third party as well. Authorization techniques in NoSQL provide authorization at higher layers only. Authorization in NoSQL allows controlling of user access to the database but it is not possible to control user access to specific data collection. Employment of weak security mechanism makes NoSQL databases vulnerable to inside attacks. They may be unnoticed due to poor log analysis mechanisms and other fundamental security mechanisms. The NoSQL Big Data systems either use password or the default system password, therefore making anybody to easily access them.

Data Privacy Issues

Data Privacy and Data security are tightly coupled aspects of Big Data. Even though security and privacy look they are related but they are two different concepts. Infrastructure level restriction which prevents or allows accessing of data or network area on authorization is referred as Security. Whereas privacy is restricting or controlling access for different authorized users to access a specific set of data. According to Kristin Lauter (2011), it is challenging to protect private data on the web. Data Privacy has become a sensitive issue with the evolution of Big Data because it increases the risk of leakage of data. In Distributed Computing environment the data provider with privacy concerns will not expose the data; on the other hand, data demander requires accurate data for analysis. It is very difficult to preserve privacy in distributed data sharing environment using available privacy-preserving mechanisms. Information Technology besides providing convenience in public's daily life it also brings the risk of leakage of data with every transaction they do online. Cyber attackers are creating hidden online markets where personal it is possible to buy and sells stolen information. The recent cyberattacks have demonstrated that there is potential harm to personal data. Because of the reasons stated above, there is a need to continuously enhance the current privacy-preserving mechanisms, which enable the organizations employing data sharing systems to take the benefit of big data analytics.

Impact of Data Mining and Analytics on Security

The data collection, storage, and usage trend are modified by Big Data analytics. Today the consumer data is turned into business intelligence and provide new insights into different industry sectors including manufacturing, financial services, healthcare, consumer goods IT and technology, professional services, pharmaceuticals, and biotechnology. Big data is helpful to predict or forecast organizations' business and to fix optimum price a product, new product development and to enhance the market. Unethical means of information mining methods are allowing gathering personal data without asking users' permission or notification (Shrivastava & Kumar, 2017). In 2013 Cloud Security Alliance published magazine published an article on Top Ten Security Big Data Security and Privacy Challenges and it states that data analytical techniques are leading to untrustworthy, invasion of privacy and decreased civil freedom. It is required to collect and aggregate data from many nodes to perform data analysis. It is challenging to secure data while providing compatibility between nodes which are working in different computing environments. There is an extensive study of Privacy Preserving Data Mining (PPDM) since years, but still, it is a challenge to apply different mining algorithms without reading confidential data. One of the best challenges in PPDM and analytics is making certain that derivation of person acknowledgeable data is not possible (Shrivastava & Bhatnagar, 2011).

Insufficient Cryptographic Mechanisms for Data Security

Data encryption and access control mechanisms ensure the end to end security to the sensitive data and allow only authorized entities to access. The existing techniques, like Attribute-Based Encryption (ABE), are not efficient and scalable. Also, the existing authentication policies need to be improved to ensure secure communication among distributed entities. Traditional Policy of encryption that encrypts everything or nothing is inefficient on large datasets since it makes sharing or searching of records either insecure or time-consuming process. Searching and filtering of encrypted data, securing an outsourced computation are the other challenges to be considered while designing a cryptography mechanism for big data. It is highly challenging to secure data through encryption when distributed file systems are used to store the big data and processed in the cloud. File-system encryption can effectively apply only to data at rest. This requires encryption and decryption of a file every time it is accessed which increases computational time. Sometimes this overhead forces users to choose between security and performance.

Insufficient Access Control Mechanisms

Node and API authentication are concerns due to the limitations and inherent vulnerabilities in the out-of-the-box Big Data Security implementations. Rouge node insertion and stolen ticket issues are at the top of the list for holes that can be exploited. Security Design Flaw: Most of the Big Data technology implementations are built keeping minimal security model in mind. Most of the services do not authenticate users.

In Big Data the data nodes themselves do not implement any access control mechanism. The traditional SQL based database systems have good access control mechanisms for users, even at the table level, row level, and cell level. Big Data NoSQL databases are lack of comprehensive access control mechanisms. It is a complex task to keep track of different roles of users along with preserving access labels during large networked analytical transformations which can be considered as the potential threat. At the same time, granular level access control implementation gives sound security, but the data may move more restrictive category, making data analysis and decision making critical.

Data Management and Integrity Issues

Insecure Data Storage and Transaction Logs

In Big Data environment the data and related transaction logs are stored in a multi-tiered storage media as it is difficult to move data manually between tiers by the manager and to have control on exactly what data is moved and when. The exponential growth of Big Data demands auto-tiering for storage management. But, Auto-tiering based data storage solutions do not keep track of where the data is stored, leading new data storage security challenges. According to Cloud Security Magazine on Top Ten Security Big Data Security and Privacy Challenges (2013), new imperative security mechanisms to thwart unauthorized access and maintain constant availability.

Auto-tiering form of storage enables automatic storing of petabytes of data based on the policies established, which may lead security challenges like unverified storage services and mismatched security policies. Also, transaction logs are to be protected. Two kinds of attacks are possible in auto-tiered environments: collusion attacks, rollback attacks.

- **Collusion Attack:** Interchange of keys and access codes between services providers may allow them to gain excessive privileges to access data for which they are not authorized.
- **Rollback Attack:** The datasets which are outdated will be uploaded back to replace current version of data sets.

Confidentiality, integrity, consistency, and data provenance are the vulnerabilities associated with big data storage. For logging and auditing, several factors create challenges in this area including policy modeling, appropriate access definitions/profiles when someone has breached your cluster and you must find ways to detect it by recording an activity.

The Transactional logs of Big Data are huge and require protection. Data Confidentiality and Integrity is also a matter of concern where encryption and signatures might be important. Authentication, authorization, and encryption may be considered as a challenge at each node since the data is stored at different distributed nodes. Securing communication between nodes, middlewares, and the user is another security concern.

Ineffective Granular Audits

The real-time security monitoring mechanisms will enable to understand when an attack can happen. But, identifying new kinds of attacks is a problem. To identify the missed attacks audit information is needed. Also, understanding the forensics, regulation and compliance reasons are required. Therefore, the auditing should focus on more granularity levels, where one has to deal with more number of distributed data objects.

Data Provenance Issues

When you find some information in big data it is difficult to know from where it has got there since there may be a chance that the data has copied from somewhere. There may be a case where the data has been edited in the copying process. So the trustworthiness of data depends on root from where it has been generated so it is a challenge to find if the data is trustworthy. Metadata of data which is generated by the different applications can be of use to disambiguate the data and also allows reusing of data. According to Craig Gentry (2015) data provenance, one kind of metadata pertains to the derivation history of a data product starting from its original sources. The programming environment of Big Data applications generates a large number of provenance graphs leaving complex metadata. Analyzing and detecting metadata dependencies for security and or confidentiality applications from such large provenance graphs are computationally intensive.

Reactive Security Issues

Ineffective Input Validation and Filtering Mechanisms

End-point Input Validation and Filtering is another challenge as the breadth of data sources and size of the data pool is large. A key challenge of data collection process is input validation: What kind of data is untrusted? And what are the un-trusted data sources? Therefore data filtering is required to filter rogue or malicious data. In Big Data GBs or TBs of continuous data is accumulated and signature-based data filtering has a limitation that what kind of behavior aspect is to be considered for filtering are challenges. Validating the data sources and finding whether data is malicious or incorrect and filter out unreliable data is really difficult. The ID cloning attack and Sybil attack can spoof multiple IDs and also feed fake data to the data collection device, as data collection devices and programs are vulnerable to attacks. Organizations need analysis and monitoring tools in Big Data framework to identify an attack at its very first sign. Security of computational elements such as Hadoop framework has two parts namely mapper and reducer and there is every possibility of leakage of sensitive information, therefore trustworthiness of these computational elements needs to be evaluated through the process of data sanitization and de-identification.

Big data applications require data collection from the variety of sources and this process involves two fundamental security risks:

1. **Input Validation:** If all data sources are known, then only data and its source trustworthiness can be evaluated.
2. Filtering of data is also one of the major concerns since Big Data applications collect huge amount data making it difficult to validate and filter data on the fly. The existing conventional signature-based data filtering techniques may not completely resolve the input validation and data filtering problems.

Ineffective Supervising Security Monitoring Mechanisms in Real-Time

Security monitoring in real time is a challenge, based on the number of alerts generated by security devices. The Big Data technologies allow fast processing of data on the fly, however, humans cannot cope with the correlated effect of these security alerts or false positives due to the shear amount of data and velocity. Therefore, techniques or tools are necessary to detect real-time anomalies, while supporting scalable security analytics.

Renu Kesharwani (2016) has summarized the big data security challenges as follows:

- The Big Data has distributed computing environment, which supports only a single level of protection and is not recommendable.
- The evolution of Non-relational databases (NoSQL) is making it difficult to keep up security solutions in Big Data with demand.
- The auto-tiering mechanism used for automatic data transfer requires additional security mechanisms and are not available.
- When any Big Data system receives huge volumes of information, validation is required to retain trustworthiness and accuracy; however, this is not always practiced.
- During data mining, unethical IT specialists can gather personal data without having users' permission or notification.
- The traditional access control mechanisms, data encryption standards and communication procedures used for security have become dated and insufficient to rely on it.
- In many organizations, the type of access controls is not instituted to divide the level of confidentiality within the company.
- The detailed auditing mechanism is not recommendable Big Data due to the large volume of data involved.
- Consistently monitoring and tracking the origins is a challenge due to the size of Big Data.

DEFENSE SCHEMES FOR BIG DATA SECURITY ISSUES

Data Management

Data Management Comprises: Data Classification, Data Discovery and Data Tagging

1. **Data Classification:** The organizations which maintain Big Data should be:
    a. Able to identify which data is more sensitive, which fields should be more prioritized for applying for cryptographic protection etc. For this purpose, the organizations should prepare a data classification matrix.
    b. Able to perform security control assessment to determine:
    c. Location of data, such as which data is to be exposed to the Internet and which data should be kept in the secure zone, Number users or systems that can access data and Security controls such as cryptography.
    d. Able to determine data value to the attacker.
    e. Data is available easily for resell by the attacker and belongs to Intellectual Property.
    f. Able to determine the impact on revenue and compliance.
    g. Determining and reporting breaches for distinct fields, loss of a particular data field such as cardholder information may affect the business and estimating cost involved in buying new security products and re-architecting the current system.
    h. Able to determine the impact of phishing attacks on personal data such as customer's email IDs or credit card information etc.
2. **Data Discovery:** Programmatically one can protect sensitive fields of structured data such as CSV and JSON files. However, for unstructured data performing classification of sensitive data and finding its location is difficult. Therefore building threat models and profiles and sharing with

Data Analysts is useful to prevent data ex-filtration activities. Conditional search routines should be built.

3. **Data Tagging:** Understanding of ingress and egress methods will help in know the end-to-end data flow. One should identify all data ingress methods including manual, automated and methods that go through meta-layer, where the file may be copied and what kind of interface is used, such as Command Line or Java APIs. Similarly, one should know all egress methods, such as reporting jobs through Hive queries, Pig jobs or exporting through Sqoop or copying via REST API etc. This will decide control boundaries and also trust zone. It is also, helpful for data discovery and access management activities.

Identity and Access Management

POSIX Style of Permissions Provides Access Controls in Hadoop Environment

1. **Data Metering and User Entitlement:** Using machine learning algorithms and access models the threshold value should be decided to access a particular data per particular user/application and thereby data metering can be performed. The access policies should be tied to data and not for the accessing methods. Attribute-based access control should be leveraged. Providing permissions is a method to leverage data attributes user and environment or location.

2. **Role Based Access Control (RBAC) Authorization:** The security administration in huge networked systems is very complex challenging to manage. Existing access control mechanism is costly and errors prone since every user are given different privileges by the administrator. The user may be able to access confidential information when he is granted privileges that exceed the need of their job role.

RBAC is becoming popular among the people who are working with big data technologies since it reduces the complexity of administration in security. RBAC is also being adopted in many commercial applications and huge networked applications. RBAC allows you give different roles for different users and give different privileges for different roles; this reduces the risk of a user being given the privileges that exceed the need for his/her job role.

Fine-grained access control can be delivered through RBAC. Data access should be managed by role and not the user. Relations between users and roles should be determined based on group memberships and rules across all data access paths.

Data Privacy and Protection

In Hadoop distributed environment data-at-rest encryption at the file level or block –level, field-level or column level encryption (application level), data tokenization, and data masking/redaction provide security.

1. **Application Level Cryptography:** Security granularities and audit tracking capabilities are enabled by tokenization and field level encryption. Through manual intervention the fields, which need encryption should be decided and where and how to enable authorized decryption.

2. **Transparent Encryption:** To prevent access through the storage medium Full Disk Encryption or HDFS layer encryption should be adopted. Employment of Data – at – rest encryption in Hadoop

will result in protecting sensitive data and keeping the disks out of audit scope. Employment of Transparent Encryption scheme at disk level makes residual data, human unreadable format when the disks are removed or deactivated from the cluster.

3. **Data Redaction or Data Masking:** Data redaction or data masking before loading data in ETL process de-identifies the Personally Identifiable Information, therefore no sensitive data in Hadoop. To keep Hadoop environment potentially out of audit scope both static and dynamic masking tools can be deployed for batch or real-time data processing.

Network Security

Network security includes data protection in-transit, authorization mechanisms, and network zoning.

1. **Data Protection in Transit:** HTTPS can prevent information disclose and elevation of privilege threats. Today's Hadoop environment is using TLS protocol to provide authentication and ensuring the privacy of communication name servers, nodes, and applications. To ensure data confidentiality the following controls should be adopted:
   a. From client to Hadoop cluster perform Packet level encryption using TLS.
   b. Between Namenode to Job Tracker and Job Tracker to Datanode apply packet-level encryption within Hadoop cluster.
   c. To prevent Sniffing attack use Lightweight Directory Access Protocol (LDAP) over SSL called LDAPS when communicating with enterprise directories.
2. **Network Securing Zoning:** To allow traffic to the approved levels segment the Hadoop clusters into Choke points such as Rack switches and thereby:
   a. End users are able to connect with only individual Datanodes, but not to the Namenodes.
   b. To control traffic in and out of Hadoop environment Apache Knox Gateway can be used and it provides per-service-level granularity.

Infrastructure Security and Integrity

The infrastructure security and integrity consist of Auditing, Secure Enhanced Linux, File Integrity Checking, Data Tamper Monitoring, Privileged user verification and Activity monitoring.

1. **Auditing or Logging:** Every unique change of Hadoop ecosystem needs to be audited and audit logs should be protected and includes the following:
   a. Addition and deletion of management and data nodes.
   b. State changes in management as well as Jobtracker and Namenodes.
   c. Activities including preventing of the addition of unauthorized node into Hadoop cluster.
   d. When data is not limited to only one of the Hadoop components, the data security leads many moving parts and results in the high percentage of fragmentation. To address this fragmentation problem the following technologies are recommendable.
      i. **Apache Falcon:** Focuses on data management and controls data life cycle.
      ii. **Cloudera Navigator:** To address log sprawl of metadata.
      iii. **Zettaset Orchestrator:** Having its own metadata collected from Hadoop components.

2. **Secure Enhanced Linux:** National Security Agency (NSA) of US created the Secure Enhanced Linux called SELinux and has Mandatory Access Control. If any user changes settings of his home directory the SELinux policy prevents other users and processes access it. It prevents command injection attacks. Even any malicious user access the root, still he will not be able to execute anything using any kind of data ex-filtration methods. SELinux makes access decisions depending on all the information available like user, type, role, and level.

REQUIREMENTS FOR SECURITY MANAGEMENT OF A BIG DATA SYSTEM

A successful big data system for organizing the security need to:

- Reduce tedious manual tasks in a routine assessment and response activities. When an issue is being investigated, the system requires diminishing the number of repetitive and manual tasks which includes executing the same operation on n different tools, toggling between consoles etc. The system should make efforts to consistently decrease the number of steps involved per incident since these tasks cannot be eradicated in an instant.
- Apply business context in order to point analysts towards the main impact issues. The securities teams should be able to map the systems they consider monitoring and able to manage back the crucial business applications and processes being supported. The dependencies between the system and the third party need to be understood along with understanding their current state of compliance and vulnerability.
- Present the analysts with only the most appropriate data. "Reducing false positives" is often referred by the security professionals. The system should eliminate the noise and provide the analysts with the pointers to work on the high impact issues. The system should provide the data aiding to highlight the what, why are the likely biggest problems.
- Supplement human knowledge. The system should extend support to the analyst for analyzing the significant critical items. This involves providing built techniques that identify the current threats as well as the high priority issues. These techniques use to recognize the current tools, methods, and procedures being used by the attacker community.
- View "over the horizon". Defending the system against the current threats is a "race against time". The system needs to be predictive and able to present early warning. By making aware of the external threat intelligence by the internal situational awareness attending the internal security team to an active defense and prevention state from a passive defense state.

HANDLING BIG DATA PRIVACY CONCERNS

According to the article, Big Data Analytics for Security Intelligence by Cloud Security Alliance Magazine (2013) the possible strategies for the Big data privacy protection can be analyzed by considering the following development strategies of the framework.

1.   The privacy policies able to access the stored data in the target platforms.
2.   The making of useful enforcement monitors for these policies.
3.   The integration of the generated monitors with the target platforms.

Big data privacy can be handled in various phases of Data generation, Data storage, and Data processing etc.

Big Data Privacy in Data Generation Phase

The risk of privacy violation can be minimized at the data generation phase by either access restriction or by falsifying data.

1.   **Access Restriction:** The data owner provides the massive amount of data if the data contains sensitive information which cannot be shared by others. For privacy preserving a few measures such as encryption tools, script blockers, anti-tracking extensions need to be taken in to account.
2.   **Falsifying Data:** In certain circumstances, in order to prevent the access to the sensitive data, data can be distorted before the data is got. In such cases, true data cannot be obtained easily from the distorted data. Data distortion can be achieved by the following techniques.
     a.   A *Socketpuppet* tool is used to hide the online individual identity. By using numerous Socketpuppets to one particular individual data, it is seen as the individual data having the place with different people. Hence, it is difficult to relate the data of different socketpuppets to one individual data.
     b.   *Mask Me* is an example of the security tool used to mask the identity of the individual. This is applicable especially in cases of the data having patients' health records, owners' credit card details etc.

Big Data Privacy in Data Storage Phase

According to the article Big Data Analytics for Security Intelligence by Cloud Security Alliance Magazine (2013) with the advancement of data storage technologies, storing large volumes of Big data is not a challenge. According to Kesharwani (2016), the major challenge is ensuring the Big data storage without disclosing the individuals' sensitive data. According to Priyank Jain (2016), the traditional security mechanisms of data protection can be categorized into four groups as the file level data security schemes, database level data security schemes, media level security schemes and application level encryption schemes.

According to Liu (2011) information availability ensures the access of the needed data to the authorized users. Therefore the primary concern of the big data storage is to ensure the privacy of the individual. For example, public key encryption (PKE) is an existing method to ensure such a requirement where the encrypted can only be decrypted by a valid recipient. User privacy in the data cloud can be achieved by any of the following techniques.

1.   **Attribute-Based Encryption:** Access control is granted based on the user's identity to have complete access to all resources.

2. **Homomorphic Encryption:** Can be carried out by IBE/ABE deployment scheme settings by updating the possible ciphertext receiver.
3. **Storage Path Encryption:** Ensures the secured big data storage in the cloud.
4. **Usage of Hybrid Clouds:** Usage of Hybrid cloud environment which is a combination of both public and private cloud environment provides a secure access to the data to a certain extent.

Big Data Privacy in Data Processing Phase

The big data privacy preservation in the data processing phase can be achieved in two phases. It is possible that the collected data contains sensitive data which affect the privacy of data owner. Therefor the first phase is intended for safeguarding this sensitive data from the unsolicited disclosure. The second phase is aimed at extracting significant information from the data without privacy violation.

TECHNIQUES FOR HANDLING BIG DATA PRIVACY

There were traditionally used techniques for providing privacy in big data. The demerits of these traditional techniques led to the introduction of advanced techniques.

De-Identification

According to Cheng (2015) and Mehmood (2016), De-identification is one of such traditional techniques of privacy preserving.

With De-identification there is an increased possibility of re-identification also. There are three types of De-identification privacy-preserving methods,

- K-anonymity
- L-diversity
- T-closeness

1. **K-Anonymity:** The K-anonymity allows maximizing data utility of data while limiting disclosure risk to an acceptable level. Therefore, it is especially suitable for privacy protection But, it is still unaided by attacks such as unsorted matching attack, temporal attack, and complementary release attack. An additional limitation of the problem is where attributes are suppressed in place of individual entries. This limitation was handled by the L-diversity approach of data anonymization.
2. **L-Diversity:** By diminishing the granularity of data representation, the L-diversity group based anonymization safeguards the privacy of the data sets. The k-anonymity model extends to l-diversity model (Distinct, Entropy, Recursive) by utilizing both generalization and suppression methods in such a way as to map any given record onto at least k diverse records in the data. The setback of this method is that it is dependent on the sensitive attribute value range. Apart from this L-diversity method also tends to skewness and similarity attack.
3. **T-Closeness:** According to Li N (2007), t-closeness is an added enhancement of l-diversity group based anonymization. The l-diversity model is extended to t-closeness model (Equal/Hierarchical distance) by handling the attribute values distinctly by considering into account the data distribu-

tion values for that attribute. The major improvement of t-closeness is that it intercepts attribute disclosure. The major setback of t-closeness lies in the increased odds of re-identification with the increased size and variety of data.

Differential Privacy

Differential Privacy is a technique which allows the user to access user data from databases where personal information of people is stored without revealing the identity of the individual. Information is distracted minimally by the database system to achieve Differential Privacy. The distraction should be minimal that it should preserve data privacy as well as provide enough useful information to the analyst.

In DP direct access to the database is not provided to the analyst. Database analyst and database are separated by an intermediate piece of software known as Privacy Guard to protect the privacy.

Identity-Based Anonymization

According to Samarati, P (1998) an open architecture for anonymization was created by Intel allowing the utilization of a wide range of tools utilized for both de-identifying and re-identifying web log records. It is found that the enterprise data has different properties to those of standard anonymization examples. This concept revealed the benefits of big data techniques when working with anonymized data. The anonymized data was found exposed to correlation attacks instead of masking the sensitive personal information.

Anonymization needs to be beyond simple masking or generalizing certain fields. To achieve valuable results Intel used Hadoop to analyze the anonymized data. Anonymized datasets need to be carefully analyzed to determine whether they are open to attack.

VARIOUS ENCRYPTION TECHNIQUES FOR PRESERVING THE PRIVACY OF SENSITIVE DATA

With the rapid growth in demand for improved security and the limitations of the ancient encryption techniques of data, the need for the advanced encryption techniques has increased. In this section, we recommend the employment of new encryption techniques like Searchable, Order-preserving and Homomorphic schemes.

Searchable Encryption

Searchable encryption provides us with the facility to search in the encrypted data. Searchable Encryption is an optimistic method of protecting individuals' sensitive data while retaining the ability to search on the server side. SE allows the search of encrypted data in the server side without information leakage in plaintext data. In addition to the security of the stored documents and keywords on the server side, the security of the query keywords should also be guaranteed in the searchable encryption scheme. Moreover, the search pattern and the access pattern should also be protected. Searchable encryption can be categorized into the main branches as Searchable Symmetric Encryption (SSE), Public-key Encryption with Keyword Search (PEKS), and Deterministic Encryption.

Order Preserving Encryption Scheme (OPES)

An OPES is a deterministic encryption technique where the encryption algorithm generates the ciphertexts that maintain the numerical ordering of the plaintexts. The main objective of the technique is to consider a target distribution provided by the user as an input and alter the plaintext values such that the alteration never changes the order while ensuring that the altered values are following the target distribution. The capability of the Order-preserving encryption technique by directly supporting the range query processing on the encrypted data without decrypting them made the technique important. This technique is exclusively designed to work with the existing indexing structures, hence can be easily integrated with the existing database systems. Without decryption, OPES directly allows comparison operations to be performed on the encrypted data.

Given a series of non-negative integers, Ozsoyoglu (2003) considered attribute-level encryption for relational databases to show that there can be a distinctively determined order-preserving function. The input distribution function is a sequence of strictly growing polynomial functions. Since this distribution method never considers input distribution, the shape of the distribution of the encrypted values varies with the shape of the input distribution.

OPES that makes the encrypted result independent of input distribution was designed by Agrawal (2004). The encrypted result of this technique is statistically indistinguishable which is achieved by introducing the "Flatten" stage.

CryptDB is a system which provides confidentiality for the applications using database management systems by exploring an intermediate design point. This system was presented by Popa (2011).

Homomorphic Encryption

Homomorphic encryption allows us to encrypt the data in such a way that performing a mathematical operation on the encrypted data and decrypting the result produces the same answer as performing an analogous operation on the unencrypted data. The homomorphism is defined as the correspondence between the operations performed on the encrypted data to those of the operations performed on the unencrypted data. This correspondence can be utilized to perform operations which are secure in the cloud. A partially homomorphic cryptosystem is a system that exhibits either additive or multiplicative homomorphism, but not both. Homomorphic cryptosystems are available in many forms which are designed to perform specific operations. A fully homomorphic cryptosystem was recently proposed by Craig Gentry (2015). Few Homomorphic Encryption Techniques are Fully Homomorphic Encryption, Fully Homomorphic Encryption over the Integers, Homomorphic evaluation of AES.

GOOD PRACTICES FOR MANAGING BIG DATA FROM A SECURITY POINT OF VIEW (ENISA-CSA,2015)

- If big data information is stocking in the cloud, the cloud provider should have good enough security mechanisms in place. Also, the provider should carry out regular security inspections and agree on fines if case sufficient security standards are not met.
- To obtain security in big data Granular auditing must be carried out. The confidentiality and integrity of the audit information are also important. The big data and the audit information are to be

stored separately. The audit information is to be regularly monitored and protected with the users' granular access controls. This can be performed by the available open source audit tools.

- Develop a proper access control policy such as allowing access to authorized people users. The access control can be handled in two ways as granting the user access and restricting the user access. Better security is provided by implementing the policy that that chooses the correct trick for a particular scenario. For providing the best access controls, CSA (2013) has suggested the following tips:
  - Normalizing the mutable elements and de-normalizing the immutable elements.
  - Ensuring proper implementation by tracing the secrecy requirements.
  - Maintaining the access labels.
  - Tracing the admin data.
  - Using SSO (Single Sign-ON).
  - Maintaining accurate data federation by using a labeling scheme.

- **Secure the Data:** Both the raw information and the result from analytics should be properly secured. Encryption should be utilized to make sure that no confidential data is leaked.

- Storage management is an important part of the Big Data security. A technique known as secure untrusted data repository (SUNDR) is used to detect the illegal modifications of the file by malicious server agents. This technique recommends the usage of signed message digests for identifying each file by a digital identifier. This is supported by many techniques such as policy based encryption schemes, encryption key rotation and key updating for lazy revocation, digital rights management (DRM) for copyright protection etc. It is better building one's own secure cloud storage over the existing infrastructure.

- **Secure Communications:** Data on transport should be appropriate to make sure its confidentiality and integrity.

- **Real-Time Security Supervising:** Access to the information should be supervised. Tools related to threat intelligence should be deployed to prevent unauthorized access to the confidential data.

- Endpoint security is vital and this can be achieved by using Mobile Device Management (MDM) by connecting only to the trusted devices in the network, performing resource testing, and using trusted certificates. Further, the techniques of outlier detection and statistical similarity detection are used for filtering the malicious inputs while safeguarding against ID spoofing attacks, Sybil attacks etc.

- The application of big data analytics is recommended by implementing tools such as Internet Protocol security (IPsec), secure shell (SSH) and Kerberos in order to handle the real-time data. Data compliance is a major task when dealing with the constant overflow of data. This overhead is can be tackled by considering the security at each level of the stack and also through real-time analytics. The implementation of the security controls at each level of the stack of the cloud, application level, and clusters can be achieved by deploying the front end security systems such as the application level firewalls and routers. Care should be taken against the attacks that try to circumvent the infrastructure of the Big Data and also the "data-poisoning" attacks (i.e., the monitoring system is tricked by the falsified data).

- Managing the data privacy in ever increasing data sets is really hard. The key for data privacy is maintaining the Scalability and Composability with the implementation of techniques such as differential privacy and homomorphic encryption. Differential privacy minimizes the record identification while maximizing the query accuracy. Homomorphic encryption provides the feasibility of storing and processing the encrypted data in the cloud. Incorporating awareness among the employees by training them on the latest privacy regulations and making sure of maintaining the software infrastructure with the aid of authorized mechanisms helps in maintaining the data privacy. Encouraging the implementation of the "privacy-preserving data composition" helps in data leakage control from various databases by monitoring and reviewing the infrastructure that is linked to the databases together.

- Mathematical cryptographic techniques were advanced in these days. Constructing a system that allows the operations such as searching and filtering on the encrypted data actually runs Boolean queries on the encrypted data. Searchable Symmetric Encryption (SSL) is one such technique. Relational encryption aids in comparing the encrypted data by matching the identifier values and the attribute values without sharing the encryption keys. The key management is made easy in the public key systems by Identity-based Encryption (IBE). This technique allows the encryption of the plain text for a certain identity. Attribute-based encryption integrates the access controls with the encryption scheme. Identification of the duplicate data in the cloud can be achieved by using the converged encryption scheme which makes use of the encryption keys.
- SSL certificates offer great security and protection. It encrypts all the communications that happen between a website and browser. Therefore SSL certificates are mandatory for web-based data transactions. The security is provided by encrypting the passwords and ensuring the end-to-end encryption by encrypting the data at rest. Apart from Secure Sockets Layer (SSL), algorithms such as Advanced Encryption Standard (AES), Secure Hash Algorithm 2 (SHA-256), RSA, Transport layer security (TLS) can also provide secure encryption.
- Data provenance is referred to as the provenance metadata originated from the big data applications. This is also the category of data that needs considerable protection. Developing a protocol such as an infrastructure access protocol that controls the access is recommended. Making use of the mechanisms such as checksums to set up regular status updates and continuous data integrity verification is also recommended. The finest practice for data provenance includes the implementation of scalable and dynamic granular access controls and also the implementation of the encryption methods.
- Secure big data environments using firewalls. Antivirus applications like Bit defender are used across various organizations who want to secure their big data repository from cyber attackers.
- End-to-end lineage tracking, entity matching, and thorough assessments can help in quickly detecting security breaches.

In summary, various security and privacy practices to be followed are shown in Table 1.

CONCLUSION

Big data is the most important area of the research problem in these days. The commercial impacts of big data have the potential to generate significant productivity growth for a number of vertical sectors. Big data presents the opportunity to create unprecedented business advantages and better service delivery. All the challenges and issues are needed to be handled effectively and in an efficient manner. The major issue is to provide great security to the big data so that the big data could be handled and man-

Table 1. Security and privacy methods

Security Mechanism	Purpose	Method
Security in Cloud Environment	Securing the data storage process on cloud	Authentication, Encryption-Decryption, and Compression
		Key Establishment, and ID based Encryption Algorithms
Hadoop Security	Security and privacy of Hadoop	Trust establishment between User and Name node, Random Encryption technique on data
	HDFS Security	Kerberos mechanism, Bull Eye Algorithm, and Name node approach
Monitoring Mechanism	Intrusion detection architecture	Maliciousness attack identification metrics
	Detection of anomalies or predicting network behaviour	Data collection, analysis, integration, and interpretation
	Detection of abnormal user behaviour	Self-assuring network control system
Auditing Mechanism	Auditing Dynamic Storage of Big Data	MuR-DPA: Top Down based on Merkle Hash Tree
Key Management Method	Generating strong keys, and authenticating data centers	Quantum cryptography algorithm and Pair-Hand protocol
	Securing group-key transfer	Online key- generation centre using Diffie-Hellman key Agreement mechanism and linear secret-sharing scheme
	Securing group -data sharing	Outsourcing conditional proxy re-encryption scheme
	Securing unstructured big data	Data analytics such as data- filtering, clustering & classification; security suit for existing security standards and as well as algorithms.
Anonymization Method	Providing privacy for sensitive fields using anonymization	K-anonymity Approaches
	Data mining with privacy preserving	Adaptive utility based k-anonymization model
	Scalable anonymization capability	Techniques such as Hybrid Top Down and Bottom Up SubTree Anonymization
	Scalable privacy- preservation for big data	Two Phase Clustering algorithm

aged with the Cloud along with the modern systems. A successful big data managed for security has a system that extracts and presents critical data for analysis in the fastest and effective way. This chapter elaborated various security and privacy issues and factors that affect the Big Data storage, processing and communication and the possible defense mechanisms. In this chapter, we presented various privacy-preserving techniques in the big data applications perspective. As far as security of big data is concerned the existing techniques are promising to progress into new vulnerable to big data arose and the necessity for securing the big data increases.

This study reveals that it may be difficult to attain big data with privacy but is not unattainable. Many issues related to the intellectual property rights, Cybersecurity, data privacy along with data integrity, Code of conduct for the big data and the exploitation liability need to be resolved.

The Big Data organizations need to employ three key security controls: Preventive, Detective and Administrative for securing Big data life cycle.

- **Preventive:** Securing the data using encryption techniques while it is at rest/motion and use of access control and identity management.

- **Detective:** Adopting auditing mechanisms to monitor anomalous behavior and to provide compliance reports/alerts about the potential problems throughout the Big Data environment.
- **Administrative:** Implementation of administrative processes and procedures for security through privileged user analysis, sensitive data discovery, encryption key management capabilities, and configuration management.

To achieve the above, the new research direction privacy-preserving data mining should be strong. In this method, data should be published with appropriate suppression, generalization, distortion, and decomposition so that privacy of individuals is not compromised and yet the disclosed data is used for analytical purposes. K-Anonymity algorithm is one of the best ways to achieve security. The data collector is not a trustworthy, hence privacy-preserving pattern publishing is needed so that sensitive information about underlying data is not revealed. Therefore, Pattern hiding method can transform the data in such a way that certain patterns cannot be derived via data mining. The Secure Multiparty Mining a distributed mining method, where the data on which mining is to be performed is partitioned, vertically or horizontally among several nodes. This partitioned data is not shared and hence remains private, but the results of mining process can be combined and shared among participating nodes.

In future, to provide highly secure Big Data environment it is recommendable to implement application security rather than device security, isolating devices and servers having sensitive data, applying reactive and proactive protection mechanisms, regular auditing, analyzing logs, and updating attack information across the organizations can help for better organization of data.

REFERENCES

Agrawal, R., Kiernan, J., Srikant, R., & Xu, Y. (2004). Order-preserving encryption for numeric data. *Proceedings of SIGMOD '04*, 563 – 574. 10.1145/1007568.1007632

Big Data Analytics for Security Intelligence. (2013). Retrieved from www.cloudsecurityalliance.org/research/big-data

Big Data and Privacy principles under pressure in the age of Big Data analytics. (2014). Retrieved from https://dzlp.mk/en/node/2736

Boneh, D., Di Crescenzo, G., Ostrovsky, R., & Persiano, G. (2004). Public key encryption with keyword search. Advances in Cryptology – EUROCRYPT '04, 506–522.

Boneh, D., & Waters, B. (2007). Conjunctive, subset, and range queries on encrypted data. *Theory of Cryptography Conference (TCC '07)*, 535–554. 10.1007/978-3-540-70936-7_29

Brakerski, Z., Gentry, C., & Vaikuntanathan, V. (2011). Fully Homomorphic Encryption without Bootstrapping. *Cryptology ePrint Archive Report*.

Brakerski, Z., & Vaikuntanathan, V. (2011). Efficient Fully Homomorphic Encryption, LWE. *Proceedings of FOCS*.

Chang, Y. C., & Mitzenmacher, M. (2005). Privacy preserving keyword searches on remote encrypted data. *ACNS 05, 3531*, 442–455.

Cheng, H., Rong, C., Hwang, K., Wang, W., & Li, Y. (2015). Secure big data storage and sharing scheme for cloud tenants. *China Communications*, *12*(6), 106–115. doi:10.1109/CC.2015.7122469

Cheon, Coron, Kim, Lee, Lepoint, Tibouchi, & Yun. (2013). Batch fully homomorphic encryption over the integer*s. EUROCRYPT,* 315-335.

Collins, T., Hopkins, D., Langford, S., & Sabin, M. (1997). *Public Key Cryptographic Apparatus and Method.* US Patent #5,848,159.

Coron, Naccache, & Tibouchi. (2012). Public key compression and modulus switching for fully homomorphic encryption over the integers. EUROCRYPT 2012, 446-464.

Coron, J. S., Lepoint, T., & Tibouchi, M. (2014). Scale-invariant Fully Homomorphic Encryption over the Integers. *PKC 2014*, *8383*, 311–328.

Differential Privacy for Everyone. (2012). Retrieved from http://download.microsoft.com/Differential_Privacy_for_Everyone.pdf

Fei, H. (2016). Robust cyber-physical systems: Concept, models, and implementation. *Future Generation Computer Systems*, 449–475.

Gentry, Halevi, & Nigel. (2015). *Homomorphic evaluation of the AES circuit* (Updated Implementation).

Gentry, C. (2009). Fully homomorphic encryption using ideal lattices. *Symposium on the Theory of Computing (STOC)*, 169-176.

Goh, E. J. (2003). Secure indexes. *Cryptology ePrint Archive*. Retrieved from https://eprint.iacr.org/2003/216.pdf

Hussain, N. I., & Saikia, P. (2014). *Big Data ppt*. Retrieved from http://www.slideshare.net/nasrinhussain1/big-data-ppt-31616290

Jain, Gyanchandani, & Khare. (2016). Big data privacy: A Technological Perspective and Review. *Journal of Big Data*, *3*(25).

Jing, Q., Vasilakos, A. V., Wan, J., Lu, J., & Qiu, D. (2014). Security of the internet of things: Perspectives and challenges. *Wireless Networks*, *20*(8), 2481–2501. doi:10.100711276-014-0761-7

Kesharwani, R. (2016, August). Enhancing Information Security in Big Data. *International Journal of Advanced Research in Computer and Communication Engineering*, *5*(8).

Lauter, Naehrig, & Vaikuntanathan. (2011). Can homomorphic encryption be practical? ACM-CCSW, 113–124.

Li, N. (2007). t-Closeness: privacy beyond k-anonymity and L-diversity. *IEEE 23rd international conference on Data engineering (ICDE)*.

Liu, S. (2011). Exploring the future of computing. *IT Professional*, *15*(1), 2–3. doi:10.1109/MITP.2012.120

Machanavajjhala, A., Gehrke, J., Kifer, D., & Venkitasubramaniam, M. (2006). L-diversity: privacy beyond k-anonymity. *Proceedings of 22nd International Conference Data Engineering (ICDE)*. 10.1109/ICDE.2006.1

McKinsey Global Institute. (2011). *Big data: The next frontier for innovation, competition, and productivity*. Author.

Mehmood, Natgunanathan, Xiang, Hua, & Guo. (2016). Protection of Big Data Privacy. *IEEE Access on Special Section on Theoretical Foundations for Big data Applications: Challenges and Opportunities,* 1821 – 1834.

Mehmood, A., Natgunanathan, I., Xiang, Y., Hua, G., & Guo, S. (2016). *Protection of big data privacy*. IEEE Translations and Content Mining.

Meyerson, A., & Williams, R. (2004). On the complexity of optimal k-anonymity. *Proceedings of the ACM Symposium on Principles of Database Systems*.

Ozsoyoglu, Singer, & Chung. (2003). Anti-tamper databases: Querying encrypted databases. *Proceedings of the 17th Annual IFIP WG 11.3 Working Conference on Database and Applications Security*.

Popa, R. A., Zeldovich, N., & Balakrishnan. (2011). *CryptDB: A practical encrypted relational DBMS*. Technical MITCSAIL-TR-2011-005, MIT Computer Science and Artificial Intelligence Laboratory, Cambridge, MA.

Porambage, P., Ylianttila, M., Schmitt, C., Kumar, P., Gurtov, A., & Vasilakos, A. V. (2016). The quest for privacy in the Internet of Things. *IEEE Cloud Computing*, *3*(2), 36–45. doi:10.1109/MCC.2016.28

Rivest, R., Shamir, A., & Adleman, L. (1978). A method for obtaining digital signatures and public-key cryptosystems. *Communications of the ACM*, *21*(2), 120–126. doi:10.1145/359340.359342

Samarati, P., & Sweeney, L. (1998). *Protecting privacy when disclosing information: k-anonymity and its enforcement through generalization and suppression*. Technical Report SRI-CSL-98-04, SRI Computer Science Laboratory.

Sedayao, J., & Bhardwaj, R. (2014). Making Big Data, Privacy, and Anonymization work together in the enterprise: Experiences and Issues. *Big Data Congress*. 10.1109/BigData.Congress.2014.92

Shirudkar & Motwani. (2015). Big-Data Security. *International Journal of Advanced Research in Computer Science and Software Engineering*, *5*(3).

Shrivastava, G., & Bhatnagar, V. (2011). Secure Association Rule Mining for Distributed Level Hierarchy in Web. *International Journal on Computer Science and Engineering*, *3*(6), 2240–2244.

Shrivastava, G., & Kumar, P. (2017). Privacy Analysis of Android Applications: State-of-art and Literary Assessment. Scalable Computing. *Practice and Experience*, *18*(3), 243–252.

Sokolova, M., & Matwin, S. (2015). *Personal privacy protection in time of Big Data*. Berlin: Springer.

Song, D. X., Wagner, D., & Perrig, A. (2000). Practical techniques for searches on encrypted data. *Proceedings of IEEE Symposium on Security and Privacy*, 44–55.

Tarekegn, G. B., & Munaye, Y. Y. (2016). Big Data: Security Issues, Challenges and Future Scope. *International Journal of Computer Engineering & Technology*, *7*(4), 12–24.

The Economist Intelligence Unit Ltd. (2012). *Big Data: Lessons from the Leaders.* Retrieved from http://www.bdvc.nl/images/Rapporten/SAS-Big-data-lessons-from-the-leaders.pdf

Top Ten Security Big Data Security and Privacy Challenges. (2013). Retrieved from http://www.cloud-securityalliance.org

Wang, Y., Wang, J., & Chen, X. (2016, December). Secure Searchable Encryption: A survey. *Journal of Communications and Information Networks., 1*(4), 52–65. doi:10.1007/BF03391580

Wiener, M. (1990, May). Cryptanalysis of Short RSA Secret Exponents. *IEEE Transactions on Information Theory, 36*(3), 553–558. doi:10.1109/18.54902

Yogesh, Simmhan, Plale, & Gannon. (n.d.). *A Survey of Data Provenance Techniques.* Technical Report IUB-CS-TR618.

This research was previously published in the Handbook of Research on Network Forensics and Analysis Techniques edited by Gulshan Shrivastava, Prabhat Kumar, B. B. Gupta, Suman Bala, and Nilanjan Dey, pages 326-350, copyright year 2018 by Information Science Reference (an imprint of IGI Global).

Chapter 99

Investigating the Determinants of IT Professionals' Intention to Use Cloud–Based Applications and Solutions:
An Extension of the Technology Acceptance

Sabah Al-Somali
King Abdulaziz University, Saudi Arabia

Hanan Baghabra
King Abdulaziz University, Saudi Arabia

ABSTRACT

Using a sample of 155 IT professionals from private and government organisations in Saudi Arabia, the authors tested a model of cloud-based applications adoption that is influenced by individual characteristics (represented by personal innovativeness in the domain of IT), organisational context (represented by the accessibility of the technology), technological context (represented by perceived vulnerabilities) and social context (represented by social image). The model explained 74% of the intention to use cloud-based applications. The findings show that accessibility of the technology, perceived vulnerabilities, individual characteristics and social image are all important determinants for using cloud applications and solutions. The findings will potentially contribute to research and practice by revealing the crucial factors that will impact IT professionals' intention to adopt cloud computing in the context of developing countries in the Arab world. Theoretical and practical implications of the findings are presented.

DOI: 10.4018/978-1-5225-8176-5.ch099

1. INTRODUCTION

In the current digital age, organisations are using advanced Information Technology (IT) applications such as cloud computing to reduce their IT operations and maintenance costs. In fact, cloud computing has changed the nature of computing and how business operates. Cloud computing (CC) can be defined as accessing of shared data and applications over a network environment without concern about ownership or management of hardware or software (Scale, 2009). CC allows organisations to use a set of IT resources such as networks, hardware, storage devices and applications) that can be provisioned and released through the web (Thompson & Havard, 2015). Moreover, cloud-based applications and solutions add value to business by reducing operating costs and increasing operational efficiency. In fact, many of the big players in the software industry such as Amazon, Google and Microsoft have entered the development of cloud services and are delivering various cloud-based services.

Recently, research trends on cloud computing have been focused on the technology, benefits, data privacy and security of cloud computing at the organisational level. However, little research attention has been devoted to explore the intention to adopt and use cloud applications at individual level and how contextual factors can influence diffusion of cloud computing applications and solutions (Opitz et al., 2013).

This paper proposes an extended model for the use of cloud computing applications and solutions by IT professionals. In fact, it is believed that compared with end users, IT professionals may show trivial differences in their technology adoption and use (Chau and Hu, 2002). In addition, IT professionals' attitudes on the basis of their beliefs and/or intention to use cloud applications have been barely studied in the literature. It is noteworthy that, the decision to use specific technology is dependent on how the technology is understood and perceived by IT professionals and practitioners. The objective therefore is to understand the factors that may influence or discourage IT professionals' intention to use cloud-based applications and solutions. Hence, this study conducts a field study to empirically demystify IT professionals' intention to use cloud-based applications by testing an extended technology acceptance model which will be used to answer the following questions: (1) What are the factors that influence the intention to use cloud-based applications and solutions by IT professionals? (2) How can existing technology adoption theories be used to model the intention to use cloud computing?

This paper is structured as follows: the following section briefly discusses cloud computing technology, and provides a picture of its types, deployment models and the state of cloud computing in developing countries. Next, in Section 3, we discuss the theoretical approach and put forward the hypotheses to be tested. In section 4, we then explain the main method employed and in the penultimate section we carry out the empirical analyses. Finally, we present the research findings and concluding remarks, as well as future research recommendations.

2. CLOUD COMPUTING TECHNOLOGY

Cloud computing is seen as the next-generation of IT architecture designed to deliver numerous computing services. Stieninger & Nedbal (2014) note that, the definition of the term cloud computing is still not clear, even for IT experts and mnagers. According to the National Institute of Standards and Technology (NIST), cloud computing is defined as "A model for enabling reliable, on-demand network access to a communal pool of configurable hardware and software resources that can be quickly provisioned and released with least management effort or interaction (Mell & Grance, 2011). By using cloud computing, users are able to access applications and services from multiple devices and customize the content they access.

Recent research found that the use of cloud-based applications continues to grow as IT professionals look for ways to routinized and delegate management activities that rob IT departments of precious time and resources (Spiceworks, 2013). The International Data Corporation (IDC) reported that the worldwide total cloud computing market will grow to reach $107 billion in 2017. On the other hand, worldwide spending on cloud services will grow from nearly $70 billion in 2015 to more than $141 billion in 2019 (IDC, 2013). Cisco Global Cloud Index (2014) predicts that, by 2019, 55% of the consumer Internet population will use cloud storage up from 42 percent in 2014 (Cisco Global Cloud Index,2014). Table 1 provides a summary for cloud readiness by region in 2015. It can be seen from the table that, North America had the most cloud traffic (1,211exabytes annually), followed by Asia Pacific (1,042 exabytes annually) and Western Europe (501 exabytes annually). Moreover, Western Europe led with the number of secure Internet servers per one million people.

2.1. Cloud Computing Services and Models

The most common classification is the (1) software-as-a-service, (2) platform-as-a-service and (3) infrastructure-as a-service. In fact, these services differ according to their flexibility and level of optimisation, that is:

1. Software-as-a-service (SaaS) allows cloud customers to take advantage of software running on the provider's infrastructure through the web in which the service is accessible from various client devices. Most SaaS applications can be run directly from a Web browser and it reduces the need to install and run applications on individual computers. Examples of SaaS would be Google mail and Google Docs, (Ataur Rahman and Masudur Rahman, 2014);
2. Platform-as-a-service (PaaS) enables cloud customers to deploy their own applications and data on platform tools, including programming tools, database management systems, servers, storage,

Table 1. Cloud readiness for consumers by region in 2015

Region	Average Number of Devices per Internet User	Internet Population (2017)	Cloud Traffic Growth, in Exabytes	Fixed Network Average Download Speeds (Mbps)	Percentage of Secure Internet Servers to Total Web-Facing Internet Servers by Region
Asia Pacific	4.1%	4,102,053,575	1,042	28.1	23%
Central and Eastern Europe	5.0%	499,710,427	191	28.3	29%
Latin America	4.4%	645,585,277	203	7.6	13%
Middle East and Africa	4.6%	1,491,094,868	77	7.0	10%
North America	10.1%	379,566,614	1,211	25.4	27%
Western Europe	7.8%	444,623,933	501	22.8	50%

Source: Cisco Global Cloud Index (2015)

and networking that are managed by the cloud provider. PaaS makes the development, testing, and operation of applications a simple and cost-effective service which eliminates the need to buy additional hardware and software. Examples of PaaS include Google's Apps and Microsoft's Azure Platform (Ataur Rahman and Masudur Rahman, 2014; Arutyunov, 2012);

3.   Infrastructure-as a-service (IaaS) finally, provides the use of a virtual computer infrastructure environment (including the network, servers, and storage systems) as a service on a rental pay-per-use basis. Examples of IaaS would be Amazon S3, SQL Azure and Amazon EC2 (Ataur Rahman and Masudur Rahman, 2014; Aljabre, 2012).

In addition to the service models, different models exist to deploy the cloud platform. According to the National Institute of Standards and Technology (NIST), the common four cloud deployment models include: public, private, community and hybrid models, each of which is addressed in Figure 1. In fact, the data that can be kept in the cloud ranges from public sources, which has less security capabilities, to private data containing extremely sensitive information.

Users and enterprises are drawn toward the cloud's promises of agility, reduced capital costs, and improved IT resources. Given that cloud computation takes place on remote servers, hardware requirements such as storage components, memory, switches and other physical computing infrastructure elements are minimal, thus resulting in lower operating and maintenance costs (Erenben, 2009). Moreover, cloud computing is a way to increase the capabilities of the existing technologies without investing in new infrastructure or buying new software. In fact, cloud computing offers sole advantages such as online delivery of software, virtual storage and high availability.

Conversely, cloud computing technology presents entirely new challenges and raises some obstacles which may slow down its use, particularly in regions coping with limited technical expertise, bandwidth, and IT resources. Potential disadvantages include the risk of services being unreachable due to insufficient power. Furthermore, cloud computing is associated with security risks and concerns relating to data ownership and intellectual property rights (UNCTAD, 2013; Greengard, 2010). In fact, individual users and organisations will not use cloud applications and infrastructure without evidence of the trustworthiness of the elements of the cloud (Abbadi and Martin, 2011).

Figure 1. Cloud computing deployment models (source: current study)

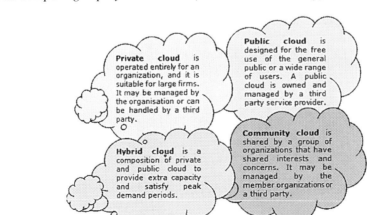

Generally speaking, cloud computing creates both opportunities and challenges for companies and IT practitioners. Given that cloud models are fast becoming a norm, and that IT professionals will be the drivers of adopting and supporting usage of such models in their respective organisations, research needs to identify the factors that promote and/or hinder adoption of cloud applications. It is this objective which is contextualized within a theoretical background.

2.2. State of Cloud Computing in Developing Countries

Currently cloud computing is an emerging innovation that enables organizations to access computing resources and services at low cost. Many businesses in developing countries become motivated to use cloud computing in which cloud applications are used in a wide range of areas, including healthcare, education and supply chain (Kabir et al., 2015). Moreover, global cloud providers such as Microsoft, Amazon and Dell are actively searching for opportunities and implementing cloud computing centers in the developing world (Kshetri, 2010). However, recent studies indicate that cloud adoption and use in developing countries is low and these economies face considerable challenges to participate successfully in the cloud economy. Challenges to adoption include: non-availability of adequate infrastructure, concerns about data privacy and security in the cloud, user resistance, lack of trust, differences in international laws, regulatory compliance concerns, and regulations and finally lack of confidence in ability and promise of the cloud (Akin et. al., 2014; Yeboah-Boateng & Essandoh, 2014, Bilbao-Osorio et al., 2013; Kshetri, 2010).

A review of the recent academic literature on cloud computing (*see Table 2*) has revealed a gap in the research regarding factors that influence the intention to use cloud-based applications in developing Arab countries from IT professionals and decision-making perspective. In fact, IT professionals are the principal stakeholders of a new technology and their acceptance and use of new technology is believed to facilitate its wider adoption among end-users (Benlian and Hess, 2011).

3. THEORETICAL BACKGROUND

There are many competing models or frameworks for studying the adoption or implementation behaviours to use new technologies. For example, the Technology Organization Environment (TOE) model (Tornatzky and Fleischer, 1990) was developed to analyze technology adoption by firms with an emphasis on the organisational characteristics and environment in which the technology is to be deployed. Another powerful model in the context of technology adoption is the Technology Acceptance Model (TAM). TAM model suggests that individual intention to use a technology is determined mainly by two beliefs of perceived usefulness (PU) and perceived ease of use (PEOU). According to Moore and Benbasat (1991), PU is similar to the term 'relative advantage' which states that an innovation is more rapidly diffused if it is perceived to be better than the innovation it is replacing (Rogers, 1983). PEOU concerns the degree to which an individual believes that using the technology in question will not require additional effort (Davis et. al., 1989). TAM has been used in many empirical studies to understand individual acceptance of new technology and software applications. Moreover, many researchers suggested extending the TAM model by adding additional factors or incorporating the model with other IT acceptance models to provide powerful models (Wangpipatwong et al., 2008; Legris et al. 2003; Lu et al. 2003). In addition, it is found that TAM can be applied to understand the behavior of both inexperienced and experienced users, with different emphasis on the determinants of intention (Taylor & Todd, 1995). Table 2 shows that a significant body of research validated the TAM model to study the adoption and diffusion of cloud computing.

Moreover, it can be seen from Table 2, that limited research has explored the factors that influence the intention of key agents responsible for taking decisions to adopt cloud applications. Hence, there is still a need to examine the factors that influence the intention to use cloud-based applications by IT professionals in developing countries.

In this study, we investigate the determinants of the intention to use cloud-based applications by IT professionals. The research model used in this study is presented in Figure 2. We proposed that the

Table 2. Studies examining cloud technology adoption/usage/diffusion in the context of developed and developing economies

Study	Theory/Context	Participants/Study Subject	Research Purpose/Research Finding
Ashtari & Eydgahi (2015)	TAM and the Human Organization Technology Fit Model/Developed economy	Undergraduate students enrolled in the College of Technology at Eastern Michigan University.	The purpose of the study was to examine the factors that facilitate the use of cloud applications among university students. The study found that, perceived ease of use, computer anxiety, computer self-efficacy, and internet self-efficacy and perceived usefulness influence the use of cloud applications in higher education.
Chen (2015)	TAM/ Developing economy	Employees, decision makers and business managers at Taiwan's enterprise companies in manufacturing and service sectors.	The study explored the factors affecting the adoption of SaaS in Taiwan. The results showed that perceived usefulness, perceived ease of use positively affects intention to use SaaS cloud computing services.
Akin et. al (2014)	Developing economy	100 IT staff, 50 para-IT staff and 50 students from ten public universities in Nigeria.	The study investigated challenges associated with the adoption of cloud computing in universities in Nigeria. The study revealed that the adoption of cloud computing has a major impact on cost, availability, low environmental impact, reduced IT complexities, mobility, scalability, efficient operability and eliminated investment in physical asset. Conversely, security risks, regulatory compliance concerns and privacy concerns were found to be critical challenges hindering the adoption of cloud in Nigeria.
Changchit (2014)	TAM/ Developed economy	585 Students at Southern United States University	The study explored students' perceptions of cloud computing and understand the factors that influence or hinder the acceptance of cloud computing. The results reveal that perceived usefulness, perceived ease of use, perceived security, perceive speed of access, and perceived cost of usage have an important role in encouraging students to accept cloud computing to enhance their learning.
Stieninger & Nedbal (2014)	TOE/ Developed economy	Experts from nine SMEs from different industries.	The study examined the factors that influence the use of cloud computing in SMEs. The analysis of the results revealed that many factors influence the acceptance and diffusion of cloud solutions. Moreover, the study concludes that cloud computing definition remains unclear even for IT professionals.
Opitz et al.(2012)	TAM/Developed economy	100 CIOs and IT managers in Germany	The study examined the technology use of cloud computing by CIOs and IT managers. The results indicate that the adoption of cloud computing by IT managers and experts are affected by social influence and image, job relevance and perceived usefulness.

Figure 2. Extended TAM model for cloud-based applications use by IT professionals

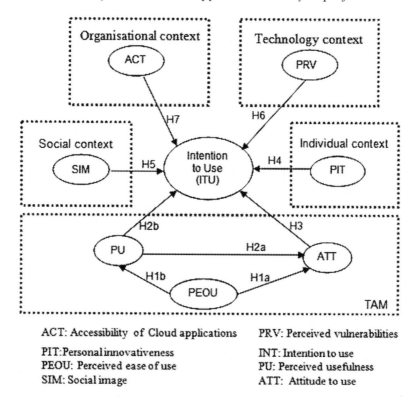

ACT: Accessibility of Cloud applications   PRV: Perceived vulnerabilities

PIT: Personal innovativeness   INT: Intention to use
PEOU: Perceived ease of use   PU: Perceived usefulness
SIM: Social image   ATT: Attitude to use

intention to use cloud-based applications is affected by external variables. Variables were grouped into four contexts or categories: technology context, organisational context, social context and individual context. First, technological context refers to the nature of the technology adopted and it looks into the degree to which cloud-based application is perceived to be free of risks or vulnerabilities. Second, organisational context, which includes: organisational traits such as system accessibility and the quality of firm's telecommunications networks available internally. Thong et al. (2002) argued that relevance, system visibility, and system accessibility are organizational determinants that influence that adoption of new innovations. Third, social context means the social pressure in which the use of cloud application is perceived to enhance one's image or status in the social domain.

Finally, the fourth context is the individual context, which includes individual characteristics of IT decision-makers. In general, it is believed that adopting decision-makers tend to be younger, better educated, and willing to try new technologies (Rogers, 1983). In general, the potential of the TAM to simultaneously examine various factors is a strong advantage for studying the use of cloud computing in the respect that cloud computing covers a broad range of applications, services, organisational contexts, and individual context (Wangpipatwong et al., 2008; Legris et al. 2003; Lu et al. 2003). Through applying TAM, this research, focuses on the views of those agents responsible for making the technological decisions surrounding the potential use of cloud computing technology. The following section proposes several hypotheses within the context of applying an extended TAM model to examine the factors that influence the intention to use cloud-based applications by IT professionals.

3.1. Hypotheses

Based on the TAM model, this study puts forward the following hypotheses with regard to intention to use cloud-based applications by IT professionals and experts.

3.1.1. Perceived Ease of Use (PEOU)

PEOU refers to the degree to which IT practitioners believe that using cloud applications and services based on the cloud would be effortless to access and utilise. Previous TAM research postulates that PEOU is an important factor and may affect both PU and ATT (Wu, 2011; Venkatesh and Bala, 2008; Venkatesh and Davis, 1996; 2000). Based on these findings, we argue that PEOU is expected to have a positive effect on attitude (ATT) and PU in the context of cloud computing. Consequently, we hypothesised:

H1a: PEOU has a positive effect on PU.
H1b: PEOU has a positive effect on the attitude toward using (ATT) cloud-based applications.

3.1.2. Perceived Usefulness (PU)

In this study, perceived usefulness (PU) is referred to as the degree to which an IT expert believes that using cloud-based applications and services will increase his or her job performance. Cloud computing is cost effective and it allows agile distribution of resources (Kondo et al., 2009; Vouk, 2008). It is believed that, perceived usefulness of cloud computing should encourage IT experts to consider using cloud computing to serve users. Referring to Wu (2011), PU is a determinant of attitude (ATT). Based on these findings, the present study hypothesised that level of usefulness of cloud application, as perceived by IT experts influenced their attitude toward adopting the technology. Moreover, many studies (Wu, 2011; Venkatesh and Bala, 2008; Venkatesh and Davis, 1996, 2000) have demonstrated and confirmed that PU is directly related to behavioural intention to use (ITU). ITU is defined as the degree to which individuals intend to use the new technology (Davis, 1989). In accordance with the TAM framework and related prior studies (Wu, 2011; Venkatesh and Bala, 2008; Venkatesh and Davis, 2000), this study posits the next two hypotheses:

H2a: PU has a positive effect on the attitude toward using (ATT) cloud-based applications.
H2b: PU has a positive effect on IT professionals' intentions to use cloud–based applications.

3.1.3. Attitude Toward Using Cloud-Based Applications and Solutions (ATT)

Attitude toward using a new technology (ATT) can be defined as the tendency to which an individual has a favorable or unfavorable manner to use the new technology (Davis, 1989). A large number of previous studies revealed strong correlations between attitudes toward using new technology such as Cloud Computing and behaviour (Kwon et al, 2014; Venkatesh and Davis, 2000; Davis, 1989). Thus, the following hypotheses were set forth:

H3: ATT has a positive effect on IT professionals' intentions to use cloud–based applications.

3.1.4. Individual Context: Personal Innovativeness (PIT)

Previous research has indicated that PIT is believed to motivate new IT adoption and it is expected to impact individual's using or rejecting new innovation (Polites and Karahanna, 2012; Venkatesh et al., 2003; Agarwal and Prasad, 1999; Ajzen and Fishbein, 1980).

Based on Agarwal and Prasad (1998)'s definition, IT personal innovativeness in this study has been defined as IT experts' receptiveness or willingness to try cloud computing and its applications and solutions (e.g. Google Apps, Cloud SQL, Cloud Social Apps). In general, a willingness to try new innovations and untested ideas is believed to lead to a favourable behaviour to use the new innovation and move from passive acceptance to enthusiastic endorsement (Huy, 1999).

Individuals who are likely to adopt new innovations earlier than others and serve as a facilitator for the adoption of new technologies are well aware of the importance of their adoption decisions to encourage others to use the technology (Agarwal and Prasad, 1998). Therefore, early adopters are found to value the positive image that they gain from the use of the new innovation. Consequently, we hypothesised that:

H4: Personal innovativeness has a positive effect on IT professionals' intentions to use cloud–based applications.

3.1.5. Social Context: Social Image (SIM)

Previous research found that social image is an important factor that affects the adoption of new technology (Venkatesh et al., 2012; Venkatesh and Davis, 2000). Social image is defined as "the degree to which use of an innovation is perceived to enhance one's image or status in one's social system" (Moore and Benbasat, 1991, pg. 195). Rogers (1983, pg. 215) argued that "undoubtedly one of the most important motivations for almost any individual to adopt an innovation is the desire to gain social status".

Previous research found that IT experts generally enjoy a high level of prestige and autonomy as a result of their technical expertise (Lim, 2008). Therefore, they are likely to be aware of the image they display as it relates to their professional status and their interactions within their social network and reference group. In fact, it is believed that individuals often respond to social normative influences to establish or maintain a favourable image with a reference group (Kelman, 1958). Moreover, an individual may perceive that a new technology is useful because the technology will convey a favourable high-status image to others and improve social status. Venkatesh et al. (2003) demystified that social influence has a vital role in the intention to adopt IT. Cao et al. (2013) conducted a study to investigate cloud computing adoption in China and found that social image influence is a major predictor for using cloud storage services in China. Thus, based on above, the following can be hypothesized:

H5: Social image has a positive effect on IT professionals' intentions to use cloud–based applications.

3.1.6. Technological Context: Perceived Vulnerabilities (PRV)

Cloud computing introduces many risks and vulnerabilities (Dahbur et al, 2011). Hashizume et al., (2013) assert that cloud computing risks and vulnerabilities involve the flaws in a system that enable an attack to be successful and has unauthorised access to all the potential resources such as network, system, or data. Leading providers of cloud computing services have suffered from vulnerabilities and risks related to data loss or suspension of service. In 2010, Symantec identified 500 browser vulnerabilities, some of which were identified as critical. Moreover, in 2009, Salesforce.com suffered an outage that locked more than 900,000 subscribers out of crucial cloud applications (Dahbur et al., 2011).

In fact, some users are anxious about the risks presented when using cloud applications and services (Benlian and Hess, 2011). These risks and vulnerabilities include hacking attacks that allow hackers to have access to important data (Hashizume et al., 2013). Cloud users express concerns about issues related to data protection, confidentiality and copyright (Yang and Tate, 2009). Data stored in the cloud can be lost due to unintended deletion by the cloud service provider.

Recent research by the Cloud Security Alliance (CSA) which looks at cloud computing and information security matters lists the following as the top risks associated with cloud computing applications: malicious attacks and data loss or damage during downloading and/or uploading (CSA, 2013). Furthermore, research found that 84% of the consumers are concerned about their data storage location and 88% of the consumers worry about who has access to their data (Fujitsu Research Institute, 2010).

We define perceived vulnerabilities (PVR) as the extent to which the IT professional believes that using cloud applications is not safe and his/her data will be disclosed and altered by an unauthorised party. In fact, IT experts will fully accept and adopt cloud computing only if they are confident that private information stored in the cloud will not be used or disclosed by the cloud provider in unexpected ways. This definition denotes a personal perception rather than any objective measurement, and assumes an IT expert's intuitive ability to assess risk.

PRV is viewed as a negative factor that can increase uncertainties and potential dangers related to adopting the new technologies. PRV thus decreases the overall ease of use (Bhatnagar et al., 2000). In fact, IT experts who perceive that cloud applications have high level of risk will have a lower intention to use cloud applications. Pavlou (2003) founds that trust and risk are crucial when uncertainty is present in the context of Internet-based innovations. Kim et al., (2008) investigate the impact of perceived risk in the context of business-to-consumer (B2C) e-commerce. The result of their study shows that consumer's perceived risk has a negative effect on consumers' intention to purchase on the Internet actual purchase decisions. Moreover, Featherman (2001) notes that extending TAM by inclusion of perceived risk may improve the models' predictive validity when investigating adoption of application service provider (ASP) systems, and other web-services. Consequently, we propose the following two hypotheses:

H6: PRV has a negative effect on IT professionals' intentions to use cloud–based applications.

3.1.7. Organisational Context: Accessibility of Cloud Applications (ACT)

Accessibility is defined as the extent to which IT experts can locate computer, telecommunications networks and Internet easily and are readily available when needed, allowing them to access cloud computing applications such as electronic mail, data storage and web applications at any time and place (Musa, 2006; Musa et al., 2005). Cloud computing applications are generally web-based and they are accessible through a variety of devices with Internet connections. These devices include desktop, laptop computers, mobile phones and PDAs. Accessibility of a technology is a vital construct and it is believed that an individual's decision to select and use new technology is a function of the extent to which the source is perceived as being accessible (Swanson, 1992). In fact, the existence of appropriate technological infrastructure greatly helps the given technology to be used to its full potential (Alampay et al., 2003).

A large body of research has established accessibility of related technologies as an important consideration when individuals are faced with decisions to select and use new technology (Musa, 2006; Musa et al., 2005; Swanson, 1992). Moreover, these studies suggest that access to basic forms of technology helps facilitate easier acceptance and adoption of modern types of technologies. Park et al., (2009) claimed that exposure to technology leads to greater usefulness and more frequent use of a technology, whereas low accessibility works as a usage barrier. Moreover, Ilie et al., (2009) assert that lack of access to a computers and Internet connection are found to be a major concern for teachers, information science scholars, librarians, and other academics. Lin and Lu (2000) reported that higher information accessibility brings about higher intention to use a new technology. Based on these findings, we hypothesised that:

H7: Accessibility of cloud applications has a positive effect on IT professionals' intentions to use cloud–based applications.

4. RESEARCH METHODOLOGY

4.1. Participants

A survey questionnaire was distributed to 259 IT experts and professionals identified as being involved in taking decisions regarding the adoption of cloud-based applications in their organisations. It is noteworthy that, in this study, we used the definition of cloud computing proposed by the National Institute of Standards and Technology (Mell & Grance, 2011), which refers to the shared applications and services that the surveyed IT professionals were using through the internet to manage application activities or to access data stored on shared servers. We distributed 195 questionnaires and we received 177 questionnaires. Incomplete questionnaires reduced the usable responses to 155. Table 3 summarises the demographic characteristics of the research sample. Of the vast majority of respondents were male (n=143, 92.3%), while a small minority were female (n=12, 7.7%). In terms of age, 57.4% of the respondents were between the ages of 18 and 25, 32.3% were between the ages of 26 and 35, 5.2% were between the ages of 36 and 45, and 4.5% were between the ages of 56 and 65. The majority of respondents – i.e., n=106 (68.4%), confirmed having 6-10 (n=49, 31.6%) and 11-20 (n=57, 36.8%) years of work experience. The surveyed respondents were generally well educated with over a third (n= 34.2%) holding a master's degree and above, and nearly two thirds of the sample (n=94, 60.6%) having a 4-year first degree. All respondents confirmed accessing and using the internet, with a third of the sample (n=46, 29.7%) indicating usage ranging from 11-30 hours a week.

4.2. Measurement Development

To ensure high level of reliability and validity of the questionnaire, a two-stage validation exercise was conducted. First, whenever possible, items selected for the constructs were adapted from previous studies (Venkatesh et al., 2012; Alvarez, 2011; Nasri, 2011; Venkatesh and Davis, 2000; Agarwal and Prasad, 1998; Taylor and Todd, 1995; Davis, 1989). The statements were assessed using a five-point Likert scale, with (1) being "strongly disagree" and (5) being "strongly agree". The final questionnaire items used to measure each construct are presented in Table 4.

Table 3. Sample profile

Respondents characteristics	Final Sample size (n =155)	Percentage (%)
Gender		
Male	143	92.3%
Female	12	7.74%
Age (yr), (%)		
18-25	89	57.4%
26-35	50	32.3%
36-45	8	5.2%
46-55	1	0.6%
56-65	7	4.5%
Education		
High School	4	2.6%
Bachelor	94	60.6%
Master	46	29.7%
Doctorate	4	2.6%
Diploma	7	4.5%
Work experience		
Less than one year	8	5.2%
1-5	29	18.7%
6-10	49	31.6%
11-20	57	36.8%
More than 20 years	12	7.7%
Company Industry		
Government Affairs	14	9.0%
Financial	24	15.5%
Education	13	8.4%
Medical	9	5.8%
Information Technology	66	42.6%
Other	29	18.7%
Internet use per week		
Less than 1 hours	3	1.90%
1- 4 h	14	9.0%
5-10 h	21	13.6%
11-30 h	46	29.7%
31-60 h	38	24.5%
More than 60 h	30	19.4%
I don't know	3	1.9%
Type of Internet connection		
Wired Internet connection	66	42.6%
Wi-Fi	59	38.1%
Mobile broadband	25	16.1%
other	5	3.2%

5. RESULTS AND DATA ANALYSIS

Structural equation modeling (SEM) was applied to test the measurement model. As illustrated in Table 5, reliability measures were all above 0.70 demonstrating sufficient internal consistency (Hair et al., 1995; Nunnally, 1978). The constructs also demonstrated adequate convergent and discriminate validity. Average variance extracted (AVE) for all constructs was above 0.5 which illustrates adequate convergent validity is adequate.

The exploratory factor analysis reveals that the items were well-associated with high loadings to signify the constructs. Table 6 presents the results for the discriminant validity of constructs and it can be seen that all items load greatly on their own constructs than on other constructs.

5.1. Results of Hypotheses Testing

The partial least squares (PLS) software package was utilized to perform the assessment of the research model (Ringle et al., 2005). Figure 3, shows the results of statistical analysis of the research framework. Moreover, the results of the estimated path coefficients (β) and R^2 value are reported in Table 7.

Table 4. Summary of the study measures

Constructs	Measures	
Perceived ease of use (PEOU)	PEOU1	My interaction with cloud applications is clear and understandable.
	PEOU2	Using cloud applications would not require a lot of my mental effort.
	PEOU3	I find it easy to get cloud applications to do what I want it to do.
	PEOU4	Overall, I find cloud applications easy to use.
Perceived usefulness (PU)	PU 1	Using cloud applications increases my productivity.
	PU 2	Using cloud applications improves my job performance.
	PU 3	Using cloud applications enhances my effectiveness on the job.
	PU 4	Overall, I find cloud applications useful in my job.
Social image (SIM)	SIM 1	Using cloud computing applications improves my reputation in my company.
	SIM 2	I earn respect from others by using cloud computing applications.
	SIM 3	Information technology decision makers using cloud computing have more prestige.
	SIM 4	Cloud computing is a status symbol in an organization.
Personal innovativeness (PIT)	PIT 1	If I hear about new technology, I would look for ways to purchase it.
	PIT 2	I usually provide new information of new technology to others.
	PIT 3	Amongst my peers, I am usually the first to try out new technologies.
	PIT 4	I like to experiment with new information technologies.
	PIT 5	In general, I am hesitant to try out new information technologies.
Accessibility of Cloud applications (ACT)	ACT 1	My organisation has speedy connectivity to the Internet.
	ACT 2	My organisation has the resources necessary to use applications based on the cloud.
	ACT 3	My organisation is able to provide cloud computing applications on dedicated hardware.
	ACT 4	I can use cloud applications and services at any time of a day.
	ACT 5	I can get help from others when I have difficulties using cloud applications.
Perceived vulnerabilities (PRV)	PRV 1	Cloud-based applications are more secure than than other applications.
	PRV 2	Cloud applications are reliable.
	PRV 3	Using cloud applications is putting data in trouble.
	PRV 4	Security issues are a concern for using cloud applications.
	PRV 5	Cloud providers keep promises that data will not be disclosed and altered by an unauthorized party.
Attitude to use (ATT)	ATT 1	I will encourage my colleagues to use cloud applications.
	ATT 2	Using cloud applications is a good idea.
	ATT 3	I find using cloud applications to be valuable in my work.
	ATT 4	Overall, my attitude towards using cloud applications is positive.
Intention to Use (ITU)	ITU 1	Assuming I can decide, I intend to use cloud applications.
	ITU 2	Given that I have access to cloud-based applications, I predict that I would use them.
	ITU 3	I will start using applications based on the cloud soon (or have started)
	ITU 4	I will strongly recommend others to use cloud applications.
	ITU 5	Applications based on the cloud are the next IT model.

Most of the path coefficients are significant at 1% level providing strong support for all the hypothesised relationships. In fact, the results indicate that H1a, H1b, H2a, H2b, H3, H4, H5, H6 and H7 are statistically significant. Perceived ease of use (PEOU) and perceived usefulness (PU) influenced IT professionals' attitudes towards using cloud-based applications, support Hypothesis H1a and Hypothesis H2a. These factors had path coefficients 0.624 and 0.765 respectively and they explained 28% of the variance in attitudes towards cloud applications use. Moreover, PEOU has significant effects on PU and this factor had path coefficients of 0.477 meaning that Hypothesis H1b is also supported.

Subsequently, the results show that PU along with the attitudes towards using cloud applications, personal innovativeness, social image, accessibility of cloud applications and perceived vulnerabilities explained 74% of the variance in the intention to use cloud-based applications. These six factors had path coefficients of 0.692, 0.515, 0.475, 0.286, -0.419 and 0.515 meaning that Hypothesis 2b, Hypothesis 3, Hypothesis 4, Hypothesis 5, Hypothesis 6 and Hypothesis 7 are also supported.

The results confirm the suitability of the TAM in explaining IT professionals' behavioural intentions to adopt and use cloud applications and solutions. In addition, the results also give support for the new variables added to the extended TAM representing the effects of accessibility, perceived vulnerabilities, social image and personal innovativeness on the intention to use cloud-based applications and solutions by IT professionals.

Table 5. Properties of the constructs

Constructs	Measures	Loading	t-value	Composite reliability	Cronbach's alpha (α)	Average Variance Extracted (AVE)
PEOU	PEOU1	0.588	46.230	0.883	0.818	0.6533
	PEOU2	0.772	48.605			
	PEOU3	0.462	55.445			
	PEOU4	0.673	62.253			
PU	PU 1	0.736	43.943	0.786	0.892	0.8345
	PU 2	0.829	45.313			
	PU 3	0.823	46.474			
	PU 4	0.704	55.151			
SIM	SIM 1	0.793	34.254	0.790	0.849	0.707
	SIM 2	0.777	38.674			
	SIM 3	0.816	33.135			
	SIM 4	0.774	37.850			
PIT	PIT 1	0.720	60.365	0.840	0.852	0.718
	PIT 2	0.767	59.541			
	PIT 3	0.694	48.307			
	PIT 4	0.802	62.124			
	PIT 5	0.587	41.765			
ACT	ACT 1	0.640	63.062	0.832	0.836	0.708
	ACT 2	0.855	51.479			
	ACT 3	0.738	47.773			
	ACT 4	0.645	52.026			
	ACT 5	0.639	48.452			
PRV	PRV 1	0.694	32.847	0.819	0.778	0.690
	PRV 2	0.651	50.286			
	PRV 3	0.740	35.480			
	PRV 4	0.732	40.549			
	PRV 5	0.626	45.892			
ATT	ATT 1	0.691	46.607	0.767	0.768	0.674
	ATT 2	0.697	61.654			
	ATT 3	0.773	54.098			
	ATT 4	0.841	57.569			
ITU	ITU1	0.734	58.549	0.816	0.899	0.688
	ITU 2	0.737	57.370			
	ITU 3	0.548	52.935			
	ITU 4	0.727	52.535			
	ITU 5	0.675	56.710			

Table 6. Discriminant validity of constructs

Construct	PEOU	PU	SIM	PIT	ACT	PRV	ATT	ITU
PEOU	**0.808**							
PU	0.466	**0.914**						
SIM	0.168	0.444	**0.829**					
PIT	0.168	0.404	0.194	**0.834**				
ACT	0.131	0.479	0.131	0.444	**0.776**			
PRV	0.432	0.338	0.209	0.265	0.302	**0.638**		
ATT	0.619	0.754	0.389	0.523	0.473	0.408	**0.876**	
ITU	0.349	0.723	0.349	0.585	0.522	0.411	0.856	**0.846**

Figure 3. Results of structural model

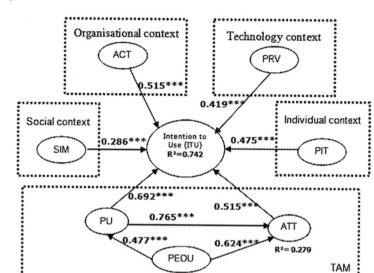

Table 7. Assessment of the structural model

No.	Hypothesis path	R^2	Path coefficient (β)	T-Value	p-Value	Supported?
H1a	PEOU → ATT	0.385	0.624	9.686	0.000***	Yes
H1b	PEOU → PU	0.227	0.477	6.598	0.000***	Yes
H2a	PU → ATT	0.582	0.765	14.334	0.000***	Yes
H2b	PU → ITU	0.475	0.692	11.462	0.000***	Yes
H3	ATT → ITU	0.260	0.515	7.152	0.000***	Yes
H4	PIT → ITU	0.220	0.475	6.384	0.000***	Yes
H5	SIM → ITU	0.076	0.286	3.562	0.001***	Yes
H6	PRV → ITU	0.170	-0.419	5.503	0.000***	Yes
H7	ACT → ITU	0.260	0.515	7.152	0.000***	Yes

Hypothesis 6 which suggests that vulnerabilities and risks have a negative effect on the intention to use cloud-based applications and services is also supported and the results strongly supported the hypothesis with negative path coefficients of 0.419.

Accessibility of cloud applications has a positive effect with path coefficients of 0.515 meaning that Hypotheses 7 is supported. This is profoundly important, and supports the belief that accessibility of cloud technology motivates individuals to use the technology and supports users in the adoption process of advanced technologies (Musa, 2006).

6. DISCUSSION AND CONCLUSION

As more and more firms implement cloud based applications and services, it is essential to study the factors that influence IT professionals and expert attitudes towards using these applications. The current study confirms the applicability of TAM to explain IT experts' acceptance of cloud based applications and systems. Our findings are partly consistent with previous technology acceptance and adoption studies and all research variables were found to have adequate reliability and validity (Cheung and Vogel, 2013; Chau and Hu, 2002). Specifically, all the relationships proposed by TAM have been tested satisfactorily and the findings demonstrate the role of perceived vulnerabilities, social image, accessibility of cloud applications and personal innovativeness on the intention to use cloud-based applications and solutions (Hashizume et al., 2013; Polites and Karahanna, 2012; Venkatesh et al., 2012; Wu, 2011; Yang and Tate, 2009; Venkatesh and Davis, 1996).

This study employed a questionnaire survey to identify the factors that influence IT professionals' intentions to use cloud-based applications and services in Saudi Arabia, one of the first Arab countries that focus on the concept of cloud computing with an investments equivalent to half the size of the technology market in the Middle East.

This study raises important implications for practitioners and organisations. Firstly, organisations would have to involve IT decision makers and experts at all stages of cloud based applications to help ensure successful implementation. Secondly, IT professionals and experts are expected to consider using cloud computing applications and solutions if it enhances job performance, productivity and does not require greater efforts to implement it. In fact, organisations would select cloud applications with no security risks and vulnerabilities. Security risks are believed to be IT executives' dominant concern in the adoption intention of cloud-based applications. Thus, IT professionals and experts will use cloud-based applications only if they are certain that confidential information stored in the cloud will not be used or disclosed in unexpected ways. Such concerns are valid ones, given that each year security firms identify thousands of software risk and vulnerabilities in Internet and PC software applications. For instance, in 2010, Symantec identified 500 browser vulnerabilities and some of these vulnerabilities were identified as being critical in nature (Symantec, 2011).

Notably, our results demonstrate that the perceived usefulness and perceived vulnerabilities were not factored into behavioural intentions to the same extent. Perceived usefulness tends to have a much stronger impact on the behavioural intention to use cloud based applications than do perceived vulnerabilities. Perceived vulnerabilities explained 17% of the variance in behavioural intention, while perceived usefulness explained 47.5% of the variance in behavioural intention to use cloud-based applications. This has important implications, as it highlights that potential failure or risks may not be the major factor in the use-or-adopt choices regarding cloud applications acceptance. Instead, opportunities and benefits seem to be more influential than risks.

Finally, our findings emphasise the necessity of conducting further research. In particular, we could start future work based on these findings. Future research may reuse the model developed in this study to explore cloud application acceptance in a larger group of stakeholders, which may include business managers and users. The results derived from such further studies may be used as a comparison with the findings of this research and thus provide a more holistic picture concerning the acceptance of cloud applications and services. Second, there is notably little research on what forces effectively influence successful cloud based application adoption by organisations (Stieninger et al., 2014). Therefore, it would be interesting to conduct future research to analyse how firms are using cloud applications to create advantage and identify business benefits and challenges of adopting cloud applications. Overall, research on this topic is very much needed. In summary, this study shows the applicability of the extended TAM to predict the factors that encourage the use of cloud-based applications and solutions by IT professionals.

REFERENCES

Abbadi, I. M., & Martin, A. (2011). Trust in the Cloud. *Information Security Technical Report, 16*(3-4), 108–114. doi:10.1016/j.istr.2011.08.006

Akin, O., Matthew, F., & Comfort, D. (2014). The Impact and Challenges of Cloud Computing Adoption on Public Universities in Southwestern Nigeria. *International Journal of Advanced Computer Science and Applications, 5*(8), 13–19.

Aljabre, A. (2012). Cloud Computing for Increased Business Value. *International Journal of Business and Social Science., 3*(1), 234–239.

Arutyunov, V. V. (2012). Cloud Computing: Its History of Development, Modern State, and Future Considerations. *Scientific and Technical Information Processing, 39*(3), 173–178. doi:10.3103/S0147688212030082

Ashtari, S., & Eydgahi, A. (2015). Student Perceptions of Cloud Computing Effectiveness in Higher Education. *Proceedings of the 18th IEEE International Conference on Computational Science and Engineering*, Porto, Portugal (pp. 184-191). IEEE. doi:10.1109/CSE.2015.36

Ataur Rahman, M., & Masudur Rahman, M. (2014). Improvements of Cloud Computing: Scenario of MDCs and LDCs. *International Journal of Scientific and Engineering Research., 5*(2), 262–267.

Benlian, A., & Hess, T. (2011). Opportunities and risks of software-as-a-service: Findings from a survey of IT executives. Decision Support Systems, 52, 232–246.

Bhatnagar, A., Misra, S., & Rao, H. R. (2000). On risk, convenience, and Internet shopping behavior. *Communications of the ACM, 43*(11), 98–105. doi:10.1145/353360.353371

Bilbao-Osorio, B., Dutta, S., & Lanvin, B. (2013). The global information technology report 2013. Retrieved from http://unctad.org/en/PublicationsLibrary/ier2013_en.pdf

Changchit, C. (2014). Students' perceptions of cloud computing. *Issues in Information Systems, 15*(I), 312–322.

Chau, P. Y. K., & Hu, P. J. H. (2002). Examining a model of information technology acceptance by individual professionals: An exploratory study. *Journal of Management Information Systems, 18*(4), 191–229.

Chen, L. Y. (2015). Determinants of Software-as-a-Service Adoption and Intention to Use for Enterprise Applications. *International Journal of Innovation and Applied Studies., 10*(1), 138–148.

Cheung, R., & Vogel, V. (2013). Predicting user acceptance of collaborative technologies: An extension of the technology acceptance model for e-learning. *Computers & Education, 63*, 160–175. doi:10.1016/j.compedu.2012.12.003

Cisco Global Cloud Index. (2015). Cloud Readiness Regional Details. Retrieved from http://www.cisco.com/

CSA- The Cloud Security Alliance. (2013). Cloud Computing Top Threats in 2013. Retrieved from www.cloudsecurityalliance.org

Dahbur, K., Mohammad, B., & Tarakji, A. B. (2011). A survey of risks, threats and vulnerabilities in cloud computing. *Proceedings of the 2011 International Conference on Intelligent Semantic Web-Services and Applications*, Amman, Jordan (pp. 1–6). 10.1145/1980822.1980834

Davis, F. D. (1989). Perceived usefulness, perceived ease of use and user acceptance of information technology. *Management Information Systems Quarterly*, *13*(3), 319–339. doi:10.2307/249008

Davis, F. D., Bagozzi, R. P., & Warshaw, P. R. (1989). User acceptance of computer technology: A comparison of two theoretical models. *Management Science*, *35*(8), 982–1003. doi:10.1287/mnsc.35.8.982

Featherman, M. S. (2001). *Extending the technology acceptance model by inclusion of perceived risk* (pp. 758–760). Boston, MA: Americas Conference on Information Systems. Retrieved from http://aisel.aisnet.org/amcis2001/148

Fujitsu Research Institute. (2010). *Personal data in the cloud: A global survey of consumer attitudes. Technical Report*. Fujitsu Research Institute.

Goundar, S. (2010). Cloud computing: Opportunities and issues for developing countries. *Diplomacy.edu*. Retrieved from http://www.diplomacy.edu/sites/default/files/IGCBP2010_2011_Goundar.pdf

Greengard, S. (2010). Cloud Computing and Developing Nations. Communications of the ACM, 53(5), 18-20.

Hashizume, K., Rosado, D. G., Fernández-Medina, E., & Fernandez, E. B. (2013). An analysis of security issues for cloud computing. *Journal of Internet Services and Applications.*, *4*(5), 1–3.

IDC (The International Data Corporation). (2013). Forecasts Worldwide Public IT CLOUD SERVICES Spending to Reach Nearly $108 Billion by 2017 as Focus Shifts from Savings to Innovation. Retrieved from http://www.idc.com/getdoc.jsp?containerId=prUS24298013

Ilie, V., Van Slyke, C., Parikh, M. A., & Courtney, J. F. (2009). Paper Versus Electronic Medical Records: The Effects of Access on Physicians' Decisions to Use Complex Information Technologies. *Decision Sciences*, *40*(2), 213–241. doi:10.1111/j.1540-5915.2009.00227.x

Kabir, M. H., & Islam, S. (2015). Detail Overview of Cloud Computing with its Opportunities and Obstacles in Developing Countries. *International Journal of Engineering Science Invention.*, *4*(1), 52–63.

Kelman, H. C. (1958). Compliance, identification, and internalization three processes of attitude change. *The Journal of Conflict Resolution*, *2*(1), 51–60. doi:10.1177/002200275800200106

Kim, D. J., Ferrin, D. L., & Rao, H. R. (2008). A trust-based consumer decision-making model in electronic commerce: The role of trust, perceived risk, and their antecedents. *Decision Support Systems*, *44*(2), 544–564. doi:10.1016/j.dss.2007.07.001

Kshetri, N.(2010). Cloud Computing in Developing Economies. *IEEE Computer Society*, 43(10), 47-55

Kwon, S. J., Park, E., & Kim, K. (2014). What drives successful social networking services? A comparative analysis of user acceptance of Facebook and Twitter. *The Social Science Journal*, *51*(4), 534–544. doi:10.1016/j.soscij.2014.04.005

Legris, P., Ingham, L., & Collerette, P. (2003). Why Do People Use Information Technology? A Critical View of the Technology Acceptance Model. *Information & Management, 40*(3), 191–204. doi:10.1016/S0378-7206(01)00143-4

Lu, J., Yu, C., Liu, C., & Yao, J. (2003). Technology Acceptance Model for Wireless Internet. *Internet Research: Electronic Networking Applications and Policy, 13*(2), 206–222. doi:10.1108/10662240310478222

Mell, P., & Grance, T. (2011). The NIST definition of cloud computing. National Institute of Standards and Technology Special Publication. Retrieved from http://nvlpubs.nist.gov/nistpubs/Legacy/SP/nist-specialpublication800-145.pdf

Moore, G. C., & Benbasat, I. (1991). Development of an instrument to measure the perceptions of adopting an information technology innovation. *Information Systems Research, 2*(3), 192–221. doi:10.1287/isre.2.3.192

Musa, P. F. (2006). Making a Case for Modifying the Technology Acceptance Model to Account for Limited Accessibility in Developing Countries. *Information Technology for Development, 12*(3), 213–224. doi:10.1002/itdj.20043

Musa, P. F., Meso, P., & Mbarika, V. (2005). Toward sustainable adoption of Technologies for human development In sub-saharan africa: Precursors, Diagnostics, and prescriptions. *Communications of AIS., 15*(33), 1–31.

Opitz, N., Langkau, T. F., Schmidt, N. H., & Kolbe, L. M. (2012). Technology Acceptance of Cloud Computing: Empirical Evidence from German IT Departments. Proceedings of the HICSS '12 (pp. 1593–1602). 10.1109/HICSS.2012.557

Park, N., Roman, R., Lee, S., & Chung, J. (2009). User acceptance of a digital library system in developing countries: An application of the Technology Acceptance Model. *International Journal of Information Management, 29*(3), 196–209. doi:10.1016/j.ijinfomgt.2008.07.001

Pavlou, P. A. (2003). Consumer acceptance of electronic commerce: Integrating trust and risk with the technology acceptance model. *International Journal of Electronic Commerce, 7*(3), 101–134.

Ringle, C. M., Wende, S., & Will, A. (2005). SmartPLS 2.0. Retrieved from http://www.smartpls.de

Rogers, E. M. (1983). *Diffusion of innovations* (3rd ed.). New York: Free Press.

Scale, M.-S. E. (2009). Cloud computing and collaboration. *Library Hi Tech News, 26*(9), 10–13. doi:10.1108/07419050911010741

Spiceworks (2013). Survey: IT Professionals Turn to Cloud-Based IT Applications to Reduce Management Headaches. Retrieved from http://www.spiceworks.com/news/press-release/2013/09-25/

Stieninger, M., & Nedbal, D. (2014). Diffusion and acceptance of cloud computing in SMEs: towards a valence model of relevant factors. *Proceeding of the 47th Hawaii International Conference on System Sciences (HICSS)* (pp. 3307-3316). 10.1109/HICSS.2014.410

Stieninger, M., Nedbal, D., Wetzlinger, W., Wagner, G., & Erskine, M. (2014). Impacts on the organizational adoption of cloud computing: A reconceptualization of influencing factors. *Procedia Technology.*, *16*, 85–93. doi:10.1016/j.protcy.2014.10.071

Swanson, E. B. (1992). Information accessibility reconsidered. Accounting. *Management and Information Technology*, *2*(3), 183–196. doi:10.1016/0959-8022(92)90015-K

Taylor, S., & Todd, P. A. (1995). Assessing IT Usage: The Role of Prior Experience. *Management Information Systems Quarterly*, *19*(4), 561–570. doi:10.2307/249633

Thompson, C. J., & Havard, B. (2015). Virtual Research Integrity. In M. Khosrow-Pour (Ed.), *Encyclopedia of Information Science and Technology* (3rd ed., pp. 6601–6609). Hershey, PA, USA: IGI Global. doi:10.4018/978-1-4666-5888-2.ch649

Thong, J., Hong, W., & Tam, K. (2002). Understanding user acceptance of digital libraries: What are the roles of interface characteristics, organizational context, and individual differences. *International Journal of Human-Computer Studies*, *57*(3), 215–242. doi:10.1016/S1071-5819(02)91024-4

Tornatzky, L. G., & Fleischer, M. (1990). *The Processes of Technological Innovation*. Lexington, MA: Lexington Books.

UNCTAD (United Nations Conference on trade and development). (2013). Information Economy report 2013: The Cloud Economy and Developing Countries. United nations publication. Retrieved from unctad.org/en/PublicationsLibrary/ier2013_en.pdf

Venkatesh, V., & Davis, F. D. (1996). A model of the antecedents of perceived ease of use: Development and test. *Decision Sciences*, *27*(3), 451–481. doi:10.1111/j.1540-5915.1996.tb01822.x

Venkatesh, V., & Davis, F. D. (2000). A Theoretical Extension of the Technology Acceptance Model: Four Longitudinal Field Studies. *Management Science*, *46*(2), 19–186. doi:10.1287/mnsc.46.2.186.11926

Venkatesh, V., Morris, M. G., Davis, G. B., & Davis, F. D. (2003). User acceptance of information technology: Toward a unified view. *Management Information Systems Quarterly*, *27*(3), 425–478.

Venkatesh, V., Thong, J. L., & Xin, X. (2012). Consumer acceptance and use of information technology: Extending the unified theory of acceptance and use of technology. *Management Information Systems Quarterly*, *36*(1), 157–178.

Wangpipatwong, S., Chutimaskul, W., & Papasratorn, B. (2008). Understanding citizen's continuance intention to use e-government website: A composite view of technology acceptance model and computer self-efficacy. *The electronic journal of e-government*, *6*(1), 55-64.

Wu, W. (2011). Developing an explorative model for SaaS adoption. *Expert Systems with Applications*, *38*(12), 15057–15064. doi:10.1016/j.eswa.2011.05.039

This research was previously published in the International Journal of Cloud Applications and Computing (IJCAC), 6(3); edited by B. B. Gupta and Dharma P. Agrawal, pages 45-62, copyright year 2016 by IGI Publishing (an imprint of IGI Global).

Chapter 100
Privacy Preserving Public Auditing in Cloud: Literature Review

Thangavel M.
Thiagarajar College of Engineering, Madurai, India

Varalakshmi P.
Anna University, India

Sridhar S.
M. Kumarasamy College of Engineering, India

Sindhuja R.
Thiagarajar College of Engineering, India

ABSTRACT

Cloud computing has given a bloom to the technical world by providing various services. Data storage is the essential factor for the users who are having or working with lots and lots of data. Cloud data storage becomes the only way to store and maintain the large data, which can be accessed from anywhere and anytime. The open nature of cloud computing leads to some security issues. With respect to the cloud data storage, the Cloud Service Provider (CSP) has to provide security for the data outsourced. Data owner will be concerned on the data correctness after outsourcing into the cloud. To verify the data correctness, ensuring the state of data at the cloud data storage is needed, which is performed with the help of a Trusted Third Party Auditor (TTPA). Data owner can also perform the verification task, but it leads to computation cost and communication costs in huge amount. This survey gives a brief on public auditing schemes to explore what are all the system models designed by various researchers.

DOI: 10.4018/978-1-5225-8176-5.ch100

INTRODUCTION

Computing technologies like distributed, parallel, mobile, grid and cloud computing become essential to process huge data in an effective manner. In the recent trends, Cloud Computing is a key computing technology for everyone in the world today, because of enormous computing resources and services are available in pay per use model. Cloud computing is a technology enabling ubiquitous on demand access to a shared pool of configurable computing resources. It also has issues such as disaster recovery, abuse and nefarious use, malicious insiders, shared technology, etc. Data security issues in cloud computing are serious in many faces. Once the user outsource the data in the cloud, then the access to that data is done by any computing devices like laptop, mobile and other devices, which is allowed with a valid identity. If the data revealed by anonymous users, then in such cases sometimes even malicious insiders give the data to the competitors.

Ensuring privacy of outsourced data and the correctness of the data are considered to be a serious issue in cloud services. The availability of data is ensured by performing data duplication in different cloud servers. Maintenance of this duplicated data such as regular data updates in a dynamic form is harder to achieve. As per the researcher's statement, the privacy preservation can be achieved using appropriate cryptographic techniques. Correctness of the data at cloud storage should be ensured to provide a reliable service delivery to users. This requires data auditing through cryptographic hashing techniques. In case of data availability, replica placement leads to difficulty in achieving the dynamicity of data. Data update and maintenance is harder in this situation. So, there is a need to overcome these problems with the appropriate techniques, in order to provide a reliable, guaranteed service delivery to the cloud users and data owners.

The survey concise the methodologies followed in the existing system or technique. Identification of problems in the existing system and the performance of that system are reviewed. The auditing task performed with the help of TTPA involves challenge and response actions. This task may be handled by the data owner, but the cost required to run the system is very large.

Integrity

In general, the state of the data needs to be consistent. Once the data is outsourced from the user, it is uploaded to the server safely. The uploaded data has been modified only by the person who is authorized or owner of that data. The unnecessary modification need to be blocked. So, the integrity of the data is needed to be verified for certain time intervals.

Cloud Based Auditing

Verifying the data integrity is a major task when considering the data amount and its location. Huge amount of data in a place may lead to such violations. Periodic verification of the data will give a success to the system. It also ensures the reliable service delivery. To verify the data integrity various cryptographic mechanisms are used. If the size of the data to verify is huge, then it is hard to perform by a normal user, since normal user can have limited number of hardware resources. This situation brings a Trusted Third Party Auditor (TTPA) to perform auditing which is also called as public auditing (Figure 1). In Cloud, public auditing is done by the TTPA where he initially gets the request from the Data Owner or the Client to perform auditing for the specific file or blocks of a file. He also receives the metadata to compute a

Figure 1. Public auditing of the data stored in cloud

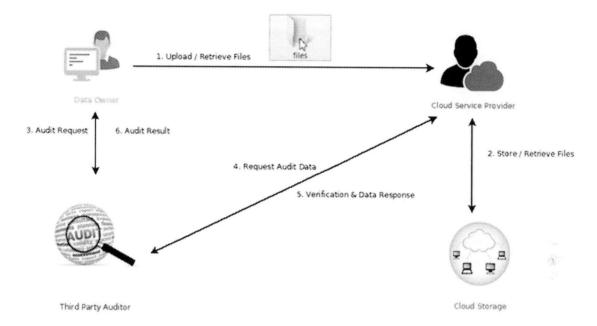

challenge to the cloud server. Based on the proposed algorithm or scheme the challenge is created and imposed to the cloud server. The cloud server then generates the proof, as a response to the challenge for the requested file or blocks to be verified and sends it to the TTPA. The TTPA compares the result obtained from the computation on proof with the values received from the Data Owner and generates the result to the Data Owner denoting whether the data is verified and correct or it has been modified.

The public auditing or integrity verification by the third-party auditor will overcome the resource overhead issues of cloud user. It also ensures the integrity of the data with such additional supports.

BACKGROUND

The data stored in the cloud server who holds all the control over the data need to store and maintain the data in a secured manner. To ensure the integrity of the data that it has not been modified by any adversary or due to any attacks or any data loss occurred by the cloud service provider. The need of integrity verification of the data stored in cloud storage by the Data Owner is to protect and prevent the data from unintended users. The privacy of the data as well as the Data Owner has to be preserved. It means that the data in cloud could contain personal details, social security numbers, health records or any sensitive data that becomes more valuable when it is into the hands of the competitor or attacker of the Data Owner who could cause harm to the Data Owner by monetary or reputation oriented commitments or personal gain of an attacker. Thus, auditing or checking of the data for its correctness and being assured that data has not been modified by anyone is done. Since not all the Data Owners are capable with large amount of resources to audit all the data in cloud, the Data Owner gives the responsibility of auditing the data to a TTPA. The third-party auditor performs auditing of the data in cloud on behalf of the Data Owner and gives the result back for further actions. The TPA gets the request from Data Owner and challenges for a file to the cloud server and cloud server generates the proof and sends to TPA. TPA verifies the values computed from both Data Owner and cloud server and generates the final integrity result. Mostly, in public auditing digital signatures are used for integrity verification. It works in such a way that the original data is performed hashing through any cryptographic hash function or hashing algorithm and the hash values are altogether signed or encrypted with the private key of the sender and sent to the receiver. The receiver uses the public key of the sender and retrieves the hash value and also computes the hash values of the encrypted blocks and compares the resulted hash values bit by bit to ensure they are equal denoting data is intact or else not. These concepts have been modernized in algorithmic approaches by various researchers and applied the same for public auditing of the data stored in cloud.

STATE-OF-ART OF PUBLIC AUDITING IN CLOUD

C. Wang et al. (2010) initiated the concept of publicly auditable secure cloud data storage services. The usage of cloud data storage is increased because of the user dependency in the data maintenance. Enterprises need to fulfill the customers need on time with efficient data management services. Cloud data storage is the key for the users in urge of data outsourcing. To do this work securely it is necessary to ensure the data security after outsourcing it. Public auditing is a mechanism provided to verify the data storage security in the public storage. Trusted users who have the knowledge to do the verification are performing the verification. The data owner gives the task to the external verifier to save the computation time at his side. This makes the data owner having more trust into the service provider. The author noted many real-time incidents on behalf of the secure cloud storage service. The concept of cryptographic techniques is not suitable for this situation. It is not possible to download the entire data for each time to do the verification. A person doing this task specifically for secure cloud data storage is a Third-Party Auditor (TPA). The Third-Party Auditor is doing the auditing task of verifying the integrity of the outsourced data. The report generated by the TPA gives the actual status of the data at the cloud storage.

There are some requirements for doing this public auditing for the outsourced data at the cloud storage. First is to minimize the overhead while performing the auditing. Second is the privacy of data, at the time of auditing. Third is to provide access to the user for performing any operations with the outsourced data. Fourth is the external verifier has the chances to do multiple tasks simultaneously. Existing methods in this arena follows some cryptographic primitives, some systematic models, some frameworks and some models. In case of data size is huge hash tree (Merkle, 1980) concepts are used. This hash tree was constructed using the hash values. The hash values of the file are used to construct the tree with smaller hashes at the leaves in the tree as child nodes. This will finally make a tree with a root node value. The root node value is used for performing the verification.

With the above approaches, there is a need for the user to download the data from the cloud storage. So, there is another concept with the use of MAC keys. The data owner has to compute such MAC keys for the whole data and store as metadata with the cloud service provider. When verification is performed the verifier asked the CSP to give a fresh keyed MAC value. The value is compared with the locally stored MAC. Each time the CSP needs to compute and give a fresh MAC key value. This is restricted in terms of number of times the calculation is done. A file is restricted with a certain number of MAC key values. By doing verification with these MAC key values the time and cost are saved. In this approach a verifier can recompute another set of MAC values. Data owner need to update the MAC values at the server side. It could cause in terms of performance issue. By doing this task, it may not support data dynamics because the keys are for the files which are already stored in the cloud storage. Homomorphic authenticator is another technique which is used for reducing the online burden of data owner (Shah et al., 2008; Curtmola et al., 2008). The metadata values are computed from aggregated set of values. In this data block is divided with a common set of blocks. The data blocks are computed with a signature for each of its own value. The blocks and the signature values are stored. The verifier can ask the cloud service provider to provide the signature values of particular file blocks. The CSP response by aggregated set of signature values to the verifier. In this approach, there is a chance for the verifier can regenerate the data from the signature values. So, this technique works well in encrypted format data only.

The random masking of blocks could ensure the block request at verification. Data operations performed by block level could improve and support the data dynamics. It can be formulated as block level insertion, updation, deletion and modification. The concept of Merkle Hash Tree (MHT) is used for supporting this requirement. The calculation of root node and the leaf nodes auxiliary authentication information is a formidable task. It requires huge communication cost and introduce newer vulnerabilities to violate data privacy. To overcome this MHT concept is linked with the homomorphic authenticator based technique. It supports operations of individual blocks. Bilinear signature is a technique used by the TPA to do multiple auditing tasks at a time. Each auditing task is considered and aggregated with signatures.

There is no mechanism to verify the actors involved in this scenario, any entity can be a malicious at any point of time. All such tasks are lacking their capacity in terms of time consideration. Performance and time are the issues in this area. The regulatory and compliance are ensuring such security of the outsourced data. Through this analysis a secure model is needed for the cloud data storage.

Q. Wang et al. (2011) described about the public verification and dynamics nature of data for the cloud computing storage security. The Classic Merkle Hash tree is used for providing salient features in public verification and the data dynamism. Existing models using the concept of Provable Data Possession (PDP) and Proof of Retrievability (PoR) to achieve data dynamics (Ateniese et al., 2007; Shacham et al., 2008). These models have the lacking in security concerns.

In public verification, any user owns the public key can be a verifier for the data integrity. To overcome the issue of signature index calculation for the data blocks each time, the index information is removed from the existing model. Calculation of hash value for each message blocks is done only with the information about the data is known. At each time of protocol execution, the tags need to be authenticated.

There are six algorithms defined for this auditing model. The algorithms are, KeyGen, SigGen, GenProof, VerifyProof, ExecUpdate, VerifyUpdate. During the setup phase the KeyGen and SigGen algorithms are performed. Public and Private key of data owner are generated by KeyGen algorithm. Signature values for the file bocks are generated and Merkle Hash Tree is constructed using the computed signature values. The client stores the file, signatures and hash value of the root node in MHT at server side. At integrity verification GenProof and VerifyProof are executed. In GenProof the cloud service provider has receiving a challenge from the verifier as random blocks signatures needed.

The cloud service provider provides the nodes auxiliary information to construct root node in MHT, hash values of blocks, aggregated signatures. With the provided values verifier compares the root hash value of MHT. If it is matched the verification is success otherwise it is not.

Dynamic operations of data are performed with block level operations as data insertion, updation, modification and deletion. The author performed security analysis by theorem proofs for Computational Diffie Hellman. Performance Analysis is performed by comparing the computation complexity at each actor's side and the cost required to do each task. The concentration is only on the public verification with data dynamics. There is no concentration given on the data privacy at this work.

C. Wang et al. (2012) proposed a public auditing system model for data storage security in cloud computing. The problem taken here is the auditor can perform the audit task without local copy of data and it never gives an online burden to user, this process doesn't bring newer vulnerabilities to this area. This model uses the concept of public key based homomorphic authenticator with random masking technique. They reviewed some existing models are using the public key based homomorphic authenticators. This technique is vulnerable to data loss. The external auditor can reveal the user data based on the linear combination of blocks. So, the author applied a random masking concept with the above technique. Related works of this paper finds information as follows. It is the first work to involve Provable Data Possession (PDP) in public auditing to ensure the possession of data at untrusted storage. This work is based on RSA based homomorphic authenticators. This scheme requires linear combination of data blocks. This leads to privacy issues. It uses Proof of Retrievability (PoR) concept used with spot checking and error correcting codes. This ensures possession of data and Retrievability. In this scheme the number of times to perform the audit task is limited and the construction of Merkle Tree construction applicable only to encrypted data (Ateniese et al., 2007) uses the PoR scheme with BLS construction. This also leads privacy issues (Ferrara et al., 2009). a scheme based on encryption and hash values is described (Shah et al., 2007; Chang et al., 2008) but this works only for encrypted data files. Author proposed a dynamic version of the previous PDP scheme. It supports symmetric key cryptography and encrypted data files only for limited number of audits (Ateniese et al. 2008).

The author stated that none of the literature review papers are fulfils the required scenario of public auditing. Four algorithms were mentioned to perform the public auditing task. Each of these algorithms is describe the task of public auditing scheme as a series steps.

KeyGen algorithm is used to generate the keys that are required to do the public auditing task. It takes some input parameters such as generators, prime value and others. Then it generates public and private key pairs.

SigGen algorithm is used to generate signatures which are for data privacy. The outcome of this algorithm avoids the data given to the auditor for auditing. Because some models designed as the auditors are requiring the copy of data. This algorithm will generate signatures for a block or set of blocks based on the user input. After getting the output from this algorithm the signature values are stored with the data in the cloud.

GenProof algorithm is used to generate proof for the requested audit task based on the details given by the auditor. This algorithm calculates hash values and aggregated signatures. A PseudoRandomFunction (PRF) is used with algorithm to generate random elements. The details got from the algorithm are hash value, signature value and random element. These details are given to the auditor.

VerifyProof algorithm is used to audit the data which are requested by the auditor based on the user requirement. Once the auditor get the required details then he immediately use this algorithm to verify the data correctness. The auditor perform comparison between the data given by the previous algorithm with the given user details.

This model is based on two basic schemes. The scheme functionalities are enhanced in this model. The schemes are:

- Pre-computed (Message Authentication Code) MAC and data files stored in the server. Set of secret keys are given to the auditor. The auditor requires some selected data blocks and its MAC values from the server. It gives an easier task because the selected blocks verification is easier than entire data verification. This introduces problems which is the auditor request data blocks for verification. It leads to privacy issues. Performance overhead are introduced such as time delay, bandwidth.

- The second scheme is an extension to the above scheme as, random message authentication code keys are chosen and MAC values are computed for the whole file block. For every audit the auditor may give some MAC keys to the server and request fresh keyed MAC values. This scheme has the problem as the keys are only fixed. It requires re-computation and re-publishing of keys. Auditor must update the status of each audit. These schemes support only with static data.

This model supports batch auditing task by utilizing the technique of bilinear aggregate signature (BLS). Based on this server sends an aggregated signature with each user id mentioned values to the auditor. The auditor checks the signatures by the user id attached. The corruption of any portion in this response will lead a mismatch. So, the author further mentioned a technique based on divide and conquer approach which is recursive one. The responses are divided into two equal halves and find which is invalid and re perform the audit as individual user data audit. The author proves some theorems for storage correctness guarantee, privacy preserving guarantee, and security guarantee for batch auditing.

Performance analysis of this work are done by measuring the cost of privacy preserving guarantee, batch auditing efficiency, sorting out invalid responses, computation time and communication complexity. The author concluded that this work is full- fledged for public auditing. The future work as extend this scheme to work in multi user setting. No error correction measures are defined in this paper. The author concentrates only on the data privacy. The public key based homomorphic authenticator with random masking technique is to overcome the linear data block identification. But not the auditing task is strengthened in terms of performance and security.

Q. Wang et al. (2012) solve the problem in public auditing and support of dynamics in remote data storage in cloud. Modified classic merkle hash tree is constructed for block tag authentication of file. For multi user data auditing, bilinear aggregate signature is used. Some existing system models are designed for checking the integrity of static data files in remote data storage (Ateniese et al., 2007: Juels et al., 2007; Shacham et al., 2008; Schwarz et al., 2006; Ateniese et al., 2008). In the case of dynamic data storage and updates the schemes are not efficient and security loopholes may arise (Ateniese et al., 2007). In the Provable Data Possession (PDP) scheme the number of queries to perform dynamic data operation is limited. The same work followed has limitation of partial support in data dynamics. Data block is identified by using a sentinel value based on the Proof of Retrievability (PoR) concept (Juels et al., 2007). Dynamic provable data possession model is proposed to support the provable updates for the data storage by using the rank based authenticated skip lists. The PDP model (Ateniese et al., 2007) utilized by eliminating the tag information and uses authenticated skip list data structure for updates verification procedure. But the efficiency is still not improved. This work has used with several system models but the scheme has limited number of operations and dynamic operations are not supported. It is based on block tag information instead of index value used in the existing schemes (Ateniese et al., 2008; Juels et al., 2007; Shacham et al., 2008). By the block tag information operation on block doesn't affect other blocks. So, the dynamicity of data is achieved. Classic merkle hash tree (Merkle, 1980) is reconstructed by select the blocks from the left to right sequence and compute root based on this sequence. So the leaf nodes are determined uniquely for operations. KeyGen, SigGen, GenProof, VerifyProof, ExecUpdate, VerifyUpdate are the six algorithms used. To overcome the problem of MAC and Signature based solutions the author went to public key based homomorphic authenticator to perform multiple auditing tasks simultaneously. Data dynamics is performed using the ExecUpdate and VerifyUpdate.

ExecUpdate is performed by the client using the File F, aggregated signature and update is a request message for modification. Update consists of Modification operation, position of block, updated message, and updated signature. The server replaces the updated block, signature, hash value and generates a new root in (Merkle Hash Tree) MHT. CSP sends a response as auxiliary authentication information, hash value of message, signature value, and the updated root. The client executes VerifyUpdate using the response send by the CSP. Then generates new root using the aggregated signature and hash value of message then perform authentication on the root value. If update is correct, proceed otherwise reject it. The client generates a new metadata and sends it to CSP for update.

At the same time dynamicity is achieved for insertion and deletion. Batch auditing task is performed by the use of (Boneh-Lynn-Shacham) BLS based aggregation signature. The author proves their work using theorem and mathematical proofs. Comparison of the work is performed with the others by using time complexity term taken by the operations such as public audit, server computation, communication cost etc., Performance analysis is shown that the scheme take merely same or less time than other works. The use of homomorphic authenticator may lead to regeneration of linear blocks by the verifier. They concentrate on the data dynamics operations as a feature. Error correction mechanism such as erasure codes is not provided.

C. Wang et al. (2012) proposed a model for the problem of public auditing mechanism by utilizing the homomorphic token with data dynamic operations and multiple auditing tasks. The author introduces a mechanism called distributed erasure coded data. This erasure correcting code used in file distribution process gives against byzantine servers (Castro et al., 2002). This scheme works with less communication overhead compared to other schemes. In data error localization the identification of server which is misbehaving. Generalized framework for existing framework via different PoR model is given as theoretical study matters (Curtmola et al., 2008). BLS based homomorphic authenticator with merkle hash tree is proposed (Wang et al., 2011) by the combination of two existing models. Another skip list based scheme is defined to provide provable data possession with full data dynamics support (Erway et al., 2009). Incremental cryptography provides a set of cryptographic building blocks such as hash, MAC and signature functions for integrity verification in dynamic data. But this scheme requires maintaining a local copy of data for verification (Bellare et al., 1994). Another scheme provided for ensure data possession for multiple replicas maintained at distributed storage system. The PDP scheme extended to cover multiple replicas. No need to encode each replica separately (Curtmola et al., 2008). By using erasure codes a backup scheme on P2P mechanism is followed to disperse data files blocks of data files across m+k peers using (m,k) erasure code. To verify the integrity peer requests, random blocks from their backup peers by using a separate keyed hash values attached on each block. It detects loss of data from free riding peers. It doesn't ensure all data are changed (Lillibridge et al., 2003). An RSA based hash defined to verify the integrity. It ensures data possession in peer-to-peer file sharing networks. It is not possible for large size files (Filho et al., 2006). A scheme proposed by applying encryption to the data. Pre computed hash keys are given to the auditor for verifying the integrity. It works only for encrypted data files and the auditors maintain their state for a long time (Shah et al., 2011; Rivest, 2007) Erasure codes and block level file integrity checks ensure the integrity of files in distributed servers (Schwarz et al., 2006).

Previous work (Erway et al., 2009) of the author gives the storage and auditing process. In this work the author gives more importance to error detection and correction. The user computes a set of verification tokens for individual vectors. Each token covers a subset of data block in random number. Token Precomputation, Correctness Verification and Error Localization, FileRetrieval and ErrorRecovery are the algorithms concentrated by the author. The algorithms are separately defined and used for error localization and recovery. The work is by utilizing the PRP and PRF. Data dynamics is achieved by block level insertion, deletion and modification. The work fully depends on the erasure correcting code to give a guarantee on the data. The scheme is proved by security analysis as detection probability against data modification where the identification probability of misbehaving server's security strength against a worst case scenario file and the performance evaluation is done for file distribution preparation, challenge token computation.

Worku et al. (2013) proposes privacy preserving public auditing protocol that prevents from any internal and external attacks and also assures the integrity of the data stored in cloud. The proposed framework has four algorithms such as KeyGen, SigGen, ProofGen and VerifyProof. In KeyGen algorithm, a security parameter is used to create a private - public key pair. It is also used to provide audit delegation to TPA to get authorized from the CSP.

In SigGen, a randomized algorithm is used to create a set of signatures for every file block using the secret key and the input file. A tag is generated to identify the blocks uniquely. In ProofGen phase, a proof for the challenge given on the specific set of signatures of a corresponding file is generated by the cloud server as shown in Figure 2.

In VerifyProof phase, the TPA or the user on receiving the proof computed by the cloud server checks with the signature and challenge and outputs the result as either True or False, where the former denotes data is verified for its correctness whereas the latter denotes that the data has been modified or lost. Here, the cloud server uses a random value to blind the original data from the TPA.

This framework also supports batch auditing where the challenges are aggregated from the request of multiple users. The server randomly selects files from each user request to compute a blinding factor and generates the proof, which is verified by the TPA for integrity verification. This approach has resulted

Figure 2. Signature based auditing

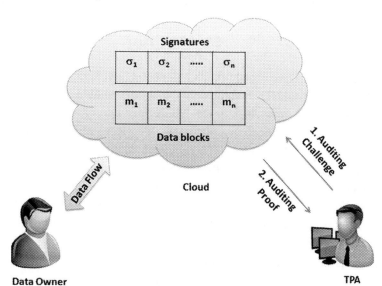

with preserving the privacy of the user data as well as it has contributed with minimum computational overhead and communication overhead as it uses BLS short signatures where less data is communicated during both data outsourcing and retrieval.

B. Wang et al. (2014) proposed a public auditing mechanism for shared data in the cloud storage. The public auditing mechanism is described with the concept of ring signatures to generate the metadata needed for verifying the correctness of shared data. The identity of the signer for every block is kept private to avoid the problems from the external verifiers. In normal case the data verification is done by downloading the data from the server and calculating the hash values for it. The calculated hash values are compared with pre-stored hash values. But this approach is not suitable for cloud data storage services. The existing models to verify the outsourced data integrity are not suitable for the shared data storage services (Bellare et al., 1999; Jackobsson et al., 1999; Kubiatowiz et al., 2009; Maheswari et al., 2000; Boneh et al., 2001; Golle et al., 2001). The scheme provided to support public auditing, correctness, unforgeability and identity privacy. Identity privacy is achieved with various mechanisms in some models as to use a globally shared private key with a group of users. The computation of key for each time a user relieving from the group introduces overhead issues. The usage of proxy to perform the middle tasks is allowed but it is vulnerable once it is compromised. Homomorphic authenticators based ring signature scheme is derived from the actual ring signature scheme (Wang et al., 2003). It supports to preserve the identity as well as block less verification.

The homomorphic authenticators based ring signature contains the algorithms such as, KeyGen, RingSign, RingVerify. The user runs the KeyGen to compute public and private key pairs. In RingSign the user computes the ring signature with the private key and randomly chosen blocks. In RingVerify user uses the public key with the blocks, then computes the signature. Compare the signature values to verify it. Security analysis for these Homomorphic authenticators based ring signature is performed with four theorem proofs.

In the public auditing mechanism or concept the author runs five algorithms as KeyGen, SigGen, Modify, ProofGen and ProofVerify. In KeyGen the user computes the public and private key pairs needed for verification. Additionally, the user generates a public aggregate key by the random elements of global parameters. In SigGen algorithm each block signature values are computed by using the private key and with the blocks of the file. Aggregated signature is calculated by using the aggregated blocks and with the public aggregate key. Modify algorithm is run three levels as insert, update and delete. To insert a new block the identifier for the newer block has computed. The signature for the blocks is updated in the storage. The total number of blocks in the shared data storage is increased by one. If any blocks want to be deleted from the storage the id and the signature are located. Then the number of blocks in the storage is decreased by one. To update a newer block to the data storage the signature for the block to update is computed and stored in the storage. The total value of the file blocks remains same.

To perform the integrity verification for the outsourced data the cloud service provider runs the ProofGen algorithm. The verifier sends a challenge to the CSP as number of blocks needed from a particular set and a random value. The CSP generates the proof by calculating the aggregated signature. The verifier runs the ProofVerify algorithm to verify the proof. With public aggregate key and with the aggregate signature the proof has been verified. Security analysis of this public integrity verification is done with three theorem proofs.

In batch auditing the algorithms used are BatchProofGen and BatchProofVerify. In BatchProofGen the verifier needs to generate the challenge which is same as sent in the ProofGen of public integrity verification. Once receiving the challenge the cloud service provider returns the proof as aggregated signature. The verifier runs the BatchProofVerify to verify the proof given by the cloud service provider. By using the private key the signatures are computed and compared. Security analysis of this batch auditing is done with two theorem proofs. Performance analysis is done in terms of computation and communication cost. By the usage of ring signatures with the homomorphic authenticators it is possible to verify the integrity of the outsourced data without retrieving the actual data from the server. Traceability and data freshness are considered as future scope for extending this work.

C. Liu et al. (2014) proposed a public auditing framework for dynamic big data storage on cloud to support efficient verifiable fine grained updates. In the existing models the authorization or authentication of the verifier at the cloud service provider is still open. It makes anyone with some necessary details can request auditing. Some works support the data updates for the fixed size blocks by utilizing the BLS signatures, if the block size is dynamic in nature, the scheme doesn't support it. The author utilizes the Merkle Hash Tree into a Ranked Merkle Hash Tree to support efficient dynamics operations of data. The actors involving in this process can authorize each other. There are some schemes defined for supporting data dynamics. The works are with random masking technology and to ensure the TPA cannot infer any information from this. But the cost required for storage and communication are comparatively huge. A rank based merkle hash tree is introduced in which each level of the tree such each node of the tree is assigned with a particular rank value. Each node contains a hash value and a rank. Compare to the binary tree this merkle hash tree contains two leaf nodes for the non-leaf nodes at each level. Parent node is constructed at each level by performing concatenation between the leaf nodes.

Block level operations in fine grained updates are performed by Partial Modification, whole block Modification, block Deletion, block Insertion, and block Splitting. The algorithms used with this framework are KeyGen, FilePreProc, Challenge, Verify, GenProof, PerformUpdate and VerifyUpdate. During the Setup phase KeyGen and FilePreProc are performed. The KeyGen algorithm outputs the public and private key pairs for signing. In FilePreProc the file is divided into set of blocks, signatures are calculated for divided set of blocks and for the entire file. The construction of ranked merkle hash tree is done with the hash values. The root node value is computed and file tag information is generated. The file tag contains the name, number of blocks and signature values. In verifiable data updation the algorithms applied are PerformUpdate and VerifyUpdate. UpdateReq is sent from user to cloud service provider. Then PerformUpdate algorithm is run by the CSP. The UpdateReq contains the type of operation such as PartialModification or Whole block Modification. The cloud service provider will update the data blocks by message, root node value and signature values. Once it is done the cloud service provider respond to the client by $P_{update.}$. Once receiving the P update the client runs VerifyUpdate with the received value and by using the public key. The client computes the root value and its hash value then perform comparison between these values. If all are true, the update is success. To verify the integrity of the outsourced data the following algorithms are performed as GenChallenge, GenProof and Verify. TPA runs the GenChallenge algorithm to request the TPA for public auditing. TPA sends challenge message with signature, ID assigned to the TPA and a random set of file blocks. Cloud service provider received the challenge from the TPA and runs the GenProof algorithm to generate the proof.

From the GenProof algorithm the cloud service provider respond to the TPA as Proof P. The cloud service provider verifies the TPA by the VID sent and with the signature sent. Upon successful receiving of Proof the TPA runs Verify algorithm. This algorithm runs by public key, challenge and with the proof received. The TPA computes the hash values and compares the root node value in the ranked Merkle hash tree. Fine-Grained Dynamic data updates are proved with a theorem. Security analysis is performed for each level by utilizing the theorems and definitions. There performance analysis is not explicitly done but the experimental evaluation is performed. This scheme shows that the fine grained updates in the big data applications are possible with security. Future scope is to ensure the confidentiality and the availability of data at the server side storage.

B. Wang et al. (2013) proposed a system model for public auditing of shared data with efficient user revocation in the cloud data storage. In the shared data storage, if a user revoked from a group it is need to sign the data blocks which are already signed by the revoked user. It is performed by the actual data is downloaded from the server and the resigning is done at user revocation. To overcome the problems in this user revocation the concept of proxy re signatures is used. In this the cloud will perform the resign of blocks instead of the user can doing this task. The shared data integrity is preserved by the signature attachment with the data where the signature is calculated by any user in the group. A user acts as a group manager to provide keys to the other users. Once a user leaves from the group, the signature generated by the user is revoked by the group manager. A common group key is shared between the group, and the key is used to sign each block of data. If a user leaves from a group, a new key is calculated and shared among the group. The system is designed to provide the following properties such as Correctness, Efficient and Secure User Revocation, Public Auditing and scalability. The homomorphic authenticators based signature scheme run with the following algorithms as KeyGen, ReKey, Sign, ReSign, and Verify. Public and Private key pairs are generated with the KeyGen algorithm. Resigning of key is done by running the ReKey algorithm. With the private key and the block to store, sign algorithm is performed. ReSign algorithm is used for signing a particular block using proxy. A particular block is verified with the public key, block value, block identifier and signature. Two theorems are shown the security analysis of this resigning process. The public auditing mechanism is performed with the algorithms KeyGen, ReKey, Sign, ReSign, ProofGen, ProofVerify. The public and private key pairs are generated and a list of user is generated and maintained by the user in a group. ReKey is performed by the cloud. In Sign private key and block identifier are used to generate the signature. In ReSign the public key, signature block, block identifier are used to generate the signature. Once it is done the user list has been updated. If a TPA wants to perform verification then ProofGen algorithm is performed. TPA sends an audit message to the cloud service provider. The cloud service provider sends the proof as signature for the requested blocks. With the received proofs the TPA compares the signatures and gives the result to the owner. The scheme is shown with security and performance analysis at each level.

Yuan et al. (2015) proposed a public integrity auditing model dynamic data sharing with multiuser modification. The model supports multi user modification, public auditing, error detection, user revocation as well as less communication and computation overhead. The existing models supports only single data owner files auditing. Some models are defined to support the multi user data. Any user can access the data at any time. But computational cost required is high and no error detection mechanism with less probability. There are some challenges in this area are an aggregation of tags with user read, write operations require each time a new set of tags and secret keys. This limits the scalability. So sharing of secret key is needed to overcome it. Revocation is a challenging issue in such security model. A PoR scheme proposed in both public and private model with a constant communication overhead. It utilizes algebraic property of polynomial (Yuan et al., 2013). By utilizing oblivious RAM a private PoR model with the support of data dynamics is derived (Cash et al., 2013). An auditing scheme derived for shared data by using ring signature based homomorphic authenticators. User revocation is not attained in this model and the overhead is increase in cost (Wang et al., 2012). The extension of the above scheme with user revocation is defined by utilizing tag and key based concept. It is possible to get the keys of user at the time of revocation. It doesn't ensure batch auditing (Wang et al., 2013). This work has two models as basic system model and threat model. In the system model, the entities are cloud server, group user and third party auditor. A master user is for a number of users on each group. The tag are generated by the master user. Shamir's secret sharing mechanism (Merkle, 1980) is utilized with user revocation. By this, an advanced user revocation model is designed. It has the algorithms such as setup, key generation, update, challenge, prove and verify. It is also defined for batch processing as batch challenge, batch drive and batch verify. Performance evaluation is performed for the factors of communication cost, update, user revocation, real time auditing of single file, and real time auditing of multiple files. This work overcomes and gives the public data auditing mechanism for multi user modification data files. The advanced user revocation method is an extra feature. It ensures error detection and resist the impersonation attack. Also batch auditing support model is defined. Authentication and aggregation of tags are used for data blocks aggregation. So the verification is easily done as aggregated one by the verifier. The author concludes that the model provides a solution for public auditing of multi data that requires less resource overhead.

Liu et al. (2015) considers that the process of public auditing without the authentication of the blocks enables the cloud service provider to create a fake proof for the third party auditor that passes the auditing process without having the intact data in cloud storage. To protect data from dishonest storage servers and to reduce the communication overhead due to the update operations performed in all replicas which is caused by updating a single block of data, a novel public auditing scheme using Authenticated Data structure (ADS) is proposed. It is based on the concept of Merkle hash tree that is constructed not only based on the file but also depends on its replicas as well as the cryptographic hash function. It involves the process of key generation, file pre-processing, data updates and verification and auditing of replicas. In this approach, initially the user and the cloud service provider decide the parameters and the hash function. To generate the keys, the client generates a primitive root of a residual set and generator value for a group. The value of generator to the power of primitive root value is considered as public key and the primitive root as secret key. Another key pair having a secret key and public key is chosen for computing the signature. Then the client stores the files as blocks in the cloud. To do so, client makes indices to the number of replicas and computes random values to form blocks. Then the Multi Replica-Merkle Hash Tree (MR-MHT) is constructed with the replica blocks. Root value of the tree is found in such a way that every node holds the value of the hash of that block, level of the node, maximum number of nodes that could be reached to leaf node and the binary value denoting left or right of the sub-tree. Using these values, signature is computed with the secret key. The authenticator value is computed for all the blocks. At last, the block, authenticator and signature are uploaded to the cloud server.

To perform updates on blocks, every time the client computes the new block values and sends to the server. Client sends the request to server mentioning the type of update as modification, insertion or deletion along with the block number and updated block. The server updates the level of the node for every insertion and deletion whereas the auxiliary information remains the same for the non-leaf nodes. On receiving the request, the server locates the corresponding sub tree and updates the root hash value and sends newly computed values to client. Client verifies with the existing values and the newly sent root value if they are equal then the blocks are said to be updated. In performing auditing, the TPA sends the challenge request with signature, block indices and random values to server that verifies the signature and computes proof with the hash of blocks, auxiliary information, authenticator value and signature that is sent to the TPA. The TPA then verifies root value, signature and authenticator value to uniquely identify the block and if all verifications are passed then data is said to be intact. Thus, auditing of multiple replicas in the cloud storage is performed. The auditing of multiple replica yields the drawback of data confidentiality as the data has not been encrypted and additional communication overhead is caused during the retrieval of data.

J. Wang et al. (2015) addresses the issues of cloud service provider who try to send an incomplete query result or a wrong query result in order to save the bandwidth or due to any resource constraints. In performing auditing process, the original data getting tampered by the third party auditor or by an adversary is protected. The handling of dynamic verification of the entire database based on the audit request is performed. In the proposed framework, initially the data owner generates master key from which three keys are created and one is used for encryption process and two keys are shared to the authenticated users. The bloom filter tree with hash functions for attributes are initialized and sent to the Arbitration center (similar to TPA).

The Data owner then finds the hash value of the attribute with total number of tuples considered and the computed hash values are placed in leaf nodes of the Merkle hash tree. The root node holds the hash value of the entire record. Encryption of every attribute is done with the key and a search tag is generated from the key and cipher text. The cipher text is sent with the signature of root value and bloom filter to CSP. To retrieve the data, the user sends the request to CSP. On verifying the signature, CSP returns the cipher text to user. User further sends the cipher text to Owner and he decrypts and sends the original message to the user. The user checks for integrity of the result and in case of error it reports the AC as reject or else it sends a message as accept after verifying the signature. Auditing process prevents the exposure of the sensitive data to cloud service provider and also protects from TPA. It checks for completeness and correctness of data retrieved as records or tuples from the cloud storage. It evaluates the strategy through security analysis and performance analysis to ensure less overhead to the Data owner.

Tian et al. (2016) derived a two dimensional data handing mechanism with dynamic hash table (DHT). It is given to the third party auditor for protecting the data process for dynamic auditing. The public key based homomorphic authenticator with random masking is utilized for privacy preservation and BLS signature used for batch auditing task. Auditing the data by the data owner is directly performed between the user and the CSP (Sebe et al., 2008; Juels et al., 2007). This requires relatively lower cost. But in case of huge size data it leads to overhead. Encryption is followed to ensure the privacy of outsourced data (Sebe et al., 2008). At the time of verifying this data, there is a chance for leaking the data content (Wang et al., 2010). An index hash table based public auditing scheme is storing the hash table information at the auditor place. So, the cloud service provider doesn't face such issues or overheads. This reduces computation overheads. This index hash table also provides a support for data dynamicity. The update operation is inefficient due to the structure of index hash table (Zhu et al., 2013). Compared to MHT and scheme of skip list, this DHT gives less communication and computation overhead. On the auditing process performed by the auditor, it is difficult to handle multiple auditing at a same time (Wang et al., 2010; Cash et al., 2013; Zhu et al., 2012). To overcome this aggregation of different data block tags produced from different users are making as single and verify it.

Dynamic Hash Table (DHT) is designed with the advantage of linked list. It is a two-dimension structure model containing file and block elements. Each file element has index number, file identifier and pointer for indicating the array elements. DHT performs file level and block level operations. Each file can have one or more number of blocks. It requires very less time for searching at the time of verification process. The dynamic data verification with privacy preservation involves setup and verification phases. In setup, key initiation, data initiation, signature generation and tag generation are performed. In verification, the flow follow as file identifier check, challenge, proof generation and proof check. Dynamic updates and batch verification models are defined with series of steps. The security analysis is performed for proving the unforgeability, resist to replacing attack, and replay attack. Computation cost at the time of setup, verification, update, batch auditing is reduced than the reviewed works. The author concluding that this work has provided with DHT which completely reduces the cost of computation at server side. Multiple auditing task aggregates BLS signature techniques from bilinear maps to perform the task at the same time. Signature of data blocks are aggregated as a single one. So, it reduces the communication cost at the verification process. This scheme proposed a hash table technique based on indexed hash table. This gives efficient data blocks updation at the time of multiple user data maintenance and the public key based homomorphic location authenticators with random masking technique ensure the data privacy. BLS signatures are provided to support aggregated tasks. It gives a newer model which overcomes the existing techniques with fewer overheads. Calculation of hash values in the DHT has taken some time in case of data size is huge with multiple user requests. So, it gives such overhead issues.

More et al. (2016) proposed a framework for public auditing that involves Data owner, cloud server and TPA. It is ensured that TPA gets zero knowledge of the data being audited. Initially, the Data owner splits the file into blocks and encrypts the blocks using AES algorithm. Then, the hash values of the blocks are generated using SHA-2 algorithm. All the hash values of the blocks are concatenated together and a signature is generated on this concatenated hash value. The Data owner stores the encrypted blocks in the cloud storage. For data auditing, the TPA receives the computed signature from the Data owner and the encrypted blocks from the cloud storage. It then computes the hash values of the blocks and the signature of the concatenated blocks. It is then compared with the signature received from the Data owner for integrity verification and generates the results to the Data owner. Though integrity is maintained, the transfer of original encrypted blocks for auditing to TPA may lead to retrieval of original data as well as it increases the communication cost and overhead to the Data owner.

Li et al. (2016) proposes two privacy-preserving public auditing protocols with lightweight computations that are able to be performed in less powerful user devices. It addresses various issues such as cloud service providers who remove the stored user data that has not been used for a long time, curious TPA who try to attain the knowledge of the user data at the time of auditing. It also addresses handling of multiple audit requests simultaneously. The overhead causing complexity in the update operations like modification, insertion or deletion operations are addressed for light weight computational power devices.

The solution approach is that, if the input is smaller in size, the basic protocol is implemented otherwise the improved protocol is used. Consider the smaller input message as a Telephone number. The basic protocol involves various phases as follows:

- **Globe Setup**: The Trusted Authority (TA) generates the global parameters. The security parameter is chosen as input to generate two generators using the bilinear map having two groups. A hash function and a secure signature scheme are chosen. It generates a private-public key pair.
- **User Setup**: The User's public and private key, certificates are generated by the TA. The User generates full private key and full public key and receives a certificate signed by the TA using his secret key.
- **OffTagGen**: The User generates the offline tags. The User chooses some random values and generates a finite number of offline tags that are stored locally with the user.
- **OnTagGen**: User generates online tags from the offline tags when data is to be outsourced. The file to be sent is split into blocks. For each block the unused tuples in the local storage of the user is used to generate online tags. They are computed to generate the final tag of the file which is sent

along with the filename to CSP and sends the signature, file name and tags to TPA. TPA checks whether the signature is valid and CSP also checks whether the online/offline signature of the file is valid.

- **Audit**: Third Party Auditor sends a challenge to CSP. CSP generates the response and sends to TPA. TPA checks for correctness. The TPA chooses certain blocks and computes values based on the indices of the blocks and constructs the challenge with the filename, indices and the computed values then sends to CSP. On receiving the challenge CSP generates the proof by hiding the block value to TPA. Then TPA computes the values and checks whether the data is intact or not.
- **Batch Audit**: TPA receives multiple audit tasks. It behaves the same as auditing but instead it takes multiple files of multiple users simultaneously and performs computation.

User performs operations such as, modification, insertion and deletion. In modification, the user modifies the file. The user chooses an unused tuple and generates an online tag and sends the modified block with file name, tags, signature and time stamp to the CSP. CSP verifies the signature of the auxiliary information and the tags. On being valid it updates the blocks and sends the updated signature to TPA. When TPA receives, it checks for signature validation and updates the tags and sends the intact information status to CSP and user. Similarly, insertion and deletion is performed.

In Improved Protocol, Merkle Hash Tree is used in every process where the leaf stores the hash values of the online tags. The signature of the root hash value is used to check for integrity whereas the operations performed in every phase remains the same. The experiment shows that the overhead and time taken to perform operations is quite low when compared to another research work as shown in Figure 3.

Figure 3. Time taken to generate tags for varying number of blocks

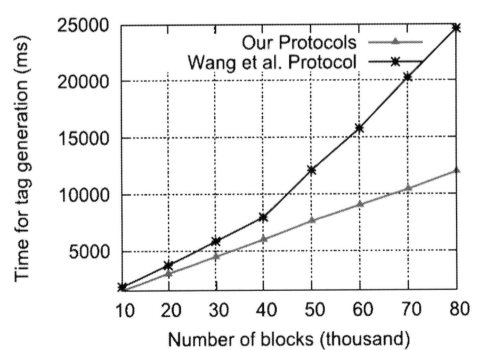

SUMMARY

The cloud service provider needs to provide a reliable service delivery to their customers. So, the correctness of data needs to be known and it is verifiable by the data owner at any point of time. This verification task is given to the Third Party auditor, who will perform the auditing task. This process also introduces vulnerabilities as such what details are needed to be given to the TPA for verification. The details which are given to the TPA doesn't give any clue about the actual data. There are some models defined for the public auditing of cloud data storage. See Table 1.

All schemes are based on the setup of four basic algorithms such as setup, challenge, generate proof, and verify proof. These four algorithms are used for verifying the correctness of data residing at cloud data storage. The existing schemes are providing solutions on the basis of signatures and key generation mechanisms. By this schemes, data stored in the cloud are in original format. No mechanisms are provided to address this issue. Preferred encryption techniques are not mentioned for the cloud data. The authorization of auditor is not followed in many schemes and the followed schemes are not strong. It is a semi trusted concept. Constructing a tree using hash values and verifying the root value is a technique followed in many systems. Hash tree construction, replicas, regeneration of code takes more computation time and it is vulnerable in some cases.

Most schemes perform auditing tasks only for the block of files. No full auditing concepts are mentioned. Mentioned system models are failure in performance issues. In some models the identity of user is secured for securing the confidential data files like government data. But the technique such as proxy based solution is not providing support. Proxies are vulnerable as it is easily compromised by an attacker. Maintaining these proxy servers is a harder task as what data given to the proxy, how the communication happen over the proxy setup is needed.

DISCUSSION AND ANALYSIS

From the analysis of the various research works discussed in this chapter, it is evident that every approach is different from each other but still the objective to ensure integrity of the data remains the same. Different parameters are compared based on the complexity and the cost incurred to achieve more security with reduced complexity. Those parameters involved in performance evaluation are communication overhead, computational overhead and time taken to perform auditing of the data blocks, to perform data dynamics operation like insertion, deletion and modification, in addition to it also finds the cost incurred to store, retrieve and verify the computed hash values for error localization and correction. From the theoretical study of the performance analysis, the computational complexity gets increased in utilizing multiplicative and exponential operations. When the local copy data of huge size is transferred between the stakeholders for integrity verification, it increases the communication overhead by continuously utilizing the maximum bandwidth. Similarly, when a small update in a block causing additional update to the entire tree of file blocks happens, it contributes greatly towards computational complexity and computational cost. The storage overhead occurs in scenario where the metadata gets increased in volume to verify the single piece of data at anytime required. Thus, an approach has to be framed that keeps an efficient trade-off between the utmost security and minimum cost with reduced complexity.

Table 1. Comparison of public auditing schemes in cloud

Comparison Factor / Paper	C. Wang et al. (2010)	Q. Wang et al. (2011)	C. Wang et al. (2012)	Q. Wang et al. (2012)	C. Wang et al. (2012)	B. Wang et al. (2013)	C. Liu et al. (2014)	B. Wang et al. (2014)	J. Yuan et al. (2015)	H. Tian et al. (2016)
Authentication	No	Yes	Yes	Yes	No	Yes	Yes	Yes	Yes	Yes
Availability	No	No	No	No	No	No	No	No	No	No
Protocol	No	PDP POR	No	No	PRP	No	No	No	No	No
Technique	No	No	PKHVARM	BLS	Homomorphic token	Homomorphic authenticator based ring signatures	Tags	Homomorphic authenticators	Tags	Dynamic Hash Table
External auditor	Yes	Yes	Yes	Yes	Yes	Yes	Yes	Yes	Yes	Yes
Encryption	No	No	Yes	Yes	Yes	Yes	Yes	Yes	Yes	Yes
Data structure concept	Yes	Merkle Hash Tree	No	Modified merkle hash tree	No	Merkle hash tree	Ranked merkle hash tree	No	No	Dynamic hash values
Signature	No	Yes	Yes	Yes	Yes	Yes	Yes	Yes	Yes	Yes
Functions	Yes	No	PRF	No	PRF	No	No	No	Yes	No
Dynamism	Yes	Yes	No	Yes	Yes	Yes	Yes	Yes	No	Yes
Batch auditing	Yes	Yes	Yes	Yes	Yes	Yes	Yes	Yes	Yes	Yes
Error localization	No	No	No	No	Yes	No	No	No	Yes	No
Data recovery	No	No	No	No	Yes	No	No	No	No	No

SOLUTIONS AND RECOMMENDATIONS

Cloud data storage and the correctness of stored data are the important considerations in the cloud arena. It is observed that public auditing schemes provide a verification mechanism for the storage data correctness. The existing system models are defined with various solutions such as cryptography based solutions, data structure based solutions, signature based solutions, key updation based solution, proxy based solution, and function models based solutions. Each model gets defined with its own concept. As a separate model defined or used, it is not possible to satisfy the problem in this public auditing. A model needed with a collaboration of two or more schemes. At each level a separate methodology is need to be defined for satisfying the security constraints. The cost and complexity mainly applies on the operations of data dynamics as well as data transferred between entities for integrity verification. Thus the metadata and the data used to perform these functionalities have to be handled in smaller size without compromising security objectives. It could certainly reduce the communication cost and overhead. At the same time, the computations should be able to be performed on the data with the anytime available sufficient resources to reduce the computation cost and overhead for the stake holders like Data owner, Third party auditor and cloud storage server.

FUTURE RESEARCH DIRECTIONS

Based on the analysis of the existing schemes, it is clear that the existing schemes are providing a limited security model for public auditing of data storage. To overcome these issues, a newer framework would be designed by providing security primitives at each level. The future framework of the auditing model will be designed and it would be completely new to this arena that holds the efficiency regarding performance and security analysis. The framework should be feasible to handle data of any size, to preserve the privacy of the data and to audit the replicas of the original file blocks for complete integrity verification. Data dynamics and batch auditing should reduce the communication cost and overhead in order to meet out its significance on implementation. It shall also meet the requirements to be adopted for real time scenario that allows to be deployed for real time implementations involving TPA for auditing. Even techniques could be proposed that satisfies the above solutions without involving any third-party auditor for integrity verification. Meanwhile, it should also be easy for the data owner to verify integrity of the data along with the cloud storage server without any overhead and security issues.

CONCLUSION

Digital data world has started to incorporate and maintain the data in the cloud data storage. Cloud data storage model helps the user to store their data without worrying about the maintenance of the data. But the data stored in the cloud data storage has the possibility of being accessed and modified in some cases such as attacks. So, it is mandatory to verify the correctness of the outsourced data. This is done by Trusted Third Party Auditor. TTPA performs verification tasks and gives the result to the Data owner. But this scheme also has some constraints or limitations to provide a secure auditing system. The Data owner can perform this task on his own but due to the time and resource required to do this task is not enough for the user, it is done by the TTPA. The existing models define various solutions or schemes to perform auditing process. But no such solutions are effective and efficient in terms of cost, security and performance. From this survey, existing system models followed for the auditing task and the problems with the models are identified. Based on the identification, the criteria to design a secure data auditing framework is studied that suits the purpose of performing an auditing task in the cloud data storage with utmost efficiency in terms of performance and security.

REFERENCES

104th United States Congress. (1996). Health Insurance Portability and Accountability Act of 1996 (HIPAA). Retrieved from http://aspe.hhs.gov/admnsimp/pl104191.html

Allmydata Inc. (2001). Unlimited Online Storage and Backup. Retrieved from http://allmydata.com

Amazon.com. 2009. Amazon Web Services (AWS). http://aws.amazon.com

Ateniese, G., Burns, R., Curtmola, R., Herring, J., Kissner, L., Peterson, Z., & Song, D. (2007). Provable data possession at untrusted stores. Cryptology ePrint Archive. Retrieved from http://eprint.iacr.org/

Ateniese, G., Pietro, R.D., Mancini, L.V., & Tsudik, G. (2008). Scalable and Efficient Provable Data Possession. *Proceedings of Fourth International Conference on. Security and Privacy in Communication Networks SecureComm '08* (pp. 1-10). 10.1145/1460877.1460889

Bellare, M., & Goldreich, O. (1992). On defining proofs of knowledge. In E.F. Brickell (Ed.), Advances in Cryptology – CRYPTO '92, (pp. 390–420). Springer.

Bellare, M., Goldreich, O., & Goldwasser, S. (1994). Incremental Cryptography: The Case of Hashing and Signing. *Proceedings of 14th Annual International Cryptology Conference: Advances in Cryptology CRYPTO '94* (pp. 216-233).

Bellare, M., & Miner, S. (1999). A forward-secure digital signature scheme. In Advances in Cryptology CRYPTO'99 (pp. 431-448). doi:10.1007/3-540-48405-1_28

Blum, M., Evans, W. S., Gemmell, P., Kannan, S., & Naor, M. (1994). Checking the correctness of Memories. *Algorithmica, 12*(2/3), 225–244. doi:10.1007/BF01185212

Boneh, D., Gentry, C., Lynn, B., & Shacham, H. (2003). Aggregate and Verifiably Encrypted Signatures from Bilinear Maps. *Proceedings of 22nd International Conference on Theory and Applications of Cryptographic techniques Eurocrypt '03* (pp. 416-432). 10.1007/3-540-39200-9_26

Boneh, D., Lynn, B., & Shacham, H. (2001). Short Signatures from the Weil Pairing. *Proceedings of Seventh International Conference on Theory and Application of Cryptology and Information Security: Advances in Cryptology ASIACRYPT '01* (pp. 514-532). 10.1007/3-540-45682-1_30

Bowers, K.D. Juels, A. & Oprea, A. (2008). Proofs of Retrievability: Theory and Implementation. Cryptology ePrint Archive.

Cash, D., Kp, A., & Wichs, D. (2013). *Dynamic proofs of retrievability via oblivious ram. In Advances in Cryptology: EUROCRYPT 2013, LNCS* (pp. 279–295). Springer. doi:10.1007/978-3-642-38348-9_17

Castro, M., & Liskov, B. (2002). Practical Byzantine Fault Tolerance and Proactive Recovery. *ACM Transactions on Computer Systems, 20*(4), 398–461. doi:10.1145/571637.571640

Chang, E. C., & Xu, J. (2008). Remote Integrity Check with Dishonest Storage Server. *Proceedings of 13th European Symposium on Research in Computer Security ESORICS '08* (pp. 223-237). 10.1007/978-3-540-88313-5_15

Clarke, D. E., Suh, G. E., Gassend, B., Sudan, A., vanDijk, M., & Devadas, S. (2005). Towards constant bandwidth overhead integrity checking of untrusted data. *Proceedings of the IEEE Symposium on Security and Privacy '05* (pp. 139–153). 10.1109/SP.2005.24

Curtmola, R., Khan, O., Burns, R., & Ateniese, G. (2008). MR-PDP: Multiple-Replica Provable Data Possession. *Proceedings of IEEE 28th International Conference on Distributed Computing Systems ICDCS '08* (pp. 411-420).

Deswarte, Y., Quisquater, J. J., & Saidane, A. (2003). Remote Integrity Checking. *Integrity and Internal Control in Information Systems, 6*, 1–11.

Dodis, Y., Vadhan, S., & Wichs, S. (2009). Proofs of Retrievability via Hardness Amplification. *Proceedings of the Sixth Theory of Cryptography Conference on Theory of Cryptography TCC '09* (pp. 109-127).

Dwork, C., Goldberg, D., & Naor, M. (2003). On memory-bound functions for fighting spam. In D. Boneh, (Ed.), CRYPTO '03 (pp. 426–444). Springer. doi:10.1007/978-3-540-45146-4_25

Erway, C., Kupcu, A., Papamanthou, C., & Tamassia, R. (2009). Dynamic provable data possession. *Proceedings of the 16th ACM conference on Computer and Communications Security: CCS'09* (pp. 213-222).

Ferrara, A. L., Greeny, M., Hohenberger, S., & Pedersen, M. (2009). Practical short signature batch verification. *Proceedings of CT-RSA, LNCS* (pp. 309–324). Springer. 10.1007/978-3-642-00862-7_21

Filho, D.L.G., & Barreto, P.S.L.M. (2006). Demonstrating Data Possession and Uncheatable Data Transfer. IACR Eprint archive.

Golle, P., Jarecki, S., & Mironov, I. (2002). Cryptographic primitives enforcing communication and storage complexity. In M. Blaze (Ed.), Financial Cryptography '02 (pp. 120–135). Springer.

Golle, P., & Mironov, I. (2001). Uncheatable distributed computations. In D. Naccache (Ed.), CT-RSA '01 (pp. 425–440). Springer. doi:10.1007/3-540-45353-9_31

Hendricks, J., Ganger, G., & Reiter, M. (2007). Verifying Distributed Erasure-Coded Data. *Proceedings of 26th ACM Symposium on Principles of Distributed Computing PODC '07* (pp. 139-146).

Hwang, M., Lu, J., & Lin, E. (2003). A Practical (t, n) Threshold Proxy Signature Scheme Based on the RSA Cryptosystem. *IEEE Transactions on Knowledge and Data Engineering, 15*(6), 1552–1560. doi:10.1109/TKDE.2003.1245292

Jakobsson, M., & Juels, A. (1999). Proofs of work and bread pudding protocols. In B. Preneel (Ed.), *Communications and Multimedia Security* (pp. 258–272). Kluwer.

Juels, A., & Kaliski, J. S. (2007). PoRs: Proofs of Retrievability for Large Files. *Proceedings of 14th ACM Conference Computer and Communication Security CCS '07* (pp. 584-597) 10.1145/1315245.1315317

Kallahalla, M., Riedel, E., Swaminathan, R., Wang, Q., & Fu, K. (2003). Plutus: Scalable secure file sharing on untrusted storage. *Proceedings of the 2nd USENIX conference on File and Storage Technologies FAST' 03* (pp. 29–42).

Kher, V., & Kim, Y. (2005). Securing distributed storage: Challenges, techniques, and systems. *Proceedings of the ACM Workshop on Storage security and survivability StorageSS '05* (pp 9–25). 10.1145/1103780.1103783

Kubiatowicz, J., Bindel, D., Chen, Y., Czerwinski, S., Eaton, P., Geels, D., ... Zhao, B. (2000). Oceanstore: An architecture for global-scale persistent storage. *SIG PLAN Notices.*, *35*(11), 190–201. doi:10.1145/356989.357007

Li, J., Krohn, M., Mazieres, D., & Shasha, D. (2004). Secure untrusted data repository (SUNDR). *Proceedings of 6th conference on symposium on Operating System Design & Implementation OSDI '04* (pp. 121–136).

Li, J., Zhang, L., Liu, J. K., Qian, H., & Dong, Z. (2016). Privacy-Preserving Public Auditing Protocol for Low-Performance End Devices in Cloud. *IEEE Transactions on Information Forensics and Security*, *11*(11), 2572–2583. doi:10.1109/TIFS.2016.2587242

Libert, B & Vergnaud, D. (2011). Unidirectional Chosen-Ciphertext Secure Proxy Re-Encryption. *IEEE Transactions on Information Theory*, *57*(3), 1786-1802.

Lillibridge, M., Elnikety, S., Birrell, A., Burrows, M., & Isard, M. (2003). A Cooperative Internet Backup Scheme. *Proceedings of USENIX Annual Technical Conference: General Track* (pp. 29-41)

Liu, C., Ranjan, R., Yang, C., Zhang, X., Wang, L., & Chen, J. (2015). Mur-DPA: Top-Down Levelled Multi-Replica Merkle Hash Tree Based Secure Public Auditing for Dynamic Big Data Storage on Cloud. *IEEE Transactions on Computers*, *64*(9), 2609–2622. doi:10.1109/TC.2014.2375190

Liu, C., Ranjian, R., Zhang, X., Yang, C., Georgakopoulos, D., & Chen, J. (2013). Public Auditing for Big Data Storage in Cloud Computing - A Survey. *Proceedings of 16th IEEE International Conference on Computational Science and Engineering CSE* (pp. 1128-1135).

Maheshwari, U., Vingralek, R., & Shapiro, W. (2000). How to build a trusted database system on untrusted storage. *Proceedings of the 4th USENIX Symposium: Operating System Design and Implementation*, Berkeley, CA, USA.

Mambo, M., Usuda, K., & Okamoto, E. (1996). Proxy Signatures for Delegating Signing Operation. *Proceedings of Third ACM Conference: Computer and Communication Security CCS '96* (pp. 48-57). 10.1145/238168.238185

Merkle, R. C. (1980). Protocols for Public Key Cryptosystems. *Proceedings of IEEE Symptoms: Security and Privacy* (pp. 122-133).

More, S., & Chaudhari, S. (2016). Third Party Public Auditing scheme for Cloud Storage. *Proceedings of the International Conference on Communication, Computing and Virtualization* (pp. 69-76). Elsevier. 10.1016/j.procs.2016.03.010

Muthitacharoen, A., Morris, R., Gil, T., & Chen, B. (2002). Ivy: A read/write peer-to-peer file system. *Proceedings of the 5th symposium on Operating Systems Design and Implementation: ACM SIGOPS Operating Systems Review OSDI '02* (pp. 31–44).

Naor, M., & Nissim, K. (1998). *Certificate revocation and certificate update.* USENIX Security.

Naor, M., & Rothblum, G. N. (2005). The complexity of online memory checking. *Proceedings of the 46th Annual IEEE Symposium on Foundations of Computer Science FOCS* (pp. 573–584). 10.1109/SFCS.2005.71

Network Technology Group. (2007). DataVault Offsite Data Backup to Completely Secure Critical Computer Data. Retrieved from http://www.ntg.com/datavault.asp

Pack, S., Rutagemwa, H., Shen, X., Mark, J., & Park, K. (2008). Proxy-Based Wireless Data Access Algorithms in Mobile Hotspots. *IEEE Transactions on Vehicular Technology, 57*(5), 3165-3177.

Papamanthou, C., Tamassia, R., & Triandopoulos, N. (2008). Authenticated hash tables. *Proceedings of the 15th ACM Conference on Computer and Communications Security CCS '08* (pp. 437–448).

Rabin, M. (1989). Efficient dispersal of information for security, load balancing, and fault tolerance. *Journal of the ACM, 36*(2), 335–348. doi:10.1145/62044.62050

Rivest, R. (2007). The pure crypto project's hash function. Cryptography Mailing List Posting. Retrieved from http://diswww.mit.edu/bloompicayune/crypto/13190

Ryoo, J, Rizvi, S. Aiken, W & Kissell, J. (2014). Cloud Security Auditing: Challenges and Emerging Approaches. *IEEE Security & Privacy, 12*(6), 68-74.

Schwarz, T., & Miller, E. L. Store, Forget, and Check: Using Algebraic Signatures to Check Remotely Administered Storage. *Proceedings of 26th IEEE International Conference on Distributed Computing Systems ICDCS'06* (pp. 12). 10.1109/ICDCS.2006.80

Sebé, F., Domingo-Ferrer, J., Martínez-Ballesté, A., Deswarte, Y., & Quisquater, J. J. (2008). Efficient Remote Data Possession Checking in Critical Information Infrastructures. *IEEE Transactions on Knowledge and Data Engineering, 20*(8), 1034–1038. doi:10.1109/TKDE.2007.190647

Shacham, H., & Waters, B. (2008). Compact proofs of retrievability. *Proceedings of the 14th International Conference on the Theory and Application of Cryptology and Information Security Asiacrypt '08* (Vol. 5350, pp. 90–107). 10.1007/978-3-540-89255-7_7

Shah, M. A. Baker, M. Mogul, J. C. & Swaminathan, R. Auditing to Keep Online Storage Services Honest. *Proceedings of the 11th USENIX Workshop Hot Topics in Operating Systems HotOS '07* (pp. 1-6).

Shah, M. A., Swaminathan, R., & Baker, M. (2008). Privacy-Preserving Audit and Extraction of Digital Contents. Cryptology ePrint Archive.

Shamir, A. (1979). How to share a secret. *Communications of the ACM, 22*(11), 612–613. doi:10.1145/359168.359176

Tamassia, R. (2003). Authenticated data structures. Proceedings of ESA '05, LNCS (Vol. 2832, pp. 2–5). Springer.

Tian, H. Chen, Y. Cheng, C. Jiang, H. Huang, Y. Chen, Y. & Liu, J. (2016). Dynamic-Hash-Table Based Public Auditing for Secure Cloud Storage. *IEEE Transactions on service computing.*

Valdes, A., Almgren, M., Cheung, S., Deswarte, Y., Dutertre, B., Levy, J., ... Uribe, T. E. (2003). An Architecture for Adaptive Intrusion-Tolerant Server. *Proceedings of Security Protocols Workshop* (pp. 158-178).

Wang, B., Baochun, L., & Hui, L. (2013). Public auditing for shared data with efficient user revocation in the cloud. *Proceedings of the 32nd IEEE International Conference on Computer Communications INFOCOM '13* (pp. 2904–2912). 10.1109/INFCOM.2013.6567101

Wang, B., Li, B., & Li, H. (2012). Oruta: Privacy-preserving public auditing for shared data in the cloud. *Proceedings of the IEEE Fifth International Conference on Cloud Computing CLOUD '12* (pp. 295–302). 10.1109/CLOUD.2012.46

Wang, C. Chow, S. M. Wang, Q. Ren, K. & Lou, W. (2013). Privacy-Preserving Public Auditing for Secure Cloud Storage. *IEEE Transactions on Computers, 62*(2), 362-375.

Wang, C., Ren, K., Lou, W., & Li, J. (2010). Towards Publicly Auditable Secure Cloud Data Storage Services. IEEE Network Magazine, 24(4), 19-24.

Wang, C. Wang, Q. Ren, K. Cao, N. & Lou, W. (2012). Toward Secure and Dependable Storage Services in Cloud Computing. *IEEE Transactions on services computing, 5*(2), 220-232.

Wang, C., Wang, Q., Ren, K., & Lou, W. (2009). Ensuring Data Storage Security in Cloud Computing. *Proceedings of 17th International Workshop on Quality of Service IWQoS '09* 10.1109/IWQoS.2009.5201385

Wang, C., Wang, Q., Ren, K., & Lou, W. (2010). Privacy-Preserving Public Auditing for Data Storage Security in Cloud Computing. Proceedings of IEEE INFOCOM (pp. 1-9). doi:10.1109/INFCOM.2010.5462173

Wang, H. (2013). Proxy Provable Data Possession in Public Clouds. *IEEE Transactions on Services Computing, 6*(4), 551-559.

Wang, H. Wu, Q. Qin, B. & Domingo-Ferrer, J. (2014). Identity-based remote data possession checking in public clouds. *IET Information Security, 8*(2), 114- 121.

Wang, J., Chen, X., Huang, X., You, I., & Xiang, Y. (2015). Verifiable Auditing for Outsourced Database in Cloud Computing. *IEEE Transactions on Computers, 64*(11), 3293–3303. doi:10.1109/TC.2015.2401036

Wang, Q., Wang, C., Ren, K., Lou, W., & Li, J. (2011). Enabling Public Verifiability and Data Dynamics for Storage Security in Cloud Computing. *IEEE Transactions on Parallel and Distributed Systems, 22*(2/5), 847–859. doi:10.1109/TPDS.2010.183

Webopedia. (2007). Data Vaulting. http://www.webopedia.com/TERM/D/data_vaulting.html

Wikipedia. Cyclic Redundancy Check. 2007. http://en.wikipedia.org/wiki/Cyclic_redundancy_check

Worku, S. G., Xu, C., Zhao, J., & He, X. (2013). Secure and efficient privacy-preserving public auditing scheme for cloud storage. In Computers and Electrical Engineering (pp. 1703 – 1713). Elsevier.

Yuan, J., & Yu, S. (2013). Proofs of retrievability with public verifiability and constant communication cost in cloud. *Proceedings of the International Workshop on Security in Cloud Computing: Cloud Computing '13* (pp. 19–26). 10.1145/2484402.2484408

Yuan, J. & Yu, S. (2015). Public Integrity Auditing for Dynamic Data Sharing with Multi-User Modification. *IEEE Transactions on Information Forensics and Security, 10*(8), 1717-1726.

Zheng, & Xu, Q. (2011). Fair and dynamic proofs of Retrievability. *Proceedings of the first ACM conference on Data and Application Security & Privac: CODASPY'11* (pp. 237–248)

Zhu, Y. Hu, H. Ahn, G. & Yu, M. (2012). Cooperative Provable Data Possession for Integrity Verification in Multi-Cloud Storage. *IEEE Transactions on Parallel and Distributed Systems, 23*(12), 2231-2244.

Zhu, Y. Wang, H. Hu, Z. Ahn, G.J. & Hu, H. (2011). Zero-knowledge proofs of Retrievability. *Science China Information Sciences, 54*(8), 1608–1617.

Zhu, Y. Wang, H. Hu, Z. Ahn, G. J. Hu, H and Yau, S. (2013). Dynamic Audit Services for Outsourced Storage in Clouds. *IEEE Transactions on Services Computing, 6*(2), 227–238.

Zhu, Y., Wang, H., Hu, Z., Ahn, G. J., Hu, H., & Yau, S. S. (2011). Dynamic audit services for integrity verification of outsourced storages in clouds. *Proceedings of the 2011 ACM Symposium on Applied Computing SAC '11* (pp. 1550–1557). 10.1145/1982185.1982514

KEY TERMS AND DEFINITIONS

Integrity Verification: Verifying the correctness of the outsourced data.

Merkle Hash Tree: It is based on the binary tree data structure in which each non-leaf nodes are constructed by the leaf nodes with hash values to construct the root node.

Privacy Preservation: Preserving the privacy of data after outsourced into the public storage.

Proxy: A computer or a machine to perform some automated tasks.

Public Auditing: Verifying the outsourced data correctness which is located at the cloud data storage.

Signature: It is generated for a file or data block by the user using any cryptographic signature generation algorithms.

Third Party Auditor: A person who is performing the auditing task or integrity verification of outsourced data based on cost or agreement.

This research was previously published in Advancing Cloud Database Systems and Capacity Planning With Dynamic Applications edited by Narendra Kumar Kamila, pages 133-157, copyright year 2017 by Information Science Reference (an imprint of IGI Global).

Section 8
Emerging Trends

Chapter 101
Advances in Information, Security, Privacy and Ethics:
Use of Cloud Computing for Education

Joseph M. Woodside
Stetson University, USA

ABSTRACT

The future of education lays in the hand of Cloud Computing given the benefits of learning delivery, costs reduction, and innovation. At the same time, the threat of cyber-attacks and security breaches are also mounting for education based organizations and are a prime target given the amount and type of personal information available. This manuscript discusses the cloud security, privacy, and ethical mechanisms required from a teacher, student, and administrator perspective.

INTRODUCTION

The future of education lays in the hand of Cloud Computing, with easy to configure hardware and software components. Utilizing Cloud Computing to their advantage, teachers, administrators, and students are able to deliver content and learn much more effectively within an integrated environment. Given the ability to access anytime anywhere, this enables teachers, administrators and students to target individual needs of students and customize educational delivery. Instead of maintaining all systems separately at each institution and in order to eliminate infrastructure that is dated by 10-20 years at most institutions, Cloud Computing offers the flexibility to delivery current learning technology for the 21st century.

In an effort to reduce costs, increase efficiency and availability, increase enrollment, and innovate with technology many educational institutions are moving to a Cloud Computing model. At the same time, the threat of cyber-attacks and security breaches are also mounting for education based organizations and are a prime target given the amount and type of personal information available. In recent example cases, financial and legal costs are estimated in the millions of dollars with several hundred thousand student and personnel records compromised. In another instance at a state university, some

DOI: 10.4018/978-1-5225-8176-5.ch101

30,000 student's social security numbers were compromised. It is estimated that many data breaches in education go undetected more than in other industries, and the impact is often realized in the forms of enrollments and endowments.

Learning Objectives

This chapter includes the cloud security, privacy, and ethical mechanisms required from a teacher, student, and administrator perspective. For cloud security, the paper outlines the access strategies, service-oriented architectures, and implementation components required to successfully utilize cloud computing in education. For privacy and ethical considerations, several federal laws have been passed to develop a minimum standard for protection of records, and must be developed with flexibility of changing technology and regulations, along with established techniques for privacy preservation.

CLOUD COMPUTING

Cloud computing enables convenient on demand access to an elastic set of shared computing resources. Generally cloud computing is broken into 3 categories of software as a service (SaaS), infrastructure as a service (IaaS) and platform as a service (Paas). SaaS is anticipated to grow the fastest and is typically what users see and interact with directly. The cloud computing market is anticipated to be nearly $200 Billion in 2020 according to Forrester, up from $58 Billion in 2013 (Seeking Alpha, 2015).

SaaS

Software as a Service (SaaS) is software that can be deployed over the Internet and is licensed to customers typically on a pay-for-use model. In some cases a service may be offered at no charge if supported from other sources such as advertisements. SaaS is quickly growing and double-digit growth of 21% is anticipated, with a forecast of $106B in 2016 (Seeking Alpha, 2015).

Cloud computing support SaaS by providing a scalable and virtualized services to the end-user via a simple web browser. A third party manages the computing infrastructure, and provides the software as a service (SaaS). Salesforce.com, Google Apps, Amazon, and Facebook provide have cloud computing offerings. Cloud computing allows organizational to reduce IT capital costs, and buy computing on an as needed basis. There are economies of scale through shared use of systems and resources by multiple customers. Cloud computing reduces the entry barriers by eliminating software distribution and site installation requirements. This also permits organizations to develop new business models and sources of revenue through on demand services (Woodside, 2010).

SOA is used as the access point for all systems through web services and XML is utilized for the data representation. SOA promises improved agility and flexibility for organizations to deliver value-based services to their customers. A service is the application of knowledge for co-creation of value between interacting entities. Service systems involve people, technology, and information. Service science is concerned with understanding service systems, and improve and design services for practical purposes. SOA includes Web service, technology, and infrastructures, and is a process that add value, reuse, information, and overall value to the business. SOA provides a commodization of hardware and software providing organizations with improved architectures and which support IT service flexibility. The SOA approaches are utilized to develop SaaS from IaaS (Woodside, 2010).

IaaS

Infrastructure as a Service (IaaS) is a method for deploying infrastructure such as servers, storage, network and operating systems. These infrastructure services are offered on-demand in a secure environment. This allows customers to utilize resources on-demand instead of purchasing the resources up front. There are a few technologies IaaS utilizes including virtualization, enterprise information integration (EII) and service oriented architecture (SOA). Virtualization creates a virtual version of a computing platform, storage, or network. Unlike SaaS users are responsible for managing the operating system components along with data and middleware (Seeking Alpha, 2015).

Additional technologies supporting IaaS include EII which describes the combination of various sources of data into a unified form without requiring all sources be contained within a data warehouse and also integration complexity reductions. The enterprise unified view must consume data that is available real-time via direct system access, and semantic resolution must occur across systems. Semantic integration or an ontology is a higher level natural language approach to combine differing pieces of information together, and in support of real-time events. A semantic information model can be constructed using Web Ontology Language (OWL) developed by W3C. (Woodside, 2010).

Most real-time architectures consist of the required data sources and a virtual or mediated data schema which is then queried by the end user or application. The systems are typically build on a XML data model and query language. EII reduces data access time, while Enterprise Application Integration (EAI) allows system updates as part of the business process to occur. Both these technologies are utilized as a best practice and combined into the concept of Enterprise Integration (EI). The EI architecture supports heterogeneous data sources such as relational and non-relational databases, flat files, XML, transactional systems, and content management systems. Information transparency is provided through the virtual data access services layer which permits real-time programming services. This architecture adheres to SOA, where business processes exist as distinct services which communicate through known interfaces. This also helps promote code re-use and more flexible IT infrastructure by allowing focus on business logic, and leaving the data tasks to the EII layer (Woodside, 2010).

PaaS

Platform as a Service (PaaS) is generally considered the most complex of the three categories of cloud computing. PaaS is a computing platform which also allows the instantiation of web-based software applications without the added complexity of purchasing and maintaining software and infrastructure. Based on market studies, PaaS is anticipated to reach $44 Billion in revenue by 2020, with 16% of overall cloud services by 2018 (Seeking Alpha, 2015). Some of the advantages to PaaS include efficiency of development and deployment cycles, capacity on demand, portability between platforms, simplified mobile application creation, and increased business value (Mehta, 2015).

Cloud Computing in the Classroom

New generations of touch enabled devices which interact via wireless networks have created a new form of learning also called the Classroom in the Cloud. Students now have an entire computing ecosystem in the palm of their hand through mobile devices such as smartphones, tablets, and laptops. Administration and installation of the infrastructure is easily setup through a wide spectrum wireless network which permits connectivity across locations with resource and Internet access using a specified user key or account. Using a Cloud-based implementation further saves administrative and maintenance costs, allowing platform and service based storage and systems. Distance learning or joint classroom learning is also enabled from local or international partners. Virtual networking, web conferencing, and whiteboard technology can be utilized to display the assignments, homework, or in class materials (Lieberman, 2013).

K-12 Cloud Computing

Cloud computing in K-12 is forecasted to comprise 25% of the technology budget and increase to 35% within the next four years. Educational institutions are leverage cloud computing, which utilizes remotely hosted servers to help reduce technology costs and reduce administration and content management costs. Other key advantages include backup capability to auto-save content to avoid any loss of documents and all accessible through the cloud. Storage also allows use of all types of content and files such as eBooks, apps, music, documents, and photos. Accessibility of information is key with access from anywhere and any device such as portable or mobile devices. The Cloud also allows collaboration between users to update, edit, or exchange ideas simultaneously. Less resources are utilized printing hard copy content, with all documents accessible electronically. Assignments and grading can also all be done online with real-time grading and quizzing (Weaver, 2013).

In a recent example, all Lincoln Nebraska Public Schools students in grades 3-12 will receive Chromebook computing devices at an approximate cost of $300 each, which rely on cloud computing and include word processing, spreadsheet and educational applications in the cloud vs. locally installed on the devices. The plan took approximately four years to date, with a 10-year $50 million plan. This plan is expected to cover nearly 40,000 students and become the largest program in the state. The name of the plan is CLASS for Connected Learning for the Achievement of Students and Staff - Technology Plan. Digital curriculum, assessments, learning goals, student collaboration, research and lab scheduling has driven the need for devices to be rolled out to all students (Anderson, 2015).

Higher Education Cloud Computing

In higher education end-users are also driving the use of the Cloud. In higher education end users or students are digitally focused and mobile adept. In a CDW survey, colleges are moving to the Cloud to increase efficiency, improve employee mobility, increase innovation, improve IT staff availability, reduce IT costs, and enable new service offerings. For applications, email, word processing, messaging, conference, communication and collaboration tools were commonly moved to the Cloud to increase employee and students productivity (Daley, 2013).

At Fairfield University, a 70 year old private institution with 5000 students, they have transformed their organization and the classroom through technology in order to remain competitive and enroll students. These technologies allow students to engage with campus activities, measure student participation and satisfaction, maintain calendars, and access the centralized portal through their cloud and mobile devices. Staff at the University have enjoyed a cloud system for streamlining various hiring and HR paperwork processes such as W-2s and paystubs. Fairfield University has also introduced an innovative classroom, one that students are looking to more closely replicates the way they use digital tools and cloud-computing outside of the classroom (Castle, 2015).

While cloud computing has many potential applications and benefits to universities, administrators will be required to educate and engage all faculty members on cloud technologies. Some examples of cloud computing at universities include campus mail and learning management system software. Unfortunately some surveys suggest that most universities will not have deployed more advanced cloud computing applications by 2019. In addition, many technology officers are still unclear on the security of clouds and uneasy with trusting third parties or vendors (Florence, 2015).

CYBER ATTACKS IN EDUCATION

Cases and Impact

It is estimated that many data breaches in education go undetected more than in other industries, and the impact is often realized in the forms of enrollments and endowments. Traced to the year 1998, a cyber attack at the University of Maryland has resulted in the loss of 309,079 student and personnel records, and estimated to result in millions of dollars in legal and related costs. The University of Maryland case unfortunately is not an isolated incident. Indiana University had 146,000 student data records vulnerable due to a staff error. North Dakota University identified 291,465 students and 784 employees whose information was on a hacked server (O'Neil, 2014). At Iowa State University, 29,780 student social security numbers were breached with data ranging from 1995-2012 (Jackson, 2014).

On average, data breaches cost $111 per record, similar to the $136 per record found in other industries. Costs to address these breaches include consultants, lawyers, call centers, websites, mailings, identity theft protection, credit checks, security projects, and legal suits. Indiana University has incurred costs of $75000 for their call center, while North Dakota State University incurred costs of $200,000 on identity theft services and call center. Another Maricopa County Community College District incurred costs estimated at $17.1 million after adding in consultant work to fix their security and legal services (O'Neil, 2014).

Methods

The image of the individual hacker in the basement no longer holds true. These individuals are being replaced by increasingly sophisticated governments and organized crime groups which create the biggest threat for education. These groups work 24/7 to compromise sensitive research, student information, and intellectual property. Methods for these attacks include passwords, social media, phishing, smartphones, and denial of service. For passwords, weak policies and ability to download sensitive information unprotected to portable devices is a common area of concern, along with outdated anti-virus software across campus devices. For social media, hackers often impersonate friends or employers that students may access and install virus or other malware tools unintentionally. Phishing utilizes personal information from Facebook, LinkedIn and other publically available sites to send a personalized communication in hopes of stealing information or installing malware. Smartphones are another common area of risk, given the wide usage and often insecure connectivity over wireless networks along with loss or theft of devices (Zalaznick, 2013). In a recent example in Kansas, distributed denial of service (DDoS) attacks also inundate a network and overwhelm the system with traffic 100 times the usual volume, causing a shut-down of state exams (Herold, 2014).

CLOUD COMPUTING EDUCATIONAL MODEL

Security Strategies

While schools see Cloud-computing as a way to gain efficiencies and improved performance, they must consider the challenges unique to each environment vs. a one-size-fits-all Cloud approach. Security is of critical importance and remains challenging as schools utilize wireless access. Approximately 33% of higher education identified potential security breaches as the biggest barrier to cloud adoption. Common components of security include browser, data, network, denial of service, location, and team monitoring (Cisco, 2012). In discussing security methods, or the tools and techniques used to prevent security issues, there are three main categories: 1. authentication and authorization, 2. prevention and resistance, and 3. detection and response (Baltzan, 2012).

Authentication and authorization deals primary with people, which is often the greatest source of security breaches. This includes people both inside the organization who may misuse or distribute their access, and people outside the organization and may include social engineering to learn access information. The danger can be diverse and can come from outsiders who are unauthorized to get the information, from insiders who are authorized users, or even from the patient himself with the misuse of technology (Baltzan, 2012).

Access threats can concern inappropriate access but can also involve modification of records which can be done by mistake, for fraud or malice. The access topic has two main perspectives: one regarding the role and the other one concerning the devices that are allowed to access the records, since both these aspects can have important implications. Disclosure threats, including data at rest and data in transit, can result in release of information due to allowance of data disclosure beyond what was intended by the act of sharing, motivated by financial gain, or to embarrass the individual (Kruger &Anschutz, 2013).

In summary, anyone with potential access information could pose a potential threat to the security of the information. Strong information security policies and security plans such as password and logon requirements can help prevent these types of issues. Authentication confirms the user's identity, whereas authorization provides a user with appropriate permissions to the environment. Smart cards, tokens, and biometrics are types of devices that improve authentication of the user and implemented in conjunction with passwords (Baltzan, 2012).

All the advantages that the information technology is bringing to the system come with multiple challenges regarding the data security and privacy. The traditional approach for data protection, the perimeter approach that described the internal network of an organization as a perimeter defined network, is nowadays obsolete due to the extended usage of mobile devices. Not only that the perimeter can no longer be defined, but the perimeter-only security ignores the inside threat that exists when an organization's staff or others with access to the organization's information maliciously or non-maliciously access or leak information (Kruger and Anschutz, 2013).

Prevention and resistance deals primarily with data and technologies including encryption, content filtering and firewalls. A firewall is a hardware or software device that analyzes information to detect unauthorized use. Content filtering prevents uses software to prevent emails and spam from being received or transmitted. Encryption requires a special key to decode the information and make the information readable; this is used for secure information such as financials or other protected information (Baltzan, 2012).

Detection and response deals primarily with attacks by analyzing suspicious activity such as password attempts or file access. Intrusion detection software will monitor and alert if patterns are detected and can even shut down part of the network as warranted (Baltzan, 2012). Organizational users need advanced tools similar to malicious users and the advanced tools being used to compromise the systems. Security Intelligence and event monitoring systems analyze network, user, application, and datasets to identify trends, behaviors, and incidents (LogRhythm, 2012).

For dataset inputs these include firewall, network, system, application, rules and other event logs. These logs are then normalized to a standard format for review. Once standardized, the data is analyzed for patterns, and alerts are generated for user review. Examples of analysis methods include aggregation and categorization of logs and events, time of events and directions, statistical log, source and host information, and top items within various categories for further detailed drill-down and analysis. Examples of analysis output include the ability to detect unusual application behaviors, unusual network connections, user behavior, network baseline deviations, and compromised credentials. Other methods analyze historical data to recreate scenarios for auditing, and also generate detailed and summary reporting output for security professionals, compliance officials, or other end users to review. Organizations are beginning to establish a security center in which monitoring and investigations occur (LogRhythm, 2012).

Physical, organizational, and technical safeguards must also be in place to ensure security. Physical safeguards include protecting facility access against unauthorized entry, as well as security workstations, transportation, and storage of media and information. However physical safeguards also apply well behind the walls of an organization. Organizational safeguards include consultant or contractor agreements, customer requirements, and policies and procedures (Iron Mountain, 2010).

Technical safeguards include unique user identification, automatics logoff, encryption, having a responsible person to authorize and verify passwords, strong passwords, locking accounts after invalid logins, and deactivating employee accounts after termination. From a mobile perspective endpoint access should also be verified and permitted or prevented from accessing the network, including monitoring and notification of an unauthorized device. Wireless threats should be detected and prevented through security policies and location tracking. Security compliance should be kept by administrators to verify personally owned and operated devices to ensure compliance (Iron Mountain, 2010).

Service-Oriented Architectures

Service-oriented architecture (SOA) is the design that permits the existence of the Cloud. The premise behind SOA is that all activity between devices are known as services which fit together in a standard way, ensuring the compatibility of the system. Cloud-computing can be categorized into three general categories of software as a service (SaaS), platform as a service (PaaS), and infrastructure as a service (IaaS). Examples of SaaS may include Office 365 for word-processing or productivity software or Apple iCloud for class scheduling to common calendar. In PaaS, vendor provides the platform components such as a computer, operating system and database, examples may include Azure, Oracle Database, or Amazon EC2. Student and administrative data can be stored on these systems and hosted remotely. IaaS consists of computing or data resources, educational organizations can utilize a service such Amazon's Simple Storage Service to increase data capacity on demand (Kroenke, 2014).

Web or Cloud applications are commonly deployed using a three-tier architecture of a server, database, and user. The user tier contains the devices and web browsers to access the web pages and display content. The server tier runs the applications and resources by managing traffic and sending and receiving web content. The database tier stores and retrieves data for the web applications and content (Kroenke, 2014).

Legal, Privacy, and Ethical Considerations

Student privacy is enforced by strict regulations and risk must be limited due to legal and compliance penalties (Cisco, 2012). With all the educational breaches the public is only notified of less than 50% of data breaches due to high risk of reputation damage. Often in other industries the cost can be tied directly to sales, though in education the costs are harder to quantify (O'Neil, 2014). Educational institutions have an obligation to protect privacy and provide ethical notification of individual impacts.

With educational data many key legal, privacy and ethical considerations are present. For example, who is legally liable for computer systems, and in cases where Cloud-computing systems are compromised, or employees or students have direct liability to loss of information. Privacy considerations include the notion that privacy is not guaranteed and public information need outweighs individual rights. In an educational setting a significant amount of personal information is collected on individuals, such as for financial aid purposes, medical insurance, grade reports, employment, and housing information. Mobile devices and remote connectivity to educational resources is also recorded and may track location and usage history (Sharda, 2014).

In an effort to address these key considerations, privacy preserving analytics may be utilized to help protect information. Organizations such as Google, Facebook, Twitter and others employ similar techniques to safeguard user information. The capability of utilizing analytics to de-identify and anonymize data helps minimize risk for misuse of information both from a privacy, legal, ethical and security standpoint (Sharda, 2014).

CONCLUSION

Trends and Future Directions

The trend is clear for educational use of Cloud-computing, and the desire to improve efficiencies and learning capabilities. However despite the capabilities, caution must be exercised to ensure proper security protocols are established within the given Cloud-computing architecture. Care must also be given to individuals to ensure their information is protected and to limit impacts to the individual as well as the educational institution. There are still many improvements that educational organizations can make with regard to security and privacy, though we are beginning to reach a turning point where the attention, resources, and strategic importance of Cloud-computing and the associated security and privacy considerations must be realized for educational organizations to be successful in the 21st century.

Many cloud computing trends have taken an enterprise-oriented direction. Many enterprise workloads have begun moving to the cloud, some technologies include AWS, Google Compute Engine, Microsoft Azure, and Rackspace. Containers are also being released to speed the deployment of application components allowing faster operationalization of cloud services. Price is another important trend that is continuing to drive low-cost infrastructures and applications. Companies such as Amazon, Azure, SoftLayer and Google will continue to maintain a top tier but also are competing with low-cost providers such as Digital Ocean now the 3rd largest hosting provider in the world based on a startup low-price model. Security is also coming to the forefront, and vendors will begin incorporating more software-defined security to protect the enterprise work and feed business intelligence to end users including surveillance agents to help in monitoring. Lastly the Internet of Things (IoT) and Big Data promise to make changes with increasing numbers of internet connected devices and increasing amounts of data generation. This promises to drive cloud computing vendors and capabilities (Babcock, 2014).

One of the latest trends that is also helping to drive cloud-computing is wearable tech such as smart watches and glasses. Shipments of 100 million wearable devices are estimated in 2014, with 485 million by 2018. To further educational learning opportunities these devices must also be incorporated into the classroom and a tremendous area of growth potential within an innovative classroom environment. With BYOT and cloud-computing in education, instead of demanding students turn off or put away technology devices, BYOT and cloud-computing captures the students use and interest of technology within an educational context (Woodside and Amiri, 2014).

The initial items released under wearable tech included watches and eye lenses, followed by fitness and health monitoring devices, then smart watches with an example being Samsung's Android powered Galaxy Gear smart watch. The smart watch allowed connections to a smartphone, health, and fitness patterns. The most recent notable entry was Google Glass, an eyewear with connection to a smartphone, GPS, voice activation, camera and video recording. These devices utilize demonstrated technology such as Wi-Fi, Bluetooth Smart, Near Field Communication and GPS (Woodside and Amiri, 2014).

When implementing a cloud computing and wearable technology strategy, a few of the best practices include development of a formal set of policies including governance, compliance, equitable access to technology, and acceptable usage. The second component includes device management and ensuring compatibility between all devices and development of the appropriate infrastructure to accommodate the increase in demand of traffic and user connectivity. The last area is security, and verifying all devices contain up to date anti-virus software and patches to prevent unauthorized access or loss of data (Woodside and Amiri, 2014).

Acceptable Usage: Existing policies must be reviewed to ensure they are compatible with cloud-computing and modified as appropriate. Individuals are still bound by acceptable use guidelines whether on personal or provided devices. Also device usage time can be restricted and not permitted at all times. Acceptable personal computing devices may include laptops, netbook, tablet, cell phone, smart phone, e-reader, iPad, iPod. Gaining devices with Internet access are not permitted (Woodside and Amiri, 2014).

Technical Support Levels: In most cases, cloud-computing support is the responsibility of the individual, and they are expected to be knowledgeable on the device's usage. The company or educational facility personnel to not provide direct support for devices. This is primarily due to the range of devices and resources necessary to provide complete support (Woodside and Amiri, 2014).

Network and Software Access: Individuals are provided with Internet access and wireless access which may be filtered, and also reduced for bandwidth. Individuals may download and install any additional applications, components, or storage as they see fit, granted any do not conflict with the ethics and acceptable use policies. This is viewed similar to public access in coffee shops, hotels, or other public access points permitted (Woodside and Amiri, 2014).

Technology Ethics and Acceptable Usage: For acceptable use, this is using technology as a privilege to improve the skills, knowledge and abilities students will require in the 21st century. One important component of cloud-computing is acceptable online behavior and safety (Woodside and Amiri, 2014).

Lost or Stolen Devices: Personal devices are used at one's own risk, loss or damage would need to be covered by the individual. Due to lack of secure storage, theft is often cited as a top reason students did not bring personal devices (Woodside and Amiri, 2014).

Staff Training: While in some cases instructors were not provided with direct training, after implementation recommends providing professional development to learn best practices and have an interactive community to share insights and expertise. An entrepreneurial spirit is encouraged along with experimentation to achieve the best results of cloud-computing and share those results with others to continuously improve (Woodside and Amiri, 2014).

Device Management: In order to ensure compatibility and consistent user experience across devices, organizations should utilize open standards. One such open web standard HTML5 is intended to allow cross-platform usage with a promise of write once and run anywhere, for example a Windows, Apple, or Android user could all access the same application across devices and platforms. This allows the developers to focus on the features and functionality rather than the conversion between platforms. Along with operating systems, screen sizes, resolutions, aspect rations, orientations, cameras, GPS, accelerometers and other features may vary by user and device. HTML5 is designed to accommodate these items through dynamically adapting to platforms variables and delivering a consistent experience. Currently the major browsers Internet Explorer, Firefox, Opera, Safari, and Chrome support HTML5 and CSS3, with full readiness varying (Woodside and Amiri, 2014).

Security: In order to ensure adequate security is in place for user of mobile devices, security methods must be employed. In discussing security methods, or the tools and techniques used to prevent security issues, there are three main categories: 1. authentication and authorization, 2. prevention and resistance, and 3. detection and response (Woodside and Amiri, 2014).

A recent initiative begun by The University of Texas at San Antonio is to create an Open Cloud Institute. This Institute would help develop degree programs in cloud computing along with working with industry partners. An initial investment has been made of $9 million, to include 4 endowed professors, 2 faculty researchers, and 10 graduate students. This combination aims to create a leadership role with key industry partners and recruit the top academics in the areas of cloud computing research (UTSA, 2015).

In upcoming years and decades many educators foresee a "virtual class" to include the nation's best teachers, professionally produced footage, TedTalks, interactive games, simulations, and formal real-time assessments for student results. Other innovations to classrooms include flipped learning, blending learning, student-centered learning, project-based learning, and self-organized learning. In flipped-learning the student learns fundamental knowledge outside of the classroom typically through videos, then once in the classroom works on projects, problems, and critical-thinking activities. In blended learning, students complete a portion of the course, this is projected to impact K-12 students to a greater extent with a projection of half of all high-school classes being offered online by 2019. In a recent TedTalk Sugata Mitra earned a $1 million award for a discussion around a school built in the cloud (Godsey, 2015).

REFERENCES

Anderson, J. (2015). Lincoln school district to become largest in state to provide computers to all students from elementary grades up. *OMaha World-Herald*.

Babcock, C. (2014). 9 Cloud Trends for 2015. *InformationWeek*.

Baltzan, P., & Phillips, A. (2012). *Business Driven Technology*. New York, NY: McGraw-Hill Irwin.

Castle, L. (2015). *Creating a New IT at Fairfield University*. Mobile Enterprise.

Cloud 101: Developing a Cloud-Computing Strategy for Higher Education. (2012). *Cisco*.

Daly, J. (2013). The State of Cloud Computing in Higher Education. *EdTechMagazine*.

Florence, L. (2015). *Universities struggle to effectively implement cloud-based technologies*. The Daily Texan.

Godsey, M. (2015). The Deconstruction of the K-12 Teacher. *The Atlantic*.

Herold, B. (2014). Kansas Suspends State Tests Following Cyber Attacks. *Education Week*.

HIPAA Best Practices Checklist: Best Practices That Go Beyond Compliance to Mitigate Risks. (2010). Iron Mountain.

IBM Cloud Services (Part I).(2015). Seeking Alpha.

Jackson, S. (2014) Data breach could affect 30,000 Iowa State students. *The Des Moines Register*.

Kroenke, D. M. (2013). *Experiencing MIS*. Boston, MA: Pearson.

Kruger, D., & Anschutz, T. (2013). A new approach in IT security. *Healthcare Financial Management Association*, *67*(2), 104–106. PMID:23413677

Lieberman, B. (2013). *Testing the Waters: Mobile and Cloud Computing for Education*. Intel.

Mehta, M. (2015). The Wisdom of the PaaS Crowd. *Forbes*.

O'Neil, M. (2014). Data Breaches Put a Dent in Colleges' Finances as Well as Reputations. *The Chronicle*.

Security Intelligence: Can "Big Data Analytics Overcome Our Blind Spots? (2012). LogRhythm.

Sharda, R., Dursun, D., & Turban, E. (2014). *Business Intelligence A Managerial Perspective on Analytics*. Boston, MA: Pearson.

UTSA announces creation of Open Cloud Institute. (2015The University of Texas at San Antonio.

Weaver, D. (2015). *Six Advantages of Cloud Computing in Education*. Technology in the Classroom.

Woodside, J. M. (2010). A BI 2.0 Application Architecture for Healthcare Data Mining Services in the Cloud. Proceedings of *The World Congress in Computer Science, Computer Engineering & Applied Computing - International Data Mining Conference*.

Woodside, J. M., Allabun, N., & Amiri, S. (2014). Bring Your Own Technology (BYOT) to Education. Proceedings of The 5th International Multi-Conference on Complexity. Informatics and Cybernetics.

Woodside, J. M., & Amiri, S. (2014). Bring Your Own Technology (BYOT) to Education. *Journal of Informatics, Systems, and Cybernetics, 12*(3), 38–40.

Zalaznick, M. (2013). *Cyberattacks on the rise in higher education*. University Business.

KEY TERMS AND DEFINITIONS

Classroom: A physical or virtual room where student education occurs.

Cloud Computing: Enables convenient on demand access to an elastic set of shared computing resources.

Education: The process of receiving or providing instruction and learning.

Ethics: A set of moral policies that governs behavior.

Legal: A set of law policies that governs behavior.

Privacy: The ability to have personal information used appropriately and without ongoing observation.

Security: A set of processes and techniques for ensuring appropriate access by individuals or systems in an effort to prevent harm.

This research was previously published in the Handbook of Research on Security Considerations in Cloud Computing edited by Kashif Munir, Mubarak S. Al-Mutairi, and Lawan A. Mohammed, pages 173-183, copyright year 2015 by Information Science Reference (an imprint of IGI Global).

Chapter 102

On Developing Fair and Orderly Cloud Markets:
QoS- and Security-Aware Optimization of Cloud Collaboration

Olga Wenge
Technische Universität Darmstadt, Germany

Dieter Schuller
Technische Universität Darmstadt, Germany

Christoph Rensing
Technische Universität Darmstadt, Germany

Ralf Steinmetz
Technische Universität Darmstadt, Germany

ABSTRACT

While cloud markets promise virtually unlimited resource supplies, standardized commodities and proper services, some providers may not be able to offer effectual physical capacity to serve large customers. A solution is cloud collaborations, in which multiple providers unite forces in order to conjointly offer capacities in the cloud markets. Supposably, both the Quality of Service and security properties of such collaborations will be determined by "the weakest link in the chain", therefore resulting in a trade-off between the monetary aggregates, cumulative capacity and the non-functional attributes of a cloud collaboration. Based on previous research, this paper examines efficient composition of cloud collaborations from the broker's perspective, considering Quality of Service and information security requirements of multiple cloud providers and users and presents an exact approach CCCP-EXA.KOM for building cloud collaborations. Furthermore, it proposes a Mixed Integer Programming-based heuristic optimization approach CCCP-PRIOSORT.KOM and provides its quantitative evaluation in comparison with prior optimal approach.

DOI: 10.4018/978-1-5225-8176-5.ch102

1. INTRODUCTION

Cloud markets promise to supply virtually unlimited capacities and services in a scalable, pay-as-you-go fashion (Buyya, R., Yeo, C., Venugopal, S., Broberg, J., & Brandic, I., 2009). Yet, specifically smaller providers may not be able to satisfy the resource and service demands of large customers on their own due to limited data center capacity and, consequently, limited range of services. A solution lies in cloud collaborations within cloud markets, i.e., the cooperation of multiple providers to aggregate their resources and conjointly satisfy user's demands. Supposably, such cloud collaborations have both Quality of Service (QoS) and information security impacts: as a user may potentially be served by any provider within a collaboration, the aggregated non-functional service attributes - e.g., availability, latency, security protection level, data center location or tiers – will be determined by "the weakest link in the chain", i.e., by a provider with the lowest guarantees.

Take the example of two providers: one provider guarantees 99.5% of availability and another provider guarantees only 99%. If these providers aggregate their capacities and related non-functional guarantees to build collaboration, the availability guarantees will be determined by the worst one - 99%.

Consideration of country-specific and industry-specific data privacy laws and regulations is another concern by building cloud collaborations within cloud markets. Since providers can reside in different jurisdictions (the European Union, Russia, Singapore, or the United States), where data privacy laws and data classification substantially differ (Carroll, M., van der Merwe, A., & Kotzé, P., 2011; Zhou, M., Zhang, R., Xie, W., Qian, W., & Zhou, A., 2010). Also regulatory requirements for banking, medical and healthcare institutions are stricter and harder with respect to confidentiality, integrity and availability of data in comparison with other public enterprises or business areas without confidential data (Ackermann, T., Widjaja, T., Benlian, A., & Buxmann, P., 2012). Therefore, the fulfillment of such requirements may not be achieved once multiple cloud providers enter cloud collaborations.

In our previous research (Wenge, O., Lampe, U., Müller, A., & Schaarschmidt, R., 2014; Wenge, O., Siebenhaar, M., Lampe, U., Schuller, D., & Steinmetz, R., 2012; Wenge, O., Lampe, U., & Steinmetz, R., 2014), we examined security risks and concerns of cloud computing with the focus on multi-clouds and cloud brokerage. We identified that multi-clouds are still very heterogeneous and the lack of security standards between cloud providers still pose obstacles in their cooperation and in cloud services exchange. Therefore, the role of the cloud broker is of growing interest. The broker's function is not trivial – he/she should bring cloud providers and cloud users together in order to satisfy their functional and non-functional requirements. Due to the mentioned lack of standards, cloud brokerage is becoming more complex, especially if very fine-grained security parameters and the entire security landscape must be considered.

Based on this scenario and our previous research, we examine the Cloud Collaboration Composition Problem (CCCP) in the work at hand. Our focus is on a broker within the cloud market, who aims *to maximize his/her profit* through the composition of cloud collaborations from a set of providers and assignment of users to these collaborations. In that assignment, QoS and security requirements, i.e., non-functional attributes, should also be considered and fulfilled. This work extends the previously introduced CCCP problem and its exact optimization solution approach with a heuristic approach that improves the computational time in the context of cloud markets.

The remainder of this paper is structured as follows: In Section 2, we give an overview of cloud markets and related regulations that must be considered by trading with cloud products. Section 3 describes information security focus within cloud markets and within cloud collaborations. Section 4 explains the role of a cloud broker in cloud markets. In Section 5, we describe the Cloud Collaboration Composition Problem (CCCP) and the formal optimization model. Based on this, the subsequent Section 6 briefly presents an exact optimization approach, called CCCP-EXA.KOM. Section 7 includes evaluation results of this exact approach. Section 8 introduces a heuristic approach, called CCCP-PRIOSORT.KOM, which is quantitatively evaluated and compared with the previous results in Section 9. Section 10 gives an overview of related work, and Section 11 concludes the paper with a summary and an outlook.

2. FAIR AND ORDERLY CLOUD MARKETS

Economic science studies allocation and usage of diverse resources. Some resources allocation approaches are managed by the price systems: low prices are very attractive for consumers, high prices provoke forced savings; high salaries are attractive for employees, low benefits encourage to innovations. But by many instances, the usage of only a price system as a market regulator is not sufficient. There are other aspects that must be considered as well, e.g., legal, ethical, and security requirements.

Furthermore, there are many markets where the price system operates, but the traditional assumption of perfect competition is not even approximately satisfied. In particular, many goods are indivisible and heterogeneous, whereby the market for each type of goods becomes very thin. How these thin markets allocate resources depends on the institutions that govern trading and transactions.

The current cloud market environments consist of heterogeneous clouds: cloud providers who sell services, cloud users who buy services, and cloud brokers who help to find the perfect match for their clients. In other words, cloud markets present the aggregate of possible buyers and sellers of cloud services and cloud resources and the transactions between them (Garg, S.K., Vecchiola, C., & Buyya, R., 2011). But the current cloud markets are not organized and supervised on the desired level, e.g., in comparison to financial or energy markets (Garg, S.K., Versteeg, S., & Buyyaa, R., 2013; Rahimi, A.F., & Sheffrin, A.Y., 2003).

The financial and energy markets are supervised by exchanges or other organizations that facilitate and oversee the trade, using *physical locations* (e.g., New York Stock Exchange (NYSE), Deutsche Börse (German Stock Exchange in Frankfurt), or European Energy Exchange (EEX) in Leipzig), or *electronic systems* (e.g., NASDAQ (National Association of Securities Dealers Automated Quotations), XETRA (Xchange Electronic Trading)).

These are also regulated by different national and international authorities and laws listed in Table 1. These laws demand compliance with data protection requirements and anti-money laundering (AML) policies in all circumstances with respect to trading (Wenge, O., Lampe, U., Müller, A., & Schaarschmidt, R., 2014; Wenge, O., Siebenhaar, M., Lampe, U., Schuller, D., & Steinmetz, R., 2012; Lampe, U., Wenge, O., Müller, A., & Schaarschmidt, R., 2012).

Lack of control or supervision is one of main concerns in cloud markets. The development of market supervision techniques and approaches for the current cloud marketplaces, to provide *a fair and orderly cloud market* – a market in which supply and demand for a product are roughly equal, is still in its embryonic stage. The trading of cloud resources within predefined cloud collaborations can be seen as *an interim solution* to provide desired supervision and information security governance (Guitart, J., & Torres, J., 2010; Gomes, E., Vo, Q.B., & Kowalczyk, R., 2012). Two main principles in the market design

Table 1. International market regulators and regulations

Law / Authority /Standard	Validity Area
German Federal Data Protection Act (GFDPA)	*effective in Germany*
Data Protection Directive (DPD)	*effective in the European Union (EU)*
the Privacy Act	*effective in the United States of America (USA)*
Conventions of the Organisation for Economic Co-operation and Development (OECD)	*effective in 34 countries*
Safe Harbor Principles	*effective for the USA-EU contracts*
the Uniting and Strengthening America by Providing Appropriate Tools Required to Intercept and Obstruct Terrorism Act (USA Patriot Act)	*effective in the USA*
Sarbanes-Oxley Act (SOX)	*effective for all enterprises that trade in the USA securities markets*
Directive 2006/43/EG (EuroSOX)	*effective for all enterprises that trade in the EU securities markets*
Basel Accords	*effective in 20 countries*
IT Fundamental Right	*effective in Germany*
the Personal Information Protection and Electronic Documents Act (PIPEDA)	*effective in Canada*
the Monetary Authority of Singapore (MAS)	*effective in Singapore and Asian-Pacific region*
Bank secrecy acts	*effective between banks and customers*
United States Code (USC)	*effective in the USA*
ISO Standards	*effective globally*
German Federal Financial Supervisory Authority (GFFSA)	*effective in Germany*
German Banking Act (GBA)	*effective in Germany*
Office of the Comptroller of the Currency (OCC)	*effective in the USA*
Federal Financial Institutions Examination Council – FFIEC	*effective in the USA*
Statement on Auditing Standards No. 70 (SAS-70)	*effective in the USA*
Binding Corporate Rules (BCRs)	*effective in the EU*
Certified Information Systems Security Professional Principles (CISSP)	*recommended globally*
Certified Information Systems Auditor Principles (CISA)	*recommended globally*
Board of Governors of the Federal Reserve System (BGFRS)	*effective in the USA*
Local territorial laws	*effective locally*

theory for the establishing of any fair and orderly market are *stability* and *incentive compatibility*. Both principles are derived from *the cooperative* and *non-cooperative game theory* and *the stable marriage problem* and found a very wide application in the world of economics (Shapley, L.S., 1955; Knuth D.E., 1996; Roth, A.E., 2002; Roth, A.E., Sönmez, T., & Ünver, M.U., 2005; Roth, A.E., 2008).

Stability encourages groups of to voluntarily participate in the market. Incentive compatibility discourages strategic manipulation of the market. The main principle of the cooperative game theory is building of coalitions between individuals (or players, or traders, or cloud providers in a market) who are eager to cooperate with each other. A game in coalitional form with *transferable utility* specifies, for each coalition S its worth $v(S)$. This worth is an economic *surplus* (a sum of money) that coalition S can generate using its own resources. If coalition S forms, then its members can split the surplus $v(S)$ in any way they want, and each member's utility equals his/her share of the surplus. This feature is called *transferable utility*. The function v is called *the characteristic function*. Furthermore, the cooperative game theory studies the incentives of individuals to form such coalitions under consideration that any potential conflicts of interest within a coalition can be solved by binding agreements. These agreements induce the coalition members to maximize the surplus (or revenue) of the coalition. In games with transferable utility, it is assumed that the individuals can freely transfer utility among themselves. The idea of stability corresponds to the idea of *Nash equilibrium* in non-cooperative game theory. In non-cooperative game theory, a Nash equilibrium is a situation such that no individual can deviate and make herself better. In cooperative game theory, a stable location is a situation such that no coalition can deviate and make its members better. That is why stability formalizes an important aspect of idealized frictionless marketplaces.

A coalition building between game players in the cooperative game theory with the purpose of increasing their benefit appears to be very similar to our idea of building cloud collaborations. Stability is one of the important drivers for involving new market participants and building collaborations. Incentive compatibility is necessary to prevent manipulations in the market and within cloud collaborations.

In our work we also assume that each cloud provider and each cloud user has his/her requirements (preferences) that must be fulfilled in any trading and transaction. For convenience, we assume that these requirements are strict. To fulfill these requirements a stable matching between market participants is inevitable. The matching is unacceptable to a market participant (provider or user) if it worse than to remain unmatched. We define the matching as stable, if all collaborations between cloud providers and cloud users are composed in the way they bring the most profit and all requirements are matched acceptably.

In (Wenge, O., Siebenhaar, M., Lampe, U., Schuller, D., & Steinmetz, R., 2012) we identified three types of cloud collaborations with respect to the security critical areas: federated collaborations, loosely-coupled collaborations and ad hoc collaborations. Security requirements, relevant for cloud partners within collaboration types can be used as *admission criteria* for cloud recourses trading within those collaboration types.

Federated collaborations assume the usage of a so-called *metapolicy*, which includes all policies of all collaborative clouds. This metapolicy reduces the possibility of the occurrence of security incidents and breaches, as all security configurations and controls are fully pre-agreed between collaborative partners.

Loosely-coupled collaborations are more flexible and cover smaller cloud regional environments, e.g., the EU, the USA, Canada; or industry specific, e.g., banks or medical institutions. In this case, country or industry specific regulations, or *service level agreements* (SLAs) can be used as a basis for their security policies.

Ad hoc collaborations do not presume any kind of pre-agreed security policies or SLAs, the signing of which can be very time-consuming and can hamper the dynamic of data transfer and service delivery. Ad hoc collaborations are the most critical ones and cannot be performed without a proper supervision and information security governance over them in the form of *a trusted security entity* (e.g., cloud broker, identity broker, etc.).

3. INFORMATION SECURITY GOVERNANCE IN CLOUD MARKETS

Information security issues are very critical in cloud computing (Kretzschmar, M., & Golling, M., 2011). Many aspects must be examined concerning security risks in the cloud paradigm: legal risks, data privacy and data protection risks, users' and providers' security levels, right to audit and information security governance processes.

Information Security (IS) governance is a significant part of corporate governance in an enterprise and strives towards the understanding of the criticality of information security, endorsing the development and implementation of security programs and their alignment with business strategy. IS governance also takes the responsibility for performance management, reporting and risk management.

In cloud computing the role of IS governance has become enormously important, as enterprises deal with off-premise services with the involvement of sometimes diverse vendors and non-enterprise employees, whose compliance and activity must be monitored and reported (Bernsmed, K., Jaatun, M.G, Meland, P.H., & Undheim, A., 2011; Yang, D., 2011). To the best of our knowledge, there are three security mechanisms to provide security governance over cloud providers: cloud certifications, cloud risk assessments, and trusted security entities.

Cloud certification sounds very promising and gives a certain sense of trust. The most cloud certificates are based on best practices security frameworks and already existing security standards, such as ISO (International Organization for Standardization), NIST (National Institute of Standards and Technology), CSA (Cloud Security Alliance) and FISMA (Federal Information Security Management Act). The main disadvantage of cloud certification is its *generality*. These certificates are not always sufficient for peculiar cases (e.g., for critical data, banking transactions, country laws) and should be adapted or extended with other security governance mechanisms (e.g., risk assessments and audit) (Bernsmed, K., Jaatun, M.G, Meland, P.H., & Undheim, A., 2011; Yang, D., 2011).

Cloud risk assessments are more granular and can be used with respect to different industries (banking, insurance, healthcare). Cloud risk assessments are also based on the existing risk assessments and are extended with specific vendor governance controls for availability, auditing and controlling. These risk assessments are provided by ISO, CSA, BSI (Bundesamt für Sicherheit in der Informationstechnik, Federal Office of Information Security in Germany), ENISA (European Network and Information Security Agency), COBIT (Control Objectives for Information and Related Technology), ISACA (Information Systems Audit and Control Association), Basel Accords, and SOx (Sarbanes-Oxley Act). The risk assessment process is very time-consuming and in case of risk acceptance procedures or a necessary risk remediation can be followed by numerous complex bilateral agreements (Papish, M., 2012; Bernstein, D., & Vij, D., 2012).

A trusted security entity concept is more dynamic, but currently does not cover all security aspects of cloud computing. It is mostly focused on identity and access management, ignoring infrastructure, network, and application security. The existing solutions, especially for ad hoc collaborations, do not cover the whole aspects of cloud security or need sufficient evidence for their implementation, e.g., monitoring and logging tools in place, or regular auditing (Wood, K., & Anderson, M., 2011; Ates, M., Ravet, S., Ahmat, A., & Fayolle, J., 2011; Goyal, P., 2011; He., Y.H., Bin, W., Xiao, X.L., & Jing, M.X., 2010; Yang, D., 2011).

Therefore, the role of a cloud broker, as a mediator, who is responsible for bringing cloud market actors together with respect to their requirements, is very important and in our research, we aim at the development of an efficient QoS- and security-aware brokerage model.

4. THE ROLE OF A CLOUD BROKER IN CLOUD COLLABORATIONS

Many environments, and especially IT environments, are still far from the perfectly competitive benchmark, as they are still very heterogeneous and without precisely specified rules that can govern trade. In such markets, the participants must be appropriately matched in order to trade with each other, i.e., a role of a broker, who provides this matching is very important and mandatory, if a cloud market must comply with market design principles. Cloud broker is also seen as inevitable market actor in the NIST (National Institute of Standards and Technology) cloud computing reference architecture (Liu, F., Tong, J., Mao, J., Bohn, R., Messina, J., Badger, L., & Leaf, D., 2011) (Figure 1).

According to this NIST conceptual reference model, the cloud broker's function consists in service intermediation, service aggregation, and service arbitrage. The NIST model defines cloud auditor as a separate market actor, who provides auditing of fulfillment of security, data privacy and QoS requirements. In our work, we unite cloud broker's and cloud auditor's functions, as they defined by NIST, and examine our cloud broker within cloud markets, who is responsible for bringing cloud market participants together under consideration of their requirements and who is also responsible for the supervision of compliance to related controls and laws during the complete trading process.

Today's cloud environments are built up of heterogeneous landscapes of independent clouds. The heterogeneity of clouds, as a consequence of still nonexistent technology, security and audit standards, presents a hurdle for a proper collaboration between clouds, necessary for the building of the cloud ecosystem and cloud marketplaces (Kretzschmar, M., & Golling, M., 2011; Corporation Essvale Corporation Limited, 2008).

The reasons for cloud collaborations can be very different: enterprise acquisitions, storage and compute power extensions, disaster recovery plans, sub-contracting and service outsourcing, the necessity for a wider spectrum of services, etc. Such cloud collaborations bring cloud providers further advantages. Besides the eco-efficiency, due to shared usage of data centers and technologies (Guitart, J., & Torres,

Figure 1. The NIST conceptual reference model

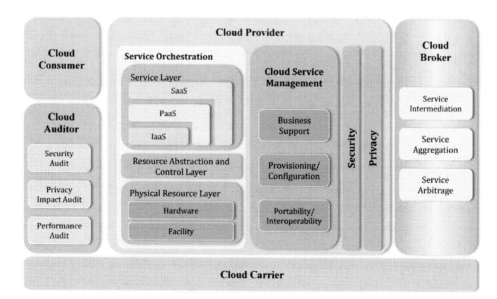

J., 2010), a better scalability and cost reduction can be achieved by the ad hoc selling of free resources and buying of additional external resources. This exchange of cloud resources forms the basis of the cloud brokerage service model (Uttam Kumar, T., & Wache, H., 2010).

Cloud brokerage enables cloud providers to find an optimally suitable match for each other, i.e., to find a collaborative partner that meets all requirements of intended cloud collaboration. These requirements may include business aspects (pricing, timelines), functional and non-functional technical aspects (compatibility, interoperability, availability), and of course non-functional legal and security aspects (level of data protection, security measures, compliance with different industrial regulations, etc.) (Uttam Kumar, T., & Wache, H., 2010; Lampe, U., Wenge, O., Müller, A., & Schaarschmidt, R., 2012; Siebenhaar, M., Wenge, O., Hans, R., Tercan H., & Steinmetz, R., 2013).

The cloud broker is the leading actor in the cloud brokerage service model, and acts as a mediator between cloud service providers and cloud service consumers, providing matchmaking, monitoring and governance of cloud collaborations (Gomes, E., Vo, Q.B., & Kowalczyk, R., 2012).

The matchmaking of security and legal requirements and especially monitoring of their fulfillment during the cloud collaboration is not trivial. The security risks tend to accelerate by entering cloud collaborations within cloud marketplaces, since collaborative partners may have different implemented security policies and standards. Therefore, two main requirements must be met to provide secure and compliant cloud collaboration - the cloud broker must perform an optimally reliable security risk assessment prior to the collaboration, or on-demand; and the cloud broker must provide the security governance during the collaboration.

The security risk assessments of cloud providers are widely discussed in the recent research, but, to the best of our knowledge, these assessments are still very time-consuming and cannot be applied to ad hoc cloud collaborations (Schnjakin, M., Alnemr, R., & Meinel, C., 2010).

5. CLOUD COLLABORATION COMPOSITION PROBLEM

As mentioned before in our work, we take the perspective of a cloud broker, who acts within a cloud market and unites cloud providers to build cloud collaborations and provides assignment of cloud users to these collaborations. So, the cloud market consists of a set of cloud providers and a set of users, formally denoted as $P = \left\{1,2,...,P^{\#}\right\}$ and $U = \left\{1,2,...,U\right\}$, respectively. Each user $u \in U$ exhibits a certain resource demand of $RD_u \in \mathbb{R}^+$ units, for which he/she is willing to pay a total of $M_u^+ \in \mathbb{R}^+$ monetary units. Furthermore, each cloud provider $p \in P$ is able to provide a resource supply of $RS_p \in \mathbb{R}^+$ units at a total cost of $M_p^- \in \mathbb{R}^+$.

QoS and security constraints, which determine requirements by consumption and provision of services, we define by the common term of non-functional constraints. Specifically, we distinguish two sets, $A = \left\{1,2,...,A^{\#}\right\}$ and $\hat{A} = \left\{1,2,...,\hat{A}^{\#}\right\}$, of quantitative and qualitative non-functional attributes. Quantitative attributes represent numerical properties, e.g., availability or latency. Qualitative attributes correspond to nominal properties, e.g., applied encryption technology, data center location, and adherence to a certain industry-specific security policy or country-specific data privacy protection controls. The cloud providers make certain guarantees with respect to the non-functional attributes. For each quantitative attribute $a \in A$, the value guaranteed by provider $p \in P$ is denoted as $AG_{p,a} \in \mathbb{R}$ For each qualitative attribute $\hat{a} \in \hat{A}$, the corresponding information is given by $\hat{A}G_{p,\hat{a}} \in \{0,1\}$. The cloud users specify also certain requirements concerning their non-functional attributes. With respect to each quantitative attribute $a \in A$, the value required by user $u \in U$ is denoted as $AR_{u,a} \in \mathbb{R}$. Likewise, $\hat{A}R_{u,\hat{a}} \in \{0,1\}$ denotes the requirement for each qualitative attribute $\hat{a} \in \hat{A}$, i.e., indicates whether this attribute is mandatory or not.

The objective of the broker is the composition of cloud collaborations, consisting of multiple cloud providers, and subsequently assigning users to them. In that process, all defined constraints must be fulfilled and *the profit maximization*, i.e., the difference between the revenue from the served cloud users and the spending on the incorporated cloud providers, should be achieved. A tangible, simplified example for a CCCP instance is provided in Figure 2. The instance exhibits four users and providers with different resource demands - supplies and non-functional requirements - guarantees, respectively. In the example, providers P_2 and P_4 form a collaboration, which enables them to conjointly serve users U_1 and U_2 under the given constraints. Both providers substantially profit from the collaboration, since their combined resource supply permits to serve larger customers and allows to achieve a higher degree of resource utilization.

6. EXACT OPTIMIZATION APPROACH CCCP-EXA.KOM

Based on the notations that were introduced in the previous section, the Cloud Collaboration Composition Problem (CCCP) can be transformed into an optimization model. The result is given in Model 1 and will be explained in the following.

Figure 2. Tangible example of a CCCP instance

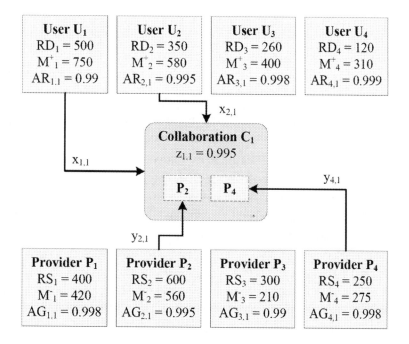

Model 1. Cloud collaboration composition problem

```
Objective function
```

(1) Maximize Profit $(x, y, y', z, z) =$

$$\sum_{u \in U, c \in C} x_{u,c} \times M_u^+ - \sum_{p \in P, c \in C} y_{p,c} \times M_p^-$$

```
so that
```

(2) $\sum_{c \in C} x_{u,c} \leq 1 \ \forall u \in U$

(3) $\sum_{c \in C} y_{p,c} \leq 1 \ \forall p \in P$

(4) $y_{p,c} + y'_{p,c} = 1 \ \forall p \in P, \forall c \in C$

(5) $\sum_{u \in U} x_{u,c} \times RD_u \leq \sum_{p \in P} y_{p,c} \times RS_p \ \forall c \in C$

(6) $z_{a,c} \leq y_{p,c} \times AG_{p,a} + y'_{p,c} \times max_{p \in P}\left(AG_{p,a}\right)$

   $\forall p \in P, \forall c \in C, \forall a \in A$

(7) $\hat{z}_{\hat{a},c} \leq y_{p,c} \times \hat{A}G_{p,\hat{a}} + y'_{p,c}$

   $\forall p \in P, \forall c \in C, \forall \hat{a} \in \hat{A}$

(8) $z_{a,c} \geq x_{u,c} \times AR_{u,a} \ \forall u \in U, \forall c \in C, \forall a \in A$

(9) $\hat{z}_{\hat{a},c} \geq x_{u,c} \times \hat{A}R_{u,\hat{a}} \ \forall u \in U, \forall c \in C, \forall \hat{a} \in \hat{A}$

(10) $C = \left\{1,2,\ldots,\min(P^\#,U^\#)\right\}$

(11) $x_{u,c} \in \left\{0,1\right\} \ and \ y_{p,c} \in \left\{0,1\right\} \forall u \in U, \forall p \in P, \forall c \in C$

(12) $y'_{p,c} \in \left\{0,1\right\} \ and \ z_{a,c} \in \mathbb{R} \ and \ \hat{z}_{\hat{a},c} \in \left\{0,1\right\}$

   $\forall p \in P, \forall a \in A, \forall \hat{a} \in \hat{A}, \forall c \in C$

To start with $x_{u,c}$, and $y_{p,c}$ are the main decision variables in the model (cf. Equation 11). They are defined as binary and indicate whether user u or provider p, respectively, has been assigned to collaboration c or not. As additional axillary decision variables, we introduce $y'_{p,c}$, which are also binary and serve as complement to $y_{p,c}$, hence indicating the non-assignment of a provider p to a collaboration c. Furthermore, $z_{a,c}$ and $\hat{z}_{\hat{a},c}$ are specified (cf. Equation 12). They are defined as real and binary, respectively, and represent the cumulative value of the non-functional property a or $\hat{a}$, respectively, for collaboration c. The variables x and y are referred to as main decision variables, since they have a direct impact on the objective function. In contrast, y', z, and $\hat{z}$ only have an indirect influence. The monetary objective consists in profit maximization (cf. Equation 1).

That is, the difference between the revenue from the served cloud users and the spending on the used cloud providers should be maximized, depending on the values of the decision variables. Equations 2 and 3 make sure that each user and provider is assigned to not more than one collaboration. Thus, the broker may opt to not satisfy certain users' demands, but also to not exploit cloud providers as part of a collaboration. Equitation 5 does not allow resource demand to exceed the resource supply. Equation 4 determines the inverse variable y' for each decision variable $y_{p,c}$. This definition is used in the following two Equations 6 and 7. They determine the cumulative non-functional values for quantitative and qualitative attributes, respectively. Both equations are formulated such that quantitative properties are given by the "worst" value among all providers in a certain collaboration, i.e., the "weakest link in the chain". Equations 8 and 9 make sure that users can only be assigned to such collaborations that make sufficient non-functional guarantees, given the users' specific non-functional requirements.

Lastly, Equation 1 defines a set of potential cloud collaborations. The underlying notion for the given definition is that no user or provider will be assigned to more than one collaboration (recall Equations 2 and 3). Hence, the maximum number of collaborations is given by the number of users or providers, whichever is lower.

We implemented the given model and evaluated the optimal approach in order to obtain an exact (i.e., profit maximal) solution. We used a Mixed Integer Program (MIP), i.e., a special form of Linear Program (LP) that features both integer (in this case, binary) and natural decision variables, and a branch-and-bound off-the-shelf optimization algorithms (Hillier, F., & Lieberman, G., 2005). The evaluation results are presented in the next section.

7. EVALUATION OF CCCP-EXA.KOM

To assess the practical applicability of our proposed approach CCCP-EXA.KOM, we have prototypically implemented it in Java 7. In order to transfer Model 1 into a programmatic representation, we use the free JavaILP framework. While this potentially permits for the application of different backend solver frameworks, we have selected the commercial IBM ILOG CPLEX framework as default due to its favorable performance (Meindl, B., & Templ, M., 2012) and its popularity in related research, e.g., (Hans, R., Lampe, U., & Steinmetz, R., 2013; Mashayekhy, L., & Grosu, D., 2012).

7.1. Evaluation Setup and Procedure

The main objective of our evaluation is to assess the required computation time of CCCP-EXA.KOM for different problem sizes. This allows us to judge the applicability of the proposed approach under practical conditions, where time constraints in the decision process play an important role. Thus, formally, we regard computation time as the dependent variable of our evaluation.

As independent variables, we include the number of considered users and providers, i.e., $U^{\#}$ and $P^{\#}$. In contrast, the number of quantitative and qualitative non-functional attributes were fixed ($A^{\#} = 1$ and $\hat{A}^{\#} = 1$); hence, they constitute controlled variables. This is justified by two aspects: First, these variables are likely also predefined in practice. Second, they do not have an impact on the number of decision variables and hence, the size of the solution space. Each specific combination of $U^{\#}$ and $P^{\#}$ results in a test case. For each test case, we created 100 specific CCCP instances with the according dimensions.

The parameter values or distributions that were used in the problem generation process are summarized in Table 2. The specifications of the nonfunctional parameters are based on the notion that the sole quantitative and qualitative attribute represent availability (a QoS aspect) and data center location in the European Union (a security aspect), respectively. Furthermore, monetary parameters were set such that higher availability results in quickly increasing values, based on the observation that each additional "nine" in the availability figure results in doubled cost (Durkee, D., 2010). In contrast, an EU data center location only leads to a moderate increase of 10%, which closely corresponds to the price difference observed for Eastern U.S. and Ireland-located Amazon EC2 VM instances (Amazon Web Services, Inc., 2013).

Following the generation, we computed a solution to each problem instance using our prototypical implementation of CCCP-EXA.KOM. In that process, we imposed a timeout of 300 seconds (i.e., five minutes) per problem instance. Based on the resulting sample of computation times for the successfully solved problems, we computed the mean computation time, as well as the 95% confidence interval.

The evaluation was conducted on a desktop computer, equipped with an Intel Core 2 Duo E7500 processor and 4 GB of memory, operating under the 64-bit edition of Microsoft Windows 7.

7.2. Evaluation Results and Discussion

The results of our evaluation, i.e., the observed mean computation times per test case, are graphically illustrated in Figure 3. As can be clearly seen, the computation times quickly increase with the problem size, i.e., the considered number of users and providers. The effect is less pronounced for the smallest two problem classes (with $U^{\#} \leq 6$ and $P^{\#} \leq 9$); in fact, for these two test cases, there is no statistically significant difference in mean computation time observable at the 95% confidence level. In absolute terms, we already find absolute computation times in the order of magnitude of one-hundred seconds

Table 2. Parameter values and distributions used in the problem instance generation. abbreviations: uni – Uniform distribution; ber – Bernoulli distribution.

Parameter	Value/Distribution
$AR_{1,u}$	*Uni(0.99, 0.9995)*
$\hat{A}R_{1,u}$	*Ber(0.5)*
$AG_{1,p}$	*Uni(0.995, 0.9995)*
$\hat{A}G_{1,p}$	*Ber(0.5)*
RD_{u}	*Uni(1000, 5000)*
RS_{p}	*Uni(1000, 5000)*
M_{u}^{+}	$\alpha_{u} \times RD_{u} \times \log_{10}\left(1 - AR_{1,u}\right)^{2} \times (1.1^{\hat{A}R_{1,u}})$
M_{p}^{-}	$\beta_{p} \times RS_{p} \times \log_{10}\left(1 - AG_{1,p}\right)^{2} \times (1.1^{\hat{A}G_{1,p}}).$
α_{u}	*Uni(1.5, 1.75)*
β_{p}	*Uni(1.0, 1.25)*

Figure 3. Evaluation results, i.e., observed mean computation times (with 95% confidence intervals) for CCCP-EXA.KOM by test case. Please note the logarithmic scaling of the ordinate.

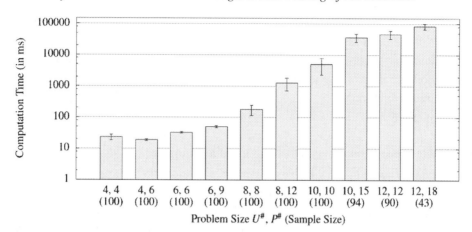

and one second respectively for the medium-sized test cases with $U^\# \leq 8$. For these test cases, increasing the number of providers increases the computation time by a factor of approximately ten already.

For the four largest test cases (with $U^\# \geq 10$ and $P^\# \geq 10$), the absolute computation times reach the order of magnitude of seconds and ten seconds. All observed increases are statistically significant at the 95% confidence level. In addition, the ratio of solved problem instances sharply drops with growing problem size. This effect is most notable for the largest problem class that involves 12 users and 18 providers, where only 43% of the 100 problem instances could be solved within the timeout period of five minutes. Given that the considered problem dimensions are still relatively small in the context of a large cloud market, it can be concluded that the practical applicability of the proposed optimization approach CCCP-EXA. KOM is rather limited.

As it has already been explained before, a broker will likely have to decide on the composition of collaborations under rigid time constraints, since users likely require resources at short notice. Hence, an important future challenge consists in the development of appropriate heuristics, which permit to trade reductions in computation time against small degradations in broker profit, and are consequently applicable to practically relevant, large-scale problem instances. In that context – apart from its potential application to small-scale problem instances – CCCP-EXA.KOM can serve as a valuable performance benchmark and we present our heuristic approach CCCP-PRIOSORT.KOM in the next section.

8. HEURISTIC SOLUTION APPROACH CCCP-PRIOSORT.KOM

Heuristic optimization algorithms (heuristics for short) seek good feasible solutions to optimization problems in circumstances where the complexity of the problem or the limited time available for its solution does not allow exact solution. The formal intractability, in the sense of NP-hardness (Jonson, D.S., 2012), of many commonly encountered optimization problems and the growing use of real-time control have made the development of heuristics a major area within operations research.

Unlike exact algorithms, where time-efficiency is the main measure of success, there are two burning issues in evaluating heuristics: how fast can solutions be obtained and how close do they come to being optimal.

As discovered in the previous section, the computation time of the proposed CCCP exact solution grows in the dependence on the number of cloud market participants and in the worst case it is exponential. In the following, we propose a heuristic optimization approach CCCP-PRIOSORT.KOM with the improved computation time.

CCCP-PRIOSORT.KOM consists of two phases:

Phase 1: Presorting of cloud providers and cloud users according to the quotients $Q_u = M_u^+ / RD_u$ and $Q_p = M_p^- / RS_p$ to provide priority lists. Thereby, the quotients Q_u are sorted in ascending order and the quotients p are sorted in descending order.

Phase 2: Composition of cloud collaborations and assignment of cloud users with the help of the greedy principle for multi-dimensional knapsack problem (Akay, Y., Li, H., &Xu, S.H., 2007).

The building of the priority lists is used as a basis for the subsequent assignment algorithm to determine in which order the cloud provider could be assigned to a collaboration; respectively, to determine which cloud users to which cloud collaboration could be assigned in the cloud market according to their resources demand. The objective of this assignment is again the profit maximization for a broker, i.e., maximization of the difference between revenue and cost.

8.1. Phase 1: Presorting

Priority list for cloud users consists of the quotients $Q_u = M_u^+ / RD_u$ (willingness to pay / resources demand) that determine willingnesses to pay for a demanded resource unit and are sorted in the ascending order, as due to the objective function, the cloud user with the best willingness to pay will be selected first.

Priority list for cloud providers consists of the quotients $Q_p = M_p^- / RS_p$ (revenue / resources supply) that determine prices for the bought resource unit and are sorted in the descending order. According to the objective function (namely, profit maximization) the cheapest cloud provider will be selected first to build cloud collaboration.

8.2. Phase 2: Assignment

Further, we apply the assignment algorithm to the priority lists, similar to the application of greedy principle to solve a multi-dimensional knapsack problem (Akay, Y., Li, H., & Xu, S.H., 2007), where the units (in our case - users) in knapsacks (in our case - cloud collaborations) are filled according to their values and the maximal weight limits (in our case - aggregated capacities).

Step 1: Search cycles. First, we search in the quotient priority lists (as our solution area) using two cycles - a search cycle in the provider list and a search cycle in the user list. We start with the cheapest cloud provider and insert the second-cheapest cloud provider to build a cloud collaboration. Then we search in the cloud user quotient priority list and insert cloud users with the best willingness to pay first, concerning the aggregated maximal capacity of cloud providers. The search runs forward with the next participants. In this step, the fulfillment and matching of non-functional requirements are not yet considered.

Step 2: Diversification. The next step in the algorithm is the diversification in cloud collaborations. As during the search cycles the cheapest cloud providers were selected firstly, it is in all probability that they also have the worst non-functional guarantees. For this reason, the probability of a successful assignment of cloud users to collaboration is very low. To avoid this side-effect and support diversification, we provide a rotation in the cloud providers' priority list: the first element will be placed at the end of the priority list. Furthermore, the cloud providers with not fulfilled non-functional requirements will be deleted from the list. During the search cycles, the valid compositions of cloud collaborations will be stored (if all cloud users and cloud providers fulfill all requirements and the profit maximization is achieved as well.

Step 3: Composition of Collaborations. Further, the mentioned above greedy principle for the multi-dimensional knapsack problem is used to replace the cloud collaboration with a lower profit by the cloud collaboration with the better profit value. Afterwards, we check whether the cloud collaboration partner can build more than one collaboration. In this case, this partner will be replaced if he can bring more profit; if not, this collaboration will be added to the solution if the objective function > 0. The complete solution - the composition - will be built with the best cloud collaborations.

The asymptotic runtime of CCCP-PRIOSORT.KOM is determined by the search cycles and the rotation step. Thereby, all cloud users $U^{\#}$ and cloud providers $P^{\#}$ will be searched once during the assignment algorithm respectively. The rotation step goes priority lists with the length P through. These steps lead to the asymptotic time $O(P^{\#^2} * U^{\#})$.

9. EVALUATION OF CCCP-PRIOSORT.KOM

To assess the improvement, we prototypically implemented our proposed heuristic approach CCCP-PRIOSORT.KOM in Java and used the same set up for our evaluation, namely, free JavaILP framework and the commercial IBM ILOG CPLEX framework. The main objective of our evaluation is to assess the required computation time of CCCP-PRIOSORT.KOM for different problem sizes and compare it with the exact optimization approach CCCP-EXA.KOM we provided before. Thus, formally, we regard computation time as the dependent variable of our evaluation. The parameter values or distributions that were used in the problem generation process are the same as summarized in Table 2.

9.1. Evaluation Results

The results of our evaluation, i.e., the observed ratio of solved instances and the ratio of the mean computation times in comparison to the CCCP-EXA.KOM approach, are summarized in Table 3. As can be clearly seen, the mean computation times are drastically improved, and even the test case (with $P^{\#} = 12$ and $U^{\#} = 18$) takes only 20.56% of the previously computation time used by the exact approach.

The ratio of the solved instances (from 100 problem instances) goes already down with the test case (with $U^{\#} \geq 8$ and $P^{\#} \geq 8$). Given that the considered problem dimensions are still relatively small in

Table 3. Evaluation results of CCCP-PRIOSORT.KOM

Test Case $(P^\#; U^\#)$	Ratio of Solved Instances	Ratio of Mean Computation Times
4; 4	89.79%	3.70%
4; 6	88.10%	5.70%
6; 6	83.15%	7.90%
6; 9	71.79%	11.01%
8; 8	66.81%	14.39%
8; 12	63.93%	15.06%
10; 10	61.19%	17.90%
10; 15	54.71%	18.45%
12; 12	53.44%	20.03%
12; 18	53.79%	20.56%

the context of a large cloud market, it can be concluded that the practical applicability of the proposed heuristic optimization approach CCCP-PRIOSORT.KOM is still rather limited. As it has already been explained before, a broker will likely have to decide on the composition of collaborations under rigid time constraints, but also with the best profit. Hence, an important future challenge consists in the improvement of our heuristic with respect to the problem reduction.

10. RELATED WORK AND COMPARISON WITH OTHER METHODS

The work on stable allocations and stable algorithms was recognized as an important theoretical contribution in the 1960s and 1970s, but it was not until the early 1980s that its practical relevance was discovered. The key contribution made Roth, A. (1984) who documents the evolution of the market for new doctors in the U.S. and argues convincingly that a stable algorithm improved the functioning of the market.

The Gale-Shapley allocation mechanisms (1962) rely on a rather abstract idea. If rational people – who know their best interests and behave accordingly – simply engage in unrestricted mutual trade, then the outcome should be efficient. If it is not, some individuals would devise new trades that made them better off. An allocation where no individuals perceive any gains from further trade is called *stable*. Gale and Shapley examined the case of *pairwise matching*: how individuals can be paired up when they all have different views regarding who would be the best match. Gale and Shapley analyzed matching at an abstract, general level. They used marriage as one of their illustrative examples. How should ten women and ten men be matched, while respecting their individual preferences? The main challenge involved designing a simple mechanism that would lead to a stable matching, where no couples would break up and form new matches which would make them better off. The solution – the Gale-Shapley "deferred acceptance" algorithm – was a set of simple rules that always led straight to a stable matching.

Chang, V. (2014) examines in his research Business Intelligence as a Service (BIaaS). BIaaS is nowadays a very helpful and important service that can process and transform collected datasets into meaningful and useful information for business purposes, and often used in business-critical servers, applications and services. The author uses Heston Model and additional APIs in the model and considers in his work the following parameters for risk and rating calculations: usability, performance, security, computational accuracy, portability and scalability. However, the primary calculation of security rating is seen as an outsourced service in the model.

Niyato, D., Vasilakos, A.V., & Kun, Z. (2011) study the cooperative behavior of multiple cloud providers in order to cooperate and support the establishment of resource pools to offer services to public cloud users. The authors present a stochastic LP game model which takes the random internal demand of cloud providers and a transferable utility into account to define and commit the optimal offer of cooperated cloud providers. In contrast to our work, Niyato et al. do not consider non-functional constraints, i.e., Quality of Service and information security requirements.

In a more recent work, Niyato, D., Wang, P., Hossain, E., Saad, W., & Han, Z. (2012)examine building coalitions between cloud providers as a novel approach to optimize the capacity expansion and maximize the mobile cloud providers' monetary benefits. The authors consider cooperative game theory and the Nash equilibrium principles in their approach and propose admission control and revenue sharing strategies for building cloud provider coalitions and a resource pool for mobile applications. The provided results illustrate improvements in cloud providers' capacity and profit maximization by entering such cloud coalitions. Similar to their previous work, the authors do not consider non-functional constraints, which are an important aspect of our work.

Gohad, A., Ponnalagu, K., Narendra, N.C., & Rao, P.S. (2013) propose a dynamic algorithm for forming self-adaptive cloud collaborations based on the identifying most appropriate healthy set of cloud provider resources (cloud provider capabilities and functional abilities at the SaaS layer), cost modeling and tenancy requirements. The approach is high-lighted with a realistic example. In contrast to us, Gohad et al. focus on ad-hoc resource provisioning, rather than the long-term formation of cloud collaborations, and do not consider security aspects. This specifically includes the cumulative security properties of cloud collaborations that were a focal point of our work.

Song, B., Hassan, M.M., & Huh, E.N. (2010) examine the problem of task selection and allocation to physical machines in the context of dynamic cloud collaborations. Their objective consists in the balancing of resource demands under consideration of different resource types, such as CPU and memory. For that purpose, the authors propose three heuristic optimization approaches, and demonstrate that a cooperative heuristic has benefits with respect to the objective of balanced resource utilization. In contrast to us, Song et al. focus on individual cloud providers and do not regard security requirements.

Mashayekhy, L., & Grosu, D. (2012) model a cloud federation formation problem based on the game theory and formulate a corresponding IP-based optimization approach. In their model, the authors consider the cooperative provisioning of VM instances and storage by federated cloud providers. Their objective consists of profit maximization combined with the formation of stable coalitions, i.e., coalitions in which cloud providers do not have a monetary incentive to switch to different coalitions. In contrast to our work, the authors only consider resource constraints, but do not regard non-functional requirements. Their work also aims at low-level VM provisioning, rather than strategic composition of collaboration.

Kołodziej, J., Khanb, S.U, Wang, L., Kisiel-Dorohinicki, M., Madanie, S.A., Niewiadomska-Szynkiewicz, E., Zomayag, A.Y., Xuh, C-Z.(2012) examine in their research the problem of minimization of the energy consumed in the processes of scheduling and execution of batch of independent tasks submitted in the grid environment. They monitor energy consumption in different grid scenarios based on the security requirements specified by the grid users. The authors define the scheduling issue as a multi-objective Independent Batch Job Scheduling problem in computer grids. Furthermore, they develop genetic-based single- and multi-population meta-heuristics for solving the considered optimization problem. The effectiveness of these algorithms has been empirically justified in two different grid architectural scenarios in static and dynamic modes. In contrast to our work, the authors consider security parameters as a sum of probabilities (a real number between 0 and 1) and use this value to calculate trustworthiness and correctness.

Lampe, U. (2013) introduces the Cloud-oriented Workload Distribution Problem. This problem concerns the distribution of a workload, which comprises multiple computational jobs, across leased infrastructure. This work assumes the position of a cloud user, who aims at cost-minimal deployment under consideration of resource constraints. On the basis of a mathematical optimization model, the author proposes the exact solution approach and the heuristic optimization approach with the improved computational time. The practical applicability and performance of these optimization approaches is demonstrated using a quantitative evaluation, based on realistic data from the cloud computing market. Furthermore, the author examines the Equilibrium Price Auction Allocation Problem. This problem refers to the allocation of Virtual Machine instances based on an equilibrium price auction scheme. Here, the research is focused on the role of a cloud provider, who pursues the aim of profit maximization. The author formalizes the problem as an optimization model, which permits to deduce the exact optimization approach. In contrast to the work at hand, the author does not consider Quality of Service and security attributes, hence, the usage of optimization models and constraints and quantitative evaluation of results is very similar.

Schuller, D. (2013) examines in his work service marketplaces and the corresponding Service Selection Problem. The author provides optimal as well as heuristic solutions to this problem under consideration of fulfillment of QoS requirements. To achieve this, the author develops an optimization framework specifying and formulating the Service Selection Problem as an optimization problem. In addition to providing the mentioned solution approach for computing optimal solutions to the Service Selection Problem, a heuristic solution method has been developed coping for scalability issues. Both approaches are thereby based on deterministic values for considered non-functional service attributes. In order to assess and reduce potentially negative consequences of differing Quality of Service, the author provides a simulation-based adaptation framework which focuses on reducing the risk of uncertainty and therewith of a potential negative impact of stochastic Quality of Service behavior. Evaluation results show that reductions in total cost up to 30% can be achieved - depending on the considered scenario - by reducing penalty costs that accrue due to the violation of Quality of Service constraints.

Lastly, Hans, R., Lampe, U., Steinmetz, R. (2013) have examined the cost-efficient selection of cloud data centers for the delivery of multimedia services. In that context, the authors propose an exact optimization approach based on IP. While their work is similar with respect to the consideration of resource and Quality of Service constraints, it focuses on a single cloud provider and does neither regard the composition of collaborations nor qualitative non-functional aspects.

In conclusion, to the best of our knowledge, we are the first to examine the profit-maximal, strategic composition of cloud collaborations under consideration of cumulative non-functional properties that result from the very formation of these collaborations, i.e., are determined by the "weakest link in the chain". Apart from the identification of that specific problem, our main contribution consists in the proposal of both an exact optimization approach, as benchmark, and our heuristic approaches. We consider security requirements and guarantees as quantitative attributes (as binary), i.e., not technically measurable. As can be found in the current research, such parameters as data center location, compliance with regulators' policies and laws are currently technically not measurable (Rittinghouse, J., & Ransome, J., 2009; Sädtler, S., 2013; Shue, L., 2013; Petcu, D., & Craciun, C., 2014) We also do not consider overall rating approaches to calculate the security level of cloud market participants and use it as a basic or admission criteria for collaboration building, as mentioned above, not all security parameters can be measured, to provide an overall security rating (Gill, A.Q., Bunker, D., & Seltsikas, P., 2011; Petcu, D., & Craciun, C., 2014) .

11. CONCLUSION AND OUTLOOK

While cloud computing promises access to virtually unlimited IT resources, the physical infrastructure of cloud providers is actually limited. Hence, smaller providers may not be able to serve the demands of larger customers. A possible solution is cloud collaborations, where multiple providers join forces to conjointly serve customers. Unfortunately, in such scenario, non-functional Quality of Service and information security properties are determined by the "weakest link in the chain", rendering the process of composing collaborations cumbersome.

In this work, we introduced the corresponding Cloud Collaboration Composition Problem with our new heuristic optimization approach CCCP-PRIOSORT.KOM, as a complement to our primary work, where we discussed the exact optimization approach for CCCP. Our evaluation results indicated drastic improvement in the computation time, but shows also that it is still applicable to small-scale problem instances, thus indicating the need for further improvements.

In our future work, we aim at the development of heuristic approaches with problem reduction and dynamic changes. In addition, we plan to extend the proposed model to cater for more complex non-functional constraints, such as conditional requirements (e.g., strong data encryption is only required if data is placed outside the European Union). Furthermore, we aim at working on cloud market design. When a market is successfully designed, many cloud market actors are persuaded to participate, thereby creating a fair and orderly market with many trading opportunities. The empirical evidences and quantitative results (e.g., results of case studies or interviews with cloud providers and cloud auditors) will extend our research scope in order to proper access and understand the functions that markets perform, the conditions required for them to be performed successfully, and what can go wrong if these conditions fail to hold. The cooperation with existing cloud markets is also on our research roadmap that can give us a possibility to gather real market data and use it to evaluate our approaches in the real-world of cloud markets.

ACKNOWLEDGMENT

This work is supported in part by E-Finance Lab e. V., Frankfurt am Main, Germany (http://www.efinancelab.com).

REFERENCES

Ackermann, T., Widjaja, T., Benlian, A., & Buxmann, P. (2012). Perceived IT Security Risks of Cloud Computing: Conceptualization and Scale Development. In *33rd International Conference on Information Systems*, (pp. 1-20).

Akay, Y., Li, H., & Xu, S. H. (2007).Greedy Algorithm for the General MultidimensionalKnapsack Problem.In Annals of Operations Research.

Ates, M., Ravet, S., Ahmat, A., & Fayolle, J. (2011). An Identity-Centric Internet: Identity in the Cloud, Identity as a Service and other delights. In *International Conference on Availability, Reliability and Security* (pp. 555 – 560). 10.1109/ARES.2011.85

Bernsmed, K., Jaatun, M. G., Meland, P. H., & Undheim, A. (2011). Security SLAs for Federated Cloud Services.In *International Conference on Availability, Reliability and Security* (pp. 202 – 209).

Bernstein, D., & Vij, D. (2012).Intercloud Security Considerations.In *IEEE International Conference on Cloud Computing Technology and Services* (pp. 537 – 544).

Buyya, R., Yeo, C., & Venugopal, S. Broberg, & J., Brandic, I. (2009). Cloud Computing andEmerging IT Platforms: Vision, Hype, and Reality for Delivering Computing asthe 5th Utility. In Future Generation Computer Systems (pp. 599-616).

Carroll, M., van der Merwe, A., & Kotzé, P. (2011). Secure Cloud Computing: Benefits, *Risks and Controls. In South Africa Conference on Information Security*, (pp. 1-9).

Chang, V. (2014) The Business Intelligence as a Service in the Cloud Future Generation Computer Systems. In Future Generation Computer Systems, (pp. 512–534).

Corporation Essvale Corporation Limited. (2008) "Business Knowledge for It in Prime Brokerage".

Durkee, D. (2010). Why Cloud Computing Will Never Be Free. *Queue, 8*(4), 20–29.

Garg, S. K., Vecchiola, C., & Buyya, R. (2011).Mandi: a market exchange for trading utility and cloud computing services. In Springer Science+Business Media. doi:10.100711227-011-0568-6

Garg, S. K., Versteeg, S., & Buyyaa, R. (2013). A framework for ranking of cloud computing services. *InFuture Generation Computer Systems, 29*(4), 1012–1023. doi:10.1016/j.future.2012.06.006

Gill, A. Q., Bunker, D., & Seltsikas, P. (2011). An Empirical Analysis of Cloud, Mobile, Social and Green Computing: *Financial Services IT Strategy and Enterprise Architecture. In International Conference on Dependable, Autonomic and Secure Computing*, (pp. 697-704).

Gohad, A., Ponnalagu, K., Narendra, N. C., & Rao, P. S. (2013).Towards Self-AdaptiveCloud Collaborations.In *Int. Conf. on Cloud Engineering*.

Gomes, E., Vo, Q. B., & Kowalczyk, R. (2012). Pure exchange markets for resource sharing in federated clouds. *Concurrency and Computation, 24*(9), 977–991. Vol. 24, Issue 9 (doi:10.1002/cpe.1659

Goyal, P. (2011).Application of a Distributed Security Method to End-2-End Services Security in Independent Heterogeneous Cloud Computing Environments.In *IEEE World Congress on Services (SERVICES)* (pp. 379 – 384). 10.1109/SERVICES.2011.34

Guitart, J., & Torres, J. (2010).Characterizing Cloud Federation for Enhancing Providers' Profit.In IEEE 3rd International Conference on Cloud Computing (CLOUD)(pp. 123-130).

Hans, R., Lampe, U., & Steinmetz, R. (2013). QoS-Aware, Cost-Efficient Selection of CloudData Centers. In *6th Int. Conf. on Cloud Computing*.

He, Y. H., Bin, W., Xiao, X. L., & Jing, M. X. (2010). Identity Federation Broker for Service Cloud. In *International Conference on Service Sciences* (pp. 115 – 120).

Hillier, F., & Lieberman, G. (2005). *Introduction to Operations Research* (8th ed.). McGraw-Hill.

Jonson, D. S. (2012). A Brief History of NP-completeness. In Documenta Mathematica.

Knuth, D. E. (1996). *Stable Marriage and Its Relation to Other Combinatorial Problems: An Introductionto the Mathematical Analysis of Algorithms*. American Mathematical Society.

Kretzschmar, M., & Golling, M. (2011).Security management spectrum in future multi-provider Inter-Cloud environments - Method to highlight necessary further development. In *5th International DMTF Academic Alliance Workshop on Systems and Virtualization Management (SVM)* (pp. 1-8). 10.1109/SVM.2011.6096462

Lampe, U. (2013) Monetary Efficiency in Infrastructure Clouds - Solution Strategies for Workload Distribution and Auction-based Capacity Allocation.

Lampe, U., Wenge, O., Müller, A., & Schaarschmidt, R. (2012). Cloud Computing in the Financial Industry - A Road Paved with Security Pitfalls? In 18th Americas Conference on Information Systems (AMCIS), Association for Information Systems (AIS).

Liu, F., Tong, J., Mao, J., Bohn, R., Messina, J., Badger, L., & Leaf, D. (2011). NIST Cloud Computing Reference Architecture NIST Cloud Computing Reference Architecture, available online www.nist.gov/manuscript-publication-search.cfm?pub_id=909505

Mashayekhy, L., & Grosu, D. (2012).A Coalitional Game-Based Mechanism for FormingCloud Federations. In *5th Int. Conf. on Utility and Cloud Computing*.

Meindl, B., & Templ, M. (2012). *Analysis of Commercial and Free and Open Source Solversfor Linear Optimization Problems*. Technical report, Technische Universitat Wien.

Niyato, D., Vasilakos, A. V., & Kun, Z. (2011). Resource and Revenue Sharing with CoalitionFormation of Cloud Providers: Game Theoretic Approach. In11th Int. Symp.onCluster, Cloud and Grid Computing.

Niyato, D., Wang, P., Hossain, E., Saad, W., & Han, Z. (2012). Game Theoretic Modeling ofCooperation Among Service Providers in Mobile Cloud Computing Environments.In *2012 Wireless Communications and Networking Conf.*

Papish, M. (2012). A method for implementing dynamic, cloud-based metadata services based on a unified content ID space across a fragmented CE ecosystem. In *IEEE International Conference on Consumer Electronics (ICCE)* (pp. 57 – 60). 10.1109/ICCE.2012.6161736

Petcu, D., & Craciun, C. (2014). Towards a Security SLA-based Cloud Monitoring Service. In 4th International Conference on Cloud Computing andServices Science (CLOSER(, (pp. 598-603).

Rahimi, A. F., & Sheffrin, A. Y. (2003). Effective market monitoring in deregulated electricity markets. *InIEEE Transactions on Power Systems*, *18*(2), 486–493. doi:10.1109/TPWRS.2003.810680

Rittinghouse, J., & Ransome, J. (2009). *Cloud computing: implementation, management, and security.* In CRC press.

Roth, A. E. (2002). The Economist as Engineer: Game Theory, Experimentation, and Computationas Tools for Design Economics, InEconometrica, Vol. 70, Issue 4(pp. 1341–1378).

Roth, A. E. (2008). *The Shapley Value: Essays in Honor of Lloyd S. Shapley.* Cambridge University Press.

Roth, A. E., Sönmez, T., & Ünver, M. U. (2005).A kidney exchange clearinghouse in New England.In American Economic Review. doi:10.1257/000282805774669989

Sädtler, S. (2013). Aktuelle Rechtsfragen des Datenschutzes und der Datensicherheit im Cloud Computing, In PIK - Praxis der Informationsverarbeitung und Kommunikation, (pp. 165–173).

Schnjakin, M., Alnemr, R., & Meinel, C. (2010). Contract-based cloud architecture. In *Iternational workshop on Cloud data management (CloudDB)* (pp. 33-40).

Schuller, D. (2013) QoS-aware Service Selection - Optimization Mechanisms and Decision Support for Complex Service-based Workflows.

Shapley, L. S. (1955). *Markets as Cooperative Games.* RAND Corporation.

Shue, L. (2013). Sarbanes-Oxley and IT Outsourcing, available online: http://www.isaca.org/Journal/Past-Issues/2004/Volume-5/Documents/jpdf045-Sarbanes-OxleSandITOutsou.pdf

Siebenhaar, M., Wenge, O., Hans, R., Tercan, H., & Steinmetz, R. (2013).Verifying the Availability of Cloud Applications. In *3rd International Conference on Cloud Computing and Services Science (CLOSER 2013).*

Song, B., Hassan, M. M., & Huh, E. N. (2010).A Novel Heuristic-Based Task Selection andAllocation Framework in Dynamic Collaborative Cloud Service Platform.In2ndInt. Conf. on Cloud Computing Technology and Science.

Uttam Kumar, T., & Wache, H. (2010). Cloud Broker: Bringing Intelligence into the Cloud. In *IEEE 3rd International Conference on Cloud Computing (CLOUD)* (pp. 544 – 545).

Wenge, O., Lampe, U., Müller, A., & Schaarschmidt, R. (2014). *Data Privacy in CloudComputing an Empirical Study in the Financial Industry.In 20th AmericasConference on Information Systems.* AMCIS.

Wenge, O., Lampe, U., & Steinmetz, R. (2014). QoS- and Security-Aware Composition of Cloud Collaborations. In *4th International Conference on Cloud Computing andServices Science (CLOSER)*, (pp 378-382).

Wenge, O., Siebenhaar, M., Lampe, U., Schuller, D., & Steinmetz, R. (2012).Much Ado about Security Appeal: Cloud Provider Collaborations and their Risks. In *1st European Conference on Service-Oriented and Cloud Computing (ESOCC)*, Springer (pp. 80-90). 10.1007/978-3-642-33427-6_6

Wood, K., & Anderson, M. (2011). Understanding the complexity surrounding multitenancy in cloud computing. In *IEEE International Conference on e-Business Engineering* (pp. 119 – 124). 10.1109/ICEBE.2011.68

Yang, D. (2011). Ad Hoc Aggregation Query Processing Algorithms Based on Bit-Store. In *International Conference on in Data Intensive Cloud Cyber-Enabled Distributed Computing and Knowledge Discovery (CyberC)* (pp. 313 – 320).

Zhou, M., Zhang, R., Xie, W., Qian, W., & Zhou, A. (2010). Security and Privacy in Cloud Computing: A Survey. In *6th International Conference on Semantics Knowledge and Grid*, (pp. 105–112). 10.1109/SKG.2010.19

This research was previously published in the International Journal of Organizational and Collective Intelligence (IJOCI), 4(3); edited by Victor Chang and Dickson K.W. Chiu, pages 22-43, copyright year 2014 by IGI Publishing (an imprint of IGI Global).

Chapter 103

The Much Needed Security and Data Reforms of Cloud Computing in Medical Data Storage

Sushma Munugala
Charles Sturt University, Australia

Ali Syed
Charles Sturt University, Australia

Gagandeep K. Brar
Charles Sturt University, Australia

Azeem Mohammad
Charles Sturt University, Australia

Malka N. Halgamuge
Charles Sturt University, Australia

ABSTRACT

Cloud computing has shifted our old documents up into the clouds, with the advancement of technology. Fast-growing virtual document storage platforms provide amenities with minimal expense in the corporate society. Despite living in the 20th century, even the first world countries have issues with the maintenance of document storage. Cloud computing resolves this issue for business and clinic owners as it banishes the requirement of planning, provisioning, and allows corporations to advance their filling system according to service demands. Medical practices heavily, rely on document storage as; almost all information contained in medical files is stored in a printed format. Medical practices urgently need to revolutionize their storage standards, to keep up with the growing population. The traditional method of paper storage in medical practice has completely been obsolete and needs to improve in order to assist patients with faster diagnosis in critical situations. Obtaining Knowledge and sharing it is an important part of medical practice, so it needs immediate attention to reach its full service potential. This chapter has analyzed content from literature that highlights issues regarding data storage and recommends solution. This inquiry has found a useful tool that can be beneficial for the development of this problem which is, 'data mining' as it gives the option of predictive, and preventative health care options, when medical data is searched. The functionality and worthiness of each algorithm and methods are also determined in this study. By using cloud and big data services to improve the analysis of medical data in network of regional health information system, has huge advancements that assure convenient management, easy extension, flexible investment, and low requirements for low technical based private medical units.

DOI: 10.4018/978-1-5225-8176-5.ch103

INTRODUCTION

Cloud computing has become one of the fastest emerging techniques in the area of information technology. Information technology has started to gain interest due to population increase and virtualization of documents in a business environment, as it gives possible solutions to this rising problems. Organizations need a sustainable filing system that copes with current demands to solve this issue, in order to serve their clients better and faster. The technology of cloud computing provides a few number of benefits. Firstly, it is convenient, with a common shared infrastructure that provides servers with storage disks, networking components with wires, switches, hubs, and routers. Secondly, the implantation of cloud allows medical related information to be available over the Internet; thereby rendering this information to make it accessible is evolutionary. A huge number of people who use the Internet inspire to reach this ultimate goal. Storage of data, with secure confidentiality, and analysis of the stored data has three important aspects that make cloud computing easy to manage.

Firstly, the information collected in the medical field is referred to as "raw data". This data is stored in the data warehouse for future use or analysis. This Data Warehouse is a collection of databases where volumes of data are stored, then used when needed. Here, the collected data can be stored both in structured and unstructured format. To convert the unstructured data into a structured format, the data needs to be clustered. In addition to the k-means cluster algorithm for clustering the unstructured data into some structured format is also revolutionary. Once the data is clustered, then we will get various patterns that are then subjected to analysis. This enhances the analysis phase by allowing various interesting patterns to rise, and consequently data is abstracted. The aforementioned Fuzzy logic technique is one of the most common methods used for the decision-making process during the analysis.

Additionally, in cloud computing, one of the major issues is security and confidentially of sensitive data. To overcome the security problems of data storage in cloud is to use an encrypted format that makes it hard for hackers to interrupt, and understand. Next, we reviewed the studies in related area about big-data clustering and analyzed cloud computing techniques in relevant medical decision-makings situations. Considering a vast amount of medical data that has been available on the Internet, the easy retrieval of data is helpful to health service providers, and particularly for specialists who need to identify diseases in depth in a limited timeframe.

Once medically relevant data has been collected from networks, it then needs to be stored in a database to precede data analysis (i.e. clustering approach) this process allows users to obtain required information. The current system allows medical organizations to share their confidential information through the Internet, and causes leaks of confidential data. The current system also does not provide sufficient techniques or functions to secure confidential data while transmitting it through the Internet. In lieu of health service providing, organizations that have faced problems when analyzing the required information about a particular medicine or disease through the Internet will also benefit from this function. To avoid these issues in the "medical data security" field, this chapter proposes a technique that will help to organize collected information from the Internet securely. This highlighted method would help these advanced algorithms to share information with others while sustaining confidentiality. Furthermore, K-means technique is used to cluster big data from the database to retrieve required medical information. Some of the necessary steps involved in Parallel clustering algorithms are based on k-means in big data; this is displayed as follows: (i) Centroid-based clustering, (ii) Density-based clustering (iii) Connectivity-based clustering, (iv) High-dimensional clustering, (v) Similarity-based clustering, and (vi) Co-clustering.

Implementing 'decision making' with cloud computing technologies in medical fields is one of the hardest parts of this process. It challenges various traditional approaches when applying design, and management of medical files in an organization or medical data centers, particularly if there are issues with security portability and interoperability. Some decision-making algorithms have been available on networks that use fuzzy logic technique in decision-making, which helps to identify the possible information about various medical data, nevertheless they have been unsuccessful. The decision-making is done based on health service providers' requirements.

The fuzzy logic concept is examined by different researchers and was suggested to make decisions as it provides better results when compared with other algorithms. Another reason for using fuzzy logic is that it is convenient because it explains the decision clearly, and it is process that can be implemented easily. One of the main challenges in ensuring "medical data security" for big data is to come up with a balanced approach towards regulation and analytics of this approach. It shows how various organizations carry out useful analytics to secure the privacy of patients. There are number of techniques available for privacy and preservation of data mining, as privacy-preserving data integration, and privacy preserving information retrieval from big data have been developed with the assurance of security. In the past few years, many organizations started to use cloud computing to store their data for this reason. Companies store confidential and sensitive data in public cloud confidently, as most organization around the world use Big Data for the purpose of decision support, and to get cloud services offered by third parties. There are many benefits of increasing the security usage of cloud computing in business. Some of the advantages are as follows; parallel computing, scalability, elasticity and inexpensive.

This study has used published articles and has compared and contracted studies to analyze highlighted trends of big data. This paper has used content analysis method to draw data from various methods in order to understand multiple aspect of the trends. The comparisons and contrasts of published scholarly articles have used different algorithms and methods that highlighted these trends. The purpose is to evaluate functionality and worthiness of each algorithm method and determined and explained possible issues and ways to overcome them.

The main issues that rises from this content analysis is the fact that, the implementation of cloud computing has various possible ways, to overcome the adverse effects of unstructured data by using cloud computing is effecatious. This chapter has used specific methods to identify trends of algorithms that compares and contrasts data by using specific tools from each research article. The aim of this chapter is to give a better comprehension of cloud computing on medical data and to identify issues that are important for future research directions. . This study has used tools to measure information sourced from articles, for example, "K-means clustering algorithm" to structure data, and encryption algorithms to specifically secure medical data.

CLOUD COMPUTING DATA SECURITY

Data security in cloud computing is massive as it gives a futuristic solution to an existing problem getting bigger day by day because of data breaches on cloud. The protection of users' privacy is the biggest challenge for cloud because it contains vast amount of information from all over the globe. Cloud provides various benefits to the organizations such as low cost security, easy access of data and less management; nonetheless it is risky to upload sensitive data on cloud which can be stolen, modified and deleted by the attackers (Svantesson, 2010). This paper presents security steps which helps an organization to secure their information, and get facilities from service providers, who are aware about some rights and policies etc., (Zhang, 2016). This study will show some basic security steps to protect cloud data as a solution.

Cloud computing provides a set of resources on the internet for user conveniences. For example, a user can store, manage and process data on cloud rather than on local server or a hard disk. Cloud computing or internet computing has also big data centers all over the world, accessible anytime, anywhere, to connect you to your business by using web-enabled devices such as smartphones, tablets and laptops. This gives users big benefits to organize and move their data on cloud because they do not need to purchase big data storage devices to store their data (Pandith, 2014). They can easily store information on cloud and authorize employees to access data by using their username and password even by sitting at home, this is called virtual office. However, to transfer data on cloud is also very risky too. This is because personal information can be stolen and used in an unethical manner (Pitchai, 2016). There have been numerous accounts of news on cloud data breaches of how hackers hack personal accounts and get sensitive data. There are number issues on cloud because of financial data, personal information, and medical data breaches that can have detrimental effect on clients/patients. Without appropriate measures to establish safety set up, and information storage it becomes defenseless against leaks and, conducive to security ruptures and assaults (Mandal, 2013).

How Data Breaches Can Happen

1. **Failure of Authentication and Authorization:** As cloud data can be accessed by anyone from anywhere if the authorization and authentication process is not strong, then data breaches can be happening.
2. **Account Hijacking:** This can be done by expert hackers who can modify data and manipulate transactions.
3. **Dos Attacks:** Denial of service attacks that slows the system or simply time out where you can just sit and wait.
4. **Exfiltration:** If the cybercriminal gets into one computer in a company then the entire medical data can be extracted (Chen, 2009).

This shows that medical data security is a significant concern in cloud environment when it guarantees approved access. Information security manages information assurance and security as this includes protection of information from being lost or decimated, tainted or altered. Rather than putting away the information locally, clients store it in cloud. This way, rightness and accessibility of information must be guaranteed. The essential worry in distributed computing is security of client information which is the biggest concern of all (Waseem, 2016).

There are many methods to secure "medical data" in cloud computing such as Encryption, digital signature, secure authorization, nonetheless, these methods have some limitations which are shown below. The best solution for storing medical data security on cloud is stated according to findings of this study that can be a "powerful solution of keeping medical data in cloud, as it is a combination of three things: Data lockdown, Access policies and security intelligence" (Kumar, 2016).

Basic security methods can be given by:

- **Encryption:** According to this study, utilizing an algorithmic plan to change plain content (data) into a non-meaningful structure is called cipher-text. The opposite procedure is decryption which decodes the data from its encoded structure back to a plain content. To avert unapproved access to plain content information, the numerical calculation requires a secret value, known as key, with a specific end goal to scramble or decode the information appropriately. Cloud encryption is utilized to safe personal data saved and handled through networks, the web, tablets and remote gadgets (Chaves, 2011).

- **Limitation:** As mentioned above the information security models need few perspectives to satisfy the assessment criteria of security systems. Also, a coordinated methodology utilizing diverse strategies for verification, security and information integrity also needs to be exploited to illuminate the pitfalls of existing frameworks.
- **Digital Signatures:** Author said it is based on asymmetric cryptography, as RSA algorithm helps to generate a private and public key which is linked together mathematically. Then this is used to private key to encrypt the hash (Kaur, 2013). Limitation- Digital signatures are products with short life nonetheless it allows to get the software verification, as the sender and receiver does not have to pay any costs.
- **Secure Authorization:** In this security step, there should be a limited number of users and all the users have to have different names and passwords to access the authorized data. These passwords should be strong and secure to avoid breaches (Hagos, 2016).
- **Limitation:** The hacker can guess or break the passwords and access sensitive data.

According to the first key-point the data should not be in readable format which provides a strong key-management, and it should be done by incremental encryption. Incremental encryption use "Collision free hashing" and "Digital signatures". Secondly, after implementing access policies, only the authorized person can get access to sensitive information. The root users or Privileged users also cannot explore sensitive data after implementing these policies. Last but not least, the security intelligence will be incorporated to produce log information of users in cloud. This helps to check the behavior of users and generate alerts against hackers.

RESEARCH ISSUES

Issues and limitations related to big data medical health organizations are described in this section: 1. online information reliability. 2. Big data management and analytics. 3. Improving data analytic techniques. 4. Integrating big data with cloud computing. 5. Security and privacy challenges in cloud computing system. 6. Query and runtime optimizing for iterative and distributed programs.7 Declarative specifications and optimizes asynchronous computations 8. Data protection 9. Administrative rights.

Online Information Reliability

Retrieving medically relevant information from the Internet is one of the hardest processes, because many people around the world use their native language to communicate. This creates some difficulty for researchers or for people in the system that retrieves data from these networks. Medical data will be extracted from different resources with different qualities. However, identifying which information source is more reliable than others is impossible and is not a natural process (Hannan 2014).

Identifying the trustworthiness of the data taken from online sources is one of the most important aspects of online research. Due to living in a knowledge-based society surrounded by high-tech gadgets, people have access to various online medical details that help online users to search and identify information about a particular medicine or disease. The drawback of this is the fact that there needs to be increased levels of privacy to assure "medical data security" for confidentiality. The growth of social media, computer technology, medical and other data sets on the Internet, basically heightens the need for a secure storage system than ever. Additionally, data mining also handles the flow of data properly and the prediction of existing relational database, considering other data mining techniques that are insufficient compared to retrieving data from the Internet.

Big Data Management and Analytics

Big data management and analytics are critical in the proposed system, because big data helps to store all information that is collected from the Internet. One of the main issues is implementing infrastructure and high-performance computing techniques for storage of big data. Managing retrieved data from multiple sources and securing access to big data is crucial and hard. There needs to be more concentration on data analytics techniques that will help to manipulate and analyze big data to extract small chunks of information (Thuraisingham, 2015).

Wang (2009) proposed a technique, which helps to increase security of Big Data that not only stores cloud nonetheless also validates the required data to perform some analytical processes. This method contributes to increase the number of cloud users, and allows them to retrieve required medical information quickly from the Internet. The author proposed a technique that helps to identify the frequently searched information from the Internet as well, and also provides natural methods to analyze medical information.

Improving Data Analytic Techniques

Data plays a vital role in the proposed system; here we use k-means algorithms to require data from big data. Using the advanced k-means algorithm can easily improve data analytics. However, developing the data analytic techniques in the proposed system provides more benefits in collecting and analyzing relevant medical data. Cloud environment provides various techniques and methods to maximize the analytics of data (P.R, 2012).

To show the exact value from the database or cloud data analysis methods or tools, there needs to be an inspection system in place or to transform the auditing progress. Author (HAN HU, 2014) states that the proposed concept to improve data analytic techniques, is as follows:

- Searching with keyword that matches several native language codes that helps to increase the search information.
- Application fields leverage opportunities presented by generous data and proposed technique which will retrieve domain-specific analytical methods to derive the intended issues.
- Using the proposed techniques in data analytics will also provide many benefits (Campos, 2010).

Integrating Big Data With Cloud Computing

"ConPaaS" provides an integrated cloud environment for big data, as it helps to minimize the complexity of cloud computing. It also offers two services in Big-data such as MapReduce and Task Farming. This tool will be very helpful for integrating both big-data and cloud (Madden, 2012). Big data mainly concentrates on achieving deep business value from various deployments of advanced analytics and trustworthy data on Internet scales in medical fields. By categorizing and accessing the application loads can be beneficial as it will inadvertently help to improve big data integration with cloud computing, as this will be ideal (Changqing 2012).

The author Chandrashekar, (2015) proposed a novel technique to integrate both cloud computing and big data, He explained how this method helps to minimize the cost, and overhead, as it also triggers rapid provisioning that gives time to market with flexibility and scalability.

Security and Privacy Challenge in Cloud Computing

Collecting data from "Internet storage manipulation" and controlling the medical data security in cloud computing environment is one of the hardest processes that results in security and privacy considerations as mentioned before. However, different methods and techniques have been proposed to handle big data in cloud computing system, as this technology provides high security for data that is stored in cloud computing (Thuraisingham, 2015).

Query and Runtime Optimization for Iterative and Distributed Programs

Runtime optimization is one of the most important processes in the proposed system as it needs to analyze the data sets that are relevant to medical data. Many operations can easily be handled with the help of proposed algorithms. K-means algorithm provides a separate way to cluster information from Big Data to allow it to configure programs that match keywords. The easiest process in this algorithm is one that can easily integrate this approach in the proposed system (Baek 2015).

First of all, the proposal of big data query, and runtime is to measure, evaluate, and compare big data systems and its architecture. To retrieve required information from the Internet is one of the hardest parts that need an algorithm query processer, which matches the information retrieved from the Internet. Wang, (2014) proposed a benchmarking method to process the query, which helps people to retrieve required information from the Internet. This method contributes to minimize security issues as well as contribute to increase the query runtime of the process in the proposed system.

Declarative Specifications and Optimization for Asynchronous Computations

Big data provides room for researchers, to retract data for their research topics in their areas. Declarative specifications which play a vital role in the proposed system gives space to concentrate more on the optimizer for asynchronous computations that leads to high success factor in retrieving relevant medical data from big-data storage (Dean, 2013).

Data Protection

To improve data efficiency many cloud environments such as Hadoop stores data without encryption or any other security methods. If any unauthorized user or hackers accesses a set of machines, then there is no way to stop them from stealing critical medical data stored in machines (Ren, 2012).

The need for an advanced technique to provide data protection in both Big Data and cloud computing seems to be the resolution. Zhang, (2010) Proposed a quick grid method to secure medical data as he developed a framework to maximize the security level of data in Big Data and Cloud computing that helps secure customers medical details as well as healthcare information. At the same time, the development of a security framework that consists of four main parts such as security governance, security management, security maintenance and security technology is still much needed. Furthermore, numerous security solutions have been proposed by researchers and developers to protect users, specifically, medically relevant information in both Big Data and Cloud Computing. Many of these researchers have proposed an identity-based encryption and proxy re-encryption schemes that helps to improve security for communication services in particular processes. Some of the existing techniques and methods that contribute to secure the system are as follows; white hat security, proof point, DocTrackr, Cipher Cloud, Vaultive and SilverSky (Agrawal, 2016).

Administrative Rights

Administrative rights are the most important aspects of the aforementioned systems because they will control all activities that flow in the system. The administrator provides access controls of users, as this method also provides a particular kind of security for both the cloud computing operations as well as data (F.C.P, Oct 6-9, 2013).

Most organizations around the world are unaware of the fact that, employees have administrative rights. The administration has access to critical information that poses a risk, and to permit employees to access sensitive documents that can lead to data theft in organizations leaving them with consequences. Employees or intruders can easily upload viruses or warm codes in the organization to steal confidential information. Therefore, providing administrative rights to particular employees to access sensitive files in an organization is one of the most crucial aspects of secure storage (Perry, 2012).

OVERVIEW OF EXISTING SOLUTIONS RELATED TO ISSUES

Computing information is also another significant aspect in the concept of storage and analysis of data. Only storing medical data securely is not enough, it also needs to be easily retrieved. So it is necessary to turn raw data into some structured format so that it will be easy to retrieve, otherwise it defeats the purpose. Brett and Hannan (2014) have used information fusion algorithm to structure raw data that is collected. They collated similar patterns that are formed by joining existing patterns and leaving out the unnecessary information behind unnoticed. This chapter demonstrates that the use of k-means clustering algorithm is needed to convert raw data into structured one, by clustering them into various patterns, can give a clear image in the data because of its patterns, and its eases retrieval. During the retrieval section of various algorithms that are used in general, here we use the fuzzy logic algorithm in the knowledge retrieval process, simply because the data is stored in a data warehouse so that is not called education.

Table 1. Comparison of research issues in big data medical health organization

Security Issues and Challenges	Concerns	Analysis and Findings	Limitation	Authors
Privacy of data transmission, data breaches. Confidentiality of data	Sensitive data expose or access while transmission	Multi-layered security where the authors compared 'CCAF multi-layered security with a single-layered approach by performing experiments. It takes more than 50 hours to secure all 2 PB information and above 125 hours to raise a caution to take control of the circumstance in the ULCC Data Centre	Time consuming and expensive process	Chang & Ramachandran (2016)
Accounts hijacking	Authorization and authentication of data	Proposed data security model	In this model all the layers have to interact with each other before starting any process.	Pitchai, & Jayashri (2016)
APIs	Management on cloud	Signals self-collected from good subjects are utilized as health information. All information is changed into binary format based on a particular quantization determination	Actions are performed on each and every layer	Bechtel (2016)
Security and privacy challenge in cloud computing	Collecting data from computer storage, manipulation and controlling of data in the cloud is difficult	Encryption Algorithms, e.g. DET Algorithms differ from one organization to other depend on security challenge. These algorithms facilitate data to be secured		Thuraisingham et al. (2015)
Data is being accessed by the unauthorized users	Certificate management, authentication breakage	Comparison between the old traditional system and three level authentication mechanisms	Three level authentication mechanisms to get higher level of cloud data security.	Sirohi & Aggarwal (2015)
Healthcare - Electronic healthcare records	Privacy sensitive health records are released to the third party in cloud	Used Anonymization With MapReduce method and anonymize health care data via generalization using two-phase clustering approach	A third party in cloud has access to healthcare records	Zhang et al. (2015) [
Healthcare - All digital healthcare industry	Regional secure data process	Raspberry Pi is a pocket-sized computer used in forensic medicine, forensic etymology	collect limit issues in future health care	Feng et al. (2015)
Malicious attacks Monitoring, management	Risk for healthcare applications	Data partitioning and scrambling - ECG signals from MIT- BIH arrhythmia database and ECG	It requires all the TCP-IP layer management and different security	Wang & Yang (2015)
Data loss, sensitive data breaches	Confidentiality, integrity and availability of data	Access control, Encryption. Cloud hosted data remains secret via encrypted transmission of data and encrypted storage of data	Account hijacking, exposer of cloud hosted data. If the private key expose, then whole data will be lost.	Devi & Ganesan (2015)
Hijacking of accounts	Cyber-attacks. Account Credential performs, Preventing Phishing attacks	Both reaction as well as preventive measures in consistence with best industry practices and international standards	This is a kind of research, analysis and prevention plan of account hijacking not a particular solution of that	Tirumala et al. (2015)
Risk of data exposure, Security of data	Untrusted third party attacks	Holomorphic encryption, the pain-text encryption done by using Holomorphic encryption before sending	Complicated algorithms used	Jain & Madan(2015)
Attacks done by malware Integrity of data, availability of data,	Limited data availability, updating of data without authority	Email-filter set up at high mode - from email setting the filter mode changed to high mode	Not applicable on vast data. Just suitable for email security	Sharif & Cooney (2015)
No authorization, No encryption	Increasing Data breaches	User errors: Methodology Encryption by complex algorithms	Training about new software, and data security by using Complex algorithm	Asaduzzaman & Jain (2015)
Password recovery, Data location, Confidentiality, Data concealment	Performance issues with cipher-text	Dynamic virtualization of software, hardware	Time consuming	Pandith (2014)
Confidentiality, authentication	Control over Information leakage. User errors	Training methods - Proper training session to train employee about new software or techniques		Gong (2014)
Authorization, authentication	Control over un-authorized access	Malicious attacks, Signatures signed on paper and scanned to save in computer then cropped to create a picture	Less effective	Kaaniche & Laurent (2014)
Improving data analytic techniques	Data plays a vital role in the proposed system. So there is a need to develop techniques used for data analysis	K-means algorithm	To cluster require data from big data	Hu et al. (2014)
Query and runtime optimizers for iterative and distributed programs.	Runtime optimization is most important and critical process that was difficult to achieve	Benchmarking Method	To minimize security issues as well as it helps to increase the query and runtime of the process in the proposed study	Wang et al. (2014)

continued on following page

Table 1. Continued

Security Issues and Challenges	Concerns	Analysis and Findings	Limitation	Authors
Online information security	The identifying truthfulness of data that is shared online	Map-reduce Algorithm	To analyze various clusters and recommend services used by other users or researchers for the same type of work	Ramamoorthy et al. (2013)
Data exposure, sensitive information leakage	Difficult to stop data exposure and leakage	Phishing attacks, Digital signatures. Less effective for huge amount of data security	Signatures signed on paper and scanned to save in computer then cropped to create a picture	Sirohi & Agarwal (2013)
Data confidentiality: Challenging multitenant environment	Remote server attaches	Virtual infrastructure provided to host services to client for its usage and management of stored data in cloud servers	Public key based framework	Barbori (2012)
Administrative Rights	They play a major role as they control all activities and flow in the system		Access permissions should be provided to particular employees to access confidential files helps to improve security level for data as well as organization benefits	Perry, (2012)
Healthcare - Covers the person suffering from Alzheimer's Disease	Current system to diagnose the patient has slight range and is not secure	A new method proposed with the long-range outdoor environment with GPS and fine-grained distributed data access control. Using location tracking technology, telediagnosis, Access using PKC	Part of data is not secure	Pramila et al. (2012)
Integrating big data with Cloud computing	The complexity of cloud increases, as there is no integration of big data with the cloud	MapReduce and Task Farming	These are used to integrate Big data and cloud, which reduces cost, overhead	Madden et al. (2012)
Healthcare	Privacy preserving for healthcare data.	Changing the data values by using noise perturbation, data aggregation, and data swapping. Spent $39.4 billion in 2008	Data masking	Motiwalla et al. (2010)
Data protection	Unauthorized users or hackers access critical data	Smart Grid Method	To maximize security level of data that helps to secure customer's personal data as well as health care information	Zhang, (2010)
Big data management and analytics	Implementing infrastructure and high-performance computing technique for storage of big data	Attribute-based Encryption	Increase security for Big data that is stored in the cloud.	Wang et al. (2009)

The data is converted into knowledge only if it is retrieved properly. By using the fuzzy logic techniques, the retrieval of data information is done in an efficient manner.

Up until now, this study has looked at, medical data storing and retrieval of stored data. The next section will talk about the importance of data transportation. The primary concern with data transportation is the tedious security requirements. The security issue is one of the threatening factors in cloud computing. There are enormous advantages in the field of cloud computing, and its main drawback is security issues. Blanke et al (2015) describes the usage of artificial intelligence to resolve security issues during the data transformation process. Using artificial intelligence, the author found that whether the medical data is transferred to the correct destination or not detecting injections or hackings during the transformation is important. On top of this, investigating various security features (Pham, 2010a, 2010b, 2011) to avoid hacking so that the system could be an interesting avenue to explore in the future to protect BigData.

Implementing artificial intelligence will be a cost consuming process, so to secure the data simply by a data encryption as well as decryption methods. DES encryption algorithm is a method used for the encryption and decryption of the medical data. Therefore, the data information stored in cloud will be retained only in the encrypted format and the encrypted data will be sent during data transfer. Even if there is a hack in between, the hacker may not find anything useful with the data retrieved, as it will not be in an understandable format because it is encrypted.

DISCUSSION

This chapter has mainly focused on exploring data storage systems from various regional health organizations. It also accomplished the exchange and sharing of medical information between different medical institutions of certain areas that have been studied after a critiquing analysis. Consequently, this chapter proposed a new framework to share medical information across the medical organizations.

At present, the information system that is used in regional health organization is still at its initial stage, and their needs to be more development to eliminate possible security and data privacy breaches. Private experts of medical information suggested that the core of regional health information is to acknowledging the importance of shared electronic health records, and electronic transmission. The accessible medical records will create a potential growth in the medical field, however, it is important to develop a sharing framework that gives attention to the security of personal details. Medical organizations share confidential information about the different diseases and patients, so in that situations, they need to enable high security for particular data transmission in a network. As a result, the emergence of cloud computing technology will bring a brand-new understanding for the development of medical information to store and retrieve confidential data.

The proposed system in this study has found that, Big Data may have many benefits to the medical organization to collect and store information about medical details of clients. Using big data and cloud computing services will significantly help to increase the assistances of decision making in the management of medical organization.

CONCLUSION

Cloud computing provides gigantic advantages, and also increases the security levels of medical data. However, there are some difficulties that still exist even after the adaptation and promotion of cloud computing. There is a strong need for an advanced higher functioning tools and approaches to secure confidentiality requirements of an industry that is growing rapidly. This research has established that Cloud computing and big data provides heightened benefits to the consumers when they adopt to improve their working process in an organization. Additionally, this study has found that, the use of cloud and Big Data services also improves the analysis of medically relevant data in the network and the regional health information systems which is based on cloud computing that has benefits such as, convenient management, easy extension, flexible investment and low requirements for low technical based personal medical units. This study recommends that the above proposed suggestions have been found by this content that will help to increase the quality of medical reports and enhance health information system and inadvertently leverage their storage systems. The extraction, containment and confidentiality of medical records need to be sustained in order to compete with the growing challenges and demands.

REFERENCES

Agrawal, V. (Accessed 2016). Securing Big Data On Cloud – Tools and Measures. Retrieved from http://www.exeideas.com/2015/09/securing-big-data-on-cloud.html

Blanke, C. A. (2015). The (Big) Data-security assemblage: Knowledge and critique. *Big Data & Society*.

Brett Hannan, X. Z. (2014, August 11-14). iHANDs: Intelligent Health Advising and Decision-Support Agent. *Proceedings of the 2014 IEEE/WIC/ACM International Joint Conferences on Web Intelligence (WI) and Intelligent Agent Technologies (IAT)* (Vol. 3, pp. 294 – 301).

Campos, L. M. (2010). Combining content-based and collaborative recommendations: A hybrid approach based on Bayesian networks. *International Journal of Approximate Reasoning, 51*(7), 785–799. doi:10.1016/j.ijar.2010.04.001

Chandrashekar, R. M. K. (2015). Integration of Big Data in Cloud computing environments for enhanced data processing capabilities. *International Journal of Engineering Research and General Science, 3*(3 Part 2), 2091–2730.

Changqing Ji, Y. L. (2012). Big Data Processing in Cloud Computing Environments. *Proceedings of the 2012 International Symposium on Pervasive Systems, Algorithms and Networks.*

Chaves, S. (2011). The Risks Issue in Cloud Computing. doi:10.2139srn.1991156

Chen, Q., & Deng, Q. (2009). Cloud computing and its key techniques. *Journal of Computer Applications, 29*(9), 2562–2567. doi:10.3724/SP.J.1087.2009.02562

Dean, J. G. C. (2013). Large Scale Distributed Deep Networks. *Advances in Neural Information Processing Systems.*

Feng, J. X., Onafeso, B., & Liu, E. (2016). *Computer and Information Technology; Ubiquitous Computing and Communications; Dependable, Autonomic and Secure Computing.* Pervasive Intelligence and Computing.

Hagos, D. (2016). Software-Defined Networking for Scalable Cloud-based Services to Improve System Performance of Hadoop-based Big Data Applications. *International Journal of Grid and High Performance Computing, 8*(2), 1–22. doi:10.4018/IJGHPC.2016040101

Hu, H., Wen, Y., Chua, T. S., & Li, X. (2014). Toward Scalable Systems for Big Data Analytics: A Technology Tutorial.

Joonsang B., Q. H. (2015, April/June). A Secure Cloud Computing Based Framework for Big Data Information Management of Smart Grid. *IEEE Transactions On Cloud Computing, 3*(2).

Kaur, M., & Singh, R. (2013). Implementing Encryption Algorithms to Enhance Data Security of Cloud in Cloud Computing. *International Journal of Computers and Applications, 70*(18), 16–21. doi:10.5120/12167-8127

Madden, S. (2012, May). From Databases to Big Data. *IEEE Internet Computing, 16*(3), 4–6. Retrieved from http://ieeexplore.ieee.org/lpdocs/epic03/wrapper.htm?arnumber=6188576 doi:10.1109/MIC.2012.50

Mandal, S. (2013). Enhanced Security Framework to Ensure Data Security in Cloud using Security Blanket Algorithm. *International Journal of Research in Engineering and Technology, 2*(10), 225–229. doi:10.15623/ijret.2013.0210033

Motiwalla, L. (2010). Value Added Privacy Services for Healthcare Data.

Muhtaroglu, F. C. P., Demir, S., Obali, M., & Girgin, C. (2013, October 6-9). Business model canvas perspective on big data applications. *Proceedings of the 2013 IEEE International Conference on Big Data*, Silicon Valley, CA (pp. 32 – 37).

Pandith, M. (2014). Data Security and Privacy Concerns in Cloud Computing. *IOTCC*, *2*(2), 6. doi:10.11648/j.iotcc.20140202.11

Perry, D. (2012). Most organizations unaware of employees with admin rights. Retrieved from http://www.tomsitpro.com/articles/administrator_rights-admin_rights-malware-IT_security_professionals,1-353.html

Pham, D. V., Syed, A., & Halgamuge, M. N. (2011). Universal serial bus based software attacks and protection solutions. *Digital Investigation*, *7*(3), 172–184. doi:10.1016/j.diin.2011.02.001

Pham, D. V., Syed, A., Mohammad, A., & Halgamuge, M. N. (2010, June 14-16). Threat Analysis of Portable Hack Tools from USB Storage Devices and Protection Solutions. *Proceedings of the International Conference on Information and Emerging Technologies*, Karachi, Pakistan. 10.1109/ICIET.2010.5625728

Pham, D. V., Halgamuge, M. N., Syed, A., & Mendis, P. (2010). Optimizing windows security features to block malware and hack tools on USB storage devices. Proceedings of Progress in electromagnetics research symposium (pp. 350-355).

Pitchai, R., Jayashri, S., & Raja, J. (2016). Searchable Encrypted Data File Sharing Method Using Public Cloud Service for Secure Storage in Cloud Computing. *Wireless Personal Communications*, *90*(2), 947–960. doi:10.100711277-016-3273-1

P.R. (2012). Third Party Data Protection Applied To Cloud and Xacml Implementation in the Hadoop Environment With Sparql.

Ramamoorthy, S. (2013). Optimized Data Analysis in Cloud using BigData Analytics Techniques. Proceedings of 4th ICCCNT.

Rathod, K. R. (2016). Cloud Computing - Key Pillar for Digital India. *International Journal of Information*, *6*(1/2), 27–33.

Ren, Y. a. (2012, October 30-November 1). A Service Integrity Assurance Framework For Cloud Computing Based On Mapreduce. *Proceedings of IEEE CCIS'12*, Hangzhou (pp. 240 –244).

Suji Pramila, R., Shajin Nargunam, A., & Affairs, A. (2010). A study on data confidentiality in early detection of Alzheimer's disease. Proceedings of the 2012 International Conference on Computing, Electronics and Electrical Technologies (ICCEET) (pp. 1004-1008).

Svantesson, D., & Clarke, R. (2010). Privacy and consumer risks in cloud computing. *Computer Law & Security Report*, *26*(4), 391–397. doi:10.1016/j.clsr.2010.05.005

Thuraisingham, D. B. (2015). Big data security and privacy. *Proceedings of the 5th ACM Conference on Data and Application Security and Privacy CODASPY '15* (pp. 279-280).

Thuraisingham, D. B. (2015). *Big Data Security and Privacy. National Science Foundation.*

Wang, L. J. Z. (2014). *BigData Bench: a Big Data Benchmark Suite from Internet Services. State Key Laboratory of Computer Architecture.* Institute of Computing Technology, Chinese Academy of Sciences.

Wang, Q. C. W. (2009). *Enabling Public Verifiability and Data Dynamics for Storage Security in Cloud Computing.* ESORICS. doi:10.1007/978-3-642-04444-1_22

Waseem, M., Lakhan, A., & Jamali, I. (2016). Data Security of Mobile Cloud Computing on Cloud Server. *OALib, 3*(4), 1–11. doi:10.4236/oalib.1102377

Zhang, T. (2010). The design of information security protection framework to support Smart Grid. *Proceedings of the 2010 International Conference on Power System Technology (POWERCON)* (pp. 1-5).

Zhang, W., Han, S., He, H., & Chen, H. (2016). Network-aware virtual machine migration in an over-committed cloud. *Future Generation Computer Systems.* doi:10.1016/j.future.2016.03.009

Zhang, X., Dou, W., Pei, J., Nepal, S., Yang, C., Liu, C., & Chen, J. (2015). Proximity-Aware Local-Recoding Anonymization with MapReduce for Scalable Big Data Privacy Preservation in Cloud. *IEEE transactions on computers, 64(8),* 2293–2307.

This research was previously published in Applying Big Data Analytics in Bioinformatics and Medicine edited by Miltiadis D. Lytras and Paraskevi Papadopoulou, pages 99-113, copyright year 2018 by Medical Information Science Reference (an imprint of IGI Global).

Chapter 104
Deployment and Optimization for Cloud Computing Technologies in IoT

Aditya Pratap Singh
Ajay Kumar Garg Engineering College, India

Pradeep Tomar
Gautam Buddha University, India

ABSTRACT

Cloud computing has proven itself and is accepted in industrial applications. Cloud computing is based on the co-existence and co-working of various technologies and services from different sources that together make cloud computing a success. Over the last few years, the Internet of Things (IoT) has been widely studied and being applied. The blending of these two efficient technologies may provide an intelligent perception about usage of resources on demand and efficient sharing. The adoption of these two different technologies and usage is likely to be more and more pervasive, making them important components of the future internet-based systems. This chapter focuses on the deployment models of cloud computing in relation to IoT. The implications of cloud computing in view of deployment are discussed. The issues for deployment and optimization related to the merger of IoT with cloud computing are raised.

INTRODUCTION

The cloud computing is a platform which originated from the convergence of utility computing, grid computing, and need for software as service. The cloud computing is a way of dealing with the deployment of computing resources externally like processing power, storage, deployed applications as a service (Stanoevska-Slabeva &Wozniak, 2010). Platform as a Service (PaaS), Software as a Service (SaaS), and Infrastructure as a Service (IaaS) are the main three service models categorized for cloud computing. These services are made available to end-user using cloud deployment models. There are four deployment models for cloud services: public cloud, private cloud, community cloud, and hybrid cloud (Victories, 2015). These deployment models are used as shared or dedicated in the organization premises or hosted externally.

DOI: 10.4018/978-1-5225-8176-5.ch104

Kevin Ashton in 1999 (Ashton, 2009) coined the term Internet of Things (IoT) for supply chain management environment. The IoT paradigm includes the things (consumer electronic appliances, sensors) as a part of the internet. These intelligent and self-configuring nodes (things) are used to create a global network to fulfill one or more purposes. This way of computation opens up new possibilities for new innovations for the realization of smart cities having best infrastructure and services to enhance the quality of life for humans. The IoT is already being used for some of the very crucial services like logistics, smart cities, and health care etc. The IoT is nowadays working on cloud computing as the IoT services led to increased demands on storage space for data, processing power, and other management services. The cloud services are matured enough in current state and are capable of providing more flexible computing and data management services for IoT. The hybrid is found to be more suitable deployment model for integration of IoT with cloud services. In general, IoT can lead to the virtually unlimited capabilities and its technological constraints are compensated by the availability of resources of cloud. In this chapter, the study of these deployment models and the optimization possibilities in relation to IoT are discussed.

DEPLOYMENT MODELS

The method of providing cloud services to end users is termed as a deployment model. To exploit the full advantages of cloud services in technical and economic respect, the cloud services are to be deployed and implemented successfully. The implementation is an activity of deployment, as only by utilizing cloud services does not make an organization different from other organizations doing business in the same domain. The other same domain organizations can also implement cloud services following as model resulting IT efficiencies. The efficient deployment of cloud services indicates the realization of distinct organizational benefits to differentiate and take competitive advantage from other organizations of the same domain (Garrison, Kim, & Wakefield, 2012). The benefits with IT-oriented success can be categorized as strategic, economic and technological benefits. The strategic benefits refer here to have full focus on organizations core activities by shifting its IT functions to cloud computing provider fully or in part. An economic benefit refers to reduces IT expenses by using cloud computing vendor's expertise and technical resources. Technological benefits refer to reduced risk and cost related to having in-house technological resources by having access to state-of-the-art technology and skilled personnel. The deployment models for the cloud services play an important role for the benefits related to strategy, economic and technological. The organization utilizing cloud services has to use some of its own IT resources and capabilities to have a required control over the resources provided by the cloud vendor. This is treated as optimizing cloud benefits.

The different deployment models for cloud services are identified in the literature (Mell 2009, Zhang 2010):

Private Cloud

This deployment model is best suited for an organization with multiple consumers. In private cloud, the services are available exclusively for a particular organization as shown in Figure 1. These cloud services deployment is owned, managed and controlled by the parent organization. The private cloud deployment is based on a cloud by an organization for its in-house users only with all services under organization's control (instead of Internet). Sometimes these cloud services are deployed by the third party or in col-

Figure 1. Private cloud

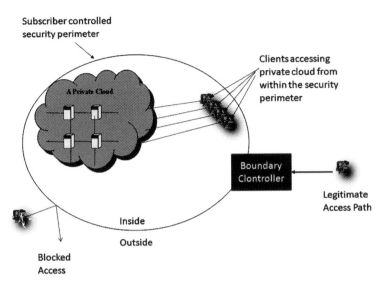

laboration with the organization in the organization premises or off the campus. A company that already own data center and developed IT infrastructure has a good choice for private clouds with particular needs around security or performance. Private cloud deployment is not a cost efficient choice of cloud services, it seems like having own building and managing it rather renting a building without concern for managing it. But in view of security, this model has tremendous efficiency. Another name given to private cloud is "internal clouds". The multi-tenancy does not affect much in an arrangement where sharing of resources and services is minimal like in private clouds. The requirement of infrastructure in private cloud deployment may be same organization premise or sometimes at the third party location. In case of on premise infrastructure the client's firewall system address secure access concern while in case of third party location the Virtual Private Network (VPN) can be a solution for secure access to cloud services. Sometimes private cloud may also demand some customized requirements. Figure 1 shows a scenario of private cloud in an organization premises.

Not only for security issues, but also various regulatory standards such as Sarbanes-Oxley (SOX), HIPAA, or SAS 70 (Papazoglou, 2008) are to be confirmed for organization data and applications. The private cloud deployment becomes a choice in such scenarios. These regulatory standards and audits may require data privacy managed. Some SaaS service models give the privilege to have a data management on their own arrangement to ensure data privacy as per organizations requirement. Some example implementations of private clouds are Elastra, Eucalyptus, Amazon VPC (Virtual Private Cloud), and Microsoft ECI data center.

Community Cloud

This deployment model is used in a scenario where organizations with shared concern work as a community for their consumers. These concerns of organizations may include security provisions, policies, and compliance considerations. These cloud services may be managed and owned by one of the organizations, group of organizations, and the third party in or off campus as shown in Figure 2. Community

Figure 2. Community cloud

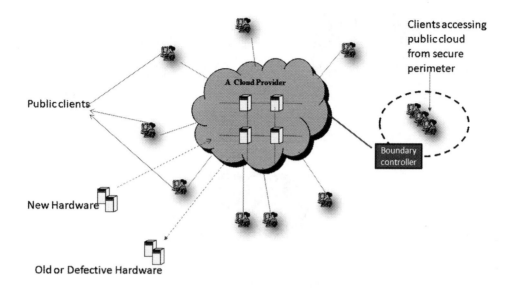

clouds can also be implemented in two ways: On-Site and outsourced community cloud. In case of outsourced deployment model, a third party cloud provider is hired to host the server side. The benefit of outsourcing is that the hired third part will be an impartial unit bound by contract rules without any preferences towards participating organizations. The high-cost factor is reduced in comparison to private cloud as in community cloud the services are shared by all the member organizations which formed a community. One good example of community cloud is United States federal government. The community cloud model is a good choice for Small and Medium-sized Enterprises (SMEs) as these SMEs can hold a complex application collaboratively by sharing services from each other otherwise it would not possible for a small organization to undertake a complex and large application.

The possible disadvantages may be like higher cost than public cloud and the fixed bandwidth and other resources are shared among all community member organizations.

Public Cloud

This type of deployment model provides services openly to the general public. It is in the true spirit of cloud hosting. Any valid user is allowed to access the cloud services via published interfaces using web browsers. This model is in good spirits of the cloud as the service provider renders services and infrastructure to all clients (Victories, 2015). In this deployment model, the user pays only for the time duration of usage like pay-per-use. One good example is the electric supply in our locality. In this deployment model, the users are not discriminated on any criteria as shown in Figure 3. The public cloud model is cost effective and does not require a large investment in infrastructure from businesses. The end user of public cloud needs not to be an expert on available services or having control over the supporting technology infrastructure.

This deployment model may be possessed, managed, and controlled by academic, business or government administrations. In this structure, the cost of deployment is shared by all the users. Good examples

Figure 3. Public cloud

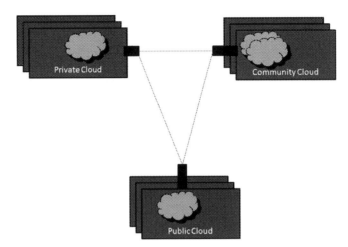

of public cloud are Google services, IBM's Blue Cloud, Windows Azure Services Platform. With least security provisions in public cloud model, the proper validation procedure at both cloud vendor and cloud client end can be implemented. Within the boundaries of operation, the cloud vendor and cloud client must identify their respective responsibilities.

The possible advantages of the public cloud include continuous uptime of services and data availability, training and technical help, on-demand scalability, optimum use of resources without wastage, cost reduction for the establishment of setup, Convenience, etc. The disadvantage of public cloud includes the lack of data security, Open-ended costs, Opacity, etc.

Hybrid Cloud

When private, community or public deployment models are merged with one another, this arrangement is termed as hybrid cloud. In this composition, each participating model remains individual entity but bound together using standard or copyrighted technology which permits data and application portability. With this arrangement, the user can increase the capability of cloud by aggregating, assimilation, and customization with another cloud service. This model may manage the workload as per need and demand. Using these hybrid arrangement organizations can use different deployment for different requirements like private cloud can be used for security oriented services and data storage along with less expensive public cloud for shared data and applications. As shown in Figure 4 this type of arrangement may be complex. Force.com and Microsoft Azure are two examples of this model.

Figure 5 represents the layered architecture of cloud services with different deployment models. The deployment models are placed at the bottom as they represent the physical infrastructure for private, community, public and hybrid arrangement (Subashini & Kavitha, 2011). There may be some other non-popular deployment models like virtual private and inter-cloud. The one layer above the bottom contains different service models which can be utilized using one of the deployment models at the bottom layer. These deployment models are at the center of cloud infrastructure establishment and are used to provide ubiquitous network, on-demand-service, multi tenancy, and measured service.

Figure 4. Hybrid cloud

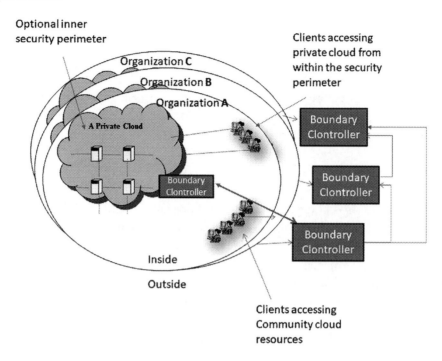

Figure 5. Layered architecture of cloud services

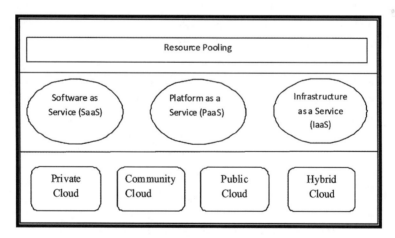

CLOUD DEPLOYMENT IMPLICATIONS

There may be some implications irrespective of chosen deployment model:

Network Dependency

For an efficient onsite or off shore cloud, a secure and reliable network is highly required. Cloud platform technologies provide technical support for the establishment of ubiquitous networking service management and its usage in the application of IoT. There is a great requirement for multi-network integration technology support in cloud services in turn to implement IoT services.

IT Skills Required by Subscribers

The cloud infrastructure will require skilled resources to manage different user devices used for accessing the cloud but in lesser number. The employees with old skills may need to update their skills as per the requirement for working in a cloud environment.

Risk From Multi-Tenancy

The risk of possible attackers is always there from a service subscriber. The "software multi-tenancy" is the term which refers to a scenario where a software instance running on a server provides access to multiple tenants (clients). This multi-tenancy risk includes security compromise and sensitive information leakage. In PaaS cloud arrangement the SaaS services are treated as tenants. Sometimes separate authorization systems are developed to handle multi-tenancy. The maximum risk of multitenancy is in public cloud and gradually reduces in the community, hybrid and Private cloud.

Data Transmission and Performance Limitations

The private cloud with on-site server deployment is always available with full bandwidth for data transmission while in other deployment models there may be limitations for bulk data requirements of client due to shared bandwidth. This kind of restrictions can be removed or reduced by provisioning high-performance and/or high-reliability networking infrastructure.

In a cloud deployment process, the security and control must be taken care of. In deployment models like public or community clouds, the organization having onsite infrastructure has the responsibility for control and security of the cloud. This arrangement is to implement a sufficient security policy that guarantees appropriate security to ensure that risk is reduced. This is not the case in private cloud deployment as it is operated and controlled by a private organization in a premise.

CLOUD AND IOT

The proposal of MIT Auto-ID Labs for Radio Frequency Identification Devices (RFIDs) system makes a way to IoT (Tao, Cheng, Da Xu, Zhang, & Li, 2014). The RFID technique is used to acquire versatile data related to location, heat, light, and sound in real time for IoT. Various other devices and techniques are used to collect information of data related to electricity, mechanics, chemistry, biology, etc using different kinds of tools and sensors like infrared sensors, laser scanner, gas sensors, and Global Position System (GPS), etc. To establish the IoT vision, various resources are required which must be efficient, secure, market oriented, and scalable. The best answer to such requirement can be the cloud computing. The cloud computing is capable of providing such services reliably by exploiting virtualized storage technologies in next generation data centers.

With support from related researches and developments, IoT evolved itself towards the integration of information space and physical world from connecting things to things. The use of cloud computing with

IoT makes it more efficient and powerful infrastructure. The sensing services from IoT stores their data on storage cloud and offers it by joining the network. The experts from a different domain can provide tools to be used in cloud computing. Like the analysts can provide data analysis software tools, data mining, and machine learning tools are provided by experts from artificial intelligence domain for creating a knowledge base, computer graphics experts can provide optimized and efficient visualization tools.

The IoT is being used in different applications background in spite of no standard and definition and uniform architecture (Miorandi, Sicari, De Pellegrini, & Chlamtac, 2012). The fast changing technology is also a constraint to set a standard for IoT architecture. These applications are smart cities, smart homes or smart buildings, smart inventory, smart business, and their implementation in environmental monitoring, product management, health-care, social security and surveillance, and so on.

A huge volume of data and communication volume is generated over cloud by IoT with very high number of devices communicating over the cloud. Such communication volume will require the deployment of competent computing devices in between IoT sensors/devices and cloud services. These computing devices mitigate the complexity and frequency of communication with the cloud. The interoperability between IoT and cloud is an issue of concern. The layered protocols and software are used to connect several nodes of IoT to cloud services. The IoT elements such as sensors, actuators, and gateways can be integrated with cloud services in data centers. There are various strategies are used to solve interoperability like the use of unique products, middleware etc. For monitoring and management of different platforms and cluster of devices, Hadoop is a choice (Díaz, Martín, & Rubio, 2016).

To enable flawless execution of various applications, exploiting full capabilities of multiple dynamic and heterogeneous resources along with the quality of service requirements of different users there is a need to improve cloud application platforms. The support of domain specific programming tools and environments is required to improve the rapid development of applications. There are some challenges related to the use of IoT and cloud in integration. These challenges are the standard for communication among IoT devices and cloud, reliability, and security.

The merger of cloud services and IoT elements would require different scheme for resource management. The resource management in this scenario would require optimization of processing scheme, resource handling for input-output, and storage management along with optimized sensor reading cycles, multi-sensor queries and shared access to expensive location-dependent IoT resources (Suciu, et al., 2013). IoT systems become complex due to the integration of cloud management techniques to manage IoT components. These cloud services play an important role as a platform for computation and data processing with management platforms for IoT.

The blending of cloud services and IoT needs a consistent software layer to be implemented between the two technologies. A cloud with IoT infrastructure must support following functions (Truong, & Dustdar, 2015):

End-to-End Engineering and Optimization

In convergence of cloud computing techniques with IoT software practitioners has to work on optimizing and developing code as per end-to-end view of the technologies involved with the due consideration of service providers for end-to-end properties. It would require creating and deploying feasible structure for IoT elements and cloud nodes as per the requirements.

Development and Production Symbiosis

There must be an arrangement in a way that reconfiguration of IoT components should not lead to interruption for running components of the application system. The system is to be configured in a manner so that it continues its develop, deploy and operation states while adding and testing IoT elements or cloud services. These systems operate critical services and should be developed in a manner so that the connection with other IoT cloud application or deployment of new element or service do not affect its live services.

Elasticity Coherence

According to Dutser et al. (Dustdar et al. 2011), the cloud's success is based on pay-per-use model. The cloud computing model supports elastic computing. As per elastic computing the required resources can be made available dynamically on demand. This process of resource management will lead to better utilization of resources. In IoT cloud environment the user is able to create and launch server instances as per their need and will be charged for only active server hours. To have such elasticity in IoT cloud system, the better coordination among cloud and IoT services to ensure coherence is required. The IoT cloud system must have well defined APIs to have runtime control on elastic competences.

CLOUD OPTIMIZATION

The main motivation for cloud computing is economic along with technological motives. The optimization of cloud computing is an activity to be followed to achieve these goals. The cloud service providers have to look forward to performing some kind of optimization of the infrastructure configuration. For optimization of a system, the following activities may be considered: monitoring, analysis, prediction, planning, and execution.

The implementation of these optimization activities to a customer by a cloud service provider is treated as local optimization. This local optimization is one of the major components of a PaaS hosting (El Kateb et al. 2014). In the current scenario, the cloud platforms focus on one-dimensional optimization like some PaaS providers provide a rule based engine to manage horizontal processing need and data storage scalability. El Kateb et al. (El Kateb et al. 2014) proposed a way to reconfigure local cloud infrastructure using a supporting tool in the form of decision-making framework. The multi-objective optimization problem can be handled using search based approaches. The authors have examined its effectiveness in the study.

The cloud with IoT also uses adaptive cloud optimization algorithms depending on the need of each deployed model. In this scenario, the cloud infrastructure is examined based on schemes for data access and storage and adapts to the service runtime with respect to cost effectiveness along with data integrity and security.

In respect to deployment of cloud services in coherence with IoT, the methods for deployment of different software components are included in cloud IoT systems at different levels of abstractions and allow continuous provisioning with procedure to configure and connect deployments. The user centric flexible and open architecture is used for IoT having cloud at its center. In such cloud centric architecture various application providers may join and share their data like wireless sensor network providers, developers, graphic designers, etc. These application providers can contribute by offering different tools related to the field of expertise. The data analyst develops compatible software tools for data analysis, data mining and machine learning tools can be contributed by artificial intelligence experts for convergence of data in to knowledge, and graphics designer can contribute by providing visualization tools.

The various applications and services contributed in cloud computing environment can be made available to users of cloud services as infrastructure, platforms or software. With the help of abstraction in cloud IoT system, the generated data by various sources with tools complexity in the background does not restrict user from exploiting the full potential of the cloud IoT system. The multiple domains of computing are integrated in cloud to build new business by provisioning scalable storage, elastic computing, and other useful tools.

CONCLUSION

In this chapter, the different models of deployment applicable for cloud computing are discussed. The private, community, public and hybrid deployment models are explained in detail. The blending of IoT with cloud computing fetches the attention hence this chapter also discussed a possible way of combining these two different technologies and the implications related to the integration of IoT with cloud services. The chapter also discusses the technical functionalities to enable both IoT and cloud services to work together with the complications involved. The scheme for cloud optimization is also discussed briefly. This blending of two heterogeneous technologies raise some research challenges like dealing with diverse quality and state of devices and technologies involved, meeting performance needs, reliability of services, privacy preservation, security, scalability, legal, and social aspects.

REFERENCES

Ashton, K. (2009). *That "Internet of Things" thing*. RFID Journal.

Díaz, M., Martín, C., & Rubio, B. (2016). State-of-the-art, challenges, and open issues in the integration of internet of things and cloud computing. *Journal of Network and Computer Applications, 67*, 99–117. doi:10.1016/j.jnca.2016.01.010

Dustdar, S., Guo, Y., Satzger, B., & Truong, H. L. (2011). Principles of elastic processes. *IEEE Internet Computing, 15*(5), 66–71. doi:10.1109/MIC.2011.121

El Kateb, D., Fouquet, F., Nain, G., Meira, J. A., Ackerman, M., & Le Traon, Y. (2014, March). Generic cloud platform multi-objective optimization leveraging models@ run time. *Proceedings of the 29th Annual ACM Symposium on Applied Computing*, 343-350. 10.1145/2554850.2555044

Garrison, G., Kim, S., & Wakefield, R. L. (2012). Success factors for deploying cloud computing. *Communications of the ACM, 55*(9), 62–68. doi:10.1145/2330667.2330685

Mell, P., & Grance, T. (2009). The NIST definition of Cloud computing. *Natl. Inst. Stand. Technol., 53*(6), 50.

Miorandi, D., Sicari, S., De Pellegrini, F., & Chlamtac, I. (2012). Internet of Things: Vision, applications and research challenges. *Ad Hoc Networks*, *10*(7), 1497–1516. doi:10.1016/j.adhoc.2012.02.016

Papazoglou, M. (2008). Compliance requirements for business-process driven SOAs. *E-Government ICT Professionalism and Competences Service Science*, 183-194.

Stanoevska-Slabeva, K., & Wozniak, T. (2010). *Grid and Cloud Computing-A Business Perspective on Technology and Applications*. Berlin: Springer-Verlag. doi:10.1007/978-3-642-05193-7

Subashini, S., & Kavitha, V. (2011). A survey on security issues in service delivery models of cloud computing. *Journal of Network and Computer Applications*, *34*(1), 1–11. doi:10.1016/j.jnca.2010.07.006

Suciu, G., Vulpe, A., Halunga, S., Fratu, O., Todoran, G., & Suciu, V. (2013). Smart Cities Built on Resilient Cloud Computing and Secure Internet of Things. *Control Systems and Computer Science (CSCS), 19th International Conference on*, 513-518. 10.1109/CSCS.2013.58

Tao, F., Cheng, Y., Da Xu, L., Zhang, L., & Li, B. H. (2014). CCIoT-CMfg: Cloud computing and internet of things-based cloud manufacturing service system. *IEEE Transactions on Industrial Informatics*, *10*(2), 1435–1442. doi:10.1109/TII.2014.2306383

Truong, H. L., & Dustdar, S. (2015). Principles for engineering IoT cloud systems. *IEEE Cloud Computing*, *2*(2), 68–76. doi:10.1109/MCC.2015.23

Victories, V. (2015). *4 Types of Cloud Computing Deployment Model You Need to Know*. IBM developer Works. IBM.

Zhang, Q., Cheng, L., & Boutaba, R. (2010). Cloud computing: State-of-the-art and research challenges. *Journal of Internet Services and Applications*, *1*(1), 7–18. doi:10.100713174-010-0007-6

This research was previously published in Examining Cloud Computing Technologies Through the Internet of Things edited by Pradeep Tomar and Gurjit Kaur, pages 43-56, copyright year 2018 by Information Science Reference (an imprint of IGI Global).

Chapter 105
Trust in an Enterprise World:
A Survey

Fotios I. Gogoulos
National Technical University of Athens, Greece

Anna Antonakopoulou
National Technical University of Athens, Greece

Georgios V. Lioudakis
National Technical University of Athens, Greece

Dimitra I. Kaklamani
National Technical University of Athens, Greece

Iakovos S. Venieris
National Technical University of Athens, Greece

ABSTRACT

Web 2.0 technologies have fundamentally reshaped everyday users' perceptions regarding online services by strengthening the importance of individual participation. This profound change is expanding to substantially affect modern enterprise operations and especially corporate information management practices. Well-established business models are upgraded to capture value from the establishment of dynamic coalitions and virtual organizations among remote stakeholders. However, these collaboration formulations dictate the concentration, use, and circulation of corporate information and sensitive personal data, and thus ignite severe security and privacy concerns. Enterprises against this background are more than willing to invest in terms cost and time in order to enforce the necessary countermeasures and thus build and maintain the trustworthiness of involved operations. This chapter studies how legislation and inherent characteristics of this new collaboration paradigm affect the qualities of trust and highlights prominent features of security and privacy protection measures that can deal with emerging trust issues.

DOI: 10.4018/978-1-5225-8176-5.ch105

INTRODUCTION

Recent advances in information technologies are fundamentally reshaping the modus operandi of online markets around the globe. Enterprises on intra and inter organizational level are moving from monolithic client-server architectures towards dynamic clouds of resources. Collaborative Web 2.0 technologies have become the leading edge of this rapid transformation and have set the foundation for the emergence of a new business operation and collaboration paradigm labeled as Enterprise 2.0. The term Enterprise 2.0 coined by (McAfee, 2006a) as the adoption of Web 2.0 services to improve knowledge workers' productivity and augment the effectiveness and competence of organizations does not necessarily embrace explicit technological tools; it rather introduces a groundbreaking model for an enterprise's knowledge structure, information management and resources sharing.

Determinants in the process of Enterprise 2.0 adoption constitute the empowerment of users, the bottom-up formulation of new processing patterns, the emergence of free-flowing collaborative engagements, and the effective guidance of possible participants (De Hertogh, Viaene & Dedene, 2011). That is, Web 2.0 initiatives call for a profound shift of dynamics from a top-down to a bottom-up business logic; business value is built collectively by knowledge workers and is not simply imposed from a small number of key stakeholders. In this context, emerging electronic transactions have become highly dynamic in their nature, while involved work and data flows are suffused over totally decentralized collaboration parties employing distinct roles in the service provision chain.

However, inherent characteristics of the 2.0 epoch described above can ignite severe trust issues among participating entities. Whereas enterprises traditionally enforce strict centralized controls regarding information access and dissemination in the context of emerging transactions, openness and collective participation attributes of Web 2.0 tend to pose significant information security and individuals' privacy risks and thus call for immediate action. In a time where European citizens declare their concerns regarding their personal data and private life protection (Gallup Organization, 2008; European Opinion Research Group, 2011), it becomes evident that it is the level of user's trust and confidence regarding these emerging technologies that can either boost their applicability and effectiveness or comprise a heavy obstacle in the way of their diffusion.

On an international level, companies involved in e-business transactions have reached this realization; while exposing their resources through collaboration initiatives the respective potential information security and confidentiality attack surface is widened. Ultimately, the key to the successful and beneficial adoption of Enterprise 2.0 is acquiring the appropriate balance between vast user empowerment and strict privilege control. Against this background, information security and privacy as means to instill trust into potential collaborators has become a salient issue for enterprises and their key personnel in the 2.0 era (Milojicic, 2008). Evidently, along with trustworthiness privacy and security measures bring commercial value to organizations, a value greatly enhanced by the fact that privacy is increasingly becoming a legislated area. Awareness of the public regarding personal data protection, strengthened by legislation on an international level, affects collaborators' online behavior when involved in commercial activities (Acquisti, 2010) and thus motivates enterprises to adopt appropriate business models. In this climate, a number of keynote information security specifications and standards issued by leading institutions further intensify the organizations' perception of trust and sensitivity about risks stemming from privacy infringement and security breaches.

Ultimate objective of this chapter is to provide a concrete theoretical and technological roadmap for trust in the 2.0 era; from privacy and security related legislation and Web 2.0 operation patterns to explicit trust requirements and from the latter to compliance through respective technical trust management approaches and solutions. Major information security standards, privacy related legislation, along with the particularization of trust in Enterprise 2.0 environments and the specification of trust requirements comprise the content of the next section. The chapter then delves into the literature and provides an overview of the most important, characteristic and influential trust inducing models. Before concluding with a short overview of the future research directions, the chapter provides an overview of the studied trust models.

BACKGROUND

Overview of the Legal and Regulatory Background

The current trend among organizations in a worldwide level towards the adoption of concrete security and privacy policies is driven by the underlying legislation. In fact, legislation provides the means for the efficient orchestration of common security and privacy mechanisms and their composition into robust holistic trust solutions. In this context, legislation compliance and technical requirements of trust frameworks obtain a linear relation.

Since user participation comprises the cornerstone of Web 2.0 principles, privacy protection becomes crucial. Undoubtedly, Directive 95/46/EC (European Parliament and Council, 1995) and complementarily Directive 2002/58/EC (European Parliament and Council, 2002) comprise the most influential statutory laws regarding privacy in the E.U. region. Disciplines of the above Directives constitute formalizations of the fundamental principles, set forth by the Organization for Economic Co-operation and Development in its milestone guidelines (OECD, 1980). The legal and regulatory requirements (OECD, 1980; European Parliament and Council, 1995; European Parliament and Council, 2002; Lioudakis, et al., 2010) that should be taken into account for privacy protection in online market environments can be summarized as follows:

- Guarantee the lawfulness of the data processing.
- Identification of the purposes for which data are processed.
- Assurance of the necessity, adequacy, and proportionality of the data processed.
- Protection of the quality of the data processed.
- Retention of identifiable data only for the period required for the fulfillment of the processing purpose.
- Notification and other authorizations from competent Privacy Authority.
- Information to the data subjects.
- Consent and withdrawal of consent from data subjects.
- Exercising rights of the data subject.
- Enforcement of data security and confidentiality.
- Processing of special categories of data is performed in compliance with the specific data protection legislation.
- Data access limitation.

- Dissemination of data to third parties and transfer of data to third countries is performed in compliance with the underlying fair data practices, the contract with the data subject and the specific provisions ruling the transfer of data.
- Supervision and sanctions by competent Privacy Authority.
- Lawful interception by competent Privacy Authority.

It should be noted that, unlike the E.U., the U.S. have retained a less holistic and cross-disciplinary approach towards privacy legislation enacting different laws for each distinct business environment. For some insights in the frameworks of the U.S. and other countries, the reader is referred to Solove's excellent essay (Solove, 2006).

Information security is defined as the protection of information from unauthorized access, usage, disclosure, and modification in order to provide integrity, confidentiality and availability. Obviously, individual privacy protection is greatly dependent on information security practices. The E.U. has therefore accordingly legislated supplementary Directives to meet requirements in individual domains such as the 1999/93/EC Directive (European Parliament and Council, 1999). More recently, Trust and Security was recognized as one of the Pillars of the Digital Agenda for Europe (European Commission, 2010a), an initiative emerged in the context of the Europe 2020 Strategy (European Commission, 2010b). This climate in favor of information security practices has turned the spotlights on popular information security standards and business best practices specifications. Driven by the original OECD privacy guidelines (1980) several information security management standards have been established in the last decade. Keynote specifications have been publicized by the National Institute of Standards and Technology (Swanson, M., & Guttman, B, 1996), the Information Systems Security Association (ISSA, 2004), the International Organization for Standardization (ISO/IEC 27002, 2005) and the Information Security Forum (ISF, 2007). Focusing on information security in different levels from a technological perspective the above disciplines converge into the following action points:

- Establishing information security policie.
- Enforcing identification and authentication.
- Enforcing access control.
- Assuring compliance with legal, regulatory, and contractual requirements of information security.

Establishing online trust constitutes the ultimate objective of all previous specifications. On the one hand, privacy principles derived from the OECD and E.U. legislative guidelines aim at protecting the user's privacy and instilling trust towards electronic transactions. On the other hand, security principles extracted from current security standards focus on protecting the most important asset of our times: information, and thus work towards motivating compliant enterprises to collaborate online. Formal pieces of documents such as the above constitute the best incentive for customers and enterprises for realizing the importance of online trust and becoming compliant with identified principles.

Trust in the Enterprise 2.0 Context

The alternation in the state of mind of enterprises regarding security and privacy enhancement measures is radical; protection technologies have turned from social added value services to be regarded as actual economic enablers. Enterprise and Web 2.0 particularities systematize this shift.

Studying the patterns of Enterprise 2.0 diffusion, Bughin (2008) recognizes that in order for companies to uphold a competitive advantage in the 2.0 era the following actions are required: loosening hierarchical structures, rewarding active and valuable participation, moving from central to "edge" competencies by means of exploiting knowledge workers outside of the corporation's boundaries and gaining the trust of customers and suppliers. Bin Husin and Swatman (2008) suggested a four-category model denoting how organizations can benefit from Enterprise 2.0 technologies including the 4Cs: Communication, Cooperation, Collaboration and Connection. These approaches in grounding Enterprise 2.0 principles converge into the following contradiction: Enterprise 2.0 frameworks can through their embedded characteristics both instill as well retrieve confidence and trust beliefs to and from their users. On the one hand, the dynamics of Web 2.0 tools, the transparency of transactions (as the collaborating party becomes an integral part of processes), the feeling of collectiveness and the user-centric nature of operations empower the user and cultivate a mood of trust towards the underlying technology. On the other hand, the extension of the service provision chain with unknown participating parties, the obscurity of collaborators' roles and responsibilities throughout transactions and the lack of central information management leading to hard to monitor work and data flows build insecurity and lack of confidence towards active involvement in operations. Hints of distrust and lack of confidence towards the emerging alteration in information building and sharing culture are prominent in recent surveys. More specifically, results of research studies have indicated that in many cases despite the great popularity of Web 2.0 tools users are not aware of risks regarding their information security (Rudman & Steenkamp, 2010). Risks and distrust reside on the enterprise side as well. By extending the user participation base and by extending collaborations outside the company's boundaries organizations in the Enterprise 2.0 era are inherently broadening their potential attack zones and become vulnerable to opportunistic and malicious behaviors. Besides, according to a Eurostat Press Release (2010) during 2009 one out of twenty enterprises in the E.U. has reported incidents involving the destruction or corruption of data due to malicious software infection or unauthorized access.

Information security and privacy protection measures adapted to the 2.0 principles can work towards this direction; protecting end-points (customers and enterprises), enhancing the privacy of involved resources and most importantly of information and eventually instilling trust to all collaboration parties. In accordance with the underlying legal and regulatory framework and the inherent Enterprise 2.0 characteristics, for the purposes of this chapter we adopt a technological perspective of trust (Ratnasingam, 2005). Technology trust is defined as the organizations' confidence founded on the belief that the underlying technology infrastructure is capable of supporting transactions according to their expectations. Dimensions of technology trust formulate the following trust requirements:

- **Confidentiality:** Means for the protection of personal privacy and proprietary information should be provided. Compliance with the legal and regulatory background described above is crucial.
- **Integrity:** Safeguard measures against improper and unwanted information modification should be enforced.
- **Authentication:** Identification mechanisms for confirming the truth regarding users' identities should be applied.
- **Non-Repudiation:** Challenging the validity of one's performed actions should be unsuccessful through the exploitation of respective acknowledgement procedures.
- **Access Control:** Restrictions on access and disclosure of information should be applied according to the enforcement of required criteria.

The above principles constitute broad definitions that mandate specific characteristics for information security and privacy protection mechanisms in the process of protecting traditional online transactions and its actors. However, Enterprise 2.0 attributes further particularize those generally accepted trust requirements. Therefore protection measures and approaches that should be promoted for adoption are those which conform to its inherent characteristics:

- **Decentralized Networks:** Services, processes and relevant information are spanned across administratively and geographically dispersed peers.
- **Independent Trust Domains:** Collaborating peers are ruled by heterogeneous security policies adapted to their own needs and requirements.
- **Dynamic Communities Coalitions:** Collaboration and information sharing in the Enterprise 2.0 context are often performed on the basis of ad-hoc and dynamic formulations of user communities.
- **User Empowerment:** Web 2.0 attributes are summarized into this key principle; moving from top-down to bottom-up business logics and thus strengthening the centrality of the user's role.

Figure 1 summarizes the adopted trust requirements applied in the context of Enterprise 2.0 operations.

MEETING THE REQUIREMENTS

Trust Issue and Countermeasures

Despite the reasonable diffusion rates of Web 2.0 among enterprises (Bughin & Manyika, 2007) a significant portion of organizations and respective employees remains quite skeptical towards Enterprise

Figure 1. Trust specification in the enterprise 2.0 context

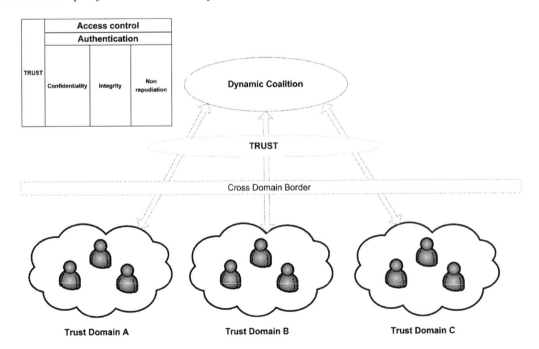

2.0 adoption. This adoption reluctance, known as the *Empty Quarter* phenomenon (McAfee, 2006b) is grounded on a variety of reasons such as the possible low interest in and fear of innovative technologies and the existence of strongly established corporate cultures. However, it is evident that information security and privacy concerns further motivate users to position themselves in the Empty Quarter (McAfee, 2008; Lin, Lee, & Lin, 2010). Consequently, trust remains in the spotlight and as Kwan and Ramachandran (2009) state: "since the raison d' être of Web 2.0 is collaboration—often with strangers—trust is the linchpin of this new continuum of participation" (p. 2). In this context, enforcing strong trust measures for addressing trust requirements defined in the previous section becomes a key issue for organizations.

Generally, security frameworks in computer science can be categorized into hard and soft security systems (Rasmusson & Janson, 1996). This conceptual categorization can be adopted in the realm of trust: hard security is achieved by traditional security mechanisms making use of concrete evidence such as digital credentials and security tokens in order to make trust decisions according to specified security policies, while soft security systems employ social control mechanisms taking advantage of metrics regarding notions such as recommendations and reputation in order to evaluate trust. Indeed, the flexibility and openness of social control measures are well suited to the dynamic and user-centric nature of Enterprise 2.0. Therefore, whereas both approaches retain their own pros and cons, hybrid models employing hard security methods on the basis of "soft information" can be applicable and effective in many risk limited cases (Varadharajan, 2009). For instance, soft security mechanisms can be crucial for the establishment of *initial trust* (McKnight, Cummings, & Chervany, 1998) among potential collaborators. Despite the usefulness of soft techniques, hard security constitutes the main target of this review. This choice, apart from being compatible with the technological perspective of trust adopted here, is not unreasonable; social control mechanisms are characterized by great volumes of uncertainty in contrast to firmness derived from "harder" security mechanisms. Recommendations and reputation metrics provided by third parties although indicative of the trustworthiness of the target under consideration are prone to opportunistic behaviors, such as distorting information and misleading partners.

Whereas the vast majority of current research surveys focuses on investigating and analyzing partial views of the trust issue (i.e., trust definition, trust by means of secure authentication, trust by means of effective authorization, trust by means of reputation and recommendations) this chapter provides an overview of trust enhancing approaches which when appropriately adopted and combined can adequately address trust requirements in the 2.0 era. Hence, goal of our review is not to provide an exhaustive view of each trust mechanism, but rather a representative description of current approaches towards security and privacy issues within the Enterprise 2.0 world. In that respect, hard security and privacy measures comprise the content of the following analysis. Investigated technologies will be presented in the context of two broad categories: trust representation and exchange and trust establishment and enforcement. The above comprise two distinct stages of trust accomplishment; the first step to trust an entity is the acknowledgement of its identity and qualities, while the second includes the determination of its privileges and the enforcement of final trust decisions.

Trust Representation and Exchange

The term trust representation and exchange in the context of a digital partnership refers to the accumulation and circulation of tangible evidence regarding information related with potential cooperating parties. Prior to being able to negotiate and establish trust relationships, entities willing to engage in collaboration need to demonstrate valid proofs of their identity and attributes. In that sense, authentication is inherently related to trust representation and exchange. Online authentication has been studied thoroughly and from different disciplines from the early beginnings of e-commerce and e-business. Generally, two forms of authentication evidence prevail in current online transactions: biometrics and digital credentials. While digital credentials employ cryptography for depicting and verifying identities and attributes, biometric authentication technologies exploit physical features of humans for their identification, such as fingerprint scanning (Jain, Ross, & Pankanti, 2006), face recognition (Dabbah, Woo, & Dlay, 2007), iris scanning (Ganorkar & Ghatol, 2007) and signature verification (Bandopadhaya, et al., 2008). Several hybrid models integrating cryptographic techniques along with biometric matchers have also been proposed (Xinyi, et al., 2011).

However effective and liable biometrics may have turned out in the process of identities recognition, respective mechanisms suffer from a number of vulnerabilities. More specifically, unlike digital identification tokens, biological characteristics cannot be without difficulty altered and revoked. Furthermore, the disclosure of biometric traits is treated with skepticism and emotional-behavioral reservations by users due to its conceptual correlation with fingerprint matching in crime investigations. Last but not least, biometric authentication inherently ignites severe privacy issues. Respective technologies can be maliciously handled for inferring further information from biological measurements such as genetic information and for effectively attacking users' anonymity (Prabhakar, Pankanti, & Jain, 2003). Hence, biometric measures fail to conform to the confidentiality trust requirement and thus are not part of our analysis.

Public key cryptography and asymmetric key algorithms can efficiently enforce integrity, confidentiality and non-repudiation and offer the possibility to authenticate the identity of entities by validating the possession of a private key associated with a known public key. This association is depicted in the form of a digital certificate. Although alternative certificate specifications have emerged over the years, the most widely diffused is found in the International Telecommunications Union X.509 standard (International Telecommunication Union, 2005). Authentication in distributed environments by the exploitation of digital certificates has been fundamentally related with two key mechanisms that prevail in the online market: Public Key Infrastructures (PKI) and Federated Identity Management (FIdM) Systems.

Public Key Infrastructure

Public Key Infrastructure (PKI) and Privilege Management Infrastructure (PMI) constitute the most influential representatives of public key cryptography employment for the creation, distribution, validation and revocation of digital certificates (depicting identities in PKIs and attributes in PMIs). The above operations comprise typical responsibilities of Certification Authorities (CAs), entities whose role in an effective PKI installation is of crucial importance since they work as the user's trust point in the infrastructure. The placement of CAs within a PKI instance affects fundamental aspects of the mechanism such as validation of certificates and cross domain trust relationships establishment. Traditional PKI schemes, such as single CAs, hierarchically organized CAs and the employment of mesh of CAs are notoriously insufficient to support large and widely distributed interactions mainly due to scalability reasons (Polk, Hastings & Malpani, 2003) stemming from heavy computations required in tracking remote users' trust points and estimating the accuracy and validity of involved digital certificates.

In order to leverage the capabilities of PKIs the concept of Bridge Certification Authorities (BCAs) has been introduced. Designed to counter traditional vulnerabilities of conventional PKI architectures BCAs and their derivatives Bridge Validation Authorities (BVAs) connect disperse existing trust domains

(PKIs), reduce certificate validation paths, equate different policies of existing corporate PKIs and thus become more adaptable to the demands of widely distributed systems. It should be noted that BCAs do not issue certificates to users and are not regarded as user trust points. That is, distinct trust domains retain their own internal PKI architecture based on traditional approaches, while a BCA facilitates their interconnection and efficient cooperation. Over the last years, several interesting solutions have been proposed for trust management based on BCA and BVA architectures. More indicative of the adherence, adaptation and acceptability qualities of BCAs in e-business are implementations put forth by acclaimed organizations on an international level:

- European Bridge-CA employs secure communication channels among businesses, banks, assurance, telecommunication companies and public authorities around Europe.
- Chinese Taipei BCA connects through certification services public and privates CAs.
- Federal Bridge Certification Authority (FBCA), which enforces secure interoperability among U.S. entities cross-certified with the FBCA.

Despite the demonstration of the above PKI success stories, many researchers argue that PKI has never met the initial high expectations of the research community for supporting the build-up of a unique global trust infrastructure. Operational and technical issues have critically obstructed the wide PKI diffusion in highly distributed and dynamic environments (Wilson, 2008). However, BCA architectures evidently constitute an important step forward. Statistics and pending attempts towards the support of large scale Bridge Certification Authorities and Bridge Validation Authorities constitute perfect examples of this PKI achievement. The fact remains, that the introduction of PKI substantially raised awareness of the public regarding the appliance of digital proofs of identities and attributes through digital certificates in online markets.

Federated Identity Management

Identity Management (IdM) systems emerged as a convenient approach towards the organized management of individual's identities and attributes. Enterprise 2.0 architectures and tools, based on users collaboration, federated work groups formulation and resources integration qualities, enlarge the need for organized online authentication mechanisms and most importantly for the management of diverse user identities. The involvement in Web 2.0 and social network communities offers a great example of users owning multiple identities, utilized in different environments and for dissimilar purposes. However, centralized and top-down logic based architectures, such as PKIs and IdMs although building the foundation for more advanced identity solutions, fail in standalone mode to conform to the dynamics of the emerging 2.0 landscape. Federated Identity Management (FIdM) systems (Shim, Bhalla & Pendyala 2005; Camenisch & Pfitzmann, 2007) supplement traditional approaches and work towards satisfying the need for an organized identification framework, by providing the means for tracking and accumulating entities' identities and attributes, stored across multiple and diverse identity management systems. A federated identity enables the user to roam seamlessly among multiple service providers, eliminates the need for numerous authentications and thus providing the comfort of Single-Sign-On, increases the portability of digital identities and leverages the flexibility of users in participating in dynamic coalitions.

A wide variety of FIdM solutions have been proposed, each handling the issue of federating identities across multiple remote trust domains from different viewpoint and discipline. In 2002, the Liberty

Alliance group proposed the Identity Federation Framework – ID-FF, which later evolved to reach its current version of ID-FF 1.2 (The Liberty Alliance Project, 2005). The key contribution of the Liberty Alliance specifications is found at the interconnection and integration of all personal information related to distinct service providers residing in the federation group into one unique federated identity. Based on the Liberty Alliance specifications, the Organization for the Advancement of Structured Information Standards formed the Security Assertion Markup Language (SAML), an XML based standard for data exchange between identity and service providers. In its current version, SAML 2.0 (OASIS, 2005) constitutes the prevalent framework for identity management in federations. Other FIdM technologies include the user-centric Microsoft's InfoCard (Bertocci, Serack & Baker, 2007), the SAML based Shibboleth (MACE, 2001) and OpenID (Recordon & Reed, 2006). The OpenID approach limits the need for multiple identities by exploiting the utilization of unique Uniform Resource Locator based identifiers. OpenID is fast evolving into becoming the default solution for secure authentication in the Internet due to its simplicity and user-friendliness. Furthermore, its user-centric nature promotes OpenID based solutions for adoption in the Enterprise 2.0 context. Nevertheless, the employment of unique identifiers and the consequent possibility of different service providers correlating users' activities are aspects that hurdle the trustworthiness of OpenID despite its wide popularity (OpenID is supported by worldwide vendors such as AOL, Google, IBM and Microsoft).

The issue of privacy uncertainty is not unusual in federated identity solutions. In fact, FIdM can ignite severe privacy issues regarding users' attributes and identities secrecy. Sharing personal identifiable data and information among service providers endangers the confidentiality of users, attacks users' anonymity and enables malicious activities such as identity theft. An interesting approach for addressing these uneasiness with FIdM is reflected in research activities proposing the exploitation of cryptography for anonymizing identification proofs. In that respect, a rapid trend towards the integration of mechanisms for the usage of pseudonyms in federated identity certificates has been built in the respective literature. Idemix (Camenisch & Van Herreweghen, 2002) an anonymous credential provider system and SPARTA (Bianchi et al., 2008) constitute indicative examples of this tendency. Furthermore, projects PRIME (FP6 IST project PRIME) and PrimeLife (FP7 IST project PrimeLife) based on digital signature schemas and cryptographic zero-knowledge proofs extend FIdM operations for achieving stronger privacy protection and effective multiple credential usage. The latter projects provide a wide variety of functionalities in the identity management area while focusing on privacy and the centrality of the user's role.

Federated identity solutions have been evolving to meet the requirements of emerging trends on the Internet leading to the concept of Identity 2.0. The most intriguing feature of this evolution, is the relocation of the user into the centre of identity management. Users in Identity 2.0 are allowed to organize and distribute their personal identifying information according to their own security and privacy preferences. Approaches that combine the utilization of pseudonyms while being compliant with the key attribute of Web 2.0 which is decentralization, constitute the perfect candidates for adoption in the realm of Enterprise 2.0. PRIME and PrimeLife attributes highlight the required qualities and reflect perfect examples of Enterprise 2.0 trust compliant solutions.

Trust Establishment and Enforcement

The term trust establishment and enforcement reflects operations taking place subsequent to the trust representation and exchange phase, that is after parties under collaboration have identified and acknowledged each other. In this phase and based on the accumulated identifying information, participants in an online partnership are called to take trust decisions and accordingly adjust their behavior. In that sense, trust establishment and enforcement operations are inherently related to authorization. Indeed, resource sharing mandates the enforcement of authorization algorithms which finalize into explicit decisions regulating the access of information on the basis of who has access rights, what kind of access privileges are acknowledged and when those privileges should be activated. Traditionally, organizations have been employing access control models and trust management technologies for these purposes.

Access Control

Trust violations in the Enterprise 2.0 world include unlawful access to respective data; in that respect access control technologies constitute highly important mechanisms for personal data protection and confidentiality enhancement. However, traditional access control models such as Discretionary Access Control (DAC), Mandatory Access Control (MAC) and Role-Based Access Control (RBAC), fail to conform to the sum of special requirements which rule trust establishment and enforcement in dynamic and complicated environments, covering only partial views of the problem. In that respect, during the last years several mechanisms have emerged extending traditional models by introducing concepts such as obligation, purpose, context, separation of duties and conflicts resolution and integrating them into their semantics.

In Purpose Based Access Control model (Byun, Bertino & Li, 2005) privacy policies allow the disclosure of information only if the purpose of the access request is related to that information, highlighting the notion of purpose. Working towards the same direction, the Purpose-Aware Role-Based Access Control model (Masoumzadeh & Joshi, 2008) defines the concept of purpose as an intermediate entity between roles and permissions in order to perform purpose aware access control decisions. Location and temporal based approaches have also been proposed. In GEO-RBAC model (Bertino et al., 2005), a complete specification of spatial constraints is utilized by means of a geometric model for the representation of objects, user positions and roles. Furthermore, the Generalized Temporal Role Based Access Control (Joshi et al., 2005) model contains significant characteristics that are related to privacy aspects. The described model supports temporal authorizations in an efficient and completed way. It also includes the concepts of dynamic and static separation of duties as well as constraints related with spatial context. In Generalized Temporal History Based Access Control Model (Ravari et al., 2010) the authorization decision is taken after the evaluation of the relevant security rules along with the temporal constraints related with the history of accesses. Moreover, the Privacy-Aware Role Based Access Control model (Ni et al., 2010) deals with the most significant attributes of an emerging family of access control models, privacy aware access control. Concepts such as purposes, obligations and conditions comprise the foundation of the model. Finally, the Organization Based Access Control framework (Cuppens & Cuppens-Boulahia, 2008) provides the means for the specification of dynamic, flexible and privacy-aware access control policies. Organization Based Access Control is centered on the concept of the Organization, i.e., the entity responsible for managing a security policy. Respective policies are modeled at the organizational level on the basis of the roles that subjects, actions or objects play in the organization.

Clearly, the aforementioned access control models take one step forward towards addressing issues of complex authorizations in online transactions. However, key characteristics of Privacy-Aware Role Based Access Control and Organization Based Access Control are better suited in the context of performing trustful Enterprise 2.0 operations. Introduced notions such as obligations and conditions in the former and organizations in the latter seem to be compliant with the specification of trust in Enterprise 2.0 provided in the previous section.

The specification patterns of the above models have been based on a single organization's point of view and thus lack formulations that could capture potential conflicts between heterogeneous security policies of disperse collaborating entities. In dynamic collaborations reconciliation and mapping methods should be applied on the security policies of distributed parties in order for an orchestrated access control decision to be extracted. Research on security policies integration and reconciliation in distributed environments has produced some interesting results. In (Hao et al., 2004) a formal framework for the hierarchical representation of security policies is provided. Hierarchies are then exploited to identify policies structures and consequently to apply an efficient reconciliation algorithm. In (Yau & Chen, 2008), the proposed policy integration solution takes into account the dynamics of collaborations when participating nodes are joining and leaving the partnership in an arbitrary fashion. While being ontology based the proposed approach utilizes a similarity based security policy adaptation algorithm and a negotiation based model for generating concrete sets of security policies which can be acknowledged and accepted by all involved participants. Authors in (He & Yang, 2009) proposed a Policy Driven Authorization Control framework for access controls in cross domain collaboration environments. The framework introduces the notion of collaboration patterns and collaboration policies in order for possible policy inconsistencies to be identified. In a recent work Sun & Chen (2011) proposed a collaborative authorization framework based on XACML (OASIS, 2004) policies. Collaborative policies are generated by applying combining algorithms on sets of binary expressions referring to XACML encoded policies and the collaboration intents of participating parties.

In our perspective, the combination of policy reconciliation and mapping algorithms with high acclaimed access control models as those described above is the ultimate key for specifying a unified collaborative access control scheme. Such integrations constitute perfect candidates for adoption in the dynamic and decentralized environment of Enterprise 2.0.

Trust Management

One of the earliest attempts in highlighting the importance of trust in highly distributed environments was trust management. Introduced by Blaze, Feigenbaum, and Lacy (1996), trust management established a general viewpoint towards building online trust, while attempting to address the problem holistically through a unified mechanism for specifying and interpreting security policies, credentials, and relationships. Trust management frameworks deal with authorization in highly distributed systems by generalizing traditional access control models and by eliminating the closed world assumption according to which all collaborating parties are known (Weeks, 2001), a perspective partially adopted in access control models described above.

Following the introduction of the PolicyMaker trust management system (Blaze et al., 1996), a variety of solutions have been proposed. The Keynote system (Blaze et al., 1999) utilized authorization mechanisms that given a set of assertions return with compliance values denoting the degree to which the request under investigation complies with written policies. The SPKI/SDSI framework (Ellison et al., 1999) emerged after the integration of the Simple Public Key Infrastructure with the Simple Distributed Security Infrastructure. SPKI enriched the SDSI with more sophisticated and distributed systems oriented authorization policies. In SPKI/SDSI, identifiers are directly bound to capabilities through authorization certificates, which can be delegated at will by their owners. The RT family of trust management frameworks includes a number of different trust management systems, starting from the role based RT0 (Li, Winsborough & Mitchell, 2001). The basic RT0 language has provided the foundation for the build-up of several follow-ups, such as RT1 and RTT (Li, Mitchell & Winsborough, 2002) for the integration of parameterised roles and separation of duties attributes and RTC (Li & Mitchell, 2003) for inserting constraints on previously integrated parameterised roles. OASIS (Dim mock et al. 2004) is another trust management solution, where users can earn their membership into role categories by demonstrating compliance with security policies of certificate authorities. The ownership of a valid role membership, represented by a relative certificate, is equal to a positive authorization. Finally, the role based Cassandra (Becker & Sewell, 2004) utilizes parameterised roles, permissions as well as role activations and deactivations.

Although not directly related to Enterprise 2.0 concepts, well known and widely deployed grid authorization frameworks such as Privilege and Role Management Infrastructure Standard (Chadwick et al., 2008), Virtual Organization Membership Service (Alfieri, 2003) and Akenti (Akenti, 2009) own useful features that can be exploited in Enterprise 2.0 oriented trust management systems. Prominent qualities of the above models are the employment of PMI attribute certificates which decouple users' privileges from their local identities and their high level of scalability when operating in the context of large virtual organizations (Jie et al., 2011).

Overview

We argue that trust in online contexts has a qualitative rather than a quantitative value. Even though several trust metrics have been proposed in the literature based on reputation, recommendations and past behavior evaluation they fail to clearly capture the notion of trust. Of course the importance of soft security mechanisms cannot be neglected; they provide fruitful information that can undoubtedly affect online behavior and most importantly found a layer of initial trust towards online transactions. From our perspective, soft security features should be utilized in combination with concrete hard measures that fundamentally create trust. This reasoning is compliant with the respective legislation as well as with keynote security specifications published by well acclaimed international vendors. In this context, trust is inherently interconnected with mechanisms which effectively establish information security and protect individuals' privacy. Obviously, trust inducing mechanisms in the Enterprise 2.0 world should be analyzed through the prism of the Web 2.0 inherent attributes.

The analysis undertaken on the basis of two fundamental online transaction phases has as its primary goal to highlight the attributes that can promote a security and privacy protection approach to be regarded as trust 2.0 compliant. User centric, dynamic aware, heterogeneity responsive and decentralized solutions clearly stand out from this investigation. Furthermore the exploitation of cryptography for ensuring integrity non-repudiation as well as for advocating strong authentication and authorization techniques is mandated. In this context, several conclusions can be drawn.

- Trust management systems provide the more holistic approach for addressing the trust issue in decentralized dynamic environments. Especially, grid oriented solutions provide features for the formulation of virtual organizations, a notion directly related to Enterprise 2.0.
- The foundation of a strong trust management system is to be found within its implemented access control model. Access control models conceptualize trust requirements and provide the basis for

enforcing explicit authorization decisions. Notions such as purpose, privacy and organization introduced in several access control models presented here are of crucial importance.

- Trust management systems and access control models capitalize on demonstrated proofs of identities and attributes in order to authorize requests. Organized circulation of digital proofs by FIdM systems, should be user centric and provide the necessary flexibility to users in order to manage their own identity profiles.
- PKIs and PMIs in their federated formation can be employed in large scale environments in order to trustfully connect independent trust domains. BCAs worldwide work towards this direction.

FUTURE RESEARCH DIRECTIONS

Undoubtedly, more than 30 years after the original OECD privacy guidelines, obtaining and maintaining trust remains vital to organizations. "Questions remain, however, as to the best combination of policies and tools to protect privacy and preserve (or restore) trust in this evolving landscape" (OECD, 2011. p. 25). Future research directions covering Enterprise 2.0 technologies involve solutions towards this direction: integration of tools. The requirement for more holistic security and privacy solutions is in the 2.0 epoch more prevalent than ever. Therefore in the future, greater interest should be shown in integrating existing innovative solutions in order to provide an holistic trust solution in the context of Enterprise 2.0 functionalities. Correlations studied among Identity Management and Automated Trust Negotiations (Bhargav-Spantzel, Squicciarini, & Bertino, 2007) and Federated Identity Management and Privilege Management Infrastructures (Bhatti, Bertino, & Ghafoor, 2007) pave the way for relative research activities.

Furthermore, one interesting trend in the trust literature refers to the association of trust metrics with risk management methodologies. While conceptually trust and risk qualities are strongly interrelated, several recent studies have built on this relationship in order to provide risk based access control features. Whereas risk management methodologies are largely active in the enterprise field, integrating risk aware security and privacy components into the Enterprise 2.0 world is of great interest.

Finally, although soft security measures such as privacy seals and reputation based security systems are not considered concrete trust frameworks and hence not a part of this chapter, when appropriately employed they can provide fruitful information as input to trust decisions. From our point of view, the combined utilization of soft and hard security mechanisms constitutes an extremely interesting approach. Some early work has already been done in this area, where hybrid models founded on the combination of vertical and horizontal trust are proposed (Lee & Yu, 2009). In the future, it is anticipated that the literature density regarding relative hybrid trust models will be greatly enhanced.

CONCLUSION

This chapter investigated the notion of trust in the Enterprise 2.0 context through a legal, regulatory, and technological perspective and has presented a variety of trust enhancing solutions found in the respective literature. Inherent characteristics of Enterprise and Web 2.0 tools along with the extracted trust requirements provided the guide for narrowing the range of investigated security and privacy enhancing solutions. The analysis undertaken while not exhaustive, provided a multidisciplinary overview of mechanisms employed in different stages of trust establishment in online collaborations and highlighted the key primitives that should characterize any adopted trust inducing technology. Results of this work can provide a useful input for extended research activities, such as analyzing selected threads of the trust issue or producing respective effective trust solutions.

REFERENCES

Acquisti, A. (2010). The economics of personal data and the economics of privacy. *WPISP-WPIE Roundtable*. Retrieved on November 3, 2011, from http://www.oecd.org/dataoecd/8/51/46968784.pdf

Akenti. (2009). *Amentia distributed access control*. Retrieved November 29, 2010, from http://dsd.lbl.gov/Akenti

Alfiery, R. (2003). Managing dynamic user communities in a grid of autonomous resources. In *Proceedings of the Conference for Computing in High Energy and Nuclear Physics*. IEEE.

Bandopadhaya, S. K., Bhattacharyya, D., Mukherjee, S., Ganguly, D., & Das, P. (2008). Statistical approach for offline handwritten signature verification. *Journal of Computer Science*, *4*(3), 181–185. doi:10.3844/jcssp.2008.181.185

Becker, M. Y., & Sewell, P. (2004). Cassandra: Distributed access control policies with tunable expressiveness. In *Proceedings of the Fifth IEEE International Workshop on Policies for Distributed Systems and Networks* (p. 159). Washington, DC: IEEE Computer Society.

Bertino, E., Catania, B., Damiani, M. L., & Perlasca, P. (2005). GEO-RBAC: A spatially aware RBAC. In *Proceedings of the 11th ACM Symposium on Access Control Models and Technologies (SACMAT '06)* (pp. 29-37). New York: ACM.

Bertocci, V., Serack, G., & Baker, C. (2007). *Understanding Windows CardSpace: An introduction to the concepts and challenges of digital identities*. Reading, MA: Addison-Wesley.

Bhargav-Spantzel, A., Squicciarini, A. C., & Bertino, E. (2007). Trust negotiation in identity management. *IEEE Security & Privacy*, *5*(2), 55–63. doi:10.1109/MSP.2007.46

Bhatti, R., Bertino, E., & Ghafoor, A. (2007). An integrated approach to federated identity and privilege management in open systems. *Communications of the ACM*, *50*(2), 81–87. doi:10.1145/1216016.1216025

Bianchi, G., Bonola, M., Falletta, V., Proto, F. S., & Teofili, S. (2008). The SPARTA pseudonym and authorization system. *Electronic Notes in Theoretical Computer Science*, *197*(2), 57–71. doi:10.1016/j.entcs.2007.12.017

Bin Husin, M. H., & Swatman, P. M. C. (2010). Removing the barriers to enterprise 2.0. In *Proceedings of the 2010 IEEE International Symposium on Technology and Society (ISTAS)* (pp. 275-283). IEEE.

Blaze, M., Feigenbaum, J., Ioannidis, J., & Keromytis, A. D. (1999). *RFC-2704: The keynote trust management system version 2*. Geneva, Switzerland: Internet Engineering Task Force.

Blaze, M., Feigenbaum, J., & Lacy, J. (1996). Decentralized trust management. In *Proceedings of the 1996 IEEE Symposium on Security and Privacy* (pp. 164-173). IEEE Computer Society Press.

Bughin, J. (2008). The rise of enterprise 2.0. *Direct. Data and Digital Marketing Practice*, 9(3), 251–259. doi:10.1057/palgrave.dddmp.4350100

Bughin, J., & Manyika, J. (2007). *How businesses are using web 2.0: A McKinsey global survey*. Retrieved November 3, 2011, from http://www.mckinseyquarterly.com/article_page.aspx?ar=1913

Byun, J.-W., Bertino, E., & Li, N. (2005). Purpose based access control of complex data for privacy protection. In *Proceedings of the 10th ACM Symposium on Access Control Models and Technologies (SACMAT 'O5)* (pp. 102-110). New York: ACM.

Camenisch, J., & Pfitzmann, B. (2007). Federated identity management. In M. Petkovic & W. Jonker (Eds.), *Security, Privacy, and Trust in Modern Data Management* (pp. 213–238). Berlin: Springer-Verlag. doi:10.1007/978-3-540-69861-6_15

Camenisch, J., & Van Herreweghen, E. (2002). Design and implementation of the idemix anonymous credential system. In *Proceedings of the 9th ACM Conference on Computer and Communications Security (CCS '02)* (pp. 21-30). New York: ACM.

Chadwick, D., Zhao, G., Otenko, S., Laborde, R., Su, L., & Nguyen, T. A. (2008). PERMIS: A modular authorization infrastructure. *Concurrency and Computation*, 20(11), 1341–1357. doi:10.1002/cpe.1313

Cuppens, F., & Cuppens-Boulahia, N. (2008). Modeling contextual security policies. *International Journal of Information Security*, 7(4), 285–305. doi:10.100710207-007-0051-9

Dabbah, M. A., Woo, W. L., & Dlay, S. S. (2007). Secure authentication for face recognition. In *Proceedings of the IEEE Symposium on Computational Intelligence in Image and Signal Processing* (pp. 121 – 126). IEEE.

De Hertogh, S., Viaene, S., & Dedene, G. (2011). Governing web 2.0. *Communications of the ACM*, 54(3), 124–130. doi:10.1145/1897852.1897882

Dim Mock, N., Belokosztolszki, A., Eyers, D., Bacon, J., & Moody, K. (2004). Using trust and risk in role based access control policies. In *Proceedings of the 9th ACM Symposium on Access Control Models and Technologies* (pp. 156-162). New York: ACM.

Ellison, C., Frantz, B., Lampson, B., Rivest, R., Thomas, B., & Ylonen, T. (1999). *RFC-2693: SPKI certificate theory*. Geneva, Switzerland: Internet Engineering Task Force.

European Commission. (2010a). *Communication from the commission to the European parliament, the council, the European economic and social committee and the committee of the regions: A Digital Agenda for Europe, L 245*. Brussels, Belgium: European Commission.

European Commission. (2010b). *Communication from the commission to the European 2020: A strategy for smart, sustainable and inclusive growth*. Brussels, Belgium: European Commission.

European Opinion Research Group. (2011). *Attitudes on data protection and electronic identity in the European Union. Technical Report Special Eurobarometer 359*. Bruxelles, Belgium: European Commission.

European Parliament and Council. (1995). Directive 95/46/EC of the European parliament and of the council on the protection of individuals with regard to the processing of personal data and on the free movement of such data. *Official Journal of the European Communities, 281*, 31–50.

European Parliament and Council. (1999). Directive 99/93/EC of the European parliament and of the council on a community framework for electronic signatures. *Official Journal of the European Communities, 13*, 12.

European Parliament and Council. (2002). Directive 2002/58/EC of the European parliament and of the council concerning the processing of personal data and the protection of privacy in the electronic communications sector (directive on privacy and electronic communications). *Official Journal of the European Communities, 201*, 37–47.

FP6 IST Project PRIME (Privacy and Identity Management for Europe). (n.d.). Retrieved November 3, 2011, from https://www.prime-project.eu/

FP7 IST Project PrimeLife (Privacy and Identity Management in Europe for Life). (n.d.). Retrieved November 3, 2011, from http://www.primelife.eu/

Gallup Organization. (2008). *Data protection in the European Union: Citizens' perceptions – Analytical report (flash eurobarometer 225)*. Retrieved November 3, 2011, http://ec.europa.eu/public_opinion/flash/fl_225_en.pdf

Ganorkar, S. R., & Ghatol, A. A. (2007). Iris recognition: An emerging biometric technology. In *Proceedings of the 6th WSEAS International Conference on Signal Processing, Robotics and Automation* (pp. 91 – 96). WSEAS.

Hao, W., Jhat, S., Livny, M., & McDaniel, P. D. (2004). Security policy reconciliation in distributed computing environments. In *Proceedings of the 5th IEEE International Workshop on Policies for Distributed Systems and Networks (POLICY'04)* (pp. 137-146). IEEE.

He, D. D., & Yang, J. (2009). Authorization control in collaborative healthcare systems. *Journal of Theoretical and Applied Electronic Commerce Research, 4*(2), 88–109.

Information Security Forum (ISF). (2007). *The standard of good practice for information security*. ISF.

Information Systems Security Association (ISSA). (2004). *Generally accepted information security principles*. GAISP.

International Telecommunication Union. (2005). *Information technology – Open systems interconnection – The directory: Public-key and attribute certificate frameworks*. ITU-T Recommendation X.509. Retrieved November 29, 2010, from http://www.itu.int/rec/T-REC-X.509-200508-I

ISO/IEC 27002. (2005). *Information technology - Security techniques - Code of practice for information security management*. ISO/IEC.

Jain, A. K., Ross, A., & Pankanti, S. (2006). Biometrics: A tool for information security. *IEEE Transactions on Information Forensics and Security, 1*(2), 125–144. doi:10.1109/TIFS.2006.873653

Jie, W., Arshad, J., Sinnott, R., Townend, P., & Lei, Z. (2011). A review of grid authentication and authorization technologies and support for federated access control. *ACM Computing Surveys, 43*(2), 12:1-12:26.

Joshi, J. B. D., Bertino, E., Latif, U., & Ghafoo, A. (2005). A generalized temporal role-based access control model. *Journal of IEEE Transactions on Knowledge and Data Engineering, 15*, 4–23. doi:10.1109/TKDE.2005.1

Kwan, M., & Ramachandran, D. (2009). Trust and online reputation systems. In *Computing with Social Trust* (pp. 287–311). Berlin: Springer-Verlag. doi:10.1007/978-1-84800-356-9_11

Lee, A. J., & Yu, T. (2009). Towards a dynamic and composable model of trust. In *Proceedings of the 14th ACM symposium on Access Control Models and Technologies (SACMAT '09)* (pp. 217-226). New York: ACM.

Li, N., & Mitchell, J. C. (2003). Datalog with constraints: A foundation for trust management languages. In *Proceedings of the 5th International Symposium on Practical Aspects of Declarative Languages* (pp. 58-73). IEEE.

Li, N., Mitchell, J. C., & Winsborough, W. H. (2002). Design of a role-based trust management framework. In *Proceedings of the 2002 IEEE Symposium on Security and Privacy* (pp. 114-130). IEEE.

Li, N., Winsborough, W. H., & Mitchell, J. C. (2001). Distributed credential chain discovery in trust management: Extended abstract. In *Proceedings of the 8th ACM Conference on Computer and Communications Security (CCS '01)* (pp. 156-165). New York: ACM.

Lin, T. C., Lee, C. K., & Lin, J. C. C. (2010). Determinants of enterprise 2.0 adoption: A value-based adoption model approach. In *Proceedings of the 2010 International Conference on Information Society (i-Society)* (pp. 12-18). i-Society.

Lioudakis, G. V., Gaudino, F., Boschi, E., Bianchi, G., Kaklamani, D. I., & Venieris, I. S. (2010). Legislation-aware privacy protection in passive network monitoring. In I. M. Portela & M. M. Cruz-Cunha (Eds.), *Information Communication Technology Law, Protection and Access Rights: Global Approaches and Issues*. Hershey, PA: IGI Global. doi:10.4018/978-1-61520-975-0.ch022

Masoumzadeh, A., & Joshi, J. B. D. (2008). PuRBAC: Purpose-aware role-based access control. In *Proceedings of the On the Move to Meaningful Internet Systems: OTM 2008* (LNCS), (vol. 5332). Berlin, Germany: Springer Berlin / Heidelberg.

Mcafee, A. P. (2006a). Enterprise 2.0: The dawn of emergent collaboration. *IEEE Engineering Management Review, 34*(3), 38. doi:10.1109/EMR.2006.261380

McAfee, A. P. (2006b). Evangelizing in the empty quarter. In *The Business Impact of IT*. New York: Wordpress.

McAfee, A. P. (2008). Some questions you might get asked. In *The Business Impact of IT*. New York: Wordpress.

McKnight, D. H., Cummings, L. L., & Chervany, N. L. (1998). Initial trust formation in new organizational relationships. *Academy of Management Review*, 23(3), 473–490.

Middleware Architecture Committee for Education (MACE). (2001). *Shibboleth system.* Retrieved November 3, 2011, from http://shibboleth.Internet2.edu/

Milojicic, D. (2008). Interview with Rich Friedrich, Dave Cohen, and Alex Dreiling. *IEEE Internet Computing*, 12(1), 10–13. doi:10.1109/MIC.2008.15

Ni, Q., Bertino, E., Lobo, J., Brodie, C., Karat, C. M., Karat, J., & Trombetta, A. (2010). Privacy-aware role-based access control. *Journal of ACM Transactions Information System Security*, 13(3), 1–31. doi:10.1145/1805974.1805980

Organization for Economic Co-Operation and Development (OECD). (1980). *Guidelines on the protection of privacy and transborder flows of personal data.* Retrieved November 3, 2011, from http://www.oecd.org/document/18/0,3343,en_2649_34255_1815186_1_1_1_1,00.html

Organization for Economic Co-Operation and Development (OECD). (2011). *The evolving privacy landscape: 30 years after the OECD privacy guidelines.* Retrieved November 3, 2011, from http://dx.doi.org/ doi:10.1787/5kgf09z90c31-en

Organization for the Advancement of Structured Information Standards (OASIS). (2004). *OASIS eXtensible access control markup language (XACML) TC.* Retrieved November 3, 2011, from http://www.oasis-open.org/committees/xacml/

Organization for the Advancement of Structured Information Standards (OASIS). (2005). *Security assertion markup language (SAML) v2.0.* Retrieved November 3, 2011, from http://docs.oasis-open.org/security/saml/v2.0/saml-2.0-os.zip

Polk, W. T., Hastings, N. E., & Malpani, A. (2003). Public key infrastructures that satisfy security goals. *IEEE Internet Computing*, 7(4), 60–67. doi:10.1109/MIC.2003.1215661

Prabhakar, S., Pankanti, S., & Jain, A. K. (2003). Biometric recognition: Security and privacy concerns. *IEEE Security & Privacy*, 1(2), 33–42. doi:10.1109/MSECP.2003.1193209

Rasmusson, L., & Janson, S. (1996). *Simulated social control for secure internet commerce.* New York: ACM Press. doi:10.1145/304851.304857

Ratnasingam, P. (2005). Trust in inter-organizational exchanges: A case study in business to business electronic commerce. *Decision Support Systems*, 39(3), 525–544. doi:10.1016/j.dss.2003.12.005

Ravari, A. N., Jafarian, J. H., Amini, M., & Jalili, R. (2010). GTHBAC: A generalized temporal history based access control model. *Journal of Telecommunication Systems*, 45(2), 111–125. doi:10.100711235-009-9239-9

Recordon, D., & Reed, D. (2006). OpenID 2.0: A platform for user-centric identity management. In *Proceedings of the 2nd ACM Workshop on Digital Identity Management (DIM'06)* (pp. 11-16). New York: ACM.

Rudman, R. J., & Steenkamp, L. P. (2009). Potential influence of web 2.0 usage and security practices of online users on information management. *South African Journal of Information Management, 11*(2).

Shim, S. S. Y., Bhalla, G., & Pendyala, V. (2005). Federated identity management. *IEEE Computer, 38*(12), 120–122. doi:10.1109/MC.2005.408

Solove, D. J. (2006). A brief history of information privacy law. In C. Wolf (Ed.), *Proskauer on Privacy: A Guide to Privacy and Data Security Law in the Information Age* (pp. 1–46). New York, NY: Practising Law Institute.

Sun, Y., & Chen, C. (2011). Towards coequal authorization for dynamic collaboration. [LNCS]. *Proceedings of Active Media Technology, 6890*, 229–240. doi:10.1007/978-3-642-23620-4_26

Swanson, M., & Guttman, B. (1996). Generally accepted principles and practices for securing information technology systems. Washington, DC: National Institute of Standards and Technology (NIST).

The Liberty Alliance Project. (2005). *Liberty alliance identity federation 1.2 (ID-FF 1.2) specifications.* Retrieved November 3, 2011, from http://www.projectliberty.org/liberty/resource_center/specifications/liberty_alliance_id_ff_1_2_specifications/

Varadharajan, V. (2009). A note on trust-enhanced security. *IEEE Security & Privacy, 7*(3), 57–59. doi:10.1109/MSP.2009.59

Weeks, S. (2001). Understanding trust management systems. In *Proceedings of the 2001 IEEE Symposium on Security and Privacy* (p. 94). Washington, DC: IEEE Computer Society.

Wilson, S. (2008). Public key superstructure it's PKI Jim, but not as we know it! In *Proceedings of the 7th Symposium on Identity and Trust on the Internet (IDtrust '08)* (pp. 72-88). New York: ACM.

Xinyi, H., Yang, X., Chonka, A., Jianying, Z., & Deng, R. H. (2011). A generic framework for three-factor authentication: Preserving security and privacy in distributed systems. *IEEE Transactions on Parallel and Distributed Systems, 22*(8), 1390–1397. doi:10.1109/TPDS.2010.206

Yau, S., & Chen, Z. (2008). *Security policy integration and conflict reconciliation for collaborations among organizations in ubiquitous computing environments. Ubiquitous Intelligence and Computing (LNCS)* (Vol. 5061, pp. 3–19). Berlin: Springer.

ADDITIONAL READING

Antonakopoulou, A., Lioudakis, G. V., Gogoulos, F., Kaklamani, D. I., & Venieris, I. S. (2012). Leveraging access control for privacy protection: A survey. In G. Yee (Ed.), *Privacy Protection Measures and Technologies in Business Organizations: Aspects and Standards* (pp. 65–94). Academic Press.

Basu, A., & Muylle, S. (2003). Authentication in e-commerce. *Communications of the ACM, 46*(12), 159–166. doi:10.1145/953460.953496

Belanger, F., Hiller, J. S., & Smith, W. J. (2002). Trustworthiness in electronic commerce: The role of privacy, security, and site attributes. *The Journal of Strategic Information Systems, 11*(3), 245–270. doi:10.1016/S0963-8687(02)00018-5

Bruno, A., Marra, P., & Mangia, L. (2011). The enterprise 2.0 adoption process: A participatory design approach. In *Proceedings of the 13th International Conference on Advanced Communication Technology (ICACT' 11)* (pp. 1457 - 1461). ICACT.

Camenisch, J., Leenes, R., Hansen, M., & Schallaböck, J. (2011). An introduction to privacy-enhancing identity management. In J. Camenisch, D. Sommer, & R. Leenes (Eds.), *Digital privacy*. Berlin: Springer-Verlag. doi:10.1007/978-3-642-19050-6_1

Cavoukian, A., & Tapscott, D. (2006). Privacy and the enterprise 2.0. In Learning, (pp. 1-26). New Paradigm Learning Cooperation.

Chadwick, D. W., Otenko, S., & Nguyen, T. A. (2009). Adding support to XACML for multi-domain user to user dynamic delegation of authority. *International Journal of Information Security, 8*(2), 137–152. doi:10.100710207-008-0073-y

Chen, J., Wu, G., & Ji, Z. (2011). Secure interoperation of identity managements among different circles of trust. [Amsterdam: Elsevier Science Publishers B. V.]. *Computer Standards & Interfaces, 33*(6), 533–540. doi:10.1016/j.csi.2011.02.008

Christidis, K., Mentzas, G., & Apostolou, D. (2011). Supercharging enterprise 2.0. *IT Professional, 13,* 29–35. doi:10.1109/MITP.2011.70

Giorgini, P., Massacci, F., & Zannone, N. (2005). Security and trust requirements engineering. [LNCS]. *Proceedings of the Foundations of Security Analysis and Design III, 3655,* 237–272. doi:10.1007/11554578_8

Gutmann, P. (2007). PKI design for the real world. In *Proceedings of the 2006 Workshop on New Security Paradigms (NSPW '06)* (pp. 109-116). New York: ACM.

Hawkey, K. (2009). Examining the shifting nature of privacy, identities, and impression management with web 2.0. In *Proceedings of the 2009 International Conference on Computational Science and Engineering* (Vol. 4, pp. 990-995). Washington, DC: IEEE Computer Society.

iDABD – European eGovernment Services. (2010). *Completion of the framework for signature validation services.* Retrieved November 3, 2011, from http://ec.europa.eu/idabc/en/document/7764

Jøsang, A., Ismail, R., & Boyd, C. (2007). A survey of trust and reputation systems for online service provision. [Amsterdam: Elsevier Science Publishers B. V.]. *Decision Support Systems, 43*(2), 618–644. doi:10.1016/j.dss.2005.05.019

Kerr, R. C. (2007). *Toward secure trust and reputation systems for electronic marketplaces.* A (Thesis). University of Waterloo, Waterloo, Canada.

Kumari, A., Mishra, S., & Kushwaha, D. S. (2010). A new collaborative trust enhanced security model for distributed system. *International Journal of Computers and Applications, 1*(26), 117–124.

Li, N., Mitchell, J. C., & Winsborough, W. H. (2005). Beyond proof-of-compliance: Security analysis in trust management. *Journal of the ACM, 52*(3), 474–514. doi:10.1145/1066100.1066103

Madsen, P., & Itoh, H. (2009). Challenges to supporting federated assurance. *Computer, 42*(5), 42–49. doi:10.1109/MC.2009.149

Murugesan, S. (2007). Understanding web 2.0. *IT Professional, 9*(4), 34–41. doi:10.1109/MITP.2007.78

Myhr, T. (2008). Legal and organizational challenges and solutions for achieving a pan-european electronic ID solution or i am 621216-1318, but I am also 161262-43774.1: Do you know who I am? *Information Security Technical Report, 13*, 76–82. doi:10.1016/j.istr.2008.06.001

Patton, M. A., & Jøsang, A. (2004). Technologies for trust in electronic commerce. *Electronic Commerce Research, 4*(1-2), 9–21. doi:10.1023/B:ELEC.0000009279.89570.27

Ruohomaa, S., & Kutvonen, L. (2005). Trust management survey. In *Proceedings of the ITRUST 2005* (LNCS), (vol. 3477, pp. 77-92). Berlin: Springer-Verlag.

Scherp, A., Schwagereit, F., Ireson, N., Lanfranchi, V., Papadopoulos, S., & Kritikos, A. … Smrz, P. (2009). Leveraging web 2.0 communities in professional organisations. In *Proceedings of the W3C Workshop on the Future of Social Networking*. Barcelona, Spain: W3C.

Shafiq, B., Bertino, E., & Ghafoor, A. (2005). Access control management in a distributed environment supporting dynamic collaboration. In *Proceedings of the 2005 Workshop on Digital Identity Management (DIM '05)* (pp. 104-112). New York: ACM.

Siponen, M. T., & Oinas-Kukkonen, H. (2007). A review of information security issues and respective research contributions. *SIGMIS Database, 38*(1), 60–80. doi:10.1145/1216218.1216224

Tapscott, D. (2006). Winning with the enterprise 2.0. In *Learning*, (pp. 1-59). New Paradigm Learning Cooperation.

Tredinnick, L. (2006). Web 2.0 and business - A pointer to the intranets of the future? *Business Information Review, 23*(4), 228–234. doi:10.1177/02663821060072239

KEY TERMS AND DEFINITIONS

Access Control: The mechanisms for allowing access to resources, systems or services to authorized persons or other valid subjects and denying unauthorized access.

Enterprise 2.0: The adoption of Web 2.0 services in business environments in order to improve knowledge workers' productivity and augment the effectiveness and competence of organizations.

Identity Management: The mechanisms for identifying individuals in a system and controlling the circulation of established identity profiles in order to deal with access to the resources in that system.

Information Security: The protection, in terms of integrity, confidentiality, authenticity and availability, of information from unauthorized access, usage, disclosure, modification, or destruction.

PKI: The sum of mechanisms for exploiting public key cryptography in order to create, distribute, validate, and revoke digital certificates.

Privacy: The claim of individuals, groups, or institutions to determine for themselves when, how and to what extent information about them is communicated to others.

Trust Management: A unified approach for specifying and interpreting security policies of a system, credentials of involved users and relationships among them.

This research was previously published in the Handbook of Research on Enterprise 2.0 edited by Maria Manuela Cruz-Cunha, Fernando Moreira, and João Varajão, pages 199-219, copyright year 2014 by Business Science Reference (an imprint of IGI Global).

Chapter 106
Challenges and Opportunities in Vehicular Cloud Computing

Zeinab E. Ahmed
University of Gezira, Sudan

Rashid A. Saeed
Sudan University of Science and Technology, Sudan

Amitava Mukherjee
Globsyn Business School, India

ABSTRACT

Vehicular ad-hoc networks (VANET) have become an important research area due to their ability to allow sharing resources among the users to carry out their application and provide services of transport and traffic management. VANET communication allows exchange of sensitive information among nearby vehicles such as condition of weather and road accidents in order to improve vehicle traffic efficiency through Intelligent Transportation Systems (ITS). Many technologies have been developed to enhance ITS. Recently, vehicular cloud computing (VCC) has been developed in order to overcome the drawbacks VANET. VCC technology provides low-cost services to vehicles and capable of managing road traffic efficiently by using the vehicular sources (such as internet) to make decisions and for storage. VCC is considered as the basis for improving and developing intelligent transportation systems. It plays a major role in people's lives due to its safety, security, trust, and comfort to passengers and drivers. This chapter investigates the vehicular cloud computing. The authors first concentrate on architectures. Then, they highlight applications and features provided by VCC. Additionally, they explain the challenges for VCC. Finally, the authors present opportunities and future for VCC.

INTRODUCTION

For the past few years, Intelligent Transportation Systems (ITS) attracted the attention of many researchers for the purpose of improving the traffic monitor, road safety, and signals utilization. Vehicular Ad-hoc Networks has been proposed as ITS environment due to its ability to managing traffic, enhance road safety using GPS information, computing power, and media. A VANET is communicating among the vehicles by using a wireless network to provide services of transport and traffic management (Whaiduz-

DOI: 10.4018/978-1-5225-8176-5.ch106

zaman, Sookhak, Gani, & Buyya, 2014). There are two components of VANET architecture: hardware and software. There are three types of communication in vehicular ad hoc network: 1.) vehicles-to-road infrastructure (V2R); 2.) vehicle-to-vehicle (V2V), and; 3.) vehicles-to-sensors (V2S) communication (Kumar, Singh, Bali, Misra, & Ullah, 2015; Eltahir, & Saeed, 2015). In the V2V, the vehicles communicate with another by using On Board Units (OBU), while the vehicles communicate in the V2R with infrastructure units like road side units (RSUs) (Eltahir, Saeed, Mukherjee, & Hasan, 2016).

Many technologies have been found to enhance Intelligent Transportation Systems (ITS). Some of the solutions to face the challenges of VANET were proposed such as Cloud computing and later than appearance Mobile Cloud Computing and Vehicular Cloud Computing (VCC) (Whaiduzzaman, Sookhak, Gani, & Buyya, 2014). In Cloud Computing, users share resources such as applications, location, and storage over the Internet. The increasing of mobile applications and mobile devices new technique appeared called mobile cloud computing to overcome shortages of Cloud Computing. Vehicular Cloud Computing (VCC) has a big effect on the ITS specially when using the resources of vehicles like computing power for instant decision making, the internet, storage, GPS, and sharing information on the cloud. VCC has many benefits such as low energy, real-time services of software, platforms, and infrastructure with QOS to passengers and drivers. And also VCC prove, better road safety, and secured intelligent urban traffic systems. The list of acronyms which appeared in this chapter is given in Table 1.

Table 1. List of acronyms

CaaS	Cooperation as a Service
CC	Cloud Computing
DaaS	Data as a service
DSRC	Dedicated Short Range Communication
INaaS	Information as a Service
ITS	Intelligent Transportation Systems
MCC	Mobile Cloud Computing
NaaS	Network as a Service
OBU	On Board Unit
PaaS	Platform as a Service
RSU	Road Side Unit
SaaS	Software as a Service
STaaS	Storage as a Service
V2I	Vehicle-to-Infrastructure
V2S	Vehicles-to-Sensors
V2V	Vehicle-to-Vehicle
VANET	Vehicular Ad-Hoc Networks
VCC	Vehicular Cloud Computing
VCN	Vehicular Cloud Network
WAVE	Wireless Access in Vehicular Environment

This chapter is organized as follows:

- Firstly, offers an overview of vehicular ad-hoc networks.
- Discusses the cloud computing and mobile cloud computing.
- Provides an overview of Vehicular Cloud Computing (VCC).
- Present and discuss about related work.
- Explains the architectures and organization of VCC.
- Focuses on the applications of the VCC.
- Discusses the challenges.
- Finally, talk about opportunities and the future for VCC.

VEHICULAR AD-HOC NETWORKS (VANET)

A VANET is a communications between the vehicles to exchange sensitive information like a condition of weather and road accidents to improve vehicle traffic efficiency through ITS. The main aim of VANET is to obtain the highest safety on the road (Sugumar, Rengarajan, & Jayakumar, 2016). Vehicles, Infrastructure Domain, and Road Side Unit (RSU) are the contents of VANET architecture (Bhoi, & Khilar, 2014). In a VANET, the communications between vehicles by using wireless equipment such as OBUs for V2V and RSUs for V2R. This communication happens when the Dedicated Short Range Communication (DSRC), which is a standard, developed by the USA, and enabled IEEE 802.11p. A VANET classified into two types based on network topologies: infrastructure-less (ad-hoc) and infrastructure-based (Cushman, Rawat, Chen, & Yang, 2016). The V2V communication is transmitting data by using broadcasting or multicasting. The broadcasting is classified into naive and Intelligent, naive broadcasting which generate the collision, but the collision is decreased when using intelligent broadcasting. In a VANET to avoid accidents or congested, the vehicle broadcasts messages called beacons (Rajput, Abbas, & Oh, 2016) contain very important information like location, direction and a speed of it. This beacon makes a VANET is attractive areas for engineers and researcher, many papers focus on a VANET application and characteristics. The VANET had many important characteristics like high mobility, a dynamic environment, and relatively low antenna heights on the vehicles and RSU (Viriyasitavatm, Boban, Tsai, & Vasilakos, 2015). These characteristics make the VANET facing more issues and challenges. However, a VANET has some shortcomings, therefore new technology appeared called a cloud computing.

CLOUD COMPUTING (CC)

Nowadays, cloud computing (CC) is an active area because delivering services to users over the internet through sharing resources such as applications and storage. In the CC, when tasks sharing by users, it can carry out their tasks fast and efficiently as well as decrease the computation time (Bajpai & Singh, 2016). Addition, the providers of cloud service manage a network infrastructure for collection the computing power enormous from a number of servers. Cloud computing has some main characteristics like (Verma, & Kaushal, 2011; Habib, Hauke, Ries, & Muhlhauser, 2012):

- Multi-tenancy or sharing of resources
- On-demand self-service
- Ubiquitous network access
- Rapid elasticity
- Measured service

CC has several features which provided advantages for a business domain such as No up-front investment, highly scalable, lowering operating cost, easy access and reducing business risks and maintenance expenses (Zhang, Cheng, & Boutaba, 2010). Moreover, it has many advantages such as connecting services, shared architecture, flexible nature, and metering architecture (Hindia, Reza, Dakkak, Awang Nor, & Noordin, 2014). The cloud computing architecture separates into 4 layers: the hardware layer, the infrastructure layer, the platform layer and the application layer, demonstrated in Figure 1. CC is categorized into four models: public, private, hybrid and community. Each of these models is divided into three service models: Software as a Service (SaaS), Platform as a Service (PaaS), and Infrastructure as a Service (IaaS) (Cardoso, Moreira, & Somoes, 2014).

MOBILE CLOUD COMPUTING (MCC)

In mid-2007, a new technique was appeared which called mobile cloud computing. and it become attractive area for business domain because of a spread use of a mobile applications with low cost. When the processing and storage for data was occurring outside of the mobile device, this infrastructure called mobile cloud computing. The applications moved from mobile phones to the cloud, to share applications, data storage and mobile computing among the mobile devices (Singh, Kaur, & Sandhu, 2015). So, the Mobile cloud computing using in a wide range of application like crowd computing, natural language processing, sharing GPS, image processing, sensor data applications, querying, sharing Internet access, and multimedia search (Fernando, Loke, & Rahayu, 2013).

Figure 1. Cloud computing architecture

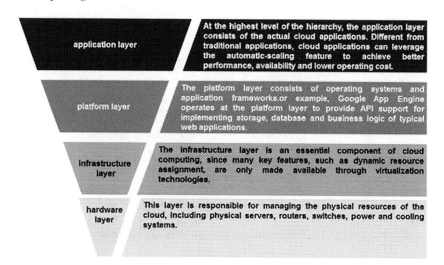

Mobile cloud computing has several advantages: a) all users anywhere and anytime; can be access to services; b) the services provide information to users such as location and context; c) Improves processing power and capacity of data storage; d) extending the battery lifetime; e) Mobile computing has found many solutions to overcome cloud computing problems (Singh, Kaur, & Sandhu, 2015; Shravanthi, & Guruprasad, 2014; Dinh, Lee, Niyatio, & Wang, 2013). Most of the mobile applications, such as mobile commerce, mobile learning, and mobile healthcare, benefited from the MNC advantages. The architecture of mobile cloud computing classified based on data centers layer and the cloud service standard model that includes Platform as a Service (PaaS), Infrastructure as a Service (IaaS), and Software as a Service (SaaS) (Singh, Kaur, & Sandhu, 2015; Fernando, Loke, & Rahayu, 2013). Although it has several advantages and services provided to users, it faces many challenges like computing offloads, low bandwidth, quality of services, and security for mobile users.

VEHICULAR CLOUD COMPUTING (VCC)

Vehicular cloud computing (VCC) is an extension of mobile cloud computing (MCC). In VCC vehicles, the resources and services could arrive in real time for information from anywhere. This makes passengers and drivers access numbers of new applications to provide various services (Othman, Madani, & Khan, 2014; Ahmad, Noor, Ali, & Qureshi, 2016). So, VCC considers the basis for improving and developing intelligent transportation systems and rich environment for researchers. Additionally, it plays a major role in people's lives due to providing safety, security, trust, and comfort to passengers and drivers. The basic objective of VCC is to provide low-cost services to drivers, and to reduce accidents, congestion of traffic. The traditional cloud computing provided services such as software, storage, and computing resources, but in the vehicular cloud appeared other services. Figure 2 shows the vehicular

Figure 2. Vehicular Cloud Computing

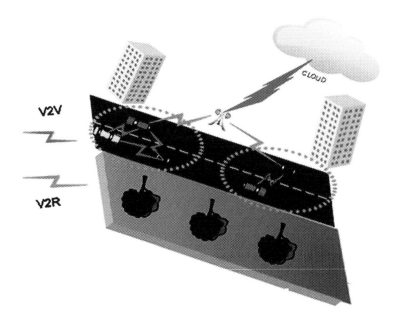

cloud computing, which exchanges information between the vehicles or between cloud data center, and vehicles for the vehicular through RSUs in order to computing or storing.

The VCC services classified into three types: 1.) Network-based services; 2.) Sensing-based services, and; 3.) Cooperation-based services (Mekki, Jabri, Rachedi, & ben Jemaa, 2016).

- **Network-Based Services or (NaaS):** Where some vehicles on the road have Internet, and it can be used by others vehicles which that haven't Internet.
- **Cooperation as a Service (CaaS):** When the driver and passengers access to the applications and use the services like a road condition, and traffic information of this type (Sharma, & Kaur, 2015).
- **Sensing-Based Services:** Where vehicles can share sensing information between them to improve the knowledge of drivers (Mekki, Jabri, Rachedi, & ben Jemaa, 2016).

The vehicular cloud infrastructure provides services to several domains such as scientific application, social networking, education, and business etc. Vehicular Clouds provide services, like Infrastructure as a Service (IaaS), Platform as a Service (PaaS), Application as a Service (AaaS), Software as a Service (SaaS), and Storage as a Service (STaaS), to vehicle when connected via OBUs to get unlimited storage and computing power (Ahmad, Noor, Ali, & Qureshi, 2016). The VCC improves the road traffic management and or by reducing the risk of life, cost and time.

RELATED WORK

Recently, Baby et al. proposed a new method known as Vehicular Cloud for Roadside scenarios (VCR). VCR architecture has separated into two types: the public cloud and private cloud communication. The main aim is to provide safety and non-safety services in vehicular applications through the public and private vehicular cloud to fulfill max benefit (Baby, Sabareesh, Saravanaguru, & Thangavelu, 2013). Chang, Yao-Chung, et al. used Software-Defined Networking (SDN) architecture to assist a vehicular cloud serving system and or by achieving highly efficient services. The design based on SDNBroker system which is an SDN application to schedules resources using the linear programming algorithm and improves network routing using Dijkstra's routing (Chang, Chen, Ma, & Chiu, 2015).

An intelligent transport system (ITS) had a high impact on people's lives because it provide several applications, safety, and other information to the passenger and drivers as well as manage traffic of vehicles. So, the author has (Meneguette, 2016) proposed VehIcular Cloud Transport Management (VICTiM) to a management a big city as well as to provide mechanisms for storage of information and allow carrying out heterogeneous communication among the several vehicles. Azizian et al (2016) proposed a new solution to solve the service delivery problem more efficiently by using VC based on transmission scheduling methods. Distributed clustering algorithm (DHCV) was used to fulfill this proposed through creating a cloud of vehicles have fixed size and regulate vehicles inside cloud according to mobility (Azizan, Cherkaoui, & Hafid, 2016). After that applied transmission scheduling methods to improve delay and throughput for the service delivery.

In (Garai, Rekhis, & Boudriga, 2015) the authors proposed a cloud Communication-as-a-Service (CaaS) have three aims in their: firstly, provide a continuous communication to vehicles when the move outside area uncovered through Roadside units, secondly overcome from resource limit, and lastly supply high Quality of Service (QoS). The architecture was separated into three layers based on a tree topology: Vehicular Cloudlet (V-Cloudlet), Roadside Cloudlet (R-Cloudlet), and central cloud (CC).

Merging vehicular social networks and mobile wireless communications became future of networks, so, Li, Ting, et al. proposed a new method to support marketers known as On Selecting Vehicles as Recommenders for Vehicular Social Networks (SV-VSNs) (Li, Zhao, Liu, & Huang, 2017). Three algorithms to improve were present efficiencies for marketers based on benefit factor, coverage factor, and geographical track to select vehicles in vehicular social networks. The obtained result was effective when applied in real traffic in some cities.

Recently, location-based services (LBS) use become widespread to assist people and make life very easy, but facing some issues such as privacy. To solve this problem, Zhu et al. (2016) suggests a new scheme called efficient and privacy-preserving LBS query scheme in the outsourced cloud (EPQ) (Zhu, Lu, Huang, Chen, & Li, 2016). The EPQ depends on the encryption mechanism especially spatial range query algorithm over ciphertext (SRQC). EPQ proved excellent for facing the most security threats, and adding an effective performance in the cloud server.

Road traffic complexity leads to one of the important issues which are a collision. Many research puts approaches to solving this issue, in (Riaz, & Niazi, 2016) offers a comprehensive study for a survey of vehicular cyber-physical systems (VCPS) from the collision-avoidance perspective. In addition to aid researchers through giving solutions to avoid a collision and understanding communication of vehicular cyber-physical systems.

VEHICULAR CLOUD COMPUTING ARCHITECTURES

The architecture of Vehicular cloud computing was based on three layers, which are: inside-vehicle layer, cloud computing layer and the communication layer, as shown in Figure 3.

- **Inside-Vehicle Layer:** Also called an on-board layer. In an Inside- vehicle layer, before establishing communication among the vehicles, firstly the vehicle sense the environment, road condition and collecting information inside the car or other parameters by using a number of sensors such as vehicles' internal sensors and smartphone sensors (Ghafoor, Mohammad, & Lloret, 2016). The collated information either store on the cloud or considered as input for other software programs in the application layer.

Figure 3. Layers of the architecture of vehicular cloud computing

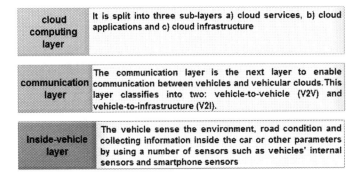

cloud computing layer	It is split into three sub-layers a) cloud services, b) cloud applications and c) cloud infrastructure
communication layer	The communication layer is the next layer to enable communication between vehicles and vehicular clouds. This layer classifies into two: vehicle-to-vehicle (V2V) and vehicle-to-infrastructure (V2I).
inside-vehicle layer	The vehicle sense the environment, road condition and collecting information inside the car or other parameters by using a number of sensors such as vehicles' internal sensors and smartphone sensors

- **Communication Layer:** The communication layer is the next layer used to enable communication between vehicles and vehicular clouds through cellular communication devices such as 3G or 4G, Wi-Fi, WiMAX, Wireless Access in Vehicular Environment (WAVE), IEEE 802.11p or Dedicated Short Range Communication (DSRC) (Mekki, Jabri, Rachedi, & ben Jemaa, 2016). The communication on this layer is classified into two: vehicle-to-vehicle (V2V) and vehicle-to-infrastructure (V2I). The connection among the vehicles needs an equipment such as On-Board Units (OBUs) and GPSs to make the internet available on moving devices. In V2V, communicate between vehicles is directly established to provide traffic safety and related applications for the passengers and drivers. Unlike the V2I where the communication is indirect among vehicles, infrastructures and the cloud to exchange Information over wireless networks like satellite, 3G (Whaiduzzaman, Sookhak, Gani, & Buyya, 2014).

- **Cloud Computing Layer:** The last layer called cloud computing layer. It is split into three sub-layers:
  ○ Cloud services.
  ○ Cloud applications.
  ○ Cloud infrastructure.

Cloud infrastructure consists of computation cloud and cloud storage. Cloud storage, which is responsible for storing all information that is collected in the on-board layer (Sharma, & Kaur, 2015). Cloud computation plays an important role in improving network performance by using computational tasks such as the health and behavior of the driver in cloud storage. Cloud applications consist of many applications and services used by passenger and driver these applications like health, human activity, and environmental recognition. Figure 4 illustrates most details for vehicular cloud computing architecture.

Several services such as Infrastructure as a Service (IaaS), Platform as a Service (PaaS), Application as a Service (AaaS), Software as a Service (SaaS), Network as a Service (NaaS), Information as

Figure 4. Vehicular cloud computing architecture

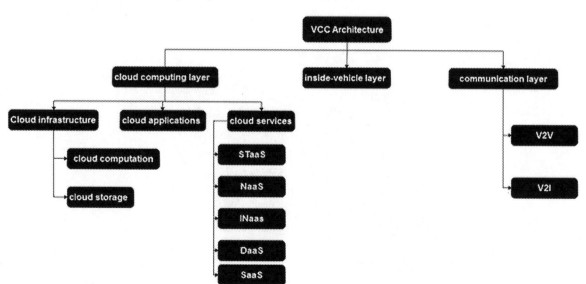

a Service (INaaS), Data as a service (DaaS), and Storage as a Service (STaaS), consider basic parts of cloud services. Several vehicles on the road, one of them have internet and another doesn't have the internet. The vehicles have internet can provide access the Internet for other vehicles that need Internet this process know as Network as a Service (NaaS) (Sharma & Kaur, 2015).

The services have permission to exchange information among the vehicles in the same cloud. Often the drivers want the important kind of information like news of large events, advance warnings, and road conditions. The Information as a Service (INaaS) response for supplying these information to a driver.

When the passenger and drivers on the road used all hardware to run the applications at the same moment, this leads to need an additional storage. So, some vehicles have a higher capacity for storage and it can provide the repository for storage to other vehicles that have low storage capability. It knows virtual network hard-disk and also called Storage as a Service (STaaS) (Mershad, & Artail, 2013).

ORGANIZATION OF VCC INFRASTRUCTURE

Vehicular cloud computing can classify into two types: static VC and dynamic VC (Ghafoor, Mohammed, & Lloret, 2016; Hussain, Son, Eun, Kim, & Oh, 2012; Olariu, Khalil, & Abuelela, 2011).

1. **Static VC:** Earlier, people spend a lot of time in shopping, airport, work, and hospital and when parking their vehicles. Most companies are thinking to take benefit from advantages of parking because those vehicles consider idle computing resources. Static VC creates center data storage when combining between a computer cluster, storage resources, and computational power of the participating vehicles. Figure 5 shown static VCC.
2. **Dynamic VC:** Dynamic formation of VC because of the high mobility of the vehicles and the speedily change among the networks. One of the vehicles on the cloud, known as cloud head, is responsible to invite all near vehicular to join for formation dynamic VC, as shown Figure 6.

Figure 5. Static VCC

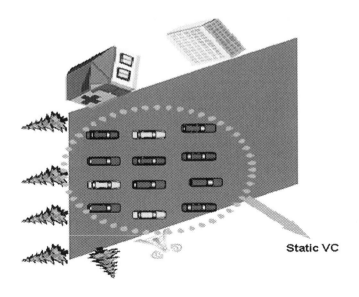

Figure 6. Dynamic VCC

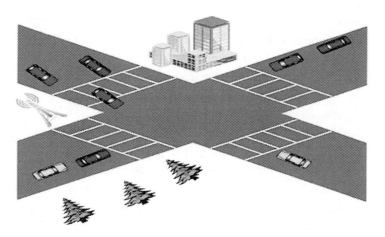

APPLICATIONS OF VEHICULAR CLOUD COMPUTING

Because of sharing resources among the vehicular and RUS with clouds, the VCC provides a vast range of applications like in an airports as a data center, traffic management, road safety message, managing parking facilities, real-time navigation, vehicle maintenance, accident alerts at intersections, parking lot data cloud, and managing evacuation etc. (Whaiduzzaman, Sookhak, Gani, & Buyya, 2014;Ghafoor, Mohammed, & Lloret, 2016; Yan, Wen, Olariu, & Weigle, 2013; Gu, Zeng, & Guo, 2013; Olariu, Elto-weissy, & Younis, 2011). The following paragraph described several applications:

1. **Road Safety Message:** It is one of the important alerts on road because the VCC contributes to road safety. Modern vehicles have a sensor, to monitor road and provide road safety for drivers and passengers, to query the state of roads such as risk, flooding areas, overcrowding, temperature, and speed, to evaluate the situation of other vehicles and alert drivers.
2. **Traffic Management:** The result of the increasing number of vehicles, the traffic management plays an important role on the road to find the best solution for several problems which face drivers and passengers such as wastes the valuable time and energy of human, threatens the health of citizens and needs the huge computational effort to be solved. One of the solutions which provide to manage the road, drivers receives reports about status for traffic (e.g., congestion) from VCs. Reduce frequent congestion is one of the important application types for traffic management. In the congestion, some drivers want to transform the road (Yan, Wen, Olariu, & Weigle, 2013). This decision depends on the last information on the vehicular and itcloud provide an efficient solution to the drivers. This information being available after calculating the impact of the local road and the cause of the congestion in the traffic flow.
3. **Real-Time Navigation:** Navigation is a static geographic map for vehicles in traditional networks, but the VCC has a virtual-reality application which the drivers can move freely without hurdles. To provide a real-time navigation for vehicles. the 3D space for interaction with the virtual environment was used.

4. **Management Parking:** In the populated areas, it is difficult for drivers to find parking space. The VCC allows drivers to book parking easily supplying near and suitable space because all information related locations parking found in the cloud.

5. **Managing Evacuation:** The disaster authority uses the model the road to monitor traffic to execute an evacuation. Therefore, evacuation events can be divided into cases where prior notice of an imminent event is provided. In the VCC, vehicles and vehicular cloud are taking part of the evacuation process to make decisions on the current situation.

6. **Data Center Configuration:** In mall, hospital, work, and the airport, the people are parking their vehicles for several hours or days. During this period, the vehicles are considered inefficient resources. Can benefit from parking to build a data center. The vehicular takes part of the cloud through connected to the Internet by cable. But one of the important challenges of parking data center structure is dynamic, because of time for arrival and spends per vehicles in parking unknown.

7. **Improving Traffic Signals:** Traffic signals have high significant on the road to assign a length of signal cycle and green phase lengths. Thus, VCs can maximize the signal system performance by making dynamic use of a vehicular network.

VEHICULAR CLOUD COMPUTING CHALLENGES

In the vehicular cloud computing, the mobility of nodes is very high and topology changes in the network frequently so appeared issues and challenges facing the VCC such as message confidentiality, trust management, securing vehicular communication, authentication, secure location information, the safety of messages, and the interoperability of different clouds. In this section, all these challenges can be discussed and concentrate on the issues correlated with ITS applications like security, traffic management, navigation systems, and congestion detection (Whaiduzzaman, Sookhak, Gani, & Buyya, 2014;Gu, Zeng, & Guo, 2013; Chaqfeh, Mohamed, Jawhar, & Wu, 2016; Aloqaily, Kantarci, & Mouftah, 2015; Ahmad, Kazim, Adnane, & Awad, 2015; Karagiannis, Altintas, Ekici, Heijenk, Jarupan, Lin, & Weil, 2011).

1. **Threats for Vehicular Cloud Computing:** All VCC components: vehicles, passengers, messages, wireless communication, and architectures need security against attackers. In vehicles, attackers attempting to access application unit and enter malware in it, while wireless communication considered between the vehicles or RSUs via V2V and V2R communication the best environment for the attackers, because it contains some vulnerabilities. The wireless communication threats classified into:

   a. **Denial of Service (DoS):** It blocks communication by using reject any members to forward important messages to other vehicles or the cloud.

   b. **Data Tempering (Modification):** In this type, the attacker objects the messages when the routes to other vehicles or RSUs and after that can modify and alter it.

   c. **Jamming:** DoS attack to make jamming in the channel for wireless communication which carries the messages.

There are also several threats like repudiation, information disclosure, and sybil attack. To provide secure vehicular cloud computing, communication takes considering requirements for security like authentication, integrity, and confidentiality.

2. **Authentication, Privacy, and Liability:** In VCC, the communication depends on the integrity of messages and authentication of the users. To increased authenticate between RSUs and vehicles in the vehicular networks, the vehicles used aliases to deception the attackers for not track their communication and activities. Also, exchange information between the vehicles requires being privacy and trust. The privacy is one of the most important challenges in VCC. Many researchers are working to find methods and solutions used to protect the privacy of the vehicles in a vehicular network. The passengers and drivers have controlled exchange information and determine, what the information open on networks, and what the information keeps private and can't broadcast on the networks.

3. **Service Delay and Location:** Because to the topology in the network changes quickly, the time and location play an important role on data packets sent by applications for vehicular networking. In VCC, the most applications depend on the information on the current location of a vehicle such as collision, congestion avoidance, and traffic status. The vehicular networks use devices like GPS, filtering, inter-cell position, and radar to check the location information. Many researchers proposed several methods to check the location information. These methods can classify into three types: active location, active location and general location (Whaiduzzaman, Sookhak, Gani, & Buyya, 2014).

In vehicular cloud computing, the delay can impact on price for service. So, the passengers and drivers are interested about service delay, because the increase of service delay leads up to increase the price for service.

4. **Confidentiality, Integrity, and Trust for Messages:** At VCC, messages split into four types: the first one using to send alerts or warning messages called short message, second known as media message, utilize when the vehicle needs services from other cloud or vehicles, Priority message is third one employed to end the warning messages, the last one acknowledge message after delivery of messages send these to confirm access. Most applications for a vehicular network focused verification and trust to provide a secure communication. Confidentiality is an important issue, all messages in the network can't read by an unauthorized user, but after encrypting the messages and allowing only access to authorized users. Therefore, the RSU registers all vehicles and users that enter the domain to increase confidentiality by using secure and encrypted communication. Furthermore, to safeguard the networks from security threats such as denial of service, forgery and jamming attack, must verify the integrity for receiving messages.

5. **Securing Vehicular Communication:** In the environment of a vehicular cloud, from the important providing secure communications to avoid attackers and reduce security holes like traffic tampering, privacy violations, forging messages, and preventing communication by utilizing cryptographic algorithms (Ahmad, Kazim, & Adnane, 2015; Falchetti, Azurdia-Meza, & Cespedes, 2015). The big problem facing the cryptographic algorithm is key management, so found a method for the solution this problem. The Vehicular Public Key Infrastructure (VPKI) is one of the methods key management to guarantee confidentiality and integrity of the message in vehicular networks.

OPPORTUNITIES AND FUTURE FOR VCC

The vehicular cloud computing plays a major role in people's lives due to traffic management and providing safety, security, trust, and comfort of passengers and drivers, so considered very rich environment for researchers. It considers the basis for improving and developing intelligent transportation systems. However, the development and improvement process still constrained by several factors such as challenges and issues for VCC. Several applications and services appeared in the last days result from exploiting the resources by the vehicular cloud. Future of VCC in next days benefits from underutilized resource and exploits it to the maximum extent such as to benefits, capacities of storage and computation which owned by modern vehicles, and time which wasted in the parking. So, some companies are thinking to rent resource from the parking to carry out some application or task.

In (Dressler, Handle, & Sommer, 2014), the authors present a new method, known Virtual Cord Protocol (VCP), depends on the benefit from parked vehicles to create a cloud for storing information and to provide network communication between the moving vehicles and the vehicle storing the requested data. The inter-domain routing techniques used to enable dynamic cloud services and to achieve the communication between the moving vehicles and cloud. W He, et al proposed a new architecture for IoT-based vehicular data clouds, by integrating several devices, cloud computing, and IOT to Share resources and exchange information among the passengers, vehicles, and roadside infrastructure (He, Yan, & Da Xu, 2014). The (He, Yan, & Da Xu, 2014) study and face two vehicular data cloud services: the first one is intelligent parking cloud service and the second is the mining vehicular maintenance data service. Although finding several challenges this method provides enormous opportunities for technology in the vehicle industry.

Wan et al (2014) proposes a context-aware architecture with mobile cloud support and two crucial service components, namely cloud-assisted Context-aware Vehicular Cyer-physical systems (CVCs). This paper studies context-aware dynamic parking service as a case study to improve QoS and the performance of CVCs. Addition, discuss the challenges and find potential solutions (Wan, Zhang, Zhao, Yang, & Lloret, 2014). It will consider this attractive field for researchers in the near future.

To benefit from sensors such as map, radar, and lidar the authors proposed a new method to detect the vehicles on the way or parked on the roadside to provide the best motion, the easiest method to pass the parked vehicle, and assuring safety for drivers and passengers (Mei, Nagasaka, Okumura, & Prokhorov, 2015). Additionally, assist drivers to make the decision to choose the smooth and safe path to avoid harassing from other vehicles.

The traffic accidents and traffic flow issues are major challenges for VCC, maybe occur when the vehicles parked on the way illegally. So, the authors presented the new system to monitor traffic and detect traffic flow to avoid accidents by using cumulative dual foreground differences (Wahyono, & Jo, 2017). The results appeared that the method is efficient and can be considered as part of the intelligent traffic monitoring system, but possibly generate false results when producing a noisy foreground image.

The nature VCC has open communication medium, fast topology changes, and dynamic. Thus, one of the key challenges is exchange information due to nature VCC can be fake and lead to sharing false information between drivers and passengers. Sharma et al (2015) presented a new method by using Elliptic Curve Cryptography (ECC) to provide security for communication to guarantee authentication, integrity, confidentiality, and privacy between sender and receiver (Sharma, Bali, & Kaur, 2015). The ECC has several advantages to against various attacks like spoofing attack, replay attack.

Huang, Cheng, et al presented new method, Privacy-Preserving Trust-Based Verifiable Vehicular Cloud Computing scheme (PTVC), to improve safety for traffic and offering services to passengers and drivers (Huang, Lu, Zhu, Hu, & Lin, 2016). The mechanism PTVC system merges between the best advantages of VCC, techniques of verifying, and requirements of privacy, to select the trustworthy vehicle among the vehicles to create a vehicular cloud. The PTVC scheme proves is effective, secure and robust against several attacks.

CONCLUSION

In this chapter, we first talked about vehicular ad-hoc, cloud computing, mobile cloud computing, and we listed all the related to vehicular cloud computing such as architecture, organization, application, challenge, and future. Firstly, we discussed architecture for VCC and then a detailed explanation of the tasks of each layer and clarification of types of services. After that, we talked about the type of organization for VCC infrastructure. Because of sharing resources among the vehicular and RUS with clouds, we highlight for applications providing by VCC like an airport as a data center, traffic management, road safety message, managing parking facilities, real-time navigation, vehicle maintenance, and accident alerts at intersections, etc. Addition, we will survey the issues and challenges facing the vehicular cloud computing resulted from high mobility and the fast topology changes in the network. Finally, we discussed opportunities and the future for VCC that can be the basis to open research directions.

REFERENCES

Ahmad, F., Kazim, M., & Adnane, A. (2015). Vehicular Cloud Networks: Architecture and Security. In *Guide to Security Assurance for Cloud Computing* (pp. 211-226). Springer International Publishing.

Ahmad, F., Kazim, M., Adnane, A., & Awad, A. (2015, December). Vehicular cloud networks: architecture, applications, and security issues. In *Utility and Cloud Computing (UCC), 2015 IEEE/ACM 8th International Conference on* (pp. 571-576). IEEE.

Ahmad, I., Noor, R. M., Ali, I., & Qureshi, M. A. (2016, September). The Role of Vehicular Cloud Computing in Road Traffic Management: A Survey. In *International Conference on Future Intelligent Vehicular Technologies* (pp. 123-131). Springer.

Aloqaily, M., Kantarci, B., & Mouftah, H. T. (2015, November). Vehicular Clouds: State of the art, challenges and future directions. In *Applied Electrical Engineering and Computing Technologies (AEECT), 2015 IEEE Jordan Conference on* (pp. 1-6). IEEE.

Azizian, M., Cherkaoui, S., & Hafid, A. (2016). An Optimized Flow Allocation in Vehicular Cloud. *IEEE Access: Practical Innovations, Open Solutions*, 4, 6766–6779. doi:10.1109/ACCESS.2016.2615323

Baby, D., Sabareesh, R. D., Saravanaguru, R. A. K., & Thangavelu, A. (2013). VCR: vehicular cloud for road side scenarios. In Advances in Computing and Information Technology (pp. 541-552). Springer Berlin Heidelberg. doi:10.1007/978-3-642-31600-5_53

Bajpai, A., & Singh, S. (2016). A survey on Security Analysis in Cloud computing. In *Proceedings of the International Conference on Recent Cognizance in Wireless Communication & Image Processing* (pp. 249-262). Springer India.

Bhoi, S. K., & Khilar, P. M. (2014). Vehicular communication: A survey. *IET Networks, 3*(3), 204–217. doi:10.1049/iet-net.2013.0065

Cardoso, A., Moreira, F., & Simões, P. (2014). A Survey of Cloud Computing Migration Issues and Frameworks. In *New Perspectives in Information Systems and Technologies* (Vol. 1, pp. 161–170). Springer International Publishing. doi:10.1007/978-3-319-05951-8_16

Chang, Y. C., Chen, J. L., Ma, Y. W., & Chiu, P. S. (2015, December). Vehicular Cloud Serving Systems with Software-Defined Networking. In *International Conference on Internet of Vehicles* (pp. 58-67). Springer International Publishing 10.1007/978-3-319-27293-1_6

Chaqfeh, M., Mohamed, N., Jawhar, I., & Wu, J. (2016, December). Vehicular Cloud data collection for Intelligent Transportation Systems. In Smart Cloud Networks & Systems (SCNS) (pp. 1-6). IEEE. doi:10.1109/SCNS.2016.7870555

Cushman, I. J., Rawat, D. B., Chen, L., & Yang, Q. (2016, August). Performance Evaluation of Vehicular Ad Hoc Networks for Rapid Response Traffic Information Delivery. In *International Conference on Wireless Algorithms, Systems, and Applications* (pp. 571-579). Springer International Publishing 10.1007/978-3-319-42836-9_50

Dinh, H. T., Lee, C., Niyato, D., & Wang, P. (2013). A survey of mobile cloud computing: Architecture, applications, and approaches. *Wireless Communications and Mobile Computing, 13*(18), 1587–1611. doi:10.1002/wcm.1203

Dressler, F., Handle, P., & Sommer, C. (2014, August). Towards a vehicular cloud-using parked vehicles as a temporary network and storage infrastructure. In *Proceedings of the 2014 ACM international workshop on Wireless and mobile technologies for smart cities* (pp. 11-18). ACM. 10.1145/2633661.2633671

Eltahir, A. A., & Saeed, R. A. (2015, September). Performance Evaluation of an Enhanced Hybrid Wireless Mesh Protocol (E-HWMP) Protocol for VANET. In *Computing, Control, Networking, Electronics and Embedded Systems Engineering (ICCNEEE), 2015 International Conference on* (pp. 95-100). IEEE.

Eltahir, A. A., Saeed, R. A., Mukherjee, A., & Hasan, M. K. (2016). Evaluation and analysis of an enhanced hybrid wireless mesh protocol for vehicular ad hoc network. *EURASIP Journal on Wireless Communications and Networking*, (1): 1–11.

Falchetti, A., Azurdia-Meza, C., & Cespedes, S. (2015, October). Vehicular cloud computing in the dawn of 5G. In *Electrical, Electronics Engineering, Information and Communication Technologies (CHILECON), 2015 CHILEAN Conference on* (pp. 301-305). IEEE.

Fernando, N., Loke, S. W., & Rahayu, W. (2013). Mobile cloud computing: A survey. *Future Generation Computer Systems, 29*(1), 84–106. doi:10.1016/j.future.2012.05.023

Garai, M., Rekhis, S., & Boudriga, N. (2015, July). Communication as a service for cloud vanets. In *Computers and Communication (ISCC), 2015 IEEE Symposium on* (pp. 371-377). IEEE 10.1109/ISCC.2015.7405543

Ghafoor, K. Z., Mohammed, M. A., & Lloret, J. L. (2016). Vehicular Cloud Computing: Trends and Challenges. *ZANCO Journal of Pure and Applied Sciences*, *28*(3), 67–77.

Gu, L., Zeng, D., & Guo, S. (2013, December). Vehicular cloud computing: A survey. In Globecom Workshops (GC Wkshps), 2013 IEEE (pp. 403-407). IEEE.

Habib, S. M., Hauke, S., Ries, S., & Mühlhäuser, M. (2012). Trust as a facilitator in cloud computing: A survey. *Journal of Cloud Computing: Advances, Systems, and Applications*, *1*(1), 19. doi:10.1186/2192-113X-1-19

He, W., Yan, G., & Da Xu, L. (2014). Developing vehicular data cloud services in the IoT environment. *IEEE Transactions on Industrial Informatics*, *10*(2), 1587–1595. doi:10.1109/TII.2014.2299233

Hindia, M. N., Reza, A. W., Dakkak, O., Awang Nor, S., & Noordin, K. A. (2014). Cloud computing applications and platforms: a survey (pp. 515–524). Academic Press.

Huang, C., Lu, R., Zhu, H., Hu, H., & Lin, X. (2016, December). PTVC: *Achieving Privacy-Preserving Trust-Based Verifiable Vehicular Cloud Computing. In Global Communications Conference (GLOBECOM)*, 2016 *IEEE* (pp. 1-6). IEEE.

Hussain, R., Son, J., Eun, H., Kim, S., & Oh, H. (2012, December). Rethinking vehicular communications: Merging VANET with cloud computing. In *Cloud Computing Technology and Science (CloudCom), 2012 IEEE 4th International Conference on* (pp. 606-609). IEEE.

Karagiannis, G., Altintas, O., Ekici, E., Heijenk, G., Jarupan, B., Lin, K., & Weil, T. (2011). Vehicular networking: A survey and tutorial on requirements, architectures, challenges, standards, and solutions. *IEEE Communications Surveys and Tutorials*, *13*(4), 584–616. doi:10.1109/SURV.2011.061411.00019

Kumar, N., Singh, J. P., Bali, R. S., Misra, S., & Ullah, S. (2015). An intelligent clustering scheme for distributed intrusion detection in vehicular cloud computing. *Cluster Computing*, 1263-1283.

Li, T., Zhao, M., Liu, A., & Huang, C. (2017). On Selecting Vehicles as Recommenders for Vehicular Social Networks. *IEEE Access: Practical Innovations, Open Solutions*.

Mei, X., Nagasaka, N., Okumura, B., & Prokhorov, D. (2015, June). Detection and motion planning for roadside parked vehicles at long distance. In *Intelligent Vehicles Symposium (IV)*, 2015 *IEEE* (pp. 412-418). IEEE. 10.1109/IVS.2015.7225720

Mekki, T., Jabri, I., Rachedi, A., & Ben Jemaa, M. (2016). Vehicular cloud networks: Challenges, architectures, and future directions. *Vehicular Communications*.

Meneguette, R. I. (2016). A Vehicular Cloud-Based Framework for the Intelligent Transport Management of Big Cities. *International Journal of Distributed Sensor Networks*, *12*(5), 8198597. doi:10.1155/2016/8198597

Mershad, K., & Artail, H. (2013). Finding a STAR in a Vehicular Cloud. *IEEE Intelligent Transportation Systems Magazine, 5*(2), 55-68.

Olariu, S., Eltoweissy, M., & Younis, M. (2011). Towards autonomous vehicular clouds. EAI Endorsed Trans. *Mobile Communications Applications, 1*(1), e2. doi:10.4108/icst.trans.mca.2011.e2

Olariu, S., Khalil, I., & Abuelela, M. (2011). Taking VANET to the clouds. *International Journal of Pervasive Computing and Communications, 7*(1), 7–21. doi:10.1108/17427371111123577

Othman, M., Madani, S. A., & Khan, S. U. (2014). A survey of mobile cloud computing application models. *IEEE Communications Surveys and Tutorials, 16*(1), 393–413. doi:10.1109/SURV.2013.062613.00160

Rajput, U., Abbas, F., & Oh, H. (2016). A Hierarchical Privacy Preserving Pseudonymous Authentication Protocol for VANET. *IEEE Access: Practical Innovations, Open Solutions, 4*, 7770–7784. doi:10.1109/ACCESS.2016.2620999

Riaz, F., & Niazi, M. A. (2016). Road collisions avoidance using vehicular cyber-physical systems: A taxonomy and review. *Complex Adaptive Systems Modeling, 4*(1), 15. doi:10.118640294-016-0025-8

Sharma, M. K., Bali, R. S., & Kaur, A. (2015, October). Dyanimc key based authentication scheme for Vehicular Cloud Computing. In *Green Computing and Internet of Things (ICGCIoT), 2015 International Conference on* (pp. 1059-1064). IEEE. 10.1109/ICGCIoT.2015.7380620

Sharma, M. K., & Kaur, A. (2015, September). A survey on vehicular cloud computing and its security. In *Next Generation Computing Technologies (NGCT), 2015 1st International Conference on* (pp. 67-71). IEEE

Shravanthi, C., & Guruprasad, H. S. (2014, May). *Mobile Cloud Computing as future for mobile applications. International Journal of Research in Engineering and Technology.*

Singh, P., Kaur, S., & Sandhu, S. S. (2015). An Overview of Mobile Cloud Computing.*International Journal of Computer and Communication System Engineering, 2*(2), 255–259.

Sugumar, R., Rengarajan, A., & Jayakumar, C. (2016). Trust based authentication technique for cluster based vehicular ad hoc networks (VANET). *Wireless Networks*, 1–10.

Verma, A., & Kaushal, S. (2011). Cloud computing security issues and challenges: a survey. *Advances in Computing and Communications*, 445-454.

Viriyasitavat, W., Boban, M., Tsai, H. M., & Vasilakos, A. (2015). Vehicular communications: Survey and challenges of channel and propagation models. *IEEE Vehicular Technology Magazine, 10*(2), 55–66. doi:10.1109/MVT.2015.2410341

Wahyono, W., & Jo, K. H. (2017). Cumulative Dual Foreground Differences For Illegally Parked Vehicles Detection. *IEEE Transactions on Industrial Informatics, 13*(5), 2464–2473. doi:10.1109/TII.2017.2665584

Wan, J., Zhang, D., Zhao, S., Yang, L., & Lloret, J. (2014). Context-aware vehicular cyber-physical systems with cloud support: Architecture, challenges, and solutions. *IEEE Communications Magazine, 52*(8), 106–113. doi:10.1109/MCOM.2014.6871677

Whaiduzzaman, M., Sookhak, M., Gani, A., & Buyya, R. (2014). A survey on vehicular cloud computing. *Journal of Network and Computer Applications*, *40*, 325–344. doi:10.1016/j.jnca.2013.08.004

Yan, G., Wen, D., Olariu, S., & Weigle, M. C. (2013). Security challenges in vehicular cloud computing. *IEEE Transactions on Intelligent Transportation Systems*, *14*(1), 284–294. doi:10.1109/TITS.2012.2211870

Zhang, Q., Cheng, L., & Boutaba, R. (2010). Cloud computing: State-of-the-art and research challenges. *Journal of Internet Services and Applications*, *1*(1), 7–18. doi:10.100713174-010-0007-6

Zhu, H., Lu, R., Huang, C., Chen, L., & Li, H. (2016). An Efficient Privacy-Preserving Location-Based Services Query Scheme in Outsourced Cloud. *IEEE Transactions on Vehicular Technology*, *65*(9), 7729–7739. doi:10.1109/TVT.2015.2499791

This research was previously published in Vehicular Cloud Computing for Traffic Management and Systems edited by Jyoti Grover, P. Vinod, and Chhagan Lal, pages 57-74, copyright year 2018 by Engineering Science Reference (an imprint of IGI Global).

Chapter 107
Future Directions to the Application of Distributed Fog Computing in Smart Grid Systems

Arash Anzalchi
Florida International University, USA

Aditya Sundararajan
Florida International University, USA

Longfei Wei
Florida International University, USA

Amir Moghadasi
Florida International University, USA

Arif Sarwat
Florida International University, USA

ABSTRACT

The rapid growth of new technologies in power systems requires real-time monitoring and control of bidirectional data communication and electric power flow. Cloud computing has centralized architecture and is not scalable towards the emerging internet of things (IoT) landscape of the grid. Further, under large-scale integration of renewables, this framework could be bogged down by congestion, latency, and subsequently poor quality of service (QoS). This calls for a distributed architecture called fog computing, which imbibes both clouds as well as the end-devices to collect, process, and act upon the data locally at the edge for low latency applications prior to forwarding them to the cloud for more complex operations. Fog computing offers high performance and interoperability, better scalability and visibility, and greater availability in comparison to a grid relying only on the cloud. In this chapter, a prospective research roadmap, future challenges, and opportunities to apply fog computing on smart grid systems is presented.

DOI: 10.4018/978-1-5225-8176-5.ch107

INTRODUCTION

Unlike conventional power systems, smart grid today is a healthy amalgamation of multiple interoperable, scalable, efficient, sustainable and secure technological domains contributing holistically towards the availability, reliability, and quality of the power generated, transmitted, and distributed to consumers. These technological domains extend beyond power systems themselves, manifesting as data management, cyber-physical security, human behaviors, mathematics, communication, and even wireless sensors. Such an interconnected smart grid can provide sustainable and reliable power delivery, ensuring availability and eco-friendly means of generating power. Integrating many renewables into the grid, at both transmission as well as distribution levels, is expected to yield an unstable grid owing to their intermittent nature. This necessitates the need for smoothing as well as optimizing the cost of operation, production, and distribution (Popeanga, 2012). Consumers have now metamorphosed into "prosumers", wherein they have gained the ability to both produce as well as consume power. With the integration of more intelligent sensors and devices on the field, largely distributed across the grid, Internet of Things (IoT) has gained prominence in this critical infrastructure as well. These devices churn data points constantly, racing to the central servers bolstered by strong and resilient communication infrastructure (Dastjerdi & Buyya, 2017). Consequently, the significance of computing in the smart grid domain must be investigated. For this purpose, three sub-domains within the smart grid will be explored in this chapter: information management, energy management, and security.

Significance of Computing in Information Management

Currently, the deluge of digital data is centrally ingested and cleansed into useful information blocks that can be processed. Many critical power system applications such as Demand Response (DR), load flow and Optimal Power Flow (OPF) analyses, fault and reliability analyses, quality assurance models, customer billing processes, direct load control, active/reactive power control and distribution planning, to name a few, depend on the veracity and validity of the information gathered from the field. This warrants the need for effective and powerful computing technologies for smart grid.

Significance of Computing in Energy Management

The existing power grid needs an optimal balance of electricity demand and supply between consumers and the utilities. The smart grid can address this requirement. Such features in a smart grid are realized by the integration of various Energy Management Systems (EMSs) such as Home Energy Management (HEM), Demand Side Management (DSM), and Building Energy Management Systems (BEMS) (Fang, Misra, Xue, & Yang, 2012). A smart grid allows various renewable energy sources (such as solar and the wind) to have the efficient management of supply and demand. In the emerging smart city and microgrid scenarios, EMS is one of the most important cornerstones. Naturally, for the efficient and continuous operation of such complex ecosystems within the grid, computation will play a crucial role. With the integration of secondary storage devices such as batteries and supercapacitors, optimal economic dispatch, peak load shaving, and other operations will be required at micro-grid level. Under such scenarios, effective distributed computing methods need to be added on top of the underlying power infrastructure.

Significance of Computing in Security

Smart grid today is a Cyber-Physical System (CPS). While historically air-gapped with cyber and physical silos, the modern grid comprises multiple interdependent elements from both cyber as well as physical realms (Harp & Gregory-Brown, 2013). The cyber realm comprises the Information Technology (IT) solutions that include data processing servers, networked operator consoles, and workstations, visualization interfaces as well as the communication infrastructure itself. On the other hand, the physical realm contains the Operation Technology (OT) solutions that include Industrial Control Systems (ICSs) like Supervisory Control and Data Acquisition (SCADA), Process Control Domains (PCDs), Distributed Control Systems (DCSs) and Programmable Logic Controllers (PLCs). While IT relies heavily on networking functionalities to pull data from different sources and visualize useful insights for the operators and analysts continuously, the OT adopts proprietary protocols and the ICSs for control and dispatch. This silo-based operating framework, however, is no longer adequate, considering the proliferation of more intelligent field sensors that discourage the concept of such a framework and are required to interweave the principles of IT and OT. However, this increased intermingling between IT and OT realms has exposed the vulnerabilities of the grid's critical infrastructure elements greater than ever before. It cannot be denied that a cyber-attack on the modern grid will have definite ramifications in the physical realm, and vice-versa. Recent successful cyber-attacks or even cascading failures on power grids across the world, such as the 2003 Northeastern United States blackout due to cascading failures (Chadwick, 2013; National Electric Reliability Commission [NERC], 2004), the 2015 Ukrainian grid blackout due to BlackEnergy3 malware (Electricity Information Sharing and Analysis Center 2016), and attacks on SCADA/ICS due to the HAVEX worm (Nelson, 2016) bear testimonies to this fact.

Most attacks target sensitive IT gateways and checkpoints, including operator workstation consoles and emails, through methods such as phishing, malware, social engineering or Denial of Service (DoS) by exploiting vulnerabilities like poor security configuration, lack of situational awareness, susceptibility of ill-informed or poorly-aware system operators, bugs in critical OT-managing software, poorly maintained Access Control Lists (ACLs), and inadequate patching and firmware updates (Wang, 2013). In response to these concerns, the National Electric Reliability Commission (NERC) has put forth several Critical Infrastructure Protection (CIP) standards for cyber-security, including those for personnel and training, incident reporting and response planning, information protection, physical security and vulnerability assessment (NERC, 2012, 2014a, 2014b, 2014c). It is imperative that to successfully ensure adherence to these standards, effective computational technologies and methods must be in-place.

Contribution of This Chapter

While existing computation tools increasingly imbibe the principles of Cloud Computing (referred to as *Cloud* moving forward), its centralized processing is counterproductive to the inherent way the smart grid is designed to function, which is distributed. The energy infrastructure requires high performance, lightweight, low latency, and distributed intelligent methods which shift significant processing and management workloads from the center towards the edge of the grid. The emerging applications that involve computations directly or indirectly need to inculcate an optimal combination of computing principles, giving way to the new paradigm of "Fog Computing", referred to in this chapter as *Fog*. Although Fog is touted to be equivalent to Edge Computing (referred to moving forward as "Edge"), there exists a little difference. While the Cloud looks at retaining its intelligence only at the central point of an infrastructure, the Edge attempts to move significant computations to the infrastructure's end devices. However, the Fog tries to strike a balance by shifting low latency, lightweight applications to the edge and high latency, heavyweight applications to the Cloud. In this case, Fog can be thought of as a combination of the Edge and the Cloud, and under such a context, the term "Fog" becomes interchangeable with "Edge". In this chapter, the word "Edge" will be used in this context unless otherwise stated.

Fog addresses the inherent drawbacks of the Cloud such as latency, energy consumption concentration, bandwidth and associated costs, and privacy. It also presents additional benefits such as localization, location-awareness, operational visibility and dynamic resource management, and fulfills business goals (Yi, Li & Li, 2015). In addition, it is predicted that the Fog utilization will have a strategic role in the motivation and design of the emerging smart grid and will increase the robustness of its communication. This chapter, hence, lays the much-needed emphasis on the distributed fog computing architecture and framework, which was initially coined by Cisco and later structured and disseminated by the OpenFog Consortium in 2015, of which Cisco is also a member (Cisco, 2015). The authors believe that this chapter will serve as a unique starting point for readers interested in further investigating the potential of Fog Computing on the future smart grid for better performance, stability, and reliability.

Organization of This Chapter

In Section II, a foundation is first laid by reviewing the traditionally employed computing tools and contrasting them with the more recent cloud computing technologies for the smart grid. Applications of Cloud to energy management, information management, and security are discussed. Section III introduces the envisioned Fog architecture for the smart grid, which involves a two-tiered approach comprising Local and Central Tiers. The introduced framework's significance and validity in energy management, information management, and security is then investigated by the authors. Section IV presents a case study to provide the context for mechanisms included in Fog by considering different power system applications that can be then validated, such as short-term Distributed Renewable Resource (DRR) generation forecasting, unit commitment and adequacy assessment for scenarios involving high penetration DRRs. The mathematical models for these applications are provided first, followed by an explanation of how the envisioned Fog model can be used to achieve their implementation. Following that, in Section V, the proposed testbed simulator is introduced and described. Further, it is shown how this testbed is used for validating the applications discussed in Section IV.

BACKGROUND: OVERVIEW OF SMART GRID AND EXISTING COMPUTING

Before introducing and discussing the proposed Fog framework, it is important to first discuss the smart grid architecture that lays the foundation for the computing models discussed in this chapter. Then, the emergent Cloud framework must be briefly discussed, since it has the precursors to Fog. To help the reader better appreciate the pros and cons of these two technologies, they are explained in the context of three major power system applications: energy management, information management, and cyber-physical security, which are also covered in the smart grid architecture discussion.

Smart Grid Architecture

It is, by now, clear that smart grid cumulatively generates continuous streams of high-dimensional, multi-variate data-points which bear the characteristics of big data: large volume, high velocity, acute veracity, diverse variety and critical validity, collectively called the "Five Vs" of smart grid big data. Although these characteristics are applicable to all forms of big data, they are more crucial for smart grid because of their direct implications on power delivery and security, as briefly investigated in Section I. Data volume refers to the size of generated data which is generally of the orders of Terabytes (TB) or Petabytes (PB) every month in most utility-operated territories. Data velocity attributes the speed with which these devices churn data observations, which ranges from the orders of a few milliseconds to one hour. Velocity can also be understood as a measure of data resolution. This augments with the concept of variety, which signifies the different sources that spawn data records. Typical sources of today's automated data generation include the Advanced Metering Infrastructure (AMI) smart meters, Phasor Measurement Units (PMUs), meteorological weather stations, and Intelligent Electronic Devices (IEDs) such as Voltage Regulators, Load Tap Changers (LTCs) and Capacitor Banks. Data veracity encapsulates the idea of data integrity and consistency, which is important for the smart grid, considering important decisions regarding power dispatch and demand response are made based on processes which use these data. Finally, data validity represents the freshness of data (Sornalakshmi & Vadivu, 2015). There are scenarios in power systems where computational algorithms must process a newly generated data almost in real-time to generate actionable results. A delay even by one minute could cause significant losses in revenue or energy. Such latency-cognizant applications need to have constant and on-demand access to data.

A conceptual architecture of the future grid in smart cities is shown in Figure 1. It comprises the physical devices and controllers at the edge level such as AMI meters, PMUs and IEDSs among others. These devices and electronic systems communicate with the Edge Computing module of the Fog, forming the Local Tier. Simple analytics and security protocols are executed at this level, with results aggregated and encapsulated with partially processed data to increase abstraction. Using designated gateways, over an efficient and available network connectivity, further bolstered by optimal routing strategies, the information is forwarded higher in the hierarchy on a need-to-compute basis. Diagnostic analysis methods such as contextualization, association mining, correlation, simple optimization and iterative processes are executed at this point. It is key to remember that as the data goes higher in the hierarchy, the processing power and scale grows rapidly as well. Thus, the nature of the data itself morphs into one that of big data. As it enters the Central Tier where the Cloud still resides, heavyweight applications come into picture. Most of these applications are legacy, being run at the utility's CCC. The applications at this level must have immense computational power, ability to run parallel processes over multiple cores, and fully exploit the robustness and flexibility of the cloud platform. It is noticeable that data gets proliferated across the two Tiers in multiple ways, thus increasing ubiquity and connectivity. This in-turn increases the attack surface of the overall smart grid. Hence, cybersecurity approaches also need to be decentralized, implemented at varied complexities in the Local as well as Central Tiers.

Cloud Computing Framework

The cloud infrastructure can empower customers to have immediate access to the data they are entitled to, via customized applications, from anywhere anytime, provided they are connected to the network.

Figure 1. The smart grid architecture and its tiers of computing

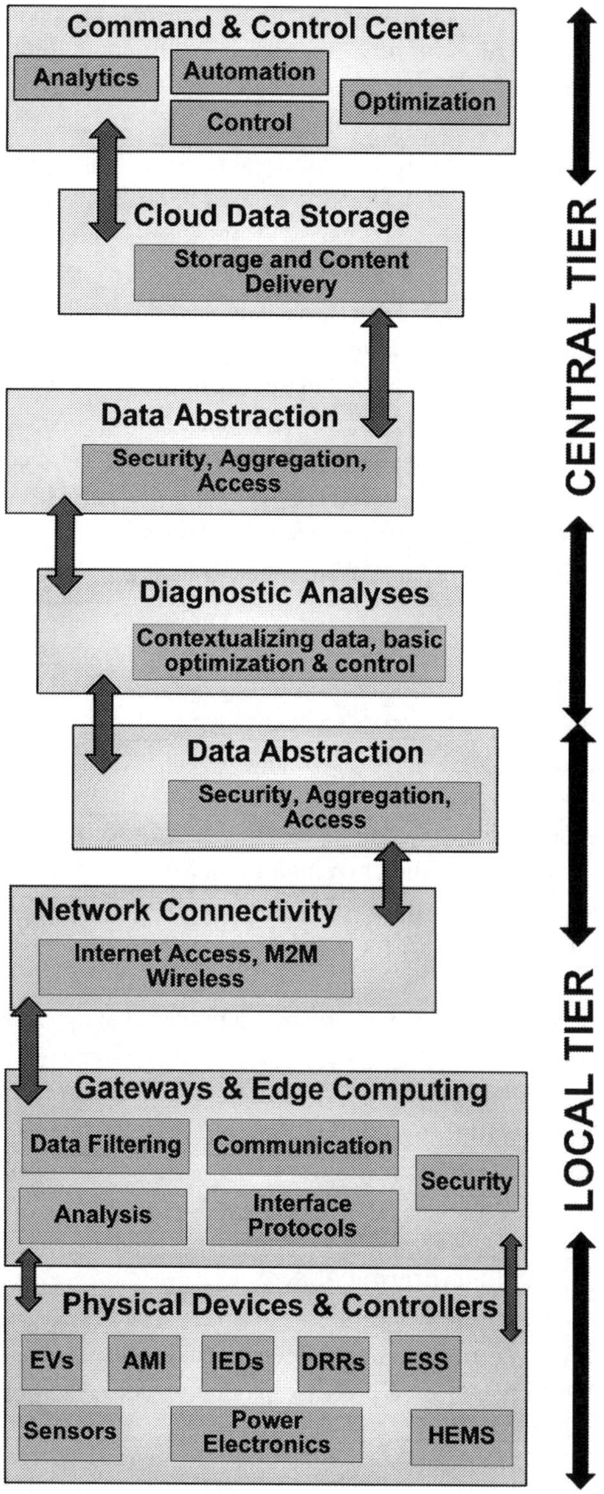

Recently, the use of cloud computing for managing and processing smart grid big data has been discussed in the literature. Nozaki, Tominaga, Iwasaki, and Takeuchi (2011) suggest administering central optimization frame and communication infrastructure using cloud computing data hubs as auxiliary cognitive radio system of smart meters. Fang, Misra, Xue, and Yang (2012) proposed a model of data management for the smart grid based on cloud computing is offered. This model exploits distributed administration for instantaneous data acquisition, recovery of real-time information as a parallel analyzer, and network-wide access. A system for decision support as well as a software for cloud computing is offered by Guo, Pan, and Fang (2012). This technology brings together consumers, energy consultants, modern web interoperable technologies, and energy service procedures. Some studies compare smart grid with the traditional power grid to recognize new weaknesses and exposures in the grid of the future. Zaballos, Vallejo, and Selga (2011) proposed an architecture for private cloud computing which can be used for supporting smart grid. An agent-based cloud-client architecture which is designed for the smart grid is introduced by in Metke and Ekl, (2010). This technology can combine storage resources and computing, and make no changes to the interior configuration or current equipment of the system. A systematic approach for smart grid virtualization at both device and substation levels is introduced. A high-level overview of devices, trust, and communication security, as well as complexity and scalability issues of the smart grid, is presented by Zhang, Wang, Sun, Green, and Alam (2011).

Energy Management

Several cloud computing methods have been proposed in the literature for energy management in the smart grid. Today, most of the utilities have an EMS which emphasizes instantaneous grid management. Global smart grid framework needs accessible software infrastructure which analyses and integrates flowing of real-time data from numerous smart meters for optimization and investigation of supply and demand curves. Cloud platforms are being well studied to reinforce such enormous data and compute-intensive, online applications. For these purposes, scalable constraints are obtainable by the cloud products to shape a dynamic and real-time software. Cloud as an essential part of this environment offers these benefits:

- The elastic operation of cloud helps to avoid inflated capital cost at the peak load, therefore it helps to cut the expenses of the utilities.
- Real-time pricing statistics and power consumption data can be shared with customers and they can take advantage of the real-time information.
- Information can be securely distributed to third party organizations through cloud facilities, in order to build smart tools to tailor end user needs.

Information Management and Communication

Currently, numerous advanced smart meters are implemented at the distribution grid. Cloud computing is a beneficial service to effectively store and process this bulky data for information management, for these reasons:

- Smart grid data analysis process matches the storage and handling mechanism of the cloud.
- In a smart grid, data distribution is a significant concern in the smart grid structure. Various can be pooled by implementing cloud computing.

- Main players of the smart grid, e.g. consumers, utilities, and microgrids, can get access to the cloud data, even though they are operating in islanded mode.
- A significant characteristic of the smart grid is two-way information and energy flow which empowers several functions and operational control systems in the smart grid, the however real-time process of smart grid behaviors can be done in the cloud platform.
- Management of massive data is complex, costly, and may be beyond the capacity of existing data management systems in the smart grid. Using a cloud-based information management system can help in encountering such drawbacks.
- A cloud-based information center can help managing huge data in a cheaper way. Moreover, the current system's ability to do such a thing have much more limitations than cloud.

Cyber-Physical Security

Smart grids can be assumed as a cyber-physical scheme which makes the physical systems (electricity) function in parallel with cyber-framework (internet). This facility as the backbone of the can communicate with the consumer appliances and also provide the backbone for service providers to absorb contents and control operations. With the presence of online connectivity, it is a big challenge to prevent cyber-attacks in the smart grid that can potentially disrupt the power supply.

To solve these problems in the smart grid expansion, a number of security mechanisms have been proposed in the literature by application of cloud computing, which are listed below:

- A security structure for power system and protection system information, established on the security of the cloud, is offered by (Yanliang, Song, Wei-Min, Tao, and Yong (2010). Security of the cloud was separated into two sections: client and server. Data are collected by the client and the actions are chosen by the server's reactions. On the other hand, On the other hand, the cloud computing is exploited by the server as a smart decision maker and distributed storage. After that, by use of the Internet, the results are transmitted.
- The security of stored data in cloud computing is guaranteed by the distributed verification protocol (DVP). The execution of the DVP protocol is appropriate for power management and data storage structures in the smart grid (Ugale, Soni, Pema, & Patil, 2011).
- Many security threats are presented by Yang, Wu, and Hu (2011), such as (a) the personal sensitive data can be accessed by the cloud supervisors, (b) security of transmission and storage of the data is in a close relationship with the cloud location.

THE FOG COMPUTING FRAMEWORK

Smart grid big data can be grouped into four broad categories: Operational, Non-operational, Event message, and Meter data. Operational and non-operational datasets are part of the grid's Energy Management System (EMS) and Distribution Management System (DMS). While Event message data corresponds to Outage Management System (OMS), the meter data belong to the Meter Data Management (MDM). These logical zones of the grid are meant to be interoperable and constantly exchange data between their layers for executing different applications. The operational data are concerned with voltage and current phasors, real and reactive power flows, DR, OPF constraints and values, and generation forecasts. Non-operational data corresponds to data on asset health, power quality, reliability, asset stressors, and telemetry. Event message data is mostly concerned with asset vulnerabilities, threats, failures, and likelihood of risks including but not limited to device flags, checksum errors, fault detection events, device logs, alert messages, and meter voltage loss information. Meter data includes the energy consumption readings, the average peak and time of day values.

The Fog framework supports an architecture that enables the processing of latency-sensitive data and computations closer to the sources of such data, instead of sending them unprocessed all the way to the cloud and retrieve results. As shown in Figure 2, the Fog framework combines both the Edge and the Cloud in a manner that increases latency top-down. At the edge of the grid are the various data source nodes which constantly generate data-points which fall into one of the four categories described in Section II. These nodes, depending on the volume and validity of the data they generate, are allocated dedicated or shared computation-rich processing nodes called "Fog nodes", all of which, along with the source nodes themselves, form the *Local Tier.* The Fog nodes could be cloudlets, smartphones, Personal Digital Assistants (PDAs) or even client computers. Latency-intensive, stream computations including preliminary descriptive analytics on the raw data could be executed at this Tier (Sajjad, Danniswara, Al-Shishtawy & Vlassov, 2016). For example, in the AMI architecture, a few hundred residential smart meters feed their data continuously to an Access Point (AP). A Fog node dedicated to this AP could check the data's quality and integrity, clean erroneous values, identify missing records and correlate them with the checksum values and device flags to create a rudimentary analysis. Data obfuscation and privacy-preserving policies could also be implemented at this Tier before the node forwards the semi-processed data to the node next in the hierarchy. Depending on the application, there could be more than one level of Fog nodes in the grid, where the data is subject to processing at each level until it reaches the Cloud, called the *Central Tier.* This Tier might not only be the central cloud. For example, an industry might have its own private cloud with which its Fog nodes interact, and the private cloud finally sends only the

Figure 2. The envisioned Fog Computing Framework for Smart Grid

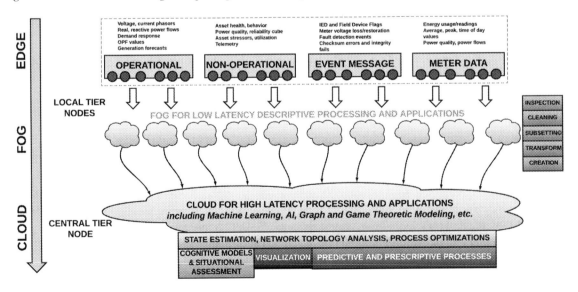

required information to the publicly managed Cloud at the center, where very heavyweight computations employing batch processing, process optimizations, state estimation and network topology analysis could be performed on the aggregated data.

As can be seen above, Fog framework has a dynamic topology, where different IoT devices could interact in different ways depending on their needs and business model requirements. This, unlike in a Cloud environment, raises significant concerns, elaborated in the following subsection.

How Fog Differs From the Cloud?

It is now time to examine the key areas where the Fog and the Cloud exhibit differences. The observations, gathered mostly from industrial white papers and technical articles in journals and proceedings, are summarized and tabulated below in Table 1 (Rao, Khan, Maschendra & Kumar, 2015; Saharan & Kumar, 2015; Yi, Hao, Qin & Li, 2015; Almadhor, 2016; Deshmukh & More, 2016; Okay & Ozdemir, 2016; Luntovskyy & Spillner, 2017). It can be concluded from this comparison that there are meritorious aspects to the Fog that the Cloud cannot compete against. At the same time, there are aspects where the Cloud has a winning hand over the Fog (Shi & Dustdar, 2016). Hence, application of Fog to one's requirement is not universally justifiable and is greatly dependent on one's business and operational requirements. However, Fog has generally found a greater applicability than the Cloud for any IoT or IoT-like ecosystem, of which smart grid is increasingly becoming a part.

Table 1. A high-level comparison between the Fog and Cloud frameworks

	The Fog	**The Cloud**
Computing Architecture Style	Distributed	Centralized
Suitable for	Lightweight, moderate-weight applications requiring low latency	Heavyweight applications that can survive medium to high latency
Latency	Milliseconds to seconds (real-time)	Minutes to days
Information Storage	Streaming (hours to few days)	Batch (months to years)
Data locality	Closer to the data sources (localized)	At a data center located away from the sources (centralized)
Framework Scope	Local to each source (device/aggregator-level)	Global scope (network or infrastructure-level)
Heterogeneity	High (different sources need to be inter-operable across varied protocols, schemas, and structure)	Low (nature of original sources does not matter as data is pooled and centrally managed)
Interactions	Machine-to-Machine (M2M)	Machine-to-Command and Control-to-Machine (MCM)
Common Application	Descriptive analytics, local control	Predictive, prescriptive analytics, global control
Partitioning	Information and applications are partitioned between Edge and Cloud for optimal processing	Information and applications are partitioned within the Cloud for optimal storage, security
Privacy	By virtue of data localization, privacy can be better guaranteed	Under public Cloud environments, privacy is still a debated concern
Maintenance	Owing to heterogeneity in protocol and topology, maintenance is difficult	Owing to its central storage and processing, maintenance is easier

The Architecture

Fog computing is introduced and defined by the OpenFog Consortium (2017) as "a horizontal, system-level architecture that distributes computing, storage, control and networking functions closer to the users along a cloud-to-thing continuum" (p. 3). This definition is holistic considering it advocates the distributed nature of Fog and the fact that it integrates the individual concepts of the Cloud and Edge, applicable the best for IoT environments. Another noteworthy aspect is its emphasis on just computing being distributed, but also storage, control and networking (communication). This implies that the Fog is a heterogeneous ecosystem where constituent devices need to be interoperable and cross-functional. It is quite different to the notion of a Cloud, where all devices engage in a unilateral correspondence with the central nodes and rely on them for all their needs. Keeping in mind these key views, the Consortium proposed the OpenFog Reference Architecture (OpenFog RA) to help various Fog stakeholders like managers, developers, and users (OpenFog Consortium, 2016). For consistency, the OpenFog RA is referred to in this chapter as the Fog architecture.

Now that the envisioned distributed fog framework has been introduced, it is time to investigate the different characteristics of the framework, namely the factors that define the Fog architecture. They also help in evaluating the performance and applicability of this architecture to a critical infrastructure like smart grid. The Fog architecture can be described by nine key characteristics which are inter-dependent and complementary in nature (Byers & Wetterwald, 2015). They have been briefly summarized below, but the authors regard them as important emerging and open areas of research.

1. **Reliability:** Like other traditional computing paradigms such as mainframe, grid, cluster and cloud, the Fog also must satisfy some of the critical standard reliability characteristics with respect to physical and computational resources (Madsen, Albeanu, Burtschy & Poentiu-Vladicescu, 2013). While physical resources include computing hardware, sensor nodes, actuator nodes and augmented smart technologies like smart inverters, IEDs and PMUs to name a few, computational resources include the models and algorithms running over the software platforms. The Fog derives characteristics from its predecessors, such as dynamic resource allocation and deallocation (see C.4), parallel processing (through its distributed nature) and virtualization. The authors refer to Madsen et al. (2013), which considers the failure of sensor nodes, lack of network coverage, failure of the platform or the network itself, or the failure of just the user interface as part of Fog reliability.

2. **Hierarchical Structure:** By definition, the Fog nodes of a particular Local Tier are designed to be as close to the end-devices as possible. For a simple infrastructure, there could be one Local Tier and one Central Tier. However, for more complex networks like the smart grid, there are bound to be multiple Local Tiers that retain operational autonomy but are interoperable with their peer Tiers. The Local Tiers higher up by a step could aggregate two or more end Local Tiers which are closely related in terms of functionality or resources. For example, in a smart community, different Local Tiers corresponding to micro-grids, the utility's distribution network, AMI meters and autonomous Electric Vehicles (EVs) can exist. These Local Tiers almost always need to interact with one another since their unimpeded operations depend on applications such as energy management, power flow analysis and direct load control. For this purpose, a medium-level Local Tier could be built which aggregates relevant information from the end-Local Tiers and handles medium-weight processes. The Central Tier (Cloud) could then conduct demand response, load profiling and customer billing

processes based on the results delivered by the different layers of Local Tiers. This hierarchical, multi-tier structure of the Fog makes it quite adaptive in nature, which cannot be achieved by Cloud.

3. **Resilience:** Resilience is an attribute of how effectively the mission-critical applications continue to run even in the event of a failure or an attack. Being distributed not only in computing, but also in storage, processing and communication, Fog architecture is one of the best approaches to ensure resiliency (Pradhan, et al. 2016). The Fog nodes are meant to be dynamic, interoperable, and hierarchical in nature. Should a Local Tier be compromised, resources for the nodes in that Tier could duly be deallocated and reallocated to the nodes in adjoining Tiers which can take over the additional load, which in-turn can be smartly distributed to multiple peer Tiers based on their own computation loads. Should the Central Tier itself be compromised, all the Local Tiers can still run critical applications as usual since they do not depend on the Cloud for them. Fog nodes usually employ checkpoints which identify the most recent "safe" mode of operation, to which they could rollback upon restoration. Replication or redundancy is another tolerance mechanism which is more applicable for a distributed framework like Fog, considering the enormity of information to be replicated at a Local Tier is much less than at the Central Tier in the event of a disaster or attack.

4. **Dynamism and Heterogeneity:** The hierarchical structure of a typical Fog framework was discussed. It follows from this characteristic that the Fog is also dynamic in nature. Due to the varying energy needs dictated by dynamic load profiles, for instance, the intermittent generation profiles of renewables installed in the micro-grid, and the inclusion of mobile smart loads such as EVs, there could be scenarios that warrant idle processing power, skewed loading of Fog nodes both within a Tier and across Tiers, etc. Sometimes, physical and computational resources become surplus or deficit. The Fog architecture is capable of dynamic allocation, deallocation and reallocation of resources to nodes across layers (Emfinger, Dubey, Volgyesi, Sallai & Karsai, 2016). The added heterogeneity of the original sources implies greater dynamism.

5. **Partitioning:** The Fog also supports the principle of data and application partitioning, where certain parts of the data generated by the source nodes are ingested at the Edge while the remaining are reserved for the Cloud. A similar concept is applicable to the applications that depend on these data. Consequently, they require to be partitioned in a manner that Fog-data is utilized by Fog-Applications and Cloud-data by the Cloud-applications (Khedkar & Gawande, 2014).

6. **Interoperability, Automation and Autonomy:** Fog is meant to be transparent and support ubiquitous computing. Interoperability of the Fog resources is critical to ensure seamless Machine-to-Machine (M2M) communications at the Tiers. The architecture also enables autonomy of resources and services for discovery and registration, management, allocation and deallocation, security (such as Authentication-Authorization-Accounting or InfoSec), and most importantly, operation. Autonomy and self-healing nature are considered the defining traits of the smart grid, and the Fog is strategically positioned to facilitate moving a step closer to fully realizing this goal. The architecture further supports the use of Application Programming Interfaces (APIs), standards and containerization (isolated execution for looser coupling) of applications for customizing nodes and Tiers, through which operational dynamism and interoperability can be automated. Automation can be additionally achieved by implementing Software-Defined Network (SDN) technologies and M2M communications like Message Queuing Telemetry Transport (MQTT) and Constrained Application Protocol (CoAP) also lend towards increased automation and interoperability. In some

cases, SDN-managed Network Functions Virtualization (NFV) can help reduce physical resource constraints and enhance load management (Gupta, Nath, Chakraborty & Ghosh, 2016).

7. **Latency and Bandwidth:** Probably the most talked about characteristic of the Fog is its low latency and high utilization of available bandwidth. It is expected that the Fog nodes within Local Tiers are energy-conservative in nature. Hence, they are resource-constrained and bandwidth-aware (Borcoci, 2016). Since many Fog nodes handle time-critical and mission-critical analyses, factors such as data validity is important. For events such as fluctuating renewable energy generation due to frequently passing clouds that might negatively impact the grid it is connected to, the associated Fog nodes have to not only smoothen the spikes and dips but must also be capable of accurately predicting these intermittencies so that secondary generation dispatch can be scheduled. For this, data validity is key, as basing results on outdated data could lead to erroneous forecast since the renewable generation values are bound to change rapidly under high penetration levels envisioned in the future. This consequently boils down to computational latency, communication latency and network bandwidth. While the first factor is dependent on the node's memory, processing power and the application itself, the second and third factors depend on the topology of the Fog, availability of resources and nature of data.

8. **Security and Privacy:** Privacy, although technically different from security, can be considered part of the whole. Fog architecture is founded upon an end-to-end approach where the nodes of the grid can interact with one another at a local level and only avail the services of a cloud when a problem requires the solution from a heavyweight computation module. Even when Fog nodes are deployed as Fog as a Service (FaaS), security is built through the concepts of Root of Trust (RoT), authorization and privacy. It is expected of Fog nodes to establish trust with other nodes and underlying assets they are tied to, by discovering and maintaining a chain of authorization, termed formally as attestation. The node closest to the end-device within the Local Tier could be the first point of security. Before passing this protected data to the next level, the node must attest its trust. As the continually processed data is handed higher up both within the Local Tiers and to the Central Tier, the nodes each add their attestations, thus establishing a chain of authorization. Owing to the dynamism of the nodes in the Fog, it is required that the physical and computational resources also be attested along with data.

9. **Agility:** It is, by now, well understood that data by itself has no meaning. For it to obtain meaning, it needs to be duly ingested, processed, computed and turned into useful information. The missing link in bringing this full circle is "context", which the Fog is also capable of achieving. Prior to processing, the original data is spurious, poorly structured, haphazardly encoded and might even contain a few missing values. This data as such is unfit for analysis and requires undergoing a series of processes, collectively called descriptive analytics, as was discussed in the introduction of Section III. However, as important as it is to format and cleanse the data, it is crucial to derive appropriate context for it as well, since most computation processes depend on data's context for providing results. The contextual understanding must expedite the ability of the models to make faster and optimal decisions that then drive broader decisions and policy management higher in the hierarchy. Once a context is established, the applications can be executed on any Fog node located on any layer of the architecture, and hence become more robust to every-day changes in data patterns or system behaviors.

APPLICATION OF THE FOG TO DEMAND MODELING FOR NETWORK

An overview of the proposed fog framework is shown in Figure 3, which considers a specific use-case of demand modeling to explain its significance. Power supply and demand in a grid are continuously changing. The challenge has become far fiercer with higher penetration of intermittent renewables. Demand modeling has taken a new turn with novel technologies to collect almost real-time load information. Demand modeling involves understanding and formulating complex mathematical models for customer behavior. The electricity demand curves are ever changing with the introduction of newer kinds of loads. To obtain a comprehensive load modeling, a two-tier fog framework is introduced. In the future smart grid, demand modeling would be required at both Local as well as Central Tiers. For example, demand modeling for a micro-grid in a community can be considered at the Local Tier, while the modeling for a larger community (like a city) falls under the Central Tier. In both scenarios, a common set of steps need to be executed. The first step utilizes historical load and weather data to achieve a platform for future dynamic load identification. The second step upgrades this model using data from Advanced Metering Infrastructure (AMI) and Intelligent Electronic Devices (IEDs). As a corollary, historical and 15 minute-interval data will be utilized to conduct large-scale studies to develop a model to predict the behavior of individual customers and then aggregate the predicted models to achieve a comprehensive demand pattern.

A similar approach is adopted on the generation side, where the available power from renewables can be accurately estimated only for shorter duration of time. To model the uncertainty of renewable resources, two main factors should be considered: 1) weather prediction, 2) the performance of the solar panels and wind generators. In this part, renewable generation is estimated as well as the bulk generations. From the total supply modeling point of view, two important generation types will be considered:

Figure 3. Schematic view for demand modeling at central and local tiers of the proposed fog framework

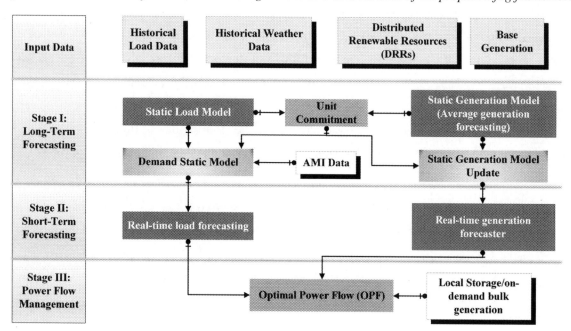

1) Bulk generations (most of the generations of this category are conventional, such as fossil fuel power plants), 2) renewables. The total generation of the first group can be calculated accurately. However, the generation estimation of renewables is not as achievable as bulk generations. In this cahpter, two influential renewables, wind and solar, are considered because of their considerable market share. The intermittency of wind and solar 1 generations helps us to achieve a better estimation of generation. Additionally, the uncertainty of these two renewable resources should be modeled based on two factors: 1) weather prediction (wind speed, solar radiation, and other weather parameters), 2) the performance of the solar panels and wind generators. This part leads to a generation model which will be utilized in the next simulations.

In order to validate the performance of the models in the proposed framework, an adequacy assessment is introduced in Section IV(C). Based on the forecasting model proposed, system adequacy can be estimated in terms of the system reliability.

Demand Forecasting

Assume that there are a set of customers C distributed over an area. By partitioning the area into n disjoint parts: $\{A_1, A_2, ..., A_n\}$, we obtain a corresponding partition of set $C = \{C_1, C_2, ..., C_n\}$ (communities of customers). The demand values of each subset C_q has been measured every μ units in time $[0, T\mu]$ for some integer T and real value μ. Then, assume that a year is divided into m parts (school time, Christmas holidays, summer break, etc.) based on the similarity of electricity usage pattern. We partition time interval $[0, T\mu]$ into m subsets: $\{I_1, I_2, ..., I_m\}$ such that I_i contains the ith part of every year belonging to $[0, T\mu]$. Additionally, every set I_i is divided to two parts: weekends I_{i1} and business days I_{i2}. Moreover, if a day is divided into d parts (again based on the similarity of electricity usage pattern during the day), we partition every interval I_{ij} into $\{I_{ij1}, I_{ij2}, ..., I_{ijd}\}$.

In addition, assume that we have the historical weather data in every area A_q over period $[0, T\mu]$. Considering that W denotes the set of different weather conditions, we partition time interval I_{ijk}, $\forall i = 1, ..., m$, $j = 1, 2$, $k = 1, ..., d$, in the following form for every area A_q, $\forall q = 1, ..., n$, $I_{ijk} = \bigcup_{w \in W} I_{ijk}^{(w,q)}$, where $I_{ijk}^{(w,q)}$ specifies the subset of I_{ijk} such that the weather condition in area A_q and time $t \in I_{ijk}^{(w,q)}$ is w.

Now, if interval $[0, T\mu]$ contains δ days, let D_v specifies the vth day of time interval $[0, T\mu]$ for every $v = 1, ..., \delta$. Additionally, consider $D(q, \tau)$ as the power demanded by the set of customers C_q measured at moment $\mu\tau$ (for every $\tau = 1, 2, ..., T$). For every interval $I_{ijk}^{(w,q,v)} = I_{ijk}^{(w,q)} \cap D_v$, if $I_{ijk}^{(w,q,v)} \neq \varnothing$, we specify five parameters: $X_1^{(q)}$ is the number of years passed since $t = 0$ (till interval $I_{ijk}^{(w,q,v)}$), $X_2^{(q)}$ is the number of weeks passed since the beginning of the ith partition of a year, $X_3^{(q)}$ is the number of days passed since the beginning of the jth partition of a week, $X_4^{(q)}$ is the temperature in area A_q and time interval $I_{ijk}^{(w,q,v)}$, and

$$y^{(q)} = \frac{\sum_{u\tau \in I_{ijk}^{(w,q,v)}} D(q,\tau)}{\sum_{u\tau \in I_{ijk}^{(w,q,v)}} 1},$$

(1)

where $y^{(q)}$ specifies the average power demanded by the set of customers C_q in time interval $I_{ijk}^{(w,q,v)}$.

Maximum Likelihood Estimator. For every subset $I_{ijk}^{(w,q)} \subset [0, Tu]$, we construct a maximum-likelihood estimator for the dependent variable $y^{(q)}$ based on the following linear model:

$$\hat{y}^{(q)} = \left[1 \; X_1^{(q)} X_2^{(q)} X_3^{(q)} X_4^{(q)}\right]\left[\widehat{\beta_0} \; \widehat{\beta_1} \; ... \; \widehat{\beta_4}\right]^T + N\left(0, \hat{\sigma}^2\right).$$

(2)

Considering that condition $I_{ijk}^{(w,q,v)} \neq \varnothing$ is only true for $v = v_1, v_2, ..., v_p$, we obtain that:

$$Y^{(q)} = X^{(q)}\beta + \varepsilon, \forall q = 1, 2, ..., n, \text{such that } Y^{(q)} = \left[y_1^{(q)} y_2^{(q)} ... y_p^{(q)}\right]^T, \beta = \left[\widehat{\beta_0} \; \widehat{\beta_1} \; ... \; \widehat{\beta_4}\right]^T, \varepsilon = \left[\varepsilon_1 \varepsilon_2 ... \varepsilon_p\right]^T,$$

and

$$X^{(q)} = \begin{bmatrix} 1 & X_{11}^{(q)} & X_{12}^{(q)} & X_{13}^{(q)} & X_{14}^{(q)} \\ 1 & X_{21}^{(q)} & X_{22}^{(q)} & X_{23}^{(q)} & X_{24}^{(q)} \\ \vdots & \vdots & \vdots & \vdots & \vdots \\ 1 & X_{p1}^{(q)} & X_{p2}^{(q)} & X_{p3}^{(q)} & X_{p4}^{(q)} \end{bmatrix}$$

(3)

In Equation 1, $y_\iota^{(q)}$ specifies the average power demanded by the set of customers C_q in time interval $I_\iota^{(w,q,v)}$, moreover, $X_{\iota 1}, ..., X_{\iota 4}$ denote the parameters on which $y_\iota^{(q)}$ is dependent, $\forall \iota = 1, 2, ..., p$. Using the maximum-likelihood method for the linear model mentioned in Equation 2, we obtain that:

$$\hat{\beta}_{ML} = \left(X^{(q)T} X^{(q)}\right)^{-1} X^{(q)T} Y^{(q)T},$$

(4)

$$\hat{\varepsilon}_{ML} = \left(Y^{(q)T} - X^{(q)}\hat{\beta}_{ML}\right) = N\left(0, \hat{\sigma}_{ML}^2 I\right),$$

(5)

$$\hat{\sigma}_{ML}^2 = \left(Y^{(q)T} - X^{(q)}\hat{\beta}_{ML}\right)\left(Y^{(q)T} - X^{(q)}\hat{\beta}_{ML}\right)^T / p.$$

(6)

Note that the ML estimator specified in Equation 2 can forecast the average power demand in an interval of few hours. However, by using the estimator repetitively and for different intervals $I_{ijk}^{(w,q)}$, we can forecast the average power demand for longer time; however, the variance of error will increase respectively. Additionally, the similar estimation model can be made for power generation. The only difference is that we don't need to partition a week into two parts. Moreover, we should partition a year into small parts based on the similarity of power generation pattern.

Short-Term Forecasting

In the previous subsection, we partitioned the interval $[0, Tu]$ into $\tilde{}\ \left(\text{md}\,|W|\right)$ subsets in the form of $I_{ijk}^{(w,q)}$ (for every set of customers C_q). Additionally, for every subset $I_{ijk}^{(w,q)}$, a maximum likelihood estimator was constructed to estimate the average power demanded by customers C_q in time interval $I_{ijk}^{(w,q)} \cap D_v$. Our ultimate goal in this section is to construct an estimator for the value of power demanded by set of customers C_q in moment $t = \tau u$ (for some integer value τ) based on ARIMA(a,0,0) model with drift $-u^{(q)}$:

$$\left[1 - \sum_{l=1}^{a} \phi_l L^l\right]\left(D\left(q, \tau\right) - \mu^{(q)}\right) = \varepsilon_\tau, \tag{7}$$

where $\mu^{(q)}$ is the average of demand value $D\left(q, \tau\right)$ in time interval $t \in I_{ijk}^{(w,q,v)}$ which is estimated by Equation 2, ε_τ is a white noise of variance σ^2, $\tau u \in I_{ijk}^{(w,q,v)}$ for some i, j, k, w, v, and L is the lag operator: $L\left(D\left(q, \tau\right)\right) = D\left(q, \tau - 1\right)$. By simplifying Equation 7, we obtain that:

$$D\left(q, \tau\right) = \left(\sum_{l=1}^{a} \phi_l - 1\right)\mu^{(q)} + \sum_{l=1}^{a} D\left(q, \tau - l\right) + \varepsilon_\tau. \tag{8}$$

By replacing $\mu^{(q)}$ with by $\hat{y}^{(q)} + \varepsilon'$ where $\varepsilon' = N\left(0, \hat{\sigma}_{ML}^2\right)$, we obtain that

$$\begin{aligned} D\left(q, \tau\right) &= \left(\sum_{l=1}^{a} \phi_l - 1\right)\left(\hat{y}^{(q)} + \varepsilon'\right) + \sum_{l=1}^{a} D\left(q, \tau - l\right) + \varepsilon_\tau \\ &= \left(\sum_{l=1}^{a} \phi_l - 1\right)\hat{y}^{(q)} + \sum_{l=1}^{a} D\left(q, \tau - l\right) + \varepsilon_\tau + \left(\sum_{l=1}^{a} \phi_l - 1\right)\varepsilon' \end{aligned} \tag{9}$$

Note that Equation 7 works only if random process $D\left(q, \tau\right)$ shows stationary behavior; otherwise, we need to use the model with moving average. In fact, assuming that process $D\left(q, \tau\right)$ is not stationary, ARIMA($a, 1, 0$) is much better for short-term forecasting:

$$\left(1 - \sum_{l=1}^{a} \phi_l L^l\right)\left(1 - L\right) D\left(q, \tau\right) = \varepsilon_\tau .$$

Consequently, we obtain that:

$$D\left(q, \tau\right) = (\phi_1 + 1) D\left(q, \tau - 1\right) + \sum_{l=2}^{a}\left(\phi_l - \phi_{l-1}\right) D\left(q, \tau - l\right) - \phi_a D\left(q, \tau - a - l\right) + \varepsilon_\tau \quad (10)$$

As can be seen, ARIMA($a, 1, 0$) model forecasts the demand value using its ($a + 1$) previous values with a white noise error. In addition, the power generation of the gth generator can also be forecast using ARIMA($a', 1, 0$). Assuming that $G\left(q, \tau\right)$ specifies the instantaneous power generated by the gth generator at moment t, we have: $\left(1 - \sum_{l=1}^{a'} \phi_l' L^l\right)\left(1 - L\right) G\left(q, \tau\right) = \varepsilon_\tau'$, or equivalently.

$$G\left(q, \tau\right) = \left(\phi_1' + 1\right) G\left(q, \tau - 1\right) + \sum_{l=2}^{a}\left(\phi_l - \phi_{l-1}\right) G\left(q, \tau - l\right) - \phi_{a'}' DG\left(q, \tau - a' - l\right) + \varepsilon_\tau' \quad (11)$$

In the following section, we analyze the adequacy of the electricity system based on ARIMA($a, 1, 0$) forecasting model.

Unit Commitment and Optimal Power Flow Problem

After long term demand and generation forecasting, we should solve the unit commitment (UC) problem. The main objective of solving UC problem is to calculate the most economical combination of all of the power generation units in order to meet estimated load (in the first stage) and required reserve for power system performance. Several constraints of generation units are considered in UC problem, such as minimum on/off time, ramping up/down, minimum/maximum generating capacity, and fuel and emission limit. The calculated power output of each generation unit will not meet the demand accurately and it needs more almost real-time scheduling to compensate the error of demand estimation. Therefore, we need the real-time generation estimation to ensure that generation meets load at each instant.

We define objective function F, of generating power from N units over a specific time horizon T. The total cost from each generator at a given period is the fuel cost, C_i, plus the any start-up costs, CS_i, that may be incurred during the period:

$$F = \sum_{t=1}^{T} \sum_{i=1}^{N}\left[C_i\left(P_i\left(t\right)\right) + S_i\left(x_i\left(t\right), u_i\left(t\right)\right)\right], \quad (12)$$

where the fuel costs, C_i, are dependent on the level of power generation $P_i\left(t\right)$. The start-up costs, S_i, are dependent on the state of the unit, x_i, which indicate the number of hours the unit has been on (positive) or off (negative), and the discrete decision variable, u_i, which denotes if power generation of the unit at time t is up (1) or down (-1) from the unit at time $t+1$. The objective function is to be minimized subject to a series of system and generator constraints. First, the system demand, $P_d(t)$, must be met $\sum_{i=1}^{N} P_i(t) = P_d(t)$.

There also must be sufficient spinning reserve, r_i, to ensure reliability. The required system spinning reserve is designated as P_r. The actual spinning reserve for a unit i is zero if the unit is off or

$$r_i = \min\left\{P_i^{max}(t) - P_i(t), r_i^{max}\right\} : \text{i.e.,} \sum_{i=1}^{N} r_i(x_i(t), P_i(t)) \geq P_r(t).$$

In order to calculate the power flows in smart grid, with high penetration of distributed renewable resources, we should solve the power flow problem. The following equations show the power flow problem formulation and constraints.

$$\text{minimize} \sum_{k} f_k\left(P_{G_k}\right) \text{over } P_G, Q_G, \text{ and } V \tag{13}$$

subject to:

$$\left|
\begin{array}{l}
P_{G_k} - P_{D_k} = \sum_{i \in N} \Re\left\{V_k\left(V_k^* - V_l^*\right)y_{kl}^*\right\} \\
Q_{G_k} - Q_{D_k} = \sum_{i \in N} \Im\left\{V_k\left(V_k^* - V_l^*\right)y_{kl}^*\right\} \\
P_k^{min} \leq P_{G_k} \leq P_k^{max} \\
Q_k^{min} \leq Q_{G_k} \leq Q_k^{max} \\
V_k^{min} \leq |V_k| \leq V_k^{max} \\
\forall k
\end{array}
\right.$$

where N is the number of buses, $\left(P_{D_k} + jQ_{D_k}\right)$ is the load value at the kth bus, and $\left(P_{G_k} + jQ_{G_k}\right)$ is the generation value at the kth bus. Additionally, if there exists a line between the kth and l^{th} buses ($k,l \in N$), the following relations also constrain the mentioned minimization problem:

$$\left|
\begin{array}{l}
|\theta_{kl}| = |\angle V_k - \angle V_l| \leq \theta_{kl}^{max} \\
|P_{kl}| = |\Re\{V_k\left(V_k^* - V_l^*\right)y_{kl}^*| \leq P_{kl^{max}} \\
|S_{kl}| = |V_k\left(V_k^* - V_l^*\right)y_{kl}^*| \leq S_{kl^{max}} \\
|V_k - V_l| \leq V_{kl}^{max}
\end{array}
\right. \tag{14}$$

The cost function f_k of generation units is as follow:

$$f_i(p) = a + bp + cp^2 \tag{15}$$

where a, b, and c are positive values. As the cost function of generation units is convex, we need potent convex optimization tools to solve this problem.

Adequacy Assessment

By assumption, we consider the maximum security for our electrical facilities (like cables, smart measurement equipment, etc.). Henceforth, the system reliability in our discussion refers to the system adequacy. In order to analyze the system adequacy, we need to use the forecasting models of instantaneous demand and generation presented in the previous section:

$$\begin{cases} D(q,\tau) = \hat{D}(q,\tau) + D_\tau \\ G(q,\tau) = \hat{G}(q,\tau) + G_\tau \end{cases} \tag{16}$$

$$\hat{D}(q,\tau) = (\phi_1 + 1)D(q,\tau-1) + \sum_{l=2}^{a}(\phi_l - \phi_{l-1})D(q,\tau-l) - \phi_a D(q,\tau-a-l). \tag{17}$$

$$\hat{G}(q,\tau) = (\phi_1' + 1)G(q,\tau-1) + \sum_{l=2}^{a'}(\phi_l' - \phi_{l-1}')G(q,\tau-l) - \phi_a' D(q,\tau-a'-l) \tag{18}$$

such that: and where D_τ and G_τ are two independent Gaussian white noises of the following covariance functions (regarding the Central-Limit theorem, the estimation errors of the instantaneous demand and generation are Gaussian processes):

$$\begin{cases} cov(s,t) = \sigma_g^2 \times \delta(s-t) \\ cov(s,t) = \sigma_d^2 \times \delta(s-t) \end{cases} \qquad \forall s,t \geq 0$$

Now, assume that community C_q uses the qth renewable power plant (DRR) to satisfy its demand. Assuming that at given time t, community C_q has stored $S(q,\ t)$ units of energy, we obtain that:

$$S(q,t) = \int_o^t \left(G(q,t') - D(q,t') \right) dt' + s_q \quad \forall t \geq 0 \tag{19}$$

such that s_q is the initial stored energy in the community. By replacing the generation and demand functions with their equivalent random processes, we obtain that: where $\hat{S}(q,t) = \int_0^t \left(\hat{G}(q,t') - \hat{D}(q,t') \right) dt' + s_q$

and $W_t = \int_0^t \left(D_{t'} - G_{t'} \right) dt'$. Since D_τ and G_τ are two independent Gaussian white noises, W_t is a Wiener process of variance $(\sigma_g^2 + \delta_g^2)$. Here is the covariance function of process W_t: $cov\left(W_s, W_t\right) = \min\{s,t\}(\sigma_g^2 + \delta_g^2)$. Moreover, $\hat{S}(q,t)$ is the expected value of the stored energy at given time t:

$$S(q,t) = \int_0^t \left(\hat{G}(q,t') - \hat{D}(q,t') + G_{t'} - D_{t'} \right) dt' + s_q$$
$$= \int_0^t \left(\hat{G}(q,t') - \hat{D}(q,t') \right) dt' + s_q - \int_0^t \left(D_{t'} - G_{t'} \right) dt' = \hat{S}(q,t) - W_t \tag{20}$$

$\bullet$ $\left[S(q,t) \right] = E\left[\hat{S}(q,t) - W_t \right] = \hat{S}(q,t) - E\left[W_t \right] = \hat{S}(q,t)$

According to the above analysis, the amount of stored energy $S(q,t)$ is equal to the summation of deterministic amount $\hat{S}(q,t)$ and the scaled Wiener process (W_t). In the rest of our analysis, we assume that the expected value of the stored energy never becomes less than the initial amount of energy (s_q); i.e. $\hat{S}(q,t) \geq s_q$, $\forall t \geq 0$. This condition can be held by providing sufficient DRRs for every community (which is designed based on long term forecasting of power demand and generation).

Here, we define the system adequacy ratio ($\rho_q(0,t)$) for the qth community as the probability that the actual stored energy $S(q,t')$ doesn't meet the low-threshold ($s_0 - \lambda$) for some $\lambda \in [0, s_q]$ and every $t' \in [0,t]$.

$$\rho_q(0,t) = \Pr\left[\forall t' \leq t : S(q,t') > s_0 - \lambda \right] = \Pr\left[\forall t' \leq t : \hat{S}(q,t') - W_{t'} > s_q - \lambda \right]$$
$$\geq \Pr\left[\forall t' \leq t : W_{t'} < \lambda \right] = \Pr\left[\sup_{t' \leq t} \{W_{t'}\} < \lambda \right] = \Pr\left[M_t < \lambda \right] \tag{21}$$

$$\rho_q(0,t) \geq \mathrm{erf}\left(\frac{\lambda}{\sqrt{2t\sigma^2}} \right) \tag{22}$$

where M_t is the running maximum process corresponding to the scaled Wiener process W_t. So, regarding the characteristics of the running maximum process, we obtain the following inequality: such that

$\sigma^2 = \sigma_g^2 + \delta_g^2$. In other words, we assume that if $S\left(q, t\right) \leq s_0 - \lambda$ (the stored energy becomes lower than some threshold in the qth community), the consumers demand will not be satisfied anymore.

If the DRR of each community is the only source of power for the community customers, the adequacy ratio will substantially decrease over time. In fact, even if the DRRs are sufficient to satisfy the customers' demand in long-term ($\hat{S}\left(q, t\right) \geq s_q$), the system adequacy cannot be guaranteed because of the white noise errors existed in the short-term forecasting scheme of demand and generation. Subsequently, we have to get help from the bulk generators located outside the community to cancel out the temporary noises and improve the adequacy ratio by generating extra energy on demand.

RECOMMENDED TESTBED FOR FUTURE APPLICATION OF FOG COMPUTING PLATFORM ON SMART GRID

To provide a context for validating the mechanisms of the Fog computing platform on smart grid, preliminary scenarios are carried out considering the sequence of failure illustrated in Figure 4 (a). In this figure, all data will be initially stored in the local storages. These data can be from distributed fault data to weather, load and irradiance data. Then command and control center will analyze the data, make the decisions, do the forecasting, perform the optimizations, and send the control signals. It has local and central sections. The IEEE 9 bus system can be used as the testbed in the proposed application, as shown in Figure 4 (b). Event 1 corresponds to a lightning strike on line 5 which leads to the operation of circuit breakers 13 and 14 and the reclosers which sense the over current. Event 2 will be a phase to phase short circuit fault on line 2.

Event 3 is a three phase to ground fault on line 3. Event3 is assumed to be an internal fault on Transformer 3 (e.g. insulation breakdown between winding and earth, transformer core fault, etc.) is occurred which results in failing of transmission lines 4 and 5. In Event 5 renewable generations (PV and wind) and/or related inverters are getting off while T3 is still faulty.

Event 1 and 2 are an asymmetric fault and Event 3 is a symmetrical fault which all three need subtransient, transient and steady state analysis from the power system point of view. To check the clearance of these 3 events, reclosers will start operating. The first reclosing attempt will be made 2 seconds after the fault happening and 2nd and 3rd attempt will be made 15 seconds and 40 seconds after Lightning. Furthermore, fault ride through controllers on PV inverters and back to back converters of wind generation system will be enabled in all 5 cases. On the renewable side, LVRT controller on the inverters will be enabled to meet the interconnection standards. Due to IEEE 1547a standard, if a voltage sag of 55% happens, it should be cleared in less than 1 second. And if the voltage sag is less than 40%, it can be cleared in less than 2 seconds. Moreover, the operation of other equipment like LTCs (Load Tap Changer), CBs (Capacitor Bank), VRs (Voltage Regulator), etc. will be studied. For Events 4 and 5 it is needed to enable the demand response and energy management control on top of all the other mentioned methods. Other important criteria which should be considered are the speed of data transmission to/from Fog storage and Fog computing center, speed of reading/writing data from/on Fog storage and speed of computational and control processes in comparison to the speed of local data transmission, local storage, and local computational an control processes.

Figure 4. (a) Network base storage and computing framework. (b) Schematic view of the Smart Grid structure based on IEEE 9 bus system.

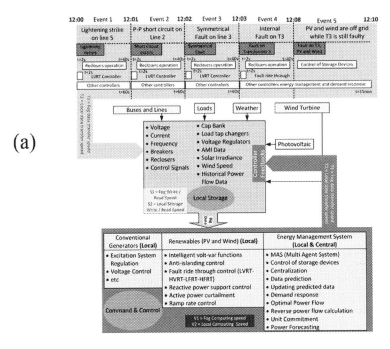

(a)

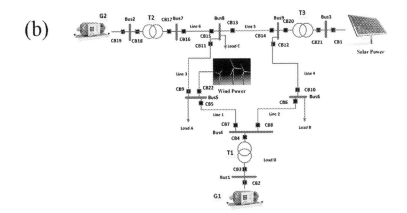

(b)

FUTURE RESEARCH DIRECTIONS

Fog computing applications are one of the most useful techniques for the future smart grid development. Beyond the previously discussed applications for the fog, various future opportunities for fog -based energy management, information management and security in smart grid are discussed below with some of the research challenges (Bera, Misra, & Rodrigues, 2015).

- The flexibility of the smart grid is a very useful feature which makes it operate with or without real-time data and energy exchange. When a fault happens in the system smart grids should be able to give-and-take energy from/to the Fog energy storage devices.
- Virtual energy storing can be proposed to keep supply and demand curve all through peak hours. For this purpose, optimization (real time and online), the control flow of energy, and prediction will be done using Fog framework.
- Controller optimization for virtual power flow which will operate in both islanded mode and normal mode with any intermittencies of renewable power generation.
- Private and public Fog can be scaled and made interoperable to encourage global deployment in smart grid
- Scheduling of data traffic to reduce information traffic percentage in Fog environment and in the smart grid.
- Dynamic interaction of Fog services by customers to improve smart grid functionality through a decentralized power delivery.
- Fault protection algorithms will be implemented in a Fog-based structure in the future smart grid systems. In this framework, different kinds of equipment will be efficiently interacting with each other and multiple optimization algorithms will be implemented.
- Data leakage can happen intentionally or unintentionally and future smart grids are supposed to distinguish planned data leak by application of Fog computing technology. Nevertheless, accidental data leakage may happen occasionally in smart grids. Therefore, future grids need to differentiate the intentional from unintentional leakages and be able to avoid the latter.
- The state estimation, enterprising, and active management of the future smart grids will be done by Fog infrastructure. In state estimation speed is a crucial factor. As the rate of renewable integration into the grid is getting high, an instantaneous state estimation response will play an important role in the future and satisfactory policies can be defined by companies that provide power for a reliable energy distribution to the customers.

CONCLUSION

In this chapter, the significance of computing for smart grid was highlighted and justified in the context of three crucial scenarios: information management, energy management, and cyber-physical security. While the existing applications for processing and managing smart grid big data rely heavily on centralized frameworks such as the Fog, they will not prove scalable, interoperable, efficient and reliable under the future scenarios such as high levels of renewable integration into the transmission and distribution networks, and proliferation of large numbers of intelligent sensors across the grid. It is expected that network latency, congestion, and subsequent reduction in consumer QoS will make the Fog a stressed ecosystem for computing. This calls for a decentralized framework that distributes computational intelligence from the Fog towards the edge of the grid, called the Fog computing. Unlike the cloud, fog is capable of exhibiting scalability and interoperability with emerging future technologies for the smart grid. The effectiveness of the Fog for the three previously considered scenarios was discussed, following which the proposed Fog framework was introduced. Models for long/short-term forecasting, unit commitment, and adequacy assessment were elaborated. These models were then applied to a prototype fog ecosystem over a standard IEEE 9-bus testbed for validation.

ACKNOWLEDGMENT

This work is supported by the National Science Foundation under Grant No. 1553494. Any opinions, findings, and conclusions or recommendations expressed in this material are those of the authors and do not necessarily reflect the views of the National Science Foundation.

REFERENCES

Almadhor, A. (2016). A Fog Computing based Smart Grid Cloud Data Security. *International Journal of Applied Information Systems, 10*(6), 1–6. doi:10.5120/ijais2016451515

Bera, S., Misra, S., & Rodrigues, J. J. P. C. (2015). Cloud Computing Applications for Smart Grid: A Survey. *IEEE Transactions on Parallel and Distributed Systems, 26*(5), 1477–1494. doi:10.1109/TPDS.2014.2321378

Borcoci, E. (2016). Fog-computing versus SDN/NFV and Cloud computing in 5G. Paper presented in DataSys conference, Valencia, Spain.

Byers, C. C., & Wetterwald, P. (2015). *Fog Computing Distributing Data and Intelligence for Resiliency and Scale Necessary for IoT the Internet of Things*. Paper presented at ACM Symposium on Ubiquity.

Cisco. (2016). *Fog Computing and the Internet of Things: Extend the Cloud to Where the Things Are*. Retrieved from http://www.cisco.com/c/dam/en_us/solutions/trends/iot/docs/computing-overview.pdf

Dastjerdi, A.V., & Buyya, R. (2017, January). *Fog Computing: Helping the Internet of Things Realize its Potential*. IEEE Computer Society.

Deshmukh, U. A., & More, S. A. (2016). Fog Computing: New Approach in the World of Cloud Computing. *International Journal of Innovative Research in Computer and Communication Engineering, 4*(9), 16310–16316.

Emfinger, W., Dubey, A., Volgyesi, P., Sallai, J., & Karsai, G. (2016). Demo Abstract: RIAPS – A Resilient Information Architecture Platform for Edge Computing. Paper presented at IEEE/ACM Symposium on Edge Computing (SEC), Washington, DC. 10.1109/SEC.2016.23

Fang, X., Misra, S., Xue, G., & Yang, D. (2012). Smart grid—the new and improved power grid: A survey. *IEEE Communications Surveys and Tutorials, 14*(4), 944–980. doi:10.1109/SURV.2011.101911.00087

Guo, Y., Pan, M., & Fang, Y. (2012). Optimal power management of residential customers in the smart grid. *IEEE Transactions on Parallel and Distributed Systems, 23*(9), 1593–1606. doi:10.1109/TPDS.2012.25

Gupta, H., Nath, S. B., Chakraborty, S., & Ghosh, S. K. (2016). *SDFog: A Software Defined Computing Architecture for QoS Aware Service Orchestration over Edge Devices*. arXiv preprint arXiv:1609.01190

Harp, D. R., & Gregory-Brown, B. (2013). *IT/OT Convergence: Bridging the Divide*. NexDefense ICS SANS Report. Retrieved from https://ics.sans.org/media/IT-OT-Convergence-NexDefense-Whitepaper.pdf

Khedkar, S. V., & Gawande, A. D. (2014). Data Partitioning Technique to Improve Cloud Data Storage Security. *International Journal of Computer Science and Information Technologies*, 5(3), 3347–3350.

Luntovskyy, A., & Spillner, J. (2017). *Smart Grid, Internet of Things and Fog Computing. Architectural Transformations in Network Services and Distributed Systems*. Wiesbaden, Germany: Springer. doi:10.1007/978-3-658-14842-3

Madsen, H., Burtschy, B., Albeanu, G., & Popentiu-Vladicescu, F. (2013). *Reliability in the utility computing era: Towards reliable Fog Computing*. Paper presented at 20th International Conference on Systems, Signals and Image Processing, Bucharest, Romania. 10.1109/IWSSIP.2013.6623445

National Electric Reliability Commission. (2012). *CIP-004-6: Cyber Security – Personnel & Training*. Retrieved from http://www.nerc.com/pa/Stand/Prjct2014XXCrtclInfraPrtctnVr5Rvns/CIP-004-6_CLEAN_06022014.pdf

National Electric Reliability Commission. (2014). *CIP-008-5: Cyber Security – Incident Reporting and Response Planning*. Retrieved from: http://www.nerc.com/pa/Stand/Project%20200806%20Cyber%20Security%20Order%20706%20DL/CIP-008-5_clean_4_(2012-1024-1218).pdf

National Electric Reliability Commission. (2014). *CIP-010-2: Cyber Security – Configuration Change Management and Vulnerability Assessments*. Retrieved from http://www.nerc.com/pa/Stand/Reliability%20Standards/CIP-010-2.pdf

National Electric Reliability Commission. (2014). *CIP-011-2: Cyber Security – Information Protection*. Retrieved from http://www.nerc.com/pa/Stand/Prjct2014XXCrtclInfraPrtctnVr5Rvns/CIP-011-2_CLEAN_06022014.pdf

Nelson, N., (2016). *The Impact of Dragonfly Malware on Industrial Control Systems*. SANS Institute InfoSec Reading Room Report.

Okay, F. Y., & Ozdemir, S. (2016) A Fog Computing Based Smart Grid Model. In *Proceedings of the International Symposium on Networks, Computers and Communications (ISNCC'16)*. IEEE. 10.1109/ISNCC.2016.7746062

OpenFog Consortium Architecture Working Group. (2016). *OpenFog Architecture Overview*. Retrieved from https://www.openfogconsortium.org/wp-content/uploads/OpenFog-Architecture-Overview-WP-2-2016.pdf

OpenFog Consortium Architecture Working Group. (2017). *OpenFog Reference Architecture for Fog Computing*. Retrieved from https://www.openfogconsortium.org/wp-content/uploads/OpenFog_Reference_Architecture_2_09_17-FINAL.pdf

Popeanga, J. (2012). Cloud computing and smart grids. *Database Systems Journal, 3*(3), 57–66.

Pradhan, S., Dubey, A., Khare, S., Sun, F., Sallai, J., Gokhale, A., . . . Sturm, M. (2016). *Poster Abstract: A Distributed and Resilient Platform for City-Scale Smart Systems*. Paper presented at IEEE/ACM Symposium on Edge Computing (SEC), Washington, DC. 10.1109/SEC.2016.28

Rao, T.V.N., & Khan, M.A., Maschendra, M., & Kumar, M.K. (2015). A Paradigm Shift from Cloud to Fog Computing. *International Journal of Computer Science & Engineering Technology, 5*(11), 385–389.

Saharan, K. P., & Kumar, A. (2015). Fog in Comparison to Cloud: A Survey. *International Journal of Computers and Applications*, *122*(3), 10–12. doi:10.5120/21679-4773

Sajjad, H. P., Danniswara, K., Al-Shishtawy, A., & Vlassov, V. (2016). *SpanEdge: Towards Unifying Stream Processing over Central and Near-the-Edge Data Centers*. Paper presented at IEEE/ACM Symposium on Edge Computing (SEC), Washington, DC. 10.1109/SEC.2016.17

Shi, W., & Dustdar, S. (2016, May 13). The Promise of Edge Computing. *IEEE Computer Society*, *49*(5), 78–81. doi:10.1109/MC.2016.145

Sornalakshmi, K., & Vadivu, G. (2015). A Survey on Realtime Analytics Framework for Smart Grid Energy Management. *International Journal of Innovative Research in Science, Engineering and Technology*, *4*(3), 1054–1058.

Ugale, B., Soni, P., Pema, T., & Patil, A. (2011). Role of cloud computing for smart grid of India and its cyber security. *Proc. IEEE Nirma Univ. Int. Conf. Eng.*, 1–5. 10.1109/NUiConE.2011.6153298

Wang, W., & Lu, Z. (2013). Cyber Security in the Smart Grid: Survey and Challenges. *Computer Networks*, *57*(5), 1344–1371. doi:10.1016/j.comnet.2012.12.017

Yang, Y., Wu, L., & Hu, W. (2011). Security architecture and key technologies for power cloud computing. *Proc. IEEE Int. Conf. Transp., Mech., Electr. Eng.*, 1717–1720. 10.1109/TMEE.2011.6199543

Yanliang, W., Song, D., Wei-Min, L., Tao, Z., & Yong, Y. (2010). Research of electric power information security protection on cloud security. *Proceeding IEEE International Conference on Power System Technology (POWERCON)*, 1–6.

Yi, S., Hao, Z., Qin, Z., & Li, Q. (2015). *Fog Computing: Platform and Applications*. Paper presented at the Third IEEE Workshop on Hot Topics in Web Systems and Technologies. 10.1109/HotWeb.2015.22

Yi, S., Li, C., & Li, Q. (2015). *A Survey of Fog Computing: Concepts, Applications and Issues. ACM Mobidata ('15)*. Hangzhou, China: ACM. doi:10.1145/2757384.2757397

Zaballos, A., Vallejo, A., & Selga, J. (2011). Heterogeneous communication architecture for the smart grid. *IEEE Network*, *25*(5), 30–37. doi:10.1109/MNET.2011.6033033

Zhang, Y., Wang, L., Sun, W., Green, R. II, & Alam, M. (2011). Distributed intrusion detection system in a multi-layer network architecture of smart grids. *IEEE Transactions on Smart Grid*, *2*(4), 796–808. doi:10.1109/TSG.2011.2159818

This research was previously published in Smart Grid Analytics for Sustainability and Urbanization edited by Zbigniew H. Gontar, pages 162-195, copyright year 2018 by Engineering Science Reference (an imprint of IGI Global).

Chapter 108
Emerging Cloud Computing Services:
A Brief Opinion Article

Yulin Yao
Anastaya, UK

ABSTRACT

Cloud Computing has offered many services to organizations and individuals. The emerging types of services such as analytics, mobile services and emerging software as a service have been offered but there is a lack of analysis on the current status. Core technologies for emerging Cloud services have been identified and presented. This brief opinion paper provides an overview of the current emerging Cloud services and explains the benefits for several disciplines. Four areas have been identified that may bring in more positive impacts for the future direction.

1. INTRODUCTION

Cloud Computing has moved in different directions due to the maturity of different technologies, easier access to data, improvement in quality of service, availability, usability and security (Buyya et al., 2009; Armbrust et al., 2010; Marston et al., 2011). However, there are different recommendations in which directions that Cloud Computing should move forward. Mobile Cloud is popular due to the rise and availability of mobile services with affordable costs (Fernando et al., 2013; Chang, 2014 a). A lot of services can be delivered online and on mobile internet so that people can receive, share and store almost information quickly and instantly. Similarly, there are different types of services such as weather forecasting and simulation which can make the public to be more aware of the extreme weather conditions, so that they can make better preparations for challenges ahead. There is a Business Intelligence as a Service which can monitor the status of return and risk in real-time and predict the market trends, so that the stakeholders can make better judgment on their investment (Chang, 2014 b; Ramachandran and Chang, 2014). Gaming as a Service (Yao and Chang, 2014; 2015) provides interactive gaming services for millions of users who can play online. The trust and friendship they have developed can be essential

DOI: 10.4018/978-1-5225-8176-5.ch108

for community building and business opportunities. Disaster Recovery and Storage as a Service (Chang, 2015 a) can ensure all big data can be protected and services to be resumed in a short of time when major accidents have happen. The benefits of doing so can allow business continuity with a minimum impacts to disruptions. There are also security concerns and improvements to ensure that all services and users are safeguarded from real attacks. There are services to blend with firewall, access control, identity management, encryption and Openstack to allow data is always protected from unauthorized access (Chang et al, 2016 a; Chang and Ramanchandran 2016). All these examples lead to the development of Emerging Software as a Service and Analytics (ESaaSA), which aim to understand the complexity behind each discipline, run simulations at the background and present the results in a way that can be understood more easily by the general public without even the background knowledge. This serves the future trends in the Emerging Cloud Computing Services, whereby Chang (2016 a) demonstrates several examples in different disciplines and explains the contributions for each discipline under his proposed "Emerging Software as a Service and Analytics" (ESaaSA).

2. CORE TECHNOLOGIES

This section explains the core technologies used by Emerging Cloud Computing Services essential for the service development, maintenance and expansion. Core technologies are as follows.

- **Database and Data Warehouse:** All the collected datasets should provide storage, query and archiving services and allow users to understand, query and synthesize datasets (Di Meglio et al., 2014).
- **Artificial Intelligence and Machine Learning:** Artificial intelligence and machine learning can compute all the mathematical models and complexity behind the scenes and ensure all results can be modeled quantitatively (Chen et al., 2014).
- **System and Software Architectures:** Modern system and software architectures should be developed to ensure all services can be efficiently functioned (Zhang et al., 2010), such as the use of API for architecture development (Chang, 2014 b).
- **Statistical Computing and Analysis:** They provide useful analysis for computational and social scientists such as the use of Organizational Sustainability Modeling (OSM) to provide useful real cases (Chang et al., 2016 b)
- **Visualization and Analytics:** Visualization and analytics can ensure users can understand scientific outputs better and easier, particularly from numerical computing to visualization and analytics (Antcheva et al., 2009; LaValle et al., 2013).
- **Predictive Modeling and Analysis:** Results of the previous data can be used to predict the likely trends and study the similar patterns and behaviors between different datasets, correlations and variables (Cohen et al., 2013).
- **Big Data Services:** Big Data services including volume, velocity, variety, veracity and value should be provided with real deployment and case studies (Chang and Wills, 2016).
- **Security**: All services must be secure and protected from hacking and unauthorized access. Large scale data analysis should be provided to know the latest trends (Chang et al., 2016 a; 2016 c).
- **Other Areas:** Other areas include the integration with the latest technologies such as Big Data and Internet of Things, whereby more users can interact with other individuals and businesses within an interactive platform.

3. DISCIPLINES RELEVANT FOR EMERGING CLOUD COMPUTING SERVICES

A growing number of disciplines can receive benefits as a result of Emerging Cloud Computing services as follows.

- **Healthcare:** All the services can allow scientists to perform their tasks better, patients to have the data secure and more meaningful analysis to be undertaken. For example, Chang (2014 c) demonstrate brain segmentation as a service service and explain the benefits to understand analysis and implications in seconds.
- **Finance:** Financial services can understand the impacts and benefits by adopting risk visualization as a service (Chang, 2014 b), Monte Carlo Simulation as a Service (Chang et al., 2014) and Business Intelligence as a Service (Chang, 2014 b) to ensure that businesses can stay competitive in understanding all the data analysis in real time.
- **Education:** Education as a Service (Chang and Wills, 2013) has been developed to study the impacts on learning and satisfaction. There are also studies to identify success factors for learning and training, whereby Chang (2015 b; 2016 b) demonstrate the effectiveness of interactive learning that can be adopted for industry and academia with selected examples in five organizations.
- **Social Networks:** Chang (2016 c) develop Social Network as a Service to understand the relationship within his network which can be taken as an example to demonstrate the effectiveness and power of the network.
- **Natural Science Research:** Emerging Services and Analytics can be used to simulate complex natural disasters, weather science and biological simulations as demonstrated by Chang (2016 a).
- **Frameworks:** Frameworks can be adapted in multi-disciplines since they introduce ethe best practices. Frameworks can provide useful insights, recommendations and case studies with positive impacts (Chang et al., 2013; Chang and Ramanchandran 2016).

4. DISCUSSION

Critical success factors are required to ensure all emerging Cloud Computing services can serve the purpose. As an opinion paper, the future direction for Cloud Computing can be influenced by the followings:

- **Business Models:** Business models need to follow the market demands to ensure businesses can stay competitive. Emerging services such as mobile services, analytics, financial apps and health checks can help organizations to improve their business opportunities, revenues, collaboration, reputation, efficiency and customer satisfaction (Chang, 2015 c).
- **Security and Privacy:** All services should always stay secure and protected against all types of attacks and attempts to steal, corrupt and destroy data. A variety of solutions should be demonstrated to provide improved level of security and privacy for all users (Mather, et al., 2009).
- **Mega Storage:** The rise of data creation, usage and arching can pose challenges since petabytes and zetabytes of data need to be taken care of on the daily basis. Intelligent ways to deal with mega storage services should be provided (Antcheva et al., 2009; Chang, 2014 d).

- **Entertainment**: Gaming, video, sports, music and related entertainment services can reach millions of users and have increased importance in the market trend and popularity (Parameswaran and Whinston, 2007; Chang, 2015 c).

5. CONCLUSION AND FUTURE WORK

This opinion paper presents an overview of emerging Cloud computing services and explains why the emerging services can provide a better quality and future-proof trends over the other traditional services focused on infrastructure. Future directions have been discussed. Our future work will include investigations of related modern technologies such as Internet of Things and Big Data, as well as how to integrate services in collaborative, secure and easy-to-use platforms.

REFERENCES

Antcheva, I., Ballintijn, M., Bellenot, B., Biskup, M., Brun, R., Buncic, N., ... Tadel, M. (2009). ROOT—A C++ framework for petabyte data storage, statistical analysis and visualization. *Computer Physics Communications*, *180*(12), 2499–2512. doi:10.1016/j.cpc.2009.08.005

Armbrust, M., Fox, A., Griffith, R., Joseph, A. D., Katz, R. H., Konwinski, A., ... Zaharia, M. (2010). Above the Clouds: A Berkeley View of Cloud computing. *Communications of the ACM*, *53*(4), 50–58. doi:10.1145/1721654.1721672

Buyya, R., Yeo, C. S., Venugopal, S., Broberg, J., & Brandic, I. (2009). Cloud computing and emerging IT platforms: Vision, hype, and reality for delivering computing as the 5th utility. *Future Generation Computer Systems*, *25*(6), 559–616. doi:10.1016/j.future.2008.12.001

Chang, V. (2014a). Measuring and analyzing German and Spanish customer satisfaction of using the iPhone 4S Mobile Cloud service. *Open Journal of Cloud Computing*, *1*(1), 19–26.

Chang, V. (2014b). The Business Intelligence As a Service in the Cloud. *Future Generation Computer Systems*, *37*, 512–534. doi:10.1016/j.future.2013.12.028

Chang, V. (2014c). Cloud Computing for brain segmentation – a perspective from the technology and evaluations. *International Journal of Big Data Intelligence*, *1*(4), 192–204. doi:10.1504/IJBDI.2014.066954

Chang, V. (2014d). A proposed model to analyse risk and return for Cloud adoption. Saarbrücken: Lambert Academic Publishing.

Chang, V. (2015a). Towards a Big Data System Disaster Recovery in a Private Cloud. *Ad Hoc Networks*, *35*, 65–82. doi:10.1016/j.adhoc.2015.07.012

Chang, V. (2015b). *The role and effectiveness of e-learning for the industry*. Lambert.

Chang, V. (2015c). A proposed Cloud Computing Business Framework. Nova Science Publisher.

Chang, V. (2016a). An overview, examples and impacts offered by Emerging Services and Analytics in Cloud Computing. *International Journal of Information Management*.

Chang, V. (2016b). Review and discussion: E-learning for academia and industry. *International Journal of Information Management, 36*(3), 476–485. doi:10.1016/j.ijinfomgt.2015.12.007

Chang, V. (2016c). A proposed Social Cloud. *Journal of Systems and Software, 2016.*

Chang, V., Kuo, Y. H., & Ramachandran, M. (2016a). Cloud computing adoption framework: A security framework for business clouds. *Future Generation Computer Systems, 57,* 24–41. doi:10.1016/j.future.2015.09.031

Chang, V., & Ramachandran, M. (2016). Towards achieving data security with the cloud computing adoption framework. *IEEE Transactions on Services Computing, 9*(1), 138-151.

Chang, V., Ramachandran, M., Yao, Y., Kuo, Y. H., & Li, C. S. (2016c). A resiliency framework for an enterprise cloud. *International Journal of Information Management, 36*(1), 155–166. doi:10.1016/j.ijinfomgt.2015.09.008

Chang, V., Walters, R. J. & Wills, G. (2013). The development that leads to the Cloud Computing Business Framework. *International Journal of Information Management, 33*(3), 524-538. doi:10.1016/j.ijinfomgt.2013.01.005

Chang, V., Walters, R. J., & Wills, G. (2014). Monte Carlo risk assessment as a service in the cloud. *International Journal of Business Integration and Management.*

Chang, V., Walters, R. J., & Wills, G. B. (2016b). Organisational sustainability modelling—An emerging service and analytics model for evaluating Cloud Computing adoption with two case studies. *International Journal of Information Management, 36*(1), 167–179. doi:10.1016/j.ijinfomgt.2015.09.001

Chang, V., & Wills, G. (2016). A model to compare cloud and non-cloud storage of Big Data. *Future Generation Computer Systems, 57,* 56–76. doi:10.1016/j.future.2015.10.003

Chen, C. P., & Zhang, C. Y. (2014). Data-intensive applications, challenges, techniques and technologies: A survey on Big Data. *Information Sciences, 275,* 314–347. doi:10.1016/j.ins.2014.01.015

Cohen, J., Cohen, P., West, S. G., & Aiken, L. S. (2013). *Applied multiple regression/correlation analysis for the behavioral sciences.* Routledge.

Di Meglio, A., Purcell, A., & Gaillard, M. (2014). CERN openlab Whitepaper on Future IT Challenges in Scientific Research.

Fernando, N., Loke, S. W., & Rahayu, W. (2013). Mobile cloud computing: A survey. *Future Generation Computer Systems, 29*(1), 84–106. doi:10.1016/j.future.2012.05.023

LaValle, S., Lesser, E., Shockley, R., Hopkins, M. S., & Kruschwitz, N. (2013). Big data, analytics and the path from insights to value. *MIT sloan management review, 21.*

Marston, S., Li, Z., Bandyopadhyay, S., Zhang, J., & Ghalsasi, A. (2011). Cloud computing – The business perspective, Decision Support Systems. *Elsevier B., 51*(1), 176–189.

Mather, T., Kumaraswamy, S., & Latif, S. (2009). *Cloud security and privacy: an enterprise perspective on risks and compliance.* O'Reilly Media, Inc.

Parameswaran, M., & Whinston, A. B. (2007). Social computing: An overview. *Communications of the Association for Information Systems, 19*(1), 37.

Ramachandran, M., & Chang, V. (2014). Financial Software as a Service – A Paradigm for Risk Modelling and Analytics. *International Journal of Organizational and Collective Intelligence, 4*(3), 65–89. doi:10.4018/ijoci.2014070104

Yao, Y., & Chang, V. (2014). Towards trust and trust building in a selected Cloud gaming virtual community. *International Journal of Organizational and Collective Intelligence, 4*(2), 64–86. doi:10.4018/ijoci.2014040104

Yao, Y., & Chang, V. (2015). Cloud gaming virtual community-A case study in China. *International Journal of Organizational and Collective Intelligence, 5*(2), 1–19. doi:10.4018/IJOCI.2015040101

This research was previously published in the International Journal of Organizational and Collective Intelligence (IJOCI), 6(4); edited by Victor Chang and Dickson K.W. Chiu, pages 98-102, copyright year 2016 by IGI Publishing (an imprint of IGI Global).

Index

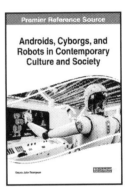

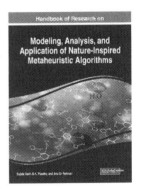

Ensure Quality Research is Introduced to the Academic Community

Become an IGI Global Reviewer for Authored Book Projects

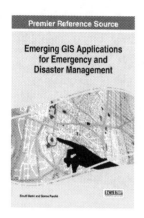
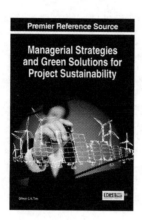

The overall success of an authored book project is dependent on quality and timely reviews.

In this competitive age of scholarly publishing, constructive and timely feedback significantly expedites the turnaround time of manuscripts from submission to acceptance, allowing the publication and discovery of forward-thinking research at a much more expeditious rate. Several IGI Global authored book projects are currently seeking highly qualified experts in the field to fill vacancies on their respective editorial review boards:

Applications may be sent to:
development@igi-global.com

Applicants must have a doctorate (or an equivalent degree) as well as publishing and reviewing experience. Reviewers are asked to write reviews in a timely, collegial, and constructive manner. All reviewers will begin their role on an ad-hoc basis for a period of one year, and upon successful completion of this term can be considered for full editorial review board status, with the potential for a subsequent promotion to Associate Editor.

If you have a colleague that may be interested in this opportunity, we encourage you to share this information with them.

Printed in the United States
By Bookmasters